Islam in the Public Sphere

Islam in the Public Sphere

Religious Groups in India, 1900–1947

Dietrich Reetz

OXFORD
UNIVERSITY PRESS

OXFORD
UNIVERSITY PRESS

Oxford University Press is a department of the University of Oxford. It furthers the University's objective of excellence in research, scholarship, and education by publishing worldwide. Oxford is a registered trademark of Oxford University Press in the UK and in certain other countries

Published in India by
Oxford University Press
YMCA Library Building, 1 Jai Singh Road, New Delhi 110 001, India

First published 2006

ISBN-13: 978-0-19-566810-0
ISBN-10: 0-19-566810-3

To

Petra, Julian, Marie, and Dinah

for their patience and encouragement

Acknowledgements

This book is based on research made possible by a grant from the (German Research Fund Deutsche Forschungsgemeinschaft) for a project titled 'Allāh's Kingdom on Earth: The Political Project of Islamic Movements in India (1900–1947)' conducted at the Zentrum Moderner Orient (Centre for Modern Oriental Studies) in Berlin during 1996–2000.

Contents

Tables and Figures

Tables

Figures

Abbreviations

AIMSF	All-India Muslim Students' Federation
AISC	All-India Sunni Conference
BLOC	British Library Oriental Collections
CP	Central Provinces
EI	Encyclopaedia of Islam
IAR	Indian Annual Register
IMDR	The Indian Muslims: a documentary record, 1900–1947, *see* Muhammad, Shan 1980
ISC	Indian Statutory Commission, *see* Great Britain 1930
JI	Jamā'at-i Islāmī, Islamic Party
JUH	Jam'īyat-e 'Ulamā'-ye Hind
JUI	Jam'īyat-e 'Ulamā'-ye Islām
JUP	Jam'īyat-e 'Ulamā'-ye Pakistān
KC	Khilāfat Conference
L/P&J/...	File classification of India Office based on department structure: Legal/Political & Judicial/...
L/P&S/...	File classification of India Office based on department structure: Legal/Political & Security/...
MEC	Muslim Educational Conference
NAI	National Archive of India, Delhi
NDC	National Document Centre (of Pakistan), Islamabad
NMML	Nehru Memorial Museum and Library, Delhi, India
TJ	Tablīghī Jamā'at
UPSA	Uttar Pradesh State Archive
BJP	Bharatiya Janata Party
VHP	Vishwa Hindu Parishad
RSS	Raṣṭriya Swayamsevak Sangh

Glossary

ahl-i ḥadīth: people of the tradition

ahl al-sunna wa-'l-jamā'a: people following the conduct of the Prophet and his community

Aḥmadīya: movement, sect in Islam founded by Mirza Ghulam Ahmad

Aḥrār: the free, noble (high-minded)

'ālim: scholar of Islamic religion and law (pl.- *'ulamā')*

amīr: leader, ruler

anjuman (Urdu): organization

anṣār: lit. helpers, those men of Medina who supported Muhammad

'aqā'id: beliefs, articles of faith

Ārya Samāj (Sanskrit): (Hindu reformist) Society of the Nobles

ashrāf: high-born, noble Muslims, in India of foreign ancestry

auliyā' (sg.-*walī*): friends of God, saints

aḏān: call for prayer (Urdu: *aẓān*)

baraka: blessing, grace (Urdu: *barakat*)

bay'a: oath of allegiance (Urdu: *bay'at*)

bayt al-māl: Muslim treasury, fisc, (Muslim) community fund

bid'a: (mainly reprehensible) innovation (in Islam), also: heresy (Urdu: *bid'at*)

birādarī: 'brotherhood', patrilineage, (endogamous) social group of north Indian Muslims

chillā: withdrawn worship (in seclusion)

crore: ten million, (anglicized, Urdu/Hindi: *krōr*)

dahrīyat: atheism

dā'ī: preacher, propagandist of Islam

dajjāl: lit. the deceiver, one-eyed monster appearing before the end of the world, Islamic equivalent of the 'Anti-Christ'

dār al-ḥarb: 'land of war', land where the law of Islam does not rule

dār al-Islām: 'land of Islam', land where the law of Islam is followed

dār al-'ulūm: 'house of sciences'—theological institution of higher learning (alt. *dāru'l-'ulūm*)

dār al-iftā': office/department for religious advice/decrees (*fatāwā*)

da'wa: propagation (of Islam), invitation (Urdu: *da'wat*)

dawla: reign, state (Urdu: *dawlat*)

ḏikr: prayer remembering Allah, Sufi practice (Urdu: *ẕikr*)

dīn: religion (of Islam)

dīnī madāris: religious schools

fatwā (pl. *fatāwā)*: Islamic religious advice, decree

fiqh: Islamic jurisprudence

fitna: split, division (in Islam), confusion, dissent, civil strife

Firangī Maḥall: lit. 'foreign palace'

ghair-muqallid: not following a law school, appellation of the *Ahl-i Ḥadīth*

ḥadd (pl. *ḥudūd)*: penal laws, Qur'anic punishment for forbidden acts against religion, lit. hindrance, impediment

ḥadīth: written tradition of the Prophet Muhammad, his companions (*ṣaḥāba*) and Medinese followers (*anṣār*)

ḥajj: annual pilgrimage to Mecca

Ḥanafī: following the law school of Abu Hanifa (699–767)

ḥarām: forbidden (in Islamic law), harmful

ḥaẓrat: here: Honorable, Excellency (address)

ḥijāb: veil

hijra: migration of the Prophet and his followers from Mecca to Medina, starting the Era Hijri; also generally migration from an un-Islamic country, *dār al-ḥarb* (Urdu: *hijrat*)

ijmā': (legal) consensus/agreement of the community

ijtihād: independent reasoning, reinterpretation, theological category of application of Qur'anic injunctions and/or Prophetic tradition (*ḥadīth*); lit. effort

iftā': giving legal opinion, through a *fatwā* (*dār al-iftā'*—legal department of a *madrasa*)

'ilm al-kalām: defensive apologetics, science of discourse (on God), theology (in Islam)

imām: prayer leader, also founder of law school, (anglicized: Imam)

īmān: faith

irtidād: apostasy

iṣlāḥ: reform of religion, of Islam, of behaviour

iṣtiṣlāḥ: methodological legal principle in Islam to establish 'public interest' (*maṣlaḥa*)

istiftā': seeking religious advice

iṯā'at (Urdu): obedience, worship

Jamā'at-i Islāmī (JI): Islamic Party

Jam'īyat-e 'Ulamā'-ye Hind (JUH): Association of religious scholars in India

Jam'īyat-e 'Ulamā'-ye Islām (JUI): Association of religious scholars of Islam

Jam'īyat-e 'Ulamā'-ye Pakistān (JUP): Association of religious scholars in Pakistan

Jazīrat al-'Arab: Arabian Peninsula

jihād: (self-)exertion in the way of God; military action with the object of expansion of Islam, 'Holy War'

Khāksār: the humble (lit. humble as dust)

khalīfa: deputy (of the Prophet), successor (pl. *khulafā'*)

khānqāh: building reserved for mystics, a Ṣūfī hospice

khilāfat: Caliphate

khān: (Pakhtun) tribal leader

khuṯba (Urdu): address, sermon

kufr: unbelief

lakh: hundred thousand, (anglicized, Urdu/Hindi: *lākh*)

lashkar: (Pakhtun) enforcement commandos, armed groups

māddīyat: materialism

madrasa: Islamic religious seminary

maḥalla: urban neighbourhood quarter (Urdu: *moḥalla*)

mahdī: leader, chosen one, saviour

maḥram: male guardian, confidant, to whom the *ḥaram* or women's apartments are open (father, son, etc.)

maktab: religious school (of primary level)

maslak (Urdu): way, conduct, school of thought

Maulānā: honorific title used for an *'ālim*, revered person (also *Mawlānā*)

Maulwī: title for learned cleric, often of lower rank (also *Maulawī*, *Mawlawī*)

madhab: Islamic law school, tradition (Urdu: *mazhab*)

mīlād-i muṣṭafā: birthday of the Prophet

muftī: judicial clerk, a person, giving a point of law, a *fatwā*

muḥaddithūn (pl.): scholars of Prophetic tradition (*ḥadīth*)

muhājirūn (pl.): refugees, (religious) migrants (Urdu: *muhājirīn*)

muḥarram: Muslim month (of mourning), *muḥarram* procession, particularly for the Shi'a

muhtamim: administrator, superintendent, or rector (of religious school)

mujāhidūn (pl.): holy warriors (Urdu: *mujāhidīn*)

munāẓara (Urdu): religious disputation

mu'tamad (Urdu): secretary

Nadwat al-'Ulamā': council of religious scholars, alt. *Nadwatu 'l-'ulamā'*

parda (Urdu): veil, seclusion of women (anglicized: purdah)

pīr: lit. old person, elder, in South Asia especially Ṣūfī guide, mentor (also *murshid*, *shaykh*) of a student (*murīd*)

qaṣba: (old) town, (traditional) Muslim quarters

qāḍī: judge (Urdu: *qāẓī*)

qiyās: (judicial reasoning by) analogy

Qur'ān: the Koran, the sacred book of Islam, as dictated by God to his messenger, Muhammad, the Prophet

Ramaḍān: ninth month of the Muslim calendar, period of fasting (Urdu: *Ramaẓān*)

Rāmlīlā: Hindu religious festival and folk theatre devoted to the life of the Hindu God Rama

ṣadr-i mudarrisīn: principal, head teacher (at the Deoband Seminary)

ṣaḥāba (pl.): companions of the Prophet Muhammad, the 'inner circle of leadership' of the first Islamic community/state

sajjāda-nishīn: lit. 'praying on the carpet', the spiritual superior of a mosque or religious endowment

salafiyya: (people following) the way of the ancestors, of the founder generation of Islam (*salaf*—the 'pious ancients')

ṣalāt: ritual prayer, benediction of the Prophet

sanad: degree

saṅgaṭhan (Sanskrit): unity

satyāgraha: civil disobedience, non-violent protest

Sayyid: Muslims of foreign ancestry in India (*ashrāf*)

sharīʿa: Islamic law (Urdu: *sharīʿat*)

shaykh: elder, Sufi guide and mentor, also part of name especially in South Asia

Shīʿa: the Shiʿa, lit. the party (of Ali, the son-in-law of the Prophet Muhammad)

shuddhī: purification

shūrā: advisory council, consultation

silsila: (Sufi) line of tradition; chain; Sufi (sub-)order

sīra: biography of the Prophet (Urdu: *sīrat*)

Sufi: mystic, ascetic

Sunna: tradition, life and conduct in the way of the Prophet (Urdu: *sunnat*)

swarāj (Hindi): independence, self-administration (under dominion status)

Tablīghī Jamāʿat: missionary movement

tafsīr: commentary (on the Qur'an), exegesis

ṯālibān (Urdu/Persian pl.): students (here: of religious seminaries), sing. *ṯālib*

tanẓīm: organization; movement of self-organization (Urdu: *tanẓīm*)

ṭarīqa: path, mystic (Sufi) order in Islam

taṣawwuf: mysticism

tauḥīd: unity of God, principle of monism/monotheism

taḏkira: biographical memoir, biography (Urdu/Persian: *tazkirat*)

umma: (global) Islamic community

ʿurs: festival in honour of a saint, also marking his death anniversary

wāʿiẓīn (Urdu): preachers (pl.)

zakāt: welfare tax, compulsory alms, one of the 'five pillars' of Islam

zamīndār (Urdu): landholder

ẓarūrīayt-i dīn (Urdu): essentials of religion

Introduction

The national movement against colonial rule in British India provided the backdrop for a general mobilization of political, social, cultural, and religious forces. A key aim was to set out the terms and conditions for a new and independent India. Every segment of society formulated its own project for a new polity and a reformed society. The question was on what ideological and political foundations would the new state be built, how would it be different from the Western colonial political system that had existed in India so far, and how would it meet the aspirations of India's divergent classes, forces, and races.

The degree of mobilization and activism by Islamic forces during the national movement is rarely acknowledged. Attention has mainly been focused on the two major political coalitions, those of the Indian National Congress and the Muslim League. The Pakistan movement led by the Muslim League eventually brought about the secession of territories in the northwest and northeast of the subcontinent where Muslims constituted the majority. Although Pakistan was fought for in the name of Islam, religious issues played little role in the movement. Islamic forces were distanced from the movement until the final stages, and the academic literature describing the nationalist struggle and the Pakistan movement largely ignored the ideas and activities of Islamic groups, which had mobilized it. This is a study of how major religious groups in Islam articulated their public position towards the national movement, the Pakistan movement, and the future independent polity.

Although Muslims represented a minority in South Asia, not exceeding 22 per cent of the population,[1] the influence of Islam was far from minimal, both for South Asia and for the Islamic world. South Asia, as compared to the Arab countries, to West or Central Asia, hosted

[1]The 1901 Census counted 21.22 per cent of Muslims in the population (Census 1901, Vol. 1, part II: 397). The Muslim share grew to 22 per cent by 1921, cf. Chapter 3, fn. 106.

the largest number of Muslims in the Islamic world. In terms of believers, South Asia continues to enjoy this prominent status in global Islam today, though this is often not realized in the Arab world and even by scholars of Islam from the West. Islamic religious groups operating in India reflected the impulses of divergent civilizational and cultural traditions with a reach far beyond their own territories.

To facilitate the comparative analysis of Islamic groups and to measure their political and public impact, the concept of the public sphere (*Öffentlichkeit*) has been applied, as formulated by the German philosopher Jürgen Habermas and subsequently developed by various new studies. For its genesis, evolution, and application see Chapter 1.

From a large number of organized and spontaneous forms of Islamic activism, of mainly Sunni persuasion, groups with an expressly religious connotation have been selected for issue-based analysis and comparative study. Grouping and classification is generally difficult. Those chosen have been tentatively grouped as (i) educational or *madrasa* movements and (ii) faith and revival movements. The former included the Deobandis, the Barelwis, the graduates and teachers of the Nadwa and Firangī Maḥall schools, and, for comparison, Aligarh; the latter comprised the Tablīghī Jamā'at, the Aḥrār, the Khāksār, the Ahl-i Ḥadīth, and the reformist sect of the Aḥmadīya. They have been profiled in Chapter 2. Shi'a activism is occasionally considered for comparison.

In order to facilitate comparison, a distinction is made between the role played by the Islamic groups in religious, political, and social affairs. Chapters 3, 4, and 5 respectively have been designed to discuss the related discourse, public activism, and institutional life of these groups.

Chapter 6 suggests conclusions on the contours of an Islamic project and the dimensions of an Islamic sphere as they emerge from this comparative analysis.

The study addresses several ambiguities, which I choose not to resolve but to emphasize. At the centre of investigation is the public role of religious groups. Here we can see how they follow the dictates of religion and the compulsions of politics at the same time. As the groups represent different schools of religious interpretation, comparison may be difficult. Yet, on the level of public activity and impact, a surprising convergence of views and tactics can be observed. As Islamic groups contest the public sphere and carve out for themselves an Islamic sphere of their own, they constantly strive for a balance between a meeting of minds and increasingly tough contestation of the common ground on which they move. When they enter the public sphere, they do so implicitly understanding that they pursue concerns of wider interests that go beyond the parameters of the group's existence. What is here called an 'Islamic project' stands for a virtual direction of change in politics and society. It feeds on very similar or shared views with a clear accentuation. Working out its main elements serves the purpose of analytical clarification and does not imply that the Islamic project was a practical programme of action pursued at any given time. In contrast, the delineation of an 'Islamic sphere' will highlight the divisive competition between these groups to rule over a common social space, the Muslim community, and more specifically, those members who were conscious of and active in matters of religion. Ambiguities also surface inside Islam. The purist and reformist approach grapples with the all-pervasive influence of Sufi-based, *pīr-* and shrine-related devotional customs[2] without ever achieving a clear separation. As far as its public face is concerned, Islamic activism appears close to religious activism of other denominations, particularly where Hindu revivalism is concerned, casting each other as public enemy. It betrays parallels with major secular movements of the time, notably the national movement with its non-cooperation and civil disobedience campaigns, from which it is partly derived.

The term 'Islamic group' is applied to these movements in a more general sense, not implying any uniform strictness in belonging. The Islamic movements under study formed social groups inasmuch as their members were marked by 'relatively stable patterns of interaction' (Marshall 1994: 207) through shared group norms and institutions where the density of the interaction varied (Fuchs-Heinritz et al.,1994: 255). As people are bound in competing and overlapping networks of interaction the Islamic groups represented only one of several concurrent states of association. Group membership was, therefore, relative and could be challenged on competing grounds. A group, movement, or party will be considered Islamic if its aims related to Islamic doctrine or the furtherance of Islamic belief, and if it was not primarily founded for political purposes. Also the terms 'activist Islam' and 'Islamic activism' are frequently used in this study. They imply active public involvement beyond personal or private contemplation, which is not necessarily political in nature. 'Islamist' is more specific and will be reserved for Islamic activists and groups aiming at the establishment of an Islamic state, or taking political control. Consequently, political

[2]From an anthropological perspective, a distinction is often made between the scripturalist Islam as preached by the religious scholars and local or folk Islam. This division is based on Robert Redfield's distinction between Great and Little Traditions (1960), creating a dichotomy that has also much influenced Clifford Geertz's interpretation of Islam (1971). This juxtaposition has created some confusion, particularly where it regarded the two strands as mutually exclusive, which they are not. Still, local forms of Islam, largely based on Sufi-inspired practices and beliefs, will be marked here as folk Islam assuming that this does not preclude reformist or scripturalist influences on Sufi-based and locally practised folk Islam.

Islam will be understood to denote Islamic activism seeking a political role for Islam in society. It presupposes direct involvement of religious leaders of Islam, of Islamic activists in a political discourse, activity, and institution-building. It is marked by the application of the religious argument to political issues. It has to be distinguished from the mere garnishing of ordinary political activity with Islamic references. Where related to Islam as a system, a set of rules and guidelines, 'Islamic' is used, while as qualification for a person's religious affiliation, 'Muslim' is preferred.

The distinction between the public and political dimensions of the Islamic project too requires clarification. Religious groups and institutions compete with each other over a share of the public sphere, a process that has political dimensions. If the focus is on control over the wider public sphere, which includes secular as well as religious manifestations of public life, the term 'public' is given preference. The term 'political' will be mainly reserved for matters directly bearing on political power. These would include connections with major political parties and the national movement, as also with the colonial government. In this sense, political life is understood to be more restricted than public life. This permits the term 'public sphere' to more comprehensively reflect the impact of forces and activities without access to political power under an authoritarian government.

The features and dynamics of the Islamic project and the Islamic sector endow the current study with more general importance. The project provides an insight into the relationship between the Islamic religious discourse and public policy, aspects seemingly irreconcilable. The sanctity and divine authority of religious discourse supply arguments for the legitimacy and temporal authority of Islamic forces within the public sphere. Although religious forces do not usually mutate into regular political parties nor dominate of the political system, their political clout is undeniable though difficult to measure.

Although this is a study of politics and the public profile of religious movements, it devotes much space to the analysis of religious discourse. It is felt that it is doctrinal discourse that negotiates the hierarchy of values and activist concepts in competition and comparison with other Islamic or religious groups and also with secular forms of social and political mobilization such as ethnic, regional, or national identity. Therefore, it is important to investigate the categories of Islamic discourse in their contemporary political context, particularly where they stake claim to public status, influence, or resources on the basis of religious doctrine. The divine attributes of religious discourse apparently sanctify the claims of Islamic activists in the eyes of their adherents and of the public at large. It is equally important to penetrate the nuanced meanings attached to political and religious categories by Islamic activists and their detractors.

These meanings reveal the programme and concept of public action of Islamic groups. This study attempts to help decode the claims to political and public status of religious activists from the Islamic sector in British India, and, by extension, in India and Pakistan today.

Much of Islamic activism conceived before independence continues to impact current activity in South Asia. The study highlights some of these connections. Also radical positions in South Asia are much based on continuity. It was before independence that radical Sunni groups started attacking views and practices as followed by Sufi-oriented folk Islam, the Shi'a on the Aḥmadīya. Radicalism is understood here as a reductionist approach that emphasizes selected and usually simplified principles pursued with extreme rigour and harshness. It does not automatically imply militancy or violence. The term 'sectarian radicalism' is used here to describe activities and views directed against religious dissenters. Although certain Sunni doctrines appeared central to the radicalism of some of these groups it is not implied that radicalism is inherent in Sunni beliefs or in Islam in general. Radicalism and militancy are understood to be a product of the ideological and political interpretation of religious doctrines, and not vice versa. Also the numbers and proportions should be kept in mind. While Islamic activism and radicalism appear prominent through the media, their adherents form a clear minority. The vast majority of South Asian Muslims follow contemplative and devotional practices of folk Islam in a local setting and show little inclination to engage in Islamic activism. At the same time, the latter cannot be discounted as insignificant. It often dominates the public perception of Islam.

Islamic activism emanating from South Asia has become a global factor. Many of the Islamic groups under study have branched out into other countries of the Islamic world and beyond. Some, such as the Tablīghī Jamā'at, have become truly global phenomena. This global dimension of the South Asian Islamic project amplifies its significance.

The usage of terms may occasionally clash with divergent local meanings. In South Asia, and in Pakistan more particularly, Sunni has come to denote followers of the Barelwi tradition (see Chapter 3, section 3.1.3), whereas here it is mainly reserved for general reference to Sunnite Islam (except where appearing in the name of Barelwi organizations). Today the Aḥmadīya sect is considered by most Sunni Muslims as outside orthodox Islam. Yet conservative Muslim leaders from the Nadwa, the association of religious scholars in India, Jam'īyat-e 'Ulamā-ye Hind (JUH), or the Muslim League considered the early Aḥmadī leaders still part of the Islamic tradition and called them a Muslim sect, despite their doctrinal differences. They will be treated as such in this study too. Islamic reformism will refer to movements following the tradition of *iṣlāḥ* as it evolved in Egypt at the end of the nineteenth century. Both terms will also be used as analytical categories. Since they relate religious demands to social change, they are preferred here over terms such as scripturalism, traditionalism, or fundamentalism. The latter often privilege the Western perspective, in their usage. Islamic reformism should not be confused with reformism of the modernist, Western variety, as contemporaries used the term reformist for 'modernists' such as Sayyid Ahmad Khan.

The primary source material has been drawn mainly from the archives of the India Office (the ministry charged with conducting Britain's relations with colonial India), now in the British Library's Oriental Collections (BLOC). The National Archive of India (NAI), the Uttar Pradesh State Archive (UPSA), the provincial archives of Pakistan and its federal National Documentation Centre (NDC) have collected comparable files. Files located at the Nehru Memorial Museum and Library (NMML) have also been consulted.[3] While documenting the aspirations of national forces, much archival material also reflected the apprehensions of the colonial administration. The authorities viewed Islamic activism primarily as a threat to 'public order'. They often classified such activity as 'pan-Islamism'. The British took great pains in tracing specific movements considered potentially 'disruptive'. Specific references are available on the Aḥrār,[4] Khāksār,[5] the Aḥmadīya,[6] the Ahl-i Ḥadīth[7] movements, the Shi'a conference,[8] the 'Silk letter conspiracy' of 1916,[9] the agitation for migration (*hijrat*) from northwest India to Afghanistan in 1920,[10] the *Moplah* uprising,[11] the Muslim volunteer movement,[12] and the Khilafat agitation.[13] In addition, the British administration produced running series of sources through its regular reports on local newspapers, on the internal political situation,[14] and on intelligence.[15] Colonial sources were accused of political bias and distortion of facts. Yet, the serial character of continuous sources mitigated such bias by limiting at least factual manipulation. Although

[3]They will be quoted here by their respective shelf numbers, preceded by the designation of their place of storage.

[4]NDC L/I/1/628, NAI Poll(I) 41–3/11, BLOC L/P&J/7/751.

[5]E.g., files no. NDC L/I/1/628–29, NDC 230; partly published in Muẓẓatar 1985.

[6]BLOC L/P&J/7/751, BLOC L/P&J/6/2002.

[7]On their connection with *mujāhidīn* colonies of the 'Hindustani fanatics' on the northwest frontier, see BLOC L/P&S/11/111.

[8]BLOC L/P&J/8/693. [9]BLOC L/P&S/10/633. [10]NDC 242, 268, BLOC L/P&J/6/1701. [11]BLOC L/P&J/6/1782. [12]BLOC L/P&J/6/1731.

[13]BLOC L/P&S/10/795–8, BLOC L/P&S/10/895, BLOC L/P&S/11/119, BLOC P/CONF/51, BLOC L/P&J/6/1696–97. [14]BLOC L/P&J/12/685–751.

[15]This series is known as the (Fortnightly) Intelligence Diaries or Reports, located, for instance, in the file groups of BLOC L/P&S/, sub-groups 7, 10, and 12.

the interests of the colonial administration dominated such reporting, liberal British traditions of government and administration allowed for the inclusion of original, unedited statements and material reflecting critical views. Descriptive and autobiographical publications by activists and followers were used to countercheck and balance reports from the files. The religious movements produced a significant amount of literature in Urdu at the time of their formation, and still do. These publications contain primary source material in the form of biographical data and descriptive material about the formative phase of the movements, which has been little used so far in West. The *Indian Annual Register* has also been helpful in documenting political and public activity by parties and organizations.[16] The same applies to local newspapers such as *Dawn*. Archival holdings of newspapers in Urdu are patchy and have been consulted mostly through the administration's native press reports.[17] The British-Indian population censuses, held at ten-year intervals, also give details about Islamic groups when the latter took on a sectarian character, as did the Aḥmadīya and the Ahl-i Ḥadīth. Although the ethnographic and statistical data thus gained have to be interpreted critically, they provide valuable insight.

Proposing a comparative approach, this study seeks to fill a gap in the research literature. It seeks to provide a political perspective on religious groups in South Asian Islam for the period immediately preceding independence.[18] The classic studies on South Asian Islam by M. Mujeeb (1967), Peter Hardy (1972), Annemarie Schimmel (1980), Barbara Metcalf (1982), and Mushirul Hasan (1985) have now become dated. Accounts written from a religious perspective such as Quddus (1989) and I. Qureshi (1974) tended to be ideologically tilted. The treatment of political and secular issues in South Asian Islam was often limited to the Pakistan movement and the issues of adequate representation for Indian Muslims versus the Hindu majority population (Shaikh 1989; Lelyveld 1978). Minault (1982) covered the Indian Khilafat Movement in support of the Ottoman–Turkish Caliphate (1918–24) mainly in the context of the nationalist and anti-colonial movement and not so much for its own political potential and consequences, whereas Qureshi (1999) concentrated

[16]For this study, the reprint of 1988 has been used (Mitra and Mitra 1988). The internal structure of the annual volumes had been somewhat irregular. They will be quoted here as *IAR* + year of initial publication/no. of part, that is, *IAR* 1920/I, etc.

[17]Such collections exist province-wise as for the United Provinces, for instance, under BLOC L/R/5/95ff.

[18]The related study by Peter van der Veer on religious nationalism (1994) treated the subject in a more general context with less focus on Islam, dealing more with prototypes and concepts than with individual movements.

on its pan-Islamic aspect. Social factors were uppermost in the mind of W. C. Smith. His well-known 1947 study on movements of Indian Islam grouped Islamic movements according to their vision of society (in favour of British culture, of Islamic culture, of a new culture of the future), and to their socio-political characteristics (progressive/reactionary) (Smith 1985). Though the study was ground-breaking at the time, the pattern of analysis was rather schematic. Later publications were more detailed and accurate in their assessments of these movements. While, for instance, Smith's harping on the 'reactionary' aspects of the thinking of Muhammad Iqbal (1877–1938) seemed overdone, his judgement of the Aḥrār was unduly optimistic (Smith 1985: 155–80, 270–75). Two more recent analytical Urdu publications are worth mentioning in this context. Iqtidar Muhammad Khan who graduated from Aligarh University gave a balanced, if partly superficial account of major Islamic movements, concentrating on the post-1947 period of independence (1995). H. B. Khan discussed the role of the Islamic religious scholars ('ulamā') in politics and in religion during the Pakistan movement (1995), representing a detailed historical study although limited in scope and reference.

Representatives of the Cambridge school of Indian history analysed Islamic movements often in regional settings (Brass 1974; Robinson 1974). Valuable additions to the regional approach were made by Tazeen Murshid's work on the Islamic discourse in Bengal (1995) and by Jamal Malik's comprehensive study of the Islamic academic culture of Lucknow in north India, and of the Nadwa madrasa, in particular (1997). While Malik opened up a wealth of source material, his interpretation could be challenged. He viewed the Nadwa madrasa largely as an agent for integrating the local intellectual Muslim élite from the traditional Muslim urban quarters, the *qaṣba*, into a 'colonial sector,' a 'colonial public sphere' (Malik 1997: 520; see also Malik 1989, 1996). Here he followed Reinhard Schulze's analysis of pan-Islamic tendencies in the early twentieth century (1990; for the elaboration of the 'colonial sector' thesis, see also Schulze 1985). Islamization and reformist Islam were depicted as responses of Muslim urban colonial society to colonial modernization. They were regarded as means to reach into sectors of society hitherto untouched by modernity and colonial rule. This approach did not differentiate between colonial domination and capitalist modernization. It effectively turned reformist Islam into an agent of colonial rule, an assessment fraught with serious misunderstanding. It could not account for the abiding anti-colonial political impulses of reformist Islam. It also neglected the early and pre-colonial trends of reformist Islam in the fifteenth to eighteenth centuries, which responded to a variety of perceived threats not necessarily colonial in nature. This approach became even more problematic when applied to developments after independence, as Malik did in his study of 'traditional' Islamic institutions in Pakistan (1996). Thus all modern developments in these countries were tarnished by their contrived descent from former colonial domination. Such a paradigm denied that independent development for the former colonial countries was possible. For the purpose of this study, the term 'colonial society' is reserved for the colonial period only. The 'colonial sector' is understood here to encompass only social and political strata and structures directly related to the exercise of colonial control and domination.

Major case studies were published on the Deobandis (Metcalf 1982), the Barelwis (Sanyal 1996a), the Nadwa (Malik 1997), the Aḥmadīya (Friedmann 1989), the Tablīghīs (Haq 1972; Masud 2000; Sikand 2002), and the Khāksār (Malik 2000; Seth 1985). For the Aligarh Movement, Christian Troll (1978) exemplarily discussed the religious concept of its founder, Sayyid Ahmad Khan (1817–98). Some of these were only initial forays into their subject (Haq 1972; Seth 1985). Others focused on the religious nature of the subject and took little account of the public and political relevance of Islamic activities. Still others concentrated on the nineteenth century and did not extend far into the period covered here (Malik 1997; Metcalf 1982; Sanyal 1996a).

This book has benefited from discussions with colleagues at the Centre for Modern Oriental Studies, Berlin, notably Albrecht Hofheinz and Lutz Rogler, and from a number of reviews and commentaries by Werner Ende, Margrit Pernau, Georg Pfeffer, Martin Riexinger, Dietmar Rothermund, and Aslam Syed. Kishwar Mustafa and Shahid Riaz checked the Urdu translations and Gareth Prosser proof-read parts of the draft for English usage. Special thanks go also to Mujeeb Ahmad from the History Department of Punjab University in Lahore, Pakistan, for references on the Barelwi movement. While their input was very welcome, responsibility for any errors rests entirely with me.

Vernacular terms are generally explained at their first appearance (where they are printed in *italics*) and in the glossary. Where it is not mentioned otherwise, general terms of Islam are given in Arabic transcription. Vernacular terms relating to the South Asian context are based on Urdu, the predominant language of the Indian Muslim discourse. For bibliographic references, transcription has been applied throughout to authors and titles of publications in Urdu or Arabic. Diacritics have only been used for technical terms on first occurrence. More common terms have been transcribed according to the English-language convention. Urdu transliteration is based on John T. Platts' *Dictionary of Urdū, Classical Hindī and English* (1884). Original texts in the Urdu vernacular have been translated by me, except where indicated otherwise. Preference is given to contextual clarity over literalism. Where this may create uncertainty the original term has been added in brackets. Parts with no more than an ornamental function have been omitted where indicated.

1 The Concept of the Public Sphere and its Evolution

1.1. THE DISCOURSE ON THE PUBLIC SPHERE AND ITS CRITIQUE

The meaning of the public sphere has varied greatly in history. The term is loaded with diverse and sometimes conflicting subtext. This study intends to review only the realm of public debate, mobilization, and participation in decision-making. This involves discourses as much as institution-building and the various means of 'going public', that is, the creation and use of public forums and media, where printing holds special significance. Derived meanings such as public buildings and public sector are not considered here.

In current political theory, the public sphere has come to be viewed as a social and political category largely through interventions by the German philosopher Jürgen Habermas. His main work, *The Structural Transformation of the Public Sphere*, published in 1962, discussed the evolution of the bourgeois public sphere in its classical form and its transformation under the influence of structural change in society (Habermas 1990). The belated (1989) translation into English helped shape discourse on the public sphere in English-language research (Habermas 1998). On the occasion of the English translation and stimulated by the political sea change in Eastern Europe in 1989–90, Habermas revisited the subject in a commentary for the East German (GDR) edition of his work in 1990 (quoted here after the English translation, Habermas 1992). He focused on the origination of the public sphere in the private realm. He saw it embodied in private citizens deliberating on issues of public concern. Habermas maintained that

> ...the bourgeois public sphere may be conceived above all as the sphere of private people come together as a public; they soon claimed the public sphere regulated from above against the public authorities themselves, to engage them in a debate over the general rules governing relations in the basically privatised but publicly relevant sphere of commodity exchange and social labour. The medium of this

political confrontation was peculiar and without historical precedent: people's public use of their reason (*öffentliches Räsonnement*) (Habermas 1998: 27; for the German original, see Habermas 1990: 86)

Yet his usage of the term was far from clear-cut, a fact belatedly recognized by Habermas himself (Calhoun 1992: 462–3). A major ambiguity resulted from the concurrent normative and descriptive usage of the concept. His normative intent was to focus on the importance of enlightened and proactive public critique, which linked his understanding of the public sphere with the fundamental project of enlightenment and reason. Habermas assumed that the institution of the public sphere stood for a given set of normative principles. These reflected a liberal and critical evaluation of public concerns and potentially egalitarian access to such discourse by private citizens and public bodies. It was characterized by autonomy from both private concerns and the structures of political and economic power.

The descriptive aspect was reflected in his portrayal of the different dimensions which the public sphere comprised: (i) a reasoned critical discourse on public affairs, (ii) the reasoning section of the public conducting this discourse, and (iii) a 'network of public communication', embodied in the 'associational life' (Habermas 1992: 423) of bourgeois society.

Another ambiguity resulted from the uneven character of the two parts of his analysis, his idealized description of the emergence of a classical public sphere in the eighteenth to the nineteenth centuries and its degeneration towards the beginning of the twentieth century. While it is the former that survived as a model concept, Habermas was more interested in the latter. He hoped to provoke efforts to rescue the progressive potential of public communication through revitalizing democratic institutions and deliberative politics. He wanted to re-establish public control over political bureaucracies and forge a new consensus about the purpose of politics and its rationalization (1998: 233–5). Therefore, any application of his thought has to consider that his intent was not to create a new concept but to write a critique of political and ideological trends in society. Also his historical analysis, which he undertook when describing the emerging classical public sphere, was considered one-sided and partly defective.[1]

[1]In an extension of the Habermasian analysis James van Horn Melton has gone into the details of the rise of the public in Enlightenment Europe, adducing much broader historical material than Habermas was able to do. There he also consciously included areas disregarded by Habermas such as women and the family, drinking in public, that is, taverns and coffee houses, and the religious pursuit of freemasonry as a nascent expression of civil society (2001: 195ff.).

Various philosophers and political scientists have since critically reviewed these ambiguities.[2] Yet despite its defects, Habermas' approach proved remarkably resilient. It provided a framework for various dimensions of ideological, social, and political change in society. Its great asset was the integrative function of discourse analysis. This explained the remarkable revival of the concept after the sea changes in global politics in 1989–90, both for current analysis and for historical research. The public sphere concept provided a set of tools to model multi-factor change. These tools included a quantitative and qualitative assessment of non-formal political and social actors, of their discourses, their interaction, and their impact. However, the application of the concept has inevitably moved away from the originator's intentions, especially as regards his pessimism over the degeneration of the public sphere and his rather selective and sometimes élitist view of its composition.

Critics argued that public institutions did not automatically lose their potential for egalitarian participation and critical discourse as feared by Habermas and the philosophers of the Frankfurt school. Several authors conceptualized means for a renewal of deliberative politics and democratic action in the West.[3] Habermas (1992) has acknowledged a remaining kernel of emancipatory potential for these institutions.

Habermas also seemed to restrict participation in the public sphere to a bourgeois, middle class, literate, male circle of individuals. Social and political analysis using the public sphere model turned subsequently to those sections of the public previously neglected. This research received much stimulation from Michel Foucault (1926–84) who exposed internal power relationships in seemingly homogenous categories of modernity. Foucault saw power as oppressive. It could prevent or limit participation and self-articulation in public discourse.[4] Although initially somewhat wary of Foucault's research, Habermas eventually acknowledged the

[2]For a recent review of critical research in German, see Heming (1997), and for a review of the term *Öffentlichkeit* (public sphere) and its related concept, including an extensive bibliography, see Hohendahl (2000), also see Michael Hog's dissertation (1990); for the English-language debate, Calhoun's conference volume still remains largely representative (1992). For a more general critical debate of political theory in this connection, see Bauman (1999).

[3]Proceeding from the Habermasian concept of the public sphere, several German-language authors have been reviewing recently the potential for democratic action and deliberative politics either through the established institutions of the political system (Lang 2001), or through other forms of participation such as 'direct democracy' (Scheyli 2000); for the English-language literature, on this aspect, see Clark (2000) and for the evolution of the public and private domains, see Edgell (1995).

[4]Cf. especially Foucault (1970, 1972). For a perceptive discussion of Foucault's analytical perspective, see Bublitz et al. (1999), in particular Lorey (1999).

connection in his 1990 essay (1992: 425). There he also accepted that more than one public may have gone into the constitution of the public sphere in the very beginning. In the process, competing public spheres may have come into existence. Since then a multitude of 'publics' has come into focus. The disadvantaged have been characterized as 'insurgent publics' (cf. Boyle 1992; Ryan 1992; Eley 1992), which refers to those striving to get a say in the public sphere hitherto denied them. Women's movements, racial and cultural minorities, and the 'lower' classes have been treated as insurgent publics since. Participation in the public sphere is now recognized as a value in itself. This has proved crucial for evaluating the public activism of Islamic groups and Muslims in a world dominated by Western capitalism, and in the local context of countries emerging from Western colonial rule or dependence.

Another key area of disagreement was the question of what constituted the public sphere. As an institution Habermas saw it mediating between the private interests and public, or state power. Yet he conceded that state affairs could not be fully excluded from the public sphere as they were increasingly conducted in public by the bourgeois state, in contrast to feudal and aristocratic tradition (Habermas 1998: 27). It is now generally agreed that the public sphere should be understood to be a more inclusive concept encompassing all but the very secretive affairs of the state and economy at one end, and the intimate affairs of individual and family, at the other. This definition emphasizes the publicness of the public sphere, unrestricted access to it, and the potential of all citizens to participate. Here, the concept of the public sphere connects to the 'open society' approach as developed by Karl Popper (1945). Keeping participation open, affairs public and transparent, is of strong and lasting normative significance. It holds out an enduring promise of democracy. Insisting on the publicness of the public sphere is a powerful corrective to competing reclusive and potentially destructive discourses. It has abiding significance also for the evaluation of Islamic discourses. Their capacity to accept internal and external dissent and mediate divisions is a potent measure for their integration into a democratic society. Keeping discourses public, open, and transparent brings insurgent actors and debates to confront their critics, a process often resulting in mediation and compromise. In the end, insurgent publics benefit as they learn to hold their own. Considering the public functions of government and economy as elements of the public sphere makes sense from several angles. Their involvement did not automatically undermine the autonomy of public discourse. Public state-sponsored activity and private-financed public engagement (endowments, etc.) have played a large role in providing an outlet for 'insurgent' publics, for alternative discourses, and for emancipatory activities supporting the causes of marginalized or underrepresented sections of society. This holds true particularly for Islamic countries.

The public sphere is also linked to another important concept, 'legitimation'. Critical public discourse is a process of 'procurement and withdrawal of legitimation' for public and political action (Habermas 1992: 452). For Habermas again, as with the 'public sphere', this category degenerated through modern and post-modern developments where true legitimation eroded or became manufactured. Post-Cold War developments belie such general pessimism, though for some developments the criticism remains valid. The end of the existential threat of the Cold War era removed its related overarching pseudo-legitimation for political systems and governments around the world. Now voters and the public relate the legitimacy of their governments much more directly to the results of government activity, whether it contributes to improving their lot or makes it more miserable. Through public exposure insurgent discourses also seek to establish their legitimacy towards their own participants and towards other discourses.

Because of its perceived autonomy from the state and private life, the public sphere concept at times appeared to be close to the 'civil society' approach.[5] While Habermas focused on critical public debate, civil society came to describe the associational life of society, its extent and intensity creating a so-called buffer zone between state and economic power on one side, and the individual on the other.[6] Today they are used to offer different perspectives on public life. Where the public sphere concept emphasizes the publicness of debate and activity, civil society looks at the level and quality of self-organization.[7]

For Habermas, many of the qualifications and limitations he introduced were meant to focus on the public sphere as an arena for qualified public opinion. Its critical thrust constituted its normative and universalist value. If participation was thrown open and its subject was interpreted broadly it was feared that the concept would be watered down and might lose its analytical value. Subsequent developments proved, however, that such

[5]The English-language edition of Habermas' work used the term 'civil society' for '*bürgerliche Gesellschaft*' where Habermas described it as the genuine domain of private autonomy that stood opposed to the state (1998: XVII, 12).

[6]Habermas also followed up on these aspects through his differentiation between the systemic worlds of power and market on one side, and the lifeworld on the other, in his *Theory of Communicative Action* (1984/87). Hohendahl discussed how this work fed back into the revival of the civil society approach after the Cold War (2000: 116). See also Heming's review of the connection between the public sphere approach and that of civil society (1997: 231ff.).

[7]For an extensive discussion of the civil society concept in relation to the Middle East, see Norton (1995).

fears were unfounded. Opening up participation did not save insurgent discourses from critical inquiries. They had to address issues they previously neglected. They faced public pressure to contribute to the improvement of social and political life, to rectify what dominant actors in the public sphere (that is, politicians) had failed to do. The public sphere turned into a maturing ground where insurgent public actors were bound to come 'of age' if they participated long enough. New social movements like the 'Greens' were a case in point. This may also apply to Islamic groups if they succeed in keeping their discourses public and transparent. Even where difficulties persist in adapting to the requirements of openness, as is the case with many radicalized Islamic groups, it is important to hold out this promise of integration into society.

This leads us to the dynamics of political mobilization. Insurgent forces may establish themselves as major actors in the public sphere if they win the endorsement of the public at large. If they fail to do so they may still derive major benefits from participation in public discourse. They use it to establish and train new élites who move out of their sub-discourse to take centre stage in conventional politics. The appointment of black members in the cabinet of the George W. Bush administration in America with its conservative agenda is an obvious example. This study will show that this holds equally true for Islamic groups.

As far as Habermas' fear that critical public discourse over time becomes ineffective and fragmented was concerned, it materialized in ways different from those imagined by him. Public critique was still possible but was less focused, less homogeneous, and took different forms. The debate was increasingly over terms of inclusion in or exclusion from the public sphere. In particular, the agenda for public critique differed in industrial societies and in the developing world. Where the former looked for ways and means to democratize the bureaucracies of the state and the economy, to involve the individual citizen and the public again in the conduct of their affairs, the latter concentrated on the composition of and unqualified access to the public sphere. This was particularly true for Islamic countries where Islamists pushed for an agenda of inclusion, yet on their own, restrictive terms. Openness and transparency were sometimes compromised in facilitating the integration of Islamist forces. This may yet have a lasting effect on the very existence of the public sphere in those countries.

A major weakness in Habermas' analysis was that he had completely ignored developments in the 'East', that is, Asia and Africa. Authors discussing this lacuna in his work criticized the single attachment of his normative approach to the Western value system. They saw it as part of the Western modernizing drive to shape the world in the image of the West. At the same time, they appreciated the heightened role of the public sphere as a significant symbol and location of public identity. Instead of one single public sphere, they emphasized that a number of public arenas existed in which political and cultural identities were negotiated. This multitude of public arenas needed to be recognized without normative prejudice as to their linkage with established forms of liberal public values and practices such as reasoning, printing, and so on. It is those forms of public activity that were often made the (Western) parameters of penetration of non-Western societies by the superior notions of enlightenment and reason. Post-modernist and post-orientalist critics also attacked the singular attachment of Habermas' argument to language. Such preference rated highly all forms of public expression emanating from a literate society. In many postcolonial Asian and African countries this was still a small élite. Given generally low levels of literacy in South Asia, this approach excluded large numbers, even a majority, from constituting a reasoning public. Appadurai and Breckenridge demanded the recognition of other forms of public expression such as body representations like arts, dance, behavioural patterns, and the mass media. The Frankfurt school generally disdained mass culture and mass politics as a process of manipulation and (blind) consumption betraying modern patterns of exploitation. Appadurai and Breckenridge argued that the public in Asia and Africa (and perhaps also in the West) should be seen not only as consumer but also as agent in all these activities, expressing itself often consciously by its predilection for certain types of public activity. Reasoning took place not only through words but also through involvement in varied mass media activities (Appadurai and Breckenridge 1995: 2–3).

Despite such criticism many scholars adopted the concept of the public sphere for analysis of conditions in Asia and Africa. Some measured their modernity[8] by the maturity of the public sphere and the emergence of civil society institutions.[9] They discussed how the cultural background influenced newly emergent élites and the quest for political power (cf.

[8]Modernity is a hotly contested term. It will be taken here to signify major epochal changes in several related fields that were initiated in the seventeenth to the nineteenth centuries with the emergence of industrial, capitalist societies, a social shift to the bourgeoisie and social middle classes, a philosophical discourse veering towards a rational-scientific world-view, and a political system emphasizing individual responsibility and representative democracy. The concomitant critique of modernity assumes there are different ways to approach the construction of a new society and polity, what Eisenstadt called divergent 'cultural programmes of modernity' (2000: 182). See also Talal Asad in his interview on modernity and tradition, which he did not regard as clear-cut stages in human social development but as long-term 'dimensions of social life' (1996).

[9]Cf. Salvatore (1997). John Esposito appropriated the term 'civil society' for the 'quiet social and political revolution' taking place in the Muslim world with the emergence of a multitude of associations in the Muslim world of the 1980s (2000: 8).

Sinha 1995). Others employed the concept of the public sphere to profile conditions in a particular country formerly dominated by a colonial power or dependent on the West (Alatas 1994; Halbach 1991; Hegasy 1997; Milner 1994; Mulder 1994; Strand 1990). They focused on efforts to gain control of the public sphere and to recapture public life, the modern forms of which were often introduced from the West. Conflicts and problems emerging from this struggle were highlighted. Lately, a number of British dissertations have applied the concept of the public sphere to colonial, South Asian, and religious history with renewed vigour (Naregal 2001; Orsini 2002; Peycam 1999; Trainor 1997).[10] It appears that the objective of entering and controlling the public sphere has turned into an emancipatory and participatory political project with a latently anti-Western dimension. While Habermas' emphasis was squarely on debate and discourse, their concern has been with the whole range of public activity and articulation. It includes the emergence of the modern communicative public sphere as a self-organizing realm in which public and political concerns were articulated. Political concerns are understood to pertain to various aspects of power and control, to the polity and the state. Public concerns articulated in this process relate to the functioning of society, including participatory aspects, living conditions, and economic prospects. In many colonial and post-colonial settings, democracy and elections are yet to be introduced on a wide scale. Religious groups and reform movements have grown into a rapidly increasing and legitimate segment of the public sphere.

It was in this context that Sandria Freitag undertook to redefine the concept of the public sphere through the term 'public arenas' (1990: 182ff.). She fully shared the critique of the limitations introduced by Habermas on the public sphere and wished it not to be restricted. In her case studies of the contestation of Muslim identity in India she highlighted the local and public nature of the process. Her emphasis was on the collective public ritual as a way of constituting and capturing public arenas.[11] When reformist Islam attempted to define public and personal

[10]In association with the International Institute of Asian Studies (IIAS) at Leiden, Mahmoud Alinejad has conducted research on 'Religion, Nationality and the Public Sphere: The Question of Reform in Iran', discussing the expanding public sphere under the influence of the policies and vision of the reformist president Khatami. There he takes a line similar to the works mentioned (IIAS Newsletter, Leiden, No. 25, July 2001).

[11]Freitag continues to inspire attempts to link the concept of the public sphere to research on South Asia. That this can be problematic becomes clear from the volume edited by Yandell and Paul (2000). The papers reveal a superficial understanding of the category. They show confusion over the meaning of the public where different connotations converge.

practice it spawned the evolution of public structures and communication. Indian Muslims submitted to these in varying degrees. At the same time, they were increasingly exposed to public definitions of Islam. Earlier, Muslim rulers had provided the public setting for such definitions. After the advent of colonial power, reformist Islam established its own public discourse drawing on the Qur'an and the Prophetic tradition, the *ḥadīth*, to provide a model of personal behaviour, which was meant to substitute for the institutions and structures previously provided by the state (Freitag 1988: 117–18). According to Appadurai and Breckenridge, the focus on 'public arenas' allowed for consideration of a multitude of factors, which could be weighted more evenly, and could avoid the more unilinear approach of a Western-dominated public sphere concept (1995: 4). It is argued here that one does not preclude the other. The imagining of 'public arenas' may be a valid and welcome addition, particularly when it brings in local factors and reflects the fragmentation of public life, geographically, socially, and culturally. Yet, there is no reason why a multitude of public arenas should not feed into a larger public sphere. This helps emphasize the interrelations of public life both in its more traditional and its modern forms, be it through pilgrimages, schools of thought, imperial administration, legal proceedings—religious and secular—or through emerging parties, reform movements, educational societies, and the like. The public sphere need not be imagined as homogenous and uniform. It may be rife with contradictions, cleavages, and segmentation while still expressing a common desire to gain control over various resources. At the same time, Appadurai is probably right that public activity in the aforementioned sense is not merely a derivative of capitalist development. Paraphrasing Chris Bayly's discussion of the production of knowledge and the 'informational order' in South Asia, public activity is itself a 'social formation', relatively independent and autonomous, and cannot be reduced to 'epiphenomena of late industrial capitalism or the state'.[12]

The nexus between public activity and the generation and diffusion of knowledge is of wider significance. For religious movements, the transmission and reproduction of sacred knowledge was an act of public engagement. Belief ceased to be a private matter between the individual and god when it came to reproducing and transmitting knowledge about God and His message.[13] It was, therefore, no coincidence that religious

[12]C. A. Bayly applied this assessment to the generation of knowledge (1996: 281). The close connection between public activity and knowledge is discussed later.

[13]The way Habermas bracketed religious belief and religious activity with the family and the personal, intimate sphere, has been criticized, among others, by Calhoun (1992: 43, fn. 16) and Salvatore (1997: 26).

seminaries and educational societies played a central role in the public activities of religious groups, including those studied here. Recently, the transmission of knowledge in religious traditions and the Islamic world has received increased attention. Nigel Crook published *The Transmission of Knowledge in South Asia* in 1996, dealing, among others, extensively with religious traditions. Francis Robinson compared religious education in the three Muslim empires of the (Turkish) Ottomans, the (Persian) Safavids, and the (Indian) Moghuls (2001: 211ff.). Michael Kemper conducted a group project for Ph.D. research students at Bochum University, Germany (financed by the Volkswagen Foundation) which studied the Islamic networks of education in the local and transnational context (2000).

Contrary to Habermas' understanding, the public sphere for the purpose of this study will also include official, that is, state-related activity where it was not part of executive government action. Under authoritarian colonial government, much of public life was entangled with the state. While Habermas saw such mutual penetration as a hindrance for the unfolding of public opinion, this could not be unreservedly applied to colonial India. Although the British-Indian colonial administration usually attempted to use its leverage over the public sphere to stifle dissent, it was often hampered by the norms of liberal governance. The grants handed out to educational institutions rarely gave it the degree of control it sought. One could even argue that much anti-colonial opposition would not have come into existence without the opportunities provided by government employment or by state grants to public institutions. The public sphere for the purpose of this inquiry will, therefore, exclude by definition only explicitly 'official' forms of organization, those tied to the executive or administrative side of government where its agents, Indian or British, had an ex-officio duty to speak on behalf of the British government in India. Even there, nominated members of the Viceroy's council carefully distinguished between official duties and their public persona as representatives of public opinion. For instance, Zafarullah Khan was a member of the viceroy's executive council in the 1930s, but at other times spoke for the Ahmadīya community and participated in Muslim League activities (cf. Zafarullah Khan 1991).

From the various interventions a more differentiated and complex concept of the public sphere emerges. In sum, public sphere will be understood here both as a normative concept and as a descriptive research tool. While the former emphasizes its critical potential and autonomy, the latter points to the interplay of discourse, institution-building, and activism creating public space for the formation, contestation, and implementation of desired values. Participation and publicness emerge as key values in the functioning of the public sphere. They highlight its emancipatory potential. Terms and extent of participation have not only functional significance, they also reflect critical debate on the participation of 'insurgent publics'. They represent groups so far restricted in their access to public discourse and life. Islamic groups in general and in colonial India in particular can be seen to represent such 'insurgent publics'. Publicness indicates that all those who participate in the public sphere accept a level of public scrutiny, transparency, and public interaction.

The application of the concept will help decode the behaviour of Islamic groups. Their mutual rivalries and contestations are difficult to understand unless seen against the goal of entering and capturing the public sphere. Given their doctrinal differences, the substantial convergence of their demands remains perplexing unless the common goals of an Islamic society and state, and the pressures of public presentation from competing non-Islamic actors are considered.

1.2. THE PUBLIC SPHERE AND ISLAM

From the point of view of political theory, it is important to emphasize that there is no single interpretation of the relationship between Islam and politics (cf. Asad 1993). Instead, a multitude of factors has shaped this relationship. Related discourse particularly intensified during the Islamic renaissance in the eighteenth century and has remained highly active through the 1980s and 1990s.

The strong political relevance of Islam is often related to the fact that its founder, Muhammad, not only revealed a religion but also created the first Islamic state. Where Christianity in its formative phase was an insurgent movement, Islam's clear political goals were articulated early through the Islamic polity. It brought into existence an administration based on Islamic principles. The regulatory and administrative functions of the Muhammadan state gave it a secular dimension, generating activities not exclusively related to faith or religious worship. The Muhammadan state went about conquering territories in the name of Islam.

Islamic authors generally deduced the normative relationship between Islam and state, *dīn* and *daulat*, from the recognized sources of Islam.[14] As sources of religious knowledge, most schools of Islam recognized the Qur'an and the traditions narrating the behaviour of the Prophet Muhammad and his associates, the ḥadīth. Of these, only the Qur'an

[14]The overriding relevance of religious doctrine and text, both for Islam and Christianity, was disputed by authors such as Talal Asad who emphasized that religious representation is intimately linked to political and social life. From this perspective the relationship of religion and state appears to be mainly a product of history (Asad 1993: 53).

and a part of the traditions, which supposedly express the will of God, were considered divine. The traditions were derived from the Sunna, the life and conduct of Muhammad and the early Islamic community.[15] The Qur'anic principles were often subjected to interpretation. Many were formulated in allegorical verse. The overriding principle to which most Islamists have recourse is the comprehensive nature of Islam as a religion to regulate the whole of life. It is generally asserted that—unlike other faiths, notably Christianity—Islam was not just a religion but also a way of life not condoning distinction between the sacral and the secular, and also between the public and the private. All forms of public expression had to be consonant with Islam. Sovereignty was delegated from God and did not belong to human beings who administer this sovereignty in His trust. All public articulations in society would, therefore, have to be measured against God's will.

A closer look at the Qur'an and the early Islamic state, however, quickly reveals that such monolithic understanding of politics in Islam was far removed from reality. The Qur'an itself reflected awareness of a society that was ethnically, culturally, religiously, and socially diverse. Several verses ruled relationships with non-Islamic religious traditions. While some pointed to the exclusive status Islam was accorded in society, others demanded tolerance and forbearance. The diversity of the early Islamic community was reflected in the Covenant of Medina, essentially a treaty between various Muslim groups of different tribal origin and Jewish groups (Hamidullah 1968; for the text see also Watt 1968: 130ff.).

A key question was the extent to which historical Islamic dynasties governed according to Qur'anic principles. Islamic specialists of religious and juridical knowledge (the 'ulamā') usually posed as guardians of the right faith. Especially in the Sunni tradition, it was claimed that at least the first four Caliphs embodied the correct tradition of the Qur'an, representing a 'Golden Age' of Islam. These claims have been disputed as Islamic rulers have often been guided by secular considerations of power, wealth, and military might, neglecting the 'ulamā'.

The relationship between normative Islam and the political sphere has, therefore, often been strained. A new phase began with Western

[15]Regarding the traditions, not all Islamic scholars regard Sunna and ḥadīth as separate sources of Islamic knowledge. The latter are believed to have been derived from the former by putting them in writing. Yet some Islamic groups, particularly in South Asia, continue making this distinction. Also the glossary entries as given in the *Encyclopaedia of Islam* do not suggest that the two terms are identical. For the ḥadīth it emphasizes the 'account of what the Prophet said or did, or of his tacit approval'. The definition of Sunna highlights the 'normative custom of the Prophet or of the early community, orthodoxy' (J. Robson '*Ḥadīth*', in EI/III: 23–8; G. H. A. Juynboll and D. W. Brown, 'Sunna', in EI/IX: 878–81).

domination over large parts of the Islamic world. Local Islamic religious élites raised the battle cry that Islam was in danger. They feared that Western penetration would challenge Islamic traditions of law and administration and that colonial rule would aid Christianity in converting the local population. While the colonial encounter proved a watershed, it was only one of several factors eroding the positions of religious élites. Other factors included economic activity, commercial exchange, and the dissipation of established forms of political authority where Muslim rulers and their administrations were undermined by internecine conflict.

The resurgence of the Islamic discourse in the eighteenth and nineteenth centuries aimed at improving this state of affairs. It sought to strengthen and reform religious education and to restore the influence of normative Islam in the legal and political system (cf. Levtzion and Voll 1987; Schulze 1990). Among Islamic élites, it was often those educated in Western institutions who participated in local public discourse on the state of politics, society, and religion. They did so through the very instruments of public expression created or strengthened by Western colonial powers: printing, public education, and public associations.

Modern Islamic discourse was dominated by categories developed by reformist Islam. Some of their interpretations went back to disputes in early and medieval Islam, although their meaning and context had often changed. However, the emergence of an Islamic public sphere cannot be explained exclusively by reformist categories and a literalist approach to written sources. A substantial part of it was equally guided by Sufi-inspired folk Islam and orally transmitted Islamic practice, often specific to a particular locality.[16] For groups following such practice analysis will often have to rely on public discourse and activity as recorded by others. Some movements, however, took a middle road. From those considered here, the Barelwis, the Firangī Maḥallīs, and the Tablīghīs were influenced by mystical traditions, but also embraced normative reformism and generated a considerable amount of discursive tracts and source material. They have impregnated folk Islam with a reformist idiom and made popular religious practices subject to rules of Islamic law and conduct (*sharīʿa*).

[16]Sufi practices and normative Islam are by no means mutually exclusive. Some forms of mystical Islam, such as orders and movements descended from the Naqshbandiyya, strive to reconcile their mystical devotion with normative Islam, in particular with the *sharīʿa* (cf. Gaborieau's work on Sayyid Ahmad Bareilly, the Naqshbandi Shaykh and co-founder of Indian reformism [2000]). Also some reformist movements of normative Islam, such as the Tablīghī Jamāʿat, tend to look for popular forms of dissemination. Yet, in terms of public representation and from an anthropological perspective, the universe of various styles of lived or folk Islam, especially in South Asia, is largely derived from mystical practices and beliefs. See here the work of Katherine Ewing (1983, 1988).

Such diversity has implications for the meaning of 'public discourse' and 'dissent' in Islam. Western interpretations of the public sphere rely for its functioning on its autonomy from established authorities, creating public space for dissent. In reformist Islam, scholars usually discourage the autonomy of public discourse from religious authority. The undivided 'lifeworld' of Muslims would be subject to religious guidance, to the rules of the sharī'a. From this perspective public discourse critical of the Qur'an would be difficult to imagine. It would be unthinkable for a religious scholar (*'ālim*) to take a public stance against explicit Qur'anic injunctions, such as the application of severe punishments for certain crimes (*ḥudūd* penalties). This would make his position in society, in the religious community untenable. Doctrinal and ritual dissent was discouraged as it was seen as weakening Islam's mission to reform one's life before God. The Islamic category *fitna* is often used in this connection, meaning dissent as much as disorder and rebellion, anarchy, split. But the historical evolution of Islamic thinking has come up with ways to solve this problem and provide means and space for public discourse and dissent, mainly through skilful interpretations of religious injunctions.

Islam and its institutions have always implicitly accepted diversity of behaviour in the Islamic public. This was recognized in the Covenant of Medina by Muhammad himself, as the treaty ruled not only relations between the Muslim and Jewish population but also between different Muslim tribes representing separate legal traditions. They agreed on ways to reconcile their tribal customs with the needs of the community, reflecting flexibility before sharī'a law became settled. The multitude of Islamic sects in the two main branches of Sunnite and Shi'ite Islam was paralleled by diversity in mystical Islam embodied by the various orders (*ṭarīqa*) of the Sufis. Between them they formed a cosmos of Islamic lifestyles, and created a de-facto transnational Islamic public sphere of great diversity, united by reference to the Qur'an and the Prophet Muhammad. Yet such diversity came at a price. This 'real existing' global Islamic public sphere was and is hotly contested on inclusive and exclusive terms—who rightfully belonged there and who did not, what were 'legitimate' subdivisions and interpretations and what were not.[17]

More interestingly, normative Islam also implicitly proceeded from an assumption of Muslim diversity of behaviour when distilling the rules of Islamic law (sharī'a) and the traditions (ḥadīth) for guidance. This

[17]On the diversity of the extending Islamic sphere see also the two-stage conversion model by Eaton for South Asia where Islam first assimilated local traditions and later encrouraged their integration with the Muslim world through a unitary reformist vision (1985).

was evident from the various categories of normative behaviour, the degree of obligation, and the punishments for non-conformity.[18] A complex system thereby arose upon which the religious scholars ('ulamā') based their religious rulings (*fatwā*) on the permissibility or legality of certain actions. Their interpretation can provide a key for flexibility and a plurality of views and lifestyles.

With regard to the autonomy of the individual and of public discourse, all actions were of special interest the performance of which, or the neglect of which, was not punished. This applied to actions of the type 'permissible/allowed' (*mubāḥ*). Here Islam recognized an area, albeit minor, where it did not want or need to interfere. The final decision whether or not to behave in the intended way without being accused of infidelity, lay with the individual Muslim. In political terms, it was up to public actors to use such differentiation or to close them to the general Muslim public. For political theory, this situation has obviously two consequences: (a) Public behaviour in Islam, even by orthodox standards of religion, need not be wholly uniform as Western and Islamist analysts often appear to suggest, for different reasons. Normative Islam gave some leeway to individual behaviour through the interpretation of religious doctrine. (b) Normative public behaviour in Islam was not fixed or immutable. The categorization of certain actions as desirable or punishable might change between different sects and legal traditions, but also over time.

Ritual-laden Sufi Islam added another important dimension to the relationship of public and private in Islam. Irrespective of the many private forms of mystical devotion not considered here, some orders practised distinctly public and sometimes ecstatic forms of worship, which very visibly intervened in the public sphere. They used public space for worship, devotion, and pilgrimage. Their rituals were deeply rooted in the social and cultural life of local communities and interwoven with secular social, political, and economic activities. They rested on a high degree of public tolerance. In spite of the emphasis on personal devotion and change, Sufi-related Islam followed a long tradition of interaction with the public sphere, albeit in a very local setting.

This does not imply that Islam in doctrine and practice placed no hurdles in the way of public articulation. It did so in many ways. Particular styles of public behaviour were required for membership of the Muslim

[18]Cf. articles by J. Schacht, '*Aḥkām*' and '*fiḳh*' (*Fiqh*), in EI/I: 257, II: 886–91, and M.B. Hooker, '*Sharīʿa*,' in EI/IX: 321–28. See also the reference material published by the Muslim Students' Association (MSA), based at the University of Southern California (USC) in the US, on internet at http://www.usc.edu/dept/MSA/law/shariahintroduction.html.

community. This is to be expected, as a religion based on normative values would find it difficult to maintain the appearance of a coherent system without setting such standards. But participation in the public sphere in Islam seemed to be more circumscribed by interpretations, context, and circumstances than by any inbuilt incompatibility or mutual exclusion. Islam has tolerated and sustained public activity to an extent seldom explored and often not noticed in the West. A case in point is Iran, where the participation of women in the public sphere has increased under the Islamic regime, and has been supported with religious arguments, battling with counter-arguments equally based on doctrinaire references.

Yet, if Islam condones a certain diversity in public behaviour, does it accept the intervention of a reasoning and autonomous public? Again, no generalized answer is possible. Islamic context has historically supported authoritarian regimes and tolerant public cultures alike, though not necessarily in equal measure. The research literature distinguished several phases for Islam going public, seeking for itself a public role in society beyond the immediate religious sphere of worship and faith. In this sense it was more appropriate to speak of a majority of political Islams (cf. Azmeh 1993) rather than of *the* political Islam.

The emergence of a modern public sphere in Islam was shaped by distinct political conditions and social circumstances in different parts of the Islamic world. Generally, it is associated with the gradual penetration of Muslim societies by capitalism—albeit in its peripheral, dependent, or colonial form—and nascent bourgeois politics. This process involved indigenous capital formation, the emergence of political reformism in line with demands for civil liberties (such as the *Tanẓīmāt* reforms of the Ottoman Empire from the 1840s), the formation of an Islamic 'associaṭional life' as part of an Islamic resurgence and renaissance (*nahḍa*), the appropriation of print technology, and the introduction or dramatic extension of public education for religious and secular purposes alike. Based on these factors, it is usually dated at the beginning of the nineteenth century. Studies such as that of Reinhard Schulze on Islamic internationalism show (mainly for Egypt) that this process was directly related to the influence of Western ideas (Schulze 1990).

Although Islam has regularly sought a public role in most Muslim countries, before the eighteenth century this usually depended on the ability or inclination of the ruler of the Muslim state to rely on religious advice publicly and the extent to which he followed it. The new activism, usually associated with developments since the eighteenth century, witnessed the emergence of a public Islamic discourse that sought a public role in debates on society and the polity *apart* from the state. As the intellectual history of Islam is unimaginable without taking into account the interaction within the Islamic world, the evolution of an Islamic public sphere was a transnational phenomenon where events and developments in various Muslim countries roughly corresponded and mutually aided or at least stimulated each other in their formation. The phases suggested here are not meant to be absolutes but represent approximate signposts to help order our imagination of the public posture of Islam and to comprehend its gradual and yet distinctive evolution.[19]

The first modern phase can be marked out by the Islamic reformism of the eighteenth century represented by the teachings of Muhammad Ibn Abd al-Wahhab (1703–92) in the Hijaz (Arabian Peninsula) and Muhammad bin Ali bin Muhammad ash-Shawkani (1759–1839),[20] and similar activity by Shah Waliullah (1703–62) in India. While some researchers emphasize common intellectual origins[21] others stress the diversity of their approach (Dallal 1993). Levtzion and Voll maintained that they presumably shared teachers in the study of Prophetic traditions (ḥadīth) and guides of the mystical Sufi networks: 'Interpersonal bonds and chains of transmission were of great importance in the study of *ḥadīth* as well as in mysticism' (Levtzion and Voll 1987: 8). These scholars received a traditional religious education supplemented by a conscious intellectual networking and refinement of the doctrinaire and philosophical underpinnings of an Islamic resurgence across borders of Muslim countries, Islamic legal and philosophical traditions. This phase was marked by a restatement of Sunni Islamic faith in a way that put the emphasis on a purification of doctrine and ritual, on increased religiosity and regular observance of worship, perceiving Islam to be in a degenerative or threatened state. This phase also saw a substantial extension of self-organization of Islam in the shape of new Sufi brotherhoods and Islamic

[19]Other researchers structured the evolution of Islamic public activity differently. Price discussed 'multiple political Islams' with reference to qualitative criteria, to the vision of society and of the polity formulated by Islamic activists (1999). Nikki R. Keddie pointed to the heterogeneity of motives and forms of Islamic revolt (1994).

[20]For a recent study, see the dissertation by Bernard Haykel (1997).

[21]On the confluence of Islamic reform movements in the eighteenth century, see Levtzion and Voll (1987). Several sources named Ibrahim al-Kurani (d. 1690), his son, the Shafi'ite Shaykh Abu'l-Tahir Muhammad al-Kurani (d. 1733), and Muhammad Hayat from Sindh (India) as teachers who between them taught many of the leading figures of the eighteenth-century reforms process, including Ibn Abd al-Wahhab, Waliullah, Abd al-Rauf al-Sinkili, and Mustafa al-Bakri (Robinson 2001: 224; see also Baljon 1986: 5–6; Sindhi 1952, quoted in Aziz 1972: 22). Also see a recent work on the history of *Wahhabi* thought by Guido Steinberg (2002).

movements. Yet, this phase had not yet produced the institutions necessary to contest the public sphere effectively.[22]

A second phase drew on this intellectual discursive capital and ushered in a period of self-organizing public Islamic activity. It was deeply marked by attempts to come to grips with the consequences of Western expansion, of increasing Western political domination and intellectual influence. Its main representatives had received traditional and Western education, the ensuing tension between which pushed them to both blend and counterpose these formative springs. Intellectuals and leaders such as Sayyid Jamal ad-Din al-Afghani (1838–97), the Egyptian Muhammad Abduh (1849–1905), the Syrian Muhammad Rashid Rida (1865–1935), and the Indians, Sayyid Ahmad Khan and Shibli Numani (1857–1914), brought into being an intellectual and social movement of Islamic reformism, iṣlāḥ, which wanted to revive the intellectual, religious, and social, but not necessarily the political fortunes of Islam.[23] Abduh demanded that the 'ulamā' address new developments from the point of view of Islamic doctrine, that they rely more on independent reasoning (*ijtihād*) and less on adherence (*taqlīd*) to the established law schools (*maḏhab*). This approach has become the hallmark of reformist Islam under the label of iṣlāḥ ever since.[24] For the Islamic discourse, the 'ulamā' saw a challenge not only from the intellectuals, but also from the mystics. Sufi movements had become an important feature of Islamic renaissance in the nineteenth century.[25] In the Arab–Egyptian context, the 'ulamā' resented the loss

[22]The Wahhabi wars of the Saud family in the Arabian Peninsula in 1797–1818 and violent local insurgencies in northwest India in the beginning of the nineteenth century, influenced by Wahhabi doctrine, did not exactly serve to contest the public sphere as they were more marked by violent intervention than by a critical discourse on the state of society and the polity. For the insurgencies of the Indian 'Wahhabis', cf. Ahmad (1966) and for the Saudi wars, see Vassiliev (1998).

[23]For a detailed discussion of the concept of iṣlāḥ in relation to South Asia, see Chapter 4, section 4.1.

[24]Some of these reformist Islamic activists called themselves *salafī*, alluding to the 'pious ancients' (*al-salaf al-ṣāliḥ*), that is, the founder generation of Islam with which they identified. This term has been more commonly used in Arabian Islam and less so in South Asia. Focus will, therefore, remain here on iṣlāḥ. Cf. P. Shinar and Werner Ende, 'Salafiyya', in EI/VIII: 900–9.

[25]A full consideration of Sufi movements in the nineteenth century would go beyond the intended and possible scope of this study, because of their reliance less on discourse and more on ritual. While the significance of ritual is not to be neglected for public articulation, this study remains centred on the understanding of discourse and as such the scholars of religion ('ulamā') play a central role in this context. Yet, as will be emphasized wherever appropriate, the 'ulamā' had never severed their relationship with mysticism while several leaders of mystical movements sought to strengthen the bonds with orthodoxy by having growing recourse to the Qur'an and the Sunna. For an insightful study of the formation of Sufi activism, see Fusfeld's dissertation on the shaping of Sufi

of control over the transmission and dissemination of religious knowledge which they saw undermined by the development of uncontrolled commercial printing of Islamic tracts (Schulze 1990: 27–30) and the new flourishing of intellectual and associational public life. While the debate on iṣlāḥ took clear shape around 1880, it was preceded by the transformation and broadening of the public discourse through printing and associational life from around the 1850s. This phase approximately lasted to the turn of the twentieth century. The respective debates in India were either contemporaneous to the Arab discourse or predated it slightly. In India, however, terms and arguments were used somewhat differently. Although Sayyid Ahmad and Shibli Numani shared many of the positions taken by Abduh they did not do so in the name of iṣlāḥ. Their position was also marked by pronounced loyalty to government. In contrast, the term iṣlāḥ was taken up by the Deoband Seminary and its theologians who as a whole inclined more to the purist position of Rashid Rida. Their position was dominated by anti-government sentiments. The dispute between Abduh and the leadership of the Azhar University was echoed by the debate between Sayyid Ahmad Khan and the founders of the Deoband Seminary, Muhammad Qasim Nanaotawi (1832–79) and Rashid Ahmad Gangohi (1829–1905) (Reetz 1988; cf. Chapter 3, section 3.1.3.).

A third phase was marked by a broadening of the 'associational life' of Islam and a concomitant radicalization of Islamic political discourse. It became more critical of Western influences and colonial rule and, crucially, it took to mapping out projects for a modern society and polity ruled by Islam. The Egyptian Hasan al-Banna (1906–49),[26] founder of the Muslim Brotherhood (al-Ikhwān al-Muslimūn, 1928), and the Indian Sayyid Abu'l-A'la Maududi[27] (1903–1979), the founder of the Islamic Party in India (Jamā'at-i Islāmī, 1941) were typical intellectuals and leaders for this period. Both organizations did seek to establish hegemony over society and the polity, aiming directly at political power, which was envisaged to come to them with the downfall of colonial rule and the advent of an independent state. It in this third phase where the articulation of religious Islamic groups in India comes under scrutiny that is the subject of this study.

The first decades after the end of World War I, which were marked by a broad process of decolonization, were dominated by nationalist and

---

leadership in Delhi between 1750 and 1920 (1981). For the Arab and West African world, see also Levtzion and Voll (1987).

[26]J. M. B. Jones, 'Ḥasan al-Bannā', in EI/I: 1018–19; for a recent analysis of the genesis of the Muslim Brothers in Egypt, see Brynjar Lia (1998).

[27]For a comprehensive review, see Nasr (1996); also F. C. R. Robinson, 'Sayyid Abū'l-A'lā Mawdūdī,' in EI/VI: 872–4.

socialist discourses in the Muslim world. When these failed to satisfy the political and social expectations of the masses, a new, fourth phase in the formation of an Islamic public sphere seemed to begin. It started, with variations, in the beginning of the 1970s, marking a revival of public Islamic activities and of the related 'associational life'. Egypt witnessed a significant upsurge of Islamist activity in the 1970s. Many groups relied on the more radical tracts by Sayyid Qutb (1906–66),[28] a major activist of the Brotherhood since the 1950s. While Egyptian President Anwar as-Sadat (1918–81) first tried to instrumentalize the Islamist opposition as a counterweight to nationalist and socialist forces, his pro-Western policies earned him the wrath of radical Islamists, leading to his assassination by them in 1981. They organized under various names in groups such as the al-Jamā'a al-Islāmīya and Tanẓīm al-Jihād. In Tunisia, the Islamists formed the Tunisian Islamic Group (al-Jamā'a al-Islāmīya bi-Tūnis, 1972).[29] The Islamic opposition to the regime of the Shah in Iran was organized mainly in exile. In Pakistan, Islamists mobilized against the nationalist policies of the nationalist Prime Minister Zulfiqar Ali Bhutto (1928–79) from 1974 onwards, culminating in the military dictatorship of Zia-ul-Haq (1924–88), which lasted from 1977 to 1988. Radical Islamic assertion in the public sphere now seemed to challenge the West-inspired system of government and politics directly.[30] It was no doubt a quest for emancipation but it relegated the discourse element to the background. Opponents were less to be persuaded and increasingly subjected to social and political pressure, and if 'need be', killed. This was a mutual violent pursuit as the mainly authoritarian regimes of West Asia and the Middle East relentlessly persecuted the Islamist opposition. Its violent suppression signalled a general inability and unwillingness of the ruling élites to follow deliberative politics. Often Islamic activists during this period claimed to represent broader interests of a critical public, demanding the introduction, or restoration, of at least a semblance of democracy.

By the end of the 1980s and the beginning of the 1990s, a new, fifth phase of public articulation of Islamic activism seemed to have begun. This was characterized by polarization between militant and peaceful forms of intervention. In many countries, Islamist politics and resistance degenerated into protracted civil warfare heavily dominated by a 'senseless' violence (if political violence can ever be sensible). It made large parts

[28]See Moussalli (1992); Kepel (1984); Haddad (1983); J. J. G. Jansen, 'Sayyid Quṭb (Ḳuṭb)' in EI/ IX: 117–18.

[29]For a review of the Islamist discourse of Tunisian Islamists, cf. Rogler (2001).

[30]For the rise of an Islamic infrastructure in Pakistan during this period, see Malik (1996).

of Muslim society suffer in Algeria, Afghanistan, Pakistan, Sudan, Egypt, and partly Iran. This development did not preclude a continued peaceful expansion of an Islamic public sphere through institution-building, through a discourse searching for alternatives to Western and secular policy-making. Four instances of this tendency are mentioned here: In the international sphere, the Organization of the Islamic Conference (OIC, Munaẓẓamat al-Mu'tamar al-Islāmī, 1969)[31] attempted to reconcile Islamic public interests with global developments offering channels for Islamic public discourse and deliberative politics. It has often been ineffectual, yet it has persistently grown into an expanding network of activities and institutions, spanning the whole Islamic world. This state-based Islamic public activity has been supplemented by the non-state international organization of the Muslim World League (MWL, Rābiṭat al-'Ālam al-Islāmī, 1962).[32] It comprises Islamic scholars and intellectuals backed by Saudi Arabia and claiming to represent the Islamic umma towards their (secular) governments. Although it expanded quickly, its influence has stagnated recently. A third direction is symbolized by the successful expansion of the missionary movement of the Tablīghī Jamā'at representing a religious, faith-driven new Islamic internationalism (Masud 2000). A fourth phenomenon is represented by the increasing Islamist networking through the Internet thereby constructing a new transnational Islamic public sphere of discourse, activism, and associational life (Eickelman and Anderson 1999). These developments seem to prove that Islamic public life grows more distinct, yet more disparate. It is still subject to major swings of fortunes not necessarily rooted in its own dynamics, yet still anchored in the global capitalist economic and political environment.

Militancy is viewed here as an outflow of activism. To what extent it can be reconciled with the public sphere as an arena for deliberative politics remains questionable. Yet militancy and political violence are linked to the functional aspect of the public sphere where it mediates access to public life and resources. Violence often comes into play where access is severely limited or hampered by entrenched social and political élites. But this self-justification or legitimation of Islam-driven political militancy is hollow as such violence is more often directed at ordinary people rather than élites resisting broader participation in the public space. Yet, local militancy has repeatedly generated political and cultural change by upsetting the local equilibrium of forces. The Wahhabi wars of the Sa'ud rulers were instrumental in securing acceptance of their

[31]Cf. the review of its history and decisions in the publications of Ellinor Schöne, notably her dissertation (1997); also cf. its website at www.oic-oci.org.

[32]See the classic study by Schulze (1990); also its website at www.arab.net/mwl.

doctrine. The *jihādī* movements in West Africa in the beginning of the nineteenth century were responsible for the spread of Islam there (Levtzion and Voll 1987: 21–38). Islam cannot be blamed for this ambiguity any more than any other religious system. While many wars have been fought in the name of Islam, there is nothing in the Qur'an and the Prophetic tradition (Sunna) that makes religious war obligatory except in cases of self-defence. The understanding of jihād is exertion in the way of God, which includes self-improvement and religious striving as much as warfare. Therefore, going to war in the name of Islam remains in the end a matter of interpretation and politics.[33]

Apparently, public activity of Islamic forces cannot be explained through a single concept. It will have to be related to functional, quantitative, and qualitative factors. Political declarations of Islamic groups have to be squared with undeclared intentions and unintended consequences. For instance, while several Islamists demand with reference to the Qur'an and the Prophetic tradition that women be strongly segregated, we have seen the emergence of an Islamic women's movement. It may bring more Muslim women into the public sphere than ever before, particularly in traditional rural societies, thereby enhancing public participation and emancipation. Yet, conditions and terms of such increased participation still require critical examination, bringing in the quality dimension.

For South Asia, Islamic political traditions in the modern period have shown a considerable variety of influences. Their concepts can be distinguished either with reference to the *subject* of Islamic public life determined by the boundaries and location of the Islamic community (local, regional, global, etc.), or the *principles* by which Islamic public life is to be governed (pan-Islamism, Muslim nationalism, modernism, etc.). Although the Qur'an relates the term community (umma) primarily to the collective presence of Muslims in the whole world, the Muslim community can also be understood to be local, national, territorial or non-territorial, and transnational/global. If Muslims are in a minority situation as in India, this adds a further dimension. It is also possible to classify these schemes with reference to the *political agency* that is envisaged to implement these schemes. Muslim activists have related themselves either to the political system and the government of India, or the whole of the Islamic world (umma), or Indian society at large, or the Muslim

[33]For a summary of interpretations of jihād from the perspective of South Asian Islam, cf. Iftikhar Malik (1998). For a more general treatment of the subject, see Peters (1979) and Firestone (1999) where they also outline the qualifications and restrictions to be placed on the conduct of jihād.

Table 1.1: Stages of the Evolution of the Islamic Public Sphere in a Transnational Perspective (Selected, Schematic)

Stage	Dominant markers of Islamic public life	Islamic militancy	Major representatives in the (Arab) Islamic world	South Asia*
Eighteenth century	Critical Islamic discourse of reformist Islam.	Wahhabi wars of the Sa'ūd rulers 1797–1818; mujāhidīn activity of the 'Indian Wahhābīs' 1820s–31	Abd al-Wahhab (1703–92) in the Hijaz	Shah Wali Ullah (1703–62)
c. 1850s–1900	Reformist movement of iṣlāḥ and salafiyya; modern Islamic associational life and Islamic printing take root; in some parts of Islamic world represented by new Sufi brotherhoods.	Muslim participation in the 'Indian Mutiny' 1857–8; renewed mujāhidīn activity of the 'Indian Wahhābīs' ending 1863; Mahdī rebellion and state (1881–98) in Sudan.	Sayyid Jamal ad-Din al-Afghani (1838–97); Muhammad Abduh (1849–1905) and Muhammad Rashid Rida (1865–1935) in Egypt; Muhammad Ahmad ibn Abdallah Mahdi, (1844–1959) in Sudan	Sayyid Ahmad Khan (1817–98); Shibli Numani (1857–1914); Rashid Ahmad Gangohi (1829–1905); Nazir Husain (1805–1902)
c. 1900–1950s/1960s	Broadening and radicalization of Islamic activism; discourse and activism related to Islamic project on society and the polity.	Pan-Islamic jihād activity in India, Afghanistan, Turkey around WW I; Khilafat Movement in India 1919–25; Muslim Brotherhood activity.	Hasan al-Banna (1906–49), Sayyid Qutb (1906–66) in Egypt; Sayyid Abd ar-Rahman al-Mahdi (1885–1959) in Sudan	Mahmud al-Hasan (1851–1920); Husain Ahmad Madani (1879–1957); Ashraf Ali Thanawi (1863–1943); Sayyid Abu'l-Ala al-Maududi (1903–79)

*See Chapters 3, 4 of this study for more references.

(contd...)

(Table 1.1: continued)

Stage	Dominant markers of Islamic public life	Islamic militancy	Major representatives in the (Arab) Islamic world	Major representatives in South Asia
1970s–1980s	Renewal and upsurge of organized public Islamic activism aimed at hegemony over society.	Islamic revolution in Iran 1979; radical Egyptian groups conduct open terror campaign, assassinate President Sadat in 1981.	(Later writings by Qutb for Egypt), Ruhallah Khomeyni (1900–89) in Iran; Rashid al-Ghannushi (b. 1941) in Tunisia; Hasan at-Turabi (b. 1932) in Sudan	Mufti Mahmud Miyan (JUI, Pakistan); Miyan Tufail Muhammad (b. 1914, JI, Pakistan); Sayyid 'Abdullah Bukhari (Imam of Jama Masjid of Delhi); Sayyid Abul-Hasan Ali Nadwi (1913–99, Nadwa Seminary Lucknow, India)
Late 1980s–2000s	Renewed global and national networking of Islamic organizations and revival movements: Organization of the Islamic Conference (OIC), Muslim World League (Rābiṭa), Tablīghī Jamā'at, Islamic organizations in the Internet.	Self-serving militancy and violence showing in insurgencies and civil war in Algeria, Afghanistan, Pakistan, Egypt, Sudan, partly Iran, India (Kashmir), Phillippines, Russia (Chechnya), China (Xienjiang), Uzbekistan (Ferghana).	Prominent militant groups: GIA in Algeria; Hamas in Palestine/Israel; Hizbollah in Libanon/Iran; Al-qā'ida in Saudi Arabia/Afghanistan	Asad Madani (b. (1928, JUH, India); Fazlur-Rahman (b. 1951, JUI-F, Pakistan); Sami al-Haq (JUI-S, Pakistan); Qazi Husain (b. 1938, JI, Pakistan); Shah Ahmad Nurani (d. 2003, JUP, Pakistan); Mulla Omar (Ṭāliban, Afghanistan)

community of India as a whole, or regional Muslim communities in different parts of India (and Pakistan). These parameters combined to produce a number of distinct Islamic political traditions for the subcontinent.[34] The most influential of these are discussed next.

(a) Moghul rule: Political Islamic discourse in South Asia often looked back to a 'Golden Age' when Islam ruled over most of the subcontinent in spite of Muslims firmly remaining in a numerical minority.[35] Muslim dynasties ruled over South Asia during the time of the Delhi Sultanate (1211–1556) and the Moghul Empire of Central Asian origin (1526–1761). Opinion differed as to what extent this era or any particular reign in it embodied a truly Islamic government. Yet, the social and political privileges that had come with Muslim dynastic rule made it difficult for the Islamic élites of colonial India to reconcile themselves to British power after the British crown replaced Moghul rule as the Imperial sovereign in 1858. Islamic activists referring to this period of glory conveniently tended to forget that it was Muslim rulers who first invited the British and handed them parts of the administration and farmed out the collection of taxes to them. But Moghul rule remained a fixed reference point for all activists pursuing politics in South Asia in the name of Islam, claiming an allegedly inherent right to exercise power over the whole of South Asia, or at least over all its Muslims. Today this is often interpreted as a right to a guardianship over all South Asian Muslims. While Pakistan and to some extent Bangladesh consider themselves as Muslim states such a claim is highly explosive with regard to India whose sovereignty it challenges.

(b) Pan-Islamism: Proclaiming Islamic solidarity with the umma has been an influential activity in the political history of India and Pakistan. The British colonial regime was alarmed at the stirrings of pan-Islamism as it threatened to undermine security and stability among colonial subjects by cutting across loyalty to the crown and across the borders of nation states and colonial territories. The British, therefore, pejoratively classified pan-Islamism as 'extra-territorial loyalty' to the holy places of Islam in Arabia and the authority of the Caliph.[36] For Indian Muslims,

[34]Authors like Moin Shakir adopted different parameters for classification. Shakir identified five types of Muslim political activity associated with a particular Muslim leader, as for him Maulana Muhammad Ali stood for pan-Islamism, Muhammad Iqbal for 'constructive revivalism', Maulana Abu'l-Kalam Azad (1888–1958) for 'synthetic nationalism', M. A. Jinnah for separatist nationalism, and Maulana A. A. Maududi for a 'neo-revivalist renaissance' (Shabir 1983).

[35]See, for instance, the typically apologetic historiographical account by Shaykh Muḥammad Ikrām in three parts, with the middle part (*Rūd-i kauthar*) especially devoted to Moghul rule (1958).

[36]Hunter 1969 (1871). There are several files from the Political & Security Department

heightened solidarity with the umma has served two purposes: (i) it was an attractive weapon against the British, who had difficulty in assessing the threat potential of religious movements. Even today this is reflected in the benefits, which are sought by Islamic activists from Islamic solidarity in a contest with the West. (ii) for Indian Muslim activists, Islamic solidarity also served to balance their minority status. Islamic solidarity always promised to strengthen the position of Islamic élites vis-à-vis the Hindu majority and its communal élites. This hope continued to influence political thinking in independent Pakistan. From the 1970s, successive regimes sought extra-regional support in the Arab and Islamic world against India. It took practical form in a Pakistani military concept, sometimes called the Central Asian or West Asian 'hinterland' option. Military analysts were planning to use these Muslim 'hinterlands' to position their reserves in case of a confrontation with India (Reetz 1993).

(c) Muslim nationalism: In the Indian and Pakistani context, this term took on a special meaning referring to the supposed existence of a separate Muslim nation in India, irrespective of its cultural and linguistic heterogeneity and the lack of a consolidated homeland or territory. On this basis Muslims strove for separate political representation for Muslims in the evolving electoral system and in the administration of colonial India. For this purpose, separate Muslim constituencies were conceived. The discourse of Muslim nationalism was far from religious. On the contrary, it was closely tied to the Western tradition of political and legal thinking as it played itself out in a contest for quotas and shares in resources. It was organized through a Muslim political party, the Muslim League (1906), which was led by the offsprings of Muslim aristocratic families and by professionals such as lawyers and doctors. Its interests were modern and bourgeois. The Pakistan Movement, which started in the 1930s under the Muslim League leader Muhammad Ali Jinnah (1876–1948), became a movement for a share of power in a future independent government. As agreement over power-sharing proved elusive, the movement became a tool for the partition of the Indian subcontinent. Jinnah eventually became the first president (governor general) of the new Muslim state of Pakistan in 1947. In the South Asian context, 'Muslim nationalism' became synonymous with separate representation, in contrast with Muslim majority countries such as Turkey. Yet, the Muslim League concept retained a certain affinity to the Turkish nationalist movement under

of the India Office archive investigating the threat of 'pan-Islam', the 'pan-Islamic party', or the 'pan-Islamic League': BLOC L/P&S/11/170, L/P&S/11/171, L/P&S/11/202, L/P&S/18/A184–6, etc.

Mustafa Kemal Pasha (Atatürk, 1881–1938).[37] Given Kemal's radical secular bent, this might be surprising. Though Jinnah ultimately envisaged the establishment of a liberal, Western-type polity, more secular than religious, this vision was not shared by the majority of the Pakistani establishment, and especially the religious scholars. A 'Pakistan ideology' was coined to reconcile this internal conceptual tension by marrying Islam and territorial nationalism.

(d) Islamic government: In contrast to Muslim nationalism, religious groups and parties of Islam preferred to focus on an Islamic form of government. This was to be based on the principles of Islamic law (sharīʿa), the Qur'an, and the Prophetic tradition (Sunna, ḥadīth). Such concepts took a practical and modern shape from the beginning of the twentieth century, particularly in connection with the Khilafat movement (see Chapter 4). The idea of a formal and sovereign system of Islamic government was not particular to India and shared discurṣive traditions with other parts of the Islamic world. In India it inspired not only the religious groups in search of a political system for an independent India, but also local insurgencies, often called jihādī movements, notably in the northwest of India, and also on the Malabar coast (the Moplah uprising of 1921). The concept has been revived time and again by Islamic parties and groups in Pakistan. The debate was given a new twist by the Afghan student militia of the Ṭālibān who claimed to have established an Islamic government in consonance with the Qur'an in which they were actively aided by Islamic groups from Pakistan.

(e) Islamic society: While the concept of an Islamic government always had a territorial dimension, the vision of an Islamic society did not necessarily relate to territory. It applied to Muslim communities wherever they lived and whoever their neighbour was. It simply demanded that every Muslim led a life according to the principles of the Qur'an. The avoidance of the territorial reference made it much less controversial in political terms as it did not necessarily imply changes in territorial status for the majority Hindu population, nor did it place any restrictions on their way of life. It was meant to be hegemonic only for Muslim areas. The creation of an Islamic society had been an abiding goal of Islamic groups and activists throughout India's history. The underlying principles were considerably sharpened in connection with the campaigns of the 1920s and 1930s (see Chapter 4).

(f) Composite nationalism: This concept proceeded from the

[37]See also the careful advances made by General Parvez Musharraf, Pakistan's military ruler since 1999, to revive this connection with Turkish Muslim nationalism in order to set himself apart from religious orthodoxy.

assumption that the Indian nation was not unitary but composite in nature, consisting of several legitimate sub-nationalisms of a regional, linguistic, or religious-cultural variety. Ethnic sub-nationalisms like the Punjabis and the Bengalis would stand side by side with Muslim, Sikh, or Hindu nationalism. They would all go into the making of the Indian nation. This was the creed of the Indian Congress Party. The concept was closely connected to secularism as understood in India. It was a belief held by many non-religious political and public actors, by the so-called 'Congress Socialists', and also by the 'Congress Muslims' who shared the view of an overriding common destiny for all groups in India. Some Islamic groups (as will be shown in Chapter 4) supported this concept, as they believed that true Islam could only be implemented on a societal level, not through a separate state. In their reading, the acceptance of composite nationalism (*muttaḥida qaumīyat*) by Muslims presupposed strong religio-cultural autonomy for Muslims. In this sense, their recognition of composite nationalism was linked to their striving for an Islamic society, for a true Islamic way of life.

The genuineness of Muslim political aspirations was occassionally doubted. Nationalist and left-leaning Muslims suspected Muslim élites of pursuing their own material and political benefit above everything else. Mushirul Hasan maintained that Muslim élites were following an illusion, claiming privileges for a separate Muslim nation which was not possible given the social and cultural diversity of India. He contended that after the creation of the Muslim League, the Muslim élites pursued a three-fold project:

> ...to trace the historical evolution of an imaginary *community*, as an antithesis to the Congress theory of Unity in Diversity; to emphasise the distinct identity and separateness of this community in order to bargain and extract concessions from the government, and to invoke Islamic symbols of unity to mount a movement that would, in its essential thrust, delink specific Muslim aspirations from the broader concerns of the countrywide nationalist struggle (Hasan 1995: 108).

The application of Western categories to political realities in South Asia often presented problems. It was fraught with misunderstandings and differing interpretations, sometimes pointing in opposite directions. One example is the meaning of secularism. It was interpreted by Mahatma Gandhi (1869–1948) and applied by Jawaharlal Nehru (1889–1964) in a sense, which aimed at equal respect and support for all religions. This was very different from the preferred interpretation of secularism in the West focused on the lack of religiosity, an increasing distance from religion, or on a strict separation of religion and state. The Gandhian interpretation resulted in state protection of religious activities. It also made political and state actors hesitant to intervene in religious conflict and tension. The political instrumentalization and exploitation of religious sentiments has thus flourished in South Asia. This interpretation of secularism and the concept of composite nationalism were political tools designed to keep together a broad coalition of ethnically and religiously diverse forces within the national movement led by the Congress. On the basis of such interpretation the concepts of secularism and Islamic society seemed no longer incompatible—if the relevant clauses of inter-religious tolerance contained in the Qur'an were invoked. Both promoted peaceful religious autonomy and coexistence. This made it possible for the Association of Religious Scholars (JUH) to accept the concept of composite nationalism and yet pursue its goal of Islamic society.[38]

Another classic misunderstanding surrounded the term modernism in relation to Islam. Politicians in the tradition of the Muslim League and the Aligarh school of thought were often called modernists at the time. This related to their acceptance of Western education, of the Western political system, and of their positive attitude towards science, technology, and economic activity. Here, the modernist label masked their orthodox social views on issues such as the participation of women or 'lower classes' in politics and social affairs. By contrast, the concepts of Islamic government and Islamic society based on religious tradition were not devoid of aspects of modernism. They attempted to tackle modernity by devising a comprehensive system of education, a system of moral improvement legitimated by the negative outfall of modern developments. The proponents of the concepts of Islamic government and Islamic society slowly but surely used modern means of communication and infrastructure in education and in politics. They thus pushed into modernity groups of society which otherwise would not have entered it so decisively.

In sum, classification of political traditions in Islam can only have conditional value. A classic opinion was expressed by William Hunter, the English administrator and scholar (1840–1900) who characterized the adherents of the Indian 'Wahhabi' movement, 'extreme dissenters'

[38]Today's heir of the JUH in Pakistan, the JUI, has moved away from this interpretation. It rejects secularism as an expression of Western and Indian hegemony designed to subdue the Islamic forces in Pakistan. Switching its loyalty to the state of Pakistan as a separate Muslim state, the JUI replaced the concept of Islamic society with that of an Islamic state. This makes it view with suspicion all attempts to introduce a secular polity in Pakistan (see debate over the demands of Interior Minister Moinuddin Haider to introduce a secular and tolerant system in Pakistan vide *New York Times*, 10 June 2000). This is in contrast to Pakistan's founder, Muhammad Ali Jinnah, who after independence advocated the creation of a secular polity in Pakistan (see Jinnah's address to the Constituent Assembly of Pakistan on 11 August 1947, in Jinnah 1976: 6–10).

with respect to social order, land-holding, and established religion. He called them 'Anabaptists, Fifth Monarchy men, so to speak, touching matters of faith; Communists and Red Republicans in politics' (Hunter 1969 [1871]: 101). His description made clear that there were no easy analogies. Assessments of Muslim political traditions had to rely on a combination of references. They demarcate trends and concepts variable in time and history.

1.3. THE EVOLUTION OF THE PUBLIC SPHERE IN COLONIAL INDIA

The outline of the evolution of an Islamic public sphere in India would be incomplete without sketching the introduction of representative politics, as it had an immediate bearing on the evolution of public bodies and on Muslim representation. The realm of political representation firmly belonged in the public sphere, even under the controlled and quasi-authoritarian conditions of colonial role. An increasing degree of autonomy in the functioning of political representation could not be denied.[39] Although 'official members'—the euphemism for state-nominated ex officio members of legislatures and governing councils—at first dominated representative bodies, they could not help responding to controversial issues publicized in the media or by representatives of native communities. The print media enjoyed a significant degree of political freedom of expression even though censorship was routinely exercised. Owners of printing presses and publications had to submit deposits to authorities, which in case of conflict were forfeited resulting in closure. While the expression of nationalist and independence-minded sentiment was generally tolerated, more radical calls for a resort to violence were usually suppressed. The same applied to publications or utterances of religious defamation likely to incite 'public hatred' and violence.

Elective principles were introduced gradually through a long constitutional reforms process in the shape of successive constitutional acts, first significantly restricting electoral participation through selective suffrage by class, property, and educational qualifications. Other restrictions related to the subject matter representative bodies were allowed to deal with. Generally, public representation arrived faster at the local and provincial level than at the federal level.

[39]For a contemporary overview of the evolution of political administration, see Blunt (1937: 74ff.); Cumming (1932). For a more recent analytical evaluation, see Mishra (1987); Rothermund (1970). For factual accounts of the constitutional history of colonial India, see Sharma (1974); Pylee (1967).

The constitutional reforms of 1919 and 1935 had a substantial effect on the formation of public opinion in India. They increased the number of voters dramatically. For the 1937 elections, the 1932 Lothian Franchise Committee raised the electoral franchise from 5.4 to 27.6 per cent, thereby increasing the electorate more than five times from 7 to 36 million people. Such franchise was still not representative of India's toiling millions. But this increase aggravated already innumerable administrative problems given that literacy stood at 8 per cent, distances were vast, the police force was limited, and the number of polling stations small. Introducing adult franchise would have required facilities for 130 million electors, a task believed to be beyond the administrative capacity of the Indian government at the time.[40] The reforms also hugely increased the number of public representatives, almost doubling their overall number between 1919 and 1935 from 1.021 to 1.982.[41] Public discourse in Parliament intensified rapidly and was complemented by intense debate in the media and the rising number of associations. In spite of the persisting restrictions on political representation, public discourse in Parliament—even though conducted in cautious verbal homilies in the British Parliamentary tradition—was critical and usually unsparing of government. When the Congress boycotted the first elections, parliamentary debate was at first limited and circumscribed. It excluded nationalist opinion, an important and ever-rising section of public opinion, demanding an immediate end to colonial rule and self-government for the country. Yet, with gradual emancipation of the (mainly provincial) parliamentary system discourse

[40]*Indian Franchise (Lothian) Committee Report 1932*, in *IAR* 1932/I: 452–71, here: 452–3.

[41]Under the 1919 constitutional act, the number of elected (+ nominated) legislators in the provinces was 86 (+25) for Bombay, 98 (+29) for Madras, 113 (+26) for Bengal, 100 (+23) for the United Provinces, 71 (+22) for the Punjab, 70 (+33) for Bihar and Orissa, 54 (+16) for the Central Provinces, 39 (+14) for Assam, and at the centre, 103 (+40) for the lower chamber, the Legislative Assembly, and 34 (+25) for the federal upper chamber, the Council of State (Pylee 1967: 57). This was a total of 768 elected and 253 nominated legislators, all together 1.021. Under the 1935 Constitutional Act, the number of legislators for the assemblies (and the newly created upper councils in some provinces) was envisaged to be 175 (30) for Bombay, 215 (56) for Madras, 250 (65) for Bengal, 228 (60) for the United Provinces, 175 for the Punjab, 152 (30) for Bihar, 60 for Orissa, 112 for the Central Provinces, 108 (22) for Assam, and at the centre, 375 for the Legislative Assembly, and 260 for the the Council of State. This added up to a total number of 2.373 whereby the number of legislators would almost have doubled. As the federal formula was not implemented due to the differences on Muslim representation, the strength of the federal legislature remained at the old levels with some adjustments, standing at 141 for the Legislative Assembly and 103 for the Council of State in 1947. This brought the actual overall number of legislators slightly down to 1.982 (compiled on the basis of Pylee 1967: 57, 61, 63, 84, 91; Sharma 1974: 310).

in the Indian legislatures became more representative of wider sections of public opinion, of 'competing and insurgent publics'. Raising of ethnic, regional, social, and religious issues was indicative of such a trend. After elections under the 1935 Constitution had brought to power governments of the Congress Party in several provinces, the issue of home rule, or independence, entered all arenas of debate. At the same time, the colonial state's authoritarian practices continued, sometimes even under Congress ministries, whose politicians had smoothly adapted to a governing position and quickly grown intolerant of public dissent.[42]

The federal question eventually grew into a major constitutional dispute over the representation of India's Muslims. Without peaceful agreement on a federal post-independence constitution, Britain unilaterally partitioned colonial India and its dependent princely states. The constitutional reforms process culminated in the Indian Independence Act of 1947. The latter did not immediately create new constitutional laws as the 1935 Act was adopted with certain modifications for the business of political government both in India and in Pakistan. The constitution of independent India was adopted in 1951 while it took Pakistan until 1956 to adopt its first constitution.

The emerging public sphere was composed of very diverse sections. The constitutional reforms process created a 'semi-official' élite public consisting mainly of the new legislators. Under conditions where (provincial) governments were not (fully) responsible to parliament they appeared to legitimate the exercise of power on behalf of the colonial government. But this linkage was mainly indirect, precisely because of persisting restrictions on representation. This situation did not prevent legislators from being critical. There were fewer lobby interests to be cared for as real access to the distribution of resources was still wanting. The lack of representative power allowed many of them rather more leeway to criticize than was possible in a full-fledged Western political system.

Besides this 'semi-official' public, political forces set up competing counter-publics. Foremost were the nationalists led by the Congress Party striving for independence. Others included minority and regional parties, especially the Muslim League. The huge mass campaigns of non-cooperation (1920–2) and of civil disobedience (1930–41) directed by Gandhi mobilized millions of ordinary Indians who in one form or

[42]See, for instance, the heavy-handed policies of the Congress ministry in the Madras Presidency under C. Rajagopalachari when it decided in 1937 to introduce the compulsory teaching of Hindi in a province dominated by Tamil and Telugu speakers. As it faced massive street protest by anti-Hindi agitators from the Justice Party, the Congress government arrested hundreds of agitators courting arrest in the tradition of civil disobedience (cf. Reetz 1997; Arooran 1980).

the other started articulating their concern in public, through an intense associational life, and more so through activism of a very organized kind. The nationalist mass mobilization was shadowed by similar campaigns by trade unions, ethnic, regional, and religious parties, by the untouchable movement, by writers, filmmakers, artists, advocates, and the like.[43] The years 1918–20 proved a watershed in Indian politics, introducing mass politics and mobilization on a grand scale. Indian nationalist public opinion had hoped to be rewarded for participation in the British war effort. Instead it was confronted with new repressive laws, the most prominent of which was the Rowlatt Act of 1919, which set into motion the first mass agitation led by Gandhi. It resulted in the infamous Jallianwala Bagh massacre where unarmed civilian protesters were mercilessly shot at in April 1919. Gandhi then masterfully combined his campaign with that of leading Indian Muslim scholars ('ulamā') for the defence of the Ottoman Caliphate, the well-known Khilafat Movement (see Chapter 4, section 4.3.3).

Beside the various streams of the nationalist movement, religious groups and forces constituted another insurgent public, claiming an expanding religious-civic public sphere. Since the so-called Indian renaissance of the early nineteenth century, religious reform movements of Hindus, Sikhs, so-called non-Brahmin groups, Christians, and Muslims had sprung up all over India (Jones 1989). They were responding to the multiple challenges of British rule, the capitalist and Christian penetration. They aimed at revising their ritual in line with what was now perceived to be modern or enlightened. Occasionally they responded to authoritative and legislative pressure by the British who had been attempting, alongside native social reformers, to outlaw religious practices such as widow-burning and child marriage. Other religious reform efforts were geared to social rehabilitation of groups seen to be especially disadvantaged by the political and capitalist transformation of society, such as the untouchables within the fold of Hinduism. Special efforts were made to improve chances for education, quickly understood to be crucial for advancement in colonial society, and for access to coveted public services. The introduction of a regular population census produced a vivid public discourse on the size of various communities. This was seen as crucial in competition for rights and privileges in all fields of public representation, and especially for services and in education. In the absence of representative government in the nineteenth century and the persistence of significant curbs on public politics in the first two decades of the twentieth century, socio-religious

[43]See the classic work by Majumdar (1962). For a comprehensive overview, see Chandra (1988).

reform movements at times provided a major outlet for the contestation of public space. From the point of view of the formation of the public sphere, this activism afforded an additional advantage in that the colonial authorities found it more difficult to suppress than regular party activity. Despite initial reform efforts in the socio-religious field, the British were mostly neutral in relation to religious activity for fear of an 'irrational' backlash with implications for security and public order.

These three major streams of public life, the 'semi-official', the nationalist, and the socio-religious, produced a rich associational life, activism, and discourse. The three segments competed with each other, and were also internally fragmented. Additionally, one has to consider that associational life did not know the kind of fixed borders common in the West. Individuals would be involved in various, and sometimes competing, forms of public activity at the same time. The Congress camp provided a vivid example of that. A significant segment of Congress leaders were rooted in Hindu socio-religious reform maintaining a separate platform from which they created and directed the Hindū Mahāsabhā (Hindu Conference, 1915). They were also counted among the central leaders of the Congress (cf. Chapter 3, fn. 105). Nehru with his secularist, left-leaning views represented a very different type of public activity within the same party. Activities of these Congress factions were competitive; their political demands were occasionally opposed to each other, even mutually hostile. And yet, these tensions were reconciled in the biographies of many leaders in both the Congress and the Hinduist movement. The same applied to Muslim mobilization. Some Islamic leaders oscillated between the Congress, the Muslim League, and religious organizations.[44]

The concept of Muslim communal representation developed through several historical stages. When the British entered India their political gaze was fixed on races and communities so manifold and so vastly different from Europe. The best way to manage them seemed to regulate their cultural and political life. Security and stability were the overriding concerns of British policy. Muslims were seen as one of the Indian races, alongside other ethnic and linguistic groups and other religious communities like the Sikhs. The British also recognized the rights of special interest groups such as industrialists, landholders, and universities seen as instrumental in securing British goals.[45]

[44]Such behaviour in the most striking manner was displayed among others by the Ahl-i Ḥadith leader Thanaullah Amritsari and Abdul Bari from Firangī Maḥall cooperating at various times with the Nadwa council, the association of religious scholars (JUH), the Congress Party, and the Muslim League. See Reetz (2001b), Robinson (2001: 145ff.).

[45]For the longest period of the time under review, the operation of the 1919 Constitutional Act between 1920 and 1937, separate representation was granted to the

Separate representation had existed throughout the nineteenth century at the level of local government when members of councils were still appointed and almost entirely 'official', that is, British and ex officio functionaries of administration. Community associations were the first public bodies to nominate members for Legislative Councils. This was subsequently strengthened through regularized community representation on legislative bodies.

From the beginning of the twentieth century, modernizing Muslim élites joined other religious and ethnic groups in claiming a greater share of the public sphere. Education and positions in the civil and military services became the coveted goal of public engagement. The obsession of the élites with quotas and numbers of representation reflected their anxiety to secure jobs for their offsprings, newly educated in Western values.

Modern Indian Muslim political separatism began with a deputation to the viceroy in 1906. The viceroy was presented with two demands:

(a) Muslims must be separately represented in all elections, whether to the Legislative Council or the local government, and their representatives must be separately elected by purely Muslim constituencies, which would not necessarily be territorial as Muslims often lived dispersed in India.

(b) Muslims should be given representation above their numerical share in the population, 'commensurate not merely with their numerical strength, but also with their political importance and the value of the contribution which they make to the defence of the Empire'.[46]

These two demands were granted by the Minto–Morley Reforms of 1909. The Legislative Council was still far from being a fully elected and truly representative parliament. It was more akin to an imperial court, a *darbār*, reminiscent of the Moghul era. In the eyes of Muslim activists such as Muhammad Ali, the reforms only partly met Muslim expectations. In a letter to the private secretary of the viceroy, he pointed out the 'fallacy, which provided for the election of "members" of our community when we asked for provision for the election of our *representatives*.'[47]

The reference to the 'political importance' of Indian Muslims pointed to earlier Muslim rule over the whole of India before the advent of British

---

Muslims in all major provinces, the central Legislative Assembly, and Council of State, to the Sikhs in Punjab, to Indian Christians in Madras, to Europeans in Madras, Bombay, Bengal, the United Provinces, and Bihar and Orissa, to Anglo-Indians in Madras and Bengal, to commerce and industry in all the major provinces, and to universities and landholders in all provinces but Assam (ISC 1930/IV: 171).

[46]'"Moslem Deputation to Lord Minto" (October 1906)', in ISC 1930/IV: 130–1; see also the memoirs of Aga Khan III (1954: 92–5).

[47]Letter dated 7 January 1909, quoted in Afzal Iqbal (1974: 53).

power. It also referred to the above-average share of Muslims in the public services, the administration, and the military, since that time. The mention of the defence contribution referred to the large number of Muslim conscripts in the British-Indian army. Muslim peoples were considered to belong to the 'martial races'. The British judged them suitable for the rewards and hardships of military service. By joining the military and police services, former bureaucratic and landholding Muslim élites sought to maintain themselves against rising Hindu élites by offering themselves as junior partners to the British. The over-representation of Muslims in the political set-up became an enduring bone of contention. Similarly, Muslims preferred a federal to a unitary principle in any independent government, so that Muslim majority areas would enjoy a measure of autonomy. This was vehemently opposed by the Indian National Congress, which was suspicious of British concessions to Muslim political demands. The federal principle and Muslim demands were seen as devices to keep India disunited and subservient even after it had received home rule or outright independence.

In addition, Muslim élites felt they constantly needed to prove their 'loyalty' to the British crown. This was particularly true of Westernized élites who wanted to be coopted into administration, participate in decision-making on par with Hindus, or at least receive their due in appointments and patronage. The issue of Muslim loyalty had arisen from the Indian 'Wahhabi' movement and the 'Wahhabi' trials. In 1871, William W. Hunter, a high-placed official in the British-Indian administration, asked the question: 'Our Indian Mussalmans: Are They Bound in Conscience to Rebel Against the Queen?' (Hunter 1962 [1861]) British official opinion believed that the advocacy of religious war (jihād) by the (Indian) 'Wahhabis' and the substantial participation of Muslim activists in the 1857 uprising against British rule marked the whole Muslim community as unreliable. The dictates of religion were blamed for this. Muslims, allegedly, could not but be disloyal to the British crown if they took their religion seriously, since these dictates implied extra-territorial loyalties to the centres of Islam. The Indian 'Wahhabis' had been persecuted, but local jihād activities continued, mainly in the northwest. Granting Muslims separate political representation just when the national movement led by the Indian National Congress was gaining momentum, was seen as nothing less than the 'pulling back of sixty-two millions of people from joining the ranks of the seditious opposition'.[48]

An important dimension of public discourse of Islam stemmed from the expansion of Muslim public life beyond the constitutional framework.

[48]Lady Minto, wife of former Viceroy Lord Minto (1845–1914), quotes this statement from a letter she received from an official in the administration of her husband (1934).

The number of Muslim associations exploded around the beginning of the twentieth century. K. K. Aziz published a compendium of Muslim public life between 1850 and 1947, which serves as a good pointer in this regard (Aziz 1993). He listed 97 major Muslim organizations (not counting provincial branches). Translocal significance can be attributed to these. He counted another 313 Muslim organizations of more local significance. This demonstrates the enormous variety of public Muslim life. The register included political, educational, religious/doctrinal, cultural, literary, and medical/social associations and societies, as well as larger Muslim political parties. Only 15 out of 97 major organizations were founded before 1900, and 130 out of the 313 minor ones, pointing to the significant expansion of the public sphere after 1900. Aziz's compilation was also important in publishing statutes and board membership lists for many associations. Yet, his listing can only serve as a quantitative marker, not an absolute measurement, as the boundaries of associational life were rather fluid. The compilation also suffers from defects and inconsistencies.[49] Most public bodies started holding annual conferences particularly after 1900. This form of activity had been inherited from the British political system. Usually held at the end of each year, the turned into, at times, tumultuous and colourful events, the so-called *tamāshā* (public performance of troupes). It became fashionable to hold them.

The crucial role of print in the formation of a public sphere and of Muslim public opinion has frequently been acknowledged. Habermas himself pointed to its potential for facilitating public discourse, but also to its degenerative impact (1990: 77–80; 257ff.; 1998: 20–22, 167ff.). More recently Benedict Anderson coined the term 'print capitalism'. He based an analysis of nationalism on the use of the print media: novels and newspapers 'provided the technical means for "re-presenting" the *kind* of imagined community that is the nation' (1983: 30). His understanding of the nation as an imagined community came close to the public sphere paradigm in the Habermasian sense. Fellow readers were tied by a common bond into a reading public. Currently, the use of new media, audio- and video cassettes, private satellite and neighbourhood television, the Internet and CD-ROMS, is transcending the limitations of a reading public and subverting its standards. Particularly in the Muslim world, their circulation is perceived as a challenge to established authority—be it the state or religious scholars—just as the advent of mass printing was 150 year earlier. Eickelman and Anderson assumed that the proliferation and fragmentation

[49]One major defect, from the perspective of research, is that Aziz does not give references for these entries. In some cases, he lists entire movements, such as the Faraizi Movement in Bengal (1993: 100ff.), the 'Silk letter conspiracy' (1993: 201), or the early Wahhabi movement (1993: 204–5), as entries.

of the media and the consuming public created new public space, including more room also in the Muslim world to conduct a variegated and perhaps critical public discourse (1999).

Printing had become common in the Islamic world by the middle of the nineteenth century.[50] India was not lagging behind in this process. By the 1820s, reformist leaders were busily printing Islamic tracts. By the 1830s, the first Muslim newspapers were being printed. By the 1880s, editions of the Qur'an and other religious books were selling in tens of thousands. In the last 30 years of the century, over 700 newspapers and magazines in Urdu were started. In Upper India, at the beginning of the twentieth century, 4000 to 5000 books were being published in Urdu every decade and there was a newspaper circulation of tens of thousands (Robinson 1996: 63). The religious groups under review here also established their own printing houses and print media (see Tables 2.1 and 2.2). This had an immediate impact on Islamic discourse.

As a result of the ascent of Muslim printing, Francis Robinson perceived religious change in three areas: (i) strengthening reformist Islam, or, as he called it, 'Islamic Protestantism', relying on a literalist interpretation and, therefore, benefiting immediately from the availability of printing; (ii) pan-Islamism which needed the press to mediate knowledge of other parts of the Muslim world to its audience in the Muslim élites; and (iii) the erosion of authority of the 'ulamā', handing religious knowledge to a much wider audience (Robinson 1996: 72–8). Yet, as Robinson had to himself concede, such change was ambivalent. Printing may have strengthened not only a particular trend, but also its counter-trends. This is more easily explained with reference to the public sphere paradigm. The 'publicness' of the discourse, which was dramatically enhanced by the general availability of the print media, led to an opening of society. Under such conditions no topic could entirely or easily dominate the discourse.[51] Reformist Islam may have relied on the printed replication of teaching

[50]On Muslim printing in colonial India and the use of Urdu, see Robinson (1996). On Muslim printing in Afghanistan, see Edwards (1993). On wider aspects of printing and press in modern Muslim history, see the following three articles in Rothermund (ed.), (1999): Herzog, Christoph, 'Die Entwicklung der türkisch-muslimischen Presse im Osmanischen Reich bis ca. 1875' (pp. 15–44); Pistor-Hatam, Anja, 'Die Presse als Instrument der Selbstbehauptung: Persische Kaufleute und ihr Beitrag zur innermuslimischen Modernisierungsdiskussion gegen Ende des 19. Jahrhunderts' (pp. 45–62); Freitag, Ulrike, 'Clubs, Schulen und Presse: Formen und Inhalte des hadramischen Reformdiskurses in Südostasien und im Südjemen (c. 1900–1930)' (pp. 63–84).

[51]This is not to say that the discourse was not weighted in favour of certain views by political and administrative power, by the property status of printing presses and the media, or by other power factors such as descent or ideological constraints.

material or religious tracts,[52] but so did deviant or dissenting movements. The Aḥmadīya[53] and the Barelwi[54] movements were cases in point. The founders of both, Ghulam Ahmad and Ahmad Raza Khan, relied heavily on print to disseminate religious tracts seen as 'heretic' by their Deobandi opponents. From the perspective of public influence, reformist Islam, understood as normative Islam, may have reaped much more benefit by setting a normative agenda, by popularizing religious norms to be revived. These were spread more easily and effectively through its network of affiliated mosques and graduates who went on to teach in other mosques. The personal network relationship engendered allegiance, a crucial difference, which was difficult to convey through print media. The same qualifications apply to the ways print advantaged the adherents of pan-Islamism. In South Asia pan-Islamism was most influential on mass publics when it was couched in sentimental terms. The examples adduced by Robinson only confirm this. Pan-Islamism's public discourse was an emotional appeal, which relied less on printed knowledge than on generating sympathy and solidarity.[55] Slogans of pan-Islamism were manipulative tools targeted at mass publics, notwithstanding the sincerity of their advocates.

The most difficult is the third point about the diffusion of religious knowledge beyond the circle of religious specialists. It may be true that wider dissemination of Islamic knowledge contributed to the intervention in Islamic discourse of those who were laymen and had not received a full traditional religious education. But in this early stage there was room for all to grow. The religious scholars ('ulamā') also made full use of printing and strengthened their hold on public Muslim life in South Asia tremendously. Advice on normative behaviour was given to the public in religious injunctions (*fatāwā*). The massive and inexpensive dissemination of printed religious tracts and decrees now made the religious opinion of legal scholars accessible to a much wider audience. As collections of fatāwā became more impersonal and public they shifted the burden of interpretation and application to the audience. This contributed to the emergence of a market-like situation in which religious beliefs were

[52]For printing on behalf of the Deobandis, Metcalf (1982: 199ff.), for the Nadwa context and the merits of publishing the organ *al-Nadwa*, see J. Malik (1997: 432ff.).

[53]See, for instance, Lavan who discussed the role of printing and publications for the Aḥmadīya (1976: 92–121, 95ff.).

[54]On the Barelwis and the role of Sunni printing presses for the Ahl-e Sunnat, see Sanyal (1996a: 82).

[55]Muhammad Ali when he addressed the issue of the defence of the Khilafat in a speech delivered at a meeting held at Kingsway Hall, London, in connection with the Indian Khilafat Delegation, on 22 April 1920 (Ali 1963/II: 35).

fragmented and increasingly privatized. Sectarian images were massively reproduced, as were images of the 'other', the 'enemy'. Knowledge of normative Islam was spreading, but so was knowledge of its divisions. While printing facilitated discourse tremendously, it involved only one form of the shared communication characteristic of an emergent public life. Others included oral communication and common action. Islam has always been a profoundly oral culture, and oral communication retains much of its importance (Graham 1987). It perhaps even increased through the intensification of associational life. Meetings where people exchanged their views were regularly held. Also street activism and missionary efforts relied heavily on oral communication.

The gradual evolution of political representation had brought into being a flourishing public sphere. While British interests and Western concepts had dominated this process, they had not precluded the emergence of an active public life rooted in nationalism, religious or cultural interests. Muslim public life played itself out both in official institutions of political representation and in private associations, discourse, and activism. Public

Figure 1.1: Intertwining of Sectors in the Public Sphere in Colonial India (Schematic)

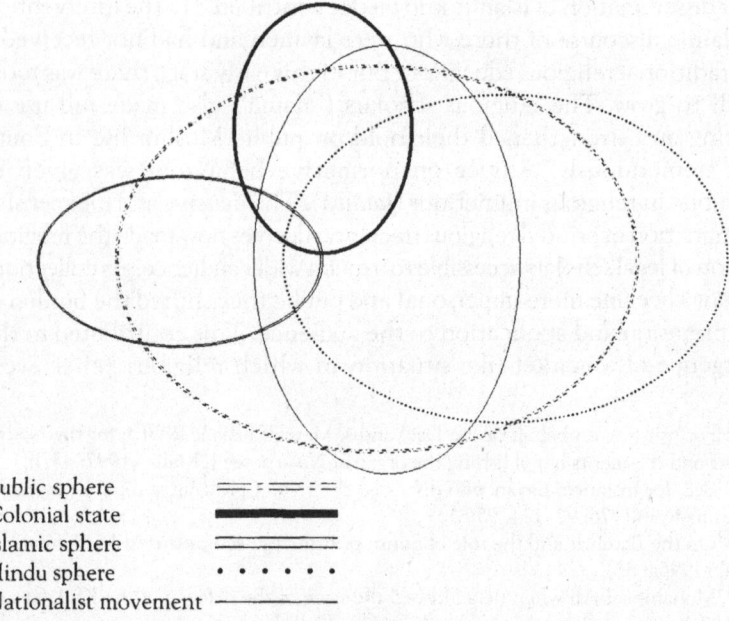

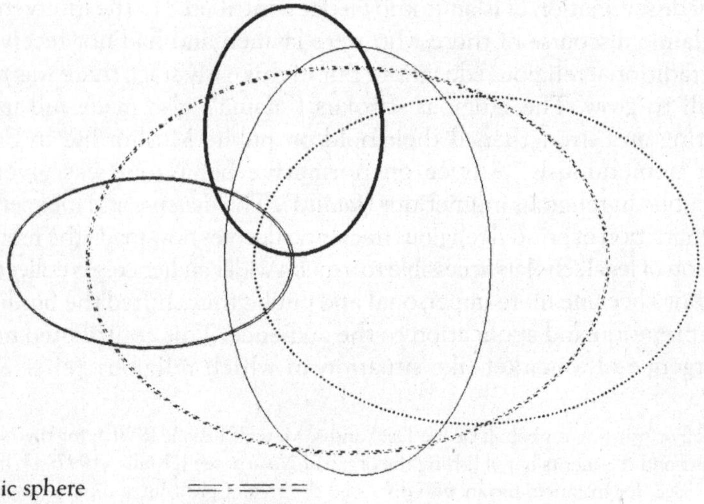

Public sphere
Colonial state
Islamic sphere
Hindu sphere
Nationalist movement

Note: The chart leaves out other 'counter-publics' besides the Hindu and the Islamic spheres to demonstrate the functioning of a fragmented public sphere with competing sectors.

life was far from homogeneous. Official public opinion competed with nationalism and other 'counter-publics' for shares of the public sphere, as schematically shown in Figure 1.1. Their territories penetrated each other as activists engaged in different forms of public activity simultaneously. Although it is often assumed that Western political principles shaped public opinion under British rule, the colonial state in reality controlled only a very limited section of the public sphere if all public activity is taken into account. Religious and cultural activity, as also nationalist activism, claimed vast public space for themselves. Competing 'counter-publics' such as the Hindu and the Islamic sector overlapped where syncretic and Sufi-influenced practices were exercised, such as worship at shared shrines. While a growing amount of activity was conducted in public, the Hindu and the Islamic spheres retained a distinct area of private worship. The nationalist sphere cut across the official and the counter-spheres.

2

The Islamic Activists and their Movements in India

Muslims constituted the largest religious minority in India.[1] Their impact on political life and on society was disproportionate in areas where they constituted the majority, that is, in Punjab, the North-West Frontier Province, Baluchistan, and Bengal in British India, in the principality of Jammu and Kashmir, and principalities of Hyderabad, Bhopal, and others. Many centres of Islamic learning and culture were in the United Provinces, still the largest and most populous province, where Muslims were in a minority of almost 15 per cent.[2] Politics was considered part of Islamic doctrine by implication. This was the perspective under dīn, the comprehensive interpretation of Islam as a way of life, in contrast to ma<u>dh</u>ab, defining it more narrowly as religious doctrine. But Islamic politics was not yet formulated as a distinct modern concept.

This changed with the rise of Muslim nationalism, which took all Muslims for members of a separate nation, *qaum*. A separate territory for this imagined Muslim nation was the aim of the Pakistan movement led by the Muslim League. As the major political movement of Indian Muslims, both the Pakistan movement and the Muslim League have been covered extensively by researchers and will, therefore, not be discussed here in detail (see Jalal 1994, Shaikh 1989). From the point of view of Islamic doctrine, the Pakistan movement was barely an Islamic movement. The Muslim League was a political party, which, beyond its Muslim subject members and its Muslim majority area concept, had rather orthodox bourgeois political ends (control of legislatures and resource allocation) and means. The Muslim League was a mainstream party based on the

[1]Other important religious minorities were the Buddhists, Christians, Sikhs, and Jains in descending order of their shares. For their percentages, see Chapter 3, fn. 106.

[2]Muslim share in the population of the British territory of the United Province in 1931 was 14.84 per cent (Census 1931, United Provinces of Agra and Oudh, Part I: 494). The given share of Shi'a is based on estimates as their number was under-reported in the statistics, cf. the Census 1921 counting only 3.5 per cent (Census 1921, Vol. I, India, Part I: 120).

British parliamentary model, complete with office bearers and conventions, programmes, and all the trimmings of Westminster-style democracy. In this it hardly represented a particularly Islamic politics. In terms of size and influence also before 1935, it remained a small, so-called leader party, representing a certain élite. It broadened its support only after the disastrous outcome of the 1937 provincial elections, when it failed to emerge as the major voice of Indian Muslims. It could not form a government in any of the Muslim majority provinces.

To study specific Islamic responses it is, therefore, necessary to look at other parties and movements and ask what constituted a specifically Islamic response to Western political categories.

Colonial India sported a great variety of Islamic parties and movements. As related to political identity, four major groups could be distinguished (Figure 2.1), although any such classification must be seen as conditional and partly overlapping:

(a) Islamic mass activism: Here large numbers of Muslims responded mostly spontaneously to political challenges through demonstrations, unrest, or riots. These were generally legitimated with a perceived threat to Islam. This category included campaigns such as the insurgencies of the Indian 'Wahhabis' or mujāhidīn; the 1921 Moplah rebellion of Muslim peasants on the Malabar coast; the Khilafat movement in support of the Turkish-Ottoman Caliph (*khalīfa*) after Turkey's defeat in World War I; the Frontier hijrat, a 1920 exodus of Muslim peasants from the North-West Frontier. Communal riots would also qualify for inclusion in this category. If mass protest was organized, it was often eclipsed by the magnitude of the mass response, which moved away from the original intention. Movements such as the Khilafat and hijrat campaigns transgressed the boundaries of spontaneous and institutionalized activism.

(b) Educational movements of Islam: These centred on lead institutions of religious learning such as the religious seminaries in Deoband, in Lucknow (Nadwa, Firangī Maḥall), and in Bareilly (Barelwis). They followed different doctrinal interpretations in the dissemination of religious knowledge. Their public influence, and also their interest in politics, was often substantial. Building up a large cross-regional following, they wielded significant social and cultural influence with political implications. The College, and later, University of Aligarh qualified for inclusion in this category insofar as it represented a distinct school of thought seeking to reconcile Islam with modern Western influences. The schools of Deoband and Aligarh in turn inspired several activist campaigns.

(c) Islamic sectarian and revival movements: They wanted to restore the original meaning of the Qur'an and the ḥadīth and were seeking to revive Islamic practice. They included the Ahl-i Ḥadīth, the Aḥrār, the

Aḥmadīya, the Khāksār, and also the *tablīgh* and the *tanẓīm* movements. Most were influenced by the legacy of Shah Waliullah and the Deoband School, although some moved away from it and set up their own agenda. Their self-definition stemmed from the prominence attached to particular Islamic injunctions or institutions and their re-interpretation, such as the centrality of the ḥadīth or of tablīgh. Their public impact derived from these concepts, which they pursued vigorously.

(d) Muslim political parties: These parties participated in mainstream politics, for which purpose they had often—but not always—been founded. They mainly operated within the parameters of Muslim nationalism and its regional variations. These parties comprised parties such as the Muslim League, the Unionist Party in Punjab, the Red Shirts in the Frontier province, the Bengal Peasants Party (Krishak Prāja) and the Jammu and Kashmir Muslim Conference under Shaykh Abdullah (1905–82). Some concurrently promoted other causes, as with the Unionist Party and the Krishak Prāja defending rural interests, or the Red Shirts and the Jammu and Kashmir Conference propagating left-leaning politics.

It was groups listed under points (a), (b), and (c) from which an Islamic response to political challenges could be expected that was largely shaped by 'internal' religious factors and not primarily by 'external' considerations. Muslim nationalists wanted to participate in colonial constitutional reforms but wanted to change the rules in their favour. The first three groups did not intend to play by the rules of the British game but were forced to respond to constitutional reforms. Popularly elected representation threatened the position of the Islamic and all traditional élites. Although their control over society had long been eroding, elected representation sealed their demise, or so it was feared. This forced them to adapt to the new system to retain local influence. As the formation of an Islamic public sphere is being studied, the focus is on educational movements of Islam and the Islamic sectarian and revival movements. They represented a structured response of Islam to change in public life and political conditions. Mass activism will be disregarded where it was spontaneous and amorphous though some campaigns, such as the Khilafat movement, will be considered for their part in institutionalized activism as and when they were pushed by Islamic groups.

The beginning of the twentieth century has been chosen as the cut-off date, as it appears that public activism of Islamic groups extended at a much faster pace thereafter, reaching a new quantity and quality in extent and density. This is demonstrated in Table 2.1 listing the great variety of forms of public life generated by the madrasa movements, and in Table 2.2, showing the same for the revival movements. In their formation of a religious associational life, the groups were marked by

Figure 2.1: Forms of Islamic Mobilization in Colonial India in 1900–47 (Schematic)

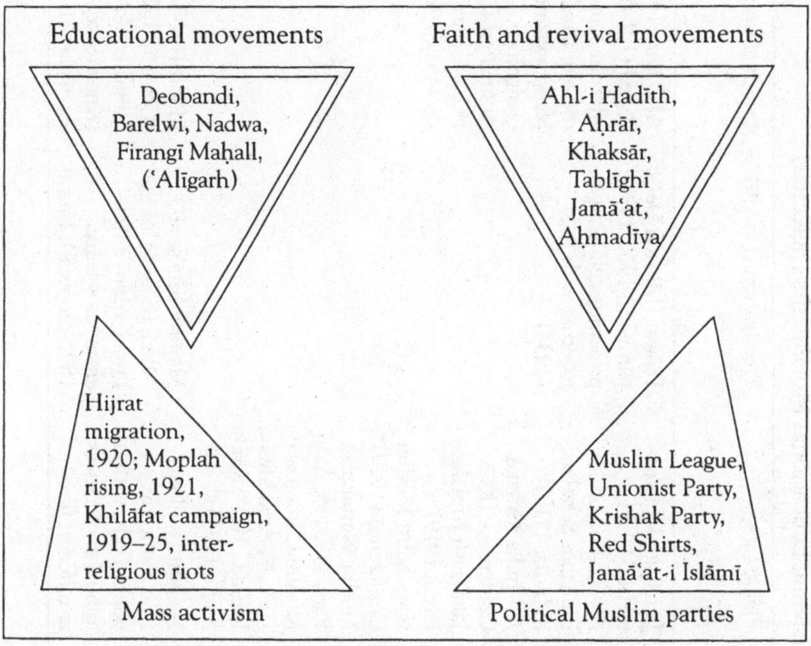

diversity and controversy, while converging on certain practices and topics of discourse. While most did not fall within the conventional understanding of sects, many showed sectarian tendencies. They were marked by pretensions of exclusivity and distinction, combining features of a religious sect and a social caste or community (*birādarī*), including endogamous trends. Yet their borders remained mostly porous. This determined their ambiguous public role, competitive and complementary by turns. Their shares of the public sphere overlapped and intertwined as some activists and institutions participated in several forms of mobilization. Figure 2.2 has been designed to help visualize this complex interaction in a simplified manner.

The study concentrated on groups, which dominated the public discourse of Islam and exerted influence extending beyond their areas of origin. This happened to be mainly the region of the classical Hindusṭan, the north Indian plains. It left out organized forms of activist Islam emerging in regions such as Bengal or south India. Such criteria for selection may appear ambivalent: The Red Shirt movement from the Frontier Province under Abdul Ghaffar Khan (1890–1988) operated not only as a political

Table 2.1: Forms of Public Life of Islamic Educational Movements (Selected)

School of Thought (*maslak*)/Lead Seminary	Education/Students	Public Life	Propagation (tablīgh)	Printing/Press
Deoband Dāru'l-'ulūm (Deoband, 1867)	Thamarāt al-Tarbīyat (Benefactors' Association of Former Graduates, 1878); Anjuman-e Mu'īn al-Islām (Helpers' Association, 1886); Jam'āyat al-Anṣār (Graduates' Association, 1909); Naẕārat al-Ma'ārif al-Qur'ānīya (Qur'anic School for English-educated Muslim Boys, Delhi, 1913); Lajnat al-Ittehād (Opposition Students' Union, 1926); Jam'īyat al-Ṯalaba (Loyalist Students' Union, 1926) Jāmi'a Millīya Islāmīya (National University, Aligarh/Delhi, 1920)*	Jam'īyat al-'ulamā-e-Hind (JUH, Association of Religious Scholars in India, 1919)*; All-India Khilafat Conference (KC, Jam'īyat-i Khilāfat-i Hind, 1919)*; Nationalist Muslim Conference (1929)*; Muslim Nationalist Party (1931)*; Āzād Muslim Conference (1942)*; Āzād Muslim Board (1942)*; Muslim Majlis (1945)*	Da'wat (Mission Department, 1907, 1934); preaching cell in Agra, together with JUH (1934)	*Al-Qāsim* (1913), *Al-Rashīd* (1914), named after the founders of the seminary, Qasim Nanotawi and Rashid Gangohi; *Al-Jamī'yat* (Delhi, 1920)*; *Khilāfat* (Bombay, 1920–35)*
Nadwa Nadwatu'l-'ulamā' (Council of scholars, Lucknow, 1893); Dāru'l-'ulūm/	Anjumanhā-ye Mu'īn al-Nadwa ([Local] societies of helpers of the Nadwa); Ṯalaba-e qadīm-e Nadwa (Old Boys Association, 1914); Anjuman-e Iṣlāḥ-ye Nadwa (Society for the Reform of the	Nadwatu'l-'ulūm—(the council as public body, with its annual conferences, as different from	Majlis-e Ishā'at al-'Ulūm (Society for the Propagation of Religious Knowledge, 1897-proposal); Iṣhā'at	Monthly *al-Nadwa* (Council, 1904); Monthly *Ma'ārif* (Knowledge, Azamgarh, 1916)

(contd...)

(Table 2.1: continued)

School of Thought (*maslak*)/Lead Seminary	Education/Students	Public Life	Propagation (tablīgh)	Printing/Press
(Seminary of the Nadwa Council, 1898)	Nadwa, 1914); Dār al-Muṣanifin (House of Writers, Authors—1914)	the seminary)	al-Islām (Programme for Propagation of Islam, 1904 proposal); Ikhwān al-Ṣafā' (Brothers of Sincerity, 1914); Dār al-Muballighīn (Preaching Department, 1938)	
Firangī Maḥall Madrasa (Lucknow, ca. 1700) Madrasa Niẓāmīya (1905–1970s); Madrasa Qadīma (1918)	Majlis-e-Iṣlāḥ (Society for [Islamic] Reform, 1910); Majlis Mu'ayyid al-Islam (Society of Supporters of Islām, 1887/1910)	Anjuman-i Khuddām-i Ka'ba (Society of Servants of the Ka'ba, 1913)*; Anjuman al-Khuddām al-Ḥaramain (Society of Servants of the Holy Places, 1925)	Bazm-i Ṣūfīya-i Hind (Organization to Revive and Reform Indian Mysticism, 1916)	*Al-Niẓāmīya* (named after Madrasa of Abul Bari, 1913); *Ikhwat* Brothers/Friends, during the Khilafat Movement, 1919)
Barelwi Jam'īyat Ahl-e Sunnat (Bareilly, ~1895); Manẓar-i	Local Anjuman-i Ahl-e Sunat and Sunni Conferences; Major local Madrasa Ḥanafiya (Patna, 1900); Madrasa Anjuman-e Ahl-e Sunnat, Jām'iya	Anjuman-e N'umānīya-e Hind (Lahore, 1887); Majlis-e Ahl-e	Anjuman-i Khuddām al-Ṣūfīya-i Hind (Servants of mysticism in India, 1901);	*Dabdabā-e Sikandarī* (Alexander's Greatness, Rampur, 1864); *Tuḥfa-e Ḥanafīya* (Memorial of

(contd...)

(Table 2.1: continued)

School of Thought (*maslak*)/Lead Seminary	Education/Students	Public Life	Propagation (tablīgh)	Printing/Press
Islām (Bareilly, 1904); Madrasa Mazhār al-Islām (Bareilly, 1937)	N'ayīmīya (Moradabad, 1910/1933); Dāru'l-'ulūm Ḥizbu'l-Aḥnāf (Lahore, 1924); annual convocation ceremonies (jalsā-e taqsīm-e asnād) at major madrasas	Sunnat wa Jamā'at (1896/1900); Anjuman-i-Anṣār al-Islām (Helpers of Islam in Support of Ottoman Empire, 1921); Al-Jam'īya al-'Āliya al-Islāmīya al-Markazīya (All-India Sunni Conference, AISC, 1925)	Jamā'at-i Raẓā-i Muṣṭafā (Society for the Veneration of the Prophet Muhammad, 1917); Jamā'at-i Ashrafiya Ishā'at al-Haqq (Society of the High-Born for the Propagation of the Right Faith); Ḥalqa-i Mashā'ikh (Circle of Great Shaykhs, 1908)*	the Hanafites, Patna, 1897); *Mashriq* (Orient, Gorakhpur); *Al-Bashīr*; *Anwāru's-Ṣūfīya* (Light of the Sufia, 1904); *Al-Faqīh* (The Jurist, Amritsar, 1918); *Yādgār-e Raẓā Al-Raẓā* (Bareilly, 1920); *Ahl-e Sunnat kī Awāz* (Voice of the People of the Sunna, 1946); *Munādī* (The Caller, Kh. H. Nizami)*
'Aligarh Anglo-Oriental Muḥammadan College (Aligarh, 1877); Aligarh Muslim University	All-India Muslim Educational Conference (AIMEC, 1886)*; Urdu Defence Association (1873)*; Anjuman Taraqqī-i Urdū (1903)*; Ikhwān uṣ-Ṣafā (Brothers of Purity, literary and students society, 1889?);	Muhammadan Anglo-Oriental Defence Association of Upper India (1893); Muslim League (1906)*; Anjuman-i Hilāl-i Aḥmar (Red		*Aligarh Gazette* (1866); *Aligarh Institute Gazette*; *Aligarh Muslim University*; *Gazette Muhammadan Anglo-Oriental College Magazine* (Student Journal, 1894)

(contd...)

(*Table 2.1: continued*)

School of Thought (*maslak*)/Lead Seminary	Education/Students	Public Life	Propagation (tablīgh)	Printing/Press
(1920)	Anjuman al-Farẓ (Duty society, 1891); Brotherhood (1892) Old Boys' Association (1899, 1907)	Crescent Mission to Ottoman Turkey 1912–13)*; All-India Muslim Ladies' Conference (AIMLC, 1914)*		
Shi'a Shi'a College (Lucknow, 1917)		All-India Shī'a Conference (1907); All-India Shi'a Political Conference (1930); Punjab Shi'a Political Conference (1939); All-India Shi'a Social Conference; All Parties Shī'a Conference		*The Moonlight*

Sources: Ahmad (1994), Ahmed (1975, 1980); Friedmann (1989); Hashmi (1989); Hermansen (2001); Inayatullah (1988); Jain (1979); Khan (2001); Lelyveld (1996); Malik (1997); Metcalf (1982); Minault (1982); Rizvi (1980); Riẓwi (1979); Robinson (1994, 2001); Sanyal (1996a).

Note: Date of foundation or (re-) activation is given in brackets. Some organizations pursued multiple objectives falling into more than one category.

Entries marked with * were founded with the assistance or at the initiative of the respective movement, but remained formally independent. Entries on Aligarh and the Shī'a are given for comparison.

Figure 2.2: Contestation of the Public Sphere by Islamic Groups

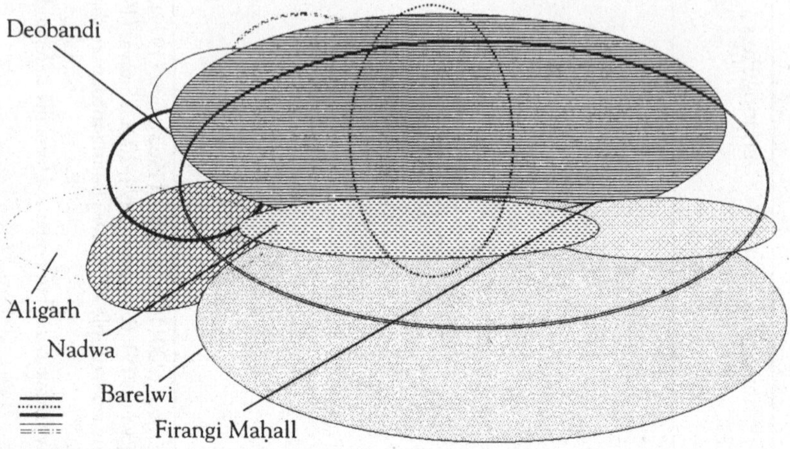

party but also as a reform movement using religious discourse. This was reflected in their appellation as Pakhtun Servants of God (Khudā-i Khidmatgarān) (Rittenberg 1988; Talbot 1990). Yet, its prime objective was not religious renewal or the revival of faith although it was not averse to using such arguments when addressing the devout Pakhtun tribes. The right-wing Muslim Front (Ittihād-ul-Muslimīn) from the principality of Hyderabad State has also not been considered (Pernau 2000). Although it had some connections with the Khāksār movement, for which it briefly acted as the local chapter, it more represented a regional struggle for the political accommodation of the Islamic élite within the State.

Although the Islamic Party (Jamā'at-i Islāmī/JI) has proved very influential in Islamic discourse and the Islamic sphere in South Asia since its foundation in 1941, it has not been considered for this study as a separate movement. During the period reviewed here it did not make much impact in public as it came into existence only shortly before colonial rule ended. Where appropriate Maududi's views will be considered subject-wise reflecting his wider importance.[3] In contrast the party had a limited influence. During most of its time of existence the JI could not break out of a certain political insularity. It gained some political clout in the early 1950s during debates on the future constitution for Pakistan under Zia-ul-Haq's military regime in the 1980s and as part of the six-party coalition MMA (Muttahida Majlis-e Amal). The incongruence between Maududi's

[3]For a comprehensive overview of the views and development of Maududi and the Jamā'at-i Islāmī, see Nasr (1996, 1994).

views and the activities of the party became even more obvious after his withdrawal from leadership (*amīr*) in 1972 and after his demise in 1979.

The JI shared these inconsistencies with several other Islamic groups. But there was also a phenomenological distinction between them. While all groups discussed here owed their inception to the renewal of religion, the ultimate objective of the JI was politics in the name of Islam and the creation of a polity on Islamic principles. This was more than a semantic divergence. In many ways the JI was an utterly modern political movement, attempting as it did to reconcile the modern requirements of state and politics with Islamic principles. It was created as an activist political party.[4] It consciously portrayed Islam as an ideology. When founded it perceived itself as an ideological party fashioned after the most successful ideological movements of the time, Communism and Nazism. Its main objective has been the creation of an Islamic state. Before independence it sought to promote conditions for such a state through reform of the Muslim intellectual élite. After independence it directed all its activities to turning Pakistan into an Islamic state. Contrary to the theological parties, it did not want to leave control over such an Islamic state in the hands of the religious scholars, the 'ulamā', but thought it necessary to establish a separate and coherent Islamic polity (Adams 1983). Such difference in perspective between the JI and the religious scholars exemplified the JI's modernity. Synthesizing different traditions and eclectic in its religious and political views, it did not base itself on a particular Islamic school of law or thought, although it remained tied to mainstream Sunni belief and of late reverted closer to Deobandi thinking. Its doctrinal eclecticism opened it to modernizing influences on questions of women's participation, technology, science, and education.[5] Although the JI remained careful not to identify with social conservatism that was argued in the name of religion, it went along with sectarian radicalism. While it did not initiate action against other sects, it acquiesced in campaigns against them or provided arguments for such campaigns. Its preoccupation with the systemic

[4]Maududi believed that the foundation of a new political party was a pre-requisite to a successful religious renewal of Islam. Masudul Hasan, *Sayyid Abu'l-'Ala Maududi and his Thought* (Lahore: Islamic Publications, 1984), Vol. 1, p. 75, quoted in Nasr (1996: 40).

[5]While on a doctrinal level, JI leaders have argued in favour of divine creation, on a practical political level they have demanded resolute strides by Pakistan in science and technology, notably to compete more successfully with India (cf. the commentary by Qazi Husain [b. 1940], 'Islamic Movement and The Global Perspective' in the party's publication *Tarjumān al-Qur'ān*, January 2000, here from their website at http://www.jamaat.org/Isharat/2000/ish012000.html). Where the Pakistani physicist Pervez Hoodbhoy regards the JI attitude with scepticism (1991), others stress the JI is pragmatically ambiguous or schizophrenic (Nasr 1994).

renewal of the polity led it to introduce stringent measures of discipline and a commando-style organization giving jihād the broadest possible political interpretation and justification as long as it served an Islamic order and was directed against a political enemy. Since the 1980s, when it extended its influence during the Afghan war, it has shown signs of developing sect-like features, controlling madrasas, mosques, and certain territories in Pakistan.

2.1. THE EDUCATIONAL MOVEMENTS

Islam in India produced a variety of forms of public mobilization that emanated from networks of religious education. They formed around a lead institution that shaped their outlook and guided adherents. The networks consisted largely of madrasas and Dāru'l-'ulūm (house of sciences).[6] These spawned a considerable number of spin-offs. The schools provided the equivalent of secondary and higher education in the theology of Islam. They are to be distinguished from the primary level of Islamic schools, the *maktabs*. Of the hundreds of schools dotting the subcontinent, the emphasis was on four schools, which established independent traditions of religious thought and education, interpretation and practice. Through their graduates they affiliated seminaries and mosques across South Asia and later across the Islamic world and beyond.

In a doctrinal sense, only the schools of the Deobandis and Barelwis represented a separate maslak (practice, way) in Islamic faith and ritual, not just separate schools of thought. Although the Nadwa and Firangī Maḥall formed into independent lines of tradition, their impact on doctrinal differentiation was limited. Firangī Maḥall attempted to preserve forms of orthodox learning in consonance with Sufi-based traditions of folk Islam. The Nadwa approach occupied an intermediate position between traditional learning and the perceived need to prepare Islamic students for a society based on Western standards that, for instance, required the knowledge of the English language. The College, and later, University of Aligarh will be considered here for its impact on Islamic discourse in India. In theological controversies it served as a modernist reference point for madrasas.

The formation of the major seminaries in the latter part of the nineteenth century represented a drive for the strengthening of faith and of formal Islamic knowledge among Muslims. Their leading scholars went public in connection with controversies over the interpretation

[6]Cf. the respective articles under '*dār al-'ulūm*' by J. Jornier and A. S. Bazmee Ansari in EI/II: 131–2.

of Islam, and religious and social reform. The scholars sought to formulate theological positions on modernizing trends among Muslims on British policy. They attempted to address reformist challenges from other communities, especially from the Hindus. The latter were well ahead in terms of adaptation to Western education and participation in public life.

2.1.1. Deoband

The Dāru'l-'ulūm came into being when a small primary school (maktab), located in the town of Deoband in north India in the Ganges plains was raised to the status of a madrasa in 1866. Comparison of Deoband with the famous Islamic Al-Azhar University in Cairo or Oxford University reflected its central role in Indian, or South Asian Islam. Its graduates included leading Islamic activists in India, and increasingly of the entire Islamic world.

Its nineteenth-century history has been aptly analysed by Barbara Metcalf in her classic *Islamic Revival in British India: Deoband, 1860–1900* (1982). The madrasa founders, Nanaotawi and Gangohi, were very conservative, notably in the famous controversy with Sayyid Ahmad Khan who was considered to be a modernizer sympathizing with the British. In the nineteenth century, the madrasa did not generate much public activism. This started changing with a new leadership largely under the influence of Mahmud al-Hasan (1851–1920). The Tripolitan and Balkan wars with Ottoman Turkey and World War I left their impact on scholars and graduates from Deoband. They instigated or participated prominently in several episodes of Islamic activism, notably the Khilafat Movement.

Theologically their leanings were purist and literalist in the tradition of Shah Waliullah. They advocated a return to the Qur'an and the Prophetic tradition (Sunna). In contrast to the Wahhabis, however, they would compromise on their adherence to their law school, Ḥanafī (after Abu Hanifa). Nor did their puritanical beliefs lead them to relinquish their connections with mystical Sufi orders of Islam, although they vehemently opposed the worship of local saints and their graves (for details see Ch. 3).

Gradually, Deoband developed all the hallmarks of a modern public institution. It institutionalized Islamic education for a wide, if not mass audience, in contrast to traditional home-based instruction. Semi-political bodies of religious scholars sprang from its fold taking up public activism in more specific ways. To these belonged an Old Boys Association (Jam'īyat al-Anṣār, 1909), and in cooperation with scholars from other schools and nationalist Muslim politicians, the All-India Khilafat

Conference (Jam'īyat-i Khilāfat-i Hind, 1919) and the Association of Religious Scholars of India (Jam'īyat-e 'Ulamā'-ye Hind, 1919).[7] After independence the movement set up its own institutions, including a separate party, the Jam'īyat-e 'Ulamā'-ye Islām (JUI), in Pakistan. Some of the latter's activities gradually grew more intolerant and militant, particularly since the Afghan war and the dictatorship of Zia-ul-Haq, although a distinction has to be made between the more radical JUI party factions, led by Fazlur Rahman (b. 1951) and Sami al-Haq (b. 1938), and the Deobandi madrasas, the majority of which remained devoted to teaching and learning. Among Deobandi doctrinal offspring in Pakistan were splinter groups involved in sectarian violence and Islamic militancy. They operated in Afghanistan, supporting and guiding the Ṭālibān, and in Kashmir through outfits such as the Ḥarkat al-Mujāhidīn (HM/Group of the Holy Warriors). Deobandi militants apparently also had contacts with the Bin Ladin network.[8] A major international conference of Deobandi scholars and madrasas took place near Peshawar in April 2001.[9]

The lead madrasa in Deoband continues to play the role of a major centre of learning and Islamic theology for Indian Muslims and the Islamic world in general. The madrasa still keeps its traditional distance from the Indian state although it is not inclined towards the openly oppositional style of its Pakistani affiliates. It remains aloof from Islamic militants, although it shares many of their ideological moorings. Personal rivalries led to a split in 1982. Maulana Marghubur Rahman was elected the new rector (*muhtamim*) in 1980 in place of Qari Muhammad Tayyib.[10] A rival madrasa of the same theological persuasion by the name of *Dāru'l-'ulūm Waqf*, headed by Maulana Muhammad Salim Qasmi, opened in 1982 in Deoband.

2.1.2. Barelwi

The Barelwi school of thought owed its beginnings to the activities of Maulana Ahmad Raza Khan Barelwi (1856–1921), a religious scholar

[7]Cf. proceedings of the Executive Committee the Working Committee (NMML B/14).

[8]The (former) leader of the HM, Fazlur Rahman Khalil, signed the appeal of Bin Ladin's group al-Qā'ida (The Base) published in 1998. It called for the killing of Americans and their allies as infidels acting against Islam (cf. the appeal 'Jihad Against Jews and Crusaders: World Islamic Front Statement' on the *Washington Post* website www.washingtonpost.com, 23 February 1998). The HM was blacklisted by the US as a terrorist organization (US Department of State Report 'Patterns of Global Terrorism—2000', at the D.o.S. website www.state.gov, Appendix B: Background Information on Terrorist Groups).

[9]*News*, 11 April 2001.

[10]Cf. the life sketch of the former rector Qari Muhammad Tayyib at Deoband's website at http://www.darululoom-deoband.com/urdu/introulema/3/g.htm.

and prolific writer from Bareilly, not far from Deoband.[11] It was first perceived as a movement in connection with an agitation against the Nadwa council and its plans to reform religious instruction between 1890 and 1900. In the beginning it was much less institutionalized than Deoband. Yet its influence radiated from the locality of Bareilly, the seat of residence of the Raza family, in a similar manner as that of the neighbouring dāru'l-'ulūm from Deoband. Ahmad Raza was guided in his activism by comparable challenges: the perceived decline of Muslim faith and practice, the growing role of 'false' and 'deviant' dogmas, and the threat allegedly posed by Christian and Hindu missionary activities.[12]

The Islam Ahmad Raza defended was the Sufi-oriented, shrine-based folk Islam of mainly rural north India. He accorded priority to the principle of adherence (taqlīd) where Muslims were called upon to stick to established traditions, and more particularly, to their law school (ma<u>d</u>hab), and to their religious mentor or guide (pīr), a function closely associated with Sufi heritage. He went to great pains to elaborate his defence of established orthodox religious order. He justified saintly intercession at graves or by a living *shaykh*, particularly attacked by purist Islamic groups. While deeply rooted in local traditions, his arguments relied on injunctions from the Qur'an and the Prophetic traditions (ḥadīth). He always wanted folk Islam to remain within the confines of Islamic law, the sharī'a. Essentially he lived the life of a religious scholar (*'ālim*), replying to queries on Islamic law and publishing religious decrees, fatāwā. At the same time he extensively engaged in devotional practices in his capacity as a pīr, granting blessings, dedicating amulets and charms, receiving and dispensing donations.

The Barelwi school of thought defined itself through the personal network of students, adherents, and disciples, following Ahmad Raza, his sons, and successors.

Their madrasa Manẓar-i Islām established in 1904 was for long less formalized than the Deoband seminary. After about 1900, the Barelwi movement became more assertive in public. Its visibility was enhanced through claims to the appellation of Ahl-e Sunnat wa Jamā'at in public discourse, for which also 'Sunni' was used as shorthand.

After Ahmad Raza's death in 1921, his two sons took over. Hamid Raza Khan (1875–1943) was appointed his successor (*sajjāda-nishīn*) in the Sufi sub-order of the Rizwis (*silsila-e-riẓwīya*) in 1915. Mustafa Raza Khan (1892–1981)[13] became the head of the Department for Legal

[11]For a comprehensive overview, see Sanyal (1996a) for the period up to the 1920s, and Sanyal (1998), for the following period.

[12]Ahmad Raza's name Barelwi derives: from the town of Bareilly.

[13]On his life, see Sayyid Muḥammad Riyasat Ali Rizwi Barelwi's biography (1980).

Consultation (*dār al-iftā'*) and a Sufi mentor (pīr) in his own right. Institutionalization of the Barelwi School made rapid progress, always trying to catch up with the Deobandis. The group produced activist offspring such as the All-India Sunni Conference (AISC) (al-Jam'īya al-'Āliya al-Islāmīya al-Markazīya, 1920), the Helpers of Islam (Anjuman-i Anṣār al-Islām, 1921) supporting the Turkish-Ottoman cause, and missionary organizations. Affiliated madrasas multiplied and expanded formal religious education among the Barelwis.

In independent Pakistan the group produced its own religious party, the Jam'īyatu'l-'Ulamā'-e-Pākistān (JUP). It emerged from the AISC at a meeting in Multan in March 1948 (Ahmad 1993: xxviii). *Sīra* and *mīlād-i muṣṭafā* conferences (to honour the Prophet) and mashā'ikh conventions, representing Sufi shaykhs and shrine keepers, became popular forms of public Barelwi representation. Led by Maulana Shah Ahmad Nurani (1926–2003) since 1973, the JUP gradually moved to a position supporting other Sunni groups on demands for Islamization of society or Islamic militancy. Since its inception the Barelwi School has visibly modernized by penetrating urban space and creating means of religious education (madrasa) and propaganda (printing presses). Yet the network of key shrines and madrasas, which serve as its backbone of influence, is still closely tied to large landholding and rural life.

In India, Maulana Akhtar Raza Khan Azhari, the grandson of Ahmad Raza, is the current successor and shrine keeper (sajjāda-nishīn) in Bareilly. The Barelwis have also not lagged behind the Deobandis in international activities. The Imam Ahmad Raza Academy is active in many parts of the Islamic world.[14] The Third International Sunni Conference was conducted in Multan, Pakistan, in April 2000.[15] International *Mīlād* Conferences are also held regularly.

2.1.3. *Nadwa*

The Nadwa was founded as a council of religious scholars ('ulamā') at a convocation ceremony at the Madrasa Faiẓ-i Amm in 1892. The meeting was convened to improve religious learning, to harmonize sectarian differences, and to reconcile religious studies with modern requirements. Maulana Muhammad Ali Monghiri (1846–1927) was the moving spirit behind the council's foundation (Hasani 1964). All major trends in Islam at the time were approached for participation: the Deobandis, the Barelwis, the Ahl-i Ḥadīth, the Shi'a, the Aḥmadīya, and the representatives of Aligarh, although the *Aḥmadīs* never participated and the Shi'is were eased

[14]Cf. the South African Barelwi website www.raza.co.za. [15]*Dawn*, 9 April 2000, at www.dawn.com.

out. As the other seminaries were slow or reluctant to implement the proposed changes, the council ultimately opened its own dāru'l-'ulūm in Lucknow in 1898. The Nadwa Movement and the attached seminaries were much more institutionalized than those of the Barelwi School. The Nadwa too established its own network of affiliated schools and support organizations. Shibli Numani, Professor of Arabic and Persian at Aligarh College, influenced the founding phase of the Nadwa seminary and pressed for reforms during his chairmanship between 1905 and 1913. In his experience, modern education at Aligarh lacked religious and cultural identity, for which educated Muslims needed to remain in touch with old learning, that is, theological instruction. In particular, he set out to reform the time-honoured curriculum of Islamic learning in South Asia, the *dars-i niẓāmī*. While the Nadwa's role was largely uneventful during the 1920s, in the 1930s and 1940s it opened to mass movements like the Tablīghī Jamā'at and to students from other regions of the Islamic world, notably Africa and Southeast Asia. From 1915 onwards, Sayyid Abdul Hayy (1869–1923)[16] took charge of the seminar as chairman of the Nadwa Council (*nāẓim*). With a short intermission, his sons Sayyid Abdul Ali (d. 1961) and Sayyid Abu'l-Hasan Ali Nadwi (1913–99) followed him in the office of chairman in 1931 and 1961. Like other seminaries, the Nadwa has had its share of internal dissent and factionalism, academic and student revolt. However, direct religious or political activism among the Nadwis, that is, graduates and teachers of this institution, was less pronounced during this period. Though the seminary was founded as a reference institution for modern Muslim learning, it could not live up to this pretence.

The associational life of the Nadwa group was dominated by annual sessions of the council of religious scholars (Nadwa) discussing both general issues of Islamic education and affairs of the seminary (dāru'l-'ulūm). Support for the objectives of the Nadwa was organized through a network of local support organizations, the Anjumanhā-ye Mu'īn al-Nadwa (Malik 1997: 426). A graduate organization of former students also came into existence (Talabā-e Qadīm-e Nadwa, 1914) (Malik 1997: 379). When the reform of the seminary activities became a hotly debated issue, the Organization for the Reform of the Nadwa (Anjuman-e Iṣlāḥ-ye Nadwa, 1914) was founded. The leaders of the seminary often used their house publication (the monthly *al-Nadwa*) and other print media (the paper *al-Hilāl*) to communicate with the public at large and Muslims in particular (Malik 1997: 374, 448ff.; see also, Table 2.1, this book).

[16]For an extensive biography by his son Sayyid Abu'l-Hasan Ali Nadwi, see Nadwi (1988b); for an overview, Malik (1997: 384ff.).

In independent India, the seminary still occupies a position of eminence, seeing itself as a guide and advisor to the Indian state in religious matters facing Muslims in India.[17] Its public face was mainly represented by S.A. H. A. Nadwi, affectionately called Ali Miyan. Its rector, Maulana Muhammad Rabey Hasani Nadwi, was elected chairman of the All-India Muslim Personal Law Board (AIMPLB) on 22 June 2002, a position through which Hasan Ali Nadwi had already exerted his influence.[18]

2.1.4. *Firangī Maḥall*

This appellation ('Foreign, or French Palace') derives from the fact that the institutional basis of the movement was laid in a building formerly belonging to a French merchant in Lucknow, the modern capital of Uttar Pradesh, and not far from Deoband and Bareilly. Emperor Aurangzeb (1618–1707) granted this building in 1694 to the surviving children of Mulla Qutbuddin Shahid Sahalwi (d. 1691), an eminent scholar ('ālim) killed by jealous rivals. His eldest son Mulla Nizamuddin (d. 1748) established a family tradition of learning and teaching, which spread over the whole of India and beyond.[19] The Firangī Maḥallīs mainly adopted private instruction in the tradition of neighbourhood teaching in the old city quarters (qaṣba). They transcended local boundaries through Nizamuddin's contribution to the reformation of religious learning. He compiled an innovative new syllabus (dars-i niẓāmī), which has dominated madrasa teaching in South Asia ever since, and more so in the religious schools of reformist Islam. Although withdrawn in demeanour and teaching style, the Firangī Maḥallīs contributed to Islamic debate and activism in the first half of the twentieth century through the activities of Muhammad Abdul Bari (1878–1926) who initiated several public associations (see the excerpt from his life sketch in Appendix I). He was both an erudite 'ālim and a pīr with a considerable following. He started the institutionalized Madrasa Niẓāmīya in 1905, which lasted into the 1970s.[20] The Firangī Maḥallīs participated in the affairs of the Nadwa Seminary in the same city, Lucknow. There were many personal bonds between these two

[17] Cf. the seminary's website at http://nadwatululama.org.

[18] *The Milli Gazette*, on the web at http://www.milligazette.com/dailyupdate/200206/20020623.htm.

[19] For a biographical dictionary of the 'ulamā' from Firangī Maḥall, see 'Ināyatullāh (1988), which was written in 1930 but published for the first time in 1988 only; on the events related, cf. ibid., 4; see also Robinson (1994: 266ff.).

[20] 'Ināyatullāh (1988: 173). For a short time at the end of the nineteenth century, a formal madrasa had existed run by Abdul Hayy Firangi Mahalli (d. 1886) (ibid., 200; Robinson 2001: 71, fn. 6).

institutions. Bari sat on the board of management of the Nadwa Seminary, (Robinson 1994: 420) although he was often critical of the passive attitude of the Nadwis and the Deobandis to the government. He played a leading role in the politicization of 'ulamā' activity from the agitation against the Balkan wars, to the Kanpur mosque incident (1913), to the beginnings of the Khilafat campaign, and the creation of the JUH in 1919 (Qureshi 1999: 88ff.). He was remarkable for his personal influence on young Muslim political activists such as the Ali brothers who became his disciples and turned to deeply religious positions. He was later eclipsed by Deoband influence and the rising star of Maulana Azad. For his activist stand, Bari faced strong opposition from a Firangī Maḥallī faction led by the brothers Abdul Hamid (d. 1932) and Abdul Majid (d. 1922), belonging to the Baḥru'l-'ulūm[21] section ('Inayātullāh 1988: 221–3). They received extensive support from government quarters to provide religious sanction against nationalist-inclined radical 'ulamā' such as Bari.

Bari also initiated broad institutional changes. He brought into being an educational society of supporters of Islam (Majlis Mu'ayyid al-Islām, 1910), a society for solidarity with the Turkish-Ottoman empire, the servants of the Ka'ba (Anjuman-i Khuddām-i Ka'ba, 1913), a Sufi conference, and periodical publications such as the *Ikhwat* (Brotherhood). This activity was partly countered by the rival Baḥru'l-'ulūm faction, which created a madrasa of its own (Madrasa Qadīma) (Inayatullah 1988: 222–3; also Robinson 1994; see also Table 2.2).

The pervasive influence of the Firangī Maḥallīs at the time can be gauged from their biographical dictionary, which listed many family members teaching across the whole subcontinent (Ināyatullah 1988). With no institutional basis, the number of actively teaching family members has since dramatically declined, but they still wield influence in local community life, and at times are also consulted by the state government of Uttar Pradesh.[22] The family is currently represented by Maulana Mufti Abu'l Irfan Firangi Mahalli, Islamic judge (*qāḍī-e-shahr*) of Lucknow,[23] and Maulana Khalid Rashid Firangi Mahalli, deputy prayer leader (*na'ib imām*) of the historic Aishbagh prayer ground (*'īdgāh*) in the city.[24]

[21]The 'Ocean of Science' the honorific appellation of Abdul Ali (1731–1810), the son of Mulla Nizamuddin at Firangī Maḥall.

[22]This was confirmed to me by Maulana Abu'l-Hasan Firangi Mahalli in an interview in Lucknow on 28 November 1998. He recounted that the chief minister belonging to the Hindu nationalist party—the Bharatiya Janata Party (BJP)—after taking office in the state, called on the head of the Firangī Maḥallī family to consult him on the political situation among local Muslims. DR.

[23]*The Milli Gazette* at http://www.milligazette.com/Archives/15052002/1505200275.htm.

[24]*The Milli Gazette* at http://www.milligazette.com/Archives/01102002/0110200265.htm.

Table 2.2: Forms of Public Life of Islamic Faith and Revival Movements (Selected)

Faith or Revival Movement (central office/mosque/seminary)	Education/Students	Public life	Propagation of faith (tablīgh)	Periodical publications/printing presses
Ahl-i Ḥadith (1864) Madrasa-yi Aḥmadīya Arah, Bihar	See under propagation	Ahl-i Ḥadīth sect officially recognized (1889); All-India Ahl-i Ḥadīth Conference (1906, 1912)	Anjuman-i Ḥimāyat-i Islām (Society for the support of Islam, Lahore, 1885)*	*Ishā'at us-Sunnat* (Propagation of the tradition, i.e. Sunna, 1877–1905); weekly *Ahl-i Ḥadith* (1903); *Ahl-i Ḥadīth* printing press (1903); *Thanā'i* printing press (Amritsar)
Tablīghi Jamā'at (1926, 1934) Bungalow mosque/Islamic centre at Nizamuddin, Delhi	Establishment/organiztation of new schools (maktab) and seminaries (madrasa) run locally	Annual congregations (*ijtimā'*) from 1940–1, no registered sect or public body	Travelling preaching groups—*Jamā'ats* from 1925–6, no separate organization	*Dar al-Ishā'at* (publication centre of the Tablīghī Jamā'at)
Aḥmadīya (1889) Jāmi'a Aḥmadīya Qadiyan → Rabwah (1948)	English high school, Madrasa at Qadiyan; primary schools in districts; Aṭfāl al-Aḥmadīya (Boys), Khuddām al-Aḥmadīya (young men); Nāṣirāt-i Aḥmadīya (girls); Lajna Amā' Allāh (women); (Religious) College (of Lahore Faction, 1914);	(Annual conferences of the Aḥmadīya in Qadiyan (1891); Aḥmadīya sect officially recognized (1900) → Ṣadr Anjuman-i Aḥmadīya (Chief Aḥmadīya society, 1906); Aḥmadīya Anjuman Ishā'at-i Islām (Society for the Propagation of Islam—Lahore faction, 1914)	Anṣār-i Allāh (Helpers of Allah, 1911); Anjuman-i Taraqqī-i Islām (missionary/propagation society, ~1915) Lajna Amā' Allāh (women's organization); Waqf-i Jadīd (Home Missionary Society); Anjuman Taḥrik-i Jadīd (Foreign Missionary Society, 1934); Nuṣrat Jahān Fund; Idāra Iṣhā'at al-Qur'ān	Weekly *al-Hukm* (Commandment, 1897); *al-Badr* (1902); monthly *Review of Religions* (1902); weekly *al-Fazl* (Virtues, 1913); *Payghām-i ṣulḥ* (Message of Peace, Lahore faction, 1913); *Islamic Review* (London, Lahore faction, 1913)

(*contd...*)

(Table 2.2: continued)

Faith or Revival Movement (central office/mosque/seminary)	Education/Students	Public life	Propagation of faith (tablīgh)	Periodical publications/printing presses
Aḥrār (1929, 1931) (Lahore)		Majlis-i Aḥrār-i Islām (Conference of the Noble in Islam, 1929); Majlis-i Markazīya-i Aḥrār-i Islām-i Hind (All-India Central Aḥrār Conference, 1932)	Sho'ba Tablīgh-ul-Islām (Department of Religious Propaganda, 1934)	*Inqilāb* (Revolution, Lahore); daily *Aḥrār* (The Noble, Lahore, 1931); *Zamīndār* (Landholder, Lahore)
Khāksar (1931–47) Headquarters at Ichhra (Lahore)	Nāẕim-e-'Alā (Supreme commander) for students appointed 1942	Majlis-i Khāksār (1926–1931) holding annual camps	Departments for Tablīgh (Propaganda) and Eḥtisāb (Press Censorship)	Official organ *Al-Iṣlāḥ* (Reform, Lahore, 1934–40); Weekly *al-Akṣarīyat* (Majority, Lucknow, 1942–43); *The Radiance Weekly* (Aligarh, 1943); *Akhwat* (Brotherhood, Aligarh); Weekly *al-Ē'lān* (Announcement, 1943); Sultān (The Sultan, Bombay, 1944)

Source: Based on Ahmed (1975, 1980); Friedmann (1989); Hashmi (1989); Jain (1979); Lavan (1976); Lelyveld (1996); Malik (1997); Mathur (1969); Masud (2000); Metcalf (1982); Minault (1982); Mirza (1975); NDC 405, 510; Qureshi (1974); Rizvi (1980); Robinson (1994); Sanyal (1996); Seth (1985); Walter (1991).

Notes: Date of foundation or (re-) activation given in brackets.

Some organizations pursued different objectives falling into more than one category.

Organizations whose entries are marked with * were founded with the assistance or at the initiative of the respective movement, but remained formally independent.

Aligarh has been included for comparison.

2.1.5. *Aligarh*

The Muhammadan Anglo-Oriental College was founded at Aligarh in 1875 on the lines of British colleges and raised to the status of a university in 1920. The institution and the school of thought it inspired are included here for their interaction with Islamic discourse and Muslim activism. As a Westernized college it was the antithesis of the madrasas of the Deobandi, Nadwa, and Barelwi variety. Its founder, Sayyid Ahmad Khan, was loyal to the British, considering this a pre-condition for Indian Muslims to hold their own against the dominant Hindu majority.

No matter how much its founder's arguments and its members' activities were couched in a modernist and pantheist spirit, Sayyid Ahmad himself emphasized the importance of religious instruction for the Muslim élite. Aligarh College and University were to provide Western education through English in a Muslim environment where the observance of religious traditions was emphasized. The works written by Sayyid Ahmad Khan on a rationalist re-interpretation of Islamic theology (*'ilm al-kalām*), mainly through his commentary on the Qur'an (*tafsīr*), played a normative role in the Islamic discourse of the time. They provoked much controversy both within and outside the college and the university. Curricular Islamic teaching at Aligarh remained basically conservative. Sayyid Ahmad and Aligarh University also inspired the creation of a number of public bodies serving the Muslim community in a modernist spirit. These included the Muslim Educational Conference (MEC, 1886) (Khan 2001) and the Muslim League (1906) (Shaikh 1989). Aligarh's early graduates, teachers, and trustees dominated much of modern public life of Muslim India (cf. Lelyveld 1996).

Today, Aligarh University continues to be a major secular educational institution for Muslims in India[25] although its educational standards cannot compete with the better Indian universities. Religious organizations such as the Tablīghī Jamā'at and the Islamic students' organization SIMI had significantly increased their activities on the campus. They created a more religion-oriented atmosphere, which grew increasingly intolerant of left-leaning and secular views that had dominated student life in the 1960s and 1970s.

2.2. FAITH AND REVIVAL MOVEMENTS

The main objective of these movements was to restore true religiosity and to enhance the relevance of Islam in daily life. The strong influence of leading personalities on the evolution of these groups distinguished

[25]See its website at http://www.amu.ac.in.

them from the educational movements, which centred on an institution. Consequently, their style was more personal and action-oriented. They explicitly contributed to the revival of Islam as a social and public phenomenon. But they also based their activities on doctrinal or religious issues. For this, they highlighted the centrality of selected Islamic institutions or injunctions, such as tablīgh and the ḥadīth. The Ahl-i Ḥadīth and the Aḥmadīya occupied a middle position between the madrasa and the revival movements. Like the madrasa movement, they fathered a new school of theological interpretation, creating (almost) a new religion in the eyes of many mainstream Muslims. Most Sunni Muslims considered the Aḥmadīya heretics. There are some who do so with regard to the Ahl-i Ḥadīth (the Barelwis). Yet, they also built a strong and close-knit social organization, which controlled its members tightly, a typical feature of the revival movements. The Ahl-i Ḥadīth were not yet as institutionalized as they became after independence and especially since the 1970s, preserving more the character of study circles of the Prophetic traditions. The activism of the Ahl-i Ḥadīth and the Aḥmadīya was very much leader-driven though, more in line with the other revival movements.

2.2.1. *Ahl-i Ḥadīth*

This movement came into existence as a relatively small circle of religious scholars bent on reforming the teaching of Islamic theology (for an overview see Reetz 2001 b). Siddiq Hasan Khan (1832–90) and Maulana Nazir Husain (1805–1902) started the Ahl-i Ḥadīth (AH) as a school of thought around 1864. In the twentieth century, it was driven by leaders such as Thanaullah (Sanaullah) Amritsari (1868–1948) and Dawud Ghaznawi (1895–1963). Under the influence of Wahhabi and Yemeni ideas, the Ahl-i Ḥadīth emphasized the need to circumvent the medieval law schools. For guidance they mainly turned to the written traditions about the life and sayings of Prophet Muhammad, the ḥadīth. They attributed the need for purification to the growing prevalence of what were perceived as un-Islamic customs among Muslims (cf. the Ahl-i Ḥadīth fatwā collection by Nazir Husain 1971). They were also concerned about Messianic movements, such as that of the Mahdī in Sudan and the Aḥmadīya in India. At the same time they retained connections to the local networks of the Indian 'Wahhabis' suppressed by the British in 1863 and sentenced in the so-called Wahhabi trials between 1868 and 1871 (Hunter 1969 [1871]). When they claimed the appellation of Ahl-i Ḥadīth they did so to underscore their devotion to religious scholarship, professing profound loyalty to British rule at the same time. Until about 1910 they actively engaged in religious reform and the renewal of instruction, also within the framework of the Nadwa council. They saw their task as providing religious knowledge and guidance in the observance of Islamic rituals. Gradually they grew into a sectarian movement with a broader following. Their regional focus was in Punjab.[26] They set themselves demonstrably apart: in doctrinal matters, they antagonized mainstream Muslims by rejecting the four Sunni law schools, and in ritual they raised frequent controversies by a manner of prayer based on a particular interpretation of some ḥadīth. By holding all-India conferences from 1912, they sought a more visible public profile. Their 'Protestantism' served them well in maintaining group cohesion. Their rigour and vigour bred institutions across India with remarkable speed. In a report prepared for the fiftieth anniversary of the Muslim Educational Conference in 1937 (cf. Khan 2001), they listed an India-wide network of madrasas, printing presses, and a plethora of religious publications—their own and vernacular translations of Arabic classics (Nausharwi 1970). While their worldly ambitions remained limited at the time, their activism was directed at shaming religious dissenters and deviant practices, as they understood them. During the reign of Pakistan's military dictator, Zia-ul-Haq, in the late 1970s and 1980s, the organization got a new lease of life and opened a large number of facilities. From the 1920s onwards, accelerating after the 1970s, it developed international connections with the Salafiya and the Wahhabiyya in Arabia, building on old networks of personal contacts with the Hijaz. Lately, they have started their own chapters in several Muslim countries. Militant activity also grew from their ranks in the shape of the Pious Army (Lashkar-i Taiba/LT], involved in insurgent activity in Afghanistan and Kashmir, although its association with the Ahl-i Ḥadīth proper was tenuous. The LT was also embroiled in the sectarian militant network in Pakistan and kept contacts with the international network of Bin Ladin.[27]

In Pakistan, the AH transformed into a political party. It joined the electoral alliance of six right-wing religious parties, Muttaḥida Majlis-e 'Amal (MMA), formed in 2001 where it was represented by its chairman,

[26]The Ahl-i Ḥadīth had grown disproportionately in Punjab (sects were not tabulated in 1901):

Census years	1881	1891	1911	1921	1931
Absolute returns	2,453	3,604	39,083	60,327	182,544
Increase over previous census		+ 46.9 %	+ 1084.4 %	+ 54.4 %	+ 302.6 %

Computed on the basis of: Census 1911, Punjab, part I: 166; Census 1931, Punjab, part I: 313.

[27]The LT was blacklisted by the US in its 2000 report on global terrorism though in a lesser category where the groups are warned but no legal action is taken against them yet. See fn. 9, this Chapter.

Maulana Sajid Mir. The AH remained a religious and educational body in India, headed by its amīr, Muhammad Yahya.

2.2.2. *Tablīghī Jamā'at*

This group started as a quietist missionary movement, devoted to spreading the message of Islam (*da'wa*) centring on the propagation (tablīgh) of correct Islamic practice and faith primarily among Muslims.[28] While Islam had not known missionary movements for most of its existence, the need was clearly felt under the impact of missionary activities by Christians and reformist Hindus in India at the end of the nineteenth century. Muslims were afraid that their numbers could significantly decrease as a result of re-conversion to the Hindu fold. Some feared for the very survival of their religious community. The heightened religious tension of the 1920s centred on the battle for the souls of so-called neo-Muslims, belonging to late-converted groups who had retained non-Islamic customs in their social etiquette. Muhammad Ilyas (1885–1944), who had close links to the Deoband seminary, directed his efforts at the Mewat region[29] near Delhi where his ancestors had also conducted religious education and preaching. He believed that special efforts were required to achieve a renewal of religious observance among Muslims. Starting individual preaching from 1926 he redoubled his efforts after 1933 when his emissaries crisscrossed the Mewat region (Nadwi 1983: 33–4). It was feared that neo-Muslim Meo tribes were becoming a major target of the Hindu reconversion activities organized by the *shuddhī* (purification) movement of the Ārya Samāj (Haq 1972). Ilyas brought inhabitants from Mewat as lay preachers (*muballighīn*) to areas of traditional and sophisticated Muslim culture and history, particularly in the United Provinces, so that they could observe for themselves correct Islamic life and practices. During these missionary tours, local Muslims were invited (da'wa—invitation, mission) to join in prayers at the local mosque where proper Islamic rituals and customs were explained to them. Gradually this approach was extended to other Muslims areas and used as a means not only to reform the travelling preachers but also the respondents in the areas visited. From the 1940s onwards, other religious groups and major madrasa movements supporting religious purism joined the tablīghī efforts to make it a true mass movement. The first reported mass meeting of the movement

[28]For a good historical review of its foundations, see Haq (1972), although he tended to be adulatory and stressed its Sufi legacy excessively.

[29]For a historical account of events in the Mewat region, and the respective tablīgh activities, see Mayaram (1997).

took place in Mewat in November 1941 in which approximately 25,000 people participated (Mayaram 1997: 155; see Chapter 3, section 3.4.4).

Today it is believed to represent the largest global organization of living Islam. Its annual congregations in South Asia attract millions. In India, the movement is led by Maulanas Muhammad Saad Kandhalawi (b. 1965), the great-grandson of Ilyas, and Zubair al-Hassan (b. 1950), his great-grandnephew. In Pakistan, the movement is led by Haji Abdul Wahhab (b. 1923). Its demonstrable abstention from politics has provoked tension with political-minded Islamic groups, such as the Jamā'at-i Islāmī. In contrast, the Tablīghīs are seen by others as preparing the ground for the spread of more radical movements.[30]

2.2.3. *Aḥmadīya*

The members of this sect are called the Aḥmadīs or the Mirzā'is after its founder Mirza Ghulam Ahmad (1839–1908),[31] or the Qādiyānīs, after its place of origin, Qadiyan in Indian Punjab. In 1889, Ghulam Ahmad started accepting disciples. He took a (Sufi-inspired) oath of allegiance (*bay'a*) from those who recognized his prophetic claims. Ghulam Ahmad assumed that new revelations he received in dreams marked him out as the 'promised messiah' whose arrival was announced in the Qur'an as heralding the end of the world. Like many of his contemporaries, and future adversaries, he was driven initially by the desire to reform practice and faith in Islam. In part, he re-interpreted Islamic dogma and incurred the wrath of the orthodox theologians through his claims to prophethood and through his renunciation of violence in 'religious war' (jihād), which he restricted to the meaning of peaceful exertion in the way of God.

The high public profile of this sect thrived on controversy. Ghulam Ahmad fuelled it often deliberately. His inheritance became a matter of dispute. Eventually Mahmud Ahmad (1889–1965), the eldest son of his second wife, prevailed—at the cost of a major split in the community in 1914. A more moderate faction under the leadership of Muhammad Ali (1874–1951) established itself in Lahore, Punjab, and henceforth this sect came to be known as the Lahōrīs. This group moved slightly back to orthodox Islam by abandoning the controversial claim to prophethood. Despite the continuous tension surrounding it, the Aḥmadīya succeeded in attracting a stable following from the professional (doctors, lawyers)

[30] Such observations were recorded by Elke Faust in her recent research in Morocco (2001).

[31] Authoritative accounts of his life from the point of view of the Aḥmadīya community were written by Muhammad Ali (1906) and Mahmud Ahmad (1924).

and new middle classes. In Punjab, it also recruited a substantial following in rural areas and among lower castes and classes.

In Pakistan, it has been subjected to continuous persecution and physical attacks by sectarian radicals (see Chapter 4, section 4.4). Prime Minister Bhutto officially declared the Aḥmadīya a non-Islamic sect in 1974. Zia-ul-Haq increased pressure on them by making public acts of worship of Islamic symbols by Aḥmadīs a criminal offence through Ordinance XX of 1984. It introduced changes to the Pakistan Penal Code by adding sections 298B and C. The so-called Blasphemy Laws of 1982 and 1986 added sections 295B and C to the Penal Code. Section 295C called for the death penalty for blaspheming the Prophet Muhammad. By 1995 under this section alone, over a hundred cases had been registered against the Aḥmadīs.[32] The city built by the Aḥmadīs for their headquarters in Pakistan on leased land in 1948 and named Rabwah, bearing Qur'anic connotations, was forcibly renamed in the late 1990s as Chenab Nagar.[33] Harassment by sectarian radicals has not prevented the Aḥmadīya from establishing branches in all Islamic and most Western countries. Today it presents itself as a close-knit missionary movement with a global reach. It is marked by strong and sometimes repressive social bonds among its members. It has created a massive stream of missionary literature translated into all major languages of the world. Since 1982 the movement has been led by Mirza Tahir Ahmad (b. 1928), who calls himself the 'Fourth Successor to the Promised Messiah' and lives in de-facto exile in Britain.[34]

2.2.4. *Aḥrār*

This group, named the 'All-India Conference of the Free in Islam' (Majlis-i Markazīya-i Aḥrār-i Islām-i Hind), came into being on 29 December 1929 when a group of pro-Congress Muslims in Punjab joined together

[32]Cf. US Department of State, Country Reports on Human Rights Practices for 1995, March 1996, quoted here after the US Embassy website in Sweden, at http://www.usis.usemb.se/human/1995/southasia/pakistan.html, downloaded on 12 November 2002. 'Personal rivals and the authorities have used these blasphemy laws, especially Section 295(c), to threaten, punish, or intimidate Ahmadis, Christians, and even orthodox Muslims. No person has been executed by the State under any of these provisions; however, some persons have been sentenced to death, and religious extremists have killed persons accused under the provisions. The blasphemy laws also have been used to "settle scores" unrelated to religious activity, such as intrafamily or property disputes' (ibid.). For 2001, see http://www.usis.usemb.se/human/2001/southasia/pakistan.html.

[33]Cf. Amnesty International, 'Pakistan: Insufficient Protection of Religious Minorities', AI document ASA 33/008/2001, dated 15 May 2001, on http://web.amnesty.org.

[34]Cf. their website at http://www.alislam.org.

to express their religious concerns in politics more forcefully (Mirza 1975/I: 83). For some time, they acted as a militant pressure group for religious Muslims in Congress. They hoped to gain stronger representation on the working committee of the party. Their most prominent leader was Sayyid Ataullah Shah Bukhari (1891–1967), a brilliant orator and charismatic leader. He was closely connected with the Deoband seminary. He had participated in the Non-cooperation Movement on the side of Congress during the early 1920s. Initially, the political stance of the Aḥrār was furiously anti-British and in favour of a cooperative Islamic society for the downtrodden. At the same time, their leaders championed doctrinal causes from the very beginning. Bukhari, assisted by religious scholars from Deoband, vigorously pursued the purification of Islam against the Aḥmadīs, Barelwis, and Shi'is. The Aḥrār leadership also included representatives of other sects, like Dawud Ghaznawi from the Ahl-i Ḥadīth and Maulana Mazhar Ali Azhar, who was of Shi'i descent, a cooperation that was based less on common doctrinal ground than on shared allegiance to the Congress.[35] The Aḥrār gained prominence in connection with the agitation for the rights of the Muslim majority ruled by a Hindu prince in the neighbouring principality of Kashmir in 1931 and in mobilizing Muslim opposition to the so-called Sarda Act, which intended to raise the age of consent for marriage (see Chapter 5, section 5.3). During those campaigns and on other occasions, they sought to mobilize forces against the Aḥmadīya sect, which they considered evil on doctrinal grounds and because of their pro-British leanings. They also sought confrontation with the Khāksār in Punjab whom they branded as conservative and communalist. They moved into action against the Shi'a community in Lucknow. They split in 1941 and the majority started moving away from the Congress, articulating a pro-Pakistan position on the eve of independence. In 1953, they instigated severe riots against the Aḥmadīya sect in independent Pakistan.[36] This did not save them from falling into oblivion in later years. They abdicated a self-conscious political role in independent Pakistan in favour of the Muslim League and most of their leading politicians migrated to other groups and parties.[37] The foundations of their religious and political philosophy are the subject of a multi-volume

[35]They participated together with Maulana Habibur Rahman Ludhiyanwi, a major Deobandi scholar and Maulana Zafar Ali Khan in the first regular conference of the Aḥrār in 1931 (Mirzā 1970/I: 146).

[36]Cf. the so-called Munir Report on the riots and Aḥrār responsibility (Munir 1954: esp. 10ff. and 187ff.).

[37]The longtime chairman of the Pakistan Democratic Party, Nawabzada Nasrullah Khan (1918–2003), was general secretary of the Aḥrār Majlis before independence. Miyan Awaiz at Aḥrār office Lahore, 10 December 2002 D.R.

publication 'The Caravan of the Free' (*Karwān-i Aḥrār*) by Janbaz Mirza (1975), a long-time activist of the movement. Today their importance is reduced to a religious pressure group of mainly local influence in Lahore under the leadership of Sayyid Ataulmomin Bukhari, the son of Ataullah Bukhari. He represents them in public protest meetings of the religious right.[38] Another group survived in Ludhiana in the Indian Punjab, the All-India Majlis-i Aḥrār Party, organized by the grandson of the erstwhile Aḥrār leader, Maulana Habibur Rahman Ludhiyanwi.[39]

2.2.5. *Khāksār*

The movement of the Khāksār (lit. dust-like, humble, from Persian) was founded by Inayatullah Khan (1888–1963), popularly known as 'Allama Mashriqi' in 1931. Although Mashriqi himself was no 'ālim, he based the arguments for his movement on a reinterpretation of Islam. In 1924, he had written a programmatic document on Islamic doctrine called the *Taḏkira*. This is normally the title of a memoir of prominent (religious) people, but used here in the meaning of an essay or treatise on the interpretation of the Qur'an (Mashriqi 1972). On a universalist note, he invited followers from all religions—with not much consequence though. He applied this non-sectarian and egalitarian approach to doctrinal issues, social problems, and racial distinctions. He assumed his objective required thorough reform and change in Indian society and even more so in the Muslim community. The main obstacle to such deep-seated change he located in the lack of a true martial spirit in Indians in general and in Muslims in particular. He considered this slackness the reason for the continued dependence and enslavement of colonial people. That is why he made physical training and fitness (*ṣalāḥīyat*) a central demand and category of his movement.

This led him to marvel at other militant movements of his time, including early Nazism.[40] Mashriqi, then in the government educational

[38]See their Lahore street protest against the US war in Afghanistan in October 2001, in *Dawn*, 10 October 2001; their membership in the Joint Pakistan-Afghanistan Defence Council of the religious scholars, coordinating jihādī activities in Afghanistan and Kashmir up to February 2002, at the JI website under http://www.jamaat.org/news/pr020302a.html; and also their participation in local teacher strikes, in *News*, 15 October 2002.

[39]Meeting of Aḥrār office, Lahore, 10 December 2002, D.R.

[40]The Dutch scholar Baljon quotes from a personal letter sent to him by Mashriqi that he had met Hitler accidentally at the Berlin National Library in 1926. Hitler allegedly told him that he knew about his work *Taḏkira* (Mashriqi 1972) and apparently he discussed Islamic jihād with Mashriqi in detail. But Baljon assumed that Mashriqi was rather more attracted 'by the energy and quick results of the fascist regimes' as he had hoped that 'such energy would save India' (Baljon 1961: 12).

department, gave practical shape to his movement with his second book, *Ishārāt*—'Directions, or the only way to make Muslims stronger and the explanation of the movement of the Khaksar' (*musalmānon ko phir tāqatvar banādene kā wāḥid ṭarīqa aur khāksāron kī taḥrīk kī tashrīḥ*) (Mashriqi 1931). He slowly but surely attracted Muslims, mainly in Punjab, the Frontier Province, and the United Provinces.[41] Muslims were drafted into a militant social volunteers' service by signing a pledge, some with their own blood. They were exposed to regular drill and paraded in central city areas where they brandished their spade (*bēlcha*), which became their tool for building, relief work, and defence. It figured as the symbol of their martial spirit and their manliness. The movement was marked by an elaborate organization, with various forms of membership and ten departments with special functions (Malik 2000: 53–4). Mashriqi was the highest authority, responsible only to the party constitution. While on tour or in the 'field' he considered himself a humble servant taking his orders from the local commander-in-chief. Membership figures fluctuated wildly, but reached their peak apparently in 1944 with an estimated 1.6 million in the whole of India.[42] Serving as guards during religious festivals and participating in disaster relief operations such as during the Bengal famine of 1943, their operations were controversial. They fell foul of the British-Indian government when the latter attempted to suppress so-called 'private armies' after 1939. They attempted to befriend the Muslim League while refusing to attack the latter's political enemy, the Congress Party, with predictable failure. The arrest of Mashriqi by the British mobilized their adherents more than its programme.

Partition and independence eventually sidelined them and made them largely irrelevant. Mashriqi formally disbanded the movement in 1947. He then founded the Indo-Pakistan Islam League (IL). Since then the Khāksār have led a radical fringe existence. Their activities revived in the early 1950s. The Khāksār continued opposing partition and any compromise on Kashmir attempting to speak for Muslims in both Pakistan and India. Mashriqi's anti-Indian stand, demanding large-scale re-distribution of territory in favour of Pakistan was found embarrassing in Pakistan also. The Khāksārs faced persecution several times. In 1958, the party was banned after it played a role in violent incidents in Kashmir and was implicated in a political assassination. The government found it necessary to control Mashriqi's political activities until his death in 1963

[41] Mathur also reported branches in Burma, Ceylon, Bahrain, and South Africa (1972: 198–9).

[42] 16 lakh was the figure quoted by government sources (Home Department [Political-Internal], No. F. 74/4/1944-Poll. (I) Pt. III, para. 6, quoted in Mathur 1972: 207).

(Malik 2000: 190ff.). In 1977, the Khāksār Party formed part of the Pakistan National Alliance opposing Bhutto (Khalilzad 1985: 665). It continues a nominal existence even today and is led by one of Mashriqi's sons, Hamiduddin Ahmad al-Mashriqi.[43] When it attempted to participate in the 2002 general elections as Khāksār Taḥrīk Pakistān its registration papers were not accepted on formal grounds.[44]

[43]In an interview with me on 29 November 2002, Hamiduddin Ahmad al-Mashriqi contended that they were continuing 'some work' not only in Pakistan but also in India, in places such as Indore and Delhi. See also their programme as circulated by their central office at 32, Zaildar Rd., Ichhra, Lahore, Pakistan.

[44]*News*, 14 August 2002: 44, '71 parties allowed to contest polls, ECP rejects documents of 58 parties.'

3

Religious Discourse and Contested Doctrines

In Islamic discourse, the concept and objective of iṣlāḥ became a standard reference point. It legitimized the public activism of Islamic groups. The meaning of the term was contested. The objective of reforming religious life, to return to 'pristine' Islam in search of solutions to contemporary problems, commanded respect and authority among Muslims. Any group wanting to maximize its impact on the Islamic public was well advised to join the drive for iṣlāḥ. Salvatore contrasted it with the more personalized reference to private forms of belief in earlier periods, summarized by terms such as *īmān* (faith). He related it to the emergence of Islam as a generalized reference scheme, which epitomized the entry of Islamic discourse into modernity (1997).

This chapter examines the relationship between the issues and the forms of public intervention over religious topics. Interventions were driven by a common doctrinal agenda, but emphasis varied, and interpretations often differed substantially. It testifies to the modernity of these movements that this process generated new traditions, which today already appear dated. What the late Afghan Ṯālibān or the Deobandi and Ahl-i Ḥadīth groups demanded with regard to the restoration of the purity of Islam was often formulated little more than a century ago and as such of rather recent origin.

This chapter assumes that religious reformism begets intervention. This notion, familiar in the literature on Christianity, should be extended to Islam as well, argued Francis Robinson in his discussion of the 'Protestantism' of Islamic reform movements and their emphasis on 'thisworldliness' (1997, 2001: 211ff.). Islamic reform sought the reformation of man and his behaviour in the spirit of the founding period of 'pristine' Islam. In reality, restoration played itself out as a process of creation. It required constant intervention in several spheres: in peoples' lives, in their religious practices, and in their beliefs. Iṣlāḥ, therefore, usually amounted to a call for social intervention. But Islamic reformism was more than an act of this-worldly engagement: it retained a transcendental, religious dimension. Pious reformists based their conduct on the assumption that an ideal state of Islam had existed: life under Muhammad was indeed marked by divine attributes and could be restored. They perceived iṣlāḥ as anathema to (Western) modernity, and sought to return public life to the traditions (Sunna, ḥadīth). Robinson rightly warned against the simple equation of iṣlāḥ with modernity.

Whether Islamists were aware of the modernity of their behaviour, of their 'this-worldly' intervention was difficult to prove. Reformists such as the Deobandis and the Ahl-i Ḥadīth must have known that their insistence on change posed a challenge to society. Their claim to be in possession of the truth was also disputed from within Islam by groups such as the Barelwis. The discourse over the direction of Islamic reform and revival was varied and contradictory, but converged on a number of issues rooted in a common agenda, the details of which were open for disputation. Central categories of Islam became hotly contested. The first part of this chapter will demonstrate the breadth of differences in interpretations. The second part will look at lines of intervention forming a religious agenda of change. The third part concentrates on the Islamic leader, a discourse full of messianic and salvational expectations (millenarianism). Part four deals with the role of missionary movements and campaigns.

3.1. THE TRUTH: CONTESTED CATEGORIES

For South Asian Islam, the term iṣlāḥ has so far attracted little analytical attention as a historical and social discourse category. The term was used more actively by some Islamic leaders, notably the Nadwa leader, Shibli Numani, and the Deobandi divine, Maulana Ashraf Ali Thanawi (1863–1943). Others like Muhammad Iqbal or the Deoband scholar, Husain Ahmad Madani (1879–1957), paid less attention to it.

For all Islamic groups in India, the correction of the defective state of Islam and Muslim life in India became the declared objective of activist Islam. But iṣlāḥ was not restricted to restoring the validity and observance of a set of principles, at least in the Indian context. All reformers starting from Waliullah emphasized the need to revive and strengthen faith and piety. This opened the way for contemplative and pietist movements in the Sufi tradition to turn to reformism. The emphasis on the corrective aspect further implied that the content and ultimate goal of correction remained open to debate. Movements soon started to disagree with one another. It was unclear whether the focus was on the Qur'an, the ḥadīth, the law schools (maḏhab), jurisprudence (*fiqh*), or custom (taqlīd). They contested the very framework of iṣlāḥ, starting from the perceived threat to Islam, to the legacy of Shah Waliullah, considered the inceptor of South Asian Islamic reformism, to the meaning of iṣlāḥ itself, to the role of independent reasoning (ijtihād), of monism (*tauḥīd*), and of the 'ulamā'.

3.1.1. Islam in Danger

It was the perceived threat to Islam that continued to inspire Islamic reformists and the founding of reformist movements. Yet their threat perception changed over time considerably reflecting the mutation of their political and social environment.[1] Roughly four different perspectives could be discerned: that of Waliullah; that of the founder generation of Deoband; those of the late-nineteenth-century movements; and those of the early twentieth-century groups. Waliullah wanted to revive the temporal and spiritual power of Islam in the wake of the rapid collapse of Mughal power and the 'rise of anti-Muslim anarchic forces of the Marathas and the Jats' as Aziz Ahmad put it (1962: 28). He appealed to Muslim princes particularly the Rohilla chief, Najib al-Dawla [d. 1790], and the Afghan ruler, Ahmad Shah Abdali to attack the Marathas. Although not intolerant, Waliullah worried that Islam, which for him was the culmination of the world's religions, would be diluted. He cited deviations resulting from cohabitation with other religions or surviving among converted Hindus. This he feared would lead to Islam's supercession (Baljon 1986).

Deoband's founders identified the threat with the abolition of the Moghul Empire in 1858 after the uprising of 1857/58 had been defeated. They were concerned about religious ritual and the lack of religious education. The town of Deoband shared the decline of other Muslim qaṣba towns, with neighbouring villages burnt down and landed property confiscated. The goal of the 'ulamā' became the creation of 'a community both observant of detailed religious law and, to the extent possible, committed to a spiritual life as well' (Metcalf 1982: 87).

Movements which formed around the turn of the twentieth century, like the Aḥmadīya[2], the Ahl-i Ḥadīth, and the Barelwis, saw the threat to Islam elsewhere. They feared Christian missionary activity; the efforts

[1] An interesting contemporary account of these perceptions is given by Andrews (1929).

[2] Ghulam Ahmad complained that 'corruption, blameworthy innovations (*bid'a*), tomb worship (*qabr parastī*), worship of Sufi sheikhs (*pīr parastī*), and even polytheism became rampant. The Islamic way of life was replaced with drinking, gambling, prostitution, and internal strife. The Qur'an was abandoned, and [non-Islamic] philosophy became the people's *qibla*.' '*Mawāhib al-Raḥmān*', in Aḥmad (1957, Vol. 19: 311), quoted in Friedmann (1989: 105).

of the newly founded Ārya Samāj to pull 'neo-Muslims' back into the Hindu fold; and splits in the Muslim community. They saw divisions among Muslims as an expression of dissent (fitna) and reprehensible innovations (bid'a), which threatened Islam's survival. All three movements were offended not only by the Deobandis' puritanism, but also each other's arguments.[3] Such perceptions were comparable with the threats perceived by Sikh and Hindu reform movements.[4] These developments have been related to the public impact of regular census operations,[5] which exposed the relative strength of communities and sparked debate about the principles of inclusion or exclusion in census categories, and in larger society.[6] Among the madrasa movements, the Firangī Maḥallīs were perhaps least driven by the sense of danger to Islam since their style of teaching and doctrinal argument was based on continuity. They too, however, were deeply affected by the decline of the Moghul empire. Most avenues of employment for their members who were graduates, including state positions like Islamic judicial clerks (*muftī*, *qāḍī*), closed. Yet they still clung to virtues of intellectual propriety and individual teaching and their networks remained remarkably wide, as Robinson maintained (2001: 79–81).

The Islamic movements which sprang up in the 1920s and 1930s, the Khāksār, the Aḥrār, and the Tablīghīs, responded to yet another kind of threat, Muslim–Hindu inter-religious tension and strife in the mid-1920s. They felt that Muslims in general and religious Muslims in particular were being eclipsed by the changes. They also feared that the worldly politics of the rising Muslim League and the Congress Party would marginalize religious Muslims and expose them to communal tension.

[3]Thus the writings of the Ahl-i Ḥadīth founder, Siddiq Hasan Khan, were marked by 'pervasive pessimism, a fear of the end of the world' (Metcalf 1982: 269; see his 'The End is Near', in Ahmad and Grunebaum 1970: 85–88). Ghulam Ahmad, the founder of the Aḥmadīya was likewise convinced that Islamic religion and society and the position of Islam had sunk to 'unprecedented depth' (Friedmann 1989: 105). Ahmad Raza Khan of the Barelwis saw many fellow Muslims failing to embracing the full essentials of religion (*ẓarūrīyāt-i dīn*), which turned them into infidels in one way or the other (Sanyal 1996a: 202).

[4]Swami Dayananda (1824–83), founder of the Ārya Samāj Movement 1875, for instance, attacked Hindu orthodoxy for weakening Hinduism from within, and causing it to fall before the challenges of 'invading Islam and the Christian British'(Jones 1976: 33).

[5]Gyanendra Pandey is typical in making this point when describing the 'pressure of the censuses, and other social and political demands of the time' in transforming the various Julāhā weaver sub-castes into a single 'community' (1996). See also Jones (1981).

[6]Among the Islamic groups under study, notably the Aḥmadīya and the Ahl-i Ḥadīth acted with an eye on the census when they engineered the inclusion of their new community appellation in the 1890 Punjab Census. For the Ahl-i Ḥadīth, cf. Reetz (2001b); for the Aḥmadīya, see Lavan (1976, 1972).

3.1.2. The Legacy of Shah Waliullah and Reformist Genealogy

Shah Waliullah formulated the concerns of the religious élite in major works such as *Ḥujjat Allāh al-Bāligha* (Peremptory Argument of God) with new clarity.[7] He had come under the influence of Arabian reformers whose ideas had also shaped the outlook of Ibn Abd al-Wahhab, with whom he was often compared. Their thinking was not, however, identical. Ibn Abd al-Wahhab was considered much more unrelenting in his puritan drive for the restoration of independent judgement (ijtihād), for monism (tauḥīd), and against polytheism (*shirk*). Waliullah was more moderate in his Puritanism. He did not completely reject the interpretive literature of the law schools, as Wahhab did. Instead he regarded them as different ways of reconciling the traditions and the Qur'anic injunctions with contemporary requirements. But he rejected blind adherence (taqlīd) to them. He favoured restoring the Qur'an and the Sunna to a place of prime importance stressing independent reasoning (ijtihād) on their basis. Aziz Ahmad saw his major practical contribution to the renewal of Islam in his promotion of the study of the Prophetic traditions (ḥadīth), hitherto neglected in India (cf. Aziz Ahmad 1962, 1964; see also Robinson 2001: 225). In practical matters Waliullah remained a follower of the Hanafi law school (fiqh). Unlike Ibn Abd al-Wahhab, he did not break with the Sufi orders. Most reformist theologians in India followed him on this point. Instead of eliminating the mystical legacy, Waliullah stressed conformity with Islamic law (sharī'a).

By their ambiguity, Waliullah's teachings inspired divergent currents of Islamic revival in South Asia. Different groups related to separate elements in his thought, which they interpreted as key: Some focused on his emphasis on the Qur'an and the tradition (Sunna) reaffirming tauḥīd, others highlighted the stress he put on the centrality of the Prophet's life and conduct. Some were more interested in his urge to remove accretions in the Islamic ritual (bid'a). Still others gave weight to his revival of the faith in terms of piety and religiosity along with an affirmation of mysticism (*taṣawwuf*) in consonance with the law (sharī'a). On this basis his legacy is still claimed by doctrinally opposed groups, such as the Deobandis, the Ahl-i Ḥadīth, and the Barelwis.

The common doctrinal and spiritual roots of reformist groups created the desire in them to construct a reformist pedigree. Many traced back their reformist endeavour to Waliullah personally, to his disciples, or

[7]For a thorough survey of Waliullah's religious thought, cf. Baljon (1986). While *Ḥujjat Allāh al-Bāligha* is Waliullah's most famous and most often quoted work, Baljon regarded his complementary work *al-Budūr al-bāzigha* (Full Moons Appearing on the Horizon) to be of even greater significance (ibid.: 13).

family members. This approach reflected Sufi-inspired techniques emphasizing lineage and descent, somewhat paradoxically put to use for the affirmation of a reformist project resting on the critique of certain Sufi practices. In a way they presented themselves as 'reformist orders' in the Sufi tradition with their Shaykh being Shah Waliullah.

The Deobandis considered Waliullah their preceptor and located all the elements of their school of thought in his teachings. These included the emphasis on the Qur'an and the Prophetic tradition, mysticism, and the commemoration of Allah (see Appendix I for the principles of Deobandi thought). The long-time rector (muhtamim) of the Deoband Seminary, Qari Muhammad Tayyib (1897–1983), explained in his introduction to the centennial history of his seminary:

> Waliullah's knowledge, taste and thought, through the medium of Shah Abdul Aziz, Shah Muhammad Ishaq and then Shah Abdul Ghani reached *Ḥujjat al-Islām*, Maulana Muhammad Qasim Nanaotawi and Maulana Rashid Ahmad Gangohi, who universalised it through this sacred institution, i.e. the *Dāru'l-'ulūm* Deoband (Rizvi 1980/I: 2).

This also applied to other groups following the tradition of Deoband, particularly the Tablīghī Jamā'at and the Aḥrār Movement. Some 'ulamā' and Islamic activists, though, questioned whether the Tablīghī Jamā'at and its founder Muhammad Ilyas were a legitimate part of the Waliullahi Movement. Their critique was based on identifying the Waliullahi tradition with political Islam and the jihādī and political activities of *Shaykh al-Hind*, Mahmud al-Hasan, and *Shaykh al-Islām*, Husain Ahmad Madani. The Tablīghīs and Muhammad Ilyas were accused of remaining aloof from their political struggle leading Muslims away from the Waliullahi tradition. The Tablīghīs took great pains to refute this allegation. One of their most popular tracts (*Irshādāt wa Maktūbāt*) attempted to demonstrate that Ilyas' programme of religious renewal was a direct continuation of the struggle of Hasan and Madani.[8]

The Ahl-i Ḥadīth too regarded Waliullah as the father of their movement, the first modern Ahl-i Ḥadīth member.[9] They underlined the close relationship between the movement's founders and the Waliullah family and disciples. Siddiq Hasan's father was a disciple of Waliullah's son Shah Abdul Aziz (1746–1824) and Sayyid Nazir Husain of Muhammad

[8]See in particular the introduction to the tract by its compiler and editor, Iftikhar Husain Faridi (Ilyās 1997: 3–4), and the new foreword for the Pakistani edition by Muhammad Abbas Shad used here, reflecting also the criticism from the Jamā'at-i Islāmī characteristic for Pakistan.

[9]Cf. the dictionary of scholars of traditions (ḥadīth) compiled in 1938 by a prominent Ahl-i Ḥadīth writer Abu Yahya Imam Khan Nausharwi (1971); see also Rahmani (1972).

Ishaq (1782–1846), the grandson of Abdul Aziz and his successor (khalīfa) (Metcalf 1982: 275–6; Nausharwi 1971; Siyalkoti 1953). Thus they constructed a spiritual-cum-genealogical Ahl-i Ḥadīth family tree. Other groups took strong exception to this approach, especially the Barelwis (Jamiyyat-i Ahl-i Sunnat [Pakistan] 1989, here Vol. 1: 9).

The Barelwis traced their doctrinal descent not from Waliullah but his son, Shah Abdul Aziz. In particular, they saw themselves in the tradition of his ḥadīth studies. Ahmad Raza has pointed out that one of the three traditions of ḥadīth studies on which the Barelwis relied for their teaching diploma (*sanad*) went directly back to Aziz. (Ahmad Raza, *Al-ijāzā al-riẓwīya*, pp. 58–62, quoted in Misbahi 1976: 33). Perhaps another reason for the Barelwis to choose Aziz as their model of religious reform was his conciliatory manner. He was reported to have concentrated on his teaching, and did not push his reformist views. His famous fatwā on the state of war (*dār al-Islām*) did not appear to have been a declaration of war. He did not seem to have been involved in jihādī activity personally. He was also reported to have condoned unorthodox devotional practices he believed harmless (Mushirul Haq 1995).

The Nadwis of the Hasani family traced their reformist credentials back to the reformist activist and Naqshbandi Shaykh, Sayyid Ahmad Bareilly (1786–1831). After Sayyid Abdul Hayy took over the school, his family highlighted their ancestors' place among his disciples. Abdul Hayy was born in Bareilly, and his original name—Sayyid Ahmad—was apparently given to him in honour of the reformist Shaykh (Nadwi 1988b: 50, note 1; see also Malik 1997: 385f.).

3.1.3. Divergent Meanings of Iṣlāḥ

In South Asia, considerable variety in reformist interpretation existed, not dissimilar to differences between Abduh and Rida in the Arab context. Iṣlāḥ stood for the objectives of the movements, which they wanted to attain. Its interpretation indicated what means the Islamic groups wanted to employ.

The Deobandis wrote down in their statutes what they regarded as the direction (maslak)[10] of their school (Dastūr-e Asāsī-e Dār al-'Ulūm, Dēoband, quoted in Rizvi 1980/I: 329–31. Cf. Appendix I). This again was a paradoxical situation: As a religious movement they resorted to non-religious means, such as the formulation of written statutes and programmes reflecting Western legal thinking, in order to define their reformist

[10] The Deobandis usually translate maslak as 'tack', which also has different connotations.

objectives.[11] Though they claimed full allegiance to Waliullah's positions, they did not take a very radical stand on reform. Independent reasoning (ijtihād) on the application of Islamic principles was circumscribed not only by the limits of their own Hanafi law school, but also by the adherence they prescribed to a guide and mentor (shaykh). This personalized form of adherence to religious precepts was called *taqlīd-i shakhṣī*. Out of seven basic principles making up the Deoband approach (cf. Appendix I), the first two pronounced the unity of law and spirituality, of sharīʿa and ṭarīqa. This was an acceptance of Sufi practices in forms legitimated by the sharīʿa and the ḥadīth. Law, that is, the knowledge of the sharīʿa, was accorded priority, but mysticism was considered indispensable for becoming a true Deobandi, as otherwise 'moderateness in morals, stability of zest and ecstasy, internal insight, mental purity and observation of reality' (Appendix I) would be lacking. The importance of conformity with the Hanafi legal school came third. Deobandis were reminded of their duty to fight false 'customs of ignorance' and 'unlawful things' (unlawful in relation to the sharīʿa). This obligation to oppose 'tergiversation and deviation' was moderated: Due consideration was to be given to the 'psychology of the milieu' and the 'contemporary familiar means' of verbal or written argument. Violence was not encouraged or condoned. Adherence to 'Qasimism' and 'Rashidism', referring to the founders of the Deoband school, was declared to be the 'temperament' of the Deoband approach, and thus part of their interpretation of iṣlāḥ (for the Deoband approach, see also Saharanpuri 1987).

The Deobandi divine Thanawi played a prominent role both in the affairs of the Deoband seminary and in the reformist discourse. His extensive writings have proved influential to this day. He has inspired many reformist Islamic movements such as the Tablīghīs and the Aḥrār. For a time, he was the patron (*sarparast*) of the Deoband seminary.[12] He was particularly active in writing on iṣlāḥ and propagating its principles. In his person, doctrinal reformism met with a broader vision of social reformism. The collections of his religious recommendations (*malfūẓāt*) (Thanawi 1984) and decrees (fatāwā) (Thanawi 1977) covered many worldly issues of immediate practical consequence. A popular compilation was called the *Iṣlāḥ al-Muslimīn*, (Renewal of the Muslims) (Thanawi 1982,

[11] Also refer to the elaborate rules governing the activities of the Khilafat conference as published in its statutes (*Dastūr-i ʿAmal*) on its objectives, composition, membership, bodies, elections, provincial branches, etc. (Aziz 1972: 338–48). The statutes of the JUH were marked by similar attention to detail, as were the rules drafted for the election of an Islamic leader for India (*Amīr al-Hind*), as partly documented in Appendices III and IV.

[12] Rizvi (1980/I: 209, 222). Thanawi held this post from 1344 till 1354 AH (1925–35).

1983). It included chapters on society, the economy, and politics. He wrote separate tracts for women (cf. Chapter 5, section 5.1) and for the propagation of Islam (tablīgh—cf. Chapter 3, section 3.4.3).

While it is often argued that the Barelwis were the antithesis of the Deobandis, the former representing folk Islam and the latter more scriptural reformist Islam, their approaches had many points in common. In principle, the doctrinal emphasis of the Barelwis on the essential unity of law and path, that is, sharī'a and ṭarīqa (Sanyal 1996a: 167) should not have given rise to any rift between the two groups. The Barelwis also insisted on adherence (taqlīd) to a given law school, much as the Deobandis did. However, they disagreed over which essentials of Islam (ẓarūriyāt-i dīn) were defined by sharī'a, ṭarīqa, and taqlīd. The key to the disagreement was innovation (bid'a). The Deobandi interpretation of bid'a would have weakened the extensive Barelwi network of shrine and saint worship in India's rural areas. The Barelwis countered by classifying the Deobandi restrictions on mystical and devotional practices as impermissible innovation, as not provided for in the Prophetic tradition (Sunna).[13]

The categories of taqlīd and Sunna symbolized the Barelwi vision of reform (iṣlāḥ). Ahmad Raza and his followers intervened in the public sphere when they believed that Muslims did not adhere to their given law school and ancestral tradition (taqlīd) and when the Prophetic tradition and conduct (Sunna) were not properly observed. Typical interventions took the form of doctrinal debates defending Ahmad Raza's interpretation or were directed at specific rituals as in the dispute over the right form of the call for prayer, *aḏān*. From the resultant campaigns, Ahmad Raza attempted to derive legitimacy for his school of Islam. During his bitter struggle against the new Nadwa council he held that all other groups were innovators (*bid'atī*) (Aḥmad Raẓā Khān, *Fatāwā al-Qudwa li-Kashf Dafin al-Nadwa* 1313 AH [1895–96]), 6, quoted in Sanyal 1996a: 222, fn. 79). He objected to the presence of all those in the first sessions of the Nadwa whom he did not regard as proper representatives of Sunni Islam. He directed his ire at the modernists from Aligarh, the Ahl-i Ḥadīth, the Shi'a, and the 'Wahhabis', his label for strict Deobandis. He complained that the Shi'a cleric, Ghulam Hasanain Kantori (1881–1918), participating in the Kanpur session of the Nadwa, did not receive a fitting response.

[13]More specifically, the Deobandis were accused by the Barelwis of attributing 'lies' to God and denigrating the Prophet. These accusations pertained to doctrinal debates about the transcendental power of God as opposed to the limited, essentially human attributes of the Prophet. Reformists argued that Allah could even lie if he wished although he voluntarily desisted from doing so. Likewise they maintained that the knowledge of the unseen, of what the future holds in store, was only unlimited in God. Both arguments were hotly disputed by the Barelwis (cf. Sanyal 1996a: 237).

In the beginning, the Aḥmadīya were also invited to attend the Nadwa sessions.[14] During his campaign against the Nadwa he set up a counter-organization in the shape of the Conference of the People in the Tradition of (majority) Sunni Islam (Majlis-e Ahl-e Sunnat wa Jamā'at) (Sanyal 1996a: 223–4). It was in this context that he used the term reformism (iṣlāḥ) when he demanded reform and purge of the young Nadwa council (ibid.: 219). While the term Ahl-e Sunnat wa Jamā'at[15] in the Qur'anic context denoted all Sunni Muslims, in the Islamic discourse of South Asia the term emphasized the conformity of the Barelwis with the Sunna. The message was that it was the Barelwis who stood for majority Islam, not the Deobandis or the Ahl-i Ḥadīth, with their aberrations and reprehensible innovations (bid'a). The appellation gained currency to the point that in South Asia it contracted to 'Sunni', otherwise applied to any Muslim following one of the Sunni law schools.

The Barelwis and the 'ulamā' of folk Islam associated with them were equally keen to be seen as reformist. A major part of the theological literature of Ahmad Raza Khan was directed at proving that the mystical practices of the Barelwis as spiritual mentors and guides (pīr) were in consonance with Islamic law or Prophetic tradition (Raza Khan 1921). This they also sought to prove in relation to their special veneration of the Prophet, to miracles, saint-worship and the possibility of intercession at graves. At the same time they ruled out practices in their mind not covered by the sharī'a, such as musical performances at certain rituals and the participation of women, in deference to the Islamic legal demand for seclusion.[16] The reformist pretensions of Ahmad Raza were underlined by his scholarly bent; he preferred to be seen as a scholar ('ālim) first and mystic (Sufi) second. This was also how his adherents perceived him. He was devoted to the collection and editing of Prophetic traditions (ḥadīth) (Misbahi 1976) and ceaseless in answering requests for religious advice (*istiftā'*) by writing fatāwā, or religious decrees (Raza Khan 1994).

The Nadwa credo focused on the reformation of education and its methods, removal of doctrinal divisions, moral improvement, and general welfare, as Abdul Hayy noted in his 1904 address to the Nadwa session (see Appendix I). While this was a general reformist programme, it reflected the careful attempt to modernize Islamic teaching within closely defined parameters. The Nadwa also organized a separate campaign to eradicate

[14]Ghulam Ahmad was invited, for instance, to attend the Calcutta meeting of the Nadwa, which he declined (*Review of Religions*, 1: 329, quoted in Walter 1991: 68).

[15]In the Urdu transcription, in Arabic: *ahl al-sunna wa-'l-jamā'a.*

[16]For a comprehensive compilation of the Barelwi doctrine (*'aqā'id*) in 1924 by the founder of the Lahore Dāru'l-'ulūm Ḥizb-ul-Aḥnāf, Didar Ali Shah, see the latter's biography by his grandson, Rizwi (1979).

'degraded customs' around 1902. All Nadwa members were encouraged to do so in the area of their influence and report on the progress made therein. They targeted singing and dancing at marriage ceremonies, excessive spending on such ceremonies and so on.

The reformist drive of the Ahl-i Ḥadīth derived from the teachings of Waliullah, especially his treatment of the four law schools (maḏhab). While Waliullah's critique gave him the freedom to draw on all of them for the solution of problems of Islamic law and conduct, the Ahl-i Ḥadīth were more literal, rejecting them outright as innovations. Where Waliullah promoted the Prophetic traditions (ḥadīth), the Ahl-i Ḥadīth drew on them as their major marker of identity. Although they shared with the Deobandis reliance on Waliullah, they did not recognize the Hanafi law school, on which the Deobandi doctrine was based. The founders of the law schools were exempt from Ahl-i Ḥadīth criticism to the extent that they were regarded as true religious divines who had learnt directly from the model of the Prophet, something that later generations could not claim. The law schools were accused of setting up their own books and leaders as rivals to the Qur'an and the Prophetic traditions (ḥadīth).[17] Islamic reformism (iṣlāḥ) for the Ahl-i Ḥadīth was primarily directed against adherence (taqlīd) to the law schools. As they denied legitimacy to the religious practice of the majority of South Asian Muslims, their intervention in the Islamic sphere brought them into direct conflict with most Islamic groups there. While they attempted to gain influence over the Nadwa project for harmonizing Islamic groups and their religious instruction, they continued to verbally attack all other groups, particularly the Barelwis, the Shi'a, and the Aḥmadīya.

The modernist perspective of Sayyid Ahmad Khan and the Aligarh School marked another 'extreme' cornerstone of the mutual reference scheme of the Islamic discourse in South Asia. His focus was not primarily on the religious reformation of Muslims or conformity with the founding principles of Islam, which was more the concern more of traditional scholars. His reformatory efforts were directed at Muslim community life. To facilitate its improvement he proposed a reinterpretation of Islam through a new theology of the Qur'an ('ilm al-kalām).[18] Although he was no 'ālim in the formal sense, his religious erudition was perhaps no less profound than that of many of his detractors, coming as he did from a background of religious family education. As he consciously promoted

[17]See, for instance, the instructive summary of the creed of the Ahl-i Ḥadīth in Siyalkoti (1953: 25ff.). Also see the collected religious rulings in Nazir Husain (1971).

[18]See, for instance, Sayyid Ahmad's speech on Islam given before the Anjuman-i Himāyat-i Islām in Lahore on 2 February 1884, in Troll (1978: 307–32).

modern education for Indian Muslims he felt compelled to contribute to the adaptation of Islam. Western science and philosophy should be harmonized with Islamic doctrine through a new set of principles for the exegesis of the Qur'an and the ḥadīth. They should provide rational arguments to satisfy the modern doubters of Islam. Sayyid Ahmad debated these principles extensively with the 'ulamā' of his time causing tremendous controversy. The essence of his arguments was his assertion that God's word (*qaul*) could not contravene God's work (*fi'l*), that is, nature. Therefore, God's message had to be consistent with the laws of nature and also with the natural disposition of man.[19] To him this was the only criterion for the truth of Islam in comparison with other religions. Similarly, God's work could not contradict reason. If God gave reason to man he could not have wanted him not to use it. To reconcile inconsistencies between God's work and word, the latter, being infallible, had to be properly understood or interpreted. This provoked an angry refutation from the founder of the Deoband Seminary, Maulana Nanaotawi (Ahmad and Grunebaum: 1970, 60–76, for Nanaotawi, 25–48 for Sayyid Ahmad). Referring to the elevated status of 'nature' in the cosmology of Sayyid Ahmad Khan, Nanaotawi coined the term *nēchārī* ('naturist') for him, which stuck to the Aligarh School through much of the controversial debates. While reformist and orthodox scholars wanted to exclude the Aligarh representatives from efforts for religious reform, the Aligarh approach was, in fact, in line with the features of the iṣlāḥ concept as represented by Abduh in Egypt. Much like the latter, Sayyid Ahmad wanted to reconcile modernity with Islam, wanted its new developments to be interpreted through the categories of Islam so that Muslims would be able to overcome their backwardness and embrace modernity without hindrance. The raison d'être of his Anglo-Muslim College, later University, was to provide opportunities for a young Muslim élite to study Western arts and sciences without being alienated from their cultural and religious background. Worship and religious instruction were, therefore, compulsory in Aligarh (Lelyveld 1996: 277) although Islamic studies were included in the curriculum as a teaching subject only at a later stage. Separate arrangements were made for Sunni and Shi'i students and for the few Hindu and Sikh students studying there (Moin 1976: 109ff.; Nizami 1995).

Graduates and teachers from Aligarh also intervened directly in the discourse among Islamic groups on the parameters of religious reform. Shibli Numani, who had received a classical religious education, was

[19]Cf. Sayyid Aḥmad Khān, *Taḥrīr fī usūl al-tafsīr* (On the Rules of a Commentary on the Qur'an), in *idem* 1961: Vol. 2, 206–7. For similarities between Sayyid Ahmad Khan's approach and the European tradition of Enlightenment, see Reetz (1988).

the Arabic and Persian professor at Aligarh before he became involved in the foundation of the Nadwa council and seminary. The Barelwis attacked him, along with Muhsin al-Mulk (1837–1907), as nēchārīs, for introducing materialism and atheism into the Nadwa council proceedings (Malik 1997). Yet, in reality Shibli took a rather conservative position. By urging the 'ulamā' in the Nadwa to recapture the lead in public life, Lelyveld felt, Shibli repudiated the foundations of the Aligarh Movement. This may have reflected more on his attempt to get the Nadwa 'ulamā' to agree to his ideas of reform.[20] Muhammad Ali was a distinguished graduate and one-time professor at Aligarh before he became a religious and political leader in the solidarity campaign for Ottoman Turkey during the Tripolitan and Balkan wars and during the Khilafat Movement. Another student, Zafar Ali Khan (1873–1956), became editor of the Urdu newspaper *Zamindār*, taking a prominent part in public discourse on Islam and its political repercussions (Lelyveld 1996: 325). He joined the religious Islamic discourse, for instance, in connection with the hijrat campaign of 1920, when he, rather opportunistically, attempted to gain mileage out of the events by suggesting it was time for a mahdī, a saviour, for Muslims in India (cf. Reetz 1995: 64). He later aligned with the Aḥrār in 1935 in the course of the Shahidganj Mosque campaign in Lahore, Punjab, where Sikhs had converted a mosque into a temple (*gurdwāra*) (Qureshi 1974: 323f.).

The reformist outlook of the Aḥrār and the Khāksār was shaped by their public activism. To them, religion was very directly a tool to achieve a certain goal in public policy, in the public sphere. But doctrinally they were at variance and politically they were rivals. They competed for a share in the Islamic sphere in the same territory, that is, in Punjab. The Aḥrār sought public influence and power for Muslims in a province where they constituted a slender majority, and for the unlimited sway of reformist Islam there. Theologically the Aḥrār derived from the Deoband school.[21] Their three-pronged policy was summarized in the words of Janbaz Mirza, that they were fighting 'in defence of Islam, for freedom (independence)

[20]Lelyveld (1996: 244). Perhaps Shibli's conservatism can be more correctly attributed to his desire to forge a compromise among the different groups of 'ulamā' so that they could be induced through the Nadwa to improve their standard of knowledge and education, which Shibli considered to be poor and failing all requirements. See his article on the scholars of Islam in the *Aligarh Institute Gazette* (14 April 1883), in Numani (1965: 13–18). There he also expressed his nuanced understanding of Sayyid Ahmad's approach by relating God's law not so much to the laws of nature as to the needs of man (13) and the 'needs of the present day' (*maujūdah ẓarūraton ko*). In order to meet these, the religious scholars have to strive for progress in religion (*maẓhab kī taraqqī*) (14).

[21]The participation of scholars from other backgrounds such as Ahl-i Ḥadīth and Shi'a does not appear to have significantly altered this, see Chapter 2, fn. 37.

of the motherland and to relieve mankind of imperialist forces' (1975, Vol. 1). From the perspective of the Congress leadership, this group led reformist Muslims to struggle against British rule. For the Aḥrār this was a corollary of struggling for the unlimited sway of reformist Islam. In doctrinal matters they moved to radical positions, opposing all ritual distinctions from reformist monism of the *salafi* variety. They took sectarian and doctrinal differences to the streets in public campaigns against groups such as the Aḥmadīya or the Shi'a. Their religious intervention in the public sphere was mainly local (confined to the Punjab) and sectarian.

The Khāksār wanted to reform Muslim behaviour and self-organization. The movement took its religious inspiration from the writings of Mashriqi. His commentary on the Qur'an did not conform to orthodox criteria and was rejected by orthodox and reformist scholars alike. Yet, in his own way he made a strong plea for reformist Islam. He summarized his religious philosophy in his 10 principles of Islam: monism (tauḥīd); unity (*itteḥād*); obedience to the leader (*iṭā'at-e amīr*); armed struggle (that is, with the sword—*jihād bi'l-saif*); struggle against the fetish of material wealth (*jihād bi'l-māl*); readiness for migration in the service of Islam (hijrat); readiness to serve God (*istiqāmat*); obtaining religious and worldly knowledge (*'ilm*); fulfilling one's moral duty (*makkāram-e akhlāq*); and keeping faith in the hereafter (*īmān bi'l-ākhirat*) (Mashriqi 1995: 237f.; 1924). For him, iṣlāḥ, or reformism, ought to be taken out of the hands of the Maulwis and directed at Muslim self-organization and self-esteem.[22] He believed that Muslims had degenerated. They required a new martial spirit (*'askarīyat*), a sort of spiritual and physical 'fitness' (ṣalāḥīyat), which should prepare them to compete with Western civilization. Worship of God (*'ibādat*) was not exhausted by prayer but had action (*'amal*) as its main component (Mashriqi 1995). Mashriqi exhibited purist tendencies in his emphasis on observance of the rules of ritual prayer and in the devotion of a substantial part of his Qur'anic commentary to strengthening faith. He lamented that the East concentrated on its spiritual heritage in a meaningless and ineffectual way. He pointed out that the West was mastering the state of practical fitness embodied in materialism, but decried the loss of spiritualism on the way. The task now for the East was to regain its strength (*taqwīyat-e nafs*) in order to reap the practical advantages of its spiritual superiority in this world, not only in the hereafter (Mashriqi 1987: 130ff.). In parts of his interpretation of Qur'anic injunctions he seemed to borrow from Sayyid Ahmad. Applying allegorical interpretations he reversed the meaning of a Qur'anic reference. Where the Qur'an said 'Ye shall have

[22]The importance Mashriqi attached to the category of iṣlāḥ also became clear from the fact that the main organ of the Khaksār was named Al-Iṣlāḥ (cf. Seth 1985).

the upper hand if ye but be believers'—meaning success flows from belief—he assumed that success and strength are an expression of belief. He elevated the 'Work of God' to a prominent place beside the 'Word of God'. He believed that modern science could be employed for the service of religion and to prove the Word of God (ibid.: 133–4).

Mashriqi consciously contrasted the ascetic piety and martial readiness of his movement with the worldly, good life-seeking habits, and the hypocritical clerical piety of the Aḥrār leaders. For the Khāksār the main priority was not battle with the British but the battle with their self (*nafs*) to overcome weakness. This process of self-reformation (*iṣlāḥ-i nafs*) included the three major aspects of Mashriqi's beliefs: simple and modest living, readiness to serve all human beings irrespective of religion, race, or colour, and physical strength. Only when Muslims were strong enough could they hope to take on the British and win, according to his projections (see also Malik 2000: 23ff.).

The missionary activity of the Tablīghī Jamā'at was geared to the reform of Muslims who had not awoken to the true meaning of their religion. Muhammad Ilyas emphasized not contentious theological issues or *masā'il* but the merits and virtues of religion, *faẓā'il* of Islam, those believed to be particularly pleasing to God and upon which all (Sunni) sects were basically agreed. For the Tablīghīs, the order of virtues in Islam can be gauged from their reading book *Faẓā'il-i A'māl*. Maulana Muhammad Zakariyya (1898–1982) from the Saharanpur Deobandi madrasa, Maẓāhiru'l-'Ulūm, compiled the work under the earlier title *Tablīghī Niṣāb*.[23] Following the sequence of chapters there, he focused on: the Qur'an; fasting during the holy month of *Ramaḍān*; preaching (tablīgh); the model conduct of the Prophet's companions (*ṣaḥāba*); prayer (*namāẓ*); God's remembrance (*ḏikr*); pilgrimage to the holy places of Islam in Arabia (*ḥajj*); charity in a spirit of sincerity (*ṣadaqāt*); and blessings for the Prophet (*durūd-i sharīf*). Their meaning was similar to the 'Six Essentials' formulated as the creed of the movement (cf. Appendix I, also see Chapter 3, section 3.4.4). Those points constituted an interesting mix. They covered the basic duties of a Muslim if he wanted to be counted among the believers, the so-called five pillars of Islam: profession of faith, pilgrimage, worship, fasting, and almsgiving. Those were non-controversial and essential duties. Their observance in general and the proper way of observance in particular

[23] Zakariyya (1975). The title was later changed to *Faẓā'il-i A'māl* (cf. Masud 2000: 81f.) of which numerous and slightly modified editions appeared from both India and Pakistan since 1928. Masud gives conflicting dates for the publication of the compilation (ibid.: 89, 253). From 1960, there is also an English edition available: *The Teachings of Islam*, Delhi: Idāra Ishā'at-i Dīniyāt.

was (and obviously is) lacking in many Muslims. Their emphasis could be regarded as a manifesto for religious reform. But Ilyas also took a stand for active reform (iṣlāḥ). The various tracts inspiring the Tablīghī movement recorded his precepts for cleansing religious and social practices.[24] Ilyas demanded the replacement of false customs (*rasmīyat*) with the correct religion (*haqīqat*). The reform of one's intention (*niyyat-e taṣḥīḥ*) would bring out the correct form of religious practice (*ā'māl kā ṣaḥīḥ rukh)* (Ilyas M 1). His doctrinal flexibility was shown by the treatment of innovation (bid'a). He castigated only 'extreme' practices (*ghāyat*) such as 'certain kinds of commemorations (*azkār*), certain spiritual [Sufi] practices (*ashghāl*) and exercises (*riyāẓāt*) etc' (Ilyas M 3). The demand for special remembrance of God and his Prophet through dikr and a special prayer for the Prophet Muhammad pointed to a Sufi legacy in Ilyas' antecedents. Yet he demanded all practices be rooted in the sharī'a. The latter was supposedly not consistent with religious feasts and festivals, Sufi poetry, or music, saint, and tomb worship as practised by the Barelwis. Muslims should live an ascetic, pure, pious, and devout life.

At first, scholars found it difficult to accept the reformist credentials of the movement as it displayed such a bewildering variety of features. After some time the doubters were won over by the visible impact the movement had not only in the Mewat region but also in small urban areas of the United Provinces and other regions. At a time when Islam seemed beleaguered this was welcome and badly needed encouragement for the reformist 'ulamā' in the quest to regain influence. Here was an example of iṣlāḥ working in reality. The success of the Tablīghīs' intervention lay perhaps in the integrative approach more than in the principles of reform. What proved to be so successful was their direct contact with believers and the ensuing mobilization effect.

The founder of the Aḥmadīya community, Ghulam Ahmad, was as dissatisfied with the deplorable state of the faith and of the Muslim community in India as contemporary Islamic reformers. For a certain period, his active and at times highly controversial contribution to religious polemics with Christian and Hindu missionaries earned him respect. Erudition was recognized in his early theological works. He formulated the basics of a reformist concept during his stewardship of the Aḥmadīya community. Members of the founder generation of the Ahl-i Ḥadīth, the Deobandis, and the Barelwis were his temporary comrades-in-arms in public debates aimed at refuting Christian and Hindu doctrines. Ghulam

[24]Cf. Numani (1993), Nadwi (1983), Ilyas (1997). That the Tablīghīs identified with the reformist concept of iṣlāḥ also became clear from their attachment to the collection of writings by Muhammad Ali Thanawi, called the *Iṣlāḥī Niṣāb*, cf. p. 160.

Ahmad demanded a return to 'pristine' Islam, wanted to infuse Muslims with new faith, and (selectively) rejected the tomb, saint, and miracle worship of folk Islam. But he also rejected the modernizing and rationalistic ideas of Sayyid Ahmad Khan. He staunchly defended the supernatural character of the revelation; special reverence of the Prophet Muhammad; the belief in the miracles, angels, and prophecies of the Qur'an; and the social customs of veiling women and polygamy—as did the Barelwis. He rejected the squabbling of the religious scholars and the divisive disputes of the law schools—as did the Ahl-i Ḥadīth. He wanted to explain the Qur'an primarily from itself and in case of a contradiction between the Qur'an and a tradition (ḥadīth) he stated that 'no authentic tradition can contradict the Holy Qur'an' (*Review of Religions*, Vol. 3: 449–50, quoted in Walter 1991: 56)—as with the Aligarh school of Sayyid Ahmad Khan. He believed in the essential unity of law and path, sharī'a and ṭarīqa, and accepted mysticism so long as it did not contradict the sharī'a.[25] In organizing his movement like a Sufi order, submitting his followers to an oath of allegiance (bay'a), he resembled leaders of more orthodox groups. Ghulam Ahmad partook in the larger reformist project to revive the fortunes of Islam and Muslims in India, but he chose provocative and ostentatious means—as with his predictions of the death of his opponents which perilously materialized (cf. Chapter 3, fn. 46), he was driven by his claim for eminence among Islamic reformers and for special status for his community. He did not use the term iṣlāḥ extensively but followed the general guidelines of the concept as much as anyone else.

3.1.4. *Independent Reasoning (Ijtihād)*

While Waliullah rejected 'blind' adherence to the law schools (taqlīd) he proposed reinvigorating independent reasoning (ijtihād) to solve problems arising from the application of the injunctions of Islam to new situations. Such an option was considered closed for mainstream Sunni Muslims: The law schools were supposed to have dealt with issues in need of clarification. After the formative period of Islamic law had ended, the qualifications of those applying independent reasoning were often questioned. Few if any were considered worthy of the title of a *mujtahid*, an Islamic lawyer capable of such reasoning.[26] From Waliullah onwards, various Islamic groups turned to the restoration of ijtihād as a tool.

[25]When Ghulam Ahmad, for instance, elaborated on the three stages of the soul to attain spiritual salvation he practically embraced interpretations of Qur'anic precepts more in line with Sufi teachings than with orthodox reading (Walter 1991: 58–9).

[26]Cf. articles on ijtihād by D. B. MacDonald and J. Schacht in EI/III: 1026–7.

Originally this was to remove late accretions in order to disinter the 'unaltered' commandments of the Qur'an and the ḥadīth. In terms of the formation of the public sphere for Islam, ijtihād provided Islamic discourse with flexibility. Many Islamic groups of the revivalist and reformist camp used it to legitimate their own group ideology. In this sense, the application of ijtihād was a very modern exercise, contributing to the articulation of a plurality of distinct public Islamic voices. At the same time, ijtihād remained for all Islamic groups a double-edged weapon: reinterpreting the dogma in the name of religion made them vulnerable to further reinterpretation by their own followers. This fear may have motivated groups accepting ijtihād to restrict it to those with sufficient religious and legal qualification. Thus limited to the élite circle of the group, to knowledgeable and committed followers, it was hoped that free reinterpretation would not undermine their standing in the Islamic sphere.

Like other categories, ijtihād was variously practised, although there was convergence on the aspect of opening up Islamic discourse to new interpretations. The narrow view of ijtihād concentrated on a solution for a problem of Islamic law. The broader approach gave freedom to reinterpret more general elements of Islamic discourse.[27] While the Deobandis were often viewed as the most persistent advocates of reformist Islam in South Asia, they accepted independent reasoning only in the most narrowly defined limits. It had to be based on the four classical sources of Islamic law, that is, the Qur'an, the ḥadīth, *ijmā'* ([legal] consensus of the community), and *qiyās* (analogy). They required not only adherence (taqlīd) to the Hanafi law school, but also to a chosen teacher ('ālim)—taqlīd-i shakhṣī (personal adherence). They left matters of judgement to the religious specialists, as they doubted the religious knowledge of the masses (Metcalf 1982: 142ff.). Yet, by promoting the study of the sources of Islamic law (of the ḥadīth in particular), they implicitly encouraged independent reasoning, if only for Deobandi adepts and graduates. Also, the formulation of a separate 'tack' (maslak) of Deobandi beliefs can be seen as exercising of independent judgement in the wider sense. One can argue that they exercised ijtihād when they elevated the views of the founders of the Deoband madrasa, Nanaotawi and Gangohi, to the rank of defining principles, literally including them in the articles of faith of the movement (see Appendix I). These distinctive principles constituted the Deobandis as a community distinct from other Sunni Muslims. In particular, the volumes of religious decrees written by Gangohi served as

[27]This is a conditional distinction as, strictly speaking, of course, all problems of Islamic practice and faith fall under the sharī'a in one way or the other.

a distinct legal standard for the movement.[28] While he claimed to have adapted nothing but Hanafi law, it was what Deobandis called the 'taste' or the 'temperament' (cf. Appendix I) that set them apart. This did not separate them from mainstream Hanafi law, but within the Islamic sphere it constituted a distinctive discourse.

The Ahl-i Ḥadīth made the reaffirmation of independent reasoning (ijtihād) the focal point of their identity by rejecting its opposite, adherence (taqlīd). Proudly calling themselves *ghair muqallid*, that is, those without a law school, they elevated their status as 'outlaws' into a distinction, turning a jibe into an honorific title. Their advocacy of ijtihād related to the special importance they gave to the ḥadīth. By accepting the Prophetic tradition without the qualifications they ascribed to other Islamic groups, they claimed a unique relationship with the Prophet and his message. Like the Deobandis, they confined re-interpretation to the sufficiently qualified. The study and knowledge of the ḥadīth being their yardstick of the interpretation of the Qur'an, the approach was de facto élitist as this knowledge was restricted only to the very learned ones.

For the Nadwa Movement, the principle of ijtihād played a special role in reconciling different sects and traditions in Islam. The establishment of a legal department for religious decrees (dār al-iftā') restored the principle of ijtihād in legal rulings independent of the various schools. For the founder member of the Nadwa, Shibli Numani, and others like Habib al-Rahman Khan Sherwani (d. 1950), who were in contact with the Salafī Movement in Egypt, ijtihād would restore direct access to Qur'anic knowledge, and would enable the modern world to be interpreted in Qur'anic categories (Malik 1997: 259, 280). Shibli deplored the outdated knowledge of the 'ulamā' who could not counter contemporary challenges to Islam (Nadwi 1943). In 1902 he demanded a new theology ('ilm-i kalām). He felt it should integrate new philosophical teachings and modern knowledge with religion as done by Islam in the Middle Ages with Greek philosophy (Jalis Nadwi and Tabriz Khan 1983/I: 302).

The Aḥmadīya, as Friedmann asserted (1989: 184–5), contributed little to the legal re-interpretation of Islam. The changes concerned three issues: the continuance of divine revelation (after Muhammad) and the resultant prophetic claims by Ghulam Ahmad and his successors; the role of the Prophet Jesus, who in orthodox Islam would be the promised one; and the rejection of a military or violent jihād (religious war). In the

[28]The international Deobandi branches today regularly quote from the *Fatāwā-e Rashīdīya* of Gangohi (1906); see, for instance, various issues of the publications *Al-Mahmood* (No. 2 of December 1999, No. 8 of March 2000) and *Al-Jamiat* (May 1998) of the *Jamīyatu'l-'ulamā'* (Kwazulu-Natal), Durban, South Africa, available on their websites http://www.jamiat.org.za and http://www.msapubli.com.

application of the sharī'a they were conservative, as in their defence of polygamy and the veil with only small modernizing modifications. Where they argued for change, as Friedmann showed convincingly, they tailored medieval traditions to suit their needs. Earlier Islamic thinkers (Ibn al-Arabi, ibid.: 73) had distinguished between legislative prophets of whom Muhammad was the last—which Ahmad did not contest—and non-legislative prophets who merely continued to receive revelations. When Ahmad claimed prophetic status for himself and made acceptance of this claim a criterion for following the true Islam, he enraged mainstream Sunni clerics. With regard to jihād, theologians before Ahmad had also limited its meaning beyond the usually accepted exertion in the way of God to defensive war. Ahmad prided himself on 'prohibiting' or 'abolishing' military warfare in the name of jihād once and for all. Those additions of Ahmad were small but of great consequence. They not only constituted a new community but provoked mainstream Sunnis by excluding all others from the 'true' fold as unbelievers.

Muhammad Iqbal, the poet and philosopher, made an influential plea for the resumption of ijtihad in a famous series of lectures on the reconstruction of religious thought in Islam delivered at Aligarh.[29] He pointed to the rebirth of the Muslim nation of Turkey as an example of how the public position of Islam and of the Muslim community in India could be strengthened. He felt that there were dangers for the Muslim community if Muslim law remained stagnant, as in Punjab, where Muslim women risked apostasy in the search for divorce.

More radical in his demands for ijtihād was Sayyid Ahmad. He rejected blind adherence (taqlīd), particularly on the example of Abu Hanifa, and all unreliable Prophetic traditions beyond the undoubtedly genuine commandments (*aḥkām-i manṣūṣa*). On this basis he remained sceptical about the *ijtihādiyāt*, the commandments worked out (after the founders of the law schools) by 'ulamā' and mujtahids on the basis of ijtihād and qiyās (cf. Troll 1978: 55, 205–6, 250). He circumscribed ijtihād by the recognized traditions and to some extent by the four law schools, in the Waliullahi tradition. Sayyid Ahmad practised ijtihād extensively by his exposition of his Qur'anic principles of exegesis while the 'ulamā' argued he was not qualified to do so (section 3.1.3).

A very modern and 'scientific' variety of ijtihād was favoured by Allama

[29]Cf. Iqbal (1930); also Masud (1995). For the lectures at Aligarh, cf. Nizami (1995: 179). That Iqbal's theological position was also influenced by Deobandi scholars is revealed in Deoband's centenary history. It points to the links between Iqbal and Maulana Sayyid Muhammad Anwar Shah Kashmiri (1875–1933) who belonged to the dissident faction purged in 1927. Kashmiri was known for his more scholarly inclinations and less for his political inclinations (Rizvi 1980/II: 51).

Mashriqi of the Khāksār movement. He wanted to integrate all Muslims and, indeed, all believers in a religious concept based on the Qur'an as the last, and the most comprehensive and authentic revelation. The Qur'an was represented as a prophetic message of action-oriented 'fitness' for this world. Now the age of 'science and evidence' afforded a unique chance to fuse the materialist and martial spirit of the west with the spiritualist legacy of the East. It was the age where 'do's and don'ts of religion can be exhibited in their true and original conception, ...their goals can be correctly fixed, (where) permanent conclusions can be drawn from them...the Divine Law and the Providential proclamation can be comprehended' (Mashriqi 1987: 134). He demanded that science be fully accepted by Islam. He felt it should be interpreted through Islamic categories. But Mashriqi went further. For him science was a means to prove the word of God. Reflecting on the rationalist debate initiated by Sayyid Ahmad Khan about the relationship between the Word of God and the Work of God, Mashriqi believed that the Work of God, that is, science, could be harnessed to increase the authority of the Word of God, the Qur'an. This would enable people to attend to the 'fundamental directive' of God, adopting as their course of action 'the real Law' by ignoring 'offshoots' and 'symbols'. He thus struck at sectarianism and mystical practices (section 3.2.4). Rephrased in very modern language, this message was not unlike the doctrinal demands of the Ahl-i Ḥadīth and the Deobandis. In his focus on the Qur'anic message he also echoed the more radical reformers of the Aligarh School, although he did not favour special status for man's reason. For him the divine message remained the ultimate arbiter of man's action. At the same time he was influenced by Western thought when he mused on the biological and racial qualities of man. He should not degenerate into a lower species from where he evolved. Man's evolutionary distinctiveness converged here with the concept of 'fitness'. This he turned against the 'effeminate' Hindus and Gandhi's strategy of non-violent action, which he thought detrimental to the interest and honour of Indians and Muslims alike (see section 4.2.3).

On a broad view of ijtihād, even groups such as the Barelwis joined the reformist and revivalist stream of re-interpretation. The Barelwis rejected independent reasoning as a legal instrument while emphasizing its counterpart, adherence (taqlīd). Yet they took to reformism practically. Their activist approach renewed religious life as it redefined doctrinal norms for their adherents. The extensively published religious decrees (fatwā) of Ahmad Raza and his sons created a specific set of norms for this school of thought. These legitimated the special veneration of the person of the Prophet and prevailing mystical practices (miracle, saint and tomb worship, annual festivals commemorating the death of local saints—*urs*) with traditional references to the Qur'an and the ḥadīth. The interpretive activity of Ahmad Raza was so extensive that his followers claimed for him the appellation of renewer of the faith (*mujaddid*).[30] This was curious for the leader of a movement claiming strict adherence to established interpretation as its strongest asset. From the point of view of creating an independent public sub-discourse of Islam, this was very extensive ijtihād indeed.

Irrespective of their doctrinal differences, almost all groups were involved in the re-interpretation of Islam. They reshaped Islamic discourse through their activism, which opened new avenues for 'practical' ijtihād. Creating educational and public organizations and holding annual conferences, was a commentary of sorts on the state of religion (see the next section). Through their public activity they were claiming an ever-larger part of the public sphere for religious interpretation. Their activity in the public sphere thus became a form of exercising their right to independent reasoning.

3.1.5. The Principle of Monism (Tauḥīd)

A distinctive feature of reformist Islam was its monism—tauḥīd, stressing the transcendent unity of God, embodied in the formula 'there is no God but God'. The opposite of tauḥīd was the association of any subject of veneration with God, sometimes somewhat imperfectly translated as 'associationism' (shirk). Monism was central to reformist discourse throughout the Islamic world. In South Asia monism was particularly significant for Islamic activists in competition with other religions, a strong contrast with the polytheism (and idol worship) of Hindu, Buddhist, and (the trinity of) Christian beliefs. Thus, it was often debated in inter-religious disputations. It was also a matter of dispute with Sufi-inspired groups and rival Islamic sects. Notably the early reformers. Sayyid Ahmad Bareilly and Muhammad Ismail (1781–1831) highlighted its importance although they did not denounce Sufi beliefs as they themselves were active Sufi shaykhs but emphasized 'correct' Sufism (cf. Metcalf 1982: 56–7). The Barelwis defended their mystical inclinations on the basis that the Qur'an and the prophetic traditions describe many miracles and acts of worship. The Shi'a and the Aḥmadīya came in for heavy criticism too. The veneration of Ali by the Shi'a was seen as undermining monism. So

[30]The appellation was claimed for him in the first formal meeting of his group, the Ahl-i Sunnat, in October 1900, see Sanyal (1996a: 226ff.). The appellation of mujaddid has, of course, broader connotations, not restricted to legal reinterpretation; cf. Chapter 3, section 3.3.

was the claim to prophethood by Mirza Ghulam Ahmad and his successors as heads of the Aḥmadīya community.

Yet, even among the more radical reformist groups, there was no agreement on what would undermine monism. What some regarded as the distinctive features of their Islamic group or sect, others attacked as idol-worship alleging that these symbols subtracted from the omnipotence of God and diminished his message. The accusation of 'associationism' (shirk) was levelled indiscriminately against others, while for their own group scholars justified respect or worship of symbols other than Allah out of expediency. The Ahl-i Ḥadīth accused those following the law schools of such impermissible 'associationism'. They argued that all other schools venerated special books besides the Qur'an and the ḥadīth while the Ahl-i Ḥadīth did not. However, they exposed themselves to the same charge as they elevated the ḥadīth to the rank of a marker, tending to idolize them, especially when refusing to distinguish between reliable and unreliable traditions.

The founder of the Khaksar Movement, Mashriqi, also interpreted tauḥīd in a distinct way. He saw inaction, passivity, and weakness as major expressions of shirk, of idol-worship (*but-parastī*), as they led to indulgence of individual desires and thus detracted from the worship of God. He also gave tauḥīd a more inclusive interpretation in relation to other denominations. He emphasized the transcendent unity of God, seeing it as a confirmation of the interconnectedness of all revealed religions. Muhammad was the last of several prophets and Islam the last and most comprehensive but by no means only true revelation. Every believer following a recognized prophet was a potential Muslim (Mashriqi 1987, 1995: 232ff.). Members of his movement were not allowed to display sectarian or class distinctions. On several occasions he tried to reach out to Hindu believers. During relief work he did not discriminate against followers of other religions. In his wider interpretation of tauḥīd Mashriqi presumably also followed Sayyid Ahmad Khan. The latter had highlighted tauḥīd as a central feature of 'unitarian' Islam. Muhammad had been the first teacher of tauḥīd comprehensible to all mankind. Even men after Muhammad could be expected to have this gift, although they would add nothing intrinsically new. The Prophet's tauḥīd was so perfect that it showed itself anonymously also in unitarian and monotheistic tendencies of other religious movements of the time (Troll 1978: 190–1). Tauḥīd was interpreted here also as an inclusive concept to unite all religions on the basis of Islam, not as an exclusive or divisive tool.

Besides the intra-Islamic debate, monism was a political argument, notably in debate on cooperation with Hindus and the Congress Party during the anti-colonial movement. Some religious scholars argued that cooperation with polytheists and idol-worshippers was impermissible. Those who condoned cooperation maintained that the Congress did not suppress and subjugate Indian Muslims and their religious beliefs while the British did. Advocates of Hindu–Muslim unity played down the significance of Hindu polytheism, while its opponents accentuated it (cf. Chapter 4, fn. 84). This became a burning issue during the Khilafat campaign and played a role during the Pakistan Movement. Ironically, those rejecting Hindu–Muslim cooperation most consistently were not those who followed strict monism in their doctrinal teachings. Although the Barelwis defended certain mystical practices such as the use of charms and amulets, Ahmad Raza staunchly argued that Hindus were idolaters (*mushrik*) and unbelievers (*kafirīn*) with whom enmity was required. On this basis he consistently opposed cooperation with the Congress during the Khilafat Movement. He believed that Hindu interference in Muslim religious practices was far from negligible, referring to intermittent inter-communal tension and rioting (Sanyal 1996a: 294ff.). Those religious scholars who in the end supported the Pakistan Movement were also not known for a principled monism, but were close to the rural-based Islam of the shrines and shaykhs, that is, the Barelwi camp. Conversely, religious scholars most proud of their monism, the Deobandis and the Ahl-i Ḥadīth, cooperated with the Congress and its Hindu members freely on the ground of their shared opposition to alien British rule. They saw the impact of British rule on religious freedom for Islam as a much graver issue.[31]

The Aḥmadīya movement accentuated tauḥīd through their critique of Hindu polytheism. This was not so much directed against (political) cooperation with Hindus, as against the Hindu reformist sect of the Ārya Samāj which laid claim to a monotheist interpretation of Hinduism elevating the role of (part of) its scriptures, the Vedas. Their missionary efforts were met by sharp criticism of nature worship among Hindus from Ghulam Ahmad (Walter 1991: 101ff.). The Aḥmadīs strongly refuted charges that they undermined Islam's monism by the Prophetic ambitions of their leaders and the worship of the latter's shrines.

This showed that doctrinal arguments were tailored to suit the needs of the Islamic groups in their capacity of public entities rather than of

[31]This dispute was rooted in differences about the evaluation of India as an abode of Islam (dār al-Islām) or a country of war (*dār al-ḥarb*) treated in detail further down in connection with the Khilafat Movement. While Ahmad Raza and the Barelwis supported the first view, the Deobandis advocated the latter opinion. The Deobandis argued in favour of cooperation with the Hindus on the basis of the Qur'anic verses 60:8/9, not prohibiting respect for those 'who fight you not for religion, nor drive you forth from your homes' and requiring to deal with them justly. Ahmad Raza alleged those verses were abrogated by verse 9:73, enjoining Muslims to strive hard against the unbelievers and the hypocrites and to be firm against them (Sanyal 1996a: 296).

religious bodies. As with ijtihād, tauḥīd opened certain avenues for those willing to reform Islam. Monism made it possible to update and modernize religious commitment as part of a more general reformation of Islam, to take a road similar to the Weberian rationalization of behaviour. At the same time, public and political competition often overrode doctrinal constraints, turning the reformist endeavour into a strategy to gain public support irrespective of the consistency of the doctrinal argument.

3.1.6. *The Central Role of the 'Ulamā'*

The agents through which the public discourse of Islam was conducted were the religious scholars, the 'ulamā'. As Peter Hardy argued, the Western challenge to Islam was intellectual and ethical rather than emotional, and capable of being countered by dialectical methods. Hence learned Muslims and scholars ('ulamā') presented themselves as the protectors of traditional Islam, rather than the Sufis (Hardy 1998: 169). The movements studied here, were all based on the activity of the 'ulamā'. Besides giving rulings on the application of Islamic law, education was their major prerogative. Some revival movements had sprung from madrasa-based groups and religious education, like the Ahl-i Ḥadīth, the Tablīghī Jamā'at, and the Aḥrār. Also, the style of religious guidance in the Aḥmadīya Movement was marked by the model of the 'ālim, explaining religious tenets and relating them to the interpretation of the Qur'an and the Prophetic tradition, commenting on the observance of religious practices and their conformity with the injunctions of Islam. Islamic learning in the Aligarh tradition was influenced by the rationalist interpretation of the Qur'an by Sayyid Ahmad Khan to which the traditional 'ulamā' were by and large hostile. Yet, inside Aligarh, Islamic learning was conducted by 'ulamā' so that their influence extended there as well. By and large, the groups reflected the heightened activism and ambitions of the 'ulamā' class. Their status was considered so important that Islamic leaders who had not completed traditional madrasa courses strove to be recognized for their religious erudition. The Khāksār leader claimed the appellation *'Allāma* (very learned person, savant), calling himself Allama Mashriqi. Also Iqbal, who had not completed traditional religious education but repeatedly intervened in Islamic discourse, accepted the title Allama. Shibli Numani and Muhammad Ali who had received traditional education without holding degree certificates found it important to be recognized as Maulanas.

The class of religious scholars was far from homogeneous and their qualifications were not universally agreed. In India's network of religious schools (*dīnī madāris*), 'ālim was a designation applied to holders of qualifications in higher religious education at approximately the B.A. or M.A. level, although duration and contents of courses varied. A learned Muslim or religious specialist usually followed a traditional syllabus of religious learning, such as the dars-i niẓāmī, or graduated from a recognized madrasa and obtained degrees of knowledge (sanad) and teaching (*ijāza*) in essential religious disciplines, or particular works only. He would normally also have recognized the consensus (ijmā') of his learned predecessors.[32] However, many reformists such as the Ahl-i Ḥadīth scholars Siddiq Hasan Khan and Nazir Husain Dihlawi rejected the consensus of earlier generations, which did not undermine their religious standing even with their opponents. Under the Moghul emperors, the 'ulamā' had been part of the decision-making élite offering legal and political advice and in charge of education. Such state employment was effectively ended after the British came to power. Religious scholars retreated to a few remaining posts in the public services of Muslim principalities, where British rule was indirect. But their interventions in the Islamic sphere were still quite versatile. Besides serving as judicial clerks (muftī, qāḍī), members of the 'ulamā' class performed a number of public roles. They ran madrasas, served as teachers for various subjects including elementary skills of reading and writing, as preachers and leaders of congregational prayers, as debaters with opponents, offered spiritual guidance as Sufi shaykhs, provided charms and amulets, or offered medical treatment in the *yunānī* (Greek) tradition (cf. Metcalf 1982: 138ff.).

The 'ulamā' had never been particularly wealthy but their social condition was becoming precarious around 1900. Marginalized by social and political developments, especially in the repression after the 1857 revolt, they were often poor, school-educated, and traditionally oriented. Hardy maintained that as a group they were drawn from the 'lower middle class of a pre-industrial society, printers, lithographers, booksellers, teachers, retail shopkeepers, skilled craftsmen and petty *zamīndārs*' (1998: 169). Such roots were not unreservedly 'pre-industrial'. In the public sphere, their affinity with printing, education, small trade, and handicraft brought them within reach of the emerging markets and public discourses, even into a position where they could initiate and shape these discourses. Here, as elsewhere, both Robinson and Hardy relied on British official phraseology in evaluating the 'ulamā'. At times this biased their work in an anti-reformist and colonial direction. But British official idiom also reflected contemporary public discourse. With stability in the Empire uppermost in their minds, the British regarded the 'ulamā' as an underclass of bigoted

[32]See P. Hardy, 'The 'Ulamā' in British India', unpublished seminar paper (School of Oriental and African Studies, 1969), quoted in Robinson (1994: 263).

fanatics sowing seeds of disaffection and even armed rebellion. The epitome of this thinking was the Hunter tract of 1871 (1969).

The British contrasted the 'ulamā' class with two other groups of activist Muslims, the so-called 'Old' and 'Young Party' (an allusion to the Young Turk Movement).[33] The 'Old Party' was considered loyal to British rule, representing the social and political status-quo. It included Muslims of public standing, usually of landed families. They either held public office or were involved in reform schemes in line with British officialdom's modernizing pro-Western thinking. The 'Young Party' consisted of political firebrands who used religion to 'subvert' the loyalty of Indian Muslims to British rule. The polarity represented a generational conflict. 'Young Party' leaders were seen as attempting to wrest political leadership of the Muslim community from the 'Old Party'.[34] The 'Young Party' stalwarts were located in the environs of the Aligarh College, either having graduated from there or occupying teaching positions. Its most prominent representatives were the Ali brothers, Muhammad (1878–1931) and Shaukat Ali (1873–1938). Both later turned to the study and observance of religion, earning the honorific title Maulana. The 'Young Party' leaders were held responsible for bringing the 'ulamā' into politics through the Khilafat movement after 1918 (Robinson 1994: 261–2). This assessment neglected the public profile, which the religious scholars gained independently during the preceding years through the contestation of their sectarian and group identities, and through their differentiated handling of central Islamic categories and concepts.

Relations between the 'Young Party' and the 'ulamā' were far from harmonious. Their contradictions reflected conflicting concerns over the emerging Islamic sphere. The Hindus' alleged success in mastering the public sphere spurred on the Young Party and 'ulamā'. The desire of the Young Party was to improve the public standing of Islam. They entered public discourse so prominently because the 'ulamā' were seen as failing. They attacked the 'ulamā' for their backwardness and their internal divisions.

A typical specimen of such criticism came from the Nadwa leader Shibli Numani. He was unsparing in his article, 'The 'Ulamā' of Islam', in the *Aligarh Institute Gazette* of 14 April 1883:

> If 'Islam feels more threatened by the philosophy of [Francis] Bacon [1561–1626] [than during classical times], why does no 'ālim learn English and study

[33]Cf. the annual official yearbook edited by Professor Rushbrook Williams (India in 1917–18).

[34]For the 'Old Party' cf. Robinson (1994: Appendix II: 390–418); for the 'Young Party', cf. ibid.: 358–89.

the new philosophy in order to save Islam from these attacks?... The educational system you advocate is utterly useless.... How mistaken are you in your opinion that the system of education current today provides for religious education. Be honest! The number of books relating to Greek philosophy (*yunānī falsafa*) that has been left in the dars-i niẕāmī, does it not outnumber the books on religion (*dīnīyāt*)?' (Numani 1965: 17)

In a second essay, Shibli dismissed those who opposed modern education on the grounds that it militated against obedience to the sharī'a: 'It is an utterly mistaken, twisted view of the matter, and the clergy (*muqqadas log*) in our country must give serious thought to this matter.' Because what these Maulanas declare to be breaches of the sharī'a, in fact were just breaches of 'the firm law of custom'. The sharī'a's 'true considerations of public interest' (*maslaḥateñ*) always moved with the times and the times moved with them (*warna sharī'a kī maslaḥateñ to hamēshā zamāne kē sāth hotī hain aur zamāna un kē sāth hotā hai*). Furthermore, they should realize how many elements of contemporary Indian Muslim life are in fact borrowed from surrounding non-Muslim cultures (ibid., 21).

Another ardent critic of the 'ulamā' was Ghulam Ahmad. Shibli and Ahmad were both accomplished theologians but not recognized as 'ālims. Friedmann maintained that Ghulam Ahmad's criticism was inspired by medieval Sufi attacks on the 'wicked 'ulamā' ('*ulamā'-i sū*'). These cast them as arrogant, pursuing worldly positions (*dunyā dārī*), quarrelling among themselves, dealing with insignificant details of the law (*sharī'at kī adnā juz'iyyāt*), occupied with external aspects of religion (*ẓāhir, maẓhab ki bīrūnī ṣūrat*), refusing to touch the 'supreme realities' of the faith (*ḥaqā'iq-i 'aliya*). He even likened them to the proverbial 'beast of the earth' (*dābbat al-ārḍ*) whose horrifying appearance heralded the Day of Judgment (Friedmann 1989: 105).

The Khāksār leader Mashriqi was adamant about the failure of the Maulwi class in guiding the religious life of Muslims and made several attacks on their wrong religion through a series of pamphlets. They contained his consecutive addresses to martial camps of his movement through the 1930s (Mashriqi 1995). He even suggested removing the word Maulwi from the dictionary and replacing it with a title for their educational qualifications, *shaykh-e fāẓil* (graduated scholar) (cf. the creed of the Khāksārs in Appendix I).

The 'ulamā' responded to such attacks. The reformist bent of the Nadwa came under heavy criticism especially from the Barelwi camp.[35] It initiated the debate over whether the tolerance of Nadwa founders towards

[35]On the Nadwa debate as pushed by the Barelwis, see Sanyal (1996a, 217–26) and Malik (1997: 482–505).

dissenting Islamic voices like the Shi'a and the Aḥmadīya portended ill. The Barelwi stance could be interpreted as defending the role and position of the traditional 'ulamā', to shield them from modernizing influences.

Time and again the 'ulamā's place in the public sphere was thrown into doubt. As a consequence, they felt compelled to reassert their public voice in the years to come. This happened in particular during the Khilafat Movement and during the foundation of the association of religious scholars, the JUH. The 'ulamā' were criticized for meddling in politics. Dissenting Muslim activists from the 'Young Party' and 'Old Party' were occasionally heard warning that the 'ulamā' were uncontrollable, that politicians should not believe that they could use the 'ulamā': by relying on them, politicians might either carry all Muslim India with them or be swept away.[36] The 'ulamā' countered by parading prophetic traditions characterizing them as heirs of the prophets. In the ḥadīth collection by Abd al-Malik Muttaqi (d. 1567), *Kanz al-'Ummāl*, it was said that 'the 'ulamā' were the lights of the earth, and the successors of the prophets, and heirs to me[37] and the other Prophets' (Muttaqi 1895: Vol. 5: 201). The usefulness of this reference as a political instrument could be gauged from the records of the JUH sessions where speakers quoted it on various occasions.[38]

According to another tradition, the 'ulamā' 'resembled the Prophets of the sons of Israel' (*'ulamā' ummatī ka-anbiyā' banī Isrā'īl*). These traditions inspired the 'ulamā' of different schools of thought. They also helped the Aḥmadīya founder Mirza Ghulam Ahmad to underline his pretensions (cf. Friedmann 1989: 92). The Aḥmadīya leader sought to shore up his contention that revelation continued even after the Qur'an and the Prophet tradition had been made known. If the 'ulamā' were directly linked to the Prophets at least some of them might be able to receive further divine communication. For the public persona of the 'ulamā' these traditions provided invaluable support. They alleged that the Prophet himself, hence God, recognized their special status. These traditions attested to their 'divine' attributes. This made their inclusion in the public

[36]Chowdry Khaliquzzaman (1889–1973) was reported to have made this warning to an intelligence agent in 1919 (Robinson 1994: 262). A similar warning was given to Shibli by his colleague Abdul Halim Sharar. When Shibli planned to elevate himself through the Nadwa to a position of leadership over all 'ulamā' as their *sartāj* (chief) or *Shaykh al-Kull* (head shaykh or mentor) in order to speed up their reformation, Sharar maintained that the 'ulamā' were uncontrollable (Malik 1997: 337).

[37]*Waraṯatī* (Arab.)—my heirs.

[38]For instance, Maulana Amrohwi quoted this tradition at the ninth session of the JUH in 1930 in support of demands for an increased engagement of the 'ulamā' in politics, in particular, in the election process (Rozinah 1981/II: 524).

sphere not only unavoidable but obligatory and their authority in public unquestionable. The 'ulamā' assumed that such references mandated acceptance of their claims by Muslims.

The reformist and revivalist groups were caught here in a dilemma, somewhat similar to the one in exercising independent judgement (ijtihād). In a way they were setting themselves apart from the orthodox, uninformed, and unreformed 'ulamā' of their time. The reformist and revivalist project was really also a project of reformation of the 'ulamā'. They needed to be improved to meet modern challenges such as the missionary activity of Hindus and Christians, the spread of atheism and materialism, of 'false' beliefs and 'corrupt' practices, of divisions and sectarianism. Yet the authority of the 'ulamā' could not be challenged. Hence each group insisted on leaving the interpretation of Islam to 'their' scholars and emphasized strict obedience to the 'ulamā' of their school or group.

Although he represented the largest reformist seminary of the time, Muhammad Qasim Nanaotawi, the founder of the Deoband seminary, demanded unquestioning obedience to the counsel of the 'ulamā'. Their authority was a reflection of the authority of the Prophet and was only mitigated by their fallibility. But it was not for unqualified individuals to pass judgement:

> It is possible for the traditionalist or exegete to fall into error so that what he says is in opposition to the plain intention of the Qur'an, but is not the office of ignorant or half-educated scholars like ourselves to investigate the points in dispute or to arrive at a reliable conclusion. It is not for everyone to comprehend (apparent) opposition between the Qur'an and some Tradition. (Muhammad Qasim Nanaotawi, '*Tasfiyat al-'Aqā'id* [Delhi 1890], in Ahmad and Grunebaum 1970: 61–2).

This position was directed against modernizers like Sayyid Ahmad Khan and his attempt to create a new theology of Islam. It reflected the monopoly of theological interpretation claimed for 'qualified' theologians. It blocked modernizers from introducing a rational interpretation of the Qur'an. As mentioned earlier, all the madrasa-based movements claimed this monopoly of interpretation. Groups not primarily linked to madrasa education enforced obedience to the leaders and functionaries rather than the 'ulamā'. This was so with the Khāksār. Nobody was allowed to give an interpretation deviating from the basic statements and scriptures of Allama Mashriqi (Seth 1985: 26ff.). Among the Aḥrār, a leader like Bukhari staked a claim to setting the norm of the discourse by his title of *Amīr al-Sharī'at*. He set himself up as the final arbiter and authority to judge the compliance of a given act or position with Islam (Mirza 1970). The Tablīghī Jamā'at also fostered unquestioning loyalty to the interpretation of Islamic tenets by its founder-leader Muhammad Ilyas and his heirs. The movement summarized the religious advice of Ilyas and later leaders through its guidance literature in fatwā style. It answered questions from believers about Islam, about correct practices of belief and observance and about the movement itself.[39] The Aḥmadīya too demanded absolute loyalty to the leader's interpretation. Dissenters were excommunicated. For their refusal to recognize Ghulam Ahmad as Prophet and Saviour, Muslims outside the Aḥmadīya sect were considered unbelievers (Friedmann 1989; Walter 1991: 150).

So the emphasis on the central role of the 'ulamā' served several purposes. It legitimated the role of the revivalist and reformist movements in the Islamic sphere. It strengthened discipline inside the groups. It underscored the claim of the movements to a more visible role for the religious scholars of Islam in the public sphere at large. The implied repercussions for Muslim politics went far. Where the Prophet had ruled over the first Muslim state in history, this place now rightfully belonged to the 'ulamā', it was alleged. It was the religious scholars and not the modernizers who had a divine right to rule the Muslim community. The modernizers had often attempted to cut the 'ulamā' down to size, and restrict them to interpreting the divine message, the Qur'an, and Islamic law, the sharī'a. But the quoted Prophetic traditions gave the scholars the right to ask for more, for a decidedly public role. The political and public self-perception of the 'ulamā' was fostered during the period under study. They created public bodies and political parties and fought elections as religious scholars. This helped blur the distinction between Islam as a religion and politics in South Asia. Yet such a development was by no means restricted to Islam. It was also much in evidence among Hindus, Sikhs, and other religious groups in India, which pursued roughly parallel lines of public engagement. Religious scholars, priests, and holy men sought public roles through bodies such as the Ārya Samāj, the Hindū Mahāsabhā for the Hindus, or the Shiromani Gurdwara Prabandhak Committee (1920), for the Sikhs.

In sum, the diversity of interpretations held by the groups was remarkable. They used central categories of Islam and reformism to define their group identity. They re-interpreted these categories freely. Reformism

[39]In particular, see Ilyas' *Malfūẓāt* (Numani 1993); his *Irshādāt wa Maktūbāt* (Ilyās 1997); his biography by S. A. H. A. Nadwi (1983); and his letters published by Nadwi (*Makātīb*, 1982). On the need to serve the 'ulamā' and treat them with respect, Ilyas was adamant. He considered their support crucial for his project as it was slow in coming in the beginning (Ilyās M 88, also 52, 135). He also quoted the tradition on the 'ulamā' resembling the prophets of the people of Israel (M 1).

became fragmented and contested. The dispute over the direction of reformism produced results that were incompatible with the doctrinal concept of reformism and more akin to innovative customs. A case in point was the construction of a reformist lineage for Islamic groups, more reflective of Sufi concerns with lineage (*silsila*) and ancestry. Such 'aberrations' could only be explained if the reformist debate was understood as a public discourse. The finding of the doctrinal truth was less central to it than the competition over public space.

But dissent and diversity did not prevent interaction among Islamic groups. All had recourse to the same categories of Islam and reformism. They shared many elements of a constructive programme, notably (i) religious knowledge, (ii) the strengthening of faith and piety, (iii) the correct and regular observance of religious rituals, including prayer and worship, (iv) the reconciliation of Islamic law (sharī'a) and path (ṭarīqa), and (v) the need for education and social rehabilitation of community members. The variegated discourse on reformism (iṣlāḥ) helped those groups to constitute themselves as separate Islamic publics.

3.2. THE AGENDA: FORMS AND LINES OF INTERVENTION

This section discusses the agenda of Islamic reformism and revivalism in India, the issues on which the reformist 'ulamā' intervened and the forms which this intervention took. Such issues arose as much from controversies as from the deliberate pursuit of the objectives of particular groups. Often an incident induced the 'ulamā' to take positions and attack opponents, often when that incident threatened an established position of influence. Intervention took on a multitude of forms: debates and public meetings; religious tracts and fatāwā; legal proceedings; preaching (tablīgh), marches and strikes; individual acts of terror; and religious mass violence. They provided different channels for the formation of an Islamic sphere. Intervention in the public sphere stayed clear of open warfare in the name of jihād, discussed separately later, but some were not at all peaceful.

At the turn of the century, religious controversies were still played out through theological disputations, the so-called *munāẓara*, which had been practised for long. The proceedings were often published in journals, the *rūdād*. This played a large part in combating Christian and Hindu missionaries. Questions were drawn up as a doctrinal challenge and opponents invited for public disputations. The founder of the Aḥmadīya sect, Ghulam Ahmad, was noted for his aggressive behaviour at these debates. He would curse his opponents and make predictions about harm that would befall them (see fn. 45, this chapter). Ahmad offered to enter a cursing contest with his Christian, Hindu, and Sunni adversaries: whoever's curses would not come true would admit and attest to the inferiority of his religion, that is, of the powers of 'his' God.[40]

In the early nineteenth century, these disputations were conducted in the salons of noble families and princely courts. By the mid-nineteenth century this genteel atmosphere had already significantly deteriorated (Metcalf 1982: 217ff.). The debates became secular public meetings in the style of Western debating societies, clubs, and parties. Discussion was increasingly tense and abusive. Metcalf believed 'these debates most emphatically did not provide an occasion for serious intellectual exchange'.[41] They often resembled a 'fair' (Ahmed 1988: 79). While they were rarely decisive, and tended to re-affirm participants' identification with their own group, this process was creating an Islamic public (or rather competing Islamic publics). These exchanges launched the formation of a modern public Islamic critique. They established a certain argumentative autonomy in relation to institutional Islam and to the state, as many debaters were standing outside established structures. In a sense these exchanges constituted an early counterpart of the literary circles of Habermas' reasoning public. Their importance subsided with the beginning of the twentieth century as new forms of exchange developed. Public meetings devoted to religious issues continued although they were now no longer conducted as structured exchanges between opposing sides. Increasing polarization of the public sphere meant that adversaries would not attend the same meeting and exchange arguments in a spirit of toleration and respect. Debates became protest meetings marked by public agitation and campaigning for particular issues. Structured exchanges were replaced by speeches and resolutions.

Controversies were also conducted by means of religious decrees, the fatāwā. Written either by individual scholars or issued by specialized departments of *iftā'*, they gave rulings by categories on the admissibility

[40]Friedmann maintained that this idea was modelled on medieval Sufi practices (1989).

[41]Metcalf (1982: 215ff.). For the nineteenth century religious polemics, see her two chapters 'Oral Debates' (1982: 215ff.) and 'The Publication of Original Writings' (1982: 210ff.) where she also attested to the growing public character of these exchanges. While she was perhaps justified in highlighting the ritualized and repetitive nature of the debates, her argument about the lack of intellectual exchange may be somewhat off the mark. It betrayed the Western categorization of intellectualism and neglected the fact that religious activism often followed ambiguous objectives, some declared and some undeclared where the undeclared were often more important than the declared ones. As she herself mentioned, for the Islamic leaders, the principle of participation and winning the contest was the real challenge which in terms of maximizing public impact and choosing the right tactics required significant political or public intellect.

of a certain practice from the point of view of Islamic tradition or the tradition of a particular school. Such rulings contributed to the standardization of religious practice among adherents of that school, and to Islamic jurisprudence. Fatāwā were published in reference editions often running to many volumes. If a ruling was extensive and covered many issues, then an essay or treatise (*risāla*) was in order. If the subject was polemical the opposing side would usually respond with another pamphlet, generating ongoing exchanges. To gain maximum impact in these broadsides, sometimes degenerating into fatwā or pamphlet 'wars', the support of scholars from the Holy Places of the Arabian Peninsula (Haramain) was sought, often through personal contacts. Here, the framing of the question (istiftā') put before the Arab scholars was significant, often determining the response. Such fatāwā would often be published in local newspapers in Urdu as a further stage of public exposure.

A third common channel of intervention—sometimes the last point of resort—were the courts of British-India. Where the rights of Muslims in the public sphere were denied on the basis of doctrinal and ritual differences, Islamic groups and their leaders increasingly appealed to the legal system. This would occur when access was hindered to places of worship, or property belonging to religious foundations (*auqāf*). Ahl-i Ḥadīth members started cases against their exclusion from certain mosques for their style of prayer. The courts often ruled in their favour. The Aḥmadīya also defended their right of access to mosques in this way, obtaining court rulings pronouncing them a regular sect of Islam.

The Barelwis even brought internal factional differences to court, as in the so-called aḏān debate, whether to make the second call for prayer from inside or outside the mosque (Sanyal 1996a: 188ff.). The 1917 case revolved around the accusation that a religious tract written by Ahmad Raza in the name of his son Hamid Raza, *Ṣadd al-firār* (Prevention of Flight), libelled the late Maulana Abdul Muqtadir, a Barelwi scholar from Badayun. The Hindu magistrate dismissed the charge, remarking that 'Muslims of the same belief ('aqā'id) were engaged in a trial of strength (*zōr-āzmā'ī*)' (Sanyal 1996a: 200). Ahmad Raza saw this as vindication. The extent to which religious discourse had already become public was clear. Rival Sunni religious groups, otherwise opposed to Hindu–Muslim cooperation in any field, accepted the verdict of a Hindu magistrate. The Barelwis demonstrated how groups relied on the modern institutions of the Western state even when clarifying religious disputes within their own ranks.

A fourth kind of intervention was preaching and religious propaganda (tablīgh). While this was generally peaceful it took various forms. Tablīgh activities were meant to stem the reconversion efforts of Hindu reformist movement directed at 'Neo-Muslims', and to improve Muslim compliance with the dictates of their religion. Institutional tablīgh activities will be discussed separately. Preaching could also take the form of public meeting convened to debate a religious issue, usually a point of doctrine or ritual under challenge. The Aḥrār, for instance, convened such tablīgh meetings to attack the Aḥmadīya movement at their main centre in Qadiyan in 1934. They did the same against the Shi'a in their *madḥ-i ṣaḥāba* campaign[42] in Lucknow, the centre of a former Shi'a principality, in 1939 (Chapter 4, section 4.4).[43] The meetings occasionally turned into street violence calculated to put maximum pressure on the adversary. The Aḥmadī and Shi'i communities were soft targets as their relations with mainstream Sunni Islam were already quite tense.

It was also the Aḥrār who practised yet another strategy of religious intervention, spreading rapidly in South Asia and by no means confined to Muslims—religious processions or marches (*yātrā*). They sent groups of volunteers (*jātha*) to enforce closure of shops (*bandh* or *hartāl*) under threat of violence simulating public support for a particular campaign issue. The Aḥrār organized a march in connection with a campaign against the ruler of the Kashmir principality in 1931. The Khāksār also practised marches in their campaigns (see Chapter 4, section 4.2.3). They were a means of pressurizing the authorities and rivals, sometimes even degenerating into violence. They have remained a feature of public contestations in South Asia to this day among Muslims and other religious groups.

Assassinations and acts of terror became increasingly common after the 1910s. They were used as forms of public protestation reflecting growing contestation of public space and sharpened resistance to colonial rule.[44] They were apparently considered effective also for proving the alleged superiority of a particular religious group, or a particular interpretation of doctrine. The alleged victims of the dire predictions of the Aḥmadīya founder Ghulam Ahmad provided a glaring example. He became famous for supposedly predicting the death of two opponents.[45] Although Ahmad

[42]Named after Sunni religious verses recited in praise of the first four Caliphs.

[43]Similar tactics were employed by the Aḥrār in independent Pakistan after 1948 when they held several public tablīgh conferences designed to incite the public against the Aḥmadīya (Munir 1954: 15–17).

[44]Prominent assassination victims of the time other than Muslim were the Ārya Samāj leader Swami Shraddhananda (1857–1926) on 23 December 1926 (*IAR* 1926/II: 107–8) and Mahatma Gandhi on 30 January1948.

[45]Ghulam Ahmad had predicted the violent death of Lekh Ram, an Ārya Samāj debater who died in 1897 (Lavan 1976: 82ff.), and of a Christian debater, Abd-Allah Atham, who died in 1896 (Friedmann 1989: 6–7, 187ff.). While in the first instance he had to defend himself before the police for his suspected involvement, which, however, could not be established, in the second case he had to defend himself before his followers as his prediction did not come true in the specified time but rather 'belatedly'.

personally was exonerated of involvement, it could never be established to what extent overzealous adherents might have assisted his predictions. The government, therefore, restrained him from making further threats. In other instances the victims were Aḥmadīs. Some of their followers were arrested and executed in Afghanistan at the orders of the Islamic court in Kabul. This was not so much individual terror as a precursor to 'state terrorism'. Two prominent Afghani Muslims accused of adhering to Ghulam Ahmad were stoned to death in 1901 and 1903. A second wave of persecutions followed under King Amanullah (1892–1960) in 1924 and 1925, tied to a rebellion in the province of Khost. One Aḥmadī, Nimatullah, was put on trial by the Islamic court at Kabul, which found him guilty of apostasy on the grounds of holding on to key Aḥmadī beliefs.[46] On 26 July 1943, the Muslim League leader Muhammad Ali Jinnah became the target of a prominent assassination attempt implicating Rafiq Sabir Mazangwi, supposedly a Khāksār follower.[47] Contemporary Sunni (and Shi'i) extremists continue religiously motivated attacks and assassinations in South Asia. Many Aḥmadīs, Sunni, and Shi'i activists still fall victim to such incidents (cf. Nasr 2000).

A review of forms of religious intervention would be incomplete without mentioning mass violence. The religious tension between Muslims and Hindus and among Muslim sects periodically exploded in wild carnage, at times bordering on civil war. The playing of loud music before mosques and the Muslim sacrificial killing of cows venerated by the Hindus were usually cited as the most common causes—or pretexts—for communal violence. Deeper social and political cleavages were thought to stand behind them (cf. Chapter 4, fn. 62). The groups studied here generally were not involved in these often-spontaneous acts of religiously motivated mass violence. The consequences of mass violence for the evolution of the Islamic public sphere will be discussed later in connection with Islamic groups' political intervention (see Chapter 4, section 4.2.2).

The issues of religious intervention interacted with great complexity: any ordered account is only an approximation. Attention is invited to

[46] *Civil and Military Gazette* 10 (Lahore, 13 September 1924), quoted in Friedmann (1989: 28). The religious verdict was spectacularly justified in October of the same year by the Deobandi scholar Uthmani (1974), see also Chapter 4, section 4.4. For central Aḥmadī beliefs, see p. 101.

[47] Cf. Mathur (1972: 220). The Khāksār leader Mashriqi vehemently denied having anything to do with the assassination attempt. A pamphlet of 1944, '*Ḥamlā*' (Attack), apparently published by the Khāksārs, argued the incident was the result of a conspiracy between Jinnah and the British-Indian government to discredit the movement. Cf. the webpage maintained in honour of Allama Mashriqi by his grandson Nasim Yousaf at http://www.allama-mashriqi.8m.com/chronology2.html.

major directions of intervention. Issues are summarized as to their argument, their impact on religious discourse, and their relevance for the public sphere.

3.2.1. Focus on the Qur'an and the Tradition of the Prophet (Ḥadīth/Sunna)

The debate on the role and place of the Qur'an and the written traditions, the ḥadīth, played a leading role in defining the agenda of several movements. It was one of the earliest lines of argument used by Islamic activists to distance themselves from previous religious practice. The Qur'an and the tradition were supposed to be the unaltered sources of Islam to which return was advocated. Discourse, therefore, started with their wider dissemination through printing and translations. Members of the Shah Waliullah family translated the Qur'an into Persian and Urdu.[48] Their first Urdu translation was followed by several others. Many Islamic groups and activists chose this medium of expression to make a strong public statement on Islam. A translation and commentary of the Qur'an in the Deobandi tradition was published by Sayyid Amir Ali Malihabadi (d. 1928) in 1896–1902 (1977–8). The Ahl-i Ḥadīth mentioned in 1937 among its religious publications five translations of the Qur'an (cf. fn. 52, this chapter). Abu'l Kalam Azad, who was close to the Deoband-dominated scholars' association JUH, published his *Tarjumān al-Qur'ān* in two volumes (Delhi, 1931, 1936). For the Barelwis, Ahmad Raza produced a translation, which was completed by Amjad Ali Azmi (*Kanz al-Imān fī Tarjumā al-Qur'ān*, 1911). The Aḥmadīya accomplished their own translations of the Qur'an into Urdu and English. The more classical versions were done by Nuruddin and Muhammad Ali respectively. After the 1914 split, the Qadiyani faction under Mahmud Ahmad felt compelled to forward its own versions (Ahmed 1977: 325). However, orthodox and reformist scholars have opposed Aḥmadī translations as defective.[49]

Many groups defined their attitude towards Islam through Qur'anic commentaries (tafsīr). The Deobandis Thanawi (12-volume edition printed in 1916, Schimmel 1980: 210), Uthmani (Bukhari 1988: 96),

[48]See the Persian translation by Shah Waliullāh, *Fatḥ ar-Raḥmān*, the Urdu translations of the Qur'an by his sons, Shah Rafiuddin (1749–1817) and Shah Abdul Qadir (1753–1827), which may also have been inspired by the Christian missionaries Benjamin Schultze (1689–1760) and Henry Martyn (1781–1812) and their Urdu translations of the Bible in 1741 and 1814, respectively (Schimmel 1975: 205–206, Martyn 1999: 93–94). For details on these early translations, see Mofakhkhar Hussain Khan (1993–4).

[49]In today's Pakistan they are not allowed to have their translations printed as they have been officially declared non-Muslims.

and Malihabadi wrote influential commentaries. Maududi's extensive introduction to the Qur'an from the 1930s, *Tafhīm al-Qur'ān* (The Meaning of the Qur'an, 1958–71) is still used extensively today by international Islamic organizations on the Internet.[50] The *Tablīghī Niṣāb* (1928 ff.), written by Muhammad Zakariyya for the Tablīghī Jamā'at, was considered to be their own commentary on the Qur'an, as numerous references in its English translation indicate. The *Taḏkira* (1924) by the Khāksār founder Mashriqi also has to be seen as a commentary on the Qur'an (cf. Baljon 1961). By the late 1930s, Ahl-i Ḥadīth scholars listed 50 Qur'anic commentaries in Urdu alone, being the medium of religious mass publication (see fn. 52, this chapter). Sayyid Ahmad Khan laid the foundation of his modernist interpretation through his seven-volume commentary on the Qur'an, *Tafsīr al-Qur'ān*, published in 1880–1904.

The traditions (ḥadīth) were difficult to popularize in the same manner. They remained hard to comprehend without commentary. But renewed study was an agreed strategy. Rashid Rida called the contribution of Deoband to ḥadīth studies a service to world Islam when he visited the seminary in 1330 AH (1912) (Rizvi 1980/I: 179–80). He said, 'If the attention of our brethren, the Indian divines, had not been lavished on the science of ḥadīth in that period, then this science would have faded out of existence from the eastern countries, because, from the tenth to the beginning of the fourteenth century Hijri, this science had reached the last stage of decay in Egypt, Syria, Iraq and Hijaz' (ibid.: 180). The Barelwis did not want to be seen lagging behind. Ahmad Raza proudly traced one chain of teaching permissions in ḥadīth studies back to a son of Waliullah (see Misbahi 1976). Abdul Bari set up a special *Dār al-Ḥadīth* for the teaching of traditions in the madrasa of Firangī Maḥall in 1916 (Robinson 2001: 163). The Tablīghī Jamā'at popularized the ḥadīth extensively for the interpretation of religious doctrine by making reading of the *Faẓā'il-i A'māl* mandatory. In matters of dress and social habits they recommended a special collection of ḥadīth, al-Tirmidhi's classic, *Shamā'il-i Muḥammadīya* (Tirmizi 1925).

By virtue of their group definition, the Ahl-i Ḥadīth put special emphasis on the study, interpretation, and publication of the ḥadīth. As they believed that the degeneration of religion stemmed from neglect of the original sources of the faith, they made the observance of the traditions and the Qur'an their sign of distinction. In a broader sense, they presented themselves as specialists in all genres of religious literature. In the report

[50]Cf. the Muslim Students' Association (MSA), at http://www.usc.edu/dept/MSA/quran/maududi/.

to the 1937 Muslim Educational Conference they presented an impressive list of scholarly works.[51]

While several reformist scholars regarded a large corpus of the ḥadīth as unreliable and some wanted to exclude traditions contradicting Qur'anic injunctions or reason, the Ahl-i Ḥadīth rejected most such disqualifications. In principle they regarded all traditions as coming from God through Muhammad and his companions, although they were not unanimous on what traditions and Qur'anic verses—if any—should be abrogated (Siyalkoti 1953: 168–72).

The Ahl-i Qur'ān[52] in turn rejected the ḥadīth as unreliable conjecture. The Qur'an alone was to be the basis of their judgement. In this they agreed with the rationalist interpretation of Islam as advanced by Sayyid Ahmad. Socially, they were more exclusive than the early Ahl-i Ḥadīth. They developed their own prayer ritual and prayed only in their own mosques. Because the Ahl-i Qur'ān attacked the status of the ḥadīth, relations with the Ahl-i Ḥadīth, which defended the ḥadīth, were especially strained. The government had to intervene to protect the life of Chakralawi, leader of the former, who had engaged in a hot controversy with Muhammad Husain Batalwi (d. 1920), member of the latter.

This tremendous flow of religious literature made public access to the Qur'an and the ḥadīth in South Asia a reality, greatly broadening the base of public discourse. The debate was now no longer limited to religious specialists knowing Arabic. These translations and their mass propagation through print were true acts of modernity, permitting individual judgement on religious issues. Recurring issues dominating the debate dealt with unclear or contradictory passages, an activity previously confined to the law schools and their legal literature. It particularly preoccupied three

[51] For a list of these publications, cf. Nausharwi (1970: 33–99). The 1970 edition used here made some corrections. The list still includes some works by Waliullah, his sons, and some of their contemporaries whom the Ahl-i Ḥadīth regard as their founding members, so the actual number of modern Ahl-i Ḥadīth publications is somewhat smaller. Nausharwi lists the following categories (number in parenthesis): translations of the Qur'an (five; one in Persian, four in Urdu), commentaries (tafsīr) on the Qur'an in Arabic (eight), in Persian (four), in Urdu (50), in Punjabi (three), notes (*ḥāshia*) on the Qur'an (17), explanations (*sharḥ*) on the Qur'an (119), on jurisprudence (fiqh) (213), on doctrine ('aqā'id) (100), on the Prophet's biography (sīra) and Islamic history (*tārīkh*) (140), works of praise and eulogy (*munāqib*) (8), on the Prophet and prophethood (*an-nabuwwāt*) (21), on politics (*siyāsat*) (15), on disputations (munāẓara) with non-Muslims (31), on the Ārya and Hindu doctrines (20), translations of Arabic books (15), on mystics (taṣawwuf) and morals (*ikhlāq*) (103), Ārya on literature and science (*ādab-o-'ulūm*) (21), on Arabic literature (32).

[52] A small splinter group of intellectuals founded in 1902 by Maulana Abdullah Chakralawi in Lahore. Some members had connections with the Aligarh School and some with the Ahl-i Ḥadīth (cf. Ahmad 1967: 120–1; Metcalf 1982: 289; Titus 1930: 190).

groups, the Aligarh school of thought represented by Sayyid Ahmad Khan, the Aḥmadīya, and the Ahl-i Ḥadith. Debates over the Qur'an and the traditions created some affinity between them, although their relationship was later hostile. Shah Waliullah attempted to reconcile seemingly contradictory or repetitive verses of the Qur'an but failed to find a satisfactory explanation in five cases (Baljon 1986: 149). Several scholars such as Sayyid Ahmad Khan, Ghulam Ahmad, and Maulwi Hakim Nuruddin (1841–1914)[53] took up the challenge (Ahmed 1977: 322).

In emphasizing the primal role of the Qur'an, the rationalist Sayyid Ahmad Khan and other reformist 'ulamā' shared the influence of Waliullah. However, they disagreed over the principles of its interpretation (see section 3.1.3). Sayyid Ahmad explained the contradictions and miracles in the Qur'anic text either by recourse to the arguments of nature or by historicizing them.[54] If a Prophetic tradition contradicted the laws of nature, as in accounts of miracles, Sayyid Ahmad saw this as a proof of their unreliability. If Qur'anic passages were in doubt he interpreted them often as allegorical expressions reflecting the historical usage of Arabic. God's message descended upon the Prophet's mind but the scriptural revelation of the Qur'an was conveyed in a language comprehensible to all, he assumed. He distinguished between the 'intrinsic value' of the revelation, which was immutable and could not but conform to nature and reason, and 'extrinsic value' whose evaluation was changing over time. Sayyid Ahmad also wanted to apply a rational standard to the traditions (ḥadīth). He dismissed outright those that contradicted commandments of the Qur'an or relied on a 'weak' chain of transmission, and also those that contradicted reason and nature. Deoband's Nanaotawi, who responded to Sayyid Ahmad in detail, believed that 'half-educated scholars' should not make such distinctions (Nanaotawi, '*Taṣfiyat al-'Aqā'id*', in Ahmad and Grunebaum 1970: 61).

[53]An early confidant of the Aḥmadī founder Ghulam Ahmad who had received a traditional religious education; for biographical details, see Friedmann (1989: 13–14).

[54]The contemporary modernist discourse on the Qur'an was broader than can be described here. Aziz Ahmad reviewed several concepts in his *Islamic Modernism in India and Pakistan* (1967). Muhsin al-Mulk, who was part of the Aligarh Movement, commented on the Qur'an in a more conservative way. While in terms of taqlīd and ijtihād he followed the views of Sayyid Ahmad Khan, he regarded the role of nature and natural law in more narrowly defined limits where supernatural agencies would not be explained away but regarded as valid 'exceptions' (ibid.: 67–9). Another variety of a modernist interpretation of the Qur'an was represented by the Islamic intellectual and bureaucrat Amir Ali whose interpretation was close to the Aligarh school, but accepted the consensus (ijmā') as a valid source of Islamic law, not as constituted by the religious scholars but by the people and the modern élite of the Muslim community (ibid.: 96). See also Muhammad Iqbal (ibid.: 148–52), Maulana Azad (ibid.: 175–85), and Ghulam Parwez (1903–85) (ibid.: 225–30).

Mirza Ghulam Ahmad framed his argument on behalf of the Aḥmadīya Movement differently.[55] For him, the Qur'an as the embodiment of the revelation was fully and wholly true and correct, without human addition. It did not contain a single word that was not true. The question of abrogating certain verses did not arise. The sequence of Qur'anic verses must also be of divine origin and have intrinsic meaning, so the repetitive parts were also deliberately revealed and essential.[56] He accepted that the figurative language of parts of the Qur'an required interpretation, but in Islamic, theological terms, and not in rational, historical, or linguistic terms, as Sayyid Ahmad had suggested. This required more than the human knowledge of the Arabic language. Only the imam of the time (see the discussion on the mujaddid), that is Ghulam Ahmad himself, could exercise this judgement. He believed the Qur'an contained the collected and full wisdom of the religion of Islam, of philosophy and the sciences, or their basis. It also contained prophesies of future events not yet fully understood. In this sense he believed that the Qur'an remained (the only revealed religious document) unaltered and complete, an understanding shared by many Islamic reformists including the founder of the Khāksār movement, Mashriqi.

Ghulam Ahmad also carefully studied the ḥadīth most of which he considered unreliable, especially where they contradicted the Qur'an, a position he shared with Sayyid Ahmad. Regarding the sources of Islam, he accorded a higher status to the Sunna, that is, the Prophetic way of life, than to the written traditions (ḥadīth), which remained to him dependent on the reliability of the transmission (Ahmed 1977: 323). But he remained critical of Ahmad's modernism, notably his endorsement of British rule and concept of union between God's work and word. The supremacy of the text of the Qur'an by-passed many traditions and the law schools: till date this remains an important strategy for the Aḥmadīya in defence of their interpretation of jihād and liberal interpretation of obligations (punishments in Islamic law—*ḥudūd*) and customs (role of women, education, etc.).

The Khāksār leader, Mashriqi, also accorded primacy to the Qur'an. He borrowed from other interpretations and like Ghulam Ahmad, considered the Qur'an immutable. Moreover, he regarded the Qur'an as a scientific document. As the Qur'an was the only revelation to have survived

[55]For a detailed exposition of the role of the Qur'an in the theology of the Aḥmadīya, see Munir D. Ahmed's contribution to the XIX German Congress of Orientalists in 1975 (Ahmed 1977).

[56]Particularly, Ghulam Ahmad's son and successor, Mahmud Ahmad, continued to investigate this line of thinking. Mahmud's desire to compose the most exhaustive and extensive exegesis of the Qur'an, planned for 30 volumes (*tafsīr-i kabīr*), was not fulfilled as he died before its completion (Ahmed 1977: 321, 324).

unaltered, it allowed science to test the authenticity of other religious books, on the assumption that conformity to the Qur'an was a measure of reliability in terms of the divine will. He believed it was invaluable in 'lifting religion to the level of science' (Mashriqi 1987: 137). To him the Qur'an was like a law of nature, which would be understood only gradually with the passage of time but could not be wrong in itself (Mashriqi 1995). All religious texts of the world were seen as the expression of one divine will of which only the Qur'an was the perfect embodiment. Between all heavenly books he saw only a 'difference in the application of the supreme directive', no difference 'of the mind's vision' (Mashriqi 1987: 135). This argument was meant to integrate religion with the modern world. They were not only compatible, but more, the Qur'an was their early product. He used this argument not to isolate Muslims from modern learning but to encourage them to master the modern world in the name of Islam. While Mashriqi shared in the critical assessment of the reliability of the ḥadīth, he too quoted extensively from the ḥadīth literature in his main work *Taḏkira* (1972/1987).

The public sphere evolved to create space for critical deliberation. The discourse on the Qur'an was almost as important in this process as the debate on ijtihād. Those who went back to the Qur'an opened the door of ijtihād by removing other layers of interpretation. Their theological and philosophical underpinnings converged. They were driven to intended or unintended historicism. Exegesis required investigation of the historical circumstances and causes of its revelation. Movements focusing on the Qur'an were accused of radicalism in their approach to Islamic doctrine, and there was interchange between groups through their involvement in public activity.

The same applied to the study of the ḥadīth, although with some significant variation. The reason was that the ḥadīth not only served radical reformist movements such as the Ahl-i Ḥadīth, they also constituted the major reference material for the legal literature of the law schools, bastions of orthodoxy and conservatism. The vast and uneven body of traditions, some reliable and some not, created a bond between all reformist and revivalist movements. All those who wanted to put Islamic learning and faith on the surer footing of the Islamic injunctions (sharī'a) needed to refer to the ḥadīth constantly. This bond was particularly clear between movements deriving from the Deoband tradition (Deobandis, Aḥrār, Tablīghī Jamā'at) or feeling close to its scholarly calling (Ahl-i Ḥadīth). Yet, the ḥadīth also played a significant role in the discourses of other movements, notably the Barelwis, the Aḥmadīya, and the Khāksār. They too supported the revival of the ḥadīth studies and quoted them when they provided valued legitimation for public arguments.

3.2.2. Veneration of the Prophet and the Legacy of Folk Islam

Debate on the Prophet and his life created another bond between all groups of Islam in different ways.[57] For folk and mystical traditions it was a legitimate means to prove a connection with the prime sources of Islam. Also, since the end of the eighteenth century, many reformist groups emphasized the Prophet's role. They united under the appellation Ṭariqa-e Muḥammadīya (The Path, Way of the Prophet Muhammad), also used by Shah Waliullah. Throughout the nineteenth and twentieth centuries in South Asia all reformist and revivalist groups, even the most radical, based claims to leadership on mystical references and the authority of the Prophet. Sufi principles enabled the groups to recruit followers and inculcate loyalty regardless of the reformist message. This was important in defining the boundaries of groups and in turning them into actors in the public sphere. It stabilized them and enhanced their autonomy from both the state and orthodox religious institutions.

The Barelwis stressed the model character of the Prophet's life and behaviour as embodied in the Sunna. These two reference points, the Prophet and his ways, structured Barelwi discourse. It allowed them to claim their share of public space from their rivals. It brought into the public sphere the Sufi-inspired and pīr-based network of devotional Islam, which was often derided by reformists for its 'corrupt' and 'backward' character, but, in fact, represented the 'silent majority' of 'real existing' Islamic practice in the subcontinent. As the Barelwi School accorded recognition to mainly rural-based practices and cultural plurality in Islam, its oppositional and quarrelsome style symbolized a defiant discourse of emancipation. Yet, the constituency of the Barelwis was limited, as they represented the organized, broadly reformist, sector of Sufi Islam. Outside the Barelwis there also existed several localized Sufi movements. Chishti Khwaja Hasan Nizami (1878–1955), for instance, operated from Delhi on similar lines, equally concerned with the reform of Sufism as with political, religious, and social activism (Hermansen 2001).

The Barelwis mostly argued their claims through references to the attributes and the status of the Prophet. They maintained the Prophet's special qualities set him apart from ordinary people, that he was not just a vessel for the divine revelation but had supernatural qualities himself, and partook in knowledge of the unseen (*'ilm-e ghaib*). They hotly contested the Wahhabi position that if God wanted to, he could have created another Prophet like Muhammad (*imkān-e naẓīr*). A similar argument revolved around whether the Qur'an was 'created', which was

[57]For literature on the cult of the Prophet, see Malik (1997: 175, fn. 81).

denied by the Barelwis.[58] They insistently refuted Christian and Hindu attacks on the lifestyle of Muhammad (particularly with regard to his marriages) and members of his family. Their concern for the Prophet was also reflected in certain rituals, such as celebrations of his birthday (mīlād), opposed as polytheistic by some reformist 'ulamā'.

It was logical to extend veneration of the Prophet to veneration of local saints, but not all Sufi shrine worship was acceptable to reformist Barelwis. Ahmad Raza set exacting standards for a shrine keeper or pīr: he should be a Sunni of good faith (*ṣaḥīḥ 'aqīdā*); have sufficient knowledge of Islamic law to solve problems without having to ask someone to interpret the sharī'a for him. He should lead an exemplary life and represent an unbroken chain of transmission (silsila) of blessing (*baraka*) to the Prophet (Sanyal 1996a: 134).

Notwithstanding the confrontation between the Barelwis and Deobandis over faith and doctrine, the Deobandi position on the Prophet was more a matter of emphasis than actual difference. They could not deny the central role of the Prophet, but God's word still retained primacy. Veneration of the Prophet also highlighted the social role of the 'ulamā', seen as his deputies.[59] But the Deobandis nonetheless attacked the external symbolism of the Prophet's veneration. They opposed mīlād ceremonies for encouraging the belief that a dead person was actually present; elevating the importance of a fixed date; and resemblance to Hindu practices.[60] Similarly, the veneration of ancestors or their shrines was condemned, particularly the anniversaries (known as 'urs) of (Sufi) saints. A classical treatise restating the Deobandi position was published in 1927 by Maulana Khalil Ahmad Saharanpuri (1987) in an exchange with the Barelwi leader, Ahmad Raza, who had attacked the Deobandis for equating certain Barelwi practices with unbelief (*kufr*).[61]

[58]Sanyal (1996a: 94), also Appendix I. Islamic reformists were divided on this count, as believing in the createdness of the Qur'an allowed reaffirmation of the principle of tauḥīd, that God was omnipotent, whereas its uncreatedness and 'pre-existence' allowed to refer all divine knowledge to the Qur'an itself as the prime and only manifestation of revelation (cf. Watt 1969: 104–5, 107–8).

[59]Cf. section 3.1.6. The point was also re-emphasized by Muhammad Qasim Nanaotawi in his controversy with Sayyid Ahmad. See Nanotawi, '*Tasfiyat al-'Aqā'id*', in Ahmad and Grunebaum (1970: 64–5).

[60]Gangohi engineered a decree opposing the observance, *Fatāwā-e Rashīdīya*, 50, 89, quoted in Metcalf (1982: 150).

[61]Ahmad Raza had equated the Deobandi School with Wahhabism in his famous 1905 fatwā *Ḥusām al-Ḥaramain* for which he had gained the support of some Arabian scholars. In order to refute these charges, Saharanpuri, somewhat ironically, set out to prove in response to a joint query of Arabian 'ulamā' that the Deobandis were not Wahhabis, or outside all law schools, but actually firm *muqallidīn*, adherents to Hanafi law, something

Customs in veneration of the Prophet were tolerated by some reformist 'ulamā' when they helped spread their own message. Maulana Thanawi used the mīlād festival on preaching missions among 'Neo-Muslims' (Masud 2000: lv). The Deobandis' were ambiguous towards Muslim saints. They branded as polytheism (shirk) the annual festival of Shaykh Abdul Qadir Jilani (d. 1166—*ghiāyrahwiñ* or the 'eleventh'). He had founded the Qadiriyya order, and was particularly honoured by the Barelwis. But they themselves acted as Sufi shaykhs on many occasions and initiated disciples into various orders. Thanawi himself was sometimes described as the most eminent Sufi shaykh in north India at the time, rivalled only by Abdul Bari (Metcalf 1992: 4; Robinson 2001: 74). The founders of the Deoband seminary, Nanaotawi and Gangohi, were initiates of mystical orders, and owed allegiance to the revered Sufi pīr Hajji Imdadullah (1817–1899).[62] He had been Shaykh to many of the reformist 'ulamā' (Metcalf 1982: 74ff.) and even after his migration to Mecca, connections between Deobandi scholars and Sufi orders went through him. The Deoband seminary maintained a Sufi hospice, as did many affiliated seminaries. Imdadullah was occasionally tolerant of 'errant' practices, and participated in a mīlād ceremony in Mecca even while he supported Gangohi's rejection of the practice in principle (Metcalf 1982: 151). Imdadullah's disciples included also Maulana Khalil Ahmad Saharanpuri, often connected with anti-Barelwi, hence anti-Sufi polemics. The Shaykh al-Hind, Mahmud al-Hasan, and Husain Ahmad Madani were his disciples too, although they advocated radical political action (Rahman 1997: 145ff.; 92ff.; 238ff.). Even Thanawi, known for his principled reformism, was Imdadullah's disciple (ibid.: 301).[63]

Imdadullah's network extended to the Nadwa council and school, including its founder Sayyid Muhammad Ali Monghiri (ibid.: 365) and Sayyid Abdul Hayy. Together with the latter's offspring these men shaped the profile of the Nadwa in the twentieth century.[64] Imdadullah also defended the Nadwa against attacks from the Barelwis (Malik 1997: 496ff.).

---

which the Barelwis themselves claimed as their major attribute. For details, see introduction (*muqaddima*) to Saharanpuri (1987: 5–14); also Raza Khan (1905).

[62]On Imdadullah and his disciples (*khulafā'*), see Raḥmān (1997), containing life-sketches of 66 khulafā' and 17 attendants (*akhwāṣ*).

[63]Thanawi hailed from the same place as Imdadullah, Thana Bhawan in U.P. He made it a special point to withdraw to the same place where Imdadullah had resided, a Sufi hospice named in his honour Khānqāh-i Imdādīyah. Reflective of their close relationship was also the fact that Imdadullah made him his 'authorized person' (*majāz*) and a spiritual successor (khalīfa) (Rizvi 1980/II: 33).

[64]Malik (1997) also named other disciples of Imdadullah like Mufti Rahim Bakhsh (b. 1855) (p. 297n), Maulwi Muhammad Hafizullah (d. 1942) (p. 304n), Khalilur Rahman (d. 1936) (p. 342n), Karamatullah Khan Dehlawi (d. 1928) (p. 492n).

The reformist pīr network of Imdadullah barely touched the Firangī Maḥall (Robinson 2001: 92). The Firangī Maḥallīs had their own resources of mysticism. Members of the family were prominent among Indian mystics and connected with major shrines, teaching the sons of many shrine keepers (*sajjādas*) at the Madrasa Niẓāmīya,[65] established and run by Abdul Bari. His disciples were well placed in north Indian Muslim élite society, including political worthies such as the brothers Muhammad and Shaukat Ali. His network transcended family traditions. He was sought after because of his prominence in all-Indian affairs, a consequence of his activity in the Pan-Islamic, pan-Turkic, and Khilafat Movements. Bari exemplifies how the Firangī Maḥallīs were changing in forms of private and public allegiance even though they were relatively untouched by reformist scripturalism. Bari also involved himself in the institutional revival of Sufism, co-sponsoring the foundation of an all-India body of coordination, the Bazm-i Ṣūfīya-i Hind in 1916 (Robinson 2001: 169, 74).

The veneration of the Prophet played a natural role in the Firangī Maḥallīs' understanding of mysticism. Abdul Bari declared that to follow the Prophet was to come near to God. 'To follow the Prophet truly is this: to follow his habits, his behaviour, his manners, his intructions so that the life of the Muslim becomes like the life of the Holy Prophet.... This is called the true Khilafat, to lose one's identiy in the being of the Prophet' (Abdul Bari, *Malfūẓ-i Razzāqī* [Kanpur 1926], 2, quoted in Robinson 2001: 83). Abdul Bari and other holy men in the family imitated the manners of the Prophet closely in dressing, eating, drinking, washing, and so on. His lineage alone had produced five saints, the most revered being Anwar al-Haq (d. 1279/1820–1) and Abdur Razzaq (d. 1307/1889–90).

The Prophet discourse was just as significant for the Tablīghī Jamā'at. Tablīghī tracts highlighted the model character of the Prophet, and sought to foster among their followers exact imitation of the Prophet and his companions. Reviving the Sunna, or ways of the Prophet, promised great rewards for the hereafter (*ākhirat*). The travelling preaching groups (jamā'at) represented the early Islamic community of the Prophet and his companions; their preaching tours (*gasht*) consciously emulated their effort to spread Islam.[66] Their recommended traditions detailed the dress, eating, and other behaviour by the Prophet and his companions as collected

[65]According to Robinson, these included the sons of the keepers from Bansa, Rudauli, Kachocha, Phulwari, Kakori, Kalyar, Ajmere, and Allahabad (2001: 73, fn. 14).

[66]Numani (1993), for example, travelling for the spread of religion is referred back to the practice of the companions of the Prophet in propagating the message of Islam (Ilyās M 92, 93); love and affection for the Prophet are highlighted in M 60; veneration of the descendents of the Prophet's family in M 58; leading a simple life like the Prophet in M 12; how the Prophet used to address people is a reference in M 101, etc.

in the classic *Shamā'il-i Muḥammadīya* by the early theologian al-Tirmidhi (d. 746). Their founding member, Zakariyya, translated it into Urdu and added a commentary (Tirmizi 1925). The silent recitation of the names of God (d̲ikr) was a Sufi practice accepted and encouraged for its conformity with recognized norms of the sharī'a. Little known is the fact that some Tablīghī leaders continued accepting disciples as shaykhs, a practice they shared with other Deobandi scholars. Devotees occasionally brought offerings to their Tablīghī pīrs. These helped them partly cover expenses of the movement. Inamul Hasan (1918–95) was reported to have maintained a wide network of disciples. He administered bay'a to groups of Tablīghī activists on the sidelines of their annual congregations by throwing a piece of cloth over them.[67] Beyond such external features it was the internal dimension of their revivalism that pointed to their Sufi antecedents. Tablīghīs were strongly encouraged to achieve their objectives through reforming their character (nafs) and purifying their intentions (*niyyat*). These directions of their activity were reflected in points four and five of their 'Six Essentials' (See Appendix I). It was easy to see why Anwarul Haq described the Tablīghī Jamā'at as an extension of Sufi traditions and therefore a Sufi movement (1972). Yet Masud strongly disagreed, emphasizing the reformism of their teachings (2000: xi).

The Ahl-i Ḥadīth believed they had direct access to the divine insight of the Prophet through the ḥadīth. This allowed them to circumvent the law schools. They argued that Muhammad received the Prophetic tradition as part of the revelation (Qur'an 53:3,4) and enjoined Muslims to follow his interpretation of the Qur'an (as captured in the Prophetic traditions) even after its revelation (Qur'an 75:19) (cf. Siyalkoti 1953: 168ff.). They did not extend their reverence of the Prophet to saints and their shrines, regarding this as aberrant.

Historical scepticism was the hallmark of modernists in the line of the Aligarh School. Sayyid Ahmad regarded prophets of all faiths as more or less equal. He extended his distinction between secular and religious aspects of Qur'anic injunctions to the life of the Prophet. Furthermore, he considered certain injunctions valid only for the time of the Prophet, a view vehemently attacked by the Deobandis. His position was more or less shared by Amir Ali (1849–1928) and Chiragh Ali (1844–95), while Shibli Numani was more cautious (Cf. Metcalf 1982: 72; for Amir Ali see Ahmad 1967: 89; for Chiragh Ali see Ahmad and Grunebaum 1970: 53; for Sayyid Ahmad Khan see Reetz 1988: 216).

[67]Interviews by the author with Tablīghī activists at Nizamuddin headquarters in Delhi on 26 October 1998 and in Aligarh in December 2001.

The Aḥmadīya here chose a middle path in their theology. While ready to examine the Prophetic traditions critically, it was important to them that no interpretation reduced the authority of the Prophet and the Qur'an, perfect and complete in every aspect. In particular, they stressed the supernatural character of the revelation and the Prophet. This was essential to support the claims of their founder, Ghulam Ahmad, and his successors, to some form of prophethood. The authority of Aḥmadīya leaders derived from the connection through their own prophesies to the Prophet Muhammad and directly to God. Yet they remained critical of 'excessive' Sufi practices not covered by the commands of the sharī'a. Pīr worship was suppressed in their communities, as were acts of 'superstition' such as the reverence of amulets (Friedmann 1989; Walter 1991). At the same time, the tomb of Ghulam Ahmad at Qadiyan became an object of veneration and a centre of pilgrimage (Walter 1991: 126).

Every movement highlighted something else in the Prophet. He and his life experience were a mirror of their own identity, legitimizing their concept of Iṣlam. The Deobandis emphasized the successorship of the 'ulamā' to the Prophet, for the Barelwis he was the object of love and mystical devotion, for the Firangī Maḥallīs and Tablīghīs he was the model of detailed emulation and imitation, for the Ahl-i Ḥadīth he was the immediate source of religious knowledge freeing them from the law schools, for the modernist Aligarh group he was a historical figure and worldly statesman. Different interpretations divided these groups but the Prophet sub-discourse also facilitated inner-Islamic communication, transcending dogmatic divisions. In India, this was even more important than in other parts of the Islamic world because devotional Islam and Sufi practices historically occupied a much larger share in practised Islam. At the same time, special emphasis on the Prophet was also driven by historical circumstance. Polemical attacks on the Prophet by Christian and Hindu missionaries since the mid-nineteenth century had left a deep trace on the psyche of Muslim religious activists and leaders. These attacks provoked a stream of literature by Muslim intellectuals defending the Prophet and raising new issues.[68]

Sufi-style action was also useful in establishing influence networks for these groups. The oath of allegiance (bay'a) strengthened the loyalty of group members, to a certain extent structuring its very membership. While the orders' influence was declining, connections among activists

[68]See, for instance, William Muir (1858), to which Sayyid Ahmad Khan directly responded (1870) and others such as Chiragh Ali (1883), Amir Ali (1922), and Shibli Numani (1953–62) by implication.

through membership endured. The master–devotee relationship (*pīr–murīd*) created emotional bonds, which helped master modern discourses and public battles. Certain orders were prevalent in different groups. The Barelwis tended to belong to the Qadiriyya, the Deobandis to the Chishtiyya and Naqshbandiyya, the Firangī Maḥallīs to the Chishtiyya–Sabriyya (Robinson 2001: 82), the Nadwis to the Naqshbandiyya–Mujaddidiyya.[69] The Tablīghīs' founder Muhammad Ilyas stood in the tradition of the Chishtiyya shaykhs.

Such preferences, however, should not be overestimated. Initiation into multiple orders became widespread from the mid-nineteenth century (Gaborieau 1986). The Deobandis took pride in being trained in all the four orders though they gave precedence to the Chishtiyya and then the Naqshbandiyya in addition to their concurrent attachment to Imdadullah (Rizvi 1980/I: 20–1). Metcalf detected a shift of Sufi allegiance from family saints to teachers, as with the Deobandis, and thought it novel. She contrasted the Deobandi tradition of becoming the disciple of one's teacher with the family tradition among the Firangī Maḥallis. However, in the Firangī Maḥallī tradition, the family saint was also a teacher. Islamic teachers often took the oath from their students. The novelty perhaps was in that the students of institutionalized seminaries such as Deoband were less marked by personal attachment or family bonds: Deoband reconstructed adherence to the seminary and movement by imposing the oath to a teacher. It turned the impersonal bond into a personal one. One could read this as facilitating the formation of modern cross-links. These promoted new group identities without foregoing the advantages of the emotional attachment involved in the Sufi allegiance to a master. Other cross-links emerged from Sufi family connections overlapping with clan structures. They too were reordered. Group leaders often constituted a sub-order resembling a religious family: the spiritual family genealogy (silsila) was linked to a particular family saint revered by all members of the family. The saint was traced back by spiritual or family descent to the Prophet and/or his companions. A typical example was the Firangī Maḥallī family. These family orders took on features of a clan (birādarī, patrilineage) or sect, notably endogamy, considered effective in reinforcing group loyalty. This feature indicated a common cultural inheritance from the Hindu caste system in South Asia. These traits have often been described from an ethnographic standpoint, but their political relevance for the formation of Islamic groups needs highlighting. Surrounding cultural and political pressure, competition in the public and the Islamic sphere, repeatedly

[69]For the Naqshbandi 'ālim Sayyid Abdul Hayy and the Hasani family, see Malik (1997: 384ff.).

set in motion a process of clan-building within these groups. In the end, the Aḥmadīs' social cohesion strongly relied on endogamy. Tablīghī Jamā'at and Ahl-i Ḥadīth members discriminated in favour of their own in marriage and social contacts. Deobandi or Barelwi affiliation was strongly considered in the social intercourse of its members although the large size of these two groups means that it could not be a sufficient marker for marital relations. That the Firangī Maḥallīs form a large family clan has already been mentioned. Aligarh affiliation may have been partly considered in social intercourse. Affiliation was less important among voluntarist activist groups like the Khāksārs and the Aḥrārs. Their group members enshrined the ideology more in task and action although they over time also converted to the clan model.

3.2.3. *Fighting Atheism and Materialism—Dahrīyat and Māddīyat*

All Islamic groups were united in perceiving atheism and materialism as a threat, although they followed different strategies to tackle it. Some feared increasing irreligiosity as part of a more general threat perception discussed earlier (see section 3.1.1). The materialist character of Western colonial power was a particular target. British separation of religion and politics had created resentment among the Muslim élites.[70] The Moghul and local law the British replaced was seen as religious law by some Muslims, even though sharī'a law was rarely enforced before the arrival of the British.

The adoption of Western culture by the Aligarh group and their teaching methods were hotly debated. Founder Sayyid Ahmad was accused of imitating the West (Nanaotawi quoted in Ahmad and Grunebaum 1970: 60–76). Religious leaders attacked the institution for producing a generation of modern Muslim leaders estranged from the roots of their own culture and too pro-Western. Islamic religious education set out to rectify this, illustrated by the approach of Sayyid Sulaiman Nadwi (1884–1953) from the Nadwa seminary in 1927. Nadwi discussed atheism (*ilḥād*) and 'Westernism' (*maghribīyat*) at the administrative session of the Nadwa convened on 5 June 1927 after the annual session in Kanpur (Jalis Nadwi and Tabriz Khan 1983/II: 369ff.). He complained that Europe's culture and civilization were spreading over the world like a flood (*sīlāb*), dispersing atheism (ilḥād) and religious hypocrisy (*zandaqa*). Indian universities and colleges could not stem this flood. Muslim youth also needed to be shown the direction for reformation (iṣlāḥ) of their beliefs and actions as Muslims. 'We don't need such higher education which separates us (*bēgānē hoñ*)

[70]Cf. the dissatisfaction of Shah Abdul Aziz with the decline of Islamic law after the British took control of Delhi in 1803, discussed in more detail in Chapter 4, section 4.3.3.

from Islamic education, Islamic traditions, Islamic nationality (*qaumīyat*) and from our religion. In this relation our recent experience is that these students become like gramophones whose hearts and brains have been filled with the feelings (*jazbāt*) and perceptions (*eḥsāsāt*) of Europe. (Instead) it is necessary that they become the future clockwork (*kal purzē*) of Islam and Islamic nationality' (Nadwi 1983: 370). The leader of the Tablīghī Jamā'at, Muhammad Ilyas, took a similar line. For him Western influences were dangerous because they could subvert the religious loyalty of Muslims:

> Friends! There is still work to do. There are two major threats quickly appearing before religion. One comes from the preaching efforts undertaken among the uneducated people by the *Shuddhī* movement. The other threat is posed by idol worship and atheism coming along with western politics and government. This should be first on your mind in whatever you do (Ilyas M 83).

A similar thought was expressed by Maulana Abu'l-Hasan Muhammad Sajjad Naqshbandi at the 1925 session of the JUH. He accused Sayyid Ahmad of being responsible for a tradition (maslak) to identify with the Christians, to rely on them, to adopt their statehood and civilization (*madnīyat*) (Rozinah 1981/I: 296).

Sayyid Ahmad originally shared some of the concerns of his orthodox critics. He thought that the Muslim youth needed to be educated in an atmosphere where their religious identity was protected despite access to Western knowledge. But traditional scholars remained suspicious of education at Aligarh. The Deobandis repeatedly tried to influence students at Aligarh and their teaching. Tense relations were driven by fear and envy. The scholars watched a relatively small contingent of Aligarh graduates take major positions in all spheres of public life from the colonial administration, to the public services, to the nationalist movement, including Congress and the Muslim League. The relationship was normalized only when a more conservative leadership took over Aligarh University. In 1940, the rector of Deoband, Qari Muhammad Tayyib, delivered a lecture at Aligarh at the invitation of the Society of Islamic History and Civilization on the subject of 'Islam and Science'. He asked: 'what is the relation between Islam and material wisdom,...what are the harms of pure materialism.' Referring to an 'authentic' prophetic tradition, Tayyib elaborated on 'human energy and capacity and its sway and domination over material powers. After making it clear that the spring of human powers was the soul, he [...] argued in a very subtle manner about spiritualism, theology, the Being of Allah and His Attributes.'[71] Regarding the

[71]Rizvi (1980/I: 234, fn. 1). A similar warning of the materialism of the modern world was formulated by the Nadwa scholar Sayyid Abu'l-Hasan 'Ali Nadwi during a

spirituality of Islam and the attributes of God superior to modern science was a position diametrically opposed to Sayyid Ahmad Khan's. The latter had conceded 56 years earlier that it was difficult to quarrel with science about the nature of the heavens and suggested the re-interpretation of the respective references in the Qur'an.[72]

While reaffirming traditional or religious education, several reformers still wanted to incorporate Western knowledge and science into Islam, or to interpret their achievements in an Islamic idiom. This demand was directed at removing the social and economic isolation into which many families of the Indian Muslim élite had fallen due to their hesitation in communicating with the British. Shibli argued in favour of reforming traditional education according to the requirements and needs of the present day (cf. Numani 1965: 16f.). His contributions to Islamic historiography were meant to meet these standards. He employed modern scientific methods of collecting evidence and scholarly arguments in order to prove the glory and superiority of Islam and Muslim history.

The need to demonstrate the superiority of Islamic and Eastern thought over the West led to another strand of argument. Western materialism was contrasted with Eastern spirituality. The founder of the Khāksar, Mashriqi, spoke for many activists when he pointed to the gap between the achievements of the West in terms of power, science, and technology, and the lack of spirituality about which Western leaders and thinkers themselves complained. Nonetheless, Eastern spirituality had not helped Eastern people to remain free from domination by the West (Mashriqi 1987: 131). Mashriqi's Qur'anic interpretations in turn triggered accusations from religious scholars. The JUH passed a resolution in 1939 confirming an earlier decision from 1924 where it accused Mashriqi of teaching atheism and heresy (*ilḥād-o-zandaqa*) (Rozinah 1981/II: 650).

Attacks on materialism and atheism were also directed against nationalism and patriotism. Conceived of as Western concepts, both were seen as threatening Muslim identity and the survival of the Muslim community. In 1910, Iqbal countered Western critics of Islam: 'I certainly do mean to attack the conduct of those who while they recognise the great value of patriotic feelings in the formation of a people's character yet condemn our '*aṣabīyat* which they miscall fanaticism' (Iqbal 1987: 18). He contrasted the defence of a territorial identity with the defence

lecture on religion and civilization at the Jām'iya Millīya University in Delhi in 1942' (Nadwi 1980).

[72] 'What is needed now is to reflect upon what "heaven" means, and for this it is necessary to work out new principles and tenets instead of simply calling to memory the worn-out and obsolete doctrines' (Troll 1978: 312).

of 'the religious idea', which 'determines the ultimate structure of the Muslim Community' (ibid.: 19).[73] The argument became more heated around 1930 when the character of the Indian nation was in dispute. Abu'l Nazar Rizwi Amrohwi warned at the 1930 JUH session: 'While in Turkey Mustafa Kemal engaged in the propagation of atheism (*dahrīyat*) and Westernism, in India the veil of "nationality" (qaumīyat) and "patriotism" (*waṭaniyat*) was thrown.' Referring to Iran, Egypt, and Turkey, he lamented: 'if you don't try to put atheism to death before it reaches its prime then the continued existence of a religious orientation will become impossible in India like in many other countries' (Rozinah 1981/II: 532–3).

At the same time, dahrīyat was read as shorthand for socialism. The Congress politician Dr Shaukatullah Shah Ansari pleaded with the 'ulamā' in his welcome address to the 1939 JUH session in Delhi that they should see the common elements in socialism and Islam. 'Every national and patriotic struggle of any oppressed nation is part of the human struggle of this era and fulfils the true historical demands of Islam', he maintained (ibid.: 623). Most 'ulamā' remained unconvinced that they should relent in their struggle against atheism, although none spoke openly at JUH meetings against socialism and communism, which were perceived as powerful instruments of resistance against the West.

Fears of 'Westernization' and atheism were most forcefully articulated by those who had been in close contact with Western ideas either in India or abroad. Among the Aligarh group it was Shibli Numani and Muhammad Ali who became staunch advocates of fighting Western influence. Shibli had imbibed Western education at Aligarh College through his association with Thomas Arnold (Lelyveld 1996: 240ff.). Muhammad Ali, together with Iqbal and the Khāksār founder, Mashriqi, had studied in England and Germany. The three of them pointed to the soullessness of the West, its lack of spirituality and excesses of material and physical possessions and values. They also brought out the fear of 'Westernization', a sense of inferiority and weakness. The Moghul civilization's greatness had quietly crumbled before the mundane and unrefined British, their trading, power politics, bureaucracy, and warfare. Tentacles of modern technology like the telegraph and the railway threw a Western 'net' over India against which it was difficult to struggle. British rule and Western media brought discussions about Einstein's theory of relativity to India's élite, heightening fears in religious minds that the West was now excising God from the universe once and for all.[74] The

[73]Iqbal dealt extensively with the threats of Westernization in his poem *Zarb-e Kalīm* (The Rod of Moses) discussed at length by Abu'l Hasan Ali Nadwi (1979).

[74]Iqbal reflected this impact in the following words: 'The theory of Einstein has brought a new vision of the universe and suggests new ways of looking at the problems common

Muslim community's fear of losing its identity grew or shrank in tandem with its feeling of siege, increasing with the spread of pan-Turkism around World War I, and when the breakdown of Hindu–Muslim cooperation in the mid-1920s led to a new wave of inter-religious riots.

While fear of Westernization and atheism was acutely felt by all Islamic groups, they drew different conclusions. Some were shrewd or prudent enough to separate the protective function of British rule from its Western attributes. British protection was sought against the Hindu majority (by the Aligarh group and the Barelwis) and against persecution by competing religious sects (Aḥmadīya). The Khāksār leader, Mashriqi, carefully distinguished between British rule and Western culture. He resisted the latter, but was neutral towards the British until his army of religious volunteers was prepared for such a battle physically and spiritually. The British distributed titles and honours to create a group of loyalist Islamic scholars ('ulamā'). The title *shamsu'l-'ulamā'* (the 'sun' of the scholars) was conferred on several prominent scholars in this way. Abdul Hamid, leader of the loyalist faction among the Firangī Maḥallis, was allegedly induced by the offer of the title to produce a favourable religious ruling during the Khilafat Movement (Robinson 1994: 271). Another holder, then Vice-chancellor of Deoband, Maulana Hafiz Muhammad Ahmad (1862–1928), opposed the anti-British tone of the joint fatwā on the Khilafat campaign (cf. Minault 1982: 80). He eventually returned the title after political pressure from the nationalists (Rizvi 1980/II: 171). The Ahl-i Ḥadīth leader Nażir Husain had also received the title in recognition of his services (Metcalf 1982: 281). Shibli Numani had received the title in 1892 (Robinson 1994: 425). While he usually protested his loyalty he tested its limits over the reform of the Nadwa council and school. Generally speaking, loyalism was dominant among religious scholars of Islam at the end of the nineteenth and the beginning of the twentieth centuries, even among many who later styled themselves as staunch fighters against colonial rule. This was partly the effect of the widespread official suspicion towards Islamic religious activism after the defeat of the Indian 'Wahhabis', or mujāhidīn. Loyalism was also in tune with public articulation and political protest in all major streams of public mobilization. Even the nascent nationalists chose the petition and the resolution as weapons, founding hopes for improvement and change on British liberalism and fair play.

These approaches treated Western influences very differently. The Deobandis wanted to replace Western institutions with an Islamic society and polity. Sulaiman Nadwi and the Tablīghī founder, Ilyas, attempted to

to both religion and philosophy. No wonder then that the younger generation of Islam in Asia and Africa demand a fresh orientation of their faith' (Iqbal 1930: 10).

curb Western influences and to keep Muslims away from them. Shibli and the followers of the Aligarh School favoured expanding Islamic thought in open competition with the West: Islam would prove the superiority of its arguments. The Aḥmadīs, Barelwis, and to some extent the Khāksār accommodated the West politically. While Western thought was roundly rejected by some, it was partly accepted by others. These differences depended as much on doctrine as it did on the degree and form of interaction of these groups with the West.

3.2.4. Fighting the Schism—Fitna

All groups shared a concern about an increasingly divided Islam. Although this discourse was connected to debates in the larger Islamic world, it was mainly a consequence of the mushrooming of Indian Islamic groups and sects by the end of the nineteenth century. The Ahl-i Ḥadīth leader, Siddiq Hasan Khan, saw in their proliferation a portent of the end of the world, a critique directed both at modernists like Sayyid Ahmad Khan and messianic movements such as the Aḥmadīya.[75] Opponents compared Ghulam Ahmad, the founder of the Aḥmadīya sect, to the *dajjāl*, the equivalent of the 'Anti-Christ', whose appearance foreshadowed the end of the world.[76] The criticism of Sayyid Ahmad was very similar to that of Ghulam Ahmad. The Sayyid and his modernist followers were accused of forming a separate sect (*firqa*), the nēchārīs, that is, those who equated nature with God. The term firqa was used widely, sometimes even for self-description. In the case of the Ahl-i Ḥadīth this had a certain self-revealing irony: they wanted to fight sectarianism but were aware that they were a new sect themselves, and a highly controversial one at that (cf. Siyalkoti 1953).

It is interesting to observe the ambivalence in the approach of these Islamic groups. Their formation and public activity made internal divisions and differences of interpretation manifest. It fragmented the Islamic sphere and increased the number of Islamic actors in the public sphere, integrating significant parts of the laity in it. Yet most groups argued

[75]Under the title 'The End is Near', he wrote in 1301 AH (1883): 'The dissensions of our world are to be found, in fact, even in religion: innumerable fitnas are increasing day by day' (Ahmad and Grunebaum 1970: 85; see fn. 3; this chapter).

[76]See, for instance, the fatwā by the Ahl-i Ḥadīth scholar Nazir Husain answering a thinly veiled inquiry about 'some scholars from the Punjab' and their views regarding the concept of the death of Jesus and the appearance of the dajjāl, which aimed at the Aḥmadīya (Ḥusain 1971: Vol. I, 12). Also, cf. the Barelwi fatwā *Ḥusam al-Ḥaramain* of 1905, quoted in Sanyal (1996a: 234), where Ghulam Ahmad is condemned in this fashion; also Masud et al. (1996: 219).

they had come into existence to heal Islam's divisions. Doubtless this defensiveness reflected guilt over the aggravation of inner-Islamic cleavages, but it also expressed real concern over the state of the umma and Muslim India in particular.

The Deobandis took pains to stress that they represented the majority following the tradition of Sunni Islam—ahl al-sunna wa-'l-jamā'a, a term that was in the process of being appropriated by the Barelwis. The Deobandis pretended that by restoring and reviving the true Islam they were uniting its followers and as such fighting the divisions in Islam. It basically meant that if every Muslim followed their brand of Islam there would be no divisions. A similar argument could be found also in the other groups.

By defending the 'silent majority' of Sunni Islam, the Barelwis claimed to be consolidating the mainstream of the faith, as opposed to the minority of 'innovators' (bid'atī) (Jamiyyat-i Ahl-i Sunna [Pakistan] 1989). The Ahl-i Ḥadīth blamed the law schools for the divisions (fitna) maintaining they sat at the roots of the dissent, which then grew over the years and centuries (Ludhiyanwi n.d.). Siddiq Hasan lamented: 'In genuine Islam there is no dissension (*fitna*) and no disruption: all these quarrels and wranglings arise from just this innovating, this taqlīd, this love of outward show, this avidity for worldly goods' (Ahmad and Grunebaum 1970: 87). The Aḥmadīs, on their part, also rejected sectarian divisions such as with the Shi'a. In turn, they and their founder Ghulam Ahmad claimed to represent the 'true' Islam excluding all other Muslims from the fold (Friedmann 1989: 185).

The Nadwa council and movement tried to transcend sectarian differences on a practical note. Through their efforts of reforming education they sought to reconcile sectarian differences. As their project addressed itself to all Islamic groups they hoped to counter divisions in Islam. Compared to other reformist endeavours, the Nadwa organizers were exceptional in inviting representatives of all schools of thought to their first sessions. But there was no unanimity on doctrinal issues for conducting business. Many members of the council were openly sectarian. Its founder, Monghiri, devoted much of his energy to countering the Aḥmadīya in his home area (Malik 1997: 349). Barelwi polemics against the Nadwa approach sharpened doctrinal awareness and sectarian concerns among the Nadwa organizers. This debate led to the exclusion of the Shi'a and the Aḥmadīya from cooperation in the Nadwa council (cf. section 3.1.3). Sunni scholars across the doctrinal divides including the Deobandis, the Barelwis, and the Firangī Maḥallīs participated in the anti-Aḥmadīya campaign of 1924–5 (see Chapter 4, section 4.4).

The Tablīghī Jamā'at played down sectarian differences. Their religious tracts made clear that they regarded the divisions in Islam as a curse.[77] Participants in Tablīghī missions were never questioned about their antecedents as long as they declared themselves to be Muslims. Yet even they could not escape the pressure of sectarian radicalism on doctrinal dissenters. When asked about certain Aḥmadī and Shi'i beliefs, the Tablīghī leaders reiterated the mainstream Sunni position without explicitly naming the dissenters or attacking them (Masud 2000). Their criticism of the worship of shrine guardians (pīr parastī) (Numani 1993, Ilyas 425) amounted to an attack on Barelwi Islam.

Mashriqi was perhaps more tolerant than other group leaders in doctrinal terms. His concept of the basic equality of all revelations made it easy for him to play down sectarian differences and even accept a token number of Hindus who professed confidence in his spiritual leadership. But in the end he remained a reformist. Searching for the true Islam, he warned against 'offshoots' and 'symbols' in his Qur'anic commentary (*Tadkira*)[78] (Mashriqi 1972). His attacks against the Islam of the Maulwis also targeted shrine-keepers (pīrs) and their dominant role in rural society.[79] He thus criticised indirectly the Aḥmadīs, the Barelwis, and the Ahl-i Ḥadīth emphasizing typical Sunni positions of his time. In his criticism he focused less on their beliefs than on their divisionary attitudes (Mashriqi 1987; Seth 1985). Mashriqi deepened differences with other groups by pursuing those who followed the 'wrong religion'. He saw enemies all around (cf. Khāksār creed in Appendix I). Other groups regarded his position as equally divisive. His radical interpretation of Qur'anic injunctions earned him the wrath of many 'ulamā' who accused him of creating a new religion[80] and setting himself up as yet another Messiah (cf. section 3.3). The JUH considered his group a threat to Islam no less than the Aḥmadīya (Rozinah 1981/II: 650).

The Aḥrār were least ashamed of celebrating their narrow radical

[77]Cf. Ilyās (M 102): 'Through this movement we should try to create conformity, peace and friendship among the followers of the religion and different religious groups, only then the differences among them can be removed' (see Numani 1993). In his *Malfūẓāt*, Ilyas stressed that the main aim of Tablīgh was to bring all Muslims around one nucleus that is the spirit of the religion (M 164).

[78]The translation of *Tadkira* as 'Warning' by Baljon (1961: 12) may reflect the intention of Mashriqi but it remains stretched, as in Urdu its principal meanings are memoir, commentary.

[79]He mocked the customs of bowing down before the shrine-keepers and sending one's wives to them (Mashriqi 1995).

[80]On the critique of Mashriqi's religious views, see the Aḥrār pamphlet by Ghulam Ghauth Hazarwi, *Mashriqī kā Ghalaṭ Maẓhab* (Mashriqi's Wrong Religion), 1936, in NDC 404.

interpretation of Islam, particularly through the activities of Bukhari. They proposed to overcome divisions in Islam by concentrating on social issues and progressive objectives. They campaigned against Shi'is and Aḥmadīs before and after independence, and with hindsight this doctrinal divisiveness undermined the credibility of their social message.

As it turned out, there were two different ways of projecting opposition to dissent. A group could present its own position as the only true one, claiming that its existence or formation laid the basis for eliminating dissent. This approach was divisive and sectarian, underlining the exclusivity of that particular group. The other approach toned down sectarian differences and incorporated universalist aspects, either within the parameters of Islam, or in relation to all religions. A rejection of the law schools was used to repudiate divisions and sectarianism. Yet, faith and truth seemed to be indivisible. Most declared their own interpretation unique and infallible, a claim that turned all dissenters into heretics, apostates, and unbelievers. Even groups socially and doctrinally as marginalized as the Aḥmadīya operated in the same way in relation to other Muslims. The fitna discourse of this period cannot be read without the concomitant claims of these groups to public influence and control over adherents. Tellingly, Islamic scholars writing on Islam's doctrinal and sectarian woes attributed dissent to the search for 'popularity' (Ludhiyanwi n.d.).

Summing up the agenda of religious intervention, one cannot fail to notice that the focus on the Qur'an and the ḥadīth united the groups as much as their interpretation divided them. While they all worked for restoring their eminence, the texts were scanned for arguments to shore up the credentials of every group. The discourse about atheism and materialism reflected their unequal and tense relationship with the West and British colonial power. Debate on divisions (fitna) negotiated mutual competition and claims over sole representation. While their intervention often worked at cross-purposes, it earned them distinct public profiles.

3.3. THE LEADER: MESSIAH AND RENEWER OF THE FAITH

A particular variety of the religious discourse was concerned with millenarian expectations and promises of salvation. While these features had been constantly present in the history of Islam, developments in colonial India endowed them with a particular flavour.[81] The advent of a Messiah promised to deliver Indian Muslims, and particularly their élite, from the status and perception of inferiority and defeat in relation

[81]On the history of messianic movements and orders, see the chapter on Mahdawiyya, *Dīn-i Ilāhī*, Rawshaniyya, and Aḥmadīya in Aziz Ahmad (1969).

to the British and an increasingly assertive Hindu majority. It was immaterial whether he was the announced Messiah or a minor one. Salvational expectations were directed at obliterating the travails of modernity and Western materialist colonial rule. In terms of the formation of an Islamic public sphere, the millenarian and salvational discourses fulfilled certain functions essential for public articulation. The discourse on the Messiah or Mahdī figure and on the Renewer of the Faith (mujaddid) provided religious, almost divine sanction for a leader of a particular group and community. It was helpful in bringing out a modern leadership in Islamic groups and in establishing a leader's authority. His leadership was modern in the sense that he combined the traditional religious sanction with modern objectives of controlling his group and achieving high public profile, 'popularity'. His renewal of the faith amounted to the creation of a particular group ideology the spreading of which was no longer (only) the propagation of the faith but the propaganda of the group's objectives.[82]

Leaders of the Islamic groups under study here aspired to various degrees of divine sanction for their leadership. They sought recognition of their erudition in the religious sciences confirming their pre-eminent status among the learned in Islam. Theological positions claimed ranged from mahdī (messiah) to mujaddid (renewer of the faith) to mujtahid (legal scholar of special distinction in Islam). Designations such as Shaykh al-Kull, Amīr al-Hind, Amīr al-Sharī'at promised leadership and guidance. Honorific titles awarded to religious scholars were the Shaykh al-Islām and Shaykh al-Hind. The titles had a long tradition, and more so in Indian Islam. Eminent epithets were selected by followers to grace their mentor and leader. The distinction we have to make here in terms of the formation of an Islamic public sphere is between the more or less casual, often inflationary award of honorific titles reflecting a certain courtly etiquette of the medieval princely states promoting religious scholarship generously, and the aspirations to a position of practical influence and control over a definite number of adherents belonging either to a particular group or to the community of Indian Muslims as a whole. In the latter sense we see a trend of refashioning theological appellation as public claims endowed with a certain degree of public, even political control.

Ghulam Ahmad made the most spectacular claim in this regard. He alleged to be the promised mahdī and mujaddid, the messiah who would come at the end of the world and save mankind and become the renewer

[82]For instance, the preface of the 1907 Deobandi tract *Al-muhannad 'alā-al-mufannad* termed the Barelwi fatwā *Ḥusām al-Ḥaramain*, written by Ahmad Raza in 1905 to which this tract responded, as 'unclean propaganda' (*nāpāk prōpagēṇḍā*) (Saharanpuri 1987: i).

of the faith.[83] He based his claim on the assumption that he was a 'shadowy prophet' (*zillī nabī*), endowed with a minor degree of prophesy, with prophetic knowledge mirroring, or 'shadowing' that of Prophet Muhammad. By this he meant the knowledge of Qur'anic secrets, which was of generally unknown aspects of interpretation. While he carefully argued that he did not want in any way or degree to cast doubts on the prophethood of Muhammad, he maintained that the Qur'an had provided for continuous revelation even though of a lesser degree than that of Muhammad. Aspiring to be a 'non-legislative' prophet he declined to have brought a new religious law to the Muslim community. In terms of the public nature of the discourse, he used his prophetic claim to legitimate his personal leadership aspirations. When the movement split in 1914, the moderate Lahōrī group reneged on his prophethood claims, which had caused tremendous controversy. Instead it claimed only the status of the renewer (mujaddid) for him (cf. Aziz 1997). Quite pragmatically, Ghulam Ahmad had 'buried' Jesus, claiming that contrary to conventional Muslim tradition (ḥadīth), Jesus was not lifted to heaven alive and waited with God for the day of final judgement when he would come to save the world from the dajjāl (deceiver), the one-eyed monster and equivalent of the anti-Christ. On the contrary, Jesus had died on earth and found his final resting place in Kashmir. Now Ghulam Ahmad was free to assume for himself the role of the messiah ascribed to Jesus. As a renewer, Ghulam Ahmad was credited by his adherents with the renewal of the Islamic faith in that he was fighting against the dajjāl of modern times, locating the evil in materialism and atheism of British-Indian civilization. He asked his followers:

> Do not wonder that Almighty God has, in this time of need and in the days of this deep darkness, sent down a heavenly light and, having chosen a servant of His for the good of mankind in general, He has sent him to make uppermost the religion of Islam and to spread the light brought by the 'best of His creatures' [i.e. Prophet Muhammad] and to strengthen the cause of the Muslims and to purify their internal condition.... The truth will win and the freshness and light of Islam which characterised it in the earlier days will be restored, and that sun will rise again as it arose first, in the full resplendence of its light (Mirzā Ghulām Aḥmad, *Fath-i Islām* [Victory of Islam, 1891], 7, 15, 16, quoted in Aziz 1997).

The discourse on the mujaddid was urged on by the debates surrounding the beginning of the fourteenth Islamic century in 1882.[84] These

[83]Other epithets claimed by him were *muḥaddath* (a person spoken to by Allah, or an Angel) and *masīḥ-i maw'ūd* (the promised messiah), for details see Friedmann (1989: Chapter 5, 105–18).

[84]Friedmann argued that in Islamic history a considerable number of persons have been awarded the title of mujaddid. 'It has been somewhat depreciated by its relatively

millenarian debates reflected the anxieties over the state of Islam in India and beyond.[85] There had been an argument going on in medieval Islam whether Islam would outlive a millennium.[86] The hope for a mujaddid was based on a prophetic tradition (ḥadīth) promising

> Allah shall raise for this Umma at the head of every century a man who shall renew (or revive) for it its religion.[87]

Other narrators of traditions added that he would be a descendant of the Prophet's family and would explain the matters of religion.[88] As none had been named or agreed upon by the 'ulamā' of the time, partly due to jealousies and rivalries among the scholars, Ghulam Ahmad believed he had a good chance to win the title. He dared the 'ulamā' to either accept his claim or name somebody else.

While Ghulam Ahmad's claim caused little surprise due to the extravagant nature of his style of religious leadership it was the pervasive spread of these claims that give reason to ponder. The claim to be a mujaddid was closely tied in with the reformist discourse. The forebear of reformist Islam in South Asia, Shaykh Ahmad Sirhindi (1564–1624), was widely known and accepted as the renewer of the second millennium.[89] Among the claimants to the mujaddid title was also the Indian reformist of the early nineteenth century, Sayyid Ahmad Bareilly (Metcalf 1982: 60). Prominent revivalists and reformists virtually staged a contest in claiming the title. No group wanted to be left behind. The disadvantage of such a contest was that the claim was often recognized by the respective group only. This was further proof of the fragmentation of the religious discourse. Among the mujaddid claimants were reformist scholars such the Deobandi founders Gangohi (Metcalf 1982: 138–9) and Nanaotawi (Rizvi 1980/I: Introduction by Qari Muhammad Tayyib) and the Ahl-i

---

extensive use, and a claim to *tajdīd* [renewal] therefore does not sound very extravagant' (1989: 109). While this may be true for the theological significance of the claim, it does not reduce the public and political relevance of such aspirations, as discussed later.

[85] Cf. the account of such fears by the Ahl-i Ḥadīth founder Siddiq Hasan Khan, 'The End is Near', written in 1301 AH (1883) and mentioned earlier (Ahmad and Grunebaum 1970: 85).

[86] Cf. E. van Donzel, '*Mudjaddid*', in EI/VII: 290 where he refers to Jalal al-Din al-Suyuti's (d. 911 AH/1505) comments on his misguided contemporaries.

[87] Abu Da'ud, *Kitāb al-Malahīm*, Chapter 1, quoted after Aziz (1997). Also quoted in Masud (2000: xix) as Abū Dā'ūd (1989: 3: 80). The subject of renewal (tajdīd) in general and in relation to South Asia is treated in Masud (2000: ix–xx) (Tablīghī Jamā'at); in Sanyal (1996a: 177–79) (Barelwis); in Friedmann (1989: 94–101) (Aḥmadīya).

[88] See E. van Donzel, '*Mudjaddid*' (EI/VII).

[89] See *Mujaddid-i alf-i ṣānī*; for a discussion of the distinction between a centennial and a millennial renewer, see Friedmann (1971: 13–21).

Ḥadīth founders Siddiq Hasan Khan and Nazir Husain (Friedmann 1989: 107). After 1900, Ahmad Raza Khan of the Barelwi School also came to be known to his followers as the mujaddid of the outgoing fourteenth Hijri century (Sanyal 1998: 642). As has been pointed out earlier, his understanding of renewal was not directed at purifying but at reclaiming conventional Islam. Maulana Maududi was also considered a mujaddid of sorts.[90] Many of them published treatises on the concept of tajdīd expounding the classical view in accordance with their own reformist pretensions (Ashraf Ali Thanawi, *Tajdīd-i ta'līm-i tablīgh* [n.d.]; Maududi, *Tajdīd wa iḥyā-i dīn* [1989]; S. A. H. A. Nadwi, *Tārīkh-i Da'wat wa 'Azimat ya'nī 'ālam-i Islām kī iṣlāḥī wa tajdīdī kōshish kā tarīkhī jaizā* [1984]).

The concept of the mujtahid—renewer of legal interpretation—was related to the mujaddid. It played a significant role in Shi'i theology. The mujtahid would be of a lower rank than a renewer of the faith (mujaddid) but way above the ordinary 'ulamā' who would normally restrict themselves by interpretation in terms of the application of the findings and commentaries of their respective law school (J. Calmard, '*Mudjtahid*' in EI/VII: 295–304). A mujtahid would be justified and expected to transcend the law schools while a mujaddid would aspire to certain divine attributes. In practice, such titles were used to negotiate a certain rank in a hierarchy of religious scholars or activists. Calmard explained: 'It is above else an honorific title applied to strong personalities. The degree of importance of each mujtahid/mujaddid thus depends most of all on his own pretensions, the appreciation accorded him by his contemporaries or by posterity' (ibid).

In Sunni theology the founders of the law schools had been among the recognized renewers of the law with few others achieving acceptance of this title. The Moghul emperor Akbar (1542–1605) made the 'ulamā' of the day sign an infallibility decree which was to give him the prerogative of an absolute mujtahid. For Sunni Islam this being an extraordinary claim, the refusal of Shaykh Jamaluddin Muhammad Jaunpuri (1443–1504) to sign the decree continued to inspire Islamic activists through the centuries. Maulana Kalam Azad, who counted the latter among his forebears, was full of admiration for him (See Faruqi 1996: 5–16). Jaunpuri had also claimed to be a mahdī, a messiah, which Azad was prepared to take in its liberal interpretation as being the guided one. It was Jaunpuri's followers who publicized this claim as a declaration that the *mahdī-i ākhir al-zamān*, the final messiah at the end of time, had arrived (Faruqi 1996:

[90]Maududi himself defined his efforts of renewal of Islam in terms of the Islamic concept of tajdīd. See Maududi, *A Short History of the Revivalist Movement in Islam* (Lahore: Islamic Publications, 1963), pp. 36–8, quoted in Nasr (1996: 56).

9). In 1913, Azad projected himself as the prophetic leader of a secret radical Muslim party, the Ḥizbullāh (the party of God), which, however, did not take off.[91] Its objective was to liberate the country with the help of religious-minded Muslims:

> For the followers of the Prophet, there can be no more ignominious death than the fact that Islam has found itself unable and helpless to educate them and lead them in a matter concerning an important aspect of their life (liberation of their country) and being disappointed with Islam they had to look lustfully towards the sucked hopes of other nations.[92]

Azad was one of those who made the connection between the theological motive of renewal and the activist concept of guidance to Indian Muslims. His focus was no particular doctrine or principle but the well-being of all Muslims. His concerns reflected proto-nationalist and secular motives. It was speculated that Azad eyed the post of a theological leader of Indian Islam, to become an imām of sorts. He was accused of deliberately constructing the argument in a way that he might also appear as the guided one, possessing a Prophet-like qualification (Faruqi 1996: 9).

Azad's aspirations have to be seen against the specific historical circumstances of the day. They were voiced through the JUH. Its founding member, the Shaykh al-Hind, Maulana Mahmud al-Hasan, died in 1920. He had been recognized among religious scholars for his services to the Muslim community by virtue of his scholarly eminence as well as his staunch anti-British position. The question arose whether a new Shaykh al-Hind should be designated and what his tasks would be. When the JUH deliberated the outlines of an Islamic system for India during the Khilafat campaign, the creation of the post of Amīr al-Hind was one option. This person, it was felt, would give direction to Indian Muslims. He would transcend sectarian differences and see to a uniform application of Islamic law perhaps assuming also the function of a Muslim chief justice (called here Amīr al-sharī'at).[93] As such it was a reformist as well as a political endeavour. Azad unsuccessfully manoeuvred to get himself selected for this post, which was never formally created.[94] Reportedly, the Firangī

[91]On Azad's concept of the Ḥizbullāh, see Douglas (1988: 114ff.).

[92]Azad's newspaper *al-Hilāl*, 9 and 23 October 1912, quoted in Ahmad (1977: 60).

[93]On the political aspects of these leadership ambitions, and for plans to set up sharī'a courts in all districts and provinces and to elect an Amīr al-Sharī'at, see Chapter 4 section 4.1.3.

[94]Cf. the documents of the JUH through 1920–21 (Rozinah 1981/I). See also Douglas (1988) on this ambition of Azad. One of his close confidants, Maulana Abdul Razzaq Malihabadi, confirmed in his memories about Azad that the latter had thought about himself as the most suitable person for such a dignified position and mentioned his own role in bringing about a consensus in Azad's favour (1960).

Maḥallī scholar Abdul Bari, the co-initiator of the Khilafat Movement, had similar ambitions as he aspired to the post of Shaykh al-Islām (Qureshi 1999: 104; Robinson 1994: 329). Before them, Shibli Numani also had at one time such leadership pretensions when he believed the Nadwa council offered the opportunity to become the leader of all 'ulamā'—in the capacity of a Sartāj and Shaykh al-kull—and thereby surpass Sayyid Ahmad Khan from Aligarh. But he was advised, among others, by Abd al-Halim Sharar (d. 1926) that the 'ulamā' were uncontrollable (Malik 1997: 337, fn. 9). From a political point of view, these ambitions may partly have been inspired by the role played by Mahatma Gandhi during the Khilafat and the non-cooperation movement against British rule. His public appearance was that of a saint and divine, revered not only by Hindus but also by many Muslims. He assumed the position of a 'dictator' of the anti-colonial movement very effectively.[95] Muslim leaders felt marginalized by Gandhi's successful public posturing. Creating a leadership post for all Indian Muslims, it was apparently hoped, would also aid their united public representation towards the Hindus and help negotiations with the British for the future political set-up of an independent India, a role which was eventually taken up by Muhammad Ali Jinnah during the Pakistan movement at the expense of the traditional segment of religious scholars.

The Khāksār founder, Mashriqi, was also influenced by the various plans to install an Amīr al-Hind. As he envisaged his movement to create a blueprint for an Islamic government in India, its leader would be the amīr of India. He based his movement on strict obedience to the amīr (*iṭā'at-i amīr*). This obedience had to be 'total, complete and absolute', as only in this way could a spiritual awakening of Muslims be achieved directed at *taqwā* (fear of God, piety), instrumental 'in fostering methodical orderliness in a race' (Malik 2000: 26–7). Critics among religious scholars alleged Mashriqi considered himself a new prophet. He thought obedience to the amīr of the time to flow from obedience to the prophet shown to him when he was still alive. What Mashriqi had apparently in mind was obedience in temporal matters, the function of the prophet as *Amīr al-Muslimīn*. But his Islamic critics argued that Mashriqi intended to give a new law (sharī'a) to the community. This confusion was partly generated by interpretation and perhaps distortion of Mashriqi's views. Baljon argued that Mashriqi's demand for obedience to the amīr was an 'application for the present that at every moment a leader of the Muslim

[95]Robinson quoted from intelligence reports where Gandhi was reported to have literally demanded from the 'ulamā' total submission to his will if he was to lead Muslims in the Khilafat movement: 'He would himself be sort of a dictator.' Report of the Commissioner of Police, Bombay, *Home Poll.* B (July 1920), 109, NAI, quoted in Robinson (1994: 315).

community should be available for the enactment of the laws of God and the Prophet' (1961: 104–5).

Circumstances suggested that the leadership ambitions of this period not only represented personal aspirations, they also reflected numerous pressures both inside and outside India. Efforts to counter Hindu reformist reconversion movements through religious propaganda (tablīgh) were qualified as renewal. Scholars and activists busy in this field such as Thanawi and the founder of the Tablīghī Jamā'at, Muhammad Ilyas, earned the title of mujaddid from their followers. They were not without pretensions though. Ilyas hinted he had received the method and message of tablīgh in a dream, not unlike the Aḥmadīya founder. Critics (from the Barelwi camp) saw this as an aspiration to the role of a (minor?) prophet. Dreams have traditionally been used in the Sufi tradition as a way of confirming divine sanction for one's activities. Ilyas was no exception while he walked the borderline between reformism and revived Sufism.[96]

JUH scholars also conferred the title renewer (mujaddid) of the day upon a foreign leader, Mustafa Kemal Pasha. Indian scholars preferred to ignore the secular bent of his policies and interpreted his efforts to revive Muslim Turkey as a religious deed of modern renewal (tajdīd). They qualified this renewal as directed at the temporal side of Islam, not its doctrinal aspect.[97] At the time the Khilafat campaign was in full swing in India. Kemal still interspersed cautious Islamic references to legitimate his claims to a national leadership position.

While Islamic theology distinctly separated the category of the mujaddid from the calls of prophesy, in practice and usage there was a fusion of attributes. The position of a renewer gave the leader a special status in his community. This status was reinforced through mystical visions. The bonds with his followers were strengthened through some form of oath of allegiance. Thus a leader emerged who mastered law and path, sharī'a and ṭarīqa. While such a broad interpretation would undermine the classical understanding of reformism in Islam, it was a clear expression of a willingness to cater to the requirements of public life.

[96]For Ilyas being called a mujaddid, see Masud (2000: 93). Ilyas' prophetic claim with reference to a dream appeared in his *Malfūẓāt* (not mentioned by Masud) where he alleged to have received a 46th part of prophethood through a dream in which he was told to preach to the people like other Prophets (Ilyas M 50). Other adepts of the movements have played this down and emphasized that this was said to highlight the origin of the method of da'wa from the Prophet and his companions. But as there was no Prophet to come after Muhammad tablīgh was a charge for the whole umma. Cf. Masud (2000: xix, xx).

[97]Cf. the presidential address by Maulana Habibur Rahman Deobandi at the 1922 Gaya Session of the JUH (Rozinah 1981/I: 138ff., here: 160).

3.4. THE MISSION: DA'WA AND TABLĪGH

Religious propaganda efforts in the name of tablīgh had been conducted for a long time, although not always under this term. In South Asia, reformists directed tablīgh activities at Muslims more recently converted, the so-called neo-Muslims, and at religious customs that were considered reprehensible innovations (bid'a). While this task made tablīgh a special concern of reformists, the spread of Islam in South Asia had also benefited from da'wa activities of the Sufi orders who had popularized the message of the Qur'an. Da'wa and tablīgh were recognized by all schools applying different interpretations. Early tablīgh efforts were often individual and largely uncoordinated. They became institutionalized mainly from 1905 onwards. In the subcontinent they took the form of non-state private associations.[98] In the Indian context, tablīgh activities claimed autonomy from the state embodying 'alien' British rule, from other religious denominations, but also from mainstream Islamic discourses, as will be shown later. As such they constituted a core area of the emerging Islamic sphere. Tablīgh activities formed a distinct discourse marked by its own method, culture, terminology, and practice. Of all public religious activities, tablīgh efforts were perhaps most clearly and recognizably based on public intervention. Reaching out to fellow Muslims and to non-Muslims required a discourse and activism that relied on a high public profile.

3.4.1. General Task of Tablīgh and Da'wa

In theological terms, da'wa was the invitation, addressed to man by God and the prophets, to believe in the true religion, Islam.[99] It also aimed at conversions. In this connection two Qur'anic verses were generally invoked using words derived from the same root as da'wa:

> Who could be a better person than the one who called (*da'ā*) toward God and acted righteously (41:33).
>
> There should be a group of people among you who call (*yad'ūna*) to [do] good, enjoining good and forbidding evil (3:104).

In the South Asian context, da'wa shared these connotations. It could be an invitation to God's way in a more general sense, but also a direct

[98]The early Muslim dynastic state often took care of da'wa efforts. The state is still involved in countries such as Libya, Egypt, Saudi Arabia, and Malaysia. Cf. table in Masud (2000: xxviii), and the annex to the introduction (ibid.: lvii–xi).

[99]M. Canard, '*Da'wa*', in EI/II: 168–70. For the Qur'anic usage of da'wa and tablīgh, see Masud (2000: xxi f. and xx f.). For a review of the history of da'wa, cf. Poston (1992: 11–45).

invitation to prayer. Based on interpretations by certain Prophetic traditions, da'wa was a duty for all Muslims. Islamic reformists were not long in reinvigorating this concept. Rashid Rida founded a propagandist school on the island of Roda near Cairo, called Dār al-da'wa wa'l-irshād (House of Propagation of [Qur'anic] Commandments) (Canard, *'Da'wa'* EI/II). The word tablīgh did not figure in the Qur'an. In the context of the Qur'anic language tablīgh should be understood as the activity and contents of the communication of God's message, the act of relaying it to others. In South Asia, and through induction into Urdu, it became synonymous with the propagation of Islam, making the message known. From this the translation as 'mission' became current. The missionary concept took a more decisive turn towards the modern public sphere when it started emphasizing meanings of 'propagation' and 'propaganda'—activities of modern public communication and the spread of ideology. Tablīgh was also used in the non-religious context for communication, spreading ideas (cf. section 3.4.3).

3.4.2. The Role of the Ārya Samāj and the Hindū Mahāsabhā

The institutionalization of tablīgh activities was substantially rushed on by the impact of the Hindu reformist movements, Ārya Samāj[100] and its later, more extremist and politically minded variants, the Hindū Mahāsabhā[101] and the RSS.[102] The Ārya Samāj developed a concept of reconversion of former Hindus, an idea alien to classical Hinduism. In practice it was mainly directed at Muslims. It could be understood as an attempt to obliterate the influence of non-Hindu civilizations on Indian history. Initially reconversion efforts were directed at Muslims and Christians who had converted recently. Later this strategy was extended to groups who had been converted several generations ago. In addition to religious purism political motives too were responsible for this movement of Hindu reassertion. It fed on the proto-nationalist idea of strengthening the Hindu identity and unity of India. It was seen as a counterpoint to Western British rule. Young Indian nationalism was heavily influenced by a nascent Hindu revivalism. This trend came to express itself for a time through a separate Hindu-nationalist wing of the Indian Congress Party

[100]Ārya Samāj (Sanskrit)—Society of Nobles, founded in 1875 by Dayananda Saraswati.

[101]All-India Hindū Mahāsabhā (conference), founded in 1915 and later led by V. D. Savarkar (1883–1966).

[102]Rāṣṭrīya Swayamsevak Saṅgh (RSS)—National Volunteers Organization, founded in 1925 by K. B. Hedgewar (1889–1940). Cf. Andersen and Damle (1987).

where some of its leaders concurrently maintained links with radical Hindu forces.[103]

The Hindu reformists repeatedly expressed anxiety over the strength of their community and its public representation. This sense of alarm was heightened by the regular decennial publication of census figures introduced by Britain in 1881, which showed much higher population growth rates for Muslims and Christians than for Hindus.[104] When it became known that the share of Hindus was decreasing, the Ārya Samāj reconversion efforts met growing support from the general Hindu public. The Ārya Samāj reinforced its reconversion campaign under the doctrine of shuddhī (purification) in 1908. It was mainly directed at so-called neo-Muslim tribes who were considered by the Ārya Samājīs to be recent converts from Hinduism. These activities concentrated on parts of Punjab, the United Provinces, and around Delhi in the Mewat region. Swami Shraddhananda institutionalized the movement in 1922 when he started special shuddhī *sabhās*. From spring 1923 on, he took up a reclamation campaign among the Malkana Rajput tribes in Agra and neighbouring districts who had been converted to Islam in the reign of Aurangzeb and earlier. The Hindu activist Dr Moonjee followed this by founding a sister movement under the name of *saṅgaṭhan* (unity) pursuing a militant reorganization of Hinduism, otherwise known for its diversity and tolerance. Excesses of violent conversions committed by enraged Muslim extremists during the so-called Moplah riots on the Malabar Coast in 1921 served as the immediate pretext for the creation of the shuddhī and saṅgaṭhan movements. Hindu nationalists had been distrustful of the Hindu–Muslim entente during the Khilafat campaign and the non-

[103]The following Hindu leaders were members and leaders of Congress: Lala Lajpat Rai (1865–1928), Hedgewar, Savarkar, Shraddhananda, Madan Mohan Malaviya (1861–1946), Dr B. S. Moonjee (1872–1948), Dr S. P. Mookerji (1901–53).

[104]Proportional share of the religious communities in 1921 and its change over 1881 (in per cent):

Hindus	Buddhists	Jains	Sikhs	Muslims	Christians	Tribals	Others
63.41	3.56	0.37	1.03	21.74	1.5	3.09	0.2
– 15	– 19	– 25	+ 41	+ 9	+ 105	+ 19	–10

Computed on the basis of: Census 1921, Vol. 1: 122–3.

For the Hindus, these anxieties were reflected in accounts by Swami Shraddhananda who was alerted to higher Muslim population growth by a friend, Colonel U. Mukherji, in 1912. The latter asserted on the basis of calculations made from statistical tables that 'within the next 420 years the Indo-Aryan race would be wiped off the face of the earth unless steps were taken to save it' (Jordens 1981: 135). The census figures were also a factor in the early debates on the foundation of Hindū Sabhās in 1906 (Mehra 1987: 304).

cooperation movement after 1919. They regarded Gandhi's reliance on the Islamic religious argument of the defence of the Ottoman Khilafat as excessive and unjustified. With reference to the prominent role of Islamic organisations such as the Khilafat Conference and the JUH, many Hindus felt that they lagged behind Muslims in terms of organization and communal awareness.[105] It was in 1924 that the distrust bore bitter fruit and Hindu–Muslim riots broke out in response to the reconversion efforts of the Ārya Samāj in Agra and other parts of Western United Provinces (Masud 2000). In a confluence of developments, the two decisive years of 1924 and 1925 saw the abolishment of the Caliphate by nationalist Turkey and the bankruptcy of the Khilafat defence doctrine in India, the foundation of the radical Hindu outfit RSS, and the expansion of the Hindū Mahāsabhā. In the face of the spiralling religious violence, British politicians felt justified in withholding further negotiations on constitutional reforms as India's population was allegedly lacking the unity of will required for relinquishment of colonial rule.

The Hindu extremist approach reproduced in the Muslim camp the stereotype fear that the Muslim community was beleaguered and under threat.[106] In extreme, the Hindu reformist argument was interpreted as an insinuation that Muslims were alien to India, foreigners, who should 'return' to where they 'came from', that is, Arabia, West and Central Asia. Hindu cultural revisionism openly championed a rollback of history.[107] These arguments have acquired a new dimension and urgency in today's India.

[105]See, for instance, demands expressed in the English-language press by Hindus that the Muslim scholars 'cannot be permitted to control public policy affecting the rights, liberties, political and economic interests of the composite Indian people in the name of their communal religion or scripture' (Letter from B. C. Pal to the editor of the *Englishman*, published on 31 January 1922, quoted in Robinson 1994: 338).

[106]For instance, Maududi became convinced that Islam was coming to its end in India until something practical was done about it (Nasr 1996: 21–2).

[107]The address delivered by N.C. Kelkar at the Hindū Mahāsabhā special session in December 1925 was very telling in this respect. There he spoke of a 'communal contest' to which Christians, Muslims, and Hindus contributed. Unlike Hindus, Muslims had 'connections and attachments outside India. ... But for this extra-territorial attachment the Mahomedans in India would not have been a great political problem. Perhaps nine-tenth of the Mahomedan population in India is made up of converts from Hinduism and they would naturally live content with their Indian setting.' The Muslim 'transcending claim to representation' was not only based on numbers and on the fact that they had once been the rulers of India but had to be 'brought into relation with the prospects however visionary or fanciful of ruling India once more'. Christians and Muslims were 'furiously nibbling not only at the fringe of Hinduism but daringly attacking at times even its heart and core'. Christians converted 2,000 Hindus a week according to Bishop Whitehead, Kelkar maintained. Revealingly, he conceded that the number of coverts to Islam 'cannot be precisely estimated. But it must be evidently a good round figure' (*IAR* 1925/II: 351–2).

Successor organizations of these reformist movements in the shape of the political BJP (Bharatīya Janatā Party), the revivalist VHP (Vishwa Hindu Parishad), and the extremist BD (Bajrang Dal) promote religious and cultural Hindu nationalism to polarize and mobilize the electorate, a policy which is seen as condoning if not encouraging acts of violence against Muslims and Christians.[108]

In turn, Hindu and Muslim reformists were united in viewing Christian missionaries as a large threat. They assumed all out cooperation between the missionaries and British colonial authorities, although the reality was more complex. Missionary activities of Christians were given wide currency through the emerging print media, even where they met with rather limited success. Muslims reacted with heightened sensitivity when Protestant conferences in Cairo (1906) and Lucknow (1911) openly declared their objective to intensify conversion efforts among Muslims (cf. Malik 1997: fn. 458).

3.4.3. *Various Organized Forms of Tablīgh*

Muslim religious activists responded to these developments with organized missionary activity. They rushed to Agra and Saharanpur to 'protect' the local Muslim population from the overtures of the Ārya Samāj and other Hindu missionaries. Local tablīgh societies started proliferating. An early such society—Jam'īyat-i Da'wat wa Tablīgh-i Islām (Society for Spreading and Propagating the Message of Islam) was reported from Lahore in Punjab in 1920.[109] Sayyid Ghulam Bhik Nairang of Ambala, a leading local lawyer, became known for his mission Jam'īyat-i Tablīgh al-Islām, also concentrated on Punjab.[110] It attempted to coordinate various local branches aspiring to be the 'central' mission. Khwaja Hasan Nizami from the shrine of Nizamuddin Auliya led the tablīgh mission in Delhi.[111]

[108]For a detailed academic discussion of current trends of Hindu nationalism, cf. Ludden (1996). On the VHP see Katju (2003).

[109]'Jamiat-i-Dawat-wa-Tabligh-i-Islam—A Mohammedan Missionary Society', in *Moslem World*, 15 (1925): 182–7. This organization was reported to have established offices in the Punjab, in Jammu (Kashmir), and in Maharashtra. Its aims included: '(1) To place the teachings of Al-Islam in their true light before Moslems in particular and non-Moslems generally; (2) Care of orphans and neglected children, irrespective of caste and creed by means of orphanages, boys' and girls' homes and industrial schools; (3) Uplift of the untouchables; (4) General relief work' (ibid.: 182).

[110]See Mathur (1968: 24); Qureshi (1974: Chapter XI: 'Disenchantment', especially 288–9). Maulana Muhammad Irfan organized the tablīgh work for the JUH among the Malkana Rajputs.

[111]Mathur (1968: 24); Minault (1982: 193–4). Nizami achieved a certain notoriety with a pamphlet detailing ways to convert Hindus to Islam, *Dā'ī Islām*, published in 1923.

While the tablīgh societies sought to counter the Hindu shuddhī activities, the saṅgaṭhan movement evoked in response the creation of tanẓīm self-defence units, laying stress on self-organization and self-help. Saifuddin Kitchlew (c. 1888–1963) started an Urdu daily *Tanẓīm* at Amritsar in Punjab in 1924 around which he organized this movement (Mathur 1968: 22). Another Punjabi, Lala Lajpat Rai, actively championed the Hindu saṅgaṭhan movement. Together with the just-mentioned Nizami and Abdul Bari, a Firangī Maḥallī scholar who also engaged in tablīgh activities, they were all former 'non-cooperators' from the Khilafat Movement, now fiercely opposing each other on communal, that is, religious, lines of division.

In order to save the spirit of cooperation, leading Muslim and Hindu politicians and religious activists met in 1923 to discuss the tension between the tanẓīm and the saṅghaṭan movements. A Unity Committee convened before the Congress special session in September of that year. Predictably each side accused the other of starting the trouble. As a way out it was suggested that all outside preachers from the region of the Malkana Rajputs be withdrawn. But they achieved no agreement as to which side should leave first. Due to the influence of religious leaders in Congress, it could not openly oppose conversion efforts. Otherwise it risked losing its support base for the nationalist struggle among the Hindu majority population. But Gandhi and Nehru made clear to the Ārya Samāj leader Swami Shraddhananda that they opposed the chosen time for such a campaign. The Ārya Samāj reclamation threatened to undermine the Khilafat and the Non-Cooperation Movements with which it coincided. Muhammad Ali emphasized the need to observe basic ethics in the conversion or reclamation process for which he referred to British political culture. He demanded an equivalent of a 'Corrupt Practices Act' to be passed, which would list and ban intolerable practices liable to incite controversy and unrest.[112] But he contributed to the controversy when he suggested that Hindu and Muslim preachers divide up between themselves the reclamation of the vast outcaste classes of Indian society (*IAR* 1923/I: 77). Such proposal was anathema to religious Hindus, and more so to reformist Hindus such as Shraddhananda (Jordens 1981: 138ff.). They considered the untouchables an inalienable part of Hindu society.

Many of the Islamic groups studied here joined the tablīgh efforts in the Agra and Saharanpur districts. At times it must have been a scramble for the souls of the Malkana Rajput tribes. No prominent group wanted

It was vehemently opposed by Shraddhananda who made it the centre of his argument about an ongoing Muslim conspiracy against Hinduism (Jordens 1981: 140).

[112]See Muhammad Ali's speech at the Cocanada Congress session on 28 December 1923 (*IAR* 1923/I: 77).

to be seen lagging behind in this undertaking. The competition was so tense that it was difficult to distinguish whether the main target was the Rajput tribes or the imagined audience of the Islamic public sphere evaluating the groups' performance in defending the faith. As such it was a clear turning point from a religious act to competitive public affirmation. It was in the context of this intense contestation of political and religious identity that after 1922–3 the tasks of tablīgh and tanẓīm were included in the agenda of most Islamic groups.

The Deoband seminary started a Department of Preaching as early as 1325 AH (1907) geared to counter the reclamation efforts of the Ārya Samāj. The 1909 Jam'īyat al-Anṣār launched by the radical Deobandi scholar Maulana Ubaidullah Sindhi (1872–1944) also considered among its aims 'to publicise, make current and universalise the effects of the Dāru'l-'ulūm' (Rizvi 1980/I: 172). The Anṣār held a grand function in Moradabad in 1329 AH (1911). Branches were established under the name of Qāsim al-Ma'ārif (Knowledge about the Views of Muhammad Qasim Nanaotawi). This designation pointed to the Deobandi priority in their propagation activity to popularize the views of their founder Nanaotawi. Pointing out his merits the annals of the seminary claimed he had 'removed the doubts which were being created by modern philosophy and [...] had developed scholastic theology to a level at par with philosophy and logic' (Rizvi 1980/I: 176). Scholarly journals to propagate the seminary's views were started—*Al-Qāsim* in 1913 and *Al-Rashīd* in 1914, named after the founders of the seminary, Qasim Nanaotawi and Rashid Gangohi (see Table 2.1). A Qur'anic school (Naẓārat al-Ma'ārif al-Qur'ānīya), launched by Sindhi and Mahmud al-Hasan in Delhi in 1913, was aimed at English-educated Muslim boys whose religious education was found wanting or nonexistent. The school served the propagation of the Deobandi variety of Islam as much as the political ambitions (see Chapter 4) of its organizers. Other ways of propagating the Deobandi message involved its graduates. They carried its legacy to faraway places and also to other countries where branches started coming up. The East and South African branches proved already strong enough to be capable of donating a considerable sum of money to the head seminary at Deoband in 1328 AH (1910). The occasion was the well-attended grand convocation ceremony of 1909 in which turbans were conferred on successful graduates. It was held after an interval of 26 years (ibid.: 173–4; 197).

Regarding the developments around Agra Deoband's leaders intervened with the Congress, and made special arrangements for preaching and the training of missionaries (Rizvi 1980/I: 204–5). For this purpose Deobandi provided for the schooling of Sanskrit and the Ārya creed. It hired Maulawi

Abu Rehmat of Meerut and one Dr Ghulam Muhammad. The latter had been on Ārya Samāj's preaching missions but had 'been affected by the beauties of Islam' during this period so much that he entered 'the pale of Islam' (ibid.: Vol. I: 207, cf. Vol. II: 243). Maulana Mirak Shah, a teacher at Deoband, headed their field office in Agra (Rizvi 1980/I: 206). The more influence the Deoband seminary gained on the JUH the more they fused their public activities. Both merged their separate field offices in Agra in 1922.[113]

The JUH had included tablīgh as one of its nine basic objectives right from its beginnings in 1920—'to propagate (tablīgh) Islam in India and in other countries'.[114] The connotation of the term was clearly 'propagation' of the faith. Often it was used together with *ishā'at*,[115] which also included printing, sometimes in combination as *tablīgh-wa-ishā'at*.[116] The JUH repeatedly grappled with the need, principles and rules of tablīgh. It felt that its tablīgh activities were not up to the central status claimed by the JUH:

> Although many '*ulamā*' are performing this service [of tablīgh—DR] at present, there is no centre for it. As the JUH is the religious guide of India and is concerned with all religious affairs, it is necessary to include the work of propaganda and publication within the aims of the *Jam'īyat* and to take action for its implementation.[117]

Maulana Madani discussed the etiquette of tablīgh and tanẓīm at the 1923 JUH session hoping to avoid acerbating Hindu–Muslim conflict over it. In consonance with Muhammad Ali, he emphasized correctness, tolerance, and peacefulness.[118] With the souring of Hindu–Muslim detente

[113]Rizvi (1980/I: 207). The JUH forced the more politically minded Khilafat Committee partly against its will to donate Rs 50,000 for the tablīgh campaign in the Agra area (*Leader* [Allahabad, 24 March and 9 April 1923], quoted in Robinson 1994: 339).

[114]See the Programme of the JUH (*Dastūru'l-'Amal*) adopted in 1920, in Rozinah (1981/I: 49); for a translation of changing versions of the programme, see Appendix II.

[115]ishā'at (Urdu)—publication; propagation; dissemination; circulation, spread, diffusion; edition.

[116]See, for instance, the presidential address by Maulana Habibur Rahman Deobandi in December 1922, a section of which was sub-titled tablīgh-wa-ishā'at (Rozinah 1981/I: 186). See also the same combination of terms in the reworked statutes of the JUH of 1939 (ibid.: 48–9, sub-clause *d*).

[117]Maulana Habibur Rahman Deobandi at the Gaya session in 1922 (Rozinah 1981/I: 186).

[118]Madani elucidated the rules for tablīgh as follows: 'During the tablīgh activities it is important to keep in mind those matters which a true and just religion considers its basic principles and foundation:

(1) Those facts, which are being propagated, have to be true and correct. (2) One should not use rude or impolite language in relation to a leader or founder of any religion.

the JUH accentuated its religious duties more strongly, as in the Peshawar session of 1927. It recalled the duty to perform tablīgh (Rozinah 1981/I: 433) and the rules of tablīgh (ibid.: 439), as discussed in the presidential address of Maulana Anwar Shah Kashmiri (1875–1933).

The resolutions of the JUH also documented the secular usage of the term tablīgh. Motion number 5 of the 1921 Lahore session read as follows:

> This session of the JUH proposes to form groups for propaganda (*tablīgh*) as soon as possible which, in various provinces of India, will spread and propagate the support for the Islamic caliphate and Ghazi Mustafa Kemal Pasha, the establishment of a system of Islamic justice (*dāru'l-qāẓa*) and other Islamic goals. The president and the secretary of the *Jam'īyat* are authorised to arrange for such groups and to dispatch them (Rozinah 1981/I: 131).

Here, tablīgh basically meant the spread of the aims and objectives of the organization. This included the political message underlying the Khilafat and non-cooperation movement as much as the religious message. The secular meaning of tablīgh corresponded with the activities of the Khilafat conference maintaining a separate department for propaganda headed by Maulana Bari (Qureshi 1999: 123)

Maulana Thanawi, who embodied the pietist side of the Deobandi School and opposed involvement in politics, conducted his own tablīgh activities in several districts of the United Provinces and around Delhi (cf. Masud 2000: liv ff.). In Saharanpur, he established an organization of tablīgh called Majlis Ṣiyānatu'l-Muslimīn (Association for the Protection of Muslims), aimed at the reform of Muslims in general. His area of activity also covered parts of the Mewat region where the Tablīghī Jamā'at later came into existence. Mewat stretched south of Delhi and was inhabited by a conglomeration of Meo tribes who had been converted to Islam in the twelfth century, although some sources contend it was even earlier (ibid.: xxx ff.). They still observed many Hindu rites and customs and counted themselves among the 'neo-Muslims.' Masud pointed to Thanawi's shrewdness and tactical sophistication in employing techniques not exactly condoned by reformist Islam. He once organized a Muslim *kithā* (story-

The Qur'an and the ḥadīth prohibit this strongly. (3) No duress or compulsion (*ikrā-o-ijbār*) should be created [through tablīgh]. (4) One should not give a position of confidence to any greedy or materially selfish person. (5) No pressure or force should be employed. (6) Moral harshness or intolerance should be avoided. These things should be made very clear. (Quoting a tradition:) Those who want can follow the true religion and those who want can harm (*halāk*) themselves'. [Follows Arabic text of the tradition] (Rozinah 1981/I: 221) On the concept of tablīgh as pursued by the Deoband seminary and the JUH see Madani, *Tablīghī Taqrīreñ* (n.d. [1927]). On his guidelines for tanẓīm, see section 4.2.2.

telling) event, and on another occasion a mīlād ceremony in honour of the Prophet's birthday. He also accepted their participation in the practice of *ta'ziya* (making models of the tombs of the Shi'i martyrs for the mourning procession in the month of *muḥarram*). These practices, doubtful as they may have been from a reformist perspective, he considered preferable to the 'neo-Muslims' becoming apostates by discontinuing their links with Islam. But these compromises would not deflect from his reformist message. Many of his reformist tracts were designed as instructions for preachers and activists. His concerns were reflected in the special course he devised for reform, his *Iṣlāḥī Niṣāb* (Collection of Texts on the Renewal of Muslims), which he compiled between 1922 and 1931.[119] Thanawi's book was also popular with the Tablīghī Jamā'at (cf. section 3.4.4). There were several parallels with Zakariyya's reading book for the TJ. Thanawi's approach foreshadowed their focus on topics such as the importance of rewards for meritorious acts, the hereafter, the concept of rights and duties of Muslims, and blessings for the Prophet (*durūd*) (Zakariyya 1975). In 1924, he devised his practical programme of da'wa called *Tafhīm al-Muslimīn* consisting of 12 points.[120] Its emphasis on correct religious practice, education, unity, self-organization, and moral improvement was of a broader meaning, not much different from programmes of other social reformers of his time. He also took special care of the educational needs of women in his reform efforts (cf. section 5.1).

The Barelwis emphasized the non-political nature of tablīgh. They rushed to Agra and Saharanpur with an organization created for this purpose in 1921, the Jamā'at-i Raẓā-i Muṣṭafā (Society Pleasing to the Prophet Muhammad).[121] In consonance with their reverence for the Prophet, their missionary efforts were demonstrably devoted to him. One may also note the play of words in the designation of the organization (Raẓā) on the

[119]The book included chapters on the life of (true) Muslims (*ḥayātu'l-muslimīn*), on proper religious conduct for which (in the hereafter) rewards could be expected (*jazā'u'l-a'māl*), on religious education (*ta'līmu'd-dīn*), on the demands of faith (*furū'u'l-īmān*), on the concept of rights in Islam (*ḥuqūqu'l-Islām*), on the duties (rights) of parents (*ḥuqūqu'l-wālidayn*), on the right behaviour and social life (*ādābu'l-mu'āsharat*), on mistakes of (common) people (in Islam) (*aghlātu'l-'awāmm*), and on finding the right way (to God) (*tashīl qaṣdi's-sabīl*). Later editions such as the one used here also included a tenth part, *zād al-s'ayīd*, dealing with the merits of blessings for the Prophet (durūd-i sharīf) (Thanawi 1990).

[120]These included *kalima*, namāz, *zakāt*, Ramaḍān, ḥajj, ta'līm, *ittifāq Muslimīn* (Muslim Unity), tanẓīm, and tablīgh against moral evils (Masud 2000: lv).

[121]See also Table 2.1. The organization continued to operate at least until 1957 (Sanyal 1996a: 92). From the Barelwi side, a number of institutions actively engaged in the preaching activities against shuddhī, reflecting also their more decentralized style of operation. For their preaching efforts in the Punjab, see the Dāru'l-'ulūm Ḥizb al-Aḥnāf of Lahore (Ahmad 1994).

name of the Barelwi founder, Ahmad Raza, who had died by this time. It was his eldest son, Hamid Raza, who formulated the Barelwi programme for tablīgh at the 1925 All-India Sunni Conference. Given the opposition of the Barelwis to the Khilafat and non-cooperation campaign, they avoided all references to these campaigns and to worldly matters in general. They pledged to counter the shuddhī movement, a task on which all groups agreed. In addition, they emphasized doctrinal aspects as they demanded preaching against 'false' teachings. For this purpose they were ready to accept a modern format. Hamid Raza suggested in 1925 that an elaborate organization and programme for tablīgh be created as part of his general programme of religious education for Muslim India. His proposals foreshadowed similar ideas by the Tablīghī Jamā'at, which were being conceptualized by its future leader, Muhammad Ilyas, at about the same time. For the Barelwis, the meaning of tablīgh was more of 'preaching'. It was to be carried out through madrasas to be set up throughout the country affiliated to a lead madrasa. Religious students would be trained in the principles of tablīgh. A select number of students as well as all teachers would be required to spend two days a week in active preaching (cf. Qadiri 1997: 146ff.). The tough stand on the rejection of Hindu–Muslim unity taken by Hamid Raza at the conference reflected the heightened communal tension and increased violence in the mid-1920s. In later years the preaching efforts of the Barelwis were deliberately contrasted with the Tablīghī Jamā'at after the latter gained more recognition. Barelwi critics made clear that they regarded the Tablīghī Jamā'at as an outflow of Wahhabi extremism (see fn. 135, this chapter).

Keeping in mind that all schools sent scholars to preach in the 'disputed territory', the 'ulamā' from Firangī Maḥall were no exception. Abdul Bari was most active here as well. Regarding the shuddhī campaign as a violation of the Hindu–Muslim understanding of the Khilafat campaign, he demanded in September 1923: 'We are determined to non-co-operate with every enemy of Islam whether he be in Anatolia or Arabia or at Agra or Banares' (Abdul Bari Papers, File 24, quoted in Robinson 1994: 339). He worked through a local tablīgh organization (Majlis Numandagam-e Tablīgh in Agra) (ibid.: fn. 4). He also sent workers of his Sufi organization, the Bazm-i Ṣūfiya-i Hind, to the field (Robinson 2001: 158). On this count the loyalists could agree with him. They felt reassured by the non-political nature of tablīgh. The preaching also provided an outlet for their opposition to Hindu–Muslim cooperation.

The attitude of the Nadwa council and seminary towards preaching was influenced by its pretensions of serving as an all-India institution for reforming normative Islam. Vague modernizing impulses of an institutional approach were reflected in the intention to form a body of regular preachers (*wā'iẓīn*). They would receive special training in debating and countering doctrinal arguments.[122] Such plans were considered as early as 1894. They were apparently modelled on the activities of Christian missionaries who had divided the country into target areas and had underpinned their conversion efforts by economic and social projects. The wā'iẓīn were to preach about correct Islamic practices; behaviour sanctioned by Islam (*ḥalāl*) or forbidden by it (*ḥarām*); reform and moral issues; the importance of trade; and the removal of 'corrupt' customs.[123] Yet, while the Nadwis recognized early the need to propagate Islam they found it difficult to implement their intentions. In 1902, another resolution was adopted. It called to work for the eradication of corrupt practices (that is, depraved customs—*rusūm-i qabīh*) responsible for the moral degradation among Muslims (Jalis Nadwi and Tabriz Khan 1983/I: 297 ff.). However, the formation of a corps of wā'iẓīn did not materialize. It was now planned to use the Nadwa support associations (Anjumanhā-ye Mu'in al-Nadwa) (see Table 2.1), which had sprung up across the United Provinces and beyond, for preaching also. Individual preaching was directed at 'degenerate' forms of Islam, particularly in areas of Barelwi influence around Rae Bareilly. Friends and sponsors of the Nadwa offered monetary rewards for each eradicated 'evil custom' ranging from Re 1 to Rs 100 per successful mission (Malik 1997: 462). In order to intensify these purification efforts, it was suggested that the Nadwa council should take direct charge of the propagation of Islam (*ishā'at al-Islām*). Shibli Numani wanted to make the council 'the centre of all religious requirements of [Indian] Muslims' with branches in all provinces (Nadwi, *Ḥayat-i Shiblī* [1943: 631 ff.], quoted after Malik 1997: 463). The task of ishā'at al-Islām, its principles and objectives, were the subject of another resolution in 1904 (ibid.: 467, fn. 155). Shibli Numani wanted to make preaching a graduation profile of the seminary. He felt that the preachers ought to learn English and Sanskrit, and study the Hindu creed from first-hand sources so that they could conduct disputes with the Ārya Samājīs at par, instead of proving ignorant or ill-informed as was often the case. For this purpose, he employed the services of a learned Hindu scholar, a pandit. Shibli pointed to the example of the religious Hindu school, the *gurukul*. He believed it provided much better education, teaching Sanskrit, English, modern sciences, and physical fitness, even though its graduates were not aspiring to become civil servants (cf. Fischer-Tiné 2003). Yet Shibli's

[122]Malik's account is being followed here (1997: 459ff.).

[123]Malik pointed to conscious efforts at the Nadwa to also engage in 'external mission'. The Nadwig were seeking the correction of the image of Islam in the minds of the English and the British-Indian administration (cf. Malik 1997: 645).

reforming efforts were short-lived and suffered from lack of support and money. A separate organization for the propagation of Islam (Markāzī majlis-e ishā'at-e Islām) proposed in 1917 did not materialize. After it was recommended in 1927, a separate department of preaching (Dār al-Muballighīn) emerged in 1938 (Jalis Nadwi and Tabriz Khan 1983/II). Eventually, the preaching activities of the Nadwa made measurable progress only after scholars such as Sayyid Abu'l-Hasan Ali Nadwi and Sayyid Sulaiman Nadwi linked up with the emerging Tablīghī Jamā'at. Both became some of its best ideologues and propagators.

To the Aḥmadīya, more than to many others, da'wa and tablīgh activities were their 'home turf'. They came into existence as a missionary movement, specializing in conversions as the only source of increasing their membership. Few mainstream Muslims would volunteer to join their ranks. From early on they developed the skills of preaching and debate, in which they received regular schooling. Their da'wa activities included several aspects, at times quite distinct. While one direction of their preaching was the recruitment of new members, another one, conducted with equal verve, was the refutation of un-Islamic beliefs. The latter often converged with preaching by mainstream Sunni Muslims. This was how it was in the beginning of their formation when they attacked Hindu reformist and Christian missionaries, and this continued to be the case in the 1920s when they rushed to the 'front' of the Rajput 'neo-Muslims' in full force. Compared to other reformist and revivalist groups, one controversial aspect of the Aḥmadīya stuck out: they were the only group becoming a target of preaching undertaken in defence of Islam by other Muslim groups—the Barelwis, the Deobandis, some leaders of the Nadwa and the Aḥrār. They were described as something of a menace, a natural calamity coming over a particular area that had to be defended against their preachings. But the exclusion of the Aḥmadīya from institutional mainstream Islam evolved only gradually. In the 1920s and 1930s they were still considered by many Muslims as deviant but not necessarily irreconcilable. After 1908, they extended their activities to South India, Bengal, Afghanistan, and England (Friedmann 1989: 15). They published several periodicals in Urdu, English and later in other international languages. Their most prominent periodical was the monthly *Review of Religions* (1902). Their missionary activities were tightly organized, including women and youth wings, a training institute, and separate outfits for Indian and foreign missionary activities (see Table 2.2). Their Kashmir campaign between 1931 and 1934 represented a particular variety of missionary activity. Kashmir held some significance in the theology of the Aḥmadīya ever since its founder Ghulam Ahmad located the grave of Jesus on Khan Yar Street in Srinagar, Kashmir. The Aḥmadīs did not choose to make this place a centre of pilgrimage as they rejected saint worship. But they directed special educational and missionary activities at Kashmir, such as a scholarship programme to bring Kashmiri boys for education to the Aḥmadī centre at Qadiyan (Lavan 1976: 146). The start of the 1931 Kashmir campaign was said to be the fulfilment of Ghulam Ahmad's prophecy that he would 'be the cause of liberation' for a persecuted people. The campaign developed into a political movement where tension was heightened with other Sunni groups battling over control of the All-India Kashmir Committee founded in Lahore and led by the Aḥmadīs in 1931–2 (ibid.: 150–4).

The Aḥrār advocated a highly politicized da'wa and tablīgh. They started a separate department of tablīgh on 22 July 1934.[124] They conducted most of their campaigns against the Aḥmadīs, the Shi'is, or Sufi customs in the name of propagating the correct faith (see section 4.4). They were self-righteous in their beliefs on which they based their assertiveness. They also adopted this approach against Muhammad Ali when they defended the 1928 Nehru Report against his opposition calling its supporters *ṯayyib* (pure and good) and its opponents *khābith* (unclean and evil) (Qureshi 1974: 307).[125]

The Jamā'at-i Islāmī also subjected its concept of da'wa to political goals. The establishment of an Islamic order (*iqāmat-i dīn*) was at its centre. Its meaning was Islamic observance, inspiring people to embrace Islam as a religion, a way of life, and a political system.[126]

3.4.4. *The Concept of the Tablīghī Jamā'at*

The Tablīghī Jamā'at requires separate treatment in this connection inasmuch as it represented the most massive, most organized, and the most successful attempt to launch preaching activities. These were, however, almost entirely directed at fellow Muslims with a negligible number of conversions of non-Muslims affected by the Tablīghīs. Their main objective was to reaffirm Muslims in their faith and to encourage or nudge them into a regular and correct observance of Islamic rites. Historically, the movement grew out of the context described earlier. In the beginning,

[124]Miyan Qamaruddin (President), Chaudhri Afzal Haq (Vice-President), Maulana Abdul Karim (General Secretary) were its office bearers. (Aziz 1993: 144).

[125]This was significant in that it undermined the standing of Muhammad Ali after he started opposing Congress politics on Muslim autonomy. He had earlier been the major spokesman of Muslim religious and political interests. After increased communal tension of the twenties he adopted more orthodox religious positions. The Aḥrār approach underlined their unprincipled manipulation of religious tenets.

[126]Nasr (1996: 28, 65). On the Jamā'at's concept of da'wa, see also Maududi (1990).

that is, between 1926 and 1934 it was no more than another programme of an individual scholar. At that time Muhammad Ilyas was pursuing his own mission. Islamic preachers had come to Mewat before, some as early as in the eighteenth and in the beginning of the nineteenth centuries. Muhammad Ilyas' father, Maulana Muhammad Ismail (d. 1898), also maintained religious connections with Meo tribals.[127] For much of the pre-independence period the movement was not called Tablīghī Jamā'at—a term which came into regular circulation only later. Ilyas preferred to call it a 'faith movement' (*taḥrīk-i īmān*).[128]

Its first institutional activity was recorded for 2 August 1934 when a meeting of village elders (*panchāyat*) was held in the Mewat region, in which 107 notables participated, including landlords and officials. Muhammad Ilyas presented to the local population his programme of action which, according to Qadiri, consisted of 15 points of religious and social reform.[129] Tablīghī sources gave different wordings of their programme but its essence comes to the same. It has been canonized in their Six Essentials (*chhē bāteñ*) (Appendix I). Priority was given to the knowledge of the essentials of Islamic belief, the so-called five pillars of Islam, and their correct practice. These were to be explained to the tribals so that they would be properly understood and not mechanically copied. Each tribe member needed to be reaffirmed as Muslim. The emphasis was on the formula of faith (*shahāda*), the knowledge and pronouncement of which in itself was sufficient to make one a Muslim, hence its practical importance for preaching and mission. Other key elements were prayer (*ṣalāt*) and commemoration of the Prophet (d̲ikr) in their correct and regular form. These required more extensive and better religious education for which old schools had to be improved and new ones founded. Muslims also needed to be recognizable as such and clearly distinguishable from Hindus by their outward appearance and customs. These included Islamic dress, together with the veiling of women (parda), and the practice of Islamic *rites de passage* such as on the occasion of marriage, birth, or death. Local customs in these matters, which sometimes entailed immense expenses, needed to be shunned. 'False' customs (bid'a) needed to be abandoned, notably the veneration of idols (shirk) of local saints or shrines, although it was legitimate to worship the saints. While these demands

[127]Sources differ on the extent and character of these connections. Masud spoke of 10 to 12 Mewati religious students at the Nizamuddin mosque in Delhi where Ismail taught the Qur'an (2000: 5).

[128]Manzur Numani's introduction to the Urdu edition of Nadwi's biography of Ilyas (1983).

[129]Muhammad Ayyub Qadiri, *Tablīghī Jamā'at kā tarīkhī jā'iza* (Karachi: Maktaba Mu'āwīya, 1971), pp. 92–3, quoted in Masud (2000: 10–11).

reflected classical concerns of Islamic reformism, the Tablīghī Jamā'at added a particular flavour to its preaching activities by its social activism. It demanded a certain civility in behaviour and mutual communication, including morality, honour, mutual respect, cleanliness, and the like. In some of the basic religious tracts that guide the activity of the movement to present day, Ilyas gave advice on details such as correct behaviour towards fellow lay-preachers while on tour.[130] This also extended to eating and drinking habits. Such advice partly mirrored a process of integrating rural Muslims submerged in the rites of folk Islam into the urban culture of reformist standards. Religious reformation was also seen to be the key to solving social ills that were blamed on Western and materialist influences. As such the Tablīghīs presented themselves as a socio-therapeutic movement that decried modernity and yet fully reflected it and responded to it in an ameliorating fashion.[131] The social reformism with regard to the Meo tribes gained the Tablīghīs acceptance from the notables and officials in the regions and increasingly from the Meos themselves. The census noted in 1931 that the Meo literacy had increased since the 1921 Census from 6 to 9 per cent 'mainly as a result of the uplift work among them' (Census 1931, Punjab, Part I: 348). Tablīghī proponents largely attribute this to Islamic missionary activity. The social climate among them was reported to have improved significantly as quarrels and transgressions of public order and behaviour decreased (Mayaram 1997: 156). It might be noted here that reformist trends in Christianity had always devoted much attention to social work and rehabilitation shaped differently in varying cultural contexts.

Islamic critique of the Tablīghīs was voiced from several sides. The Jamā'at-i Islāmī led by Maulana Maududi accused it of leading Muslims away from the political struggle for an Islamic state, nowadays most pertinent in connection with events in Afghanistan, Kashmir, and Central Asia (cf. fn. 129, this chapter). The Barelwis argued that the Tablīghīs

[130]For instance, a proper use of language is advised (Ilyas M 20, 74); arrogance is to be shunned (M 79); money to be spent wisely (M 13). See Chapter 5.

[131]I beg to disagree here with the otherwise highly valued work of Khalid Masud who repeatedly argued that the Tablīghīs, their literature, and their ideology reflect a worldview 'content with pre-modern life patterns and ideas, [... regarding] modernity as a way of life hostile to them as 'ulamā', and, therefore, a threat to Islam' (2000: 83). While this may be true with regard to their perception and intent it is only part of the truth in relation to their impact of which they were not oblivious. As I have discussed their modernity and contribution to change elsewhere I quote: 'Although they claim otherwise, the change they desired was not towards restoring tradition as it was known. They constructed a new religiosity of the industrial age for which its counterparts in the western world were well known, including groups such as the Salvation Army, Jehova's Witnesses, or the New Age religious cults' (Reetz 1999a: 97).

represented Wahhabi extremism in disguise. They maintained that the Wahhabis also began on simple premises of faith, prayer, and morals, taking an extremist turn later. The Barelwis feared they would become the target of Tablīghī reformism.[132] The Barelwis also attacked their main reading book *Faẓā'il-i A'māl* (Zakariyya 1975) for allegedly using unreliable traditions. The Ahl-i Ḥadīth resented the spread of the Hanafi law school doctrine by the Tablīghīs, taking this as a deflection from the claimed focus on the Qur'an and the ḥadīth.[133] So far such criticism could not make a significant dent in their seemingly continuously growing popularity.

In the beginning the Tablīghī Jamā'at used the tracts for religious reform written by Maulana Thanawi, the *Iṣlāḥī Niṣāb* (1990), before their own reading book was ready. Even today Thanawi's books are thought meritorious by many sympathizers of the Tablīghī Jamā'at.[134] Although Thanawi was initially reluctant to support the Tablīghī Jamā'at, he was widely identified with it by others. The Barelwis and Ahl-i Ḥadīth alleged the TJ was a vehicle for the propagation of Thanawi's Deobandi views at their expense (Masud 2000: 94–5). This would allegedly acerbate divisions (fitna). Over time the Tablīghī reading book *Faẓā'il-i A'māl* advanced to the status of an icon within the movement. Reading from it at gatherings and to family members became their major form of religious education (ta'līm).

With regard to their religious task, it was the rather innovative method of the Tablīghīs, that was responsible for their unparalleled success. From the point of view of the public sphere they privileged oral communication and personal contact going somewhat against the trend towards mediatic diffusion of knowledge. Their emphasis on meritorious acts (faẓā'il) and rewards was very effective for motivation. It contrasted with the usual way of the 'ulamā', which was mainly threatening sanctions. This was complemented with a deliberately non-controversial approach to debate. It combined steadfastness with their almost proverbial equanimity that had worn down opposition on many occasions. Participants were instructed to treat friend and foe alike, to always be friendly, to not be put off by hostility or negative responses from the audience, to not despair if the

[132] In independent Pakistan they challenged the Tablīghīs by creating their own da'wa organization, Da'wat-i Islāmī, led by Maulana Muhammad Ilyas Qadri and closely modelled on the Tablīghī Jamā'at (cf. http://www.dawateislami.net).

[133] Talibur Rahman, *Tablīghī Jamā'at kā Islām* (Rawalpindi, 1992), quoted in Masud (2000: 95). For another critical appreciation by the Ahl-i Ḥadīth not considered by Masud, see Qasim (1990).

[134] My interviews in November 1997 at the Lahore University of Management Sciences (LUMS, 6 November 1997) and the Tablīghī Jamā'at centre at Nizamuddin, Delhi (26 October 1998).

Muslims were slow or unwilling to reform (cf. Numani 1993). Their tolerance was demonstrably limitless although tested on doctrinal principles it would not withstand inquiry as they, by and large, shared the inhibitions against deviant practices and sects (Numani 1995, Ilyas M 3, also see section 3.2.4). On the conceptual side, another important element of the Tablīghī Jamā'at was the emphasis on the role of the hereafter and the paradise. This was in consonance with their demand to forgo worldly and material pleasures and think of the reward of good acts in paradise. Ilyas explicitly demanded the propagation of the advantages of paradise 'so that the followers can imagine the merits and rewards of joining the Tablīghī movement and may forget the worldly loss caused by their engagement' (Ilyas M 67). He explained:

> The true Muslim has not been sent into this world to defend the vices and lustful urges of the body, which turns this world into paradise (for those who want to live like that), but to resist them and to obey God's commands, even if this may turn this world for the pious Muslim (*momīn*) into a prison. If we also support and tolerate vices like the infidels and turn this world into a paradise for ourselves then we will stand accused of usurping the paradise of the infidels. In this situation the right of the victorious will not be on the side of the usurper, but you will incur God's displeasure (Ilyas M 37).

While such orientation pointed towards withdrawal the Tablīghīs needed to live and act in this world. Ilyas was quite clear about worldly duties, which should not be neglected. He stressed the importance of preaching to the leaders of the community, to traders and the like, to accept the rich as they were. The Tablīghīs were not to renounce them but to inspire them to live in accordance with the dictates of Islam and spend their riches for the glory of religion (Ilyas M 5, M 104, M 135). Ilyas' practical strategy also targeted community leaders and religious scholars. He understood he could neither neglect them, nor allow his followers to alienate them, even if some did not meet the moral and spiritual criteria of his movement (cf. fn. 40). The broader perspective of social reformism (within the limits of iṣlāḥ) was reflected in the separate attention devoted to the status of women and poor sections of society where the influence of the teachings of Thanawi was felt.

But Ilyas also gave the desired pietist withdrawal a practical twist. Preaching tours became the hallmark of the movement where people were taken out of their daily routine to devote energy and time to the spirit of Islam. This separation or withdrawal, he came to believe, was a precondition to make headway in the reformation of Muslim society. Although he apparently did not invent the tours and rounds (gasht) (cf. Masud 2000: 7–8), Ilyas nevertheless was responsible for turning them into a systematic approach. Out of this he developed the obligation for every member to devote as much time as possible to these preaching tours, first in his own locality, then in areas further away.

From the perspective of the formation of the public sphere, the minute prescriptions of behaviour for the intending preachers set up a ritual and culture of the Tablīghī Jamā'at quite of its own. It may have the potential to turn it into a separate community taking on sect-like features over time. Less pronounced before independence but more visible today, it also showed signs of endogamy amongst its more committed regulars.[135] The Tablīghī Jamā'at established a remarkable autonomy of their public discourse both in the Islamic sphere and in the public sphere at large. Their discourse was equally critical of the state and the forces of the market. Their attitude towards individual rights remained ambiguous though. They were known to organize and exert religious and social pressure on their followers, and more so on their regulars, often in a significant degree. Yet, as far as is known, they made no forced recruitment nor did they keep people in their ranks against their will. Many observers both in the Islamic and the secular camp were apprehensive of their activities (cf. fn. 31, Chapter 2). Still their potential to contribute to the emancipation of Muslim masses within specified parameters cannot be neglected. They offered choices to the average Muslim looking for avenues of religious activities. They opened a door to the world for Muslims from rural areas and underprivileged strata. As such the Tablīghīs met the criteria of a civil society formation.

Several aspects appear to be common to the propagation and preaching efforts of the various groups. The institution-building gave the preaching efforts a new direction. Groups shared the anxiety that much had to be done to counter the religious activities of Christians and Hindus effectively. Individual efforts were felt to be wholly inadequate. Attempts were made to set up specialized departments or institutes for this purpose. What was sought was in effect a professionalization of preaching. Special training for this purpose was given extra attention. The inclination to study the creed of the Ārya Samāj through special teachers reflected a spirit of open-mindedness. This contrasts with the situation in the 1930s and today when sectarian radicals often do not consider it worth studying the views of the opponent in detail but limit themselves to rejecting 'false' views and applying social and physical pressure against them.

[135]This information is partly based on my interviews in Delhi (1998) and Lahore (1997), and is partly owed to a recent observation made by Naveeda Khan working on 'The Construction of the *Jalil Maulvi*: Religious Debates in Contemproary Pakistan' at Columbia University, New York.

The modernization of preaching also entailed heightened competition and a growing divergence in the propagation efforts of those groups. Every group became known for its own daʿwa. They increasingly focused on the reaffirmation and reproduction of the group's views. The modernization introduced a greater variety of means for propagation purposes. This included the dissemination of printed publications and periodicals. Traditional forms also remained, such as working through graduates of the seminaries and their networks, and making use of festivals and public ceremonies.

The so-called external mission, directed to non-Muslims, developed slowly but decisively. Groups such as the Deobandis, the Nadwis, and the Aḥmadīya systematically emphasized their global ambitions. They supported the creation of foreign branches and regular networking with them more visibly after around 1910. Several groups were anxious to influence the Christian West, first of all the British. This ambition ranged from correcting the image of Islam in the minds of British administrators[136] to attempts at converting British people to Islam. The Aḥmadīya gained prominence when several Irish and English persons joined their ranks between 1910 and 1913, among them Lord Headley (Friedmann 1989: 15). Undoubtedly the British were attracted to their creed by the evocation of a peaceful jihād. The continuous professions of loyalty to British rule on the part of the Aḥmadīya in India must also have helped considerably.

Another consequence of the modernization of preaching was the reinterpretation of tablīgh and daʿwa in consonance with public and political needs. This was particularly notable after the beginning of the Khilafat campaign in 1919. The organizational efforts to put preaching on a systematic footing were to be implemented by setting up branches over as large a part of India as possible. Several groups aspired to an all-India guiding role (the Deobandis, the Nadwa, the JUH). These branches were seen not only as representing the groups' aims and objectives but also as precursors of an infrastructure of an Islamic society or polity for Muslim India. The eradication of 'corrupt' or 'false' practices was to lay the basis of an Islamic order guided by correct religious behaviour and piety. This could only be achieved by intense propagation efforts. Some groups (Aḥrār, Jamāʿat-i Islāmī) used preaching unreservedly to pursue narrow political goals, turning tablīgh into a variant of ideology.

[136]See for instance the activities of the Nadwa in 1910 recounted by Malik, where the Nadwis conducted a special campaign to check and revise English textbooks with relation to Islam (Malik 1997: 465–6). See also the efforts of the Ahl-i Ḥadīth to 'clear' the name of the former mujāhidīn and those not following any law school (*ghair muqallidīn*) of suspicions of disloyalty to British power in India resulting in the introduction of the appellation Ahl-i Ḥadīth as a group designation for all official purposes.

The appearance of a public face of Islam contributed to rising mass awareness of religious dictates among Indian Muslims, or at least among its traditional and newly emerging élites. Whereas conflicting interpretation of religious doctrine dominated the formation of a public Islamic sphere from towards the end of the nineteenth century (c. 1880s), this new-found religious self-consciousness was to translate into mass action with the beginning of the twentieth century, after 1905 and more so after 1920. The politics of Islamic mass activism were to dawn on India.

(See overleaf for Table 3.1)

Table 3.1: Doctrinaire Preferences in the Public Discourse of the Islamic Groups in Colonial India (Schematic, Selected)

Islamic groups	Iṣlāḥ—what is understood by Islamic reformism	Taqlīd—adherence to what tradition is required	Bid'a—which innovations are regarded objectionable and worth intervention	Enemies in doctrine (groups no.)
1. Deobandis	Raise status of Qur'ān and ḥadīth, reform yourself and society.	Ḥanafī law, personal mentor (taqlīd-i shakhṣī); fiqh interpretation by group leaders (fatāwā).	Saint, shaykh, and tomb worship; miracles; excessive veneration of the Prophet.	5, 2, 11, 8, 6
2. Barelwis	Revive and establish ways of the Prophet (Sunna).	Ḥanafī law, including mystic legacy, saint, shrine and tomb worship; India is *dāru'l-Islām* requiring loyalty to government; fiqh interpretation by group leaders (fatāwā).	'Denigration' of the Prophet, of mystic knowledge, of tombs and saints, of the rulings of of the law schools (taqlīd).	5, 6, 11, 1, 8, 3, 7, 13, 12
3. Nadwa	Harmonizing differences between Islamic groups and promoting religious education.	Ḥanafī, though open to other law schools in principle.	(Gradually moved to:) Saint and tomb worship, miracles, excessive veneration of the Prophet.	(11), (8)
4. Firangī Maḥall	Raising level of (abstract, individual) religious education.	Ḥanafī, accepting reformist and mystic legacy; own curriculum (*dars-i niẓāmī*).	Undue purism, 'literalism;' (partly also) political, worldly activism.	8, (12), (13)
5. Aligarh	Reconcile religious education and learning with modern world.	Qur'ān, contradictions resolved without help of ḥadīth and law schools; books of the leader of the group.	Taqlīd to law schools, fitna.	1

(contd...)

(*Table 3.1: continued*)

Islamic groups	Iṣlāḥ—what is understood by Islamic reformism	Taqlīd—adherence to what tradition is required	Bid'a—which innovations are regarded objectionable and worth intervention	Enemies in doctrine (groups no.)
6. Ahl-i Ḥadīth	Establishing study of and conduct based on (written) Prophetic traditions (ḥadīth).	Qur'ān, contradictions resolved without help of law schools; emphasis on ḥadīth, (in practice; Ḥanbalī/Wahhābī); fiqh interpretation by group leaders (fatāwā)	Taqlīd to law schools, fitna, saint worship.	2, 8, 11, 5, 7
7. Tablīghī Jamā'at	Improving and propagating (tablīgh) religious education, religious practice (ṣalāt), and faith/piety (īmān), leading model Islamic life through 'internal mission'.	Ḥanafī; emphasis on ḥadīth and Sunna, details about ways of the Prophet and his time; books of the leader of the group (*Faẓā'il-i A'mal*).	Non-Muslim (Hindu) practices in worship, ritual, appearance 'extreme' practices and rituals in Sufism; sectarianism (fitna).	12, 13, 6, 2, (8), (11)
8. Aḥmadīya	Revive Islamic belief and practice; lead model Islamic life through active participation in the affairs of the (sectarian) community; expand membership through compulsory prolysetization ('external mission').	Qur'ān, contradictions resolved without help of ḥadīth and law-schools; divine authority of the leader of the community and his tradition (books); India is dāru'l-Islām requiring loyalty to government; supernatural character of revelation confirmed (against Aligarh).	Saint and tomb worship; 'excessive' Ṣūfī practices (*chillā*), violent jihād ('*ghaziism*') 'backward' social and religious customs (untouchability); sectarian and law school distinctions (fitna).	12, 13, 5

(*contd...*)

(Table 3.1: continued)

Islamic groups	Iṣlāḥ—what is understood by Islamic reformism	Taqlīd—adherence to what tradition is required	Bid'a—which innovations are regarded objectionable and worth intervention	Enemies in doctrine (groups no.)
9. Aḥrār	Organizing Muslims for the improvement of their status: in society in general and in Punjab in particular, against British rule.	Ḥanafī; Qur'ān, ḥadīth, sharī'a (in the often literal and controversial interpretation of their Amīr al-Sharī'at, A. Bukhāri)	(Repudiation of false doctrines:) Aḥmadīya; saint, shaykh and tomb worship; Shī'a; Hindu reformists.	8, 2, 11, 12, 10
10. Khaksār	Abiding by the basic rules of Islam and the worship of one God (tauḥīd); setting up a disciplined and physically fit (ṣalāḥīyat) body of pious and obedient Muslims in an Islamic state; leading a virtuous and ascetic life through worship and physical exercise.	Qur'ān; contradictions resolved without help of hadīth and law schools; commands and books of the leader of the group unquestioningly.	Renounce distinctions in race, class (wealth), sect (fitna); reject law schools and ḥadīth; 'effeminate' Hindu influence in renouncing violence.	9, 12, (8), (2), (6)
For comparison:	Religious reformism.	Adherence.	Objectionable innovation/ practice	
11. Shī'a	Revive Shī'a religious doctrine and role of Shī'a clerics (mujtāhids).	Shī'a doctrine.	Western modernism, unbalanced by religion education porating Muslim traditions.	12, 13
12. Hindu	Emphasize monotheism of	Vedic scriptures and principles	Syncretic practices, incorpora-	Targeting Islam and

(contd...)

(Table 3.1: continued)

Islamic groups	Iṣlāḥ—what is understood by Islamic reformism	Taqlīd—adherence to what tradition is required	Bid'a—which innovations are regarded objectionable and worth intervention	Enemies in doctrine (groups no.)
reformists (Ārya Samāj)	Vedic scriptures; egalitaria-nism; social relief and reform: re-admission of converts, rehabilitation of widows, ban on child marriage.	of Āryā Samāj organization; books of the leader(s) of the group.	ting Muslim traditions.	Prophet, Christia-nity, but no specific groups.
13. Christian missionaries	Stress superiority of Christian teachings, on points of doctrines, social egalitarianism and economic progress, incorporate local ritual where possible.	Centrality of the Bible.	Giving undue weight to local traditions in ritual, to former social stratification of converts (caste, untouchable, etc.).	Islam and Hinduism as a whole, targeting no specific groups

Sources: Ahmed (1994), Ahmed (1975, 1980); Friedmann (1989); Hashmi (1989); Hermensen (2001); Inayatullah (1988); Jain (1979); Kher (2001), Lavan (1976); Lelyveld (1996); Malik (1997); Mathur (1969); Masud (2000); Metcalf (1982); Minault (1982); Mir za (1975); NDC 405,510; Qureshi (1974); Rizvi (1980); Rizwi (1979); Robinson (1994, 2001); Sanyal (1996a); Seth (1985); Walter (1991).

Notes: Statement on doctrinal enemies: numbers in brackets () + – Groups affiliates are excluded from cross membership but not openly opposed/attacked. Table stresses what the groups emphasized. Mentioning one category in relation to one group, for instance, sharī'a, does not mean that other groups necessarily repudiated the sharī'a, but that this group undertook special (public) activities directed at elevating the shari'a. See the claim of the Aḥrār leader Bukhari to the status of Amīr al-Sharī'at (Mirza 1970).

Given the varied meanings the groups attached to doctrinal categories, the terms iṣlāḥ, taqlīd, bid'a have been used here in a wider sense to symbolize three different forms of intervention in the Islamic sphere by these groups: (i) a constructive intervention, summarized under iṣlāḥ, (ii) a 'destructive' intervention, summarized under bid'a, (iii) a 'conformist' intervention summarized under taqlīd, although the terms stand also for narrow technical meanings in Islamic theology.

4

Public Action and Political Meaning

This chapter will seek to explore the public and political dimensions of Islamic activism as pursued by the groups under study here. Their intervention in politics will be understood as activities to establish a certain measure of control over the public realm, over decision-making and resource allocation. Discourse, activism, and institution-building proceeded hand-in-hand. They partly emanated from religious debates analysed in the foregoing chapter and partly took on a new quality. The involvement in public action and politics confronted Islamic groups with a number of choices they had to make while responding to upcoming events. They had to decide whether to stay with traditional forms of patrimonial rule or to go along with participatory and representative politics. Inter-communal tension forced them to address the needs for defence and self-defence, whether to respond to attacks against Muslims with submission or to show assertion. Not all were agreed on how to bring about change and renewal, whether to engage in all-out activism, right up to using violence and insurgent warfare, or to bank on internal change through contemplation. In consonance with the growing militancy of the political climate, sectarian radicalism was on the rise pitching demands for exclusion of religious dissenters against traditions of tolerance. These were stark choices with a long-term impact on the public face of South Asian Islam.

4.1. PARTICIPATION OR PATRIMONY: ON THE OUTLINES OF A POLITY

Tracing the change of attitude in matters of participation and participatory politics for Islamic movements was more than merely recording one aspect of their public discourse and activity. Participation signally embodied the formation of modern political attitudes. It marked the transition of influence and decision-making from hereditary structures based on descent and wealth to the emancipation of the individual or groups of individuals, who become empowered to make choices about political priorities. These choices could potentially give decision-making and resource allocation new direction. They accommodated change in society and in the political system. This was known to be one of the prime foundations of democratic systems of government. Therefore, the acceptance or implementation of participatory principles of public policy by Islamic groups became a major indicator of their capacity to contribute to a democratic system. Although participatory politics by no means guaranteed that the will of the individual or of the majority was actually translated into political action they opened the possibility for such a development. More significantly, in the present context, the introduction and gradual acceptance of (majoritarian) participatory politics changed the focus of political and social actors. It contributed to a deep-going change in the political culture of society. In contrast to patrimonial conditions, in participatory politics, leaders of opinion, of society, or of wealth could no longer take it for granted that their own personal opinion or decision was accepted and enforced in representation of society or a whole political class. They needed to seek legitimacy for their decisions to a new degree. It was no longer sufficient that they provided their own arguments for legitimating their politics. Such legitimacy had to come from a significant proportion of those ruled, of society at large.

According to classical and reformist Islam, the locus of political authority was not the people at large but God. While there was no unanimity on who finally represented God's trust on earth, the choice would be some form of theological leader or leadership, a position filled either by one or more religious scholars, or a single leader (īmām, *Amīr al-Mu'minīn*, Caliph). He would fuse theological and political authority and receive advice from the scholars of religion and other leaders of the community on the basis of consultation (*shūrā*). Some Islamic reformers interpreted this form of government as being not different except by nomenclature from pluralist Western parliamentary democracy. They stressed Qur'anic injunctions arguing in favour of dissent and tolerance in matters of faith.[1] Such interpretation was still an exception, though. The majority of traditional religious scholars ('ulamā') tended to limit the privileges of parliament and rights to dissent. Their favoured form of government would incline towards autocratic rule with a leader exercising some form of patrimonial leadership. It was, therefore, not without wider significance that Islamic groups in colonial India showed the need and

[1]See, for instance, the position of as-Sadiq al-Mahdi (b. 1935) from the Sudanese Umma Party and Rashid al-Ghannushi (b. 1941) from the Tunisian Islamic Movement as discussed by E. Schone (2001: 165ff.) and L. Rogler (2001: 210ff.). 'Islam and Gesellschaft in Sudan. Selbstverständnis und politisches Konzept der Umma Partei', in Reetz (ed.), 2001a, pp. 153–71.

desire to reflect and incorporate principles of participation. This related to the conduct of their internal affairs, discussed in section 4.1.1. It was also reflected in the form of their association with political life, including elections to legislative assemblies as the most formal embodiment of participatory politics, which is discussed in section 4.1.2. Principles of an Islamic polity emanating from the discourse are reviewed in section 4.1.3.

4.1.1. Participation Inside—The Public Conduct of Internal Affairs

Participation broadened mainly as a response to various influences on the workings of Islamic institutions. The introduction of British law compelled groups to accept formal rules of functioning. Legal regulations for trusts and associations required a certain transparency and accountability. The formulation of statutes and their implementation acquired a key role for all public bodies, including madrasas. This process generated debates on how to fill leadership positions; what principles of admission and educational policy to adopt; how to proceed with the expansion of activities and the construction of new buildings; and, most importantly, how to deal with finances such as contributions, student fees, grants, and expenses. Religious schools and trusts had to submit to accountability also in earlier periods. It was always a fusion of the 'laws of the land' and principles of the sharī'a that governed their conduct of affairs. Yet, now more than ever, British, meaning non-Islamic sources of law, determined the business of these schools and institutions. Now school administrators (nāẕim) needed to be qualified in the application of these laws. The rules had an impact on the composition of advisory bodies and administrative councils. They had to reflect specialized knowledge, experience, financial qualifications, local patronage and so on. The obligation of annual reports was an effective instrument for ensuring transparency. Regular sessions of administrative bodies and the recording of their decisions were other important features. These conditions were to guarantee against fraudulent interference. Their financial basis needed to be sound to ensure against bankruptcy. Under the operation of Western law, these schools could be taken to court like any other institution. The legality of affairs was to ensure against legal injunctions that would bring the work of the schools to a standstill or close them down on formal grounds. As has been mentioned in connection with doctrinal differences, such litigation had increased measurably by the end of the nineteenth century.

It was particularly the statutes that provoked important and enduring disputes.[2] The statutes determined the direction of the associational life

[2] See debates on the statutes of the Nadwa in 1913–15 (Malik 1997: 359ff). For Deoband, see the changes in the statutes effected under the patronship of Thanawi in

of the respective institution to a significant degree. These debates reflected shifting doctrinal, political, and social concerns.[3] The leader-driven movements of the revivalist camp, particularly the Khāksār, the Aḥrār, and the Tablīghīs, were less riven by dissent over internal business. If the Aḥrār and the Khāksār faced court action it was not so much due to their conduct of internal business but their public activities, which were found objectionable either by their adversaries or by the government. They were also less vulnerable to litigation as they did not represent significant material values or interests unlike the trusts, on which religious schools often depended. While such bureaucratic procedure was quite normal for an institution like the Aligarh College, it was certainly a visible innovation for a madrasa such as Deoband. Irrespective of tension generated in mutual relations between the Aligarh School and the madrasas on doctrinal grounds, the latter in their practical administrative business, in fact, shadowed the Aligarh institution very closely.

This had a direct impact on the internal culture of the Islamic institutions. Reporting the composition and business of advisory boards made the articulation of competing interests public. It contributed to a measure of openness unknown in traditional institutions. It allowed for intervention by individuals and groups in the operation of these institutions through the legal system. This enforced openness also benefited the British. They remained well-informed of trends and acts of potential 'disloyalty', not only through its extensive network of covered intelligence agents, but through the very public conduct of the affairs of these institutions. It also allowed them to influence their work and to enforce obedience. Government grants to educational institutions such as madrasas were a favoured means of controlling them. The Deoband seminary made it a point to forego any government aid and grant to ensure its complete independence. The nomination of trustees—where the (local) government was involved—was another such instrument. So was the award of titles and honours and also pensions. At the same time, the system of government

1345 AH (1927) when in the wake of the student unrest the powers of the management were strengthened by creating an executive council (*majlis-e 'amla*) of the general council (*majlis-e shūrā*), which would also regularly supervise the administration (Rizvi 1980/II: 238). See here also the abolition of the post of patron in 1354 AH as discussed later. For Aligarh, see the issues leading to the formation of the reforms inquiry committee of 1927 (Rahimtoola Commmission) in Nizami (1995: 139–49).

[3]See, for instance, the changing statutes of the Association of Religious Scholars, JUH, which reflected different priorities, where formulations allowing for Hindu–Muslim cooperation and a multi-religious society over the years gave way to distinctly communalist feelings and anxieties and a more single-minded Islamist interpretation of nationalism, society, and the basic tasks of the JUH. Cf. the statutes of January 1920 and of May 1939, in Appendix II.

favours was never so centrally planned, controlled, and executed as to allow the implementation of a uniform policy towards the religious Islamic institutions. Local connections and networks often played a much more decisive role and British colonial authority in this connection was rather more decentralized and general than focused and specific.

As a result of the new legal and administrative developments, participation in the affairs of the madrasas, and partly other groups, was opened to more than the old narrow circle of theological and public leaders that had founded and directed them in the beginning. Not that the latter became dependent on a public vote, but they were less surely footed where they neglected public opinion even within their own institutions, a development which many found difficult to accept or to adapt to.

A good example demonstrating these trends was the campaign by Shibli Numani to assert himself against the conservative elements on the Nadwa council in 1912. He faced increasing resistance against his plans to introduce certain reforms and new projects in the Nadwa. Maulana Azad supported him openly through his newspaper *Hilāl* although he could not prevent his defeat in the internal wrangling. Shibli stepped down from his Nadwa post in July 1913. Eventually, Azad's intervention through his paper contributed to a reform of the Nadwa's working procedures in 1914 and 1915. In this process, the statutes were also revised. Shibli demanded, in particular, that elections become more representative. The members of the managing committee of the council should not, he felt, usurp all powers. A reform committee decided to revive the practice of electing the chairman of the council (nāẕim) by the full membership of the council. Representatives of the Muslim League Party, the Aligarh Movement, the Muslim University Committee, and the Himāyat-e Islām organization participated in efforts to resolve the differences. Arguments in favour of broader democratic participation by Council members in decision-making were formulated in the name of implementing the Islamic principles of consultation (shūrā) and consensus (ijmā'). During the internal struggle, the reforming forces relied on a reforms committee founded for this purpose in 1914, the Anjuman-e Iṣlāḥ–ye Nadwa, which operated in conjunction with Maulana Azad (Malik 1997: 356–9; 374ff.). For our purpose it is important that the reforms committee conducted up to 50 public meetings through branches it set up throughout the Muslim quarters of the neighbouring areas. Although Malik argued that power later gravitated back to the traditional forces in the Nadwa, it appears that the influence of the new structures and conditions could never be rescinded.

Similar controversies beset the working of the Deoband Seminary. Maulana Ubaidullah Sindhi conceived his Jam'īyat al-Anṣār in fairly wide terms, intent on setting up branches all over India working also for an Islamic society.[4] Inside the seminary, he hoped to get support from the association for his plans to reform the curriculum. He was interested in more modern topics, particularly in teaching modern Arab history to further pan-Islamic ideas. His detractors regarded this as a profanation and politicization of religious teaching. In the conflict which ensured, Sindhi had to leave the seminary, although he remained in touch with Mahmud al-Hasan and Maulana Madani there.[5] In the mid-1930s, differences developed over the proper administrative management of the seminary and the post of patron. The council of the school, called the Majlis-e Shūrā,[6] had to refer decisions to the patron in case it was divided on issues. The patron could force the shūrā to reconsider its majority decisions in case he was dissatisfied and gave good arguments against the decision. This post was held by the Shaykh al-Hind, Mahmud al-Hasan, until his death in 1920. In 1344 AH (1925) the majlis selected for this post Maulana Ṭhanawi who agreed after some initial hesitation. The relationship between the majlis and the patron was regularized in 1345 AH (1926). However, dissent over this post renewed a year later. The majlis faction opposing it interpreted reliance on a patron as 'helplessness of the majlis', calling it 'unneedful'. Instead, this majlis group pleaded 'to make the majority opinion as the pivot of decision' (Rizvi 1980/I: 222). A resolution of the majlis in Rajab, 1354 AH (1935) finally accepted Thanawi's resignation and requested him 'to cast his shadow always on the *Dāru'l-'ulūm* with his pious invocations and lofty favours'.[7] The political context of the removal of Thanawi from his post was to be seen in the debate over the merits of participation in politics. The majlis' decision was not only meant to reassert its democratic powers. It also supported political involvement of the seminary. Thanawi had opposed that, as he wanted

[4]'He (Sindhi) wanted to make the Dāru'l-'ulūm a centre of national organization politically of which the first step was the establishment of the Jam'īyat al-Anṣār' (Rizvi 1980/II: 44).

[5]Minault (1982: 28). Whether Sindhi was the moving force behind this initiative or Hasan, is not clear. Sindhi alleged he followed Hasan's orders (Sindhi 1970: 67; see also Sarwar 1967: 27–9). The conflict was also mentioned in his biographical sketch in the Deoband centenary history volume (Rizvi 1980/II: 44).

[6]For the history and powers of the Majlis-e Shūrā, see Rizvi 1980/II: 235ff. The council originally consisted of 7 religious scholars. The number stood at 18 at the time of the centenary celebrations. Its members ought to be drawn from all over the country. Out of these, at least 11 ought to be religious divines; the remaining ten members should be such persons who may have insight and expertise in administration and educational matters (Rizvi 1980/II: 235–7).

[7]*Rudād-e Majlis-e Shūrā* (30th *Rajab*, 1354 AH), quoted in Rizvi (1980/I: 222).

the school to concentrate on educational issues. Most majlis members found this difficult to accept at the time of nationalist and anti-colonial fervour in the country (cf. Nasr 2000).

The controversies over the implementation of participatory principles—or democratization—revealed the deep factionalism in these institutions. Most groups were split between a sometimes only comparatively more oppositional faction being (named first) and the loyalist. The Nadwa Seminary had the Shibli and the Khalilur Rahman Khan factions opposing each other. For the Deoband Seminary there was the pro-activist faction consisting of Sindhi, al-Hasan, and Madani, opposing the moderate leadership of the seminary. This cleavage was later followed by another split in the faculty in connection with the student revolt (discussed later in this section). At Firangī Maḥall there occurred a split between adherents of Abdul Bari and the Baḥru'l-'ulūm faction led by the brothers Abdul Hamid and Abdul Majid. The latter strongly objected to the extreme line taken by Bari over the Balkan wars and resigned from his Madrasa Niẕāmīya. They created, with government assistance, a madrasa of their own (Robinson 1994: 270–1). Among the Barelwis a certain polarization took place between the scholars and the pīrs of Badayun and the immediate followers of Ahmad Raza.[8] In Aligarh, the factionalism forced one pro-vice-chancellor from office (Dr Ziauddin) as a result of a reforms committee enquiry although he was later elected vice-chancellor. Factions were known from the Aḥmadīya when the Lahore group split off from the more loyalist parent body in 1914. Family rivalries beset the Aḥrār and the Ahl-i Ḥadīth. No major splits occurred among the Khāksārs and the Tablīghīs. Besides competition for influence and resources, this factionalism had also political overtones. The British openly instigated the polarization between a loyalist and an oppositional party. At times, they aided their supporters very directly with money, titles, property deeds, and pensions. From the political point of view, though, this intervention on the part of the British mostly backfired. The polarization often strengthened the radical or reforming party or helped it carry out its plans.

The democratization of the administration of Islamic schools was decisively pushed forward by student politics. Aligarh, Deoband, and the Nadwa saw incidents of student unrest, expressing itself in student strikes. These started on minor occasions but went on to express larger conflicts of interest pitting one faction against the other. The students were usually associated with the reform side. Reforms generally sought to achieve greater

[8]See for instance the a<u>d</u>ān debate, cf. f. 118.

transparency in decision-making and to strengthen the powers of the councils. Students also demanded a greater say in the affairs of the school. Old Boys' Associations and students' organizations were founded in order to implement such designs. As Aligarh, Deoband, and the Nadwa were founded on the express notion of loyalty, these strikes represented an extraordinary development. They questioned not only the patriarchal order of the founder generation of the schools, they were also potentially anti-colonial and nationalist in character as the British, who qualified them as 'rank sedition' viewed any form of unrest with suspicion and alarm.[9]

Aligarh pioneered the student strike in 1887 in a rather traditional form where the issue over which the strike started was very conservative. Aziz Mirza, secretary of the Siddons Union Club, a rather official and loyalist institution, was its leader. The protest was directed against restrictions on upper-class students (*ashrāf*) to discipline their local servants, in particular, through corporal punishment (Lelyveld 1996: 266–7, 338). The strike reflected resentment at the pervasive influence of English professors and Western culture. In response, college regulations were tightened on the personal insistence of Sayyid Ahmad Khan and through the Trustee Bill of 1888 cementing western influence. English teachers were now allowed to serve permanently on the staff and were paid their full expenses by the school (ibid.). The next student strike was more in line with the oppositional style of the rising nationalist movement. In 1907, on the occasion of an exhibition, a student had an altercation with a policeman. He used a stick against the policeman for which he was punished. When the students opposed the penalty in public, the 'ring leaders' were expelled from college. On this occasion the students resorted to the dramatic act of taking possession of the college and the boarding house. They stated that the college was theirs and there was no reason why they should leave it. In the end the dining hall and the college were closed down for some time.[10] Another students' strike occurred in 1936 against the suppression of nationalist activities at the college led by Ali Sardar Jafri and Jalil Abbasi (Hasan 1998a: 196, fn. 25). The subject reflected the changing tide of events. Nationalist students were pitched against the All-India Muslim Students' Federation (AIMSF). Alligned with the Muslim League, the latter acted as a conservative pressure group for the Pakistan movement and was to extend its influence to Aligarh. The AIMSF demanded the

[9]This was the formula used by Governor Meston when commenting on an article in the Nadwa academic journal advocating violent jihād in 1915 (Meston on 22 April 1915, in Nadwa file, 47f., quoted in Malik 1997: 358).

[10]Mir Wilayat Husain, '*Zātī Diary kē Chand Waraq*', *Aligarh Magazine*, Special Aligarh Number (Aligarh, 1953): 54–5, quoted in Iqbal (1974: 46–7). See also Moin (1976: 134–5).

removal of teachers holding 'socialistic' and 'atheistic' ideas. As a result, a few radical teachers were dismissed, some were told to fall in line, while others were eased out of administrative positions to be replaced by loyalists. Further demands included the removal of 'dangerous books', the re-introduction of parda (veiling) in order to strengthen a visibly Islamic identity of the Aligarh School, creating what Mushirul Hasan described as an atmosphere of 'religious frenzy' (ibid.).

The strike at Deoband started with the formation of a students' organization, the Lajnat al-Ittihād (Party of Unity) in 1344 AH (1925). It took exception to certain practices in the kitchen and was directed mainly against Maulwi Gul Muhammad Khan who was in charge of the kitchen and other administrative affairs. During the annual examination in the month of *Sha'ban* of 1344 AH (1926), Khan was manhandled, for which five students were rusticated, and the others warned. The students' party was declared illegal and considered a 'source of interference in the administration' (Rizvi 1980/I: 210). Unexpectedly, the disturbances not only revived the following year but also engulfed the whole faculty. One of the teachers, Maulana Anwar Shah Kashmiri, delivered two speeches at the local mosque in support of the students' demands and was joined by a number of other teachers.[11] Strikes and instances of manhandling, which seemed at variance with the self-proclaimed ethos of the seminary, nevertheless recurred. The response of the administration was twofold. The dissenters among the students and teachers were dealt with firmly through strictures and censures, not dissimilar to the colonial government's attitudes, and were eased out over time. The new rector, Tayyib, diffused the practical issues when he took office in 1348 AH (1929) and regularized administrative affairs, introducing *en lieu* a meal ticket system. The Deoband incident was remarkable for several reasons. The autonomous formation of a students' party was a daring act, which betrayed the politicizing influence of the nationalist movement. The sequence of events also appeared to suggest that the students' strike had pushed forward the reforms within the seminary. During the time of the crisis, the administrative rules of the seminary were reviewed with the patron, Thanawi, chairing the meeting. Again the same twin response was witnessed. An attempt was made to clamp down on dissent—giving wider powers to the management in this review process. At the same time, steps were taken to remove genuine grievances—a five-member executive committee of the majlis

[11]Besides Maulana Anwar Shah Kashmiri, the following teachers were believed to belong to the dissenting group sympathizing with the students, and who had to leave the Deoband Seminary, at least temporarily: Maulana Mufti Aziz al-Rahman, Maulana Shabbir Ahmad Uthmani, and Maulana Siraj Ahmad (Rizvi 1980/I: 211).

was appointed that would regularly attend to administrative matters and inspect the Dāru'l-'ulūm from time to time (Rizvi 1980/I: 211). Another remarkable feature of the protest was the reported violence, one of the few instances when such cases were reported from the tightly controlled environment of the religious schools. Student protest also continued in the years to come and continued to be a recurring feature before independence.[12]

At the Nadwa School, the link between students' strike and internal reform was even more obvious. Shibli Numani was reported to have instigated the students against the conservative administration when he was forced to step down from his office in 1914 (Malik 1997: 365–6). The strike was planned much in advance. Its leaders wanted to make the dissatisfaction of students very public so that wider circles would take notice of it. In 1913 they challenged the decisions of the managing committee of the council such as those concerning the abolition of three educational posts (*mu'tamad*) and the restrictive admission policy, which put at a disadvantage socially weaker applicants. The students demanded the convening of a national inquiry committee into the affairs of the seminary. The abolition of the mu'tamad posts was opposed by them because it helped strengthen the hand of the conservative new chairman, Khalilur Rahman Khan, the major opponent of Shibli. He was a timber merchant by profession and needed to rely more on the administrative powers of his office than on his intellectual clout. He was seen as having usurped the post in the wrangling of 1913–4. The actual students' strike started over an incident where a student was alleged to have insulted one of the teachers in February 1914. For this he was expelled. A third of the students signed a petition demanding his reinstatement. The management rejected the demands. In particular, it argued that a students' petition was not included in the legitimate forms of intervention in the statutes. It was also pointed out that a strike contravened the Islamic definition of the relationship between students and teachers, which was to be marked by obedience. The latter accusation was made the subject of a fatwā against the striking students, never to be published however. In this time of unrest, Maulana Azad staunchly defended the students through the columns of his paper *Hilāl*. His support also helped to blunt the Islamic critique as he was considered an authority on the doctrine and interpretation of Islam. He countered the arguments of the management with his own accusations that the new management neglected the demands of the sharī'a (ibid.:

[12]Maulana Muhammad Afzal-ul-Haq Johar Qasmi, '*Dāru'l-'ulūm kē dō Sāl: 1940–41*', published in 14 installments between December 1998 and January 2000 starting with *Tarjumān Dāru'l-'ulūm* (Deoband, 1998, no. 12), pp. 47–54.

372–4). An earlier strike had occurred in 1910 in response to the growing factionalism within the school, although it was a comparatively minor affair. The Nadwa student strikes were remarkable for their political nature and for the fact that they apparently were the first to take place in a religious school.

Anti-government student unrest was at the root of the foundation of the National Islamic University (Jām'iya Millīya Islāmīya) on the premises of the Aligarh College in 1920.[13] It first operated in a makeshift arrangement. It opened on the premise that it provided true Islamic education in a nationalist spirit. It was later to function on an expressly secular basis in independent India. Aligarh was targeted by the Jām'iya Millīya project because it refused to renounce government support.[14] As part of the Khilafat and non-cooperation movement, educational institutions were called upon to renounce government grants and affiliations. Deoband from its very inception had done so and solely relied on private money. Student agitation forced such a (temporary) decision on the Nadwa in 1920. This form of student politics was stretching the points of religious involvement to the overtly political joining in a much broader stream where the religious motive was one among many different factors feeding the nationalist movement.

These incidents of internal reforms, debates, cleavages, and student politics dealt with the consequences of modernity. They demonstrated that it was a difficult struggle involving a shift in the mental outlook of leaders and participants from the personal and patrimonial to the collective, national, and democratic. Islamic arguments were freely tailored to suit the needs of the activists. Their soul-searching poured out into factionalism. While new avenues and ways were opened, old structures and networks were not necessarily defeated. Many complained that the old influence-peddling of school leaders resumed after these crisis situations and continued unabated afterwards. Yet, the terms of reference changed and broader interests had to be considered in the conduct of educational affairs.

The pervasive and enduring influence of family and clan structures in the schools and movements demonstrated how limited success was. Over time, most groups came to be ruled by the descendants of a particular family or leader. All of them wanted to break with conventional ways of leadership when they started. Yet, they found it more convenient and practical to allow certain families and clans to monopolize control over

[13]For an overview of the establishment of the Jām'iya Millīya, see Mohammad Talib, 'Jamia Millia Islamia: Career of *āzād ta'līm*', in Hasan (1998a: 156–88).

[14]Local government had granted a Rs 500 allowance per month in 1908 for secular (*duniyāwī*) subjects. It was discontinued on 15 November 1920 (Jalis Nadwi and Tabriz Khan 1983/II: 53, 272).

their affairs. It would be too simplistic to write this off as a degenerative moment in the formation of these groups. Often the family model of leadership was legitimated with reference to Sufi chains of transmission (silsila) of spiritual power, or grace (baraka), in which ancestors played a significant role. The ancestors were naturally closer to the original inceptor of the spiritual tradition than the current generation and thereby highly valued for symbolizing the mission of the group. Handing down the leadership from the father to the son or some other descendant would guarantee the continuation of this tradition and the transfer of this spiritual power. The Sufi model in turn, as was discussed earlier, was instrumental in ensuring cohesion and loyalty among functionaries and members of the movement. Such extra source of loyalty—spiritual power in addition to normative religion and worldly ties—was apparently the more important in the contest of the Islamic groups in the public sphere. The groups had to keep united for survival and maximum impact in the Islamic sphere. These conditions furthered the re-emergence of family ties whenever the opportunity arose.

The Firangī Maḥall group was the one that most naturally and most openly relied on its extensive family network. They were the offspring of Mulla Qutbuddin. 'They trace(d) their ancestry through the great scholar and mystic, Khwaja Abdullah Ansari of Herat to Ayyub Ansari, the Prophet's host at Medina' (Robinson 2001: 70). The group was by definition an extended clan of the Ansari family. Over the years it had tended to become endogamous. The Firangī Maḥallīs made no secret of their devotion to the family tradition, as they openly cherished Sufism along with normative Islam (Inayatullah 1988).

When Sayyid Abdul Hayy took charge of the seminary as chairman of the Nadwa council (nāẓim) in 1915, he established a firm hold of the Hasani family on the institution, with his two sons soon following him in the office of chairman. They traced their line of tradition (silsila) back to Hasan ibn Ali, grandson of the Prophet, after whom they took the name Hasani (cf. Jalis Nadwi and Tabriz Khan 1983/II: 158ff.; Malik 1997: 390, 421, 385; Nadwi 1988b).

The Deoband seminary was also not free of clannish influences. The descendants of the family of the founder, Qasim Nanaotawi, kept a strong hold on the school throughout its history. His son, Maulana Hafiz Muhammad Ahmad (1862–1928), had stood at the helm of Deoband affairs for 30 years (1895–1925). His grandson, Qari Muhammad Tayyib, continued this tradition for more than 40 years (1929–82). When he was appointed first pro-rector in 1341 AH (1922), the council recounted the progress made by the seminary under his father. The argument used at that time is instructive for our analytical purpose.

Because of the progress made

> ... the obligation devolves upon the well-wishers of the *dāru'l-'ulūm* in general and on the *majlis-e shūrā* in particular that the administration of the *dāru'l-'ulūm* should be entrusted to a member of this family on the condition of ability and capacity so that the spiritual grace which has been helpful and useful in the advancement of the institution may continue.[15]

Family rule over Deoband resulted in intense factionalism with competing claims to resources and posts by family members and their opponents. These conflicts came to a head around 1980. Members of the Qasimi family were pitched against the relatives of Husain Ahmad Madani. Tayyib was forced from office in a rather disgraceful manner immediately after the centenary celebrations of the seminary. Members of the Qasimi family allegedly laid claim to the coveted post of chief executive, which was resisted by the Deoband management at the behest of the Madani family. As a result, Qasimi family members established a rival madrasa calling upon the courts to freeze the funds of both institutions. Maulana Marghubur Rahman has since asserted his position through his connections with Maulana Asad Madani, who heads the JUH, to whom he is related by the marriage of their children.[16] The rival Qasimi institution continued to function in the name of Dāru'l-'ulūm Waqf on new premises in Deoband.

Aligarh College and University were no exception either. Although aspiring to a secular and modernist mode of operation, the same clannish tradition emerged. Sayyid Mahmud succeeded his father Sayyid Ahmad Khan. The latter's grandson, Ross Masud, served as vice-chancellor of the institution.[17]

For the Barelwis, the transition of leadership from Ahmad Raza Khan to his eldest son, Hamid, and then to his younger son, Mustafa, was a natural succession. The Barelwis had always emphasized the importance of handing spiritual power down the family line. For them no particular conflict arose out of this. As their movement tended to be more decentralized, control over various schools and other institutions seemed to be more widely spread (Sanyal 1998: 645). On the contrary, Ahmad Raza made the transition as formal as possible when he appointed Hamid Raza Khan his shrine keeper in 1915 well before his death. As such he consciously established himself in his lifetime as a saint in a new line of

[15]'Register *tajāwiz-e majlis-e shūrā* (1340 AH)', in Rizvi (1980/I: 217).

[16]Based on information from interviews with Deoband graduates in January 2004. See also Nadvi (1986: 42); for earlier similar conflict, see ibid.: 39f.

[17]Nizami (1995: Chapters I, II, VII). See also the quarrel over the succession to Sayyid Ahmad Khan in 1889, which went in favour of his son Sayyid Mahmud when they were accused of treating Aligarh University as a family property (Lelyveld 1996: 270–2).

succession (silsila). Over time, Ahmad Raza's tomb became a shrine in its own right. As a place of pilgrimage it became more popular by the year. For the Sufi adepts who would seek out Hamid and Mustafa it was important to be sure that they too possessed the same power to grant blessings (baraka) as their father did. The formal succession of authority in the family was, therefore, instrumental for full recognition of their public roles.

From among the revivalist movements those following the Sufi style of transfer of power most closely were the Tablīghī Jamā'at and the Aḥmadīya. Before Muhammad Ilyas died he decided to make his son Maulana Muhammad Yusuf (1917–65) his successor (khalīfa). The movement's literature also referred to the special transition of spiritual power that took place on this occasion.[18] It reportedly instantly transformed the hitherto unwilling or disinterested son Yusuf into a leader. When he led prayer the next day, his aura made clear to all those present that he was now in confident command of the movement (Haq 1971: 161f.; Nadwi 1983). The Aḥmadī case was slightly more complicated. Ghulam Ahmad had chosen as his successor a close comrade-in-arms from the founding days of the movement, Maulwi Hakim Nuruddin. He was his first recognized spiritual disciple and successor (khalīfa) and took charge of the movement in 1908. Due to his early death in 1914 he was followed by Muhammad Ali. But Ghulam Ahmad had also consciously groomed his son Mahmud Ahmad for an eminent position in the movement. Mahmud though could not take it up immediately due to his young age. When he laid claim to the title of head of the community, the movement split up. Its Lahore wing came into being following Muhammad Ali. Adherents of the latter were less inclined to recognize a hereditary leadership for the community fearing it would further acerbate the isolation of the movement (Lavan 1976: 98ff.). Significantly the rules of the Aḥmadīya organization had stipulated that every head of the community would serve until his death and he himself would appoint his successor. This established a patriarchal leadership principle, which was at odds with many democratic elements in the movement.

The Ahl-i Ḥadīth was more heterogeneous in its genealogical composition. Their radical reformist claim of rejecting all law schools was more of an idealistic title descending from supposedly superior thinking. Yet, as the spread of the movement was partly very local with distinct centres of influence, these local regions saw the formation of Ahl-i Ḥadīth family trees.[19] The sectarian features they developed along with their social

[18]The Sufi expression given by Haq is *intiqāl-i niṣbat*—relocation of attribution (1971: 161).

[19]There was a preponderance of the Ghaznawi family in the Punjab Ahl-i Ḥadīth, for instance. I owe this suggestion to Martin Riexinger and his dissertation (2004).

distinctions and endogamous tendencies also contributed to the formation of extended clan structures and family trees.

The Aḥrār and the Khāksār movements laid comparatively less stress on a family succession in the leadership at the time. Their strongly political nature was responsible for this making their existence less permanent. Yet, when they were reduced to a fringe existence in independent Pakistan, it was again family relations that ensured their survival if only of a nominal character. The Khāksār leader Mashriqi's son Hamiduddin represents the party in today's Pakistan, just as Bukhari's son, Ataulmomin, represents the Aḥrār. The fact that the question of succession of leadership was not dealt with earlier might have contributed to the decline of the two parties.

4.1.2. *Participation Outside—The Public Life of Associations, Politics and Elections*

The religious scholars who were the major driving force behind the Islamic groups changed their position on public activism with the times. They remained largely aloof from public life during the first half of the nineteenth century when their involvement was limited to a dwindling number of public service positions on law and education, while a few of them took up militant activity in local jihād movements. During the next phase that started with the defeated uprising of 1857–8 and lasted approximately up to 1910, the scholars gave priority to the educational reconstruction of the religious spirit of the Muslim community. This activity led them inexorably into the public sphere. In this race the traditional scholars were overtaken by the 'modernists' of Sayyid Ahmad Khan and friends. The latter mainly used two public bodies for their purposes. The Muslim Educational Conference was devoted to finding ways for bringing Muslims up to the standard of other communities by providing them with better and more education. The Muslim League Party provided the political backing.

Around this time a distinct politicization and radicalization of Muslim public opinion took hold. Incidents of a supposed violation of religious rights of Muslims were used to express hostility towards British rule. Pan-Islamic concerns tinged by anti-British sentiments were growing. In the eyes of many Muslim activists, the Tripolitan and Balkan wars of 1911–13 led to a conflict between the Caliph residing in Turkey and the Christian rulers of India, the British. By this time, the 'ulamā' had started organizing themselves in educational and sectarian groups. They resented being shut out of public life. In order to challenge the hold of modernists on Muslim opinion, scholars steered religious groups to more public activity.

One form of this was the holding of annual conferences taking the cue from other public bodies.[20] Since everyone scrambled for a place in the public eye, public conferences were considered important as they also ensured extensive media coverage. The proliferation of the vernacular print media, notably in Urdu, was particularly valuable for the Islamic groups.

The development of an independent and sprawling associational life among the Islamic groups formed an important element and phase of their transformation into modern public bodies. Tables 2.1 and 2.2 provide an overview of the range of public bodies created by them. From among the religious bodies, the most early and regular associational life was organized by the Nadwa council and seminary. This was not surprising since the Nadwa started in 1893 as a coordinating council, which was an explicit public association, while the related seminary came into existence only some years later in 1898. Consequently, it was one of the first religious organizations to start publication of its proceedings and reports in a regular manner. The Nadwa partly constituted a response to the modernist Muslim Educational Conference. The associational life of the Deoband Seminary was more hesitant in the beginning. Its founder generation had eschewed unnecessary publicity in favour of devotion to teaching and study. This changed rather dramatically after the turn of the century under the influence of a few scholars with a highly activist outlook such as Ubaidullah Sindhi, Mahmud al-Hasan, and Madani. Their resort to public activism was ignited by the difficulties in achieving changes in the ways of teaching from inside the seminary. At their initiative and with their participation a number of projects were started, such as the Graduates Association (1909), the Qur'anic School at Delhi (1913), and the Association of Religious Scholars (1919) (see Table 2.1), which carried the Deobandi thought into the public realm and ultimately into politics. In the beginning, educational concerns still dominated their activism. Political concerns and schemes became more important by the time of World War I. Polarization and tension deepened between the cautious non-political and pro-British line of the Deoband administration and the activities of the group around Hasan and Sindhi. The latter was expelled from Deoband as an 'infidel' and both were engaged in a political intrigue against the British, in the 'silk letter conspiracy' (cf. section 4.3.5). This did not stop the latter from pursuing further anti-British schemes from a position of 'Islamic socialism'.

[20]The Tibbi (Muslim Health) Conference started in 1906, followed in 1910 by the All-India Ayurvedic and Unani Tibbia Conferences; the All-India Shi'a Conference met first in 1907. Others were Urdu Conferences for Muslims from Punjab, the United Provinces, and Bengal in 1910, to name but a few early ones with relation to Muslim public life (cf. Aziz 1993).

In Afghanistan, he associated himself with a recently formed 'Provisional Government' in exile and helped found a branch of the Congress Party. The Congress government in the United Provinces only lifted the ban on Sindhi's return in 1937 and he returned the following year (1358 AH).[21]

But Deoband also had to submit to the demands of public associational life. The convocation ceremony, which had not taken place for 26 years, was held once again in grand style in 1909 (Rizvi 1980/I: 173). From that year on annual ceremonies were held. Also the council sessions were marked by more regularity and openness to the public, partly through the publication of its record in the rūdād. The most influential public association ever created by the religious scholars of Islam was the JUH, which in the beginning was a truly joint endeavour of various schools of thought. The Firangī Maḥallī scholar, Abdul Bari, worked together with Sulaiman Nadwi from the Nadwa, the Ahl-i Ḥadīth scholar, Thanaullah Amritsari, and the Deobandi divines, Mahmud al-Hasan and Madani. Scholars from Deoband dominated the proceedings since 1922. Its first and long-time president (1919–38) was the eminent Deobandi 'ālim Mufti Kifayatullah (1875–1952) (Bukhari 1988: 117ff.). Deoband and the JUH shared some facilities, as in proselytization (tablīgh). Deobandi scholars were also heavily engaged in the activities of the All-India Khilafat conference (1919), which oversaw the campaign for the defence of the Ottoman Caliphate. The same Mufti Kifayatullah moved a resolution to boycott the British peace celebrations at the 1919 Khilafat conference in Delhi (Bukhari 1988: 117). Another Deobandi 'ālim deeply involved in Khilafat activities was Maulana Madani. He was prosecuted and arrested (1921–3) for supporting the Karachi resolution. In fact, the JUH was founded on the sidelines of the 1919 Delhi Khilafat conference. Their organizational structure was very similar and shadowed that of the big parties. The Khilafatists also organized annual conferences, a central all-India Khilafat Committee and several provincial chapters holding their own provincial Khilafat conferences and running their provincial committees. Khilafat committees were, at least at the height of the campaign, jointly administered by Muslim League activists, Muslim functionaries of the Congress, 'nationalist' Muslims (in contrast to 'communalist' Muslims), and by JUH scholars (Qureshi 1999: 96, 121ff., 169, 470–1).

For the Barelwis, associational life often developed out of their doctrinal differences with other schools of Islam and their perceived need to assert themselves in the Islamic sphere. Most of their public bodies were created to counter existing reformist organizations or to defend

[21]See Rizvi (1980/I: 228).

themselves. From the perspective of our evaluation of the public sphere, their public activism was directed at claiming their own share of the Islamic sphere, which they felt the Deobandis, in particular, were denying them. To counter the Nadwa they started convening sessions of their Ahl-e Sunnat conference in 1896. Their missionary society Jamāʿat-i Raẓā-i Muṣṭafā meant to balance the JUH, particularly in contrast to the latter's cooperation with the Hindus. The 1921 Anjuman-i Anṣār al-Islām was set up as a loyalist response to the oppositional Khilafat conference (cf. section 4.2.2). In view of the apparent political success of the JUH, the Barelwis also felt the need to convene a more political-minded gathering, the All-India Sunni Conference in 1925 (Qadiri 1997, 1999). The founding session at Muradabad elected Pir Jamaat Ali Shah (1840–1951) as president and Maulana Sayyid Muhammad Naimuddin Muradabadi as general secretary (*nāẓim-i aʿlā*) (Qadiri 1997: 85). It was the example of a meeting turned into a public body. It held three major sessions before independence. It was instrumental in organizing Barelwi support for the Pakistan movement in the 1940s. Part of Barelwi associational life developed in close connection with worship activities at shrines. Larger shrines constituted traditional centres of pilgrimage. The annual festival of the saints (urs) was a convenient occasion to meet likeminded scholars, shaykhs, and pīrs.[22]

The Firangī Maḥall group would perhaps have stayed aloof from public activism by virtue of its very traditional and personal style of operation but for Abdul Bari. Due to his enormous charisma and his towering personality, he succeeded in drawing the Firangī Maḥall into Islamic politics. Yet, other members of the seminary, like the Baḥru'l-ʿulūm faction, followed with great hesitation. As has been mentioned, Bari pioneered Islamic activism through several of his initiatives. He revived the Majlis Mu'ayyid al-Islām and ventured into political territory with his Anjuman-i Khuddām-i Kaʿba (cf. section 4.2.1). His friendship with the Ali brothers dating from 1913 appeared to be most productive for Islamic activism. In 1918 he led a delegation of scholars to the Muslim League conference. He contributed significantly to the inception of the Khilafat Movement, with its offspring, the Central Khilafat Committee and the JUH (Robinson 2001: 154ff.).

For the Ahl-i Ḥadīth, being more a sectarian affiliation by the turn of the century than a public body, the convening of the All-India Ahl-i

[22]In 1909, Sufi pīrs started to meet at the annual ʿurs ceremony at the famous shrine of Muinuddin Chishti (1141–1236) in Ajmer for consultations. Local Sunni conferences convened in the 1920s in Karachi, Bareilly, and Muradabad under the name of Anjuman-e Ahl-e Sunnat (cf. Sanyal 1996a: 89–90 and *passim*).

Ḥadīth Conference was a rather surprising act. It did not necessarily derive from its earlier, mainly scholarly activity. Yet, at a closer look, their leaders tried to assert their influence in public bodies very pointedly. They exerted a rather strong influence on the affairs and debates of the Nadwa pushing forward reformist educational concerns and at several junctures supporting the reformism of Shibli. They had earlier gained a strong foothold in several local Islamic educational organizations, among them the influential Anjuman-i Ḥimāyat-i Islām (Society for the Support of Islam, 1885) in Lahore. This was due to the influence of Thanaullah Amritsari who for them played a similar role as Bari did for the Firangī Maḥall. He involved himself deeply in several public activities, sat at the Nadwa council, worked in the Muslim League, helped found the JUH, and worked for the Congress Party in the 1920s. He had also initiated the Ahl-i Ḥadīth conference back in 1906, which started convening regularly after 1912 (Reetz 2001b: 92–3).

The Aḥmadīya shared in all these forms of public associational life and developed them even further. The reason for their reliance on an extensive network of associations lay in the legal status derived from their registration. It gave them a measure of security and protection for their religious activity otherwise not easily available in the face of their growing isolation and the ongoing controversies with the mainstream Sunni groups. The first of such bodies was their annual meeting at the seat of their group in Qadiyan, which became a sort of an annual pilgrimage for many faithful. It served to reaffirm them in their faith against all adversities and helped their ideological indoctrination. As such it was less public than directed inwards (Friedmann 1989). But most of their other associations were public, and fiercely so, as they sought out confrontation with and conversion of doubting and inquiring non-Aḥmadī minds. This tallied with their obligation that every Aḥmadī was given a target of converting to their faith at least one person per year (Ahmed 1980).

The Aḥrār and Khāksār—as they were founded at a later time, in 1929 and 1931 respectively—came into being immediately in a dual capacity as religious groups and registered public associations while other groups took some time in going public. There was almost a full convergence of their public life with their religious activities. A third common dimension of their formation and activity was their militancy. They understood themselves to be more 'soldiers of Islam' than ordinary believers. Their militancy was not yet of the terrorist variety although it included street actions and deliberate and planned violent confrontations.

With regard to the formation of the public sphere it was important that most Islamic groups relied on a locally highly diversified public life. Most of them sported a significant number of local branches proliferating across India. These often took the character of a pervasive support network. Before the Barelwis formed all-India bodies there existed dozens of local Sunni conferences and continued to do so afterwards. The same was true of the many local ḥadīth conferences. The seminaries created extensive local support networks. The Nadwa had its local helpers' associations and so did the Deobandis (see Table 2.1); the latter also had an ever-growing number of affiliated local mosques mainly in north India, but also beyond. The Firangī Maḥallī network operated through family members and graduates taking up teaching and clerical positions across India and abroad. Those networks laid the foundation for expansion beyond the borders of India. Today, many of them aspire to a global reach. The networks were first extended to neighbouring countries such as Afghanistan. They then expanded to areas where expatriate Indian Muslim communities existed, as in East and South Africa where the Deobandi branches emerged early on. Islamic groups started connecting more frequently with Arabic countries in the 1920s, thus creating another channel for the proliferation of their influence and networks.

Beyond developing public forms of associational life, the 'ulamā' also discussed taking part in formal politics. This discussion did not make much headway before the 1919 Government of India Act. Beyond educational concerns they were mainly busy with pan-Islamic activism. After the creation of the Muslim League, a reconciliation of religious scholars and modernists was attempted. This contributed to the Hindu–Muslim accord of 1916 between the Congress and the Muslim League on constitutional reform, which came to be known as the Lucknow Pact. It envisaged separate electorates and a scheme of special Muslim representation in the legislatures.

The Khilafat and non-cooperation campaign started in 1919 declared a boycott of elections to the new legislative councils, which were to be held every three years starting from 1920. The intention of non-cooperation was to make impossible a government of India that relied on the assistance of the Indians. The campaigns wanted to make the British realize that their rule of a tiny minority over the vast majority of the Indian people rested entirely on the latter's cooperation. The fatwā of non-cooperation (cf. section 4.3.3) given by the 'ulamā' of the JUH provided doctrinal arguments why British rule was un-Islamic and why it was prohibited under Islamic law to cooperate with the enemies of religion.[23] This fatwā also prohibited 'council entry' as the participation in elections to the legislatures and in their legislative business came to be known in the print media.

[23]On speeches of Islamic activists such as Maulana Azad, Muhammad and Shaukat Ali, Dr Ansari, and Maulana Salamatullah in the course of the Non-Cooperation and Khilafat campaign, cf. UPSA Boxes 58, /A, /B.

During the Khilafat and non-cooperation campaign the JUH was politically aligned with the Congress Party. In the course of 1923 when the next council elections were approaching differences emerged. In January, the Swarajist Party[24] favouring a dominion status for India formed within the Congress and threatened to split off. This party was in favour of participation in the elections. Its members wanted to use the legislatures to put pressure on Britain to grant a dominion status to India immediately. Apparently, there was also a social background to these developments. Nationalist representatives of the new professional classes were eager to put an end to the boycott campaign and use the privileges and chances that would be available with the new constitutional reforms of the 1919 Act to further their own social status.

The same situation applied in the Islamic camp. As many as 78 candidates in the 1923 council elections held titles such as maulawi or maulwi. Their participation ran counter to the JUH policy opposing Muslim candidatures in 1923.[25] Yet few religious scholars of repute participated, one maulana (Muhammad Amin, Central Provinces) and one shamsu'l-'ulamā' (Rafiuddin Ahmad Imamuddin, Bombay). The title of maulwi pointed more to the lower ranks of the clergy. The largest contingents of maulwi candidates came from the small district towns of Bengal, Bihar and Orissa. As Maulana Madani in his address to the 1923 annual JUH session indicated, there were requests for a separate fatwā legitimating council entry, in case the scholars were not ready to withdraw or modify their non-cooperation fatwā (cf. section 4.3.3). He argued that the Congress was well within its rights as a secular organization to change its laws and programmes according to circumstances. The interpretation of Islamic law, which was embodied in the fatwā, could not be changed at a whim since the sources of Islamic law were considered immutable. Some proposed that participation in the elections should be used to block the seats, he recounted. Deputies should then resign before taking oath.[26] Others recommended entering the councils and opposing the government from within. If this opposition proved ineffective, they would leave the councils. Now it appeared that those were only pretexts. The new argument

[24]Its full name was Congress Khilafat Swarājīya Party, led by C. R. Das; about 110 members of the All-India Congress Committee signed its manifesto (*IAR* 1923/II: 1).

[25]Other appellations included shaykh, nawab, sayyid, shams-ul-'ulamā'. There were seven such candidates from the United Provinces, seven from Punjab, 12 from Bihar and Orissa, one from the Central Provinces, 11 from Assam, two from Madras Presidency, five from Bombay Presidency, 33 from Bengal (UK Parliamentary Papers 1924, Cmd. 2154).

[26]This had been the compromise position temporarily held by the executive committee of the JUH in November 1922, although the 1922 annual JUH session rejected council entry in Gaya in December the same year (*IAR* 1922/I: 941).

was that the councils should function properly in order to 'work for the rights of the community/nation (*farīqānā ḥuqūq*)' (Rozinah 1981/I: 224).

> But from the point of view of Islamic law (*sharī'a*) this cannot find support. Even if the community interests are being defended (in the councils) one would be forced to support (British) policies of enmity to Islam, of aggression and violence. The Qur'an says...you should support each other in virtuous deeds and kindness and not in reprehensible acts and misdeeds. As this is emphasised in so many different places in the Qur'an in strong words...there is no reason why a *fatwā* should confirm the legality of council entry (ibid.: 224–5).

The argument about the rights of the community (farīqānā ḥuqūq) was apparently adapted from the Congress Swarajist Party's intention to work from within the councils for India's freedom. These early differences between the Congress and the JUH have rarely been discussed in academic literature. But the hesitation of the 'ulamā' to join the councils was also based on the state of affairs in the Khilafat campaign by the end of 1923. The campaign had lost some of its arguments after the Treaty of Lausanne was concluded, which granted part of their demands regarding the future status of the Ottoman Caliphate. But they were not easily convinced to give up their hopes for the revival of the Caliphate.

Muslim voters' participation significantly increased between the 1921 and the 1923 elections. This may have been partly due to the boycott call for the 1921 election by the non-cooperation and Khilafat campaign. However, it is remarkable that Muslim voter participation was well above average in 1923 while it was significantly below average in 1921.[27] Apparently, Muslims followed the election boycott pronounced by the Khilafat and non-cooperation campaign more faithfully than other communities. The formation and articulation of a Muslim public and of an Islamic public sphere took a huge leap at the time.

At the 1925 session of the JUH, Maulana Abu'l Hasan Muhammad Sajjad Naqshbandi made a long argument in favour of political involvement of the 'ulamā' as a lesson to be drawn from the abolition of the Caliphate. The success of secular nationalism in Turkey was interpreted as an outflow of Western ideas. Naqshbandi saw the reason for such developments in the neglect of politics by the 'ulamā'. They had left the field open to

[27]For the United Provinces, for instance, average voter participation compared to the overall number of electors was 33 per cent in 1921 whereas for Muslim urban seats it was 9 per cent and for Muslim rural seats 28 per cent, showing a much stricter observance of non-cooperation by Muslim urban voters. In 1923, these figures had changed to 42.2 per cent for average voter participation, 49.1 per cent for Muslim urban seats, 54.8 for Muslim rural seats. The same pattern could be observed in other provinces with separate Muslim constituencies (UK Parliamentary Papers 1927, Cmd. 2923).

other forces and influences inimical to religion. This had to be corrected by active participation in future elections. Political positions needed to be used to advance the demands for an Islamic system, an Islamic society for Muslim India, and of course also needed to include demands for independence, as this was a precondition for following the dictates of religion. Summing up the situation, Naqshbandi warned:

> The situation of the world of Islam and especially events in India with which we are faced, their grounds and causes as much as their results and consequences give Muslims bad news of tremendous magnitude. If we do not very soon take care of Islam and of Muslims then rest assured that Islam and Muslims will be uprooted by the forces of idol-worship. Together with this I'm equally certain that if any force in India exists at present that can give protection from all this destruction it is only the *Jam'īyatu'l-'Ulamā'*. Because, whatever misfortunes are besetting Muslims it is only for the non-observance (rejection) of the *sharī'a*. If it is ever possible to repel them it is only through strict adherence to the *sharī'a* (Rozinah 1981/I: 245).

The anxiety of the 'ulamā' reflected the heightened inter-religious tension in India between Muslims and Hindus, the tremendous increase in 'communal' riots in 1924–5, in combination with the reclamation campaign of the Hindus reformist group, the Āryā Samāj. Those were aggravated by developments in Turkey. Islam, as they saw it, lost its last temporal powers of military might and political influence. The élite of India's Muslim minority had often felt the need to look for extraneous support against the non-Muslim majority in its own country. Now they feared they were left defenceless at the mercy of the majority. 'Had the '*ulamā*' and learned men of religion remained active in politics, the situation would not have reached such a state where the modern-educated intellectuals regard the Caliphate as impractical and unnecessary', Naqshbandi lamented (ibid.: 257). While there was much literature on the conventional issues of Islam, on judicial matters, the biography of the Prophet (sīra) and some on the principles of Islamic government (*imāmat*), the religious experts had largely neglected the sphere of politics, he complained. In particular he resented that there were few works on Islamic governance (*niẓām al-Islām*) (ibid.: 259). It was important and reflected the changed circumstances of 1925 that Naqshbandi did not relate the participation of the 'ulamā' in politics to the removal of British rule, as was done earlier, but to the establishment of an Islamic system. He suggested a number of principles for an Islamic system, which will be detailed in section 4.1.3.

The 1937 elections under the Government of India Act, 1935, were the first to be contested on a party basis.[28] The JUH, the Majlis-i Aḥrār,

[28] The Congress was victorious. After receiving assurances that the governors would not act as rival centres of power it assumed office in six provinces in July 1937. Due to the

and the Muslim Conference cooperated with the Muslim League in setting up a joint Muslim Parliamentary Board, nominating candidates for Muslim constituencies. Apparently, due to the mediation of the JUH some understanding was reached between the Congress and the Muslim, League (cf. Qureshi 1974: 348). The language of their manifestos was similar, emphasizing secular goals of making India a free and welfare state. For this purpose they would cooperate in the provincial legislatures and form coalition governments where the Muslim League expected a share of seats according to the proportion of the Muslim population in that province. Candidates of the Muslim Board fared poorly in these elections and the Congress secured absolute majorities in five provinces with options for Congress ministries in several other provinces. The Congress' domination was particularly ill-received by the Muslim League in the United Provinces where it achieved a better representation and its board candidates captured 27 out of 64 ordinary Muslim seats (Taylor 1972: 360).

Talks for a coalition ministry in the United Provinces broke down over the Congress' demand that Muslim League members joining a coalition ministry give up their independence and sign the Congress pledge. It was from that moment really that the Muslim League and the Congress went in different and even opposite ways, leading to the break-up of the country. The spurned Muslim League took up the cause of grievances of the Muslim minorities under provincial Congress ministries. I. H. Qureshi described the ensuing internal manoeuvrings in the JUH arguing that by isolating office bearers more independent of Congress pressure (Mufti Kifayatullah and Maulana Ahmad Said) and installing leaders more willing to compromise (Maulana Hifzur Rahman Seoharwi and Maulana Bashir Ahmad from the United Provinces), the JUH was made to accept this change of heart on behalf of the Congress. What Qureshi was suggesting, in fact, was that Seoharwi and Bashir Ahmad personally gained from a Congress ministry in the United Provinces,[29] so

parliamentary defeat of the Muslim League ministry in the North-West Frontier Province, a Congress ministry took office there in the same month. A Congress-led coalition was set up in Assam in 1938 (for detailed results see Taylor 1972: 346ff.; UK Parliamentary Papers 1937, Cmd. 5589). The Congress ministries resigned in 8 provinces in 1939 due to differences over India's status in the British war effort against Germany. The Congress resented that Britain had automatically committed India to the war effort against Germany without consulting its political representatives.

[29]A relative of Maulana Hifzur Rahman Seoharwi, Maulana Hafiz Muhammad Ibrahim was elected to the United Prvoinces legislature and became a minister of the United Provinces cabinet after he left the League. Maulana Bashir Ahmad allegedly received big contracts for his brick mill under the Congress ministry (Qureshi 1974: 350). See also M. Hasan for the circumstances of Khaliquzzaman when he changed sides and turned from a Khilafatist and Congressman into a Muslim Leaguer out of anger over these machinations (1998a: 199).

that they were practically bribed into accepting the isolation of the Muslim League. Maulana Kalam Azad led negotiations on behalf of the Congress, while Maulana Husain Ahmad Madani of Deoband (and a JUH leader) was apparently also in the picture.

The Muslim League did not succeed in establishing its credentials as the sole representative of Indian Muslims in those elections. It secured only 106 (plus five specialized mandates) of a total of 482 ordinary Muslim seats.[30] Its numbers were even surpassed by two regional outfits, the Unionist Party from Punjab and the Praja Party from Bengal, together totalling 130 seats. Still the League emerged as the single largest Muslim party with some real organization and structure. The religious scholars dabbling in politics did not succeed in playing an independent political role. The Aḥrār Party had won five seats: three Muhammadan Rural seats in Bihar and two Muhammadan Urban seats in Punjab. Local Muslim representation included the Muslim Party in Assam (24 seats), a motley collection of small groupings; the Muslim Parliamentary Board (Rauf Shah Group) in the Central Provinces (eight); and the Muslim Progressive Party in Madras (one) (Taylor 1972: 346ff.). Religious political demands for the introduction of elements of an Islamic system could not be advanced. The 'ulamā' became increasingly sandwiched between the two opposing party blocks. Maulana Azad on behalf of the Congress had offered the scholars an understanding that they would be given greater leeway on administering elements of an Islamic system for the Muslim community, particularly in relation to Muslim personal law in interpreting the sharī'a, if they supported the demands of the Congress on keeping independent India united. The 'ulamā' had hoped that the Congress would give them charge of a Muslim legal system and appoint Muslim judges (qāḍī) from among them. While such a prospect seemed enormously attractive to the 'ulamā' (as a renewed area of potential employment and, therefore, significance) it never materialized (Qureshi 1974: 346).

The Congress and the 'ulamā' allied with it tried to challenge the Muslim League assertion that it was the sole representative of Muslims in India. They floated nationalist Muslim organizations such as the Nationalist Muslim conference with provincial branches headed by Maulana Azad in 1929 (*IAR* 1929/II: 350–1). Those ran parallel to the Muslim conferences supporting a pro-League position. Pro-Congress bodies created for participation in elections included the Muslim Nationalist Party (*IAR* 1931/I: 295–307); the Azad Muslim Board (*IAR* 1942/I: 334f.) and Azad Muslim Conferences (*IAR* 1942/II: 110); the Nationalist Muslim

[30]These included the unspecified Muhammadan Urban and Muhammadan Rural constituencies (Taylor 1972).

Parliamentary Board and Muslim Majlis in 1943–5 (*IAR* 1943/II: 299; *IAR* 1945/II: 163f). But their influence among Muslims remained negligible. Attempts by the pro-Congress 'ulamā' to coordinate Muslim public opinion in view of the constitutional reforms process through the All-Parties Muslim Conference were boycotted by the Jinnah League (*IAR* 1928/II: 409–17). The JUH made a last-ditch attempt to prevent partition with its so-called Madani formula at its Saharanpur session in 1945. Resolution 11 proposed the acceptance of a national government at the centre with strong safeguards for Muslim interests through the upper house of Parliament where Hindu and Muslim members would have parity representation of 45 each with 10 seats for minorities. The government would not be able to pass any bill which was opposed by two-thirds of the Muslim members. The same parity approach would be applied to the nomination of Supreme Court judges (Rozinah 1981/II: 823).

The pro-Congress 'ulamā' from the JUH had gone far in their opposition to the Pakistan scheme and Muslim League politics. In a fatwā, Mufti Kifayatullah considered the demand for Pakistan injurious (*muẓir*) to Muslims as it disregarded the interests of those who had to remain in a minority in India proper.[31] Madani called the Muslim League a reactionary party (*raj'at-pasand*) and severely criticized its religious credentials (Rozinah 1981/II: 811–13).[32] The Aḥrār 'ulamā' opposed the Pakistan scheme and partition on similar lines in 1940 (Mirza 1975/IV: 288–89). Several attempts were made to reconcile the 'ulamā' and the Muslim League. But the League took the same uncompromising attitude as the Congress. When Kifayatullah on behalf of the JUH approached Jinnah in 1940 for cooperation the latter demanded that JUH scholars resign their membership of the Congress and join the Muslim League. Kifayatullah allegedly agreed on condition that the Muslim League radicalize its demands for an independent India, which Jinnah refused (Qureshi 1974: 357f.). The JUH was not alone in failing to get a sympathetic hearing from the big party blocks of the Congress and the Muslim League. The same fate befell the Khāksār's, the Aḥrār Party, and the All-Parties Shi'a Conference when they tried to negotiate their relationship with the two. Other minority groups also faced this problem, among them the Akali Dal representing

[31]For the facsimile of the handwritten fatwā see Qadiri (1997: 63). Madani made a similar argument saying that the demand was not in the best interest of the Muslims (*mufīd nahīñ*) (see facsimile in ibid.: 59). For an early rejection of the Pakistan scheme by the JUH, see their 1942 session where Madani's statement caused an uproar in the audience (*IAR* 1942/I: 330f.).

[32]In 1945, Madani made yet another proposal to reconcile various Muslim interests on the basis of a united free India (Rozinah 1981/II: 821–3). But he was unable to impress the Muslim League and its allies.

the Sikhs and the Pakhtun party, the Khudā-ī Khidmatgarān, also known as the Red Shirts.[33] The struggle for power and the prospects of an independent India were now dominating the dynamics of political developments. The League and the Congress were building their blocks as mighty and cohesive as possible.

With the Pakistan movement gaining momentum, a small group of Deobandi scholars split off from the JUH under the leadership of Maulana Shabbir Ahmad Uthmani (1885–1949). They set up the Jam'īyat-e 'Ulamā'-ye Islām (JUI/Association of Religious Scholars of Islam) on 31 October 1945. The JUI recognized that the Muslim League was the 'only representative political organisation and spokesman of Muslim India capable of delivering goods on behalf of the Muslim nation'.[34] Although representing only a section of the reformist 'ulamā', it was able to convene several large meetings mobilizing scholars from various schools of thought. Deobandi, Barelwi, Ahl-i Ḥadīth, and Firangī Maḥallī scholars attended their Lahore meeting of January 1946. Maulana Muhammad Zahir Qasimi,[35] the grandson of Nanaotawi, the founder of the Deoband School, was one of the main attractions of the Conference. The party eventually migrated to Pakistan and became the public body and political party of Deobandi scholars there (cf. Hasan 1997: 92ff.).

The Muslim League also mobilized religious leaders of popular and Sufi-based Islam, the pīrs and *mashā'ikh*, especially in Punjab.[36] In 1946 they formed a committee of pīrs and mashā'ikh, which included reformist shrine keepers such as the pirs of Golra Sharif (Sayyid Ghulam Muhyuddin), and Zakori Sharif (Muhammad Abdul Latif).[37] Although the respective

[33]For the Aḥrār, see *IAR* 1944/I: 240–41; for the Khāksār, Mathur (1972: 218ff.); for the Shi'a conference, see *IAR* 1944/II: 230, 1945/I: 160–2; for others cf. Reetz (1997).

[34]Resolutions of the All-India Jam'īyat-e 'Ulamā'-ye Islām Conference, Calcutta, 31 October 1945, *Freedom Movement Archives* (Karachi), Box No. 56, quoted in Hasan (1997: Appendix C, 345).

[35]He called upon Muslims to support the Muslim League as 'the *millat* is involved in a life and death struggle, when enemies of Islam have challenged the integrity of the millat, are openly denying the very existence of Mussalmans as a separate nation, are trying to wipe out all the fundamental principles that go to distinguish Islam from heresy, are making nefarious designs to enslave the Muslim nation and are out to destroy the very idea of establishing an independent Muslim state' (*Freedom Movement Archives* [Karachi], in Hasan 1997: 92, fn. 172).

[36]On the support of religious leaders of the Barelwi orientation for the Pakistan Movement in Punjab, see David Gilmartin, 'Religious Leadership and the Pakistan Movement in the Punjab', in Hasan (1993: 196–229).

[37]The Muslim League published an impressive list of shrine keepers and 'ulamā' supporting the campaign of its candidates in its election propaganda leaflet *Ḥaẓrat Ṣūfīya-e Kirām kā Elān-i Ḥaqq: Sirf Muslim League kī Ḥimāyat Karo* (Declaration of Truth by the

Muslim League poster also contained the names of three Deobandi and two Ahl-i Ḥadīth scholars (Qadiri 1997: 41), the vast majority followed the Barelwi School, which through its All-India Sunni Conference (AISC) had supported the Muslim League since around 1937 and the Pakistan demand when it was made in 1940. An impressive 500 mashā'ikh, 7000 'ulamā', and 200,000 followers gathered for the third AISC session in April 1946 in Banares (Qadiri 1997: 252). On its eve, the AISC had published a joint fatwā on Pakistan (ibid.: 338). Even then the pro-Pakistan 'ulamā' of various schools did not unite. In 1946, the AISC session in Karachi dubbed the split-off JUI led by Maulana Uthmani as Congress 'fifth columnists' (ibid.: 330ff.).

Due to the war the next elections to the Central Legislative Assembly and the Provincial Assemblies under the 1935 Constitutional Act were not held until 1945–6. The polls established the League in a position of superiority regarding Muslim constituencies. In the Central Legislature it got 40 seats compared to 303 for the Congress (*IAR* 1946/I: 229). The League now staked its claim to a national status, which brought it into the temporary national government with the Congress. In the Provincial Legislatures it secured 426 out of the 482 ordinary Muslim seats, a more than fourfold increase over 1937. The Congress gained an outright victory in six provinces and was able to form ministries in eight. The JUH and other Muslim parties—all representing a pro-Congress orientation—remained marginalized even though they increased their presence significantly: The JUH secured nine seats; the Aḥrār got one, the Nationalist Muslims six, and the Momin Conference five. Remnants of the Punjab Unionist Party managed to secure 20 seats (Kuwajima 1998: 216–32). Central legislators convened separately as the two blocks embarked on parallel constitution-making. The Islamic groups were unable to influence the character of both independent India and Pakistan when partition was effected on 14 August 1947. Congress-dominated legislators adopted an 'Objectives Resolution' in consonance with the Congress creed on 22 January 1947 (Mehra 1987: 154). In Pakistan's Constituent Assembly, the JUI joined other religious parties in campaigning for the 'Objectives Resolution' of 1949, which laid down Islamic guidelines for a future constitution of Pakistan, thus hoping to ensure that it would become a truly Islamic state (cf. Khan 1995b: 141).

Venerable Sufis: Reserve Support for the Muslim League), Publicity and Information Department: Punjab Muslim League; see facsimile of different versions in Qadiri (1997: 42–4); also cf. Hasan (1997: 92–3).

4.1.3. *Proposals for an Islamic Polity*

The public activism of religious scholars was accompanied by an increasingly public discourse on the contours of an Islamic system for India's Muslims. It was closely linked to the one led on the Indian nation. The nation discourse questioned whether Muslims constituted a separate nation, the Muslim League position, or formed part of a composite Indian nation, the Congress position (cf. section 4.3.2). Most religious scholars argued that the Muslim League's demands for Muslim nationalism were worthless unless backed up by the implementation of an Islamic system. Therefore, the Muslim League faced much resistance from the scholars of Islam. The Congress on the other hand, promised much more autonomy and influence for the dictates of religion if the scholars of Islam supported its demands for a united India in which Muslims would work and live with other religions and cultures. The Islamic system proposed by the scholars of the JUH was non-territorial in nature, concentrating on principles and elements applicable to all Muslims in India irrespective of their place of residence. One element of this plan was the creation of an office of a leader of all Indian Muslims, the Amīr al-Hind, or Amīr al-Islām, a post to which various people had aspired (Maulana Azad and Abdul Bari, among others).[38] To some extent the amīr was also to be assigned temporal powers relating to justice, education, etc. This would amount to a parallel administration for Indian Muslims.

At the Lahore session in November 1921, Maulana Azad pleaded with the JUH for the creation of such a post. Yet, he could not convince the scholars to elect him. In view of the controversy, a sub-committee was constituted to discuss the powers and duties of an amīr. It consisted of the Maulanas Kifayatullah (the JUH president), Subhanullah, Sayyid Murtaza Hasan, Muhammad Fakhar, Abdul Majid, Muhammad Sajjad, and Abdul Halim Siddiqi (deputy nāẓim of the JUH) (see Appendix III). The most Azad could get was a commitment to discuss the report of the sub-committee at the Badayun session of the JUH executive committee in December 1921 (Rozinah 1981/I: 132). At the December 1922 session at Gaya, the speaker Maulana Habibur Rahman Deobandi (d. 1929) prevaricated on the issue. While he stressed the urgency of appointing an amīr for India, he indicated that the decisions of the sub-committee, which by then had already debated the issue, might not be practical. The speaker personally gave preference to the election of provincial amīrs first so that the scheme could be tried out there. If there was a failure in one province it could be compensated in another. Yet, he feared that if there

[38]On the theological aspects of these leadership ambitions, see section 3.3.

was failure on the all-India level the scheme would be finished 'for ever' (Rozinah 1981/I: 185). The meeting also felicitated Azad for his special services to the JUH, for his patience in the face of arrest. This prominent mention seemed to be a trade-off for the refusal to elect him as Amīr al-Hind (Rozinah 1981/I: 185). The report was not acted upon at the February 1922 executive meeting 'for want of a quorum' (Hardy 1971: 32).

But the project continued. Maulana Naqshbandi dwelt at length on the principles of an Islamic system in his 1925 JUH address (Rozinah 1981/I: 245ff.). Maulana Anwar Shah Kashmiri discussed the duties of an amīr or Islamic chief justice (qāḍī) in his 1927 address to the JUH meeting (ibid.: 431). While no agreement was achieved on this post and suitable candidates for it, the JUH had designated Maulana Madani as Shaykh al-Islām in 1921. This was an honorific title and yet it laid claim to some sort of spiritual all-India authority. In this Madani was perceived as the worthy successor of Mahmud al-Hasan who had been recognized as Shaykh al-Hind (Rizvi 1980/II: 155). More concrete was the designation of an Amīr al-Sharī'at who would become a sort of an appellate authority for the application of Islamic law. Again, this post received no formal endorsement and no appointment on an all-India level was made. This was so notwithstanding certain individual claims by Islamic activists such as the Aḥrār leader Bukhari who was called Amīr al-Sharī'at as a form of honour in recognition of his erudition in the field of Islamic law. The most concrete form of such a post was achieved when the JUH set out to nominate a provincial Amīr al-Sharī'at. In 1922, the JUH felicitated its Bihar unit for nominating a provincial Amīr al-Sharī'at hoping to fill this post for all provinces and then elect an all-India supreme judge of Islam (*IAR* 1923/I: 942).

Maulana Naqshbandi addressed the issue in 1925 by drawing lessons from the abolition of the Ottoman Caliphate. He looked for a solution in the broader context of establishing an Islamic system (Niẓām-i Islām). As he saw the doubting and hesitating attitude of modern-educated Muslim intellectuals as the main reason for the collapse of the Caliphate, he planned to change Muslim public opinion systematically so that it would favour the establishment of an Islamic system. For this purpose he suggested a systematic step-by-step approach:

1. First of all compile all rules and regulations of an Islamic system (*niẓām-i islām*) with utmost order and refinement keeping in mind the following issues:
    a. All principles of an Islamic system (*shar'ī uṣūl*), which are necessary for establishing the power of the Caliphate in the whole world of Islam, should be compiled in detail without any fear or apprehension.

b. Any modification of principles (of what constitutes an Islamic system) can be done to the extent that it does not upset any basic principle (of Islam).
c. The rules of an Islamic system shall be compiled on the basis of priority and sequence and will then be included in the form of essential conditions (*majbūrī ḥālat*).
d. The compilation of the rules of the (Islamic) system will not only be based on the pronouncements of the eminent jurists (*fuqahā*), experts of tradition (*muḥadithīn*) and theologians (*mutakallimīn*), but each principle will (only) be included after its essence is established and its conformity with public interest (*uṣūl istiṣlaḥ*) considered.

2. A detailed commentary will be written on the Islamic system after it has been prepared in the aforesaid manner which will clarify the contents and assessment of every point in the light of the *sharī'a*, which will demonstrate their advantages and also point out to the harm that their rejection may cause.

3. The principles of the Islamic system and its commentary will be published in large numbers in Arabic, Urdu, and English and the whole world of Islam will be invited to discuss and implement it.

4. To defend against the ills I mentioned earlier, the basic meaning of patriotism (*waṭanīyat*) and its limits should be explained in the light of the *sharī'a* and should also be discussed with rational arguments (*'aqlī dilā'il*). And it should be made clear that these concepts (words) are wrongly interpreted today. And these treatises should (also) be published in Urdu, Arabic and English to make them available to the Muslims of the world so that the educated sections of all classes of the Islamic world can benefit from it (270).

5. A permanent journal should be published on the issue of public interest in Islam (*istiṣlaḥ*) which discusses what really is common interest (*maṣlaḥat*), how many (different) meanings does it have and what meaning does Islamic law give to common interest (*maṣlaḥat*) and how many different degrees of it exist. And from the point of view of different degrees of public interest (*madārij-e maṣāleḥ*), what commandments exist (in Islam) to tolerate which form of common interest. The objective of the journal is to remove misconceptions about what common/public interest is acceptable (in Islam). That this misconception is not removed is responsible for the fact that the *'ulamā'* and the modern-educated intellectuals are not coming together at one centre, but the gulf between them grows ever wider day by day. Hopefully this journal will also be published in three languages which will be a great help in understanding and publicizing the system of the Caliphate.

6. Delegations will be sent, taking the blueprint of the Islamic system and its commentary to all Muslim countries, and especially to the independent and free countries, to obtain from them after thorough discussions a sincere promise and agreement on its implementation. After obtaining a confirmation about the correctness of the principles of the Islamic system there will be one last consultation about this matter—just as Abdur Rahman bin Uf did during the establishment of the third Caliphate with his companions. After such

Islamic consultation the Islamic Caliphate can rely on a strong system and the whole world of Islam will be bound together by one way of conduct.

7. These treatises and journals will be made obligatory in the religious schools (*madāris*), schools and colleges of different levels. It will be attempted to make these journals obligatory in the educational system of all countries of Islam so that those evil ills do not grow in our youth and that the education about the Islamic system will remain a strong defence against them (Rozinah 1981/I: 271).

Once such a comprehensive system of consultation had produced a uniform understanding of an Islamic system, implementation seemed to be a much easier matter. Even if formal implementation of a political system was not achieved, the consultation process was expected to strengthen the religious spirit in the Islamic world and to undermine the influence of secular intellectuals. Naqshbandi was careful not to prejudge the contents of such a system. His emphasis on the public nature of the required discourse was revealing. This he apparently regarded as the quintessential condition for its acceptance by the modern, educated Muslim intellectuals. It reflected the influence of debates on transparency and democracy. Naqshbandi believed that the Islamic approach was inherently superior. The reasons for its defeat in the struggle for the Caliphate were not rooted in the doctrinal argument, but rather in its insufficient explanation, popularization, and propagation. Interestingly, he demanded that Islam equip itself with 'rational' arguments in order to convince the doubting intellectuals. His proposal envisaged an avant-garde role for Indian Muslims in the Islamic world, which he saw essentially failing in its duty to assure that Islam be equipped not only with spiritual but also temporal powers.

Naqshbandi explained how he envisaged an Islamic system to be set up in India. This vision was marked by the same comprehensiveness and lengthy process of consultation. He believed that 'if these (principles) were implemented the Islamic system would be spread throughout India very quickly':

1. General agreement or majority opinion should be reached on a single person who must be a scholar and senior authority on whose hand everyone should take an oath of allegiance (*bay'a*) with honesty and deep sincerity of the heart. He should be given the Qur'an and Sunna in his hands. And strengthen his hand to follow the Qur'an and Sunna and keep an eye on those who oppose the Qur'an and Sunna.
2. An (Islamic) administrator should be appointed in every province and district.
3. A responsible man and a knowledgeable person (regarding Islam) should be appointed in every city, village, neighbourhood and tribe.

4. Their duties should be fixed in accordance with the Qur'an and the Sunna and the guidance of the great Imams and Islamic jurists.
5. The Islamic Authority (Emirate, *i.e.* the *amīr*'s administration) should create a Muslim fund/treasury (*Bayt al-Mal*), open a department of religious justice (*maḥakuma-e qaẓā*), set up a department of public benefit (*maḥakuma-e monāf'a*) and start other departments to meet further economic needs (Rozinah 1981/I: 309).

The first step for an Islamic polity, in his opinion, was consent. Once this had been achieved he believed it was binding on all Muslims. The first task of an Islamic polity was to ensure the fulfilment of religious duties of Muslims. The leader of the community (amīr) had to submit to a system of checks and balances. Un-Islamic behaviour was not to be condoned either by the masses or by their leader. In cases of violation, social pressure and means of enforcement were to be used. The main areas of responsibility of an amīr pertained to administering community finances, religious justice, social relief, and rehabilitation. One of the main hurdles in the way of implementation of these schemes was the lack of funds. This was recognized by Naqshbandi and by many others. He suggested that this problem could be overcome by the mobilization of public resources, by the collection of funds, only if pursued energetically enough.

After responsible government was introduced at the provincial level under the 1935 Government of India Act, the JUH scholars were alarmed. Despite political pressure and mobilization there was no reservation for Muslims. Instead, the principles of majority rule and democracy were adopted, which were seen as perpetuating the minority status of Indian Muslims. The JUH pushed its proposals for an Islamic authority (*Naẓārat-e Umūr-e Sharī'a*) with renewed vigour. It believed that the elected provincial governments, seen as forebears of a national government, had a duty to grant Muslims their due share of freedom. Its 1939 session adopted a resolution rephrasing most of their earlier demands with a more practical bent. It demanded the appointment of a commissioner of Islamic affairs (Nāẓir-e Umūr-e Islāmīya) with cabinet rank. He would look after Muslim charitable endowments (auqāf); head a system of qāḍī justice; give advice on foreign policy with reference to international Islam; supervise religious education; and coordinate legislation on Muslim personal law. In order to enshrine Muslim rights in the constitution the JUH proposed to prepare a 'draft law on the basis of the principles of cultural autonomy' (Rozinah 1981/II: 637). But the implementation of these demands made no headway. They were restated in 1942 when Madani demanded the office (naẓārāt) of sharī'a affairs be anchored in the future constitution so that it could initiate laws for Islamic education, for communal and economic reform and development of Muslims without interference from the government (Rozinah 1981/II: 744).

The JUH principally understood its task to be that of a trailblazer in this regard. It constantly laid claim to a central representation of Indian Muslims. At the same time its speakers were alarmed that it could not bring about even minimal changes. Several problematic topics were regularly raised almost every year. These included the schemes for propagation (tablīgh) both of the objectives of the JUH and of Islam in general. Hindu–Muslim unity was another topic regularly discussed. In 1925, Naqshbandi warned that Muslims should not give up their independence at the cost of friendship with Hindus and start adopting reprehensible practices bordering on unbelief (kufr). Also political factionalism featured prominently which as a category fused with doctrinal dissent (fitna).[39] Naqshbandi strongly warned against new divisions and the emergence of ever-new groups. If this factionalism was not stopped it was unclear what would happen to the Muslim people and its custody of Islam in future. 'All these groups make dissension and discord their mark of distinction arguing that the nation and the community can best be served with the help of this or that group and that by rallying their members they can guard Islam and the Muslim nation against those dangers so that the internal and external attacks of the Jewish and Christian and all other enemies of the community and the nation will be stopped forever. I humbly submit that this thought is absurd as we have seen through the experience of more than 50 years and what results this has yielded is well known. If you crave for more of such experience you can have it' (Rozinah 1981/I: 298).

Alluding to former Moghul rule, the Khāksār leader Mashriqi envisaged an Islamic government over the whole of India built on a new, modern basis, ruling a multi-religious society. He imagined that his movement would build the administrative foundations of such a government. The designation of administrative departments through which his movement operated was indicative. They covered almost all aspects of government from finance to administration to secret services to (religious) propaganda (tablīgh) to politics.[40] His self-defence units and voluntary organizations

[39]On the doctrinal aspects of fitna, see section 3.2.4.

[40]These departments were listed by Malik as follows: (1) *'Azl-o-Nasb* (Establishment Department), (2) *Khidmat-i Khalq* (Social Service), (3) Bayt al-Māl (Exchequer), (4) *Adānī-o-Ajānib* (Record and Information office), (5) *Naẓm-o-Nasq* (Administration Section), (6) *Taḥrīr-o-Eḥtiṣāb* (Censorship Department; in 1939, a new department called *Maḥkama-i Taḥrīr*, a sort of press agency, was organized; both these departments were amalgamated), (7) *Farmiayshat* (Audit and Disbursing office), (8) *Tazīr* (Magistracy, divided into two parts, a Secret Service, called *Sālār-i Zabt*, and a magistracy, headed by the *sālār-i jabr*), (9) *Tablīgh*

were to carry out tasks of government. Its members had to submit to its own courts. They intended to collect the Islamic welfare tax (zakāt) and distribute it to the needy. They issued promissory currency notes as remuneration for their activists. These notes were to be cashed from the Khāksār treasury, Bayt al-Māl, at some future point in time, perhaps in an independent and Islamic India under Mashriqi's leadership (Mashriqi 1995: 260ff.; Mathur 1972: 212–16). For Mashriqi, physical training and daily parades of his Khāksār soldiers were the quintessential condition for the implementation of an Islamic system, as they would make Muslims superior to the British and the Hindus. Muslims, he felt, should strive to get in this world what they were promised for the hereafter, in paradise. Instead of wailing they should act to improve their lives. On this count religious scholars accused him of adopting heretical beliefs. He was removing the transcendental nature of Islam, they thundered. Worship ('ibādat) should not be directed at this world but at the hereafter, and not at physical prowess but at spiritual salvation, otherwise it would stop being an act of religion (Malik 2000: 41ff.).

A comparable accusation was levelled at Maududi. When he developed his concept of an Islamic system, the iqāmat-i dīn, it was an Islamic polity and government to the attainment and strengthening of which all religious activity was to be subservient. Scholars such as S. A. H. A. Nadwi from the Nadwa Seminary strongly criticized him on the grounds that he directed worship ('ibādat) at the creation of the polity. This contravened the basic understanding of Islam that worship had to be directed towards salvation in the hereafter. Perhaps it was no coincidence that Maududi mentioned that he felt influenced by the Khāksār leader who he said was the only one attempting to set up an Islamic system through an Islamic army. Maududi, of course, was much more refined in his theological and political views than Mashriqi. He placed less, if any, emphasis on an Islamic army. But the common element of practical, this-worldly interpretation of an Islamic polity was obvious (Nasr 1996).

The Barelwi concept of an Islamic order was first detailed in a fatwā issued by Ahmad Raza in 1913.[41] Initially written in response to pan-Islamic sentiments in support of Ottoman Turkey, he outlined a programme of economic, social, and religious action for Indian Muslims. They should, he felt, strive to become self-sufficient. For this he suggested four-fold action: Muslims should (i) refrain from taking their disputes to court, except for those limited matters where the government had a right to intervene,

(Publicity Department), (10) *Maḥkama-i Siyāsat* (Political Department, established in the mid-forties) (2000: 54–5).

[41] *Tadbīr-e falāḥ wa najāt wa iṣlāḥ* (Course for Prosperity, Salvation, and Reform), Bareilly: Hasani Press, 1913, quoted in Sanyal (1996a: 281 fn.); see also ibid.: 283–4.

and instead submit them to Muslim judges from the community (qāḍīs); (ii) buy whatever they needed from other Muslims, keeping money within the community, supporting Muslim traders, and becoming self-reliant; (iii) wealthy Muslims should open interest-free banks for their fellow Muslims; and (iv) all Muslims should acquire religious education, knowledge of their faith, and act on it.

The Barelwi approach shunned the elaborate organizational structure and the constitutional legalism characteristic of the Deobandi and JUH schemes. No separate Islamic authority was envisaged. Instead, the responsibility of reforming life according to the dictates of religion lay with every individual Muslim. The centre of change was local action. Ahmad Raza's programme aimed at increased autonomy of Islam in a multicultural environment. It sought to make Muslims less dependent on the Westernized state and on the dominating Hindu community. At the same time, the directions of change sought were also close to the heart of the reformists: implementing Islamic law; religious education; and an interest-free economy.

The Barelwis expressed further ideas on an Islamic order in the context of the AISC. The programme suggested there in 1925 by Ahmad Raza's son Hamid was based on his father's 1913 fatwā. Hamid elaborated the programme in relation to tablīgh, religious education, and social policy, suggesting a multi-tier structure and network (see Chapter 3, section 3.4.3 and Chapter 5). This was a departure from the less formal programme of his father though. It indicated the growing awareness of the need for self-organization. The thrust of his programme for an Islamic order was to strengthen Muslim community life. The focus of attention had now shifted to those regions where Muslims were well represented. Those were the majority areas destined to become the core territories of the future Pakistan. They included the regions where the Barelwi brand of Islam found much support, in Sindh, Punjab, Bengal, and, to a lesser degree, the Pakhtun Frontier province. As such, his support for the Pakistan movement appeared to be aiming at a regional solution to the reformation of Muslim community life. Other Barelwi scholars were less sure that partition and the creation of a separate Muslim state would bring the solution. In this connection, Sanyal pointed to the position of Mustafa Raza, the younger son of Ahmad Raza. He supported those scholars who argued against a separate state on the grounds that it would cause the severance of relations with those disciples who would migrate to the future Pakistan (Sanyal 1998: 648, fn. 37). The Barelwi vision of an Islamic order for India emerging from these initiatives focused on the Islamic quality of life and the local influence of their networks rooted in the traditional centres of pīr- and shrine-based Islam.

Where the Barelwis supported the Pakistan scheme they demanded that the future state be guided by the Qur'an and Sunna only. In his presidential address to the 1946 Banares session of the AISC, Sayyid Muhammad Ashrafi Jilani reminded the League that 'the AISC understood Pakistan to be an independent state where the principles of Islam (*sharī'a islāmīya kē' muṭābiq fuqahī uṣūl*) will not only guide the community but lead to establishing an Islamic government, which, in short, will be an example of the *Khilāfat-e Rāshida*'. The Speaker called for building Pakistan first on a piece of land, but not to rest before it extended to the entire world (Qadiri 1997: 277). This implied not only support but also a stern warning to the Muslim League not to deviate from the path of setting up an Islamic government. The Barelwis were not alone in their demand for an Islamic Pakistan. When talking about a rapprochement between the Deoband School and the League on the eve of independence, Muhammad Hifzur Rahman told Jinnah that the JUH regarded the decisions of the Muslim League as unwise 'from the Islamic point of view' (Jinnah Papers/I, part I: 412–13). The Aḥrār demanded the same during unsuccessful merger talks. They passed a resolution on 'divine government' (*ḥukūmat-i ilāhīya*) in April 1943 signalling an equidistance from the Congress and the League (Mirza 1975/V: 362). Qureshi recounted that the support of a number of 'ulamā' for the Pakistan scheme was founded on the hope that it served the 'glory of Islam' (1974: 366).

Designing and creating an Islamic polity for an India under colonial rule where Islam was in a minority was undoubtedly an enormous challenge. The public discourse, which the Islamic scholars conducted, was urged on by the political and religious insecurity and tension faced by the Muslim minority. The cultural and social characteristics of the respective Islamic group and its élite equally shaped this discourse. Four models of Islamic government could be distinguished:

(a) The Deobandi reformist approach, broadly supported by the Aḥrār, the Tablīghī Jamā'at, and the Ahl-i Ḥadīth, aimed at a non-territorial solution. It envisaged spiritual perfection and a separate religious administration for Muslims in a united India. It favoured an Islamic authority with limited and circumscribed attributes of power and enforcement, for the collection and redistribution of resources.

(b) The Khāksār and Maududi regarded the concept of the JUH as too hesitant and impractical, although both aimed at extending Islamic government to all Indian Muslims regardless of their location, a major reason for their temporary opposition to the Pakistan movement.[42] Instead,

[42]On the adaptation of the JI to the reality of Pakistan, see Nasr (1996: 41ff.). The JI continued to oppose the state of Pakistan, which it did not regard as sufficiently Islamic

they demanded that an Islamic government be set up with full powers and control, either by force (Khāksār) or by persuasion and education of the Islamic élite (Maududi). In their vision, India would somehow resume the tradition of Imperial Moghul rule and be governed by an Islamic system making provisions for other religions and cultures.

(c) The third approach, formulated by the Barelwi School supported Islamic life in its more local dimensions, with full rights for mystical traditions alongside reformist practices. It practically favoured regional autonomy for an Islamic government. Opposition to the coalition of the Congress and the Deoband divines led them to support the Pakistan movement, in which many Barelwi leaders saw a promising opening to a territorial solution of the issue of Islamic government. Out of this position grew the demands for the fourth model.

(d) Pakistan should become an Islamic state with a religious polity. This could be called the fourth model although its difference from the foregoing was more in extent than in distinct paradigm.

Out of political expediency Jinnah prevaricated on the issue, although he made clear that he never had in mind for Pakistan to become a theocracy.[43] He was a constitutionalist first and wanted Pakistan to become a strong Muslim welfare state where the minorities would enjoy equal rights with the Muslim majority: 'You may belong to any religion or caste or creed—that has nothing to do with the business of the State' (Jinnah 1976: 9). Jinnah had preserved room for manoeuvring by keeping his distance from the scholars for most of the time. Only when the 1946 elections were to decide the future partition of India on the basis of Muslim majorities, a strong Muslim League needed religious leaders and scholars to win the elections to ensure the implementation of the Pakistan scheme. Demands by the JUH scholars directed to the Muslim League in 1947 to act only after consultation with the religious scholars on the religious propriety of its political schemes were roundly rejected.[44]

The confusion about the role of religion in the polity of Pakistan persists to this day. The first three models reconstructed themselves within the parameters of Pakistan. The Barelwi approach largely retained its politically withdrawn, regional, and local orientation. The Deobandi approach pursued spiritual perfection and a religious administration for

---

to be legitimate. Still it accepted the rules of the political process (constitutional debate, elections) in which it participated although not always very successfully.

[43]'But make no mistake: Pakistan is not a theocracy or anything like it' (Jinnah in a broadcast to Australia on 19 February 1948, in Jinnah 1976: 60).

[44]See the exchange of letters between Maulana Hifzur Rahman and Jinnah between March and May 1947, in Jinnah Papers/I, part I: 412–13, 487–8, 679–80.

the whole of Pakistan. The Jamā'at-i Islāmī continued to follow a hegemonistic concept aimed at taking over the reins of the state.

Islamic groups veered towards participation not by self-conscious choice but by reaction and adaptation. Groups such as the Deobandis and Barelwis viewed as traditional today were not static at all. They allowed their members to follow participatory principles both inside and outside their institutions. Those who resisted such change were often conservative although theologically less radical. They mostly relied on political and sometimes economic or financial support from the British. Schemes for an Islamic polity reflected the various pulls of theological paradigm, geography, and client support. The Islamic project was marked by an astonishing ignorance of political reality and a lack of practicality. While it reflected the influence of ideas of democracy and participatory politics, it was clearly designed to control notably the dissenting sections of Muslim society in India, the so-called modern, educated intellectuals, if need be, through pressure and coercion. Indian Islam wanted to make good for the loss of its spiritual attraction by building a system that could spread, propagate, and control religious beliefs and practices more efficiently and with a certain force. The argument was conducted with references to the Qur'an and the time of the Prophet. But the aspirations and strategies were clearly modern, reflecting the desire to harness the products and experiences of modernity for the purpose of countering modern influences.

4.2. ASSERTION OR SUBMISSION: ON DEFENCE AND SELF-DEFENCE

Defence in the wider sense of the term was another major motive for Islamic groups to move into action. The perception of threat was pervasive and constituted a major theme of reformist and revivalist Islam as shown earlier. Whereas the Islamic discourse on participation was largely reactive in nature, the defence discourse, in contrast, was offensive and activist. It was the feeling of imagined as much as real injury that hurt and, therefore, required response. Invariably there was an overlapping with forms of religious intervention. For our purpose, four distinct forms of defence activity have been identified in South Asian Islam at that time. What the British called undifferentiated pan-Islamism was often the intention to invoke (i) Islamic solidarity in the defence of the rights and causes of Muslims, which were seen to be violated. This was first ignited by the Tripolitan and Balkan wars of 1911–13 where Ottoman Turkey was seen to be wronged by Western powers. It continued in the Khilafat campaign after 1919. The Tablīgh movement (see Chapter 3, section 3.4) was also a movement for the defence of Muslims, here against (re) conversion efforts of the Āryā Samāj and the Hindū Mahāsabhā. Its sister movement, tanẓīm, took a more pro-active stance aiming at (ii) the self-organization of Muslims. A more tangible threat to the security and lives of Muslims developed in the shape of (iii) communal riots. Here violence was perpetrated by both Muslims and Hindus. Both communities for specific reasons felt that they were at the receiving end. The endurance of such violence and attacks contributed to the (iv) rise of self-defence societies a task partly performed by the Khāksār and the Aḥrār.

4.2.1. Defence of Muslim Causes—Islamic Solidarity Abroad and in India

Following on the educational and doctrinal debates of Islamic groups, the defence of Ottoman Turkey was the spark that ignited political awakening and activism among Islamic scholars. The first public associations addressing themselves to both the Islamic sphere and the public sphere at large were devoted to solidarity with the Ottoman Empire.

One of the first was the Red Crescent Mission (Anjuman-i Hilāl-i Aḥmar) to Ottoman Turkey organized in 1912–13 by Dr M. A. Ansari (1880–1936) and Shaukat Ali.[45] Ansari was a medical doctor who had practised in England and entered politics at the behest of the Ali brothers. When he organized the mission he connected with Aligarh College of which he later became a trustee. The project was vented in the *Comrade* newspaper started by the Ali brothers in 1912. A group of Muslim doctors and assistants went to the Turkish front of the Balkan war as a medical mission. The project was well received by the government. The viceroy saw the departing mission off. Its work on the front was purely medical. It was also the first successful salvo of pan-Islamic politics, of public Islamic activities. Funds for the mission were raised across India. At Deoband, scholars gave religious verdicts (fatāwā) in its favour, students printed them on posters and sent them out 'in millions...to every nook and corner'[46] of the country. Students and staff contributed the enormous amount of Rs 65,000 (Rizvi 1980/I: 180). In fact, the seminary contributed so much that it had difficulty in tiding over the next year in terms of administrative expenses, which was only made possible by an extraordinary increase in the grant made by the princely state of Hyderabad (ibid.: 182).

The need to help Ottoman Turkey was intensely felt by Islamic scholars. When the Deobandi Shaykh al-Hind, Mahmud al-Hasan went on the

[45]Participants of the mission included Chaudhry Khaliquzzaman, Dr M. A. Ansari, Dr M. N. Ansari, Shuaib Quraishi, Abdur Rahman Siddiqi, and Bashiruddin Ahmad (Robinson 1994: 207 fn. 3).

[46]This may be a somewhat extravagant claim.

ḥajj in 1915 he used this opportunity to present Turkey with a dreadnought for its navy bought by subscriptions (Minault 1982: 37). He thus hoped to gain Turkey's support for a scheme of a Muslim uprising against British rule with the help of Afghanistan: the notorious 'silk letter conspiracy' (cf. section 4.3.5). This was an ill-fated endeavour, resulting in the arrest of the conspirators and the internment of Hasan on the island of Malta for the entire length of the war.

The next prominent project in India involving religious scholars was the Anjuman-i Khuddām-i Ka'ba in 1913 (Minault 1982: 35). It was organized by Abdul Bari from Firangī Maḥall and Shaukat Ali, the Aligarh-educated elder brother of Muhammad Ali.[47] The Ali brothers were attached to Abdul Bari also because they regarded him as their religious pīr. The organization had 16,000 members in 1915. Its original design was to protect the holy places of Islam in the Arabian Peninsula from Western encroachment. Thinking on similar lines as the Deobandi scholar Mahmud al-Hasan, the Anjuman-i Khuddām-i Ka'ba felt that Turkey ought to be helped by providing it with funds to buy military hardware (dreadnoughts, airships). This intention appeared to be impractical and did not materialize. Its statutes concentrated on the preaching of harmony at the holy places and facilitation of communication with these.[48] This basically meant collecting funds so that poor Muslims could afford to go on pilgrimage (ḥajj). Shaukat Ali made efforts to run a Muslim shipping company breaking into the European monopoly on pilgrim travel. He seemed to have made an impact bringing relief to intending pilgrims. The closure of the ḥajj route as a result of World War I was an additional stimulus for his efforts (Robinson 1994: 211). The Anjuman set up an administrative hierarchy down to the district and circle level, an approach later to be replicated by the JUH and the Khilafat Conference. The activists on various levels moved effortlessly and seamlessly from one project to the next. Public activism became institutionalized. The design of the Anjuman was rather grand and included a pledge, a uniform, and pension funds for activists (ibid.: 209). Besides the Firangī Maḥallīs, religious scholars from Badayun also joined the Anjuman, representing Barelwi activists. They were marked by their opposition to British rule in contrast to Ahmad Raza's loyalism. Deoband only grudgingly approved the scheme, more because of its success than out of conviction. Its vice-chancellor of the time, Maulana Habibur Rahman, was wary of potential disloyalty.

[47]Other prominent members of the Anjuman included Dr M. A. Ansari, the Wikar-ul-Mulk, former secretary of Aligarh college, Ajmal Khan (cf. Minault 1982: 36). For the Anjuman's programme, cf. Landau (1990: 346–50).

[48]For the statutes, see Robinson (1994: 208, fn. 4).

The British refused to grant government endorsement to the Anjuman in spite of Abdul Bari's anxious efforts. Most of the lofty aims (transfer of money to Turkey, building schools, helping orphans) were neglected, except for the assistance to *ḥajjīs*.

Though the Ka'ba society was started on the impulse of helping the Ottomans it ended with relief efforts for Indian Muslims. It was a training ground for future campaigns of Islamic solidarity with an eye on the all-India level. It was followed by the so-called Kanpur Mosque incident of 1913, which in contrast grew out of the Indian context although it also invoked pan-Islamic references.[49] The campaign was another outflow of the activism of the Ali brothers prepared on the pages of the *Comrade* newspaper. Muhammad Ali had been fighting a propagandist campaign through his paper against the demolition of old buildings and the levelling of graveyards in Delhi, which he saw as a deliberate removal of the vestiges of Moghul rule. When the Kanpur municipality in the neighbouring United Provinces decided to remove the attached wall[50] of a mosque for construction work on a new road, Muhammad Ali first pleaded with the governor of the Unied Provinces to reverse the decision. The administration refused to budge and the campaign unleashed subsequently surpassed everything that the British had expected.[51] Fatawā were issued to prove that the wall was an integral part of the mosque and as such sacrosanct. Street agitation began. A mass demonstration of Muslim weavers (julāhā) produced a violent riot. The police clamped down on the protesters with a heavy hand killing several Muslims. All Muslims in India protested, irrespective of whether they were modernists or traditionists, intellectuals or religious scholars. The trials of the rioters turned into public meetings. It took the intervention of the viceroy to pacify the protesters and rehabilitate the arrested activists. A compromise was struck with regard to the wall: it was to be rebuilt in such a way that it would also allow for the construction of the new road.[52] Religious activists from the groups

[49]During the campaign the small and rather insignificant Kanpur mosque came to be likened to the 'hundreds of mosques...destroyed in Macedonia' and 'the tombs of Imam Raza...desecrated in Meshed' (*Muslim Gazette* [2 June 1913], quoted in Freitag 1990: 210).

[50]The attached wall was the washing place used for ablution before prayer at the local mosque. This mosque was part of the fish market, and, therefore, called the *machlī bazār* mosque.

[51]Besides the Ali brothers, the major activists were the Raja of Mahmudabad (1879–1931), Mazhar-ul-Haq (1866–1929), and Azad Subhani (1884(?)–1957).

[52]On the dynamics of the Kanpur Mosque agitation, see Freitag (1988), also Freitag (1990: 210ff.); on the connection with Aligarh College affairs, see Moin (1976: 246–63); for an agitational tract of the Kanpur campaign, see Nizami (1913), containing poems, letters, and articles condemning the alleged cruelties of the local police of Kanpur.

studied here were also partly involved. The protest memorial of May 1913 was signed among others by Abdul Bari of Firangī Maḥall and Habibur Rahman of Deoband (Robinson 1994: 213 fn. 6). Shibli Numani from the Nadwa was credited with sympathy towards the agitators (Malik 1997: 367). The Aḥmadīs differed in their attitude to the agitation. It was supported by Khwaja Kamaluddin (1870–1932) and opposed by Ghulam Ahmad's son, Mahmud Ahmad, reflecting their respective oppositional and loyalist styles of action (Walter 1916: 68).

A few Islamic activists, partly modern-educated, and a handful of religious scholars had managed to nudge the Muslim community to a high degree of militancy and public preparedness. Robinson mentioned that Muhammad and Shaukat Ali in particular symbolized a new breed of Muslim public activists: 'They were men who gained their living entirely from politics. They were financed from three sources: political journalism, subscription and the patron' (1994: 185). In 1915, Shaukat Ali was accused of improper management of fund finances. As Robinson put it, 'they lived well on the proceeds of pan-Islamic politics' (ibid.: 187). Fund-raising for Islamic causes had become a popular pastime. Similar problems occurred with other funds raised by the Ali brothers. The funds in which they were involved between 1907 and 1920 included the 'Bayt al-Malk Fund', collected to send Raja Ghulam Husain, the organizer of the 1907 Aligarh student strike (discussed earlier), to Europe for higher studies, the Turkish Relief Fund, the Kanpur Mosque Fund, the Ghalib Tomb Fund, and the Hamdard Debenture Fund (ibid.: 187, fn. 1).

The British saw much of the activity of the younger generation of activists rooted in a generational struggle for ascendancy in the Muslim community and in public life. To dislodge older and more moderate leaders, the younger ones used

> invective, a multiplication of racial grievances,[53] and opposition to the Government. By invective they beat down the attempts of the older-fashioned, moderate but extremely sensitive leaders of the community to resist their domination. By racial grievances they hope to unite the Muhammadans in allegiance to themselves. By opposition to the Government they believe, that they will eventually wring out concessions which will prove to their community that they, and not the loyalists, are the leaders who may profitably be followed.[54]

From here it was a direct road to the Khilafat agitation where the Ali brothers again closely cooperated with Abdul Bari, although several other

[53]Racial grievances apparently meant here religious concerns directed at the cohesion of the community, as British officialdom used the terms 'race' and 'racial' very loosely in the connotation of ethnic and religious group.

[54]Minute by the governer of the United Provinces, Governor Meston on the Kanpur Mosque affair, *Home Poll.* A (October 1913), 100–18, NAI, quoted in Robinson (1994: 215).

religious scholars and Muslim activists were also involved. It was then that the Barelwis who had only partly supported the earlier campaigns decided to set up their own organization in this field, the Anjuman-i Anṣār al-Islām (Sanyal 1996a: 315), which was to concentrate entirely on religious solidarity instead of adopting the oppositional and confrontational attitude of the Khilafat Movement. Ahmad Raza had opposed the Ka'ba society because of its implied anti-British orientation. He couched his objection to the Ka'ba society in religious vocabulary. To him resistance to British rule was 'impermissible opposition' (*nā-jā'iz mukhālafat*) that violated the contractual obligation of Muslims.[55] He also felt that society associated Muslims of poor faith (*bad-maẕhabī*), his synonym for Deobandi scholars, with the leadership of the Anjuman. He detailed his views in a fatwā and in newspaper articles. There he also criticized the Anjuman for frittering away money of poor Muslims without achieving anything.[56]

4.2.2. *Defence of Muslims Against Conversions and Communal Riots*

Defending the religious identity of Muslims against conversions and secularization was another important plank of public activism. Tanẓīm was the name of a movement devoted to self-organization of Muslims. Tanẓīm activities were understood as the pro-active, 'worldly' side of tablīgh and da'wa. It was also the name of an organization founded by Dr Saifuddin Kitchlew in 1923. It stopped short of evolving into a permanent body like the Khāksār and the Aḥrār, although its activities resembled their's in many ways. Religious scholars were less involved in tanẓīm than in tablīgh. Kitchlew had a Khilafatist and Congress background.[57] He held radical religio-nationalist views opposing council entry and demanding that Muslims should join Gandhi's campaign for reactivating hand-spinning as a means to boycott the import of Western clothes. Such views were not shared by all Muslim leaders. Many favoured council entry and rejected Gandhi's spinning campaign as irrelevant for Muslims since the hand-woven cloth was less common among them than among Hindus.

In the face of growing religious tension and rioting, the defence of Muslims became a practical requirement. Until then there existed no special arrangement to take care of victims of violence, of their material

[55] This related to the debate on India being a land of Islam (dār al-Islām) or of war, of the infidels (dār al-ḥarb). Ahmad Raza believed Muslims were free in British India to follow their religion and, therefore, contractually bound to the ruler (cf. section 4.3.3).

[56] *Dabdabā-e Sikandarī* (11 August 1913), pp. 5–6, quoted in Sanyal (1996a: 280ff.).

[57] Cf. his biography by his son Taufiq Kitchlew (1987). He was among the accused in the Karachi trial (1921) along with Muhammad Ali as he had seconded the resolution moved by Ali, which called on Indians not to serve in the British-Indian army.

and spiritual rehabilitation. This was the task the tanẓīm movement was originally charged to carry out. It later aimed at organizing the internal affairs of the Muslim community in a more systematic way. This came close to the idea of Islamic government in India. Kitchlew tried to mobilize the substantial authority and resources of the Congress and the Khilafat Committee for the tanẓīm movement. He laid out a practical programme of action before the Central Khilafat Committee in Delhi on 24–5 June 1924. He demanded that members of the movement should open primary schools in mosques, prepare textbooks for schools, issue sermons (*khuṭba*) to be read in mosques, enforce punctuality in prayers, establish technical and commercial colleges, supervise the Muslim endowments (*waqf*), collect the Muslim welfare tax (zakāt), arrange for the relief of widows and orphans, and start Muslim cooperative societies and banks.[58]

Kitchlew travelled across India to spread his concept of tanẓīm and to encourage local Muslims to start volunteer organizations for this purpose. His main centre of activity, however, was Punjab. There he also closely cooperated with the radical Sikh organization, the Akali Dal, in their nationalist activities. Much like the early tablīgh activities, tanẓīm, according to Kitchlew was a very localized affair. Freitag described this phenomenon for Kanpur where the tanẓīm movement spread in the Muslim neighbourhoods (*moḥalla*) of the old city districts (qaṣba). These were small volunteer organizations (*anjuman*) where young Muslim men came together to hold processions in the neighbourhood. They shouted slogans that regular prayers and Islamic customs should be observed. To dissenters, they would apply measures of social boycott. For instance, they would not attend the funerals and feasts of those families. These processions were sometimes held when they felt challenged by large-scale Hindu festivals such as *Daśahrā* and the large *Rāmlīlā* processions. Some of the organizations would also have their members wear uniforms if resources permitted. They engaged in physical exercises, training in wrestling and staging mock fights with batons and swords. On occasion these activities could turn into large processions. In the case of Kanpur, the Muslim mill hands, who otherwise were not a regular part of these tanẓīm activities, joined in on weekends turning these processions into massive, and at times violent, displays of communal self-assertion and self-consciousness.[59]

The role of the religious scholars in this connection was to give 'religious

[58]NAI Home Department (Political Branch) note, dated 4 October 1924, quoted in Mathur (1968: 22). For a similar statement by Kitchlew at the December 1924 Khilafat conference, see *IAR* 1924/I: 491.

[59]Cf. the description of tanẓīm activities in Kanpur, in the United Province, for the 1920s and 30s by Sandria Freitag (1990: 230ff.).

guidance' on the matter. Yet, the argument of religious scholars was difficult to tell from the politician's position. Maulana Madani discussed the need for tanẓīm in his presidential speech at the 1923 annual JUH session:

Since from every angle the Muslim community (*jamā'at*) is so degraded it has no form of organisation whatsoever. There is no special system (*niẓām*) for economics, for education. There is no control on the forces of society and commerce (trade—*tijārat*), not on probity (*diānat*) and agriculture. There is no system to correct the moral flaws. Neither the compensation of material damage or of bodily harm [from communal riots?] nor spiritual rehabilitation is taken care of. That's why it is extremely necessary that Muslims make special arrangements for all their requirements. These should consider all necessities of life and all kinds of development needs, material and physical. But this should not mean under any circumstances that we aim at supremacy over our compatriots (*hamsāiyā qaumoñ par*) or disgrace them, and we should adopt no such position or practical policy, which would create such doubt. The objective of this activity should be only our own reformation (*iṣlāḥ*) and to meet ('prevention'—*daf'*) our own requirements and needs (Rozinah 1981/I: 223).

Kitchlew's demand in 1924 sounded very similar to the ones made by Madani in 1923. The major difference between Madani's statement and that of Kitchlew's was the former's call for moderation, as he demanded that the culture of other communities in India should be respected. This cautious approach was a reflection of a consistent position held by Maulana Madani. He had made similar demands with regard to the conduct of tablīgh activities (cf. Chapter 3, fn. 120).

The JUH continued discussion of tanẓīm in connection with its plans for an Islamic authority in India (*Imārat-e Sharī'a fī al-Hind*) (see section 1.1.3). Maulana Naqshbandi highlighted the need to make further progress in this direction in 1925. For him it was the JUH that was called upon to undertake the organization of Muslims. He felt it should take the form of an Islamic authority with its branches extending all over the country. But he also conceded that it could not make any progress due to lack of agreement. He pointed to the provincial efforts as a temporary solution of the problem. It is there that he saw Kitchlew's initiative fit in with the larger plan of the JUH (Rozinah 1981/I: 304ff.).

Religious scholars were also less involved in communal riots. These were mostly led by local politicians and men of public influence, such as traders, butchers, and so on. The most common causes were mutual complaints about certain public rituals and festivals, which the other side found offensive. Muslims easily felt provoked by loud music and merry-making at Hindu processions and festivals. Hindus regularly took offence to cow slaughter and its symbolism as they revered the cow as divine incarnation.[60] However, the sensitivity to such 'provocations' varied greatly. At times Muslims and Hindus joined in each other's most popular processions, Muḥarram and Rāmlīlā with their own contributions. At other times the same symbolism almost sparked off civil wars. The sensitivity and readiness to take offence closely followed the ups and downs of political and religious mobilization. Where Hindu organizations actively pursued their reclamation campaign this created a tense situation. Such places often became the scenes of inter-communal violence. But Muslim leaders were also responsible for the breakout of violence. If they had not drawn public attention to isolated incidents of conversion, whipping up religious fervour, violence could often have been avoided. As such, both sides shared responsibility. In this sense, religious scholars were indirectly involved in these developments, on the agitational side, not in its execution. But they could also not ignore incidents of conversion and communal riots. Commenting on them, the 'ulamā' articulated common anxieties. They also believed that the climate of conversion and riots undermined public support for their anti-colonial policies of cooperation with the nationalist movement and its Hindu representatives.

The numbers of communal riots started picking up from 1923. They reached a high point in 1925–6.[61] This created a particularly awkward situation for those religious scholars who had involved themselves in the Khilafat campaign by creating a Hindu–Muslim entente and supporting close relations with the Congress. The organizers of the Hindu extremist campaigns of shuddhī and saṅgaṭhan, Lala Lajpat Rai, Pandit Malaviya, and Swami Shraddhananda were all active members of the Congress leadership (cf. Chapter 3, fn. 105). But so was Kitchlew who had organized

[60]The rise of the 1925 incidents was attributed to the Muslim festival of *'Id al-Bakr* connected with slaughtering sacrificial animals, in India mostly cows or calves, which were led in procession to the sacrifice. These processions were prohibited in 1924 in view of the tense situation but were allowed again in 1925 when the incidents occurred in Delhi, Calcutta, and Allahabad. The Hindu Rāmlīlā festival at the end of September 1925 caused a serious riot in Aligarh with a great loss of lives. The Calcutta riot of April 1926, in which Āryā Samājis were involved, caused 44 deaths and 584 injuries in the first flare-up and 66 deaths and 391 injured several days later with a third phase in July causing 28 deaths and 226 wounded. The playing of (loud) music (as part of Hindu processions) before mosques was a cause for offence in the Calcutta riot leading to a temporary ban of playing music before mosques by the Calcutta administration. See also the summary article 'The Tide of Communalism' in the 1926 yearbook of the *Indian Annual Register* (*IAR* 1926/II: 75ff.). For a discussion of the two most frequently named causes of riots—cows and music—see Flynn (1981).

[61]Ibid. For an overview of official statistics on communal riots up to 1929, see the Government of India Memorandum on 'Communal Disorders' (ISC 1930/IV: 95–120). According to this despatch, in 1922–9 approximately 450 lives were lost and 5.000 persons received injuries (ibid.: 106). The actual figures may have been somewhat higher.

the counter-movement of tanẓīm. This constellation encouraged Islamic critics of the JUH scholars to press for a much stronger articulation of religious demands and rights. They felt that the 'ulamā' should no longer care for the sensitivities of Hindu élites, and make it clear that the Hindu-Muslim entente cannot become an embrace where Muslims were suffocated. Although the riots were difficult to control and to manage, and public leaders from all camps were well aware of it, some Islamic groups accused JUH scholars of connivance with Hindu extremism by their cooperation with the Congress.

With passing time, the JUH and the Khilafat Conference grew more determined and terse in their responses. At its 1926 special session in May convened under the impact of the terrible April riots in Calcutta, the Khilafat Conference directed all Khilafat committees to respond to communal tension directly. They were directed to either help settle differences or depute volunteers to be present on the scene of disturbances to 'render every moral and material support to the Moslems whose rights, interests, lives and property might have been endangered or suffered owing to communal dissensions or disturbances'.[62] The saṅgaṭhan campaign of the Hindū Mahāsabhā was condemned as a 'wrong and short-sighted policy, prejudicial to the prosperity and liberation of the country, [...] exhorting the Muslims to keep their feelings carefully under control and spend all their energies on the constructive programme of purification, improvement and strengthening of their community'. The 'inter-communal tumults were not only extremely injurious to the participants themselves but also stood in the way of attainment of self-government'. The more aggressive tone, which came to dominate Muslim meetings, also marked the intervention of Shaukat Ali. While demanding that both communities should live in a state of friendship, he advised that in case of an attack by the Hindus or any other community on the Muslims they should 'pay back in the like manner' (*IAR* 1926/I:413). Advocating tablīgh, Muhammad Ali prayed that one day he would convert Mahatma Gandhi to Islam. The impact of the Calcutta riots was felt so strongly that the Khilafat Conference amended its creed, adding to it clause (d) to 'safeguard the religious, educational, social, economical and political interests of Indian Mussalmans and to reforms and organise them'.[63] Using the word 'brethren' in relation to Hindus provoked noisy objections (*IAR* 1926/II: 78, I: 411).

[62]Resolution proposed by Maulana Zafarul-Mullick at the Delhi session of All-India Khilafat Conference on 8 May 1926 (*IAR* 1926/I: 412).

[63]Originally the Khilafat creed contained three objectives: (a) defending the Khilafat; (b) defending the Arabian Peninsula and the Holy Places of Islam; and (c) striving for the attainment of swarāj (independence). Cf. *Dastūr-i 'Amal Jam'īyat-i Khilāfat-i Hind* (Bombay: Khilāfat Press: n.d.), quoted in Aziz (1972: 338).

Tension was heightened tremendously when news of the assassination of the Āryā Samāj leader Swami Shraddhananda on 23 December 1926 reached the public. At the same time, it had a partially sobering effect on the climate of mutual recriminations and attacks.

The Barelwis were in the forefront of the critics of the JUH and repeatedly demanded an end to its cooperation with the Congress. While they had already formed their rival organizations for tablīgh, they discussed their political and religious response to the heightened tension at the 1925 Muradabad session of the AISC (cf. section 4.1.1). In his welcome address, Hamid Raza Khan displayed much bitterness over the pro-Hindu course of the Khilafat Committee and the JUH. He rejected any form of Hindu–Muslim unity as it had allegedly proven harmful to Muslims. The latter, he felt, had been forced to give up their identity in order to embrace the Hindus. He pointed out how Muslim leaders had started preaching against beef, Muḥarram processions, and the public recitation of the shahādat. Scholars standing steadfast to their beliefs and cooperating with government were put under unbearable pressure. Recounting quotations from the Qur'an and the traditions he emphasized that there could be no unity with 'idolaters', the by-word for Hindus. He similarly rejected unity with other Islamic sects, as this would undermine the identity of mainstream Muslims. He took exception to the very goal of freedom itself since *swarāj* (independence) would amount to Hinḍu *rāj* (rule) destined to be harmful to Muslims.[64] To save themselves from riots Muslims were advised to maintain vigilance and peace everywhere. If preparations for a riot were noticed government needed to be informed. Muslims were advised to locally organize and watch over investigations after riots so that no anti-Muslim bias would come into play (Qadiri 1997: 153–77). A 1930 AISC meeting in the province of Bengal appealed to Muslims to remain aloof from Congress politics. Another resolution criticized the JUH scholars as being puppets in the hands of the Hindus. Similar sentiments were expressed at an AISC meeting in Gujarat in the same year (Qadiri 1999: 53–5). From the Barelwi perspective, the defence of Muslims was to take place through their local communities. The shrine-keepers (pīr) saw to it that these communities stayed closely knit. But the Barelwis were also less affected by communal violence as they mainly resided in rural areas and smaller localities while communal rioting mostly occurred in the inner city areas of the district towns.

The Muslim arguments closely shadowed the Hindu rhetoric. Taking as a background the deplorable incidents of rioting and violence during

[64]This position changed when the Barelwis came around to supporting the Pakistan movement, which was accepted as a form of independence devoid of Hindu domination.

the so-called Moplah disturbances of 1921, where Hindus were forcibly converted and Hindu women raped, Pandit Malaviya, Congress politician and leader of the newly founded Hindū Mahāsabhā, defended his campaign for Hindu self-organization and defence in 1923:

> After working for a long time in the service of the public he (Malawiya) had come to the only one conclusion on the question of Hindu-Muslim unity—it was that each should feel that the other was strong enough to ward off successfully any unjust attack by the other and thus alone would harmony be maintained (*IAR* 1923/I: 943).

For reformist Hindus, the saṅgaṭhan movement also gave a new push to their social reformism, which faced stiff opposition from Hindu orthodoxy when the abolition of child marriage, for instance, was pursued. Hinduism was renowned for its internal divisions and sectarian groupings. Hinduism, in fact, thrived on its heterogeneity. Therefore, Hindu reformists regarded greater unity of action among Hindus a prerequisite for a political role of Hinduism, for the social rebirth of the Hindu religion, and for fighting the long-standing discrimination of untouchables and low-caste Hindus. Conflict with the Muslims gave them a welcome opportunity to exemplify the internal and external threats Hindus allegedly faced.

The external threats that Hindu politicians pointed out referred to select historical experiences with Muslim invasions of India, and particularly of its northern plains. The bogey of the fanatical Muslim tribesmen charging down the Khaiber through mountain passes from Afghanistan and the Pakhtun areas to the Gangetic plains to attack, plunder, and rape Hindus was regularly raised to great effect. In the same vein, Muslim leaders and scholars repeatedly projected a certain measure of strength of their minority community by making ample references to pan-Islamism, to alliances with Afghanistan, Iran, and Turkey in order to withstand the pressure of the Hindu majority. Events in the recent past had refuelled Hindu anxieties. The 1914–16 'silk letter conspiracy' of radical Islamic scholars and activists from India, Afghanistan, and Turkey was well remembered as it had sought to restore Muslim rule against the British, thereby hoping to defeat the Hindu majority. In 1920, the Islamic campaign for migration to Afghanistan (hijrat) had followed a similar strategy. Certain Congress Muslims, Khilafat activists, and Islamic scholars[65] had started it toying with the idea of inducing the amīr of Afghanistan to challenge British rule over India. The amīr had gone on a third war with Britain in 1919 with disastrous consequences for Afghanistan and was now looking for a face-saving way out. The 'Afghan' threat to

[65]Abdul Bari, Maulana Azad, cf. Reetz (1995) and Chapter 5, section 5.3.4.

India's unity also played a role in the mid-1920s when the extension of constitutional reforms to the Pakhtun province in the northwest frontier was discussed. Staunch opposition persisted on communal lines against the amalgamation of the Frontier province with Punjab. Muslim activists argued that this would dilute the Muslim character of the Frontier province. In the heat of the debate proposals were made to partition India into a Muslim north with pan-Islamic links to Afghanistan and a non-Muslim south.[66] The Hindū Mahāsabhā presented Afghan and other foreign connections of Muslims as 'external threats'. In their eyes this combined with the 'internal threat' of Hindu 'weakness' in the face of Muslim determination (*IAR* 1925/I). This stereotyping of Muslims by Hindu leaders was bitterly resented. Muslim leaders severely criticized the political and historical revisionism of Hindu leaders aiming at the removal of Muslim influences on India's history and culture. Maulana Muhammad Ali stressed in 1926 that the Khilafat Movement did not work for Afghan rule in India but for swarāj, which had occupied him all along. Maulana Husain Ahmad highlighted the external connections invoked by Hindu leaders, as the Maharaja of Nepal had been invited to preside over the Hindū Mahāsabhā session.[67] He stressed that no foreign leader had done so in any Muslim meeting (*IAR* 1926/I: 411).

4.2.3. *Self-Defence of Muslims*

In another parallel, the defence discourses of Muslims and Hindus were suffused with references to their physical weakness in the face of the other community and of British rule. Muslim and Hindu reformists shared a belief widely held in élite circles at the time that physical laxity and the influence of vegetarianism on Indians were responsible in large measure for their weakness and their enslavement by the British. Muslims also felt that British rule 'emasculated' them. This fear was repeatedly voiced in connection with restrictions on carrying weapons, which had long been a tradition with Muslim tribal populations of the Pakhtuns, for instance. The Sikhs and the Hindu Gurkhas advanced analogous arguments in relation to carrying ritual weapons. There was a significant confluence

[66] In 1925, the Hindu leader Lajpat Rai quoted the Pakhtun representative of a local Islamic Anjuman, Sardar Muhammad Gul Khan, *in extensio* when the latter gave evidence to a reforms enquiry committee. Khan repeatedly referred to an Islamic League of Nations to which the Pakhtuns should belong. He demanded, rather prophetically, a partition of India on communal lines where the territory north of the city of Agra should be made over to the Muslims and the south to the Hindus (*IAR* 1925/I: 381–2).

[67] This was done to underline the Hindu character of the whole of South Asia as Nepalese kingship drew some legitimacy from Hindu doctrine also.

of symbolism in these discourses. Colonial rule was seen to have undermined their manliness (cf. Fischer-Tiné 2001). This had to be rectified by resorting to a strict reformation of behaviour, by purification, by following a path of radical religious and social reformism. Both Hindu[68] and Muslim[69] groups demanded to combine religious with physical education and to promote the traditional gymnasiums for this purpose. British power was effectively projected through the symbols of army, police, and volunteer movements such as the Boy Scouts. While these groups were allowed to train, wear uniforms, stage parades, and carry weapons, the British viewed the local volunteer organizations with suspicion. Their concern was no unexpected burst of manliness on the part of Indians but the challenge well-trained volunteers could pose to British rule as 'private' armies.

The volunteer movement had developed in India out of a combination of being 'servants of God' and 'servants of the public', blending the tradition of employing guards and ushers at religious festivals, which existed well before the arrival of the British, and the distinct model of the Western volunteer organizations. Activities such as regular physical exercises and training, parades and uniforms, held great attraction and social prestige particularly for young men. With the rising tide of the national and anti-colonial movement, all camps and major parties saw to it to have such party troopers of 'toughs and roughs', who could push through the party agenda against adversaries, if need be, with pressure and violence. For a time, the Congress and the Khilafatists supported the activities of an All-India Volunteers' Conference meant to coordinate the formation of volunteer groups in all Indian provinces for the purposes of the Non-Cooperation and the Khilafat Movement.[70] This method of political

[68]For the Hindu discourse, see, for instance, the programme of the Hindū Mahāsabhā as announced by Lajpat Rai in 1925 which in clause 4 included the demand to 'organise gymnasiums for the use of Hindu youngmen and women' (*IAR* 1925/I: 381). This was a constant theme of the Hindū Mahāsabhā. Its leader Dr Moonjee referred in its 1927 annual session to the Hindus being weak in comparison with the Muslims who 'with a better physique had shown a better instinct for politics and higher independence of thought' (*IAR* 1927/I: 417). See also the movement by Swami Shraddhananda to establish a reformed Hindu religious school, the gurukul, which amongst other aims, sought to inculcate a spirit of physical resilience in its students. In contrast to religious Muslim schools, it also taught modern sciences and English. Cf. Jordens (1981: 66–102); see also Fischer-Tiné's discussion of the Kangri Gurukul in his dissertation (2003).

[69]JUH resolution no. 7 of its 1927 session demanded the inclusion of physical exercise in madrasa education (Rozinah 1981/I: 454). In 1946 the AISC made the demand on behalf of the Barelwis for physical education and the creation of gymnasiums (*akhāṛ ā*), as they had traditionally served the younger generation for gaining physical strength (Qadiri 1997: 274).

[70]See the reports on the volunteer conferences in Cocanada in 1923, presided over by Jawaharlal Nehru (*IAR* 1923/I: 211–9); in Kanpur in 1925, presided over by T. C. Goswami

mobilization, of physically contesting the public sphere, came to be refined and extensively practised since the mid-1920s. Sandria Freitag described the change in tactics employed by volunteers following the example of the Kanpur riots in 1913 and 1931 (1990: 230ff.). The 1913 agitation developed in a classical manner with demonstrations growing in size and leading to the involvement of ever more people. Here, the violence was sparked by attempts of police to control these crowds. By contrast, the 1931 agitation representing a 'new generation' of activism was spearheaded by a group of Congress volunteers who enforced agitation and a strike on an unwilling town threatening merchants and forcing down the shutters of markets. This method of enforcing a strike by violence, the hartāl, has since become a standard political weapon in the hands of all major political and religious forces across South Asia.

It is against the background of these discourses on weakness and manliness, defence and self-defence that the Khāksār Movement rose to fame after 1931. From among the movements included in this analysis, it was the quintessential self-defence organization (NDC 403–5). Its founder Mashriqi was the principal of a college in Peshawar. The formation of the movement was apparently prompted by the beginning of the Congress-led Civil Disobedience Movement in Peshawar in the Frontier Province. A demonstration in the Qiṣṣa Kahānī Bazār in April 1930 resulted in a confrontation with armoured cars of the military. Several of the unarmed agitators were killed when unprovoked firing started. This created a huge outcry from the public. Pakhtun tribes marched to Peshawar and the colonial army was drawn into regular battle bombarding their villages mercilessly (cf. BLOC L/P&J/6/2003; BLOC L/P&S/12/3125; Rittenberg 1988). In the Frontier Province, the Khāksār became the rivals of the Red Shirt movement led by Abdul Ghaffar Khan who supported the Congress. In Punjab, they acted opposite the Aḥrār who had formed slightly earlier (December 1929).

It was the feeling of helplessness and defencelessness in the face of brute power as applied by the colonial authorities in the Peshawar incident that pushed Mashriqi to implement his scheme of Muslim self-defence units. Outwardly, the appearance of the movement was military, that of a 'private army', the term used by the colonial administration for militant volunteer movements engaging in drilling and parading. Yet, the principles

(*IAR* 1925/II: 362–5); in Gauhati in 1926, presided over by Motilal Nehru (*IAR* 1926/II: 381–83); and in Calcutta in 1931, presided over by H. S. Suhrawardy (*IAR* 1931/I: 308). The latter also convened an All-India Muslim Volunteers' Conference. They demonstrated how prominent leaders were involved in directing the activities of the movement (cf. BLOC L/P&J/6/1731; BLOC L/P&J/8/678–79).

of the rules and structure of the Khāksār organization made clear that there was a strong religious motive involved. There was a deep-going connection with Mashriqi's religious views as expressed in his treatise *Tadkira*. He supported the regular parading and training exercises with references to Islamic tradition. As understood by him, Islam was another name for militancy ('askarīyat) and soldierly tradition (*khudā kī faujeñ*), for a spirit of sacrifice (*jānbāzī*) (Mashriqi 1995: 105, 132ff., 153). The spade (bēlcha), which had been made into a symbol of the movement, was supposed to have been used by the Prophet in digging the ditch in the battle of Azhab (in 5 AH). As such he considered the shovel Sunna, that is, a tradition of the Prophet.[71] More precisely, it was the aesthetics of pious soldierly asceticism that tremendously attracted Mashriqi and shaped the culture of the Khāksār (cf. their creed in Appendix I).

His interpretation of Islam also included the requirement of self-organization and the need for a devoted, humble, and selfless life in service of the people. With hindsight, the movement made its major impact by assembling and training hundreds of thousands of young Muslim men. This increased their level of organization and self-esteem. The few organized campaigns undertaken by the Khāksār were mainly acts of defiance. In 1939, their first conflict with the authorities occurred in Lucknow in the United Provinces. Mashriqi rushed there to offer his services of mediation in a religious conflict between Shi'i and Sunni groups. The conflict had been partly instigated by the Aḥrār, considered the archrivals of the Khāksār. When Mashriqi's services were rejected, his followers used the spade (bēlcha) against the Aḥrār in the ensuing scuffle. This led to a confrontation with the police and their externment from the province. Another conflict developed on the eve of the annual Muslim League session in Lahore in March 1940. The Khāksār defied a ban by the Punjab government on the display of shovels and on military marches. By that time, the colonial government had resolved to take more stringent measures against volunteer organizations. Suppressing 'private armies' was considered legitimate, as World War II had commenced. This led to the arrest of Mashriqi and to repeated temporary orders of some provincial governments declaring the Khāksār an unlawful association. The third campaign of the Khāksār was devoted to opposing the restrictions, fighting for the release of Mashriqi and other leaders. In extent and duration, this was their single largest campaign. The war and a resumption of oppositional agitation by

[71] To this Maududi is reported to have retorted that it was not a shovel that the Prophet used but a mattock. Use of the shovel was the Sunna (tradition) of Hitler and not of the Prophet. Cf. Maulana Maududi, '*Khaksār taḥrīk aor Mashraqī*', *Al-Furqān* (*Ṣafar/Rabī'-ul-Awwal* 1395 AH), quoted in Malik (2000: 43, fn. 19).

the Congress through the 'Quit India' movement in 1942 made it especially difficult for the Khāksār to regain their legal status.

In short intervals of legitimate activity, the Khāksār continued their militant camps, which was their major form of self-organization and enjoyed great popularity among Muslim youth. Makeshift soldierly settlements with tents and parading grounds were set up where parades were held, drilling exercises in uniforms imparted, and mock battles with shovels staged. After their ban, the military aspects were more camouflaged and partly conducted in a concealed form. In line with their vocation of militant public service, the Khāksār also offered themselves for disaster relief operations in which they mostly worked locally. Their major activity in this regard was undertaken in 1943 when they were given charge of running famine relief camps in the province of Bengal, partly with support from the local government. As the Khāksār also implemented here their universalist principles they included Hindus in their care. This was fiercely opposed by both the Hindū Mahāsabhā and the Muslim League. On the personal advice of the Muslim League leader Jinnah, the Muslim premier of Bengal ordered the closure of the Khāksār camp. This annoyed Mashriqi so much that he sent a telegram on Jinnah's birthday making a token present of the dead bodies of 600,000 famine destitutes to Jinnah (Mathur 1972: 218).

Mashriqi showed here some of his political naivety and adventurism. While he was driven by a certain idealistic concept of reconstructing Muslim society in India on militant lines, he got caught in the polarization of public activism between the Congress and the Muslim League. With a bias against the Congress Party, Mashriqi navigated a difficult zigzag course between the two rivals. His criticism of the Congress appeared to be very closely related to his militant understanding of Islam. The Congress and its creed of non-violence, as introduced by Gandhi, represented to him unsuccessful methods. More than that, non-violence and the tactics of Gandhi, whom he considered to be an 'effeminate' leader, embodied to Mashriqi an unworthy and degrading attitude, representing to him all the reasons for the weakness and defeat of the Indians by the British. This opposition to the Congress did not translate into a principled support of the Muslim League. In fact, Mashriqi opposed the League's 'two-nation theory' based on the existence of separate Muslim and Hindu nations and its call for a territorial separation of Muslim majority territories.[72] But his opposition to the Congress led his local branches to drift towards Muslim

[72]Mashriqi argued this secured the rights of 4 crore (40 million) Muslims at the cost of leaving 6 crore in India. It neglected the cultural and historical traditions of the Muslim nation. If a separation was to take place at all, it would have to be much more comprehensive. From this position, he worked for the inclusion of further Muslim territories of India into Pakistan, including first of all Kashmir, although not to great effect (Malik 2000: 179; 190ff.).

League support. A huge, organized, and seemingly idle militant Muslim force such as the Khāksār was regarded by Jinnah as a rather practical political utility, which would come handy in the power struggle with the Congress. The Khāksār were occasionally persuaded to act as guards on the occasion of Muslim League conferences. But the two could not eventually come together. Jinnah insisted that the Khāksār when joining the Muslim League should give up their organization, something totally unacceptable to Mashriqi. He also did not want to give up the right of the Khāksār to serve all communities whereas Jinnah insisted that they should serve only Muslims and among them only the Muslim League.[73] The League finally created its own party soldiers called the National Guards and so no longer needed the Khāksār's. A similarly negative answer was given to the Khāksār by the British when Mashriqi offered to send 50,000 members immediately to the war front provided he could retain control over them (Mathur 1972: 230).

As developments towards the mid-1940s made the Khāksār increasingly irrelevant, Mashriqi undertook frantic efforts to secure a political role in the transfer of power at the dawn of independence. Since he had once commanded a huge force, which now quickly dwindled away, he still mistakenly believed he had his original bargaining power. When communal tension picked up in connection with the partition he suggested to both Nehru and Jinnah that they place their forces at his command so that he could unite both the communities and lead them into a free India. When Mashriqi created a separate political department in his movement in 1945, he hoped to be able to make a dent in the forthcoming elections in 1946 among the Muslim electorate, apparently without success.[74] He preached Hindu–Muslim unity as a precondition for independence and demanded that his followers contact all major parties, including the Congress, the Muslim League, the Hindū Mahāsabhā, and the Communist Party. They were required to explain the importance of his movement to these parties (Mathur 1972: 212). He also made brief contact with the Indian National Army led by the radical Congress politician, Subhash Chandra Bose (1897–1945). He even contacted his arch-enemies, the Aḥrār, for negotiations. In 1947, Mashriqi formally disbanded the Khāksār organization. During partition his organization

[73]For this purpose, the League adopted an anti-Khāksār resolution in 1943 stipulating that the moment the latter entered the field of politics beyond religion their relations would be severed. Their relations reached breaking point when in July 1943 an attack on Jinnah was ascribed to a Khāksār activist (Mathur 1972: 218–19).

[74]Mashriqi held secret talks in March–July 1947 with some tribal Pakhtun leaders who did not want to become part of Pakistan. He proposed the creation of an Islamic government under his leadership (Malik 2000: 180ff.).

in Punjab was reported to have locally cooperated with the Muslim League, supporting some of its militant actions and helping the victims of communal violence and dislocation (Malik 2000: 179; cf. Seth 1985: 103ff.).

The Aḥrār were a self-defence organization only in a limited sense. They projected the demands of a certain regional (Punjab) and religious (Muslim) élite dissatisfied with the Congress. They started as a Punjab Muslim caucus in the Congress mobilizing Muslim support. It was suspected that their conception was the result of shrewd calculation by Maulana Azad who looked after Muslim issues in the Congress leadership. Aḥrār leaders soon went their own way in choosing points of intervention. Their programme was less comprehensive than that of the Khāksār. Their argument was often couched in radical political rhetoric. Instead of organizing Muslims for religious or social reformation, they went on the offensive in selected militant campaigns against the Aḥmadīya and the Shi'a where they picked the doctrinal and political issues with their opponents in order to gain maximum publicity. (These activities are discussed in section 4.4. as an example of Islamic radicalism.) Besides the party organization, the Aḥrār had a separate volunteer corps that was also organized on military lines, the Jaish-e Aḥrār (Army of the Aḥrār, sometimes also called, the armies—Juyūsh). As they wore red clothes they also called themselves the Red Shirts (*surkhpōsh*) in honour of the famous Frontier movement. (Mirza 1975/I: 149–50). Emulating the Khāksār's choice of the spade, they chose the axe as their weapon in 1939 (Mirza 1975/IV: 62). The JUH decided to have its own volunteers in 1940 (Resolution 12/1940: Rozīnah 1981/II: 701). The Khaldī Fauj was another Muslim volunteer force, which achieved some notoriety. It was the tanẓīm effort by Hasan Nizami who was also active in tablīgh (Malik 2000: 43). The National Guards formed by the Muslim League played a notorious role during the partition in 1946–7 (Jalal 1994: 231, 263). Obtaining volunteers had become an element of fierce competition among all political and religious groups in colonial India. It reflected the growing power struggle at the dawn of independence and the throttled state of politics. Their deployment had an anti-colonial dimension as much as a sectarian direction. It helped bestow recognition on militancy and violence as a recognized and legitimate means of contestation of the public sphere.

The Islamic discourse on defence and self-defence was strong and influential. Dealing with the defence of religious identity, it concerned all Muslims. Opinion was more unanimous and its appeal was often emotional. Issues like the threat of conversion were difficult to ignore. There were attempts to argue that conversion and community organization were legitimate tasks of all religious communities, which should be recognized.

This point was made not only by Muhammad Ali, and Kitchlew, but also by the Hindu Congress leader Malaviya.[75] They felt that it should be conducted in a spirit of peace and tolerance. The public sphere, however, had changed too much for that to happen. This was precisely one indicator of the transformation of religious groups and forces into agents of the public sphere. Religion was no longer a personal affair. It could not be left to individual Muslims of the Malkana Rajputs to decide if they wanted to stay in the category of 'neo-Muslims', become 'proper' Muslims, or become Hindus. The challenge was not to the conscience of one individual. The challenge was from one group—the Hindu reformist group, the Āryā Samāj and its offspring, the Hindū Mahāsabhā—to Islamic reformist groups. The latter had to respond to this challenge as a group, as an agent in the public sphere by public activity. Islamic leaders were quick to grasp the significance of the defence discourse for the elevation of the identity of Islamic groups. They did not care too much that its consequences were cataclysmic and at times disastrous.

The 'other' side, Hindu reformism, acted in a similar way. The magnitude of the cultural and religious revisionism pursued by the Hindu reformists was enormous. Hindu reformists repeatedly declared that they regarded nine-tenth of Indian Muslims as converts, with one-tenth of 'foreign' origin who ought to be sent back to their countries of 'origin'. They demanded that all former Hindus be taken back into the Hindu fold.[76] By this, Hindu reformists demanded nothing less than the removal of Islam from India, which had been residing there and interacting with Hinduism for centuries. This public posturing of the Hindu reformists was driven by similar social and political processes that were spurring on Islamic forces. They responded to the modern challenges of capitalist change, colonial rule, and the prospects of an independent India the nature and outlook of which was still to be determined. They were anxious to transform Hinduism from a mental and devotional concept into a religious and social, and ultimately a political force. The religious perspective served the purpose of representing the authentic, indigenous, the inner self against the 'alien,' foreign domination of Western Christian civilization through colonial rule and global capitalist hegemony.

[75]For Muhammad Ali, see his speech at the Cocanada Congress session on 28 December 1923 (*IAR* 1923/I: 77); for Kitchlew and Malaviya, see Kitchlew (1987: 48).

[76]Malaviya stated at the 1923 Hindū Mahāsabhā session: 'There are 48 million of Muslims in India of whom not more than fifty lakhs (5 million) are those who have come from outside. The rest were converted from Hinduism. Theirs is a proselytising religion while our religion has closed the doors for those who want to come to our fold' (*IAR* 1923/I: 133). See also Kelkar's statement at the 1925 session, quoted in Chapter 3, fn. 109.

The Islamic defence discourse could be divided into (i) a local, cultural response, the tanẓīm activity triggered by Kitchlew's scheme; (ii) a long-term, more centralized approach of Muslim self-organization as embodied in the efforts of the JUH to create an Islamic authority for India (*Imārat-e Sharī'a*); and (iii) the creation of self-defence units and volunteer bodies engaging in physical and military training to defend Muslims in communal tension or other conflict. The first type of response differed from the third in that it was more amorphous, less stable. The Khāksār who almost formed a full-fledged defence force exemplified the third type.

4.3. ACTIVISM OR CONTEMPLATION: FROM ENGAGEMENT TO JIHĀD

While the defence discourse appealed to the emotional level, to the 'inner self' (nafs), to the core features of what it meant to be a Muslim, the discourse on activism, on a public and political role for Islam, dealt much more with the 'outer self', the public face of Muslims and Islam in India. It was dominated by an oppositional style. The debate on activism was also different from the one on participation and participatory politics. Participation aimed at potentially legal and constructive involvement, the intent to play by the rules, whereas activism pursued the objective and demonstrated the capacity to challenge British rule over India. The discourse of political activism as presented in this chapter, therefore, discusses religious and political arguments in favour of oppositional and confrontational commitment and the action undertaken to translate it into practice.

Here we will concentrate on five lines of argument and action. The first one aimed at the choice that Islamic groups and leaders had to make between a pietist and an activist position. This choice was by no means easy to make nor self-understood. Second, 'the nation' discourse presented a similar dilemma. It put 'composite nationalism' against the two-nation theory as pursued by the Muslim League. Seemingly worldly, this debate also concerned religious leaders and implicated doctrinal positions. But it was primarily pan-Islamism that moved from contemplation to radical action. In this connection the meaning of the third, pan-Turkism and activities in defence of the Ottoman Khilafat, are discussed. Although these were transnational issues, they were essentially fought as internal Indian campaigns. In contrast, fourth, other pan-Islamist concerns were more focused on areas outside India constituting a separate sub-discourse. Fifth, the meaning of jihād, especially where it involved militant warfare for Islam, was another hotly contested issue of the time that shaped the public face of Islam back then as it does today.

4.3.1. Piety vs. Political Engagement

As has been mentioned earlier, political activism was not something that was implicit in the outlook of reformist Islamic scholars in India, and in the Deoband Seminary in particular. Before Mahmud al-Hasan, Ubaidullah Sindhi, and Husain Ahmad Madani left their imprint on the activities of the seminary, an attitude of studied loyalism towards British rule prevailed. Most of the religious scholars devoted their energy to the need of rehabilitating the Muslim community. This aimed at the revival of religious knowledge and education to strengthen its self-identification. It was also directed at the restoration of its place in the public realm as a valued and recognized community in the face of the British attacks on Wahhabism and on alleged Muslim proclivities to militant warfare and opposition to British rule in the form of jihād.

The Maulanas Madani and Thanawi represented opposing perspectives on the role of politics in religion. Madani symbolized the activist approach whereas Thanawi prioritized the acquisition of religious knowledge and pious reformation of the self. The activist faction was only gradually ascending. Madani had learnt politics from his teacher and mentor, the Shaykh al-Hind, Mahmud al-Hasan. The latter had been the first student at the Deoband Seminary, and had received personal instruction from its founder, Nanaotawi. After being a teacher he was gradually promoted to the post of principal in 1890 (Rizvi 1980/II: 133). He had inspired two students in particular, Ubaidullah Sindhi and Madani. When Hasan got himself involved in plans to support Ottoman Turkey and became a party to the 'silk letter conspiracy' (see section 4.3.4.) in 1914–16, Madani accompanied him on the ḥajj to Mecca, where Hasan was arrested by the Sharif of Mecca (Husain ibn Ali, 1852–1931) and handed over to the British who interned him in Malta. The faithful Madani not only kept Hasan company during internment but also wrote a prominent travelogue on their fate, containing their views on their political schemes for which they had been arrested.[77] Hasan contributed to the foundation of the Khilafat Conference, but he died soon afterwards (1920). While a debate started on whether to appoint a leader of Islam in India (Amīr al-Hind) and who would be the suitable candidate (cf. section 4.1.3.), Madani was nominated Shaykh al-Islām by the JUH. It was there that Madani's influence was felt most strongly. He presided over its fifth and the twelfth to fourteenth sessions.[78] But he also ascended to the highest post at Deoband

[77] *Safarnāmah Shaykh al-Hind* (Travelogue of the Shaykh al-Hind), Madani (1974); on this episode see also Miyan (1976, 1988).

[78] Rozinah (1981/I, II: passim). Apparently Metcalf erred in her account, contending Madani presided over the ninth to twelfth JUH sessions (1982: 108).

when the activist faction gained the upper hand. He was elected its principal in 1927, a post he held until his death in 1957 (ibid.: 155). During this period he had always championed a strong public role for Deoband. He remained a committed ally of Congress and gave his religious verdicts accordingly. He supported the Khilafat campaign and the non-cooperation fatwā, refuted counter-arguments, opposed the 'two-nation theory' and defended 'composite nationalism' (see section 4.3.2.). Above all, he enjoined Muslims living peacefully together with Hindus if their religious rights were secured.

On this he was opposed by Maulana Thanawi who had been a mentor, Sufi shaykh, and patron for Deoband and most of its teachers in the 1920s and 1930s (cf. Chapter 3, fn. 12). But this opposition should not be seen in overly simplistic terms. Madani was also considered to be a very learned man. He was widely valued for his erudition and his teaching of ḥadīth. And he was much inclined to practical action. Thanawi, in contrast, was of an academic bent, writing many works on a great variety of religious subjects. But he was also practical in working for religious and social reform among Muslims and launching different schemes for schools and tablīgh societies. They would not attack each other personally. Their difference lay in their views of what ought to be done to save Islam and Muslims in India. Thanawi believed that the road to success lay through the inner perfection of Muslims and the strengthening of their faith and religious practice. Madani thought Muslims should not wait for this state of perfection to arrive but act immediately. In particular, he considered action for ending British rule over India a prerequisite for restoring Islam to eminence in the life of Indian Muslims. The comparative political radicalism of Madani was complemented with relative moderation in doctrinal matters.[79] On the other hand, the cautious attitude of Thanawi on political issues was balanced by a very principled position on doctrine, earning him the name of a reformist of repute. His position there at times bordered on the rigid. Thanawi resolutely opposed the Congress and saw no good in cooperating with it.[80] He abhorred politics for their ostentatious

[79]See, for instance, his advice on the rules for tablīgh and tanẓīm where he demanded that the religion of non-Muslims should be respected and that factual truth and circumspection should prevail (see Chapter 5, section 5.2.2).

[80]Thanawi believed that the Congress wanted to throw Muslims out of India (*Malfūẓāt*, p. 192, quoted in Thanawi 1983: 518). He opposed the Congress method of courting arrest in the non-violence movement (*satyāgraha*) (ibid.: 522). He rejected all movements that were not purely religious (*khāliṣ maẕhabī*), therefore there was no obligation to participate in them (ibid.: 524). He contended the English regarded Muslims as their major enemy because their differences were religious, whereas their differences with the Hindus were political and would be over, once these were solved (ibid.: 517).

and superficial character, features he regarded to be at variance with true Islam. For this reason he initially opposed the tablīgh movement of Muhammad Ilyas. Yet when he saw change in the religious attitude of 'neo-Muslims' happening before his eyes, his practical mind was convinced.

This difference of opinion and cleavage was also played out in connection with the student strike at Deoband (see section 4.1.1.). Thanawi had argued that students should concentrate on their (religious) studies. When the rules of administration were revised and the post of patron abolished, Thanawi had to concede defeat. The Deoband faction of teachers that had to leave apparently sympathized with him (cf. fn. 12, this chapter). With Shabbir Ahmad Uthmani it also included the future leader of the pro-Pakistan JUH wing. The differences in the positions of Madani and Thanawi appear so significant that with hindsight analysts speak of separate factions, even traditions, named after them. S.V.R. Nasr interpreted much of the internal developments among the Deobandis in Pakistan and India after independence in terms of a struggle between the successors of these two factions (Nasr 2000: 169ff.). In particular, it was assumed that the Madani faction was and is inclined towards jihādī forms of struggle. When Pakistan came into being, Uthmani dominated the central leadership of the Deoband School there. But the Madani faction retained particular influence in the Pakhtun tribal areas of the Frontier Province and in Karachi where its seminaries were located, which supported close links with the Afghan Ṭālibān. It is alleged that nowadays the Madani faction has gained the upper hand in Pakistan and India.[81] It remains debatable to what extent it is justified to associate militant trends with Madani. It seems more plausible to argue that the two positions were the result of conflicting sources of 'ulamā' activism reflecting tension between their scholarly beginnings and their social and historical roots.

4.3.2. Two-Nation Theory or 'Composite Nationalism'

A similar tension could be discerned in the 'nation' debate. Religious scholars and Muslim activists intensely debated the issue whether Indian Muslims, in spite of their heterogeneous cultural and linguistic composition, constituted a separate nation (qaum) or belonged to a united but 'composite' nation that represented multicultural India. The significance of this nation discourse derived from the enormous importance of the nationalist movement. Religious scholars had considered nationalism among the

[81]Other factors beside the Madani–Thanawi factionalism may be more pertinent for the evaluation of internal trends in the Deoband schools of India and Pakistan such as the different social and political trajectories of the two countries.

vices of Western and materialist influences (cf. section 3.2.3f.). Partly this also led them to reject the idea of a separate nation of Indian Muslims. Advocates of the idea of a separate Muslim nation in India belonged to the Aligarh school of thought created by Sayyid Ahmad Khan that brought the Muslim League into being. Religious scholars viewed with anxiety how this faction adopted the concept of Muslim nationalism for the League, and later for the Pakistan movement. The 'ulamā' believed, and to some extent perhaps rightly so, that the choice of these terms meant the advocation of a worldly, secular direction for the future state of Pakistan, something to which the religious scholars could not agree. When the Muslim League moved the Pakistan concept to the forefront of its policies in the late 1930s it openly clashed with religious scholars.

The majority of reformist scholars did not believe in a territorial concept for an Islamic society. They regarded it as deviation and heresy when principles other than submission to God and worship were advanced to the top. The scholars of Deoband, of the Nadwa, and of Firangī Maḥall were not convinced that the Pakistan concept would result in an Islamic society. Neither was Maududi who wanted much firmer institutional guarantees for an Islamic state—although in principle he supported the idea that Islam could and should be enforced through the state, something which other reformist scholars also rejected.

The JUH and Husain Ahmad Madani in particular defended cohabitation between Muslims and Hindus within the framework of 'composite nationalism'—muttaḥida qaumīyāt. The latter, together with Maulana Azad, pointed to relevant verses in the Qur'an, which promoted religious tolerance. Arguments for cooperation between Hindus and Muslims were largely based on references to Sura *Al-Mumtaḥina* (60), verses 7 to 9, demanding tolerance towards those non-Muslims who did not fight against Islam.[82] Another major line of argument was based on the famous Covenant of Medina, the only known secular document related to the Prophet. The document stipulated the rules of peaceful

[82]In the course of the Khilafat campaign, the following verses from the Sura *Al-Mumtahina* (60) were quoted in support of cooperation with the Hindus:

It may be that Allah will grant love (and friendship) between you and those whom ye (now) hold as enemies. For Allah has power (over all things); And Allah is Oft-Forgiving, Most Merciful (Verse 7).

Allah forbids you not, with regard to those who fight you not for (your) Faith nor drive you out of your homes, from dealing kindly and justly with them: for Allah loveth those who are just (Verse 8).

Allah only forbids you, with regard to those who fight you for (your) Faith, and drive you out of your homes, and support (others) in driving you out, from turning to them (for friendship and protection). It is such as turn to them (in these circumstances), that do wrong (Verse 9) [Yusuf Ali].

cooperation not only between different religions but also between different Muslim tribes. The covenant was concluded between the Muslim groups of Quraish, the *muhājirīn*, and the anṣār, and the Jews of Medina. Madani argued that Muhammad by this treaty built a united nation and community (*muttaḥida qaum aur muttaḥida umma*) (Madani 1972: 30). Maulana Anwar Shah Kashmiri assumed that this covenant demonstrated that it was possible to make agreement with non-Muslims provided autonomy was secured in matters of religion (ibid.: 31). The agreement also supported common defence actions and obligations against non-Muslims. The so-called treaty Jews were entitled to assistance on behalf of Muslims. They were not to be persecuted. It was assumed that these conditions would now apply to cooperation between Muslims and Hindus against the British. The advocates of this policy apparently regarded the joint non-cooperation fatwā as a kind of agreement akin to the covenant (cf. section 4.3.3). The JUH discussed this issue several times and elaborated the clauses of the covenant. Maulana Anwar Shah Kashmiri dealt with its contents in detail at the Peshawar session of 1927. Because of the severe communal riots between 1923 and 1927, Muslims felt the agreement with the Hindus was violated. For this they faulted radical Hindu nationalists from the Hindū Mahāsabhā (Rozinah 1981/I: 404ff.).

Mushirul Hasan maintained that the JUH position of communal harmony was influenced by al-Afghani who had earlier advised the Egyptian Muslims to take pride in their pre-Islamic past in order to create a common bond of solidarity against foreign rule. He also pointed to Afghani's article in the Indian Muslim journal *Mu'allim-i Shafīq*, which 'evoked not only the universal Islamic but also national sentiments with special emphasis on Hindu–Muslim unity'. Even when talking to a primarily Muslim Indian audience, he appealed to the glory of the Indian Hindu past to create an effective basis for solidarity against the foreigner (Hasan 1985: 7).

How Madani was pushed to take a public stand on this issue was instructive for the battle lines in the public Islamic discourse at the time. When Madani addressed a public meeting in December 1937 in Delhi, he thought the existence of a joint nation of Muslims and non-Muslims was permissible in the face of hostility from a third side, that is, the British, and would not contravene basic injunctions of Islam. But he reserved the right to investigate the issue more thoroughly. The correspondent of a paper, sympathizing with the Muslim League, reported his remarks in a twisted way. Allegedly Madani had stated that 'nowadays nations [are] formed on the basis of native lands, no longer on the basis of religion.' Madani had used these words, not to describe his own position, but to characterize British policies with regard to the national movements of the Arabs and Turks under Ottoman rule, which the British had validated with reference to ethnocentric nationalism. In the paper it was made out that this was his own opinion with regard to India and Indian Muslims. As this news item was reported all over India by the Muslim press, Madani soon came under attack from all sides. Most devastatingly, Muhammad Iqbal, the famous poet and politician, responded with an acerbic couplet in which he accused Madani of holding views in contravention of the dictates of Islam. Iqbal was known for his support for the Pakistan scheme encouraging the Muslim League to take a more offensive stand on this issue. Madani responded by writing the doctrinal treatise on 'Nationality and Islam' (*Muttaḥida qaumīyat aur Islām*) where he adduced traditions (ḥadīth) and Qur'anic references to support his view (1972). He based much of his argument on the Covenant of Medina and how it embodied the practice of governance over a multi-cultural and multi-confessional state.

In contrast, the Barelwis and religious scholars opposed to Congress politics rejected 'composite' nationalism. At the 1946 AISC session in Atawah, the Barelwi leader Sayyid Misbah al-Hasan denounced 'the role of those who in the garb of religion conquer the mind of Muslims with the evil idea of "composite nationalism"' (Qadiri 1997: 243). It was suspected that this was a tool in the hands of the Congress and Hindu politicians to make Muslims subservient to their interests. Yet, the Barelwi concept of Pakistan was not identical with the Muslim League approach as they emphasized the creation of 'an independent (*āzād*) government of Islam and Qur'an in one part of India' (ibid.: 276).

4.3.3. *Pan-Turkism and the Khilafat Movement*

Internal Pan-Islamism largely played itself out as Pan-Turkism. This seemed to be directly related to the minority status of Indian Islam seeing the Ottoman Empire as a source of support and comfort. Yet, the identification of reformist Islamic movements in India with the fate of the Ottoman Caliphate developed gradually. Attention of reformist religious scholars in India to the role of the Caliphate was said to have started with Shah Muhammad Ishaq when he migrated to Mecca in 1841. Since then the 'ulamā', following the teachings of Waliullah, and later that of the Deobandis continued to champion the cause of the Ottoman Caliphate (Ahmad 1964: 63; see also Sindhi 1952). In the minds of British officialdom this raised doubts about the loyalty of Indian Muslims, and notably of those in the reformist and radical tradition, that is, the Indian 'Wahhabis'. It was feared that they owed allegiance not to the Queen but to the Ottoman Sultan and Caliph. Since several reformist Islamic clerics and Muslim princes had been associated with the 1857–8 uprising, and many of them were pushed into exile in the Hijaz, the fear of disloyalty continued to colour British perceptions of Muslim affairs in India. The new Islamic institutions and organizations were all measured against their capacity to foment disloyalty or instil loyalty to British rule in Indian Muslims.[83] But before 1900, the interest of Indian Muslims in the Ottomans and the Hijaz remained rather limited to a small circle of clerics and activists. This changed drastically with the advent of the new century. The victory of Japan over Russia in the Russo-Japanese War of 1904–5 was seen as a triumph of Asia over the greatest European colonial power after Britain. If Japan could be a great power, why not India, Muhammad Ali asked:

> Are young nations that learn their political lessons from older nations ever grateful? Japan stands today as a living example of ingratitude. In reality, it is the old problem which civilisation and enlightenment, liberally diffused, are inevitably bound to raise up against themselves. England must now cheerfully pay the penalty of her generous impulses (Ali 1963/I: 13).

In 1909, when the Young Turks forced Sultan Abdul Hamid to step down, the ensuing debate whether they were Turks or Muslims touched many a nerve in Muslim India. 'The Turk who felt himself to be nothing but a Muslim and a member of a Muslim State was now on the horns of a dilemma. The more the State lost its traditional features, that is, the more the religious and political features of the State became separated and the more the State was portrayed as a political association of the *millets*, the more the members of the *ummet* of the Turks found themselves in a vacuum.' (Iqbal 1974: 51)

The abolition of the partition of Bengal in 1912 gave another fillip to the public debate on Muslim identity. The partition of the Bengal presidency in 1905 had created a Muslim majority province of Eastern Bengal and Assam where the 15 eastern districts of Bengal were united with Assam and Chittagong. The British had engineered the partition out of expedience. The objective was to stifle the growing nationalist (Congress) movement, which to a large extent had its roots in Bengal. When the partition of Bengal and consequently the separate 'Muslim' province of East Bengal were abolished in 1912 it came as a rude shock to Muslim public opinion. Many were radicalized through this experience. Pointing to the successful Congress-led agitation against the partition of Bengal, a British intelligence officer noted that from this Muslim activists 'derived the conclusion that agitation was the way to success'.[84] It legitimated the instrument of agitation and public opposition among Islamic activists who previously had preferred to stress their loyalty to

[83]For the Governor of the United Provinces, MacDonnell, fearing the disloyalty of the Nadwa in 1899, cf. Malik (1997: 343). See also various British references to the issue of loyalty when the Shi'a College was opened in 1907, and later in 1923 (ibid.: 270).

[84]F. H. Vincent, 'History sheet of Muhammad Ali' in Iqbal (1974: 87).

British rule. Hence it was seen as no coincidence that agitation picked up among Islamic circles precisely after 1912. The medical mission led by Dr M. A. Ansari and the Ali brothers to Ottoman Turkey during the Balkan Wars in 1912–13 was the first public activity in this direction (cf. section 4.2.1). On his return to India, Ansari assured his audience at the Mohammedan Anglo-Oriental College at Aligarh, that the spirit of the Turkish nation was not dead and asserted that the most important result of the medical mission was a fusion of minds between Turkey and India (cf. Bamford 1974: 113).

Efforts discussed here such as the 1913 Anjuman-i Khuddām-i Ka'ba; the ill-fated 'silk letter' scheme organized by Deoband's head teacher, Mahmud al-Hasan, and two of his students, Ubaidullah Sindhi and Husain Ahmad Madani, were further steps in the direction of aiding the Ottomans including the collection of money for arms and plans for an anti-British uprising. Sindhi's moves for a graduates' association of the Deoband seminary (Jam'īyat al-Anṣār) were interpreted by the British intelligence as a wish 'to spread over India a pan-Islamic and anti-British movement through the agency of Maulwis trained in the famous Deoband school'.[85] But, as mentioned, this was still a minority position then, as the loyalist Deoband administration did not see eye to eye with such campaigns until the mid-1920s.[86]

Matters got considerably more complicated when Ottoman Turkey officially joined World War I on the side of Germany on 29 October 1914. Now the British regarded any expression of solidarity with the Ottomans as an act of treason. British officials did not take lightly the sentiments of Indian Muslims as they formed a significant share in the armed forces, in some branches more than 50 per cent, far exceeding their share in the population.[87] Muslims, particularly from the northwest, like the Punjabis

[85] The 1918 Sedition (Rowlatt) Committee's Report, quoted in Bamford (1974: 122).

[86] It was even suspected that the arrest of the Shaykh al-Hind, Mahmud al-Hasan, in 1916 was made possible due to secret information furnished by the management of the seminary to British intelligence. The Deoband centenary history volume goes to some length to refute this allegation (Rizvi 1980/II: 143ff.).

[87]

Army branches	Percentage of Muslims (in %) in the Indian Army by	
	January 1914	January 1919
Cavalry	48	45
Infantry	31	
Artillery	55	33
Sappers and Miners	40	
Transport Corps	89	57
Indian Army Total	40	

Based on Ellinwood and Pradhan (1978: 188–9).

and the Pakhtuns, had been targeted for recruitment more regularly as they were considered among the 'martial races' of India (like the Sikhs and the Gurkhas). Since the British war effort in parts substantially relied on the British-Indian army,[88] Muslim sentiments in India could indeed become a matter of political and security concern.

British administrators in India were therefore highly conscious of the explosive potential of Turkey's entry in the war.[89] In order to placate Muslim public opinion they made an official declaration that the British war effort would take cognisance of Muslim susceptibilities regarding the Holy Places of Islam and the role of the Caliph.[90] The wording of

[88]Almost one million Indian troops served in major theatres of war:

War theatres	No. of troops
France	132,496
East Africa	46,906
Mesopotamia	588,717
Egypt	116,159
Gallipoli & Salonika	9,366
Aden & Persian Gulf	49,700
Total	943,344

Government of India (1923: 96–7).

By 31 December 1919, 121,598 Indian soldiers died, were wounded, missing, or had become prisoners. This was a proportion of casualties comparable to the major combatant nations (ibid.: 176).

[89]While the Muslim élites largely remained loyal it was the small group of Urdu journalists and Muslim activists led by Muhammad and Shaukat Ali from which the British anticipated trouble. They were therefore interned (cf. Brown 1978: 30–1).

[90]Declaration by the Government of India on behalf of the Governments of Britain, France, and Russia on 2 November 1914: 'In view of the outbreak of War between Great Britain and Turkey, which to the regret of Great Britain has been brought about by the ill-advised, unprovoked and deliberate action of the Ottoman Government, His Excellency the Viceroy is authorised by His Majesty's Government to make the following public announcement in regard to the holy places of Arabia including the holy shrines of Mesopotamia and the port of Jedda, in order that there may be no misunderstanding on the part of His Majesty's most loyal Muslim subjects as to the attitude of his Majesty's Government in the War, in which no question of religious character is involved. These holy places and Jedda will be immune from attack or molestation, by the British naval and military forces so long as there is no interference with the pilgrims from India to the holy places and the shrines in question' (*IAR* 1921/I: 161–2). The British Prime Minister Lloyd George claiming to speak on behalf of the whole Empire stated: 'We are not fighting to deprive Turkey of Constantinople, or of the rich and renowned lands of Asia Minor and Thrace which were predominantly Turkish racially' (ibid.). He added though that the Arabs were 'entitled to a recognition of their separate national condition' (Minault 1982: 52). For the JUH position on the broken pledges, see Mahmud al-Hasan at its second annual session in Delhi in November 1920 (Rozinah 1981/I: 61). On the pledges see also Reetz (1995: 18ff.). For British arguments, see the viceregal message to Muslims in India, in *The Times of India Illustrated Weekly* (Bombay, 19–20 May 1920), pp. 28–9.

this declaration ultimately became a subject of bitter political dispute between Islamic leaders and the British. Muslim leaders and Islamic clerics regarded these statements as pledges allegedly violated by British action. Matters were made worse by the fact that the progressing war saw the forces of the Ottoman Empire suffer major defeats. Indian Muslim troops had substantially contributed to the Palestinian campaign of the allied powers under General Allenby, had helped capture Ghaza, Jerusalem, Jordan, Damascus, and finally Aleppo. On 19 September 1918, the Turkish commander surrendered. The armistice, which came into force on 31 October, brought Allenby's campaign to an end. Initially India's participation in the Mesopotamia campaigns was not very successful[91] and was temporarily suspended on 29 April 1916 amidst heavy Indian losses. Eventually, however, the campaign led by General Marshall led to the capture of Baghdad on 11 March 1917. To add insult to injury, Indian Muslims in significant numbers had helped a Western, Christian power to defeat their Caliph and capture some of the holy places of Islam. General Allenby exploited the underlying symbolism to the hilt when he entered Damascus on a white horse taking symbolic revenge for the wars of Saladin. The British prime minister acknowledged Allenby's contribution to the 'last of the crusades' publicly in parliament.[92]

After the war Britain acted not particularly wisely when it announced that major wartime restrictions on public life would remain in force through the so-called Rowlatt Bill. This provoked the first major post-war campaign, the Rowlatt Bill agitation led by Gandhi. When the peace terms by the Allies for Ottoman Turkey were announced, they appeared to Muslim activists to be the seal of surrender aimed at the dismantling

[91]'From start to finish the Mesopotamia campaigns were mainly fought by the Indian Army, were largely administered and supplied from India and were closely connected politically and economically with India.' Cf. Charles Lucas, *The Empire at War* (Oxford, 1921), Vol. V, 316, quoted in Pati (1996: 56).

[92]Lloyd George stated in August 1919: 'The name of General Allenby will be ever remembered as that of the most brilliant commander who fought and won the last of the most triumphant crusades. It was his good fortune by his skill to bring to a glorious end an enterprise which absorbed the chivalry of Europe for centuries. We forget now that the military strength of Europe was concentrated for generations upon this purpose in vain and a British army under General Allenby achieved it, and achieved it finally.' Here quoted after Aziz 1972: 110. This passage was repeatedly quoted at the time, cf. the newspaper *Mussalmān* (Calcutta, 5 March 1920), in *Report on Indian Newspapers and Periodicals in Calcutta 1920*, NAI; by Hakim Ajmal Khan (1863–1927) in his presidential address to the Amritsar session of the All-India Muslim League in December 1919, in IMDR/6: 104, and by Muhammad Ali in a meeting addressed by the Khilafat delegation at Essex Hall on 20 March 1920, ibid.: 213.

of the institution of the Caliphate. This brought them out in the open conceiving a movement for the defence of the (Ottoman) Caliphate and for Muslim control over the Holy Places of Islam in the Arabian Peninsula, issues that concerned them as part of the Islamic world. On political grounds alone this movement was hard to explain, as it sought to defend a defunct empire far away from India's shores against the resistance of the former Ottoman subjects. It appeared more to be a reflection of the guilt felt by the Muslim élites on having contributed to the downfall of this Islamic institution through their loyalism to the British crown. That support had earned them neither influence in Indian politics nor self-esteem. It, therefore, demonstrated once more to the religious-minded Muslims the fallacies of loyalism towards the secular western state when the interest of their religious community was totally disregarded.[93]

But it was also a political opportunity that the Muslim activists could not allow to pass by. Doctrinal and political impulses were fused. Addressing the Muslim League session in December 1918, M. A. Ansari redefined the limits of the Holy Places in order to justify a movement in support of the defeated Ottoman Empire. He quoted from the traditions of Islam to prove that the whole of Arabia, Palestine, and Mesopotamia was included in the Jazīrat al-'Arab[94] from which all non-Muslim influence must be removed. This reliance on a religious argument for a political purpose brought a 'nationalist' Muslim like Ansari into conflict with the nationalist aspirations of the Arabs opposing Ottoman rule. The Sharif of Mecca (Ali ibn Husain 1879–1935) was denounced for his revolt against the Ottoman Sultan after he had recognized him as the unquestioned Khalīfa of Islam (Bamford 1974: 132).

The campaign and the all-India organization for the defence of the Khilafat were orchestrated by Abdul Bari of the Firangī Maḥall, the Ali brothers, M. A. Ansari, and, at a later stage, Gandhi. The latter wanted to merge it with his intended campaign of non-violent non-cooperation designed to make rule over India by British bureaucracy impossible if the subjects of this rule dissociated themselves from it. This essentially involved a boycott of social, political, educational and legal state institutions, including courts, (legislative) councils, government-aided schools, honours, titles, and official functions.[95] Gandhi apparently hoped that making Muslim grievances cause for civil unrest would ensure a working coalition of Hindus and Muslims. This would make the campaign invincible as it would bind together the majority Hindu community and the largest minority.

[93]On the loyalist responses by Muslims to the war effort see also Pati (1996: 15ff.).
[94]In a more literal sense the term referred only to the Arabian Peninsula.
[95]It was launched by the Congress in September 1920.

While the details of the Khilafat movement have been dealt with in various other works (cf. Abbasi 1982; Bakshi 1989; Bamford 1974; Minault 1982; Niemeyer 1972; Qureshi 1999), we will focus here on the stand taken by the religious movements. The religious scholars' main instrument for the conduct of the movement was a religious decree, giving theological sanction to the envisaged acts of non-cooperation (*tark-e muwālāt*). This decree, or fatwā, was remarkable in that it represented a united decision countersigned by several hundred scholars from a variety of schools and traditions.[96] It was, therefore, called the joint decree or *muttafiqa fatwā*. Its guidelines were adopted at the 1920 JUH meeting in Delhi (Rozinah 1981/I: 76–7). It was for the first time that religious scholars had come together on one platform in India to formulate religious arguments in support of an overtly political cause. Previously, of course, the 'ulamā' had also pronounced jihād on one or the other occasion. But those had been mainly local incidents with little 'national' meaning supported by individual scholars only.

Mahmud al-Hasan who drafted the initial text of the fatwā maintained in 1920 (Rozinah 1981/I: 65) that non-cooperation was a dictate of religion directly derived from the Qur'an: 'O ye who believe! Take not my enemies and yours as friends (or protectors),—offering them (your) love' (60:1, Yusuf Ali). The question that was to be answered from a religious point of view was what kind of cooperation (muwālāt) was allowed with the British, who were considered among the enemies of religion by their actions against the Caliph, their occupation of the Holy Places of Islam, and their support for non-Muslim control over these.[97] The fatwā also sanctioned collaboration with Hindus in the Khilafat campaign, as cooperation with infidels who were not at war with Muslims was allowed.

The term muwālāt was taken in its two major aspects, love (friendship) and help (cooperation). The argument was based on a fatwā by Shah Abdul Aziz on cooperation with infidels dating from the beginning of the nineteenth century. In matters of religion, friendship with infidels was considered to be kufr (unbelief). This would apply where Muslims were in danger of giving up their faith or being converted to Christianity. Aziz stressed that cooperation with the enemies of Islam was forbidden (ḥarām). This aspect was particularly important for the non-cooperation movement. Any Muslim who in spite of his knowledge of these commandments maintained this muwālāt would be considered a great sinner. Here the authors based their arguments on the Qur'anic injunction, 'And do not

[96]In his defence speech at the Karachi trial on 29 September 1921, Muhammad Ali put the figure of 'ulamā' who signed the joint fatwā at 500 (*IAR* 1922/I: 274).

[97]For the wording of the fatwā, see Hasan (1921), for a translation see Bamford (1974).

collaborate in sin and transgressions' (5:2). Therefore, Muslims who cooperated with Britain, or with British rule in India, would be considered cooperating with the enemies of Islam as long as Britain was seen to violate the commandments of Islam, such as ensuring the religious sanctity of the shrines and Holy Places of Islam in the Jazīrat al-'Arab.

This line of argument was closely linked to a much older doctrinal dispute on the question of whether or not India under British rule could still be considered a land of Islam (dār al-Islām) where religion could be freely practised, or a land of war (dār al-ḥarb) where this was not the case. This issue had also agitated Shah Abdul Aziz when British rule—and its legal system—came to dominate India, and notably, when Delhi came under British control in 1803.[98] Reformist scholars who opposed British rule have traditionally maintained that India under the British was dār al-ḥarb whereas those wanting to stress their loyalty maintained that India was dār al-Islām where the freedom of faith was guaranteed (cf. Qureshi 1999: 177ff.). In the latter case, relations between the British and Indian Muslims would be of a contractual nature where Qur'anic injunctions were invoked disallowing Muslims to break such a contract. Any opposition against recognized contractual rule by non-Muslims was rebellion (fitna) despised by classical Islam.

The Deobandi school of thought and reformist scholars standing in its tradition maintained that India was definitely not dār al-Islām. Therefore, an obligation existed to oppose British rule. At the 1927 JUH session in Peshawar, Maulana Anwar Shah Kashmiri did not go so far as declaring India dār al-ḥarb. Instead he proposed to classify it as *dār al-īmān*, the abode of faith, where Islam was maintained within the community. In this situation it was the task of the JUH to guide India's Muslims in the fulfilment of the dictates of religion. To him the Covenant of Medina exemplified what kind of action one can take in such situation and what agreement can be made with non-Muslims (Rozinah 1981: 403f.). Yet, as has been indicated earlier, in every seminary school, there

[98]Cf. Haq (1995). Aziz's fatwā stated, inter alia: 'In this city [Delhi] the rule of the *Imāmu'l-Muslimīn* is not in force, and the rule of the Christian officers (*ḥukkām-i naṣārā*) is in force with impunity. What is meant by the enforcement of the orders (*aḥkām*) of kufr is that the infidels are acting as rulers in administration and management of the affairs of the subjects, in the collections of revenue and dues, and taxes on commerce, in checking highway robbery and theft, in deciding disputes and enforcing penalties for crimes. It is of no significance if they do not interfere in the observance of some Islamic rites, e.g. the Friday and the two *'īd* prayers, the *aẓān* and sacrifice of cow, because these things do not hold any value in their eyes. They demolish mosques without any hesitation. Without their permission no Muslim or *zimmī* can enter this city and its environs. And if they do not object to the entry of visitors (*waridīn*), travellers (*musafirīn*) and traders (*tujjār*) in their domain, it is because of their own interest...' (ibid.: 38–9). See also Hunter (1969 [1871]: 207–10).

was a loyalist group opposing such attitude on the grounds of maintaining that India was a land of Islam. As has been noted, scholars professing the latter views were often rewarded handsomely for such service by titles, land deeds, pensions, and grants for their mosques or madrasas.

The Barelwi leader Ahmad Raza Khan was perhaps among those who did not need such materialistic encouragement. He had always maintained that India was dār al-Islām. In addition he also regarded the support for the Turkish-Ottoman Caliph as overdone. Ahmad Raza had already stressed in 1913 that the Turks should first of all help themselves (Sanyal 1996a: 282). In this, he relied on the Qur'anic verse, 'Verily never will God change the condition of a people until they change it themselves (with their own souls)' (13:11, Yusuf Ali). He believed that the Caliph could justifiably only hail from the people of the Prophet, that is, from the Arab tribe of the Quraish. Regarding the boycott demands, he believed that instead of reacting negatively to British authority and institutions Muslims should concentrate on strengthening their own community from within.[99] While he opposed political action on behalf of the Khilafat Conference and the JUH, he gave in to pressure to act in support of Turkey with the creation of the Anjuman-i Anṣār al-Islām. The organization was accused of being sponsored by the government to neutralize the influence of the JUH and the Khilafat Conference.

The Aḥmadīya Movement tried to steer a middle course. The majority faction of the Qadiyanis, headed by Mahmud Ahmad, consistently favoured a loyalist position. But sympathies with the Khilafat Movement existed too. Being invited to the Allahabad Khilafat Conference in June 1920 by Abdul Bari himself demonstrated that the Aḥmadīs were still considered by its Muslim organizers to represent a sect of Islam. Mahmud Ahmad explained in an article why they disagreed with the Khilafat Movement:

> ... Religiously speaking we do not admit owing any allegiance to the Sultan. We hold that only a successor of the Promised Messiah is entitled to be the Spiritual Head of the Mussalmans, and as for our temporal Sovereign we recognise only the Power under whose rule we live.[100]

In contrast, Zafarullah Khan, who headed the Aḥmadī delegation to the Allahabad conference, believed that support for Turkey was necessary:

> Even such Muslims as Shi'as, who could not from their religious point of view accept anybody outside their own Imams as *Khalīfa* and the *Aḥmadīs* who could not accept anybody outside their own Movement as their religious leader, did lend support to

[99] See his programme of economic, social, and religious action as proposed in his fatwā of 1913, *Tadbīr-e falāḥ wa najāt wa iṣlāḥ*.

[100] *Review of Religions* (December 1919), 18, 401–2, quoted in Lavan (1976: 133).

the Khilafat Movement because, undoubtedly, Turkey represented to a very large extent the secular strength and prestige of Islam (Zafarullah Khan 1991: 15).

This compromise position, though reflecting widespread concerns of all politically minded Muslims, was dictated more by the desire to secure the position of the Aḥmadīya community within the larger Islamic sector. It also mirrored the Aḥmadī priority to ensure allegiance to their own Khalīfa, their head of the Aḥmadīya community.

As political conditions in the 1920s changed fast, scholars came under increasing pressure to modify or abolish their joint fatwā. The JUH from where the fatwā had emanated posed as the religious guardian of the decree. For quite some time it staunchly refused to give in to pressures and change the fatwā in line with demands of expediency. Its representatives argued that since those were commands of religion, they were based on the immutable injunctions of the Qur'an and could not be adapted to short-term exigencies. Change was notably demanded in connection with council entry and, later, in connection with the worsening of Hindu–Muslim relations (cf. section 4.1.2). A paradoxical situation developed when the religious scholars continued to advocate non-cooperation with the British while the Non-Cooperation Movement had already been suspended and abolished by Gandhi and the Congress. Formally it was only abandoned by the JUH when the Khilafat Conference ceased to exist[101] and the new constitutional act of 1935 was about to introduce representative government at the provincial level.

4.3.4. *Pan-Islamism and International Politics*

Indian Muslims were also drawn into the international aspects of pan-Islamic politics going beyond Pan-Turkism.[102]

Before the politicization of Islamic activism in India in the 1910s, connections between Indian religious scholars and the Islamic world were mainly conducted at an individual level. Scholars went to the Hijaz and took temporary residence there, keeping in contact with visiting compatriots of the same sectarian affiliation in India. The pilgrimage (ḥajj) to Mecca provided the best and most regular opportunity for such connections. One such external network has already been mentioned—the devotees of Hajji Imdadullah, the reformist Sufi Shaykh, who resided

[101]According to Aziz, publication of the news on the Khilafat proceedings ceased in 1933 (1972: 337). The last Khilafat conference on record was held in 1936 (Qureshi 1999: 413).

[102]For the early stages of Pan-Islamism in India, see Qureshi (1999, notably pp. 9–87); for a more general treatment of Pan-Islamism, cf. Landau (1990); Schulze (1990).

in Mecca. He, like others, had migrated to Mecca as a result of the failed uprising of 1857–8 and the subsequent suppression of Muslim activism (Qureshi 1999: 18f.). Another channel was provided by the links the Ahl-i Ḥadīth maintained on the subject of ḥadīth studies with several schools and scholars in the Hijaz. For a time, their Indian centre at Bhopal served as an attraction for Arabian scholars, many of whom took courses from there (cf. Steinberg 2002: 115–20).

Characteristic for the time after 1900 was the tendency of these links to become more formalized. Some of the Islamic groups started foreign branches and dependencies—the Deobandis, the Ahl-i Ḥadīth, the Nadwa, the Aḥmadīya, and the Tablīghī Jamā'at. Obvious links pointed to Afghanistan, but also to the Middle East and Arabia, besides places where Indian migrant communities lived such as East and South Africa, Britain, and Germany. Reformist scholars from Arabia had only sporadic contact with Indian counterparts. The Syrian Rashid Rida, who had travelled to India and contacted Deoband, the Nadwa and the Ahl-i Ḥadīth, was one of the more well-known.

Contacts picked up in connection with the international Islamic conferences. They were convened to debate the succession of the Caliphate. The Khāksār founder, Mashriqi, participated in the Egyptian Khilafat conference in May 1926 on the basis of the international fame of his Qur'anic treatise *Taḏkira* (Malik 2000; Schulze 1990: 77). Another issue, which gained prominence, was the status and sanctity of the 'Holy Land', that is, the holy places of Islam in the Hijaz. These issues got entangled with political and religious events in the Hijaz. When Ibn Saud (1880–1953) took control of the Hijaz in 1925 and threw out the Sharif of Mecca who was despised for his close contacts with the British, Indian scholars and Khilafatists applauded only half-heartedly. Many were anxious about the consequences of Wahhabi plans for Mecca and Medina. The Wahhabi militias of the Ikhwān and Wahhabi clerics were quick in moving against pilgrims worshipping at graves and other 'idols' in the 'Holy Land'. They set about demolishing domes and mosques built over graves, levelling the graves of members of the Prophet's family and his companions (cf. Steinberg 2002: 521-2, 535–42).

To gain support for his rule over Hijaz, Ibn Saud held out the promise that an Islamic World Congress would decide his fate. Three Indian delegations participated in the World Muslim Congress (al-Mu'tamar al-Islāmī) in Mecca in June–July 1926 representing the Khilafat Conference, the JUH, and the Ahl-i Ḥadīth.[103] However, their expectations were

[103]Sulaiman Nadwi, Muhammad Ali, Shaukat Ali, and Shuaib Quraishi participated on behalf of the Khilafat Conference; Muhammad Kifayatullah, Ahmad Said, Abdul

betrayed. Ibn Saud used the Congress to solidify his reputation in the Islamic world without making any concessions. The strong Indian participation was motivated by two issues, the fate of the Caliphate and the demolition drive against shrines and graves. It was particularly the latter issue that deeply divided religious scholars in India as worship at shrines and graves constituted an important element in the Sufi legacy of Indian Islam. Rumours abounded in India about the impending destruction of the Ka'ba and the Prophet's grave. Through his Anjuman al-Khuddām al-Ḥaramain, Abdul Bari of the Firangī Maḥall led a campaign in defence of the *Ka'ba*. In this he was opposed by Muhammad Ali, his long-time disciple and friend, a rift that did not heal in his lifetime. Muhammad Ali renounced his spiritual allegiance to Abdul Bari on the day when Ibn Saud declared himself King of the Hijaz (13 January 1926). Within a week Abdul Bari breathed his last (Robinson 2001: 146ff.). Ali considered support to Ibn Saud important because the latter opposed the Sharif of Mecca, a British ally. The JUH and the Khilafat Conference passed several resolutions expressing their anxiety on events in the Hijaz. The JUH argued that the united power of Muslims should take charge of the protection of the holy places,[104] a demand aiming at the internationalization of the status of the Hijaz, which was resolutely resisted by Ibn Saud. The more radical Khilafatists like Hasrat Mohani (1875–1951) suggested that the Hijaz should become a republic over which a 'Khalīfa in council' would rule in which India claimed due representation, a view subsequently not endorsed by the session (*IAR* 1925/II: 342ff.). This position was considered so extreme that Mohani's speech was expunged from the records on the insistence of Muhammad Ali and Maulana Kalam Azad (ibid.). The wish to give the new Islamic Congress more weight led the Khilafatist Ansari to open an Indian branch of the Mu'tamar on the sidelines of the Khilafat Conference proceedings in 1927 (*IAR* 1927/I: 424).[105]

The Khilafat leader Shaukat Ali became involved with the Islamic Congresses on a more regular basis. He participated in the Palestinian Islamic conference in 1928 where it was decided that he together with al-Husaini, ath-Thaalibi (1874–1944), and Rashid Rida would sign the invitation to the new General Islamic Congress (al-Mu'tamar al-Islāmī

Halim as-Siddiqi, and Bashir Ahmad Uthman for the JUH; Thanaullah, Hamid Allah, Abd-al-Wahid al-Ghaznawi, and Ismail al-Ghaznawi for the Ahl-i Ḥadīth (Schulze 1990: 82).

[104]Cf. the respective JUH resolution in 1926, in Rozinah (1981/I: 377). The JUH also took note of the deteriorating security situation during the Ḥajj of 1926 (ibid.: 375).

[105]Before partition the Mu'tamar did not make much impact in India. Cf. Qureshi (1999: 412).

al-'Āmm) to be held in Jerusalem in December 1931.[106] Its main issue was Palestine and plans for the establishment of a Jewish state there. In general, Indian delegates participated in growing numbers although they had little effect on the proceedings.[107] After the Ottoman and Turkish cause had exhausted itself in the 1920s, protest against the settlement of Jews in Palestine was one of the major causes taken up. It was shared across doctrinal divides by the Aḥrār, JUH, Barelwis,[108] and the Muslim League. The JUH passed resolutions on Palestine in 1931, 1939, and 1942 (Rozinah 1981/I: 612, 652, 752). In the War Resolution of its 1939 session, the JUH compared German actions in Poland with the 'barbarities in Palestine at the hands of the so-called British democracy' (*IAR* 1939/II: 353).

The meandering path of religious and political alignments in the Islamic world often left the scholars confused. The intention was to support movements aiming at the freedom of Islam, and also at freedom from foreign rule. Yet uprisings were short-lived and their character often unclear. The scholars expressed solidarity with the Moroccans fighting under Abd al-Karim for the 'Republic of the Rif'[109] in resolutions passed at JUH sessions in 1922 and 1925 (*IAR* 1923/I: 942; Rozinah 1981/I: 319). They warned Britain against undue pressure on Egypt in retaliation for the shooting of a British officer, Listak (Rozinah 1981/I: 317): 'Every wrong done to Egypt would be felt by $7^1/_2$ crores [75 million] of Indian Muslims, as deeply as if the wrong had been done to them. The present policy would cause an awakening among Egyptians in the same way as Jallianwala had caused among Indians' (*IAR* 1924/II: 510). The JUH and the Khilafatists also supported Turkey's bid to retain control over Mosul, which went against the interests of another Muslim state, Iraq.[110] In 1946, Islamic

[106]A seven-member delegation of the Indian Khilafat Committee participated in Jerusalem: Ghulam Rasul Allah (journalist, Lahore), Ghulam Rasul Kabir, Hafiz Abdur Rahman (notable, Peshawar), Abdur Rahman as-Siddiqi, Zahid Ali (Director General, Islamic Aid Committee), Muhammad Iqbal, Shaukat Ali, and Muhammad Shafi Daudi (Schulze 1990: 100).

[107]Schulze's analysis is not necessarily reflective of this as he is generally deficient on evaluating the impact and the situation of South Asian Muslims. See, for instance, his remarks on the 1949 Islamic Congress in Karachi and the split of the Muslim League into an Indian and a Pakistani wing. He mistakenly called the latter an example of the failure to revive transnational concepts of the umma in the face of state-oriented policies. After partition the Muslim League evinced little practical interest in pursuing 'transnational' ambitions (Schulze 1990: 110).

[108]For Barelwi resolutions on Palestine, see for instance the AISC sessions in May 1930 in Bengal (Qadiri 1999: 54), or the Palestine Day meeting on 26 October 1945 (ibid.: 200).

[109]For an overview, see Woolman (1969).

[110]Cf. the 1925 JUH session (*IAR* 1925/II: 509); for the Khilafat Conference, see ibid.: 345.

groups expressed solidarity with the people of Java and Indonesia. The AISC maintained their only fault was that they clung to their Sunni beliefs and refused to give them up (Qadiri 1997: 263).

A more political subject where religion only played a marginal role was solidarity with Indians abroad. The Khilafat Conference passed respective resolutions with regard to South African Indians in 1925 (*IAR* 1925/II: 344–5) and the Muslim League in 1924 and 1939 (*IAR* 1924/II: 479; 1939/II: 345–6). The All-India Muslim Conference appreciated the efforts of South African Muslims at its Lahore session in 1929 (*IAR* 1930/I: 346). The Congress Party and other public bodies expressed similar support for Indians in Kenya and South Africa.[111] In a way, this activity shadowed international politics of the time, particularly in the Socialist and Communist camp. The Socialist International and its Communist pendant often expressed solidarity on global issues at their conferences.

Indian Muslims also invoked pan-Islamic sentiments in order to justify their connections with Germany in World Wars I and II. In connecting with Germany they were joined by radical Indian nationalists, who had maintained an active Berlin bureau before World War I and through the 1920s. German propaganda authorities from the military used the offices of prominent German orientalists to win the sympathies of Indian Muslims. When Hitlerite Germany prepared for global domination it also started courses of the Waffen SS (military police) to train Islamic clerics for the war front.[112] Indian nationalists led by Bose formed a contingent of the Indian National Army (Āzād Fauj) in which a substantial number of Muslims participated.[113]

The Khilafat issue had served as an eye-opener for Islamic groups. Giving practical shape to ideas of Islamic solidarity became an important element of their intervention in the public sphere. Pan-Islamism developed from a religious call and vocation into a dimension of politics and international affairs. The common denominator of these activities for Indian Muslims was their attempt to gain support in the Islamic world for the solution of local or regional problems, often in relation with the minority status of Muslims in India. A second direction comprised common action on the basis of opposition to Western colonial rule. A third dimension of international interaction was the contestation of

[111] *IAR* (1925/II: 322). The issue of Indians in South Africa was discussed from a contemporary perspective in *IAR* (1925/II: 121ff.).

[112] For details see Peter Heine, 'Die Mullah-Kurse der Waffen-SS', in Höpp and Reinwald (2000: 181–8).

[113] They never had a chance to fight in or near India but were dispersed by the retreating war front. For details, see Weidemann and Günther (2000).

the meaning of Islamic reformism, where ḥadīth studies and controversy surrounding shrine worship were noticeable topics.

4.3.5. *Engaging in Jihād*

The discourse on dār al-Islām or dār al-ḥarb, whether India was a land suitable for or inimical to Islam, also influenced the discourse on jihād. Religious scholars conducted it with particular intensity. It was judged on similar criteria: those who considered India dār al-ḥarb advocated open warfare against British rule in the name of religion while those who considered it dār al-Islām pronounced themselves in favour of cooperation and loyalism. Originally, as has been mentioned, regarding India dār al-ḥarb did not signify that the only or intended approach was to wage war on Britain. Shah Abdul Aziz's fatwā on this issue most likely reflected first of all the curtailment of Islamic institutions in legal matters. Where the writ of Islam no longer extended because of British law, or where it was hedged by many conditions, Islam could not be freely pursued.[114] Subsequently reformist scholars and activists, such as Aziz's student Sayyid Ahmad Bareilly and his nephew Muhammad Ismail, perhaps deliberately, contributed to the misunderstanding that encouraged, even demanded, violent jihād against the British. Although Aziz may have inspired them, the military activity of the Indian 'Wahhabis' actually started only after his death. Their movement, first directed against the Sikhs and later against the British, was eventually defeated by the British in the 1870s.[115]

From there, we see a split in the jihād discourse. One section of Islamic activists sporadically continued militant activity, mainly in the Pakhtun tribal belt of northwest India. Other religious scholars adopted a loyalist position. They came up with arguments as to why jihād could or should no longer be conducted by violent means. They reasoned that jihād in terms of the Qur'anic language meant first of all exertion in the way of God, including the perfection of the inner self, which they regarded as the 'spiritual' or 'greater jihād' while taking up arms in jihād was considered the 'physical' or 'lesser' one.[116] Even where Muslims resorted to militant warfare in the name of religion, several conditions had to be considered first. If it was warfare against unbelievers, they first had to be

[114]Cf. fn. 100, this chapter, From this conflict eventually a separate Muslim personal law emerged, cf. Chapter 5, section 5.3.

[115]On the early activities of the Indian 'Wahhabis' and the court cases against them, cf. Pearson (1979). See also the three classical historiographical works in Urdu by Ghulam Rasul Mahr, who was a follower of the Ahl-i Ḥadīth (1954, 1955, 1956).

[116]Cf. E. Tyan, 'Djihād', in EI/II: 538–540; for the South Asian discourse see Malik (1998).

given the choice of converting to Islam voluntarily. Violent jihād could also be abandoned on the ground of social and economic disabilities of the local population. The most radical advocates of a non-violent interpretation of jihād were the Aḥmadīs. They made it a point to 'abolish' violent jihād, or ghaziism as it was sometimes called.[117] While Ghulam Ahmad went to the extent of completely rejecting violent jihād for the present time, his other colleagues limited themselves to hedging it with several conditions. Among those who considered jihād inapplicable at the turn of the century were scholars from the Ahl-i Ḥadīth,[118] the Aligarh tradition,[119] and the Nadwa.[120] Also, moderate Deobandi scholars such as Habibur Rahman considered it to be a peaceful task.[121] The Barelwis, who regarded India dār al-Islām, did not advocate it either. But these pronouncements had to be taken with a pinch of salt. Their argument may have been doctrinal but their motive was public and political, very much geared to the public sphere. They wanted and they needed to prove their loyalty to the British to be recognized by them and not be persecuted. Whoever among religious scholars advocated jihād was considered by the British to preach 'rank sedition'. It was entirely political motives which decided why those advocating almost similar positions on jihād around

[117]On the Aḥmadī point of view regarding jihād, see Friedmann (1989: 165–80).

[118]The answer (fatwa) given by Nazir Husain whether it was legitimate to do jihād in India was typical: 'It is not hidden from the master of the exalted sharī'a (Islamic law) that with regard to the conditions making jihād lawful two inevitable issues have to be considered: one, the absence of peace and security, of treaty relations and agreement between the people of Islam and the adversaries; two, an excess of power (*shaukat*), an abundance of strength (*quwwat*), vigour (*qudrat*) and armoury (*salāḥ–o-ālāt*) for jihād. In India, this grief, strength, spirit and weaponry is absent (*mafqūd*) while relations of trust and treaty exist so that the conditions for jihād are lacking in this region and conducting jihād here would be a means of slaughter (*halākat*) and rebellion (*ma'ṣiyat*)' (1971, Vol. III: 285).

[119]Sayyid Ahmad Khan treated jihād as an expression of the historical tradition of defensive warfare, arguing that all the military expeditions of the Prophet (*maghāzī*) were defensive. Cf. *Tafsīr al-Qurān*, Vol. IV, 45, 106, 110, quoted in Ahmad (1967: 50–1). Chiragh Ali argued in a similar manner (ibid.: 62).

[120]In connection with his discussion of the *jizya* tax, Shibli Numani regarded jihād as always defensive (Ahmad 1967: 83).

[121]This applied to the more loyalist 'ulamā' who dominated Deoband's administration until 1920. This position was exemplified by its founder Nanaotawi who regarded jihād as one of those categories whose inner meaning was revealed but whose outer form was left to the believer's discretion (Metcalf 1982: 142–3). Maulana Habibur Rahman was also considered to be of a similar moderate disposition (Rizvi 1980/II: 173f.). In contrast, Mahmud al-Hasan, their head teacher and later vice-chancellor, held an unapologetic and classical position on jihād being 'rationally necessary for the welfare and betterment of human society' (quoted in Ahmad 1967: 108). His student Madani believed jihād to be compulsory to regain freedom but thought that in India it could only be conducted in a non-violent way, and in alliance with the Hindus (ibid.: 189).

the turn of the century, later opposed each other viciously with reference to doctrinal matters. The Ahl-i Ḥadīth and Deobandis attacked the Aḥmadī position, so did the Barelwis, although less militantly. It attested to the political nature of the treatment of jihād by religious scholars that their attitude towards religious war went through similar historical phases as the exposition of violence by other political, religious, and social forces in India. While loyalism and the writing of petitions ruled the day until about 1910, agitation and violence became widespread across the board thereafter.[122] Mass agitation was adopted from the 1920s, not only by the Congress-led movement, but also by regional forces (Sikhs, Pakhtuns) and social agents (trade unions, peasant movement).

Where jihād continued in South Asia, it was largely concentrated in pockets of Pakhtun tribal areas. It took the form of mainly tribal insurgencies against the representatives of the government. This activity combined with other political and religious developments. The Afghan wars against British India were accompanied by tribal warfare dressed in Islamic slogans of jihād. The first major activity of all-India importance was the 'silk letter conspiracy' in 1914–16.[123] It was named after a set of letters written on yellow silk and later intercepted by British intelligence. As mentioned earlier, religious scholars from the Deoband Seminary supported contacts with activists who had withdrawn to the tribal areas where they believed they enjoyed a safe haven as policing of these areas and the enforcement of law could be achieved only with difficulty and in a very limited way (which is the case to this day). The conspirators hoped to implement a scheme according to which an Islamic army (*Hizb Allāh*) was to be formed with the support of the Turkish Sultan. They received the backing of the Sultan's Military Governor in the Hijaz, Ghalib Pasha. The army headquarters were to be based at Medina, the Indian contingent at Kabul, and the Deobandi head teacher, Mahmud al-Hasan, was to be its general-in-chief. Other local centres were to be established at Constantinople and Tehran (BLOC L/P&S/10/633). The conspirators connected with radical nationalists (Raja Mahendra Pratap, 1886–1979)[124] and Islamic socialists (Maulwi Barkatullah, 1870–1928)[125] who shuttled between the Frontier Province and Kabul. But another, more problematic destination

[122]On resort to political violence in India, see the classical assessments of the time made on behalf of British officialdom in Kaye (1926), Tegart (1932). These analyses classified all nationalist activity as terrorism where it resorted to violence.

[123]For the 'Silk letter conspiracy', see BLOC L/P&S/10/633; BLOC P/CONF/50; Miyan (1976, 1988); Madani (1974); Government of India, Sedition (Rowlatt) Committee 1918.

[124]Rizvi (1980/II: 138, fn. 1). On Pratap's activities, see also his autobiography (1947).

[125](Ibid.: fn. 3). On the influence of 'Islamic socialism' at the time, see also Hasan (1998a: 194–5).

of their travels was Wilhelminian Berlin where they hoped to receive support to overthrow British rule in India. With this intention they also contacted a German–Turkish military mission, which had arrived in Afghanistan in 1915. Some of the radicals had established a 'provisional government' of India led by Pratap, which hoped to rule over India in the event of a successful battle.

Not only were Islamic militants closely involved in these efforts, they also provided sanctuary for these activities in the tribal areas. Descendants of the Indian 'Wahhabis', renamed 'Hindustani fanatics' by the British and known among followers as the 'mujāhidīn'—had established two colonies in Pakhtun territory where they played host to the conspirators when they came to India. They were located in Smasta (Yaghistan) and Chamarkand (Bajaur).[126] These mujāhidīn in turn were associated with a large but loose network of religious scholars in various parts of India who collected money for jihād. From a doctrinal and political perspective, this network was primarily affiliated to the Ahl-i Ḥadīth,[127] although the Deobandis and the JUH network were also sympathetic towards them.[128]

In 1920, radical Islamic activists from the JUH and the Khilafat camp, joined by local peasants from the Frontier and the Punjab, staged a protest migration to Afghanistan, which came to be known as the Indian hijrat (cf. Reetz 1995; BLOC L/P&J/6/1701). The organizers believed they could put pressure on the British if they threatened to provoke a mass exodus from India. Their argument was that India had become dār al-ḥarb, where in view of the 'Khilafat wrongs' they were unable to practise Islam freely, which put them under obligation to migrate to a dār al-Islām, a land where Islam was free. This they assumed was neighbouring Afghanistan. For selfish reasons the Afghan amīr encouraged them in this belief. He tried to improve his bargaining position vis-à-vis the British. In India some Islamic activists in turn hoped for the amīr's intervention or banked at least on his support for the liberation of India. The amīr even flirted with the idea that he could eventually become the new Amīr al-Muslimīn or Caliph of the Islamic world. Not surprisingly, the campaign turned out to be a disastrous misadventure. Of the more than 35,000 Indian Muslims who took to the road to Afghanistan, more than half died en route of exhaustion or fell victim to marauding tribesmen. Afghanistan,

[126]See BLOC L/P&S/11/111; Reetz (2001b); Baha (1979).

[127]Ahl-i Ḥadīth historians maintained that the inception of the Ahl-i Ḥadīth conference in 1906 was owed partly to the need of addressing the problems faced by the frontier mujāhidīn (Nadwi 1988a: 29).

[128]Still these groups were not united in support of the mujāhidīn. Loyalists such as Siyalkoti from the Ahl-i Ḥadīth, or the (few) Barelwi members of the JUH were more cautious.

soon overwhelmed by the prospect of supporting such a massive influx of refugees, closed its borders. In the end, the British were approached to rehabilitate the returnees and show leniency with the organizers. Maulana Azad and Abdul Bari, in particular, initially invoked religious decrees in support of the hijrat, although neither of them actually participated in the migration. The whole campaign was organized as a massive peaceful display of avoidance protest. The naivety of the organizers cost the participants dearly. Still, in spite of its failure, it served to strengthen the network of Islamic activists. Maulana Azad who had been among the main instigators became a prominent Congress politician. Abdul Ghaffar Khan, who participated as a column leader, went on to lead the Red Shirt movement later. They learned mainstream politics through radical activism.

The concept of jihād served several other occasions of this period when religious scholars attempted to mobilize adherents and public opinion. The Khilafat movement was also seen as a form of crusade or jihād. The organizers were particularly irked by Gandhi's insistence on non-violent methods when they discussed its concept and the conditions for his support for the project. They regarded this as an emasculation of the Muslim spirit of jihād. Although the organizers of the Khilafat organization and the JUH were known as close allies of the Congress, they reflected this dissatisfaction as they often disregarded Gandhi's advice. Thus they reacted stubbornly to Gandhi's abolition of the Non-Cooperation Movement in the face of violence. The refusal of the JUH to change or abolish the joint fatwā could be seen in this light.

The campaign of the Aḥrār in Kashmir in 1931–4 directed against both the Hindu ruler and the Aḥmadīya, who had started the Kashmir campaign first, was also treated and popularized as jihād. The Muslim League took refuge in the jihād concept only at a very late stage, perhaps because of its uneasy relationship with religious scholars. When the so-called Direct Action Programme was started in 1946–7 by the militant units of their National Guards it was perceived as a jihād of sorts and often amounted to terrorizing the local population (*IAR* 1946/II: 70, 66ff., 182ff.). By then religious sanction of their volunteers' army could be obtained as some scholars hailing from those areas, which were going to form Pakistan, had joined the bandwagon of the Muslim League.

In sum, Islamic activism got the upper hand over contemplation during this period. While there was no linear mutation of activity, a certain sequence of time could be observed. The more contemplative and loyalist mood of the early period gave way to activism between 1910 and the 1930s. Apparently colonial rule served as an important trigger. It was, therefore, closely tied to the nationalist movement. But it followed distinct trajectories, which pointed to different objectives shaped by religious concerns in India and in the Islamic world. The religious argument appeared more opportunist and as a catalyst rather than as the major cause and ultimate aim. Militancy seemed to rise in proportion to mounting pressure on Muslim minority rights in colonial India. While the vast majority of Indian Muslims continued to live their peaceful lives it paved the way for the emergence of an extremist project of sectarian groups.

4.4. EXCLUSION OR TOLERANCE: ON THE EMERGENCE OF SECTARIAN RADICALISM

While in the beginning of the 1920s the public articulation of Islamic sentiments was primarily directed against British rule, the breakdown of the Hindu–Muslim understanding and increasing tension between the two communities led to a growing emphasis on religious concerns. Islamic leaders began to feel that cooperation with the Hindus against the British had not improved the situation for the Muslim élites. It did not increase their say in political matters. Islamic groups were not able to implement their religious demands.

Since the mid-1920s, a perceptible radicalization of Islamic groups was noticeable. It is discussed here exemplarily in relation to the Aḥrār and their most prominent religious leader, Ataullah Bukhari. The Aḥrar came into being as a group of political-minded, supposedly left-wing 'ulamā' in 1929. They emerged from the remnants of the Punjab Khilafat Committee, which was disbanded the same year (Mirza 1975/I: 83). The group clashed with the Ali brothers over the Nehru Report and other issues. The brothers had roundly rejected the recommendations of the Nehru Report as inadequate to safeguard Muslim rights. But it was also a question of personal rivalry and control over the Khilafat Conference organization and its funds (*IAR* 1928/II: 401–8; also Qureshi 1999: 405ff.). Bukhari's evolution as a religious leader allows us to trace the stages of the gradual radicalization of some 'ulamā' (Mirza 1970). In 1920, he founded the Azad High School in the city of Gujrat in Punjab in response to calls for independent education (āzād ta'līm) during the non-cooperation movement. At the time political and social concerns were still dominant in his activity. Maulana Azad opened the school showing the early closeness between the two (Mirza 1970: 51). Bukhari later supported the Hijrat movement of 1920. He participated in Khilafat activities in Rawalpindi and Lahore, going to jail from 1921 to 1924. Immediately after his release, he took active part in tablīgh activities directed against the Hindu reclamation campaign (shuddhī). From then onwards, doctrinal concerns weighed more heavily on his activism. He justified the anti-Ka'ba movement by the Wahhabi Saudis in 1925 (ibid.: 86; see also section 4.3.4). In this, Bukhari was resolutely opposed by Abdul Bari from the Firangī Maḥall, defending Sufi Islam in India. But he was also opposed by Muhammad Ali, who in spite of his political support for Ibn Saud did not go along with Bukhari's doctrinal radicalism. Bukhari again attacked Sufi Islam while assisting a Muslim candidate (Dr Muhammad Alim) in his election campaign in Lahore in 1926. For this he exploited an address of loyalty signed in 1918 by pirs and 'ulamā' of Punjab after World War I in gratitude to the British war effort. In the course of the campaign he paid no regard even to his own spiritual guide, Pir Mehr Ali Shah (1859–1937), the pir of Golra Sharif in Punjab, whom he attacked (ibid.: 99). Bukhari and the Aḥrār launched another attack on the leaders of Sufi Islam in the Shahidganj mosque agitation in Lahore in 1935. The agitation concerned a dispute over the appropriation of the mosque by Sikhs. Pir Jamaat Ali Shah, a prominent Barelwi leader and a representative of Sufi Islam, led this agitation. Here the Aḥrār cooperated with the police to force out rival agitators from public meetings.[129]

Before Bukhari helped create the Aḥrār, he took part in a major campaign of the 'ulamā' against the Aḥmadīya in 1925. The persecution of several Aḥmadīs in Afghanistan in 1924–5 had created a great stir in public opinion, and also evoked considerable protest. Indian scholars came to the 'rescue' of the anti-Aḥmadī position of the Islamic court in Afghanistan. In October 1924, the Deobandi scholar Shabbir Uthmani published his tract on legal arguments qualifying apostasy committed by Aḥmadīs and justifying the killing of apostates.[130] Bukhari joined 250 'ulamā' in signing a fatwā by various 'ulamā' against the Aḥmadīya, published in the journal *Al-Faiẓ* where Mirza Ghulam Ahmad was termed a non-believer (*kāfir*) and apostate (*murtadd*), the same applying to all those who obeyed him. No religious or worldly relations, according to the fatwā, should be kept with them (ibid.: 91). This fatwā was signed by 'ulamā' from the Deobandi, Barelwi, and Firangī Maḥallī traditions. The event helped forge an extremist coalition against dissenters. Their self-identification was based on the narrow interpretation of Sunni doctrinal beliefs. The foundations of an extremist consensus had been laid during activism for tablīgh and tanẓīm in the preceding years. They had served not only to oppose Hindu extremism but also to strive for doctrinal purity on terms of exclusion. But Bukhari did more than just that. He literally sought out the confrontation with the Aḥmadīs. He challenged them at

[129]Mathur (1972: 114ff.). On the Shahidganj mosque agitation, cf. Gilmartin (1988 and 1993).

[130]Uthmani 1974 (1924). Starting from the 1953 riots, this tract has served to legitimate the persecution of Aḥmadīs in independent Pakistan (cf. Munir 1954).

their public meetings and in their campaigns in 1920, 1925, 1927, 1931, and 1934. In 1925, he personally confronted the Aḥmadī leader Mahmud Ahmad at a public meeting in Lahore. In 1927, in an agitation in Lahore named Taḥrīk-i Shātam-i Rasūl (Movement Against Those Who Rejoice in the Holy Prophet's Misfortune),[131] he convened public meetings to demand legislation that would make abuse of the founders of religion a criminal offence, aiming at both the Āryā Samāj and the Aḥmadīya. In 1931, together with his new movement, the Aḥrār, he decided to take over the Kashmir agitation launched by the Aḥmadīya against the Hindu prince and his autocratic methods there.[132] In 1934, he conducted a public prayer meeting at the very seat of the Aḥmadīya in Qadiyan, heaping insult and abuse on them, which ultimately led to the issuance of prohibition orders and his arrest.

In 1939, the Shi'i élite and community of Lucknow became another target of Bukhari's attacks. Here he intervened in an ongoing dispute between Shi'i and Sunni groups. Both groups whipped up public attention by reciting controversial religious verses in public. The Shi'is did so in the tradition of *tabarra*, cursing the first three Caliphs after the Prophet, and *tawallā*, praising *ahl al-bayt*, the Prophet's family, and especially Ali, the Prophet's son-in-law, who allegedly was deprived of his right to succession by deceit. In a counter-tradition of madḥ-i ṣaḥāba, the Sunnis recited verses praising the four right-guided Caliphs. In 1907, a committee had ruled that both groups enjoyed an equal right to do so, a fundamental reversal of the dominance of Shi'i custom in this formerly Shi'i princely state centring on Lucknow. Now equality was no longer acceptable to the ascending Sunni middle classes, all the more as nothing much had changed in the hold of the traditional landed Shi'i élites on Lucknow's society (Freitag 1990: 263ff., esp. 271f.).

[131]The agitation was sparked by the publication of a controversial Āryā Samāj tract, *Rangilā Rasūl*, attacking the Prophet Muhammad on matters of his personal life, polygamy, etc. The tract was written in factual style with detailed references to authorities of research and of Islam. Muslim leaders, and also Gandhi, resented that the publisher was not punished, a feeling severely accentuated after he was acquitted by the Punjab High Court of 'intention to create ill-feeling between classes' in 1927 in a case first instituted by the government. The judge weighed considerations of public tranquillity against those of freedom of expression, as legislature could not be expected to entirely block the critical consideration of religious history (*IAR* 1927/I: 90ff.).

[132]The Aḥmadīs had managed to take control of the Punjab-based All-India Kashmir Committee, which in 1931 launched a campaign against the Hindu ruler of the Jammu and Kashmir principality for the removal of 'grievances' among the Muslim majority of his subjects (cf. Lavan 1976: 145–63). For the Aḥmadīya, the Kashmir campaign was an unusually activist expression of their missionary activities (cf. also Chapter 3, section 3.4.3).

Public tension was obviously less to do with religious competition than with mounting social and political pressures. The Aḥrār apparently represented 'in the main the urban Muslims, who are jealous of the ascendancy of wealthy landowners in the Legislature and Executive'.[133] They opposed the traditional hold of rural-based, non-reformist Muslim élites over Punjab, epitomized by the rise of the Unionist Party to power in the 1937 elections. Constitutional reforms after 1919 had opened up contest and participation in a variety of ways and notably through legislative elections. This development combined with the huge magnitude of the national movement. Islamic leaders, much as any other public activist, now drew their legitimacy from a considerably broader and activated public. The moment communal relations worsened and cost the lives of several hundred people, it became difficult to continue with previous policies of Hindu–Muslim cooperation if they wanted to retain their influence. Instead they explored issues of religious and communal identity to secure their standing. In this they reacted very similarly to Hindu or Sikh or Pakhtun leaders. They behaved like politicians who wanted to maximize influence and power by shoring up support among members of the public.

But the radicalization of Islamic activism as much as any religious public activism was—and is—a double-edged sword. While it was meant to create public support under specific circumstances, it changed the rules and parameters of public religious discourse. Religious radicalization was bound to narrow down choices, both politically and with regard to the interpretation of Islam. The radical project deliberately targeted deviating readings. In consequence, the number of issues seen as deviant kept increasing. Enemies of religion became countless and a siege mentality set in.

By the mid-1930s radical groups such as the Aḥrār targeted minorities such as the Aḥmadī and the Shi'i groups on a regular basis. Not only did these actions manipulate dissatisfied and frustrated believers, they also made use of the dismal social and economic situation and exploited local cleavages.[134] The Aḥrār tried to give their actions a 'progressive' political and social colouring. Attacks on the Aḥmadīya were portrayed as attacks

[133]Cf. Punjab Fortnightly Report for the first half of November 1931, *Home Political*, file 18/11/31, NAI, quoted in Hasan (1993: 213).

[134]The evidence presented to the Cawnpore (Kanpur) Inquiry Committee instituted by the Congress after the 1931 Kanpur communal riots suggested overwhelmingly that the Muslim middle class felt 'slighted' in promotions, that they saw this as a sign of Muslim powerlessness and systematic subjection to discrimination. Cf. *Commission of Inquiry Report on the Cawnpore Riot of 1931*, *Evidence*, in BLOC L/P&J/7/75 for 1931, 422–36, quoted in Freitag (1990: 233).

on a British ally,[135] those on Shi'i Muslims in Lucknow were made to look as attacks on the privileged establishment of the city and the former Shi'i principality. The Kashmir campaign was supposedly directed against feudal autocracy of the Hindu administration and the suppression of ordinary Muslims. Congress used the Aḥrār as its storm troopers on Muslim political issues. This worked to the advantage of both sides. The Aḥrār wanted to increase the influence of religious Muslims in the Congress and its working committee. The Congress wanted to curtail the influence of the Muslim League among Muslims. Maulana Azad, the prominent Congress politician, was said to have engineered the Aḥrār's emergence and coordinated some of their activities. This pointed to the regrettable encouragement that religious militancy received from political parties for short-term gains.

But the radicalization of Islamic politics was not limited to the ascendancy of the Aḥrār Party. It also took hold in the JUH. Gradual changes in its programmatic documents were indicative of such development. In 1939, the JUH in its new programme pointedly dropped references to shared (*mushtarika*) beliefs and rights of all Islamic groups, the defence of which was included in its first programme of 1920.[136] The new programme reflected the growing intolerance not only towards reforming or non-orthodox sects and traditions such as the Aḥmadīs, but also towards the Shi'a (Rozinah 1981/I: 41, 48–9). This change was also reflected in the dropping of another buzzword, 'political', from the aims and objectives (*āghrāẓ-o maqāṣid*). While initially an important task was to provide political leadership,[137] the adjective political was pushed to the background and finally dropped in 1939. Guidance in matters of Islam took a much more conspicuous place now. Instead of a more passive approach as in the beginning, the task of 'defence' was prominently added in 1939. A more

[135]This referred to staunch Aḥmadī loyalism towards British rule. It was largely prompted by the hostility of other Sunni groups towards the Aḥmadīya. Only the government would, at least partly, protect them as the British attempted to pursue a policy of freedom of faith. Also, some Aḥmadīs still enjoyed outstanding positions in public life, the most prominent of which was Sir Zafarullah Khan who at the height of the Kashmir campaign in 1931 was elected President of the Muslim League and also officiated as law member (minister) at the Viceroy's Executive Council (the British-Indian Government) in 1932. Cf. Zafarullah Khan's memoirs (1991).

[136]The relevant clause (c) first read: 'To obtain and defend the shared/agreed religious rights (of all Muslim sects and traditions—DR) and to meet the joint religious and patriotic needs.' In 1939, clause (c) was changed: 'To obtain and defend the religious and patriotic rights and needs of Muslims'; dropping the word joint (mushtarika) which enjoyed a symbolic significance in the JUH discourse (Rozinah 1981/I: 48–9; see Appendix II).

[137]This contrasts with the position taken by Minault in her classic study on the Khilafat Movement in which she asserted that the JUI was largely non-political and almost entirely focused on religious guidance (Minault 1982).

active position was also taken on the reform of Muslims and the propagation of Islam (tablīgh), reflecting not only the growing influence and success of the Tablīghī Jamā'at and its concept, but also the perceived need of less passive conduct in this area in the face of growing communal tension (Rozinah 1981/I: 41, 48–9). The JUH also defended the anti-Shi'a campaign of the Aḥrār in Lucknow (as discussed earlier). It repeatedly passed resolutions emphasizing the rights of Sunnis to engage in the praise of the Prophet's companions (madḥ-i ṣaḥāba) in public places. It demanded the release of prisoners and urged the Congress to give orders to the United Provinces Government for lifting any restrictions on the movement.[138] Differences with the Aḥrār were also discussed, but they pertained mainly to coordination. The 1939 and 1940 JUH sessions confirmed its condemnation of the Khāksār Movement as a fitna not less dangerous than the Aḥmadī beliefs (Rozinah 1981/II: 650–1, 702).

The hardening of sectarian positions among some sections of the religious scholars, the deliberate and provocative revival of anti-Aḥmadī and anti-Shi'i conflict went hand in hand with the hardening of political positions of the Congress and the Muslim League camps. The provincial ministries elected in 1937, which introduced representative political government in India, were short-lived. Congress ministries resigned in eight provinces in 1939 over India's war commitment (cf. fn. 30). When the Congress reneged on an agreement with the Muslim League to form a coalition government in the United Provinces with its small but prominent Muslim minority it created a great stir in Muslim élite circles. The Muslim League paid back in kind and started a dramatic campaign about the 'atrocities' against Muslims under the Congress government in the United Provinces and Bihar.[139] For them, this reflected the arrogance of power displayed by the Congress in anticipation of its rule over independent India, as also its unwillingness to share power with a seemingly ill-prepared and unimportant contender.

Another important development in this context was the penetration of Aligarh's Muslim University by the Muslim League after 1936. Jinnah called Aligarh the 'arsenal of Muslim India'.[140] The League and its student volunteers helped create a situation of communal intolerance at the university, leading to purges of teachers and students who held left-leaning views or sympathized with the Congress. Islamic symbolism and religious instruction were strengthened at the University. Khaliq Nizami recounted

[138] Cf. JUH Resolutions No. 25/1939, in Rozinah (1981/II: 651); No. 6/1940, in ibid.: 698–9; No. 17/1945, in ibid.: 826.

[139] A Muslim League inquiry committee published the 'Pirpur Report' used by the League in its Pakistan propaganda to much effect (All-India Muslim League 1939).

[140] Cf. Hasan (1998a: 188–220); for Jinnah's quote see ibid.: 205.

the circumstances of the resignation of the Vice-Chancellor, Dr Ziauddin, in 1947. When he realized that Pakistan was in the offing and Aligarh would remain within the Indian Union by geographical logic, he demanded that Aligarh University withdraw itself from the political forefront. The students heckled him over this and drove him from one room to another, till at last he locked himself up in a toilet. He was forced to write a letter of resignation there (Nizami 1995: 224).

The Muslim League resorted to the deliberate mobilization of religious scholars in 1945–6 only when the next elections were approaching to which mainly Barelwi scholars responded. At the 1946 AISC session in Banares, the speaker, Sayyid Muhammad Ashrafi, whipped up sectarian passion by arguing that attacks on Sunni Islam were made in the name of Sunni beliefs in order to throw Sunnis out of their homes in India.[141] He referred to the Saudi Wahhabis; to those electing an unrepresentative Amīr al-Sharī'at, attacking thereby the Deobandis;[142] to those denying the 'Finality of Prophethood'—meaning the Aḥmadīs; and to those using the name of the Prophet's family to conduct campaigns such as the madḥ-i ṣaḥāba, taking a swipe at the Aḥrār (Qādirī 1997: 263–5). The slogan was that Sunni Islam was in danger, and that the survival of Islam in the subcontinent had to be decided now or never.

The sectarian slant of Islamic radicalism subsided slightly in the wake of partition. Activists faced the squeeze of political polarization. As Pakistan increasingly appeared to become a reality, all those Islamic groups that had aligned themselves with the Congress were desperate to manoeuvre themselves either to a position of neutrality or into the Muslim League camp. The theologically more radical (Deobandi, Ahl-i Ḥadīth) or more consistent (Tablīghī) groups benefited from partition by relocating to Pakistan whereas the Barelwis continued to flourish in local territory where they enjoyed traditional support—Punjab and Sindh in Pakistan, and Uttar Pradesh in India. Although sectarian radicalism was at odds with Muslim League doctrines and policies, the theological underpinnings of Pakistan provided it with a legitimate course. Mainstream politicians were soon tempted to make use of its mobilizing potential to advance their factional interests.[143]

[141]This argument relied on the Barelwi claim that they represented all Sunnis, following which all others 'pretending' to be Sunnis made 'false' claims.

[142]He attacked Deobandi plans to elect an Amīr al-Sharī'at in Saharanpur in 1945, as also the formation of a Sunni board by Deobandi 'ulamā' for the United Provinces in Lucknow (cf. Qadiri 1999: 375ff.).

[143]There is evidence that the local Muslim League under Mumtaz Daultana in Lahore in 1953 gave the Aḥrār tacit support to conduct their anti-Aḥmadīya campaign, cf. the Munir Report (Munir 1954: 261ff.).

The project of an Islamic state, an Islamic society, scored only a token victory during the formation of Pakistan. Its Islamic character subsequently became a matter of much political conflict and hot dispute. The concepts of intervention as pursued by the Islamic groups suffered defeat at partition as they were sidelined by secular power politics. Their major achievement remained the strengthening of their organizations and their infrastructure, the elaboration of their concepts and strategies, the training of their scholars and leaders. This formed the basis of Islamic interventionism not only in modern Pakistan, but also in local developments in India (Kashmir, Hyderabad, etc.).

5

Social Commitment and a New Society

A third area of targeted intervention for the religious Islamic groups was the social sector. In this chapter attention is focused on three areas where specific discourses were conducted and campaigns supported: education, law, and welfare. Again, as mentioned in connection with other activities, the Islamic groups were taking to fields of intervention in which secular and non-Islamic religious groups were already busy. They reflected the needs of a society embroiled in a deep and painful process of capitalist transformation. The objective of this process was the adaptation to new requirements. The competition between religious and social communities for a greater share in the economic resources and a higher social status had marked education as a key factor. This had much to do with the central role employment in public services played for the Muslim élites. Successfully passing the entrance examinations to these services was seen as a cherished goal as much by young Muslims as by their non-Muslim compatriots. The reformulation and introduction of elements of an Islamic legal system was partly a response to problems encountered by Muslims in their dealings with the British legal system, in questions of marriage, property rights, and inheritance. But drives for Islamic legal codification were also convenient causes for Islamic activists to whip up public opinion and set up an agenda for change. This was seen as a safe avenue to make the influence of Islam felt without disturbing relations with other communities. Collecting public funds for the social needs of the community was an old Islamic tradition. What had originally been an instrument of fiscal policy of the state in Moghul India or in early Islamic history now became a means of mobilizing additional resources for the community to make up for its relative backwardness in comparison to others. A more practical reason to set up community funds (bayt al-māl) was to finance group activity, community organizations—an Islamic bureaucracy. Controversy often raged between those who benefited from such funds and the Muslim public-at-large. Accusations of embezzlement of funds were rife and plagued many projects.

These sub-discourses were intended to chart the contours of an Islamic society that would embody the ideals of the founder generation of Islam, the salaf or 'pious forefathers'. The Islamic groups separately and collectively were trying to recreate the community of early Islam in the way they established relations within their groups and in the way they envisaged a true Islamic society. In India, where Islam was a minority religion, this was a much more difficult enterprise than in a Muslim majority country. For many, therefore, a model community of Islam was not bound to a particular territory, but to a group of people or to society as a whole.

5.1. ISLAMIC OR SECULAR SOCIETY

The desire of Islamic groups to present their group or movement as a blueprint for the revival of the early Islamic community believed to have existed under the leadership of the Prophet was an important aspect of public religious discourse. This early community was considered to have been ideal. Notably, the collective life of the companions of the Prophet, their character, and their mutual intercourse were considered virtuous and perfect. Many modern ills of society were blamed on the lack of this spirit. Consequently, an important strategy of Islamic movements lay in the revival of this spirit and the reconstruction of the Islamic community. They laid down principles for guidance to its members to ensure success. These usually related to the Prophetic traditions as embodied in Sunna and the ḥadīth, which were frequently held up for emulation. In these they invariably emphasized different elements.

The Deobandis referred to the Sunna of the Prophet in clause (3) of their principles characterizing their 'tack' (maslak) of faith (cf. Appendix I). It was to dictate the behaviour of all Deobandis in word and deed. This aimed as much at the internal mindset as at the external way of behaviour in dress, food habits, communication, and the like. The term associated with that was adab, meaning civility or refinement, and pointed to the Moghul tradition of courtly etiquette. The school refused state grants and prided itself on living on donations. Education, including books, was free for students. For the deserving small stipends were handed out. The emphasis was on obtaining knowledge. The Deoband historiography commented with sad disdain on the trend to measure education in terms of employment. Deoband's reluctance to seek government recognition for the degrees it awards its students even today is presented as a desire to pursue knowledge over worldly gains.[1] In contrast, Pakistani seminaries

[1]Rizvi (1980/II: Chapter VI, 196ff.). In spite of this posture, the degrees are, in fact, recognized by several universities. Cf. fn. 16, this chapter.

benefited from a decision of the military government of Zia-ul-Haq to recognize the equivalence of degrees from religious schools if they met certain standards (Malik 1996). The personal ethics of Deoband could be gauged from various life sketches of Deobandi scholars in the centennial history volume, and from the particular qualities they emphasized. The famous Deoband scholar, Thanawi, for instance, was praised for his simple manners and for the fact that he received only a token salary. He supposedly earned no money from the several books he authored. This was done deliberately so as to keep the publications cheap and available to all knowledge-seeking Muslims (Rizvi 1980/II: 33–5). Such characteristics of a simple and pious life of devotion to religious knowledge and faith were also emphasized in the life of scholars of the Firangī Maḥallī tradition (Robinson 2001: 78ff.). The Nadwa scholars regarded themselves more as modern professional specialists in religion. Regular remuneration as well as state grants were seen to be a normal affair, although under student pressure during the Khilafat Movement the Nadwa temporarily had to forgo government grants (Chapter 4, fn. 15).

The Barelwi scholars were deeply embedded in their mainly rural network of devotees and lived largely on their donations. These were at times considerable and allowed some pīrs to accumulate substantial riches. Many pīrs doubled as huge landowners (Pir Mehr Ali Shah and Pir Jamaat Ali Shah, for instance). But Ahmad Raza and his sons did not use the substantial flow of resources to their personal advantage. In this they demonstrated their reformist bent to show that for them the interests of the community came first. They freely donated and distributed huge amounts of cash and valuables when on preaching tours. They visited believers and communities to ameliorate the lives of the poor and destitute among their devotees. The ceremonies to honour the Prophet and the sīra conferences on his life were welcome occasions to paint a vivid picture of his community for emulation, although this picture was much more free-flowing, miracle- and custom-laden than the respective image evoked by the Deobandis (Sanyal 1996a, 1998). At the same time, its public representatives made demands to shun expenses on feasts and improve the life of the community through self-reliance, religious education, and mutual economic assistance.[2]

Deobandi asceticism also deeply influenced Maulana Muhammad Ilyas who founded the Tablīghī Jamā'at. Living in the tradition of the Prophet's companions formed a substantial part of the internal culture of the Tablīghīs. They devoted much time and effort to emulate even minute

[2]Cf. the speech of Hamid Raza at the 1925 All-India Sunni Conference, especially pp. 177ff.

details of the behaviour of the Prophet as relayed to them by tradition. Their emphasis on the correct Islamic etiquette became clear from their six basic principles of how to conduct the movement (see Appendix I). The intention to reform the behaviour of Muslims participating in their preaching tours and to model them in the image of the assumed ideal conduct of the Prophet and his companions was reflected in their attention to proper behaviour during these tours. Elders were to be respected. Everyone was to be consulted before taking action. One was to be free to speak one's mind, but not without consideration of seniority and sincerity of intentions. The leader of the preaching group was not to enjoy particular privileges but serve as an example of proper behaviour by joining in the menial works necessary during the tour, and so on. More specifically, Ilyas himself was occasionally likened to the companions of Muhammad (ṣaḥāba). His biographer S.A.H.A. Nadwi referred to a statement attributed to the Shaykh al-Hind Mahmud al-Hasan that when he saw Ilyas he was reminded of the ṣaḥāba (Nadwi 1983: 8). Discussing this comparison further, Maulana Mufti Sayyid-ur-Rahman, in his introduction to the Tablīghī tract *Irshādāt wa Maktūbāt*, stressed two aspects of the companions—their God-fearing attitude and their humane qualities. These were also present in Ilyas, whose mission included dismantling the system of oppression and externalism and erecting the building of the divine, spiritual kingdom (Khilafat) (Ilyas 1997: 14). Ilyas was god-fearing and a friend of humanity. Rahman referred to a saying of Ilyas where he emphasized the universal rights of all people in Islam, of children, wives, parents, neighbours, and of all creatures of Allah. The rights of God and the rights of the believers (*ḥuqūq al-'abād*) both flowed from God's commandments. While God would forgive the curtailment of his rights, he would never do so in relation to His believers. That is why utmost care and consciousness had to be shown in their implementation (Ilyas 1997: 14).

Ilyas devoted special attention to character formation of the participants of the Tablīghī groups. Emphasis was put on self-denial, a self-effacing attitude, and on self-control. This showed in advice such as

- to refrain from showing off while doing good (Ilyas M 6);
- that one should exercise self-assessment and not hurry to pass judgement on others (Ilyas M 9);
- to spend money in the right way, balanced, within the limitations set by God and without being stingy (Ilyas M 13).

The technique of self-denial had proven to be a very effective strategy in dealing with adversaries. It left the onus of being wrong on the other and claimed high moral ground for whatever one demanded. The instructions for preaching illustrated its practical importance. Ilyas demanded the following:

- to show patience and yet passion, to be humble;
- to interact with the local pious and intellectual people;
- to accept hardship on the road of preaching;
- not to get disheartened by a negative response, or by not getting the right attention even from the pious and learned (Ilyas M 25–30).

Starting from the correction of the behaviour of Tablīghīs, Ilyas devoted attention to the reformation of society as a whole to which his movement felt called to contribute. This concerned the eradication of un-Islamic behaviour such as drinking or gambling to which his groups paid attention in their rounds (gasht) of the neighbourhood. There they acted as a kind of neighbourhood watch, not unlike a 'religious police', exerting soft but unrelenting social pressure on the unwilling or non-performing. This also concerned the wider outlook on society. Ilyas gave specific instructions about the interaction of Tablīghīs with different classes of society (Numani 1993: *passim*). They were not to isolate themselves from society but remain in touch with their origins, their calling in society. People were not to give up their vocation for tablīgh work. Tablīghī activity was to remain a temporary occupation if it was to be successful in reforming Muslim society at large. Ilyas demanded that special consideration be shown to the wealthy sections of the community. Their contribution was to be sought and respected. This demand reflected a certain tension between the asceticism of the movement and the need to draw in people of influence who could help to win over the local community. Repeatedly Ilyas demanded respect towards the 'ulamā' and insisted that the Tablighi groups work through them when touring distant localities. This demand responded to a certain disdain among Tablīghī workers for the 'ulamā' in relation to whom they often felt superior in their religious fervour. The 'ulamā' had their own problems with the movement. At times, as mentioned earlier, they found it difficult to accept its innovative and formalistic character. While the Tablīghīs did not emphasize so much a blueprint for a new society, or suggest a definite structure, they upheld a number of principles and a mode of conduct. Although short on specifics, they strongly promoted the ideal of a model community of the Prophet's time.[3]

[3]I beg to differ here with the otherwise insightful analysis by Barbara Metcalf (1996: 57). There she asserted that the Tablīghīs are marked by 'the total absence of a utopian vision or programme in the movement', that 'there is no attempt to establish a saintly community.' This is not only far-fetched but also incorrect as it totally disregards the wide-ranging counsel and recommendations of Muhammad Ilyas on the reformation of society, as discussed here.

The Khāksār vision of society pointed in a similar direction. Addressing the members of their annual congregation in 1936, the so-called Gujrat Camp, Mashriqi stressed that 'if today you want to see the practical implementation of the Qur'an on earth the Khāksār movement appears as its correct if somewhat dim picture'. It was through the everyday activities of its honest and sincere members that this picture became clearer by the day. 'Our mission (*da'wa*) is that the *Khāksār* soldier in the spiritual and religious context of today lays his sincerity, his service to humankind, his love, his rejection of sectarianism, his soldierly capabilities, his humane solidarity, his obedience to the *amīr*, his discipline, his organizing capabilities, his leadership qualities before God, and due to his true rejection of idols and his principled monism (*tauḥīd*) becomes a thousand times (degrees) better Muslim than the others' (Mashriqi 1995: 50). Soldierly asceticism in religious interpretation inspired the daily operation of the movement with the objective of improving the individual Muslim and society as a whole.

The social ideal of the Aḥrār, a Deobandi offspring, was formulated on an egalitarian basis, reconciling the Islamic reformist message with radical anti-British and anti-capitalist rhetoric. However, their leaders' activism was very urbane and mostly devoid of asceticism. Their functionaries were known to live and eat well, allegedly on the donations of their followers, which were rarely accounted for. Their social background was Punjabi middle-class and well-to-do peasantry (Smith 1985: 270–1). The Ahl-i Ḥadīth were quite heterogeneous in the composition of their leadership in those days as well as today. Some like Abdullah Ghaznawi (d. 1881) represented the ascetic tradition. Others reflected the growing popularity of the sect among traders and up-and-coming commercial élites, embodied by Thanaullah Amritsari. The latter was known to dress well. Yet, their social ideal was informed by their reformist intentions. It was pragmatic and knowledge-seeking. They resolutely opposed ostentatious expenditure on ceremonies, such as marriage. As a group they branched out of the cities into the districts of the Punjab where they tended to cluster in commercially more developed regions.[4] Still others coming from the jihādī background of the Pakhtun frontier tribes were poor to the point of being ragged.

The Aḥmadīya, being mainly popular among the middle classes, were known for their modest lifestyle. They also cultivated some form of asceticism.

[4]In 1911, the highest numbers of Ahl-i Ḥadīth were registered for the districts of Ferozpur, Lahore, Gurdaspur, Amritsar, Gujranwala, and Sialkot in descending order (Census 1911, Punjab, part I: 168). Riexinger pointed to the emergence of '*Ahl-i Ḥadīth* villages' in the Punjab districts of Ferozpur, Gujranwala, and Lyallpur (2004).

Their social reformism was ambiguous. They discouraged discrimination on the basis of gender, notably in matters of education and other public social activity, although they advocated veiling in the traditional Islamic way and a continuance of polygamy. They encouraged broad-based community welfare for the needy and disadvantaged, although they remained conscious of social group and former caste status. Their view that Islam encouraged 'rational views and scientific research' (Walter 1991: 152) helped shape a practical and industrious outlook among community members encouraging them to engage in modern trends and occupations in society. This brought them closest to the rationalism of the Aligarh School with which they shared this stimulation of industrious activity.[5] The organizational structure was characterized by Islamic institutions comprising a Caliph and a shūrā, that is, an advisory council, which endowed the functioning of the movement with a combination of patriarchic authoritarianism and participation (see Chapter 4, section 4.1.1).

The enhancement of the social role of women was another issue promoted by Islamic reformists. But women's self-articulation in the Islamic sector was barely noticeable before independence. By and large, the Islamic groups were male-dominated communities. And there was no uniformity in the way they dealt with this issue. There were traditional forms of influence for women, particularly from the wealthy sections of society. Islamic reformists such a Abdul Bari from the Firangī Maḥall were admired in the women quarters, the *zanānā*—separated rooms for the female members of the household living in ritual seclusion (Robinson 1994). From there activists received support—financial, social, and political. The Ahl-i Ḥadīth in their beginnings were promoted by a Muslim princess, Begum Shahjahan of Bhopal (1868–1901) (cf. Khān 2000; Preckel 2000). She was married to Siddiq Hasan Khan. Social reformers such as the Deobandi Thanawi had taken a special interest in promoting women's rights from an Islamic perspective. To redress the lack of religious knowledge among them, he compiled a popular religious reading book for women, the *Bihishtī Zewar* (Jewellery of Paradise) (Metcalf 1984, 1992). Women were called upon to be model mothers and wives. Religious traditions were invoked to guide them in this. The Tablīghī Jamā'at followed a similar approach, but less actively during the colonial period. In Mewat the emphasis was on women observing the veil and seclusion to mark themselves off from non-Muslims. The Tablīghīs expected women to support the household while the men were away on preaching tours. This could be trying for the household as families had to do without their

[5]On the sociology of the Aḥmadīya, see also Ahmed (1980).

breadwinner, creating at times precarious situations. Women's activities in reformist Islam have taken a new turn since the 1970s. The Tablīghīs started women's circles for religious education. Tablīghī women go on preaching tours accompanied by a male guardian (*maḥram*), aiming at other women only. Their groups convene inside houses where conditions of gender segregation are ensured, listening to male preachers from another room or from behind a curtain. Metcalf maintained that the Tablīghī ritual challenged traditional gender roles. All preachers while on tour must share equally in household duties—just as women do in their families (Metcalf in Masud 2000: 50ff.). The Jamā'at-i Islāmī went on to found special religious schools for girls.[6] The Aḥmadīya were the only group that systematically administered religious and secular education to girls and women before independence. They also organized women in a separate women's wing (Table 2.2). The changing attitude towards women was also reflected in the practice of the Chishti Sufis Khwaja Hasan Nizami and Hazrat Inayat Khan (1882–1927). The former published reformist-inspired treatises and magazines for women and also included some among his khulafā'. The latter, mainly operating in the West, initiated only women to the position of Sufi teachers (*murshida*) in his branch (Hermansen 2001:342ff.).

An integral part of the reformist and revivalist ethics for most groups was to cut down expenses on life cycle ceremonies. Feasts on the occasion of birth, death, or marriage rituals were universally opposed. These demands, however, did not always go down well with followers and could never be strictly imposed except for a movement like the Aḥmadīya and the Tablīghīs where internal social control was at the highest level. For some groups their members were recognizable in outward appearance. Their manner of address,[7] language, and vocabulary, their style of dress marked them off from others by specific details. This in particular applied to the Tablīghīs, many of whom could be recognized from far by their canonical clothing. It was based on the traditional dress of north Indian Muslims, which consisted of baggy trousers and a loose shirt (*shalwār/qamīṣ*) where the trousers in reference to the Prophet's ways would end above the ankle.

The groups displayed visions of themselves as model communities and examples for society that were in part conflicting and yet common on

[6]Cf. Lynsey Addario, 'Jihad's Women', *New York Times Magazine*, 21 October 2001, at http://www.nytimes.com/2001/10/21/magazine/21WOMEN.html.

[7]Beyond universal forms of address such as *ḥaẓrat* the Barelwi leaders often used barādarān (brethren—Qadiri 1997: 212ff.). The Khāksār leader Mashriqi addressed party workers as *Khāksār sipāh*' (Khāksār soldiers) (Mashriqi 1995: 38ff.) or simply *musalmānō* (Muslims) (ibid.: 43ff). Among Tablīghīs, *bhaī* (brother) is often used like a regular address (field research of the author).

a number of issues and traits. They displayed their intention to get rid of Western consumerism and materialism. A moralist stand was taken to deal with the outfall of capitalism and 'Westernization'. Values were to be re-emphasized, human relations to be strengthened to regain their warmth and closeness. But the models always implied some form of 'social engineering', applying concerted social pressure on Muslims who would not agree with them. As such, their attitude was marked by a distinct, very modern ideologization. While all groups accorded priority to religious education, secular education and economic programmes were conspicuous by their absence in their agendas. No concept for an Islamic economy was discernable. Demands focused on the share of Muslims in the economy. The JUH called on them to engage in trade at par with the seemingly more successful Hindus in order to stop the 'moral degradation' of Muslims (Rozinah 1981/I: 455). It took the side of Muslim businesses and workers when it perceived them to be disadvantaged.[8] The Barelwis,[9] the Khāksārs,[10] and the Tablīghīs[11] encouraged economic relations among group members to promote self-reliance, a concept little suited to stimulate growth in the larger society. The Aḥmadīya (cf. Bhatia 1982) and partly the Ahl-i Ḥadīth (cf. Malik 1996; Riexinger 2004) were exceptions in that they regarded economic success as tantamount to doing good work in this world for their salvation in the hereafter.

The images of the model communities reflected the social roots of these groups. A pervasive lower-middle-class service mentality characterized many 'ulamā'. Their social ideal appeared to be a well-educated, well-behaved, pious and humble clerk. This should not be surprising given the fact that many of their leaders came from a background of government service or had grown up in close contact with government servants. The founders of Deoband, Nanaotawi, and Gangohi were influenced by Delhi College, a government institution where Nanaotawi's uncle Mamluk Ali (1789–1851) served. The college was believed to have significantly influenced their concept of religious education in Deoband (Metcalf 1982:

[8]See the 1945 JUH resolutions on solidarity with workers of a local cigarette factory and with transport businesses feeling threatened by government monopoly (Rozinah 1981/II: 826–7).

[9]At the 1925 AISC session Hamid Raza demanded a new loan policy calling on Muslims to grant loans to their own co-religionists to save them from (Hindu) moneylenders (Qadiri 1997: 189–90). The 1935 AISC President, Sayyid Jamaat Ali, urged all Muslims to engage in mutual trade irrespective of their craft (ibid.: 242).

[10]Mashriqi called on the Khāksārs to purchase goods first of all from other Khāksārs who on such deals should make the least profit (Mathur 1972: 197).

[11]Ilyas is quoted as saying that god-fearing behaviour such as proper treatment of offspring or engaging in trade (buying and selling) within the limits of God's commandments would also amount to remembering God (Ilyas M 78).

71ff.). Shibli was a teacher at Aligarh. The Khāksār leader Mashriqi was principal of a college. Mirza Ghulam Ahmad was a low law clerk (Mathur 1972: 103). The other social tradition the leaders embodied was religious learning handed down from father to son, an atmosphere of personal, private piety. Ahmad Raza, Muhammad Ilyas, and Abdul Bari from the Firangī Maḥall exemplified this tradition. It betrayed deep Sufi roots and produced strivings for emotional solidarity and identity. These two influences, government service and personal piety, shaped the outlook on society of most of the leaders. However, with passing time, the social background of the adherents diversified. Over the decades they created separate milieus of their followers. These in many ways also grew socially distinct. The Deobandis started attracting the lower middle classes from urban and rural centres. A stronger rural influence was discernable in the Barelwi élite, which depended variously on incomes from land, trade, teaching, the voluntary contributions of followers, or combinations thereof (Sanyal 1996a: 68ff.). The Ahl-i Ḥadīth were well represented among traders and other commercial people. The Aḥmadīya attracted the new professional classes (doctors, lawyers, government servants, etc). These distinctions were not exclusive but they nevertheless contributed to rival images of model communities shaped by their respective social background.

The reference to the 'model community' of early Islam remains a powerful symbol also in the political and religious discourse of today's Pakistan. Its military ruler, General Pervez Musharraf (b. 1943), urged Islamic clerics in June 2001 to concentrate on making Pakistan a 'model society':

> ... There is a need to establish a model Islamic society as was set up by the Holy Prophet (PBUH). He said the Holy Prophet (PBUH) brought a revolution through Islam and established a society where there was justice and equity in the society, no rich or poor and nobody had supremacy over the other due to race, colour or creed. There was total harmony and co-operation (*The News*, 7 June 2001).

For Musharraf, this reference was not directed against the Westernization of Pakistan but against its internal weakness, social and economic. He emphasized that Muslim Pakistan cannot be strong if it remained vulnerable with regard to its economy, law and order situation, sectarian dissensions, and violence. In the end the context of any reference to the model society of the Prophet decided over the direction of the changes intended.

5.2. RELIGIOUS OR NATIONAL EDUCATION

With the advent of the national movement, the idea formed that the new, future independent India also needed a new type of citizen, one who was not marked by a slave mentality towards British colonial rule and the West but by a national conscience. British Western education was seen to be inherently failing in this duty. National and religious activists remembered all too well the famous minute on education delivered by the former member of education of the Government of India, Thomas Babington Macaulay (1800–59), in 1835, in which he pleaded to make English-language education mandatory in India. He wanted to shape a class of Indians in the image of British citizenry. For the non-cooperators and religious activists, national education as opposed to government or English education was the answer. By this definition national education was conducted in the vernacular and based on Indian values.[12] It was to be āzād ta'līm (free, independent education). What this embodied was not easy to determine. For Islamic reformists the answer was clear: Muslims could have no other national education but a religious one. The parameters of national education from the perspective of reformist Islam in India will be discussed in connection with the reform of the curriculum of the madrasas—the debate on the alternative between national and religious education, the introduction of mass education, and the need for education to contribute to poverty reduction.

5.2.1. *Reform of Curriculum*

The need to reform the teaching curricula of the Islamic seminaries was voiced by the end of the nineteenth century by several activists. As indicated earlier, the madrasas were believed not to meet the requirements of the time. The qualification of the 'ulamā' was found wanting. And, more significantly, they were seen to be evading the new questions and issues with which their faith was confronted: the ascent of Western science, secularism, and materialism seemingly undermining the foundations of faith. The impact of these developments on the world had to be explained in Islamic terms whereas the 'ulamā' of the day were running away from

[12]Dr M. A. Ansari, addressing the All-India Muslim League 1920 session, reviewed the progress of the movement for national education, recounting the course of events in Aligarh, leading up to the foundation of the National Muslim University (Jām'iya Millīya) there. He lauded its sister organization, the National University at Ahmedabad, with Mahatma Gandhi as its Chancellor, the student protest at the Khalsa (Sikh) College, the Islamic College and the Hindu University, and also the decision of the Nadwa Board of Management to refuse government grant, stating further: 'There is a great future for the education on National lines and if Non-cooperation does nothing more than removing the evils of the present system of education it shall have fully justified its inception' (*IAR* 1921/I: 225–6).

these issues.[13] In particular, the village cleric, the *mullā*, was seen to be uneducated and superstitious. The Islamic activists accused the scholars of being busy with their petty squabbles about finer, and to them increasingly remote points of doctrine, which did little to help Islam survive in the modern controversial world.

The main directions of change applied to the choice of books being taught, to the manner of instruction, to the inclusion of modern subjects, including history, and to the need to study the English language. Teaching in South Asian madrasas of the Hanafi rite was dominated by the curriculum developed by the founder of the Firangī Maḥall, Mulla Nizamuddin, the dars-i niẓāmī.[14] At the time of its inception in the seventeenth century, it represented a reformist effort to bring teaching up-to-date with the latest achievements in the field of the rational sciences, the *ma'qūlāt*, in which logic, philosophy, various branches of mathematics, and medicine were included. In contrast, the *manqūlāt*, or the transmitted sciences, included knowledge obtained from divine sources, including the exegesis of the Qur'an (tafsīr), traditions (ḥadīth), and law and jurisprudence (sharī'a, fiqh). Arabic grammar and syntax were considered essential to understanding the latter group of subjects. Theology could be put in either category depending on the amount of speculative philosophy involved in its teaching (Nayyar 1998: 217f.; Robinson 2001: 213ff.). The emphasis on rational sciences was thought necessary at the time as madrasa graduates were employed also in non-religious posts as general administrators or state functionaries. The teaching of Islam through the madrasa system was often criticized. Students did not encounter the classic works of Islamic knowledge in their pure or original form. Most were being taught through voluminous commentaries, glosses, and notes on the classics. This led to an increasingly abstract and impractical debate in madrasas isolating students from political and social realities.

One major effort to change this situation was undertaken through the Nadwa council where initially scholars from all sectarian backgrounds united to face this challenge. They had hoped to develop a teaching project agreed upon by all that could be spread throughout South Asia at least and would help remove these flaws (Malik 1997; Zaman 1999). They wished to contribute to doctrinal reconciliation and the formulation of modern Islamic answers. However, those plans were immediately undermined by controversies between the Deobandis, the Ahl-i Ḥadīth,

[13] Sayyid Ahmad Khan argued this point forcefully in a 1894 letter to Muhammad Ali Monghiri. Cf. *Aligarh Institute Gazette* (6 April 1894), quoted in Jalis and Tabriz Khan (1983/I: 114–15). Shibli Numani also advocated this position (ibid.: 303f.).

[14] For a comparative discussion of the madrasa curricula used in the Ottoman, Safavid, and Moghul empires, including the dars-i niẓāmī, see Robinson (2001: 211ff.).

the Barelwis, the Shi'is, and the Aḥmadīs. One solution to this dilemma was the foundation of a new madrasa by the council, the Nadwa Seminary. Reformist views took the upper hand there. Few changes were introduced in religious teaching. But the Nadwa included the study of modern history, current spoken Arabic (in contrast and in addition to the classic Arabic of the Qur'an), and English. The manner of instruction was reformed, stimulating debate and the articulation of views. At the same time, extreme views or purges of dissenting sectarian views were avoided. The outlook remained largely conservative and modestly open.

The necessity to change was equally hotly debated at Deoband, as has been indicated earlier. The forces of resistance were much stronger here. Efforts by the group of Ubaidullah Sindhi and others to introduce the teaching of modern Arabic history in order to further the spirit of pan-Islamic solidarity were thwarted around 1910 (Sarwar 1967: 27–9; Sindhi 1970: 67). Proposals to teach English never materialized before independence due to the lack of funds. Attempts to give students vocational training in addition to religious training did not bear fruit until 1945 when a separate craft and industry department (*sh'obā dār al-ṣanā'e'*) was created (cf. section 5.2.4). Religious teaching remained largely unchanged.[15] The current curriculum contains an optional one-year programme of modern sciences and English. The Deoband centennial history written from a contemporary perspective (1980), still seeks to defend the concentration on religious subjects. The arguments in its support have changed little. With reference to Deoband's founder, Nanaotawi, it is argued that modern subjects were being taught by other schools while it was the want of religious education that had resulted in the creation of the Deoband School (Rizvi 1980/II: 211–13). To keep it this way, Deoband still considers it necessary to remain completely independent of the government of the day, in terms of funding, affiliation, and recognition of degrees.[16] The JUH as an umbrella organization of clerics had raised

[15]For a comparative view of the curriculum of Deoband and the traditional dars-i niẓāmī, see Hashmi (1989: 50–3). This comparison makes clear that the Deoband curriculum is almost entirely based on the dars-i niẓāmī with an added number of commentaries on each subject. Arab literature and history appear to be the only 'modern' subjects at the secondary level. At the primary level though secular knowledge is integrated with the 'Urdu curriculum.'

[16]Nevertheless, as Akhlaq Ahmad pointed out, the Deobandi 'ālim degrees were recognized as equivalent to the BA in Arabic, Islamic, or Persian studies awarded by the Aligarh Muslim University, the Al-Azhar University at Cairo, and the Madina University at Madina (1985: 28). The Jām'iya Millīya and the Hamdard University in Delhi recognized them as intermediate level school-leaving certificates provided that applicants pass additional tests in the English language. (Based on interviews conducted by the author in Delhi and Deoband in February/March 2004.)

the issue of reforming the madrasas several times. It demanded the reorganization of the the syllabus and its revision so that it would meet the requirements of reform and change in the present time (Rozinah 1981/I: 453; 1981 II: 755). A training institute for graduates of religious schools was to be established in 1945 to give them instruction in current affairs (ibid.: 818). A major initiative was taken in 1939 when provincial governments started operating. The JUH saw them as an early embodiment of national rule and demanded that they should promote religious education, something that the colonial government had persistently refused to do (ibid.: 636–7). The education programme as pursued by the Ahl-i Ḥadīth concentrated on the texts of the traditions (ḥadīth). For this, they were often accused by the Deobandis of unnecessary 'literalism'. The Deobandis sought to avoid this by their emphasis on rational argumentation in the maʿqūlāt subjects. The Ahl-i Ḥadīth had actively cooperated in the proceedings of the Nadwa council. There they tried to establish the writ of reformist Islam when the issue of curricular reform was discussed.[17] Their reform efforts were extensively documented in connection with the fiftieth anniversary of the 1937 educational conference (Nausharwi 1970). The report detailed the number of publications and the madrasas under their control or influence.

The Firangī Maḥallis had always been more flexible at combining attention to the reformist and Sufi heritage. Teachers, therefore, had more choice in the books they could select. The personal and small-scale style of teaching changed little, except for the madrasa initiated by Abdul Bari. There he introduced not only formal courses but also compulsory modern subjects such as arithmetic, algebra, geometry, and geography on the lines of government schools with outside inspections and regular examinations (Robinson 2001: 152). Local madrasas representing the Sufi- and shrine-related tradition had been created since the late nineteenth and early twentieth centuries. They organized into the Barelwi network more formally well after other traditions had already grouped around various lead seminaries. In 1904, Ahmad Riza consented to the foundation of the Madrasa Manẓar-i Islām, known more often as the Madrasa Ahl-e Sunnat wa Jamāʿat. This madrasa was attended by 200 students around 1920 (Muradabadi in Sanyal 1996a: 74). Ahmad Raza's brother, Hasan Raza (1859–1908), and his elder son, Hamid Raza (Qadiri 1997), laid the foundations of a systematic Barelwi approach to

[17]Two of their leaders participated in the Nadwa founding session of 1894, Muhammad Husain Batalwi and Muhammad Ibrahim Arwi (d. 1901). Malik believes that the Ahl-i Ḥadīth partly dominated the Nadwa council proceedings around the beginning of the twentieth century (1997: 251).

religious instruction. Early teaching in Ahl-i Sunnat madrasas, like the Madrasa 'Āliya in Rampur, founded in the eighteenth century, would have more closely resembled the style described by Barbara Metcalf for the Firangī Maḥall:

In...the famous Farangi Mahal in Lucknow, family members taught students in their own homes or in a corner of a mosque. There was no central library, no course required of each student, no series of examinations. A student would seek out a teacher and receive a certificate, a sanad, listing the books he had read, then move on to another teacher or return home (1982: 94).

A more specific educational scheme for the Barelwis was expounded in the presidential address of Hamid Raza at the 1925 All-India Sunni Conference at Muradabad (Qadiri 1997: 146–150).[18] It revealed that the Sunni Conference was conceived as a complex body for religious and political guidance. It envisaged a hierarchical system of madrasas affiliated to the al-Jam'īya al-'Āliya, the Urdu shorthand for the Sunni Conference, at the national level. Children were to be taught the basics of Islam (*Islāmī qā'edā*) and the Qur'an. For general religious education (dīnīyāt) they were to read Amjad Ali's *Bahār-i Sharī'at*,[19] and if some qualification in Urdu was required, Habibullah's history. Arithmetic was to be taught, as also the skill to write properly. The speaker considered it extremely important to provide for the education of girls. Beside dīnīyāt, they were to be instructed in needlework and housekeeping. Special consideration was to be given to the Islamic rules for gender segregation (parda). Elderly people and workers who had little time for studies would be given separate lessons in reading the *Bahār-i Sharī'at* at their convenience. Separate madrasas would provide religious instruction for an hour each day to students attending English-language schools. Selected religious graduates would form a writing board (*maḥkuma-e taṣanīf*) and compose new teaching material according to the requirements of the day that would take special note of religious controversies (fitna, *ikhtilāf*). All madrasas would have a Dār al-Iftā', although important fatāwā would have to be approved by the al-Jam'īya al-'Āliya before being issued. Preachers (wā'iẓ), teachers (*mudarris*), debaters (*munāẓir*), and legal clerks (muftī) would also be trained under the aegis of the al-Jam'īya al-'Āliya. The scheme, however, was never carried through.

More advanced views held by Islamic reformers such as Shibli Numani,

[18]There are several inaccuracies in the references made by Sanyal to this speech (1996a: 308f.) quoted here after the original source.

[19]The 18-volume collection of fatāwā written by one of Ahmad Raza's close followers (khalīfa) and widely used among the Barelwis (Amjad Ali 1983).

that modern sciences should be taught to give Islamic answers to the questions they raised, could not be implemented.[20] This problem has remained acute to the present day. It is no coincidence that the reform-oriented military regime of General Musharraf in Pakistan developed a plan for 'model madrasas'[21] in which computer science, English, and other modern skills would be taught so that their graduates no longer need to restrict their search for employment to the Islamic sector. The lack of modern education in the madrasas is seen as a factor facilitating the proliferation of extremism and religious violence (cf. also Saigol 1999).

However, the discourse with regard to the reform of madrasa education was, by and large, a derived discourse that had started with a general focus on the education of Indians under colonial conditions. For the Muslim community, the debate was pioneered by the modernists, by Sayyid Ahmad Khan and the Aligarh School. Its adherents expressed their views through the Muslim Educational Conference (MEC), which continued to be an influential body well into the 1930s of the twentieth century, although its effectiveness was limited. It was the prime mover behind the establishment of a Muslim University, which materialized in Aligarh in 1920. The MEC's main objective was to overcome the relative backwardness of the Muslim community in education. It sought to help provide for facilities in consonance with Islamic religion and culture. The MEC also promoted the education of Muslim girls and women, even from families observing segregation. A girl's school was opened in Aligarh in 1906, which later acquired residential facilities. The MEC also concerned

[20]After studying the features of religious instruction in Islam since the time of the Prophet and its current practice in different Islamic countries, he was quite clear about what he felt was lacking. He apparently disliked the fact that it was a prescribed curriculum, which had become immobile through the vast adage of commentaries and through the manner of instruction. He missed the opportunities for students to travel more, to engage in universal disputations, along with their teachers, to embrace all branches of knowledge, including the natural sciences, in the service of the revealed message of the Qur'an. He would have preferred that local politicians and administrators were better versed in religious scholarship. He would also not want to restrict religious learning to mosques and the specialized class of 'ulamā'. Cf. '*Qadīm ta'līm*', in Shibli Numani, *Maqālāt* (Azamgarh: Dāru'l-Musanifīn, 1955), Vol. 3, pp. 78–90, quoted in Grandin and Gaborieau (1997: 149–50). Shibli's ideal was Imam Abu Hanifa, as his biography *Sīra al-Nu'mān* suggests, a scholar with a penetrating, imaginative, and original mind, trained in rational theology and philosophy. Shibli also introduced to the Nadwa new ways of learning he had picked up at Aligarh: debates, essays, speeches, which invigorated his students (Malik 97: 351).

[21]Cf. the announcement of the Minister of Religious Affairs Ghazi about the new scheme of model religious schools of which the government planned to set up three in the beginning (*Dawn*, 24 August 2001). Religious seminaries see this intention as a serious threat undermining their independence; see the commentary by the rector of the prestigious Deobandi madrasa attached to Binuri Mosque at Karachi, Mufti Nizamuddin Shamzai, in *Zarb-i Mumīn* (31 August 2001), p. 3 (14).

itself with curricular reform at Islamic schools. In 1937, it formed a separate section for them, the *sho'ba madrasa-i islāmīya*, over which Maulana Madani from Deoband presided (Khan 2001: 210). The MEC shared the opinion that oriental and Islamic instruction 'should be made to conform to the needs of today instead of those of a by gone day' (ibid.: 203). The MEC cooperated with the government to modernize religious education. Granting government aid to these schools was made conditional on teaching secular subjects prescribed by the Department of Public Instruction. It demanded the equivalence of Arabic certificates from recognized madrasas and the exchange of graduates between the latter and the Muslim University of Aligarh (ibid.: 210).

The moderate views of Sayyid Ahmad Khan were surpassed in radicalism by Muslim reformers such as Badruddin Tayyabji (1844–1906), Amir Ali, and Muhammad Ali. Tayyabji founded the Anjuman-i Islām (1876, Bombay) for south India. In contrast to Sayyid Ahmad, he supported the Indian National Congress. Unlike Ahmad, he also favoured women's education: in his presidential address to the Muhammedan Education Conference of 1903 he urged Muslims to remove restrictions on women's education as he thought the Qur'an did not approve of these (Ahmad 1985: 163). Amir Ali advocated liberal education for Muslims in eastern India. He had set up a Central National Mohammedan Association (1877) in Calcutta for his activities. Standing aloof from the Congress, he was more radical in terms of social reform than Sayyid Ahmad, supporting not only education of Muslim women but also 'mixed marriages' between different religions. This was vehemently opposed by Sayyid Ahmad (*Eminent Mussalmans* 1981: 145–6). Muhammad Ali was one of the few who went as far as demanding free and compulsory primary education at the 1910 Muslim League session.[22]

Aligarh and Deoband had occasionally tried to establish contact in the field of religious instruction and knowledge. Although there existed outright hostility between its founding leaders, Nanaotawi and Sayyid Ahmad Khan, Deoband apparently felt that it needed to make more impact on the graduates of Aligarh. This was an implicit recognition of the increased social and political role the old boys of Aligarh were destined to play in the administration of British India, but also in the national movement. If these leaders were deficient in the knowledge of Islam this would bode ill for the fate of religion and of the Muslim community at large. With growing communal polarization Aligarh felt compelled to devote more attention to religious instruction. Before 1920, it was organized

[22]'The best form of freedom is free education and the most pleasing compulsion is compulsory education.' Cf. *Muslim League Documents*, 209, quoted in Afzal Iqbal (1974: 56).

as an extra-curricular activity when the college was still affiliated to the University of Calcutta and later to that of Allahabad (Moin 1976: 109ff.). Once the institution at Aligarh was declared a university, theology became part of the curriculum and a compulsory subject for Muslim students. A separate department, and eventually a faculty of theology (1944) was established. Yet Sunni and Shi'a clerics teaching there could not match their counterparts in the established madrasas as they were not known for original research or particular academic rigour while their views were marked by mainstream conservatism (cf. Lelyveld 1996: 240). Such deficiencies also plagued the Departments of Arabic and Islamic Studies (Nizami 1995: 106f.) even though some of the early proposals had envisaged that Aligarh should take Deoband's place in this field, applying Western methodology to this subject.[23]

5.2.2. *True National Education*

The alternative of religious versus national education was most demonstrably formulated in the course of the non-cooperation movement in the 1920s. The boycott of educational institutions affiliated to the government and regularly receiving official grants spurred the creation of national schools which were meant to replace government schools. Some of these schools undertaken as temporary, makeshift projects in the beginning came to stay as regular institutions. For the Islamic groups national schools were first of all schools where religious instruction would be writ large, schools devoted to spreading the spirit of Islam although not necessarily madrasas. Such schools were created for the primary and secondary levels. Most of the later Khilafatists were at a time engaged in such efforts.[24] These schools were being founded even earlier as part of a

[23]Early in 1904, Theodore Morison (1863–1936) argued that a school for advanced Arabic Studies should be established at Aligarh to win the support of orthodox Muslims in the campaign for the University. Being the centre of learning in northern India, Aligarh was the proper place and not the Dāru'l-'ulūm at Deoband or the Nadwatu'l-'ulamā' of Lucknow (Khan 2001: 85).

[24]National schools were not an entirely new phenomenon. They had earlier appeared in connection with the protest movement by the Congress against the partition of Bengal between 1905 and 1911. The 'Society for the Promotion of National Education in Bengal', for instance, founded 50 national schools, which disappeared after the unification of Bengal (Hashmi 1989: 16). Muslim activists in the Pakhtun tribal belt founded āzād (free) schools. For instance, Fazl-i Wahid, also known as Hajji of Turangzai (b. 1885), supported this scheme between 1908 and 1915 and through the 1920s. Mostly these were madrasas or maktabs seeking to teach a purified Islam to Pakhtun children. In the early 1920s, Abdul Ghaffar Khan, the Pakhtun leader and a disciple of the Hajji, did likewise with his Anjuman-i Iṣlāḥ-i Afghānīya (Afghan Reform Society). Cf. Government of India,

philanthropic educational drive to improve the educational standards of the Muslim community. Another meaning of the term national was to serve the Muslim community in India as a whole—the millat. Major Muslim educational institutions like Aligarh, Deoband, or the Jām'iya Millīya attempted to create affiliated networks,[25] which would be free from colonial or state supervision and non-Muslim control.

The most prominent project in this regard was the creation of the Jām'iya Millīya Islāmīya, most often translated at the time as national university' although the choice of words also indicated the Islamic connotation. It was opened on the premises of Aligarh College on 29 October 1920 in response to the refusal of the trustees of Aligarh to 'nationalize' their college by giving up government grants.[26] In the beginning, it included open-air public classes at Aligarh during the Khilafat campaign. The opening speech was held by the Deobandi 'ālim and Shaykh al-Hind Mahmud al-Hasan who had just returned from wartime internment at Malta. There he emphasized to the students the importance of guidance in Islamic matters:

Those amongst you who are well informed will know that I have never given a religious decree (*fatwā*) considering the study of a foreign language or of the sciences and arts of other nations as *kufr* (unbelief). But without doubt I've said that the final impact of English education is such that according to our observation

---

Who's Who in the Peshawar District, corrected up to 1 January 1931, confidential (Peshawar: H. M. S. O., 1931), in BLOC L/P&S/20/B296/10, 1, for the entry on Abdul Ghaffar Khan, and 12, for the Hajji. Although not a cleric himself, Ghaffar Khan was an associate of the group hatching the 1916 'Silk letter conspiracy'. Visiting the Deoband Seminary in 1969, he confided to the students: 'Sitting here we (together with Mahmud al-Hasan) used to make plans for the independence movement as to how we might drive away the English from this country and how we could make India free from the yoke of slavery of the English' (Rizvi 1980/I: 391; for the 'Silk letter conspiracy, see also Chapter 4, section 4.3.4). Consider also the foundation of the Āzād High School by the Aḥrār leader Bukhari (Chapter 4, section 4.4).

[25]On attempts to make the future Aligarh University the core institution of an independent Muslim educational network, see Khan (2001: 88–90); on Deobandi affiliations, see section 5.2.3; on institutions affiliated to the Jām'iya, see Mohsini (1986: 47).

[26]Muhammad Ali wanted to combine 'the separate elements of the common Indian nationality and Islamic millat and brotherhood'. Cf. Mohammad Sarwar, *Maẓāmin-e Muḥammad* 'Alī (Delhi, n.d.), part I, 254, quoted in Hasan (1985: 97). Ali argued against mixed hostels and education for Muslims and Hindus in a speech made in 1904. There he outlined the blueprint for a Muslim University which Aligarh college was meant to become (Nizami 1995: 252). This position though was less prompted by opposition to Hindus than by his anxiety to establish firm reasons for a separate Muslim University. At the time he was taking issue with arguments that there was no inherent necessity for a distinctly Mohammadan institution advanced by one Mr Hydari, a Muslim scholar in the Netherlands. Therefore, Muḥammad Ali wanted to prove that it would be Aligarh's distinction to further Muslim character-building.

people become influenced by (dyed in the colour of) Christianity, or mock and abuse their religion and their co-religionists with atheist taunts, or begin to worship the government of the day. For a Muslim to stay aloof from such education will be good.

The forward leaders of our nation have done right in asserting the feeling that this is an issue of overriding importance for the Islamic *umma* (community). Without doubt, [in] those educational institutions attended by Muslims where modern sciences are being taught, if the students become ignorant of the principles and practice (root and branch) of their religion and neglect their national feelings and Islamic duties and where the support of their nation (*millat*) and their communities (*qaumeñ*) has reached a very low level, I understand those educational institutions have become an instrument of undermining (weakening) the strength of Muslims. That's why the opening of this Free University was announced which will stay free of the assistance and influence of government and the whole set-up and course of which will be based on Islamic attributes and national feelings (Miyan 1976: 58).

It was clear that Aligarh to the religious scholars was the epitome of the spread of secularism and materialism among the Muslim élite. For them to provide national education to these secularized students meant to give them Islamic religious education so that they would be grounded in their own cultural tradition. Religion was seen as the core element of national identity, not only by Islamic, but also by non-Islamic religious activists. Hindu reformers were running their gurukul schools on comparable lines (cf. Chapter 4, fn. 70; Fischer-Tiné 2003). A Hindu National University had opened in 1917. To the government the Jām'iya was a project founded on anti-colonialism. After much delay it hastily brought into operation the Muslim University Act for Aligarh in December 1920 to steal the thunder of the Jām'iya and placate Muslim community leaders.

Muhammad Ali and some of his friends did not envisage that the Jām'iya would become a permanent institution. Camping on the Aligarh ground, they felt more like religious migrants, muhājirīn, and the faithful followers of the Prophet, *anṣār*, who lay in wait for victory at Mecca (Talib in Hasan 1998a: 163). The irony of the matter was that the Jām'iya Millīya project eventually evolved into a staunchly secular institution where Muslim identity was cultivated from a nationalist, left-leaning political perspective.[27] Founding principles of the Jām'iya included educational

[27]In the beginning the Jām'iya was a mixed project of religious fervour and agitation. Muhammad Ali who was the principle driving force behind the project recalled that 'our day began with a full hour devoted to the rapid exegesis of the Koran' (Hasan 1998b: 77). In a private letter, he conceded: 'Students from other Colleges also came to us, and before long almost all decided to suspend their usual literary studies "in the year of peaceful revolution" and got practical training in propaganda regarding the Khilafat and attainment of swarāj (or self-government)' (Iqbal 1974: 237).

freedom; coexistence of religious and worldly sciences; Urdu as vernacular medium of instruction; patriotism and composite nationalism; professional training; and simplicity and economy in its administration (Mohsini 1986: 37). They were amended in 1928 and 1938 stipulating that no assistance from the government should be accepted; and that all religious traditions should be treated equally. The Jām'iya also started classes for basic, adult, and professional education (ibid.). The university continued to play this role after independence, becoming a permanent institution located in Delhi.[28] The controversy over the religious identity of the school revived in the 1990s when its nationalist Muslim rector Mushirul Hasan was boycotted and prevented from fulfilling his duties by radical Islamic student organizations.[29] There was always a certain ambiguity between the secular and religious orientation in the activities of the Jām'iya Millīya. Its long-time rector Zakir Husain (1897–1967) pursued concepts for a radically new approach to primary education, the so-called Wardha Scheme (Oesterheld 2001, see also next chapter). This scheme was severely criticized not only by the JUH 'ulamā', but also by the MEC (*IAR* 1939/I: 381f.; ibid./II: 425ff.). While they shared its social thrust they feared its grounding in Gandhian philosophy and Hindu rhetoric, calling it a plan aimed at 'denationalising Muslims' (ibid.: 425). To educate children in the spirit of *ahiṁsā*[30] regarding all religions equally true was not acceptable (Rozinah 1981/II: 642). At the same time. Zakir Husain was known as a devout Muslim. He admired the effective practice of the Tablīghī Jamā'at in spreading religious knowledge to a large number of people through its preaching tours in some of which he apparently participated. He was also in regular contact with the Nadwa scholar S. A. H. A. Nadwi.[31] It is believed that Husain devised his scheme with an eye on egalitarian concepts of Islam.[32]

Proceeding from the Jām'iya Millīya project, Deoband pursued the line of religious national education further. Its scholars were invited on advisory missions to Afghanistan and the Muslim-Indian principality of Qalat where the rulers asked for their opinion on suitable national education and its compatibility with religious instruction. On all these occasions Deoband 'ulamā' argued in favour of a curriculum in which 'the religious science would be given due weight along with modern science

[28]For a detailed and balanced review of its history and structure, see Mohsini (1986).

[29]Cf. his commentary, Mushirul Hasan, 'A Symbol of Syncretism', *Indian Express*, 17 May 2000.

[30]Derived from the Sanskrit; avoiding violence and respecting all forms of life.

[31]On the interest taken by Zakir Husain in the work of the Tablīghī Jamā'at and his personal relationship with Muhammad Ilyas, cf. Nadwi (1975/II: 62–84, here 69).

[32]Cf. the biography of Zakir Husain (Faruqi 1988, esp. 204–11).

and social necessities'. This was thought necessary to remove 'that gulf of "educational dualism"' so that, as the Deoband historian puts it, 'by the gathering of both the old and modern educational tendencies at one point of union, an effort be made to create the unity of knowledge and thought in the community' (Rizvi 1980/I: 233).

In other words, religious instruction was considered a national duty, a prerequisite to achieve national unity. Otherwise, unity would supposedly be threatened by the dominant Western education and orientation of an élite that was increasingly about to turn its back on religion. The Deobandis did not have to impose their views on the rulers of Afghanistan and Qalat. Although their proposals were not formally adopted, the ruler of Qalat and an influential section of the royal Afghan household were believed to share this perspective.[33] This approach was complemented by the British. They in turn patronized government-financed madrasas to promote Arabic and Oriental learning on Western lines. The Madrasa 'Āliya in Calcutta was the most prominent of them (Zaman 1999).

5.2.3. Mass Education

Reformist Islam represented a new mode of dissemination of knowledge. By creating institutions and frameworks for the transfer of knowledge in the shape of large college-type seminaries complete with hostels, reformist 'ulamā' emulated the Western educational system. This new approach reflected the rise of mass education, a very modern feature of society. In fact, the 'ulamā' introduced religious mass education, which was to have a lasting effect on the nature of Muslim society in India. The number of madrasa and dāru'l-'ulūm founded between 1865 and 1899 (and still existing today) was 24 in the area of the United Provinces, where much of the activity of the madrasa movements concentrated, and six in Bihar, the next most important provincial centre. Between 1900 and 1946, these figures increased to 98 and 89, respectively (Qamaruddin 1994: 81). The number of students at the Deoband Seminary increased dramatically. For the year 1945–6, 1,160 students were enrolled, which was roughly the same number of students to have graduated from Deoband between 1867 and 1912—approximately 1,000 students (ibid.: 286; Rizvi 1980/I: 174). The number of students enrolled annually at Deoband has

[33]Maududi was engaged in similar activity. He prepared a plan for religious education at the behest of Nawab Salar Jang (1889–1949) for the princely state of Hyderabad in 1932. He was greatly disappointed when his proposals were not taken notice of. This convinced him that Muslim princely states could not rectify the state of Islam in India. This conclusion turned him to more modern forms of the revival of Islam (cf. Nasr 1996: 27).

regularly surpassed 1,500 since 1960,[34] and reached 3,504 in 2003–04.

The Deobandi network of affiliated madrasa has grown tremendously. Deoband admits that it has difficulty in keeping track of all religious schools founded in its tradition. It had formally affiliated 1173 madrasas, mainly in India, in March 2004. [35] A list made in 1973 carries the names of 608 such schools in India of which 228 are located in the United Provinces, although it is believed that their number is actually more than their double. For Pakistan, a 1971 survey gives a number of 915 madrasas of Deobandi orientation as compared to 458 of the Ahl-i Ḥadīth, Shi'i, and Barelwi tradition (Rizvi 1980/I: 364). It is perhaps safe to assume that today, that is, at the beginning of the twenty-first century, more than 2,000 Deobandi madrasas of varying size exist in Pakistan and India each. Latest official figures put the overall number of degree-level madrasas in Pakistan at 5,900 with about half a million students. Out of these, 2,550 are said to operate in Punjab, with 780 of them supposedly affiliated with the Deobandi tradition. There are 650 religious schools with about 100,000 students in the Frontier Province and 700 seminaries with about 50,000 students in Baluchistan. The great majority of the two latter groups are supposed to be connected with the Deoband tradition.[36]

The number of students at the Nadwa Seminary remained stagnant for much of the time for which its fuzzy profile may have been responsible. While attendance varied between 50 and 100 around the turn of the century, it stood at 69 in 1946 (Malik 1997: 325–31; Qamaruddin 1994: 286). The Nadwa Seminary extended its influence through its graduates taking up posts in religious institutions, including madrasas, in government service, and in the private sector. Their 'modernist' advantage over Deobandi graduates was their knowledge of English and their proficiency in spoken modern Arabic. However, they faced difficulty in getting full recognition from traditional 'ulamā' (Zaman 1999). The MEC also promoted religious mass education. It got particularly involved in primary education striving

[34]For a detailed statement of students enrolled, graduated, number of teaching staff between 1866 and 1976, cf. Rizvi (1980/II: 337ff). The 2003–4 data were provided by the Department of Education (Daftar-e Ta'līmāt) during field research in Feb–Mar 2004. DR.

[35]Rābiṭa Madāris 'Arabīya (RMA), Deoband, provided during field research in 2004. DR.

[36]Kamran Khan, 'Situation Tense in Religious Heartland', in *The News* (Karachi, 18 September 2001), at its website www.jang.com.pk/thenews/. Depending on the size of the religious schools considered, estimates vary considerably. Goldberg assumed that some 10,000 schools are teaching approximately 1 million students in Pakistan. Cf. Jeffrey Goldberg, 'The Education of a Holy Warrior', in *The New York Times Magazine*, 25 June 2000, at http://www10.nytimes.com/library/magazine/home/20000625mag-taliban.html.

to improve the quality of maktabs, of mullā or Qur'an schools, and also of madrasas (Khan 2001: 208f.). Between 1917 and 1922 alone, the number of such maktabs rose from 3,000 to 21,000 and their pupils from 9,000 to 21,000 (ibid.: 211).

Mass education was a mode of operation to which scholars with a more pronounced Sufi perspective such as the Barelwi and Firangī Maḥall could only slowly be converted. The Barelwi leader Ahmad Raza, for instance, was educated at home. He still represented the way of folk religion dealing with the dissemination of knowledge, the informal way of education. After independence, and even more after the rule of General Zia-ul-Haq, the Barelwis engaged themselves much more strongly in the field of seminary-based education. They created a whole new network of seminaries reflecting the modernist trend. This may also explain why doctrinally the differences between Deobandis and Barelwis, particularly with regard to the 'enemies' of Islam, have narrowed down greatly since then.

Given this massive expansion of the infrastructure of religious education, religious beliefs could now be reproduced in a standardized manner on a large scale. The mass attendance of the seminaries also helped the respective movements to recruit dedicated followers. As most madrasas were affiliated to one or the other (sectarian) tradition, their networks were crisscrossing the country. Followers were not simply recruited on the basis of personal choices but were growing into these groups socially, often from an early age, as young as five. That is how madrasa education in the subcontinent produced a dedicated mass following of the madrasa movements. This also applied to some of the revival movements such as the Ahl-i Ḥadīth, the Tablīghī Jamā'at, and the Aḥmadīya. Their leaders and functionaries used to attend particular, selected madrasas, which created specific graduate networks. The traditional way of receiving education, from the hand and mouth of the elders, was combined, fused with the new way of institutionalized mass education. The deep social and cultural local roots of the seminaries explain to some extent why these groups take on features of endogamous castes or sects, capable of reproducing themselves not only intellectually but also socially and biologically.

5.2.4. Development and the Eradication of Poverty

Two educational projects supported by the Islamic groups included a distinct development component, the Jām'iya Millīya scheme and the Tablīgh Jamā'at campaign among the Meo tribes. Others such as the Deobandis contributed to this objective by their way of teaching.

The Jām'iya Millīya wanted to provide *basic education* to the masses through the Wardha Scheme. It centred on Gandhi's proposal to provide primary education in rural areas through some form of productive manual work, a system which would be self-supporting by producing and selling basic goods to pay for the expenses of teachers (*IAR* 1937/II: 346). As mentioned earlier, Islamic scholars and Muslim League followers were strongly opposed to this. Nationalist Muslims, however, supported the project seeing it as an important element of national education. The rector of the Jām'iya Millīya at the time, Zakir Husain, wanted to execute it through the Jām'īya (Oesterheld 2001). For this he also drew on the experience of Islamic groups such as the Tablīghī Jamā'at. He was attracted to their way of dissemination of religious knowledge to the masses. Zakir Husain was appointed chairman of a committee to frame a syllabus. His report to the National Education Conference 1937 detailed the development aspects of the scheme on a nationalist, non-denominational basis (*IAR* 1937/II: 451ff.).

The Tablīghī Jamā'at devised a new way of providing religious instructions through door-to-door contact and by the word of mouth. This brought religious knowledge to the common people and to those who would normally not be receptive to it. This could well be a model for *informal education* as a means to bring education to the masses and break the hegemony of state-based and colonial or Western education. At the same time, this educational work was seen as a civilizing mission. Before Ilyas intervened with his movement, the Meo tribes were considered ridden with social evils such as constant infighting and ignorance, etc. It was alleged that as a result of the intervention of the Tablīghī movement the social climate improved considerably and the development standard grew significantly. In fact, Ilyas not only organized the improvement of their religious education but also intervened to settle long-standing disputes between their lineage and territorial sub-groups over stolen animals and women (Sikand 1996: 210ff.). The work done by Ilyas among the Meos was preceded by a general increase of *social activism* on behalf of Islamic groups. The 1931 Census noted that literacy among the Meos had increased since 1921 from 6 to 9 per cent 'mainly as a result of the uplift work among them' (Census 1931, Punjab, part I: 348). Prior to Ilyas' tablīgh activities, this involvement culminated in the so-called Alwar Movement. There the principality of Alwar ruled by a Hindu prince became the target of missionary efforts by the Aḥrār, the Muslim League, and the JUH.

The Deobandis also took up the question of how Islamic education could contribute to development efforts and to the eradication of poverty. As the schools in the Deoband tradition waived tuition fees, provided books, and sometimes offered hostel accommodation, many Muslims from low-income groups in rural areas and small towns felt attracted to start a career through these schools. Entrance was easier and involved almost no expenses. The centennial history of Deoband emphatically stressed the contribution of the seminary to *making education universal*, meaning to remove restrictions with regard to wealth, ethnic or racial background, and age. It painted these as pioneering efforts in the field of education (Rizvi 1980/II: 217ff.). The spread of religious instruction was believed to help eradicate illiteracy. But the rapidly increasing number of graduates, notably of the Deobandi schools, posed a problem as to where they would find employment. The Islamic sector, although growing, was not yet big enough to liberally provide graduates of Islamic schools with employment. The vocational training schemes at the Deoband Seminary were meant to help solve the problem. Skills taught in one-year courses included tailoring, book-binding, making flower arrangements, manufacturing of hold-alls and suitcases. They still continue today, although they did not prove to be very effective. The centennial history made clear that Deoband addressed the bread issue only reluctantly. Only those crafts were considered acceptable which suited the intellectual and religious disposition of scholars and students.[37]

While the 'ulamā' mostly regarded material and monetary considerations inconsistent with true religiosity, proponents of the Aligarh tradition were more explicit in their development orientation. Sayyid Ahmad had always followed a utilitarian approach that better education should improve chances for Muslims to get jobs, which in turn would raise their overall prospects and self-esteem as compared with other denominations. The MEC, as mentioned, took much interest in furthering religious schools of the primary level to combat illiteracy. Not only Aligarh, but also the Islamic groups were seen as vehicles for social advancement, depending on the perspective of followers. The Ahl-i Ḥadīth and the Aḥmadīya, for instance, attracted members of the new professional classes. Through their unorthodox doctrinal views both represented a break with the courtly and administrative culture of Moghul India from which the 'ulamā' class had sprung, thus opening a niche for a radical re-interpretation of social priorities. Muslims from rural areas regarded the Deobandi, Nadwa, and Barelwi schools, as also the Tablīghī, Khāksār, or Aḥrār activities, as a road out of their social and geographic marginalization.

5.3. ISLAMIC OR SECULAR LAW

Islamic groups led by the madrasa movements contributed in a variety of ways to the dissemination of Islamic legal norms. The enormous increase

[37] Rizvi (1980/II: 244f.). Also www.darululoom-deoband.com/urdu/departments/show.php?dept=darussanae.gif at their website.

in madrasas multiplied the numbers of the departments of Islamic law, which were created in most seminaries. Deoband introduced a separate department of religious decrees (dār al-iftā') in 1310 AH (1892). This in itself was an omen of the new developments. While earlier religious scholars would entertain requests for a legal opinion (istiftā') in their individual capacity, they now seemed overwhelmed by the mass of requests coming in. The annual records of Deoband stated:

Due to the fame of the *madrasa*, legal queries (*istiftā'*) came to it abundantly from far-off places and the teachers do not have so much off-time as to write the replies thereof without harm to their teaching work. A great object in teaching religious sciences is also this that the common Muslims may know the legal propositions (*masā'il-i shar'ī*) and there may be facility in ascertaining the truth; hence, with a view to expediency, it was decided that Mawlawi Aziz al-Rahman [d. 1928] pro-vice-chancellor, be appointed for the *iftā'* service so that the common Muslims may have no difficulty in obtaining fatwas (Rizvi 1980/I: 156).

This trend resulted in further institutionalization and division of labour, elements of a modern organization of society. '... By the first decade of the twentieth century, almost every Muslim educational or political organisation had established a *dār al-iftā*'' (Masud, Messik, and Powers 1996: 197). They represented a readily available source of reference on Hanafi law, even for the British courts:

Although British judges generally did not interfere in the religious matters of the subject population, they occasionally invoked the notions of equity and justice to circumvent traditional laws that they could not endorse with good conscience. Attempts to reform Islamic law were rarely initiated by the judiciary, and British legislative attempts to reform the law were vigorously resisted by Muslims. In this case, the reform of Islamic law was initiated by the Muslims themselves through the institution of *ifta'*, which was systematically organised, using modern modes of communication to increase its popularity among the masses (ibid.: 197).

The increased publication of collections of fatāwā, reaching a much wider public since the beginning of the century, created a new sphere of Islamic legal mass communication. The fatāwā issued from Deoband alone between 1329 and 1396 AH (1911–76) numbered 439,336 (Rizvi 1980/II: 242). Others were similarly active. They put Islamic legal norms on a hitherto unknown public footing.

But the hybrid legal situation existing in British India remained unsatisfactory for Muslim activists. Judges selectively applied the community law governing individual cases and/or customary law as collected for this purpose in conjunction with British-Indian legal acts.[38] Muslim

[38]For clarification it should be added here that in legal terms India was—and is—not understood to be a country where Islamic law applied *per se* but only as much as was

activists wanted to remove 'disabilities' of the Muslim community, mainly those experienced by the Muslim élite in matters of inheritance and marriage law. The first campaign was devoted to the revision of legal provisions on Muslim family endowments, the auqāf.[39] According to the Muslim law of inheritance, Muslim landed estates were divided up among the inheritors. This was fraught with the danger of undermining the economic viability of the estate. The family would not be protected and have sufficient income. Muslims had traditionally sought to remedy the situation by concluding legal trust deeds, turning the estate into an endowment (waqf), clearly stipulating who would benefit from it and who not, and who would administer it.[40] The technically neutral legal British system had allowed legal challenges as were undertaken by bickering family members against such trust deeds. As a result, the courts often overturned the deeds, leading to a division of property and eventual decline of family fortunes. This development was seen to further undercut the status of Muslim landed families, who were considered a social pillar of Muslim culture in India by many Muslim activists. Their decline supposedly directly contributed to the decline of Muslim culture and influence under the British. It also removed sources of patronage for religious institutions and cultural activity. Muslim activists had long considered it necessary to introduce legislation to remedy this situation. Sayyid Ahmad Khan made a prominent move in this direction. In 1877, he proposed a first draft for 'A Law of Family *Waqf* for Muslims'. In his proposal he suggested that Muslim landed families be more careful in drafting these deeds and be fully aware of the legal consequences. He objected to intervention in the administration of established funds that supported traditional religious education, even if such intervention were to benefit 'modern' education such as the Aligarh College founded by him. He believed that the auqāf were founded to teach the Qur'an, theology, and Persian. 'The people who created them had a right to see their bequests carried out to the letter' even after their donors died. In 1908, Shibli Numani got himself involved in a campaign to launch a new legislation on this subject. For this purpose, he mobilized the 'ulamā' and invoked references to the sharī'a. He elicited a fatwā from them to clarify whether

stipulated by statute law. This was done through specific laws directing judges to apply select Muslim law to cases where both parties in a proceeding were Muslims.

[39]This passage broadly follows Kozlowski (1985: Chapter 6).

[40]According to the 1913 Waqf Act, such endowment was created by the 'permanent dedication by a person professing the Mussalman faith of any property for any purpose recognised by the Mussalman law as religious, pious or charitable' (Section 2). Such would be a public endowment. There was also the possibility of a private endowment for the settler's own family and his descendants (Manek 1961: 105, 114).

a trust deed could be sustained on the basis of Islamic law. The 'ulamā', although divided on finer points of interpretation, unanimously concluded that there was nothing in Hanafi law to contradict the institution of waqf and, therefore, the validity of such trust deeds. They denied the right of Hindu and British judges not trained in the sharī'a to pass judgement on such issues, a right that properly belonged to the 'ulamā' only. The issue was taken up by Muhammad Ali Jinnah in 1910. He was then still an aspiring lawyer and a newly elected Muslim member of the Bombay Council, the local parliament. A year later, he introduced the 'Mussalman Waqf Validating Bill'. Again Shibli mobilized the 'ulamā' and Muslim public opinion in support of the act. A deputation he organized in November 1911 included three religious scholars, Abdul Bari from the Firangī Maḥall, Muhammad Husain from the Deoband Seminary, and Maulwi Rafiuddin. In the end, Jinnah succeeded in overcoming opposition to the act. It passed into law unanimously on 17 February 1913. The Waqf Act was further amended in 1930 to give it retrospective effect so as to secure private endowments concluded earlier and now challenged by dissenting family factions (Verma 1986: 946).

While these Waqf Acts extended recognition also to endowments created for personal and familial benefits, the 1923 'Mussalman Waqf Act' dealt only with those created for religious, pious, or charitable purposes and not for the benefit of the creating person or his descendants.[41] It was the 1923 act that occupied the Muslim Educational Conference (Khan 2001: 214f.). In 1929 Abul Kasim sought to revise it through an initiative in the United Provinces Legislative Council. At issue was the level of control over the propriety of financial transactions by administrators (mutawallī). Islamic reformists had earlier sought to increase control so that funds were not misused for personal benefits but would be put at the disposal of the community.[42] However, where the government was seen to gain too much control over the religious endowments this was regarded as un-Islamic. Therefore several 'ulamā' opposed the revision of the 1923 act as contrary to shari'a law.

Two further legislative initiatives were taken with regard to Muslim Personal Law and the dissolution of marriages. Both can be broadly regarded as reformist projects. The initiation of the 'Muslim Personal Law (Shariat) Application Act, 1937' was mainly prompted by disadvantages faced by Muslim women in matters of inheritance. Under customary law of various territories, tribes, and castes, courts had often granted women less rights

[41]For a review of waqf legislation in South Asia before 1947 and after, cf. Rashid (2002, esp. 63ff.).

[42]Cf. Resolution No. 23 by the JUH 'ulamā' in 1927 (Rozinah 1981/I: 460).

as inheritors than was required under sharīʿa law. The new act supported arguments by judges that customary law had to be abandoned where it modified Qur'anic injunctions. Muslims could not be expected to follow orders at variance with their religion. For Muslims this would constitute an act of infidelity 'such as would render the individual concerned liable to civil punishment by the *qāḍī* in this world and to eternal punishment in the next'.[43] The act laid a broad basis for the application of Muslim personal law, for which it identified 10 areas: (i) intestate succession; (ii) special property of females; (iii) marriage; (iv) dissolution of marriage; (v) maintenance; (vi) dower; (vii) guardianship; (viii) gifts; (ix) trusts and trust properties; (x) waqfs, other than public charities and religious endowments (Manek 1961: 12). Records of debates of the Central Indian Legislature indicated that tempers were flaring high over the very need to have this piece of legislation enacted. Sayyid Ghulam Bhik Nairang who had made a name for himself through his missionary activities (tablīgh) in Mewat and the United Provinces, strongly 'objected to anyone considering it unfortunate that the Muslims wanted to be governed by their own sacred laws' (*IAR* 1937/II: 99). And Maulwi Zafar Ali Khan argued 'that without the Bill there was the danger of Muslims losing their solidarity and national unity. He appealed to the Congress Party to vote for the Bill and thus show that they were prepared to allow Muslims to follow the *sharīʿa*, otherwise they had not the right to talk of mass contact' (ibid.). That the bill eventually passed without much opposition, also from Hindu members of the assembly, indicated that Congress indeed attempted to strike a deal with the religious section of Muslims, with religious scholars. In exchange for their support for a united India they would receive support for the application of the sharīʿa if only on a select basis. The character of the law as an act of religious Islamic reform was not only diluted by its codification into statute law, but also by exempting from its application several territories marked by conservative social relations such as the tribal areas on the northwest frontier.[44] Although the tribes prided themselves on being Muslim, tribal custom nevertheless had the upper hand over Islamic literalism there.

The reform of the prevailing practice of dissolution of marriages constituted an even thornier issue for Islamic religious activists. By the mid-1930s the practice was spreading that Muslim women who wanted to get a divorce resorted to the public renunciation of the Islamic faith.

[43]This was poignantly formulated in a case judgement in 1953 (Manek 1961: 15).

[44]Ibid.; see also the text of the law in Verma (1986: 966ff.), excluding the North West Frontier Province, a reference later changed to all category B states under the constitution of independent India.

Since this constituted an act of apostasy, such marriages automatically stood dissolved. Islamic reformers such as Maulana Thanawi were anxious to find ways to provide Muslim women with recourse to dissolution of marriage that would not force them out of the faith. Thanawi, therefore, actively supported the preparation of the 'Dissolution of Muslim Marriages Act, 1939'.[45] It enabled women to file for divorce while it removed apostasy from the grounds for it.[46] Exempted from this was a situation where a woman re-embraced her former faith if she had converted to Islam previously. During the debate in the Indian legislature, Muslim members sought to press for special powers of a Muslim judge, a qāḍī. This was apparently connected with hopes by Muslim clerics to regain some control over the legal system. This would have given an enormous fillip to the employment of graduates of Islamic schools (madrasa), improving the standing of religious scholars in society. But the select committee that reviewed the bill rejected the revival of the qāḍī system and the respective clauses were removed. During the debate, Sayyid Ghulam Bhik Nairang and Sayyid Murtaza, Muslim members of the Legislative Assembly, also opposed curbs on the performance of marriages for minor girls by their father or guardian. They argued that a father would normally not act in a manner detrimental to the interests of the girl. When their amendment was pressed for free voting in the assembly it was defeated, indicating that Muslim members must have considered such curbs necessary (*IAR* 1939/I: 105). Apparently such circumspection on behalf of fathers and guardians was not taken for granted. It showed that Islamic reformism needed to be reconciled with social conservatism prevailing among Muslim leaders. Still the bill left many unsatisfied. The British Law Member criticized that far from being a measure of advance the bill really went back to ancient practice (*IAR* 1939/I: 112). The JUH 'ulamā' protested that the act gave powers to a non-Muslim judge to cancel the *nikkāḥ* (marriage) of Muslims as the law failed to instate qāḍī courts (Rozinah 1981/II: 753). They alleged the law thus became detrimental to religion and dangerous for Muslims. It would make the dissolution of marriages ineffective. Women remarrying under the law were liable to commit ḥarām (Rozinah 1981/II: 753).

Muslim public opinion responded with a campaign of its own to a piece of legislation not explicitly directed at Muslims, the 1929 Child

[45]For a detailed description of this debate, cf. Khalid Masud, 'Apostasy and Judicial Separation in British India', in Masud (1996: 193–203).

[46]Section 4 explicitly stated that 'the renunciation of Islam by a married Muslim woman or her conversion to a faith other than Islam shall not by itself operate to dissolve her marriage' (Manek 1961: 212).

Marriage Restraint Act. It was moved by Harbilas Sarda, and, therefore, called the Sarda Act (*IAR* 1929/II: 127ff.). This act was introduced from a position of Hindu social reformism and sought to restrict the social evil of child marriage. For the purposes of this act a girl was considered to be a child if under 14 years of age, a boy if under 18 years of age. Muslim leaders were enraged that the application of this act was not limited to Hindus but was made universal. It was interpreted as interference by British rule in the conduct of the religious life of Muslims.[47] They alleged that this custom was alien to Muslim groups and tribes. In the Indian legislature, Abdul Haye declared that Muslims were opposed to the principle of the measure (*IAR* 1929/II: 130). Maulwi Muhammad Shafi declared in the same debate that 'while he believed in social reform he considered the evil of early marriage [...] not as great as other evils. The greatest evil was illiteracy and the speaker desired to know what had been done to eradicate it' (ibid.). The Muslim poet and politician Iqbal angrily intervened and joined the broad-based Muslim opposition to the act. Nehru publicly replied to Iqbal in a pointed fashion quoting figures from the latest census that in some areas Muslim child marriages had actually surpassed the number of Hindu child marriages.[48] Therefore, there was no reason for this agitation. It served no other purpose but to bring Muslim public opinion behind Islamic groups and Muslim parties. Indeed, all major Islamic groups, the JUH, in particular, made references to this law and decried its grave 'injustice'.[49]

[47] A separate campaign on this issue on these lines was conducted in the Frontier Province by the otherwise left-leaning radical Muslim reforms movement of the 'Red Shirts', also known as the 'Servants of God' (khudā-i khidmatgarān), led by Abdul Ghaffar Khan. Cf. his speeches during the campaign for Civil Disobedience in 1930, in Ramu (1992). Resistance to the law was interpreted as resistance to British rule and, therefore, worthy of civil disobedience. The British regarded these activities as part of Congress strategy to mobilize public opinion. A secret government memorandum stated in 1931: 'An alarming aspect of the recent Congress activities at Peshawar was the attempt to stir up trouble among the tribes. Congress agents spread among them false versions of the contents of the Child Marriage Act, and found the cry of Government's hostility to the Moslem faith an easy means of rousing discontent among the practical half-civilised population living near Peshawar. These activities are said even to have extended across the border' (BLOC L/PS/12/3125 Coll 23/4, file page 87).

[48] Nehru pointed to the report of the Age of Consent Committee of 1928 and the 1931 Census results demonstrating that in some provinces such as Bihar and Orissa, Muslim population groups had actually surpassed the Hindus in the number of child wives under the age of 10 per 10,000 of the population. In 1931, these figures stood at 583 among Muslims and 432 among Hindus. Cf. Census 1931, Bihar & Orissa, part I: 165. For Iqbal's and Nehru's arguments, cf. Iqbal (1995).

[49] For the opposition of the JUH to the Sarda Act, see, for instance, their Resolution No. 2 of the 1930 session, attacking British interference in the administration of Islamic law (Rozinah 1981/II: 579). The presidential address delivered by Shah Muinuddin Ahmad

Controversies such as over the Sarda Act fuelled more general doubts. The Barelwis took a very critical line in 1946 when Maulana Gilani Kachh'chhawi delivered the presidential address and roundly attacked the laws on waqf, marriage dissolution, and the Sarda Act. He criticized Muslim deputies in the councils for engaging in law-making on British conditions instead of defending Islamic law. Islam was presented as if it was incomplete and had no law by itself. The government, he felt, should give Muslims their department of Islamic justice (*dār al-qaẓā'*) and charitable Muslim endowments should be used for the purposes designated to promote religious and not atheist education. In sum, all Islamic institutions, he felt, needed to be reinvigorated to meet their original tasks, the madrasas to teach religious sciences (dīn), the Sufi hospices (*khānqāh*) to disseminate religious knowledge ('ilm), and the mīlād congregations to propagate the faith (tablīgh) (Qadiri 1997: 273–4). The JUH 'ulamā' were also dissatisfied with the state of law-making. In particular they noted with anxiety that the Government of India Act 1935 made no provisions for Muslim rights, for the protection of Islamic law, religion, or culture. Their desire to anchor these principles in the constitution of independent India spurred them into initiating legislation on cultural autonomy of Muslims providing for an Islamic authority and a commissioner for Islamic affairs as discussed earlier (Rozinah 1981/II: 637f.; see p. 193).

From the perspective of the public discourse of Islam the period under review witnessed decided intervention in the legal sphere. Major legislative projects were pursued to fuse Islamic legal provisions from the sharī'a with British-Indian statutory law. The projects reflected the desire to secure the social and cultural foundations of religion (waqf law) and to ensure that key elements of personal law for Muslims were guided by Qur'anic injunctions. This was seen as a measure to shore up solidarity of the Muslim community. Here religious scholars acted hand in hand with moderate or modernist Muslims such as Iqbal and members of the legislative assembly. The rule of the sharī'a, or rather perceived attacks by the government and its British backers, appeared to be an emotive issue capable of creating broad-based ideological and political support. From the point of view of an Islamic project three points appear to be relevant. First, in the field of Islamic law Islamic groups displayed a surprising readiness for change in their reform projects. Although much of the legal advice given by the religious scholars from the fatwā departments tended to be socially conservative, they contributed to the evolution and reform of Islamic law (cf. Masud et al. 1996; also Baljon 1996). This development

Ajmeri also dealt extensively with the subject stressing how the British have increasingly abrogated or altered Muslim law since their arrival. Marriage is portrayed as an essentially religious subject where no other institution should have authority (ibid.: 560ff.).

contradicted the often repeated assumption that Islamic law was immutable and simply had to be guarded or defended. They de-facto exercised ijtihād in a big way. Second, Islamic law served these groups as a convenient trigger for public mobilization. Third, it reflected some limited desire for social reforms and the solution of practical problems encountered by Muslims. This was visible in the codification of the Muslim marriage act.

At the same time, the intervention in the legal field by religious groups proved to be as ambiguous and potentially divisive as their activism on other issues. From an Islamist perspective the results remained contradictory, selective, and patchy. The reformist intentions by Deoband-related groups were not shared by the Barelwis defending the status quo. From a secular perspective, Islamic groups strengthened the application of religious norms. They advanced the segregation of Muslim personal law. This strongly heightened religious awareness in legal matters. They thus effectively counteracted the integration of Muslims in Indian society. This contributed to a significant polarization in matters of legal reform in independent India in cases where the rights of Muslim parties under Muslim personal law were less secure than under general statute law. This was famously made clear by the Shah Bano divorce case in 1986 (Engineer 1987; Gani 1988). A Muslim divorcee had been granted comprehensive maintenance on the basis of general statute law against which the husband protested.[50] Islamic religious groups took this case to the streets demanding to uphold the requirements of Islamic law and the resultant limitations. The Congress government led by Rajiv Gandhi (1944–89) gave in to these demands to secure continued electoral support from its 'Muslim constituency'. It decided to enact a special law, the Muslim Women [Protection of Rights on Divorce] Act, 1986, to protect Muslim personal law where in conflict with legal statute.

5.4. ISLAMIC SOCIAL RELIEF OR WELFARE SOCIETY

Development concerns were forced on the 'ulamā' by the realities of the day. They were confronted with mass poverty, social inequalities, and widespread discrimination. If the government was not capable of devising

[50]The 'finer' legal point of the situation relates to the fact that maintenance for a divorcee is awarded under Section 125 (2) of the Criminal Procedure Code, which is uniform for all communities in India. In contrast, in civil law there exists separate Muslim Personal Law (MPL) as enacted by the 1937 Sharī'a Law Act. Engineer maintained that the 1986 bill drafted by the MPL board consisting of Islamic clerics and government servants demonstrated a woeful lack of knowledge of Islamic law as the bill created a situation for Muslim women in India that was socially and financially less protected than that stipulated by Qur'anic injunctions and Islamic jurisprudence (1987).

means for successful poverty relief or if its efforts in this field were to be criticized effectively, Muslim clerics needed to suggest alternative ways of solving social problems. These requirements only slowly dawned on them. That they did matter became evident from their proposals for an Islamic society as discussed for the JUH in Chapter 4, section 4.1.3. The creation of a community fund (Bayt al-Māl) was a standard demand. Various groups interpreted its role differently. For the JUH it was the budget to run the envisaged Islamic Authority in India. The Khāksār primarily financed their campaign activities from their Bayt al-Māl. But the JUH 'ulamā' also pursued a broader reformist agenda reflecting the purist Deoband approach. Preventing 'moral degradation' (*ikhlāqī pastī*) of Indian Muslims was a major issue for them. They saw it primarily related to slackness in observing the dictates of religion. They raised their voice against exorbitant expenses on wedding and funeral ceremonies (Resolutions No. 3/1926 in Rozinah 1981/I: 375; Resolution No. 8/1927 in ibid.: 454); the custom of asking for and giving bride money (Resolution No. 10/1927 in ibid.: 455); borrowing loans on interest (Resolution No. 8/1927 in ibid.: 454); sectarian enmities (Resolution No. 19/1927 in ibid.: 458); and a Western lifestyle undermining the Islamic way of life (Resolution No. 22/1927 in ibid.: 459). Social problems for them were also related to the status of Indian Muslims in society. They opposed discrimination between highborn (ashraf) and low groups (*razīl*) in relation to trade and industry in the tradition of the Hindus (Resolution No. 5/1940 in Rozinah 1981/II: 698); and they attacked government for classifying some Muslim groups as *kamīn* (menial, low-caste) (Resolution No. 9/1942 in ibid.: 754).

The Barelwis also discussed a detailed social policy, which was even more concerned with the allegedly unequal social status of Indian Muslims. Hamid Raza spelled it out in his welcome address to the 1925 Sunni conference. He related the miseries of Muslim society to the dependency on Hindu moneylenders while losing their hold on traditional sources of economic support such as landed property and public service. He suggested ways by which Indian Muslims could promote their economic welfare: instead of working in poorly paid government service or as servants to Hindu employers, they should start their own trading businesses, no matter how small. He proposed a scheme to stimulate savings among Muslims. They should create a provident fund (*zakhīrā-e qarz-e ḥusn*) or an Islamic treasury (bayt al-māl) (Qadiri 1997: 186–7). For this he advised Muslims to put aside some of their earnings to buy land at the earliest opportunity. Even if a man had inherited land, he should earn enough to buy himself some more. He advised everyone to save money for their children from the time of their birth. A paisa a day would add up to a lot in 15 years. One should also cut down on expenses, avoiding lavish wedding feasts. Better still, a man should not marry his child into a family that wanted to have a feast that would involve borrowing money. Every village should have a provident loan society (*anjuman-e qarẓ-e ḥusn*) formed from among the villagers, deciding whether or not a person was eligible for a loan and how to deal with repayment problems. He thought these loans should be interest free (Qadiri 1997: 188). These demands were remarkable for several aspects. They underlined the reformist pretensions of the Barelwis by arguing against excessive marriage expenses. His ideas on village loan societies were very similar to the modern-day micro-credit system. And self-reliance, which was used as a political weapon against the British in the boycott of foreign goods, was to be directed against Hindu merchants. It is interesting that the Khāksār also picked up this idea and advised Khāksār members to preferably buy their goods from a fellow Khāksār. Here self-reliance had an even narrower focus, the same group, not just the community. Also the Tablīghīs were reported to prefer commercial dealings with fellow members of the movement.[51] These demands and practices echoed the boycott of British goods, organized by Congress and other anti-colonial protesters at various times. They were not much reflective of social attitudes and composition of Islamic groups.

The social dimensions of the Islamic project in South Asia have so far not been much explored in research. In their combination of education, law, and development they added to the constructive potential of an Islamic project. The concept found its most visible application in modern Pakistan. Islamic education, legal facilities, and welfare administration (zakāt) were partly regulated and significantly expanded. Under the regime of Zia-ul-Haq they became tools for interference in the Islamic sector in exchange for an Islamization of the state sector. However, these attempts to foster a kind of 'state' Islam could not significantly modernize the Islamic sector. The main noticeable effect has been a further indoctrination and ideologization of segments of society while the standard of state services has gone down. This has been furthered by the continued disunity among the different Islamic sects and traditions. But a revision and correction of these developments is now politically sensitive and difficult to achieve.

[51]This trend may be more of recent origin as there is no detailed information available on this count for the pre-independence period. Tablīghī leaders are reported to have discouraged it fearing the isolation of their movement. Based on field research—DR: cf. chapter 3, fn. 139.

6 Conclusion

The Islamic groups taken into consideration for this study represented a great variety of mobilization forms among Muslims in colonial India. They were united by their desire to take advantage of a gradual opening of society and politics under the conditions of capitalism and nascent forms of popular representation. In all their diversity, their responses were marked by similar lines of argumentation and activity. They attempted to capture the public sphere by re-interpreting central categories of Islam to justify, motivate, and legitimize their intervention. They were driven as much by the desire to revive religious faith as by the intention to carve out for themselves and their groups a place in a rapidly changing political and social environment, to find their place in the new society.

It is important to highlight the dualism and ambiguity these groups displayed. This applied as much to their formulation of an Islamic project of society and politics as to their contestation of the public sphere. In some ways these groups were engaged in a common project, but in others they were in competition. The two categories of the 'Islamic project' and the 'Islamic sphere' afford different perspectives on their evolution, views, and activities. This conclusion is organized around the questions arising from these two perspectives:

a) To what extent did the Islamic groups follow a common Islamic project? What were its contours and how did it evolve?
b) To what extent were they part of the modern public sphere as defined in the introduction?

The first set of questions explores the common features of the groups, while the second looks at their heterogeneity.

6.1. ISLAMIC PROJECT

The Islamic groups studied here developed a variety of responses to the changes in their political, social, and economic environment based on a re-interpretation of Islamic injunctions. These responses together formed the Islamic project, which comprised a re-interpretation of the social, political, and economic reality of colonial Britain in Islamic terms. It represented a social and political utopia based on Islamic principles. These were Islamic not only in a general historical or civilizational sense, they were religious, tuned to the spiritual and salvational side of Islam. It is important to stress the responsive or reactive nature of the Islamic project of these groups. They responded to a dislocation of Muslim élites closely connected to the dying Moghul administration in British India, to a growing marginalization of the religious, cultural, and intellectual élites of Islam patronized by the Muslim landed aristocracy and in the courts of the princely states. This social, cultural, and economic dislocation developed into a militant political confrontation during the 'Wahhabi' insurrections in the early nineteenth century, and even more so during the 1857–8 rebellion when some Muslim clerics played a key role in fomenting and legitimating unrest. Islamic groups were also responding to the deep-seated transformation of society brought about by the spread of colonial capitalism. The concomitant increase in the influence of Western ideas and concepts of society was perceived by religious activists as materialist and atheistic. As such it was inimical to religion in general and Islam in particular. The resulting sense of siege among Islamic groups was heightened by religious competition, first of all from Christianity with its associations with the British and also from the native Hindu majority. Both were seen as dominating public activity at the expense of Islam.

The Islamic project was responsive, but it also gradually evolved. As social conditions changed in colonial India, so did the Islamic response. The sequence of chapters in this study broadly reflects the sequence of events. In terms of religious, political, and social reflection, three phases can be distinguished, although these overlapped and varied from group to group. In the first phase, that is, from the middle of the nineteenth century, concerns of religious knowledge, identity, and practice dominated the discourses and activism of established and newly emergent Islamic groups. The public sphere was contested over religious doctrine. This proved tremendously divisive as common debates and discourses emerged. At this stage the Islamic project expressed the readjustment of an Islamic religious élite to (i) its fall from power and (ii) the emergence of colonial capitalist society, whose mechanics and values were regarded as imported, imposed, and alien to traditional understanding of society.

In the second phase, from around 1905 to the 1920s, groups took to public and political activism in search of a political role for Islam both in India and in relation to other parts of the Islamic world. In this they reacted to colonial politics by Britain and other Western states towards the Islamic nations. The fate of the Ottoman Empire in the Balkan wars of 1911–13 and during World War I, the fortunes of Islamic Afghanistan during this period and thereafter, radicalized Indian Muslims and Islamic groups. They interpreted the ignominious defeat of Islamic nations at the hands of Western powers as a sign of their own disadvantaged and marginalized position in India. Islamic groups related these events to their resistance against British rule and against perceived domination by representatives of the majority Hindu community. The apparently irreconcilable twin objectives of fighting for political and religious identity brought Islamic groups into frequent and shifting conflict with each other, with adversaries and potential allies. During this period the Islamic project was marked by (i) competitive self-organization and (ii) increasing militant activity. The former developed a rich public and political associational life devoted to religio-political objectives. The latter was understood partly as self-defence against inter-religious violence, partly as military (jihādī) activity against British and Christian rule over India.

A third phase set in during the 1920s, marked by increasing attention of Islamic groups to the parameters of an Islamic polity and an Islamic society. These ideas were generated by activism around the new political and social order in prospect after independence. Debate over the new India was accelerated by the anti-colonial nationalist movement led by the Congress and the Muslim League. Islamic groups contributed various concepts aimed at securing their identity and independent operation, elevating Muslim interests in the multicultural context of India and strengthening religion in a secularizing environment. At this stage, ideas of an Islamic polity and society took concrete shape, as in the discourse conducted by the association of religious scholars, the JUH. Islamic groups pursued, despite their diversity, an Islamic project that was still reasonably cohesive. Although most clearly formulated by the JUH, most groups supported one or the other, if not all demands:

a) Installing an Islamic leader for India (Amīr al-Hind fī al-Sharī'a) and selecting provincial leaders (Amīr al-Sharī'at) who would look after the implementation of Islamic law (sharī'a).
b) Establishing a parallel Islamic administration to administer Islamic justice through Muslim judges (qāḍīs); to collect and distribute Islamic welfare taxes (zakāt); to create a community fund (bayt al-māl) alleviating the economic plight of Muslims; to look after charitable Muslim endowments (auqāf); to give religious and legal guidance through decrees (fatwā); to help solve doctrinal conflicts among Islamic groups fighting sectarianism and divisions (fitna).

c) Strengthening, harmonizing, and updating religious education, mostly through madrasas, as a counterweight to secular education and as an expression of true national education.
d) Creating a system of religious propaganda and missionary work (tablīgh) complete with separate education of special preachers, to make Muslims more religious, fighting secularism and materialism, and to withstand pressure from Hindu and Christian missionaries.

Annual conferences, regular publications, and printing presses were considered essential for political articulation. Islamic solidarity, an overriding concern of all the groups, brought into existence a multitude of organizations and funds to support the Ottoman Empire and Afghanistan. There was also a noticeable trend to reflect political, defence, and security needs in the organization of these Islamic groups. For this purpose separate posts and departments were created. The most elaborate example was provided by the leadership structure of the Khāksār movement.

Another common feature was volunteer groups and militant guards. These operated in the name of religion but actually protected party and group interests. There was a tendency for all Islamic groups to have their own guards who would then compete with each other. This reflected the need to overcome the perceived weakness of these groups, of Muslims in India in general, to stand up to the 'enemies of Islam'.

In all proposals for Islamic government and society we note some common structural aspects relating to the situation of Islam in India:

a) The minority status of Indian Islam influenced the concepts of all Islamic groups, playing itself out in a pervasive sense of inferiority and fear. Growing inter-religious tension produced a language of hatred and emotional incitement. This was counteracted in part by a still influential culture of a shared civilization where the religious values of the other side were studied and counter-arguments carefully formulated. The experience of most Muslims across the vast diversity of rural and urban India was still one of (partly syncretic) coexistence. Yet, the breakdown of cross-communal links was becoming more visible: separatism bred alienation and a growing readiness to resort to violence.

b) Political cleavages tended to be argued in doctrinal terms. Attitudes were polarized between opposites. One camp held political positions that tended to be anti-colonial, anti-state, or even confrontational (jihādī). In contrast, the other one was more contemplative in outlook, favouring a loyalist, pro-status quo, or integrative stance. The first camp included groups mostly in favour of a more reformist and literalist interpretation of Islam: the Deobandi, the Ahl-i Ḥadīth, the Aḥrār, the Khāksār (and, by extension, the Jamā'at-i Islāmī). The second contained groups that were rooted in mystical practices and concepts or drew on them to a significant degree such as the Barelwis and the Firangī Maḥallis; as also the Tablīghīs and the Aḥmadīya. Politically, the Nadwa were inclined to the first camp while the Aligarh School tended to identify with the second.

The contours of an Islamic project were created by a variety of interventions in the public sphere on behalf of the Islamic groups. These are grouped according to their major directions.

a) In terms of religious intervention, the reformist discourse (iṣlāḥ) formed the basis of the re-interpretation of Islamic categories to accommodate changes in politics and in society. This was not only true of movements inclined to 'literalism' but also applied to movements representing 'devotional' Islam such as the Barelwi. As all of them stood on the ground of the Hanafi school of law their doctrinal differences may have appeared marginal (one exception is the Ahl-i Ḥadīth, which rejected all law schools). Yet as pointed out earlier, these theological disparities combined with differing attitudes towards colonial rule and opposing ways of conduct in the public sphere. Of course, the pattern was more complex, but this generalization serves as a rough guide to the intricate meandering of religious, political, and social loyalties. The Islamic groups formulated their religious intervention in the way best suited for legitimating their group aims and the parameters of their separate existence. For this, they exercised their religious intervention in the public sphere by:

(i) Re-interpreting the Qur'an and the traditions (ḥadīth). While each group highlighted their prime importance, it selected a different element in the heritage to promote. The Deobandis combined primal sources with established tradition and the views of their leaders, in a conservative way. The Barelwis drew on miracles and wonders as related in the scriptures. The Ahl-i Ḥadīth stressed the Prophetic traditions. The adherents to the Aligarh tradition strove for a rational view of God and his work. The Aḥmadīya believed in continued revelation. The Tablīghīs stressed the propagation of the faith.

(ii) Emphasizing the role of the Prophet and the associated discourse of love and veneration. This held special importance for popular (Sufi) Islam and the Barelwis. More 'purist' groups still shared this veneration, which was deeply embedded in the long cultural tradition of South Asia, where syncretic and mystical elements have always played an important part.

(iii) Conducting a special 'leader discourse', focusing on the role of the saviour (Messiah) and the renewer (mujaddid). This provided the leaders of these groups with special legitimation as they aspired not only to the position of a religious leader but of a 'renewer of the faith' with almost divine attributes. This made it much easier to control these groups and assert leadership.

(iv) Propagating Islam through tablīgh and da'wa. All movements and discourses pursued this objective and—a remarkable innovation—it brought into being an institutionalized missionary society, the Tablīghī Jamā'at. This activity served to shore up the correct faith and proper religious practice among Muslims and particularly converts. As such it kept group members united. It also allowed groups to expand their influence at the expense of other Islamic groups and non-Muslims.

(v) Conducting the (potentially militant) self-organization of tanẓīm. This gave Muslims self-esteem, although it often proved illusory in the face of mounting social and political pressure. It contributed to drawing battle lines against dissenters and 'unbelievers' more clearly.

b) Political intervention revolved around the discourses of:

(i) Participation. This operated in two ways: claims to public representation penetrated the internal structure of the Islamic groups; simultaneously they themselves sought a share in public representation by gradually joining the electoral process.

(ii) Defence and self-defence. Islamic groups mobilized Muslims where their interests were perceived to be neglected or where they became the target of religious violence.

(iii) Activism and militancy. This legitimated mass activism in defence of Islamic institutions and the (Ottoman) Caliphate. Violent military activity (jihād) was also conducted in the tribal areas of India against British rule in India and beyond.

(iv) Sectarian radicalism. Dissenters and 'unbelievers' were targeted, partly for opportunistic political gains as symbolized by the activism of the Aḥrār against the Aḥmadīya, the Shi'a, and representatives of folk Islam (Sufis).

c) Social intervention concentrated on the areas of:

(i) Education, supporting religious over secular instruction as the true national education and introducing religious mass education with far-reaching consequences.

(ii) Law, strengthening Muslim legal segregation by selectively codifying Islamic law within the British legal system and providing Muslims with regular and standardized religious guidance through decrees (fatāwā) made available in the public domain through printing.

(iii) Welfare. This included promoting regular and institutionalized welfare activity by religious trusts; encouraging economic self-reliance and the boycott of 'enemy' businesses belonging to the British or Hindus. The creation of a community fund or an Islamic exchequer (bayt al-māl) appealed to all groups, although with little practical consequence.

The interventions of Islamic groups were directed at different recipients: at the colonial state, the national movement dominated by the Congress, and the public representatives of the Hindu majority community. These interventions thus formed a dialogue between the various discourses associated with these recipients. The Islamic discourse addressed itself to Western ideas of reform, to nationalism, socialism and the cultural nationalism of other communities (Hindus, Sikhs, etc.). As a result, many Islamic arguments mirrored those of the colonial state, the major parties, and other religious groups. Arguments about doctrinal purity were equally used to express national identity by Hindu reformists from the Āryā Samāj; and by Sikh, non-Brahmin, and (later) Tamil movements.[1] Discourses on the sanctity of leaders were also fashionable among Congress followers highlighting the divine attributes of Gandhi; within the Sikh movement in relation to Master Tara Singh (1885–1967), leader of the Akali Dal; or within the Āryā Samāj with regard to Swami Shraddhananda. Militant party guards and the volunteers' movement proliferated across the political landscape. Religious reform movements of the Hindus, Sikhs, or Christians shared with Muslims the concerns for a social rehabilitation of their communities: all saw themselves as disadvantaged by colonial policy, which motivated them to start special religious schools, welfare schemes, and so on.

Although details of the content and form of the Islamic project were intensely debated and contested between Islamic groups, their differences could not prevent a common discourse on Islamic government or society. Mushirul Hasan argued that 'the pan-Islamic ferment in the early 1920s had already heightened religious consciousness, reinforced the community's perception of being unified and cohesive, and made it susceptible to appeals made in the name of religion' (Hasan 1998a: 198). Islamic groups agreed on most of the essential points, such as the position of an amīr, the need for a separate Islamic administration, for religious education and guidance, for self-defence and offensive activity (jihād). Their differences were geared to the public sphere, rather than stemming from fundamental religious beliefs.

[1]For related discourses of reformist movements in relation to Hindu revivalism, to the Tamils, to the Christians, Muslims or the Sikhs, see Jones (1991).

Discussion on the Islamic project continued in independent Pakistan and India. In Pakistan it gained particular prominence in relation to the discourse on the Islamization of society. This debate was first conducted around the creation of an Islamic constitution. The Objectives Resolution adopted in 1949 served as the main instrument in that process. This debate intensified under Pakistan's Islamist military dictator Zia-ul-Haq. His legislative initiatives sought to integrate selected principles of the sharīʿa into the political, legal, educational, and welfare system of the country. In that he broadly followed the Islamic project as formulated before independence, even though he heavily leaned on the West and the US in particular. He actively considered making himself an Islamic leader of Pakistan, of the authority of an āmīr. He reconstituted the parliament as an advisory council (majlis-e shūrā). Religious education was broadened and subsidized. Observance of religious rituals was made obligatory in public offices and in the media (cf. Reetz 1987: 181–9; Malik 1989). While this process strengthened Islamic structures and institutions, it found only limited acceptance with the public at large. Yet it Islamized the public discourse to an extent where the expression of any public opinion became tied to the Islamic idiom. Formerly secular or nationalist parties, such as the Pakistan People's Party, had to adopt Islamic rhetoric extensively. The dominant political feature of this Islamization process was autocracy. This significantly undermined the foundations of the process and discourse of democracy. Civil governments elected afterwards had to submit to the guiding hand of the military and bureaucratic leadership, which still heavily relied on Islamist values. This particularly applied to its relations with its neighbours and in regional conflicts (Kashmir, Afghanistan).

Islamic groups in Pakistan revived the debate over the Islamic project in connection with the emergence of the Deoband-inspired Ṭālibān forces in Afghanistan in 1994. When they established the government of the Islamic Emirate in 1997 they did so in close consultation with Deobandi groups in Pakistan who advised them on their religious politics. Since then the Ṭālibān debate on the Islamic project veered to a more extreme interpretation of the Deobandi tradition, in contrast to most of its history, characterized by moderation and balance.[2] Research done by Bernt Glatzer held prolonged civil warfare responsible for the deformation of tribal Pakhtun ethics. It appeared that conditions of civil war in Afghanistan and among extremist groups in Pakistan as well as continued military rule advanced the growing distortion of Islamist principles adopted for the Islamic project. If the debate on an Islamic project in Pakistan is ever to

[2]Cf. Reetz 1999b; Bernt Glatzer, 'Zum Politischen Islam der Afghanischen Ṭālibān', in Reetz (2001a: 173–82).

return to moderation and tolerance, a restoration of lasting representative democracy seems to be indispensable. Only democracy has proved to be able to undermine the influence of more extremist interpretations of Islam and related militant activity. This was proven time and again by the poor performance of religious extremists in most of Pakistan's parliamentary elections.[3]

In India, the debate on an Islamic project reflected the continuing need to deal with the minority situation. The local Muslim élites were considerably weakened through partition and the resultant migration. Local and regional concerns dominated the issues taken up in a much-fragmented discourse. Islamic groups and secular Muslim politicians repeatedly debated whether to form a joint political party of Indian Muslims; how to further develop Muslim personal law; how to accelerate the educational, social, and economic uplift of Muslims, large parts of which were seen as belonging to an economic underclass; how to promote communal harmony and avoid tension, particularly in the light of ascendant Hindu nationalism; and how to combat a growing trend of militancy in regional and religious conflict across India.[4] From the groups studied here, all continue in today's India, albeit in their more contemplative, and sometimes very local incarnations. Many, however, have gained new support and significantly extended their networks, as the growth of the madrasa system is roughly comparable to that of Pakistan. While the JUH has been much reduced in size and influence, the Deobandi madrasa network and the Tablīghīs appear to be the most successful ones of those studied. None of them takes formal part in politics though. While most reformist groups had continued their informal support for the Congress, attention has recently shifted back to securing the religious rights of the community. Attendance of religious functions and participation in group activities by many lower and middle class Muslims seem to have grown considerably, a trend largely in line with similar developments among Hindus and in other communities. Revived inter-communal violence,

[3]This has not been disproved by the strong performance of the religious parties in Pakistan's parliamentary elections in 2001, as their share of votes has not significantly increased (Reetz 2003).

[4]Many current debates are well documented on the pages of the *Milli Gazette*, Delhi (here: online edition); see for example, 'Community News: 8-point memorandum on Deoband', 3 (18), 16–30 September 2002; 'Jamiatul-Ulama-e-Hind's agitation', 3 (23), 1–15 December 2002; 'Community News: Madrasa Registration Unacceptable', 3 (14), 16–31 July 2002; 'Mammoth Protest against Gujarat Carnage', 3 (10), 16–31 May 2002; 'Ulama Call for Boycot of US Goods', 2 (21), 1–15 November 2001; 'Jamaat-e-Islami Favours Inter-faith Dialogue', 3 (22), 16–30 November 2002; 'Community News: Jamiat-e-Ahle Hadith Calls for Gujarat relief', 3 (13), 1–15 July 2002; 'Community News: Tablighi Jamaat also Under Attack', 3 (14), 16–31 July 2002.

continued social marginalization, and strengthened Islamic networking seem to be the main motivating factors in relation to the Islamic groups.

6.2. ISLAMIC SPHERE

The activities of Islamic groups studied here helped create a sub-sector of the public sphere, a distinctly Islamic sphere in colonial India. This Islamic sector was constituted by institutionalized activity, formalized public discourses, and booming associational life. Yet how could religious arguments, intrinsically so personal and often intimate, be turned into a public tool of articulation, self-affirmation, and organization? The answer lay in the growing disparity between religious message and public calling. Their debates, activism, and institutional life became increasingly self-referential or directed at Islamic rivals. Many religious arguments became dissociated from key religious beliefs as they reflected the influence of public pressures. Groups such as the Ahl-i Ḥadīth, the Aligarh School, the Aḥmadīya, and the Khāksār, sharing a critical attitude towards the law schools and opposition to sectarian divisions, regarded each other as public enemies. The Barelwis who defended the diversity of Islamic ritual and custom proved least tolerant of other Islamic groups all of whom they attacked during the Nadwa debate. The Deobandis, who were seen as staunch defenders of a purist Islam, doctrinally restricted a possible re-interpretation of Islam by the narrowest confines and proved more traditional and orthodox than others in practical matters of Islamic behaviour. This proved that these groups acted not only as religious groups but also simultaneously as self-conscious public actors, as agents in the public sphere.

The reason was that in addition to their religious concepts they represented very specific non-religious interests. They embodied so-called insurgent publics of Muslims and of Muslim élites, who, in a disadvantaged minority position, felt they had no significant voice in the colonial polity's decision-making and would have even less in independent India. Religious activity was often a convenient cover for public and political activity that would otherwise have been quickly restricted by colonial authorities. British understanding of the consequences for public order, security, and stability made it difficult for them to suppress religious activism. They exercised special care not to inflame religious passion, but sought to defuse it through deliberate control of religious extremism.[5]

[5]This becomes clear from their policy of extensive proscription of religious pamphlets inciting hatred and discontent, a regulatory policy tool, which they used frequently. Cf. the list of proscribed literature held by the India Office Library (India Office Library and Records

While religious arguments looked to founding principles and traditions of Islam, they did so in vastly differing ways. It is, therefore, difficult to assert that they set out to preserve traditional religion or traditional Muslim society. On the contrary, all intended to change existing paths in society and religion. This interventionist activism brought them into conflict with British rule, but also with competing social and political agents within and outside Islam. It constituted their role as public actors, contributing to the formation of the public sphere and helping shape an Islamic sphere as a sub-sector of it.

Yet, if they were not traditional in the proper sense, were they modern? Often the products of modern, (partly) Westernized education themselves, the leaders of the Islamic groups borrowed modern methods of mobilization, organization, propaganda, and mass activism. However, interpretation of their activity as 'this worldly' in the Weberian sense has to be qualified. It is difficult to rationalize their world-view convincingly or clearly. Although they intervened in 'this world' (in order to gain salvation in 'the other') they often did so in total disregard of political, social, and cultural realities. They embraced modernity without actually having a fully operative constructive programme to shape modernity itself. Their activism should not be understood as the outflow of an Islamic project of modernity. At best it reflected modernity, and most of these groups would not have come into existence in this form but for modernity.

Not surprisingly, they often failed in their objectives. They could not replace secular education for all Muslims by religious education—although they succeeded in broadening and strengthening the infrastructure and practice of religious education. They could not stem the ascent of secular, materialist, and atheist values in politics and society—although they organized religious values in persuasive, defiant, combative, and militant forms hitherto unknown in Indian Islam. They could not protect the Ottoman Empire or Afghanistan—although they used these solidarity campaigns to strengthen their own political and public positions. They could not implement projects of an Islamic polity and society, nor even achieve agreement on their content among Muslims. But Muslim leaders and politicians learned to use these arguments to great effect in conventional politics, where the issue of Muslim minority rights became firmly established.

1976). That the British did not universally apply this principle but only where it suited them politically is evident from their attitude towards the Aḥmadīya sect. As the latter was expressly loyal to British rule, the British went to great length to defend its freedom of expression although they were aware of the disruptive potential of Aḥmadī beliefs for public order in Muslim areas where Sunni mainstream Islam dominated (Friedmann 1989; Lavan 1976).

Thus there was a disjuncture between intended goals and unintended consequences, between declared objectives and undeclared aspirations. As their achievements consisted mainly of undeclared objectives and unintended consequences it is hard to argue for a coherent Islamic project of modernity. At best this was a utopian vision. One area was particularly left out of consideration. The concepts relating to economic activity advanced by organized religious Islam were mainly traditional, such as the prohibition of interest in loans, or injunctions to engage in welfare activity (zakāt). No concept emerged of how an Islamic society or polity could economically sustain itself. The Deobandis and Barelwis demanded that Muslims take to trading, but mainly to become economically less dependent on Hindus. Hamid Raza from the Barelwi group came close to an economic vision when he demanded the creation of village loan societies, very similar to today's micro-credit systems. Yet his voice was a lonely one and never acted upon. No ʿālim dared consciously embrace capitalist entrepreneurship. Rather, subsidies from princely states and wealthy individuals were seen as the potential basis of the Islamic sector. The leaders of the Islamic groups, especially the religious scholars (ʿulamāʾ), could not free themselves from the mentality of a service class for which the application of religious dictates and the pursuit of religious knowledge were self-sufficient objectives. This occasionally combined with militant defiance, lashing out at those who questioned this self-reflexive and introspective piety. The attitude of defiance reflected another major social pillar of Islam in the subcontinent, the culture of the Muslim tribes in the northwest, in the Pakhtun areas, and Punjab, which had long defied the centralized state or structured political power. The ʿulamāʾ class, which was so central in the reform and revival movement of Islam, was unable to outgrow its social roots in the pre-capitalist era. This was occasionally attempted. The Aḥmadīya, the Aligarh faction, and some members of the Ahl-i Ḥadīth made moves in the direction of marrying religious values with social and economic modernity. However, these resulted in accusations of deviation, heresy, and apostasy: groups and individuals leaving the mental space of the early social foundations of the ʿulamāʾ class were instantly excommunicated.

It can be argued that the social immobility of the ʿulamāʾ class has been at the core of the emergence of strands of sectarian extremism and militancy. Defiance against seemingly superior adversaries was stiffened by the difficulty of reconciling the contradictions of this confrontation: Islamic groups based their activism on the inherent superiority of Islam, and fought adversaries who represented unbelief (kufr) and heresy. Yet they drew on the political and economic resources of a highly effective system based on capitalism and public representation. This ideological penetration of Islam combined with the social immobility of the 'ulamā' class locked Islamic discourse and activism into a closed circle of self-referential argument and action. Radical Islamic activism fed on the discontent of Muslims with social and political conditions. It could not offer them a constructive or realistic alternative in socio-economic terms. Islamic activism amounted to a permanent opposition unequal to the task of governing society, when it would have to deal with plurality and discontent from a position of responsibility. In this, Islamic groups reacted very much like other ideological groups on the political left and right. Islamic activists also benefited from the debilitating effects of colonial rule on their societies. The colonial state transferred capitalism in a selected and mutilated form, combined with oppression and violence so that the masses found it difficult to see the advantages of the new social and political system.

There was not only a disjuncture between intended goals and unintended consequences, or between the social basis and mentality of the religious scholars and the expectations and requirements of the political environment. There was also a clear disjuncture between public activism and the religious message itself. The modernity of the groups' operation in the public sphere was marked by key changes in the operation of communication, of their discourses. This adaptation created substantial problems for their religious vision. Participation in the public sphere was achieved only through compromises on the religious agenda.

a) In their *religious* intervention, groups accommodated concepts not present in their established religious discourse. They took to activities counter to their own established traditions. The Barelwis, for instance, were rooted in a Sufi Islam, which was often home-oriented, diffuse and heterogeneous. Yet they took, albeit belatedly, to the same forms of bureaucratic self-organization as more consciously reformist groups by establishing institutional madrasa, and public and political associations. The Deobandis became synonymous with political activism and radicalism, although they had set out as a pietist institution and movement exclusively devoted to education and learning. The Khāksār leader Mashriqi could never follow up his elaborate system of Islamic demands as his movement's major public activity was confined to defiant protest against arrest, prohibition, and official restrictions.

b) In their *political* intervention, this disjuncture was marked by religious verdicts (fatawa) on political issues. Inasmuch as these commented upon political events rather than elucidating points of religious doctrine, this was a remarkable innovation. The united fatwā of religious scholars issued during the Khilafat Movement was unprecedented. Another such disjuncture was noticeable when the Islamic groups, though haltingly, integrated principles of public and political life in the operation of religious institutions. The groups made concessions to democratic principles by granting greater rights to assemblies (shūrā) and accommodating protest movements and student unrest. They also made compromises on public representation, which they had originally opposed outright. While its principles were often rejected on religious grounds, quite a few scholars participated in elections as individuals. More surprising in this respect was the transformation of some Islamic groups into political parties (the JUH, the Khāksār, the Aḥrār, and later the Ahl-i Ḥadīth).

c) In their *social* intervention, this disjuncture appeared in the application of new methods to religion, such as institutionalized mass education. Groups also exploited Western legal principles and courts to achieve religious goals, for example, by taking religious rivals to court over doctrinal disputes, or by initiating legislation to create a separate Muslim personal law in India.

These contradictions show how participation in the public sphere was capable of fracturing religious discourse and the Islamic community. Islamic groups could only become more prominent through participation in the public sphere at the expense of their religious cohesion. They could achieve religious purity and the renewal that was the ultimate goal of their increased activism only by entering the doctrinally and ritually 'impure' public realm. This was also evident from the 'hybrid' cultural nature of their leaders. Not only had many of them received a 'mixed' education of modern and traditional religious schooling, some had also gained first-hand knowledge of British administration as they were connected with government service.

While these cleavages existed in a more or less veiled form before independence, they were accentuated afterwards. It was only after World War II that Western societies began to realize their democratic welfare potential. The same advantages did not materialize in the Islamic world. Through the Cold War, socialism and nationalism were held in the Islamic world, including Pakistan and India, to be potential remedies against social inequities. By the end of the Cold War, both were discredited, and disaffected Muslims turned again to religious concepts. Here, the circle almost seems to close: there is strong continuity with colonial discourses, forms of intervention, and self-organization. The social immobility of the 'ulamā' class is still visible and still feeds the discontent. The position on economic activity has been somewhat modified in the face of global capitalism. Limiting capitalist economic activity is still a cherished goal, as can be seen in the most recent campaign to force the Pakistan government to convert the whole banking system of the country to Islamic (that is interest-free) principles. However, parts of the 'ulamā' class have reconciled themselves to global economic activity as a source of income needed to resist the common 'enemy'. Internally, Islamic activism relies increasingly on support from merchants and the professional 'service' classes of lawyers, doctors, intellectuals, and most significantly on the growing student population. Islamic 'brains trusts' have intensified discussion of an Islamic economy. A more comprehensive and rational view[6] of the world in Islamic terms may be slowly emerging.

Yet, these trends have had little effect on the defiant posturing and self-serving religiosity of many of these Islamic groups in their current incarnations. This can be seen in Pakistan, and to some degree in India, among the Deobandis and the Tablīghī Jamā'at movement. It also applies more broadly to the vast array of religious Islamic parties, welfare organizations, and jihādī groups making up the Islamic sector in Pakistan. Two developments have sustained this psychological stalemate.

One is the strengthening of the Islamic sector in Pakistan in the 1970s and 1980s. The other is the lapse of the Cold War international system, with the associated resurgence of regional conflicts involving Muslims, notably Israel–Palestine and Kashmir. Under the Islamist military dictatorship of General Zia-ul-Haq, the Pakistani state intervened in the Islamic sector. For example, new regulations institutionalized the collection of the Islamic welfare tax (zakāt) through which Islamic religious schools (madrasas) were generously supported. Their number greatly increased in this period, not least because of the financial and political support of the West. The US, in particular, used them as a conduit for recruits and arms to help it in its war in Afghanistan against the Soviet Union. Today, the organized Islamic sector in Pakistan commands the allegiance of perhaps 10 to 20 per cent of the population. About 10,000 madrasas and their roughly 1,000,000 students constitute its backbone. The Islamic sector is nowadays fairly self-sufficient, a serious occupational alternative for the Pakistani youth. In India, the Islamic sector has also grown disproportionately, particularly by the dynamic expansion of madrasa education, although it has remained much weaker as an attractive social alternative.

A second factor has equally strong repercussions in Pakistan and in India's Muslim community. The Islamic élite felt forsaken by the West after the end of the Cold War and the Afghanistan conflict. The relationship with the West and the US underwent drastic re-evaluation. The US foreign policy during the first Gulf War was a catalyst for fears that the US would unilaterally impose a new world order at the cost of

[6]Rational is here more understood as a goals–means relationship and not as another expression for reason, as opposed to faith, implying that from a religious perspective also a rational world-view is potentially possible and desirable.

non-Western countries, and the Islamic world in particular. This world order might serve to exclude Muslim countries from political decision-making and from global resources unless they toed the US line. Western opposition to Islamic militancy was believed to imply opposition to Islam as a whole. In both the US and the Islamic world, new ideological battle lines were drawn by conservative cultural essentialists. Pakistan was no exception.[7] Many religious scholars in India shared in the ideological underpinnings of these positions, although from a much less activist position.

These two developments contributed to a preservation of the ideological defiance and social immobility of the 'ulamā' class. It no longer saw the need to adapt to a changing world; indeed, it saw its beliefs confirmed by international developments. This climate of confrontation and polarization has also served to freeze the Islamic project of modernity. Tackling modern problems from an Islamic perspective requires new concepts and views, but these are drowned in a confrontationist attitude. The elaboration of an Islamic project of modernity will have to continue if Islamic groups and their infrastructure are to be integrated in Pakistani and Indian society and face the challenge of globalization. This would seem to be as much in the interest of the Islamic world as of the West.

The value of the concept of the public sphere lies in analysing non-conventional political actors such as religious Islamic groups in terms of their impact on politics and the public sphere. The concept reveals the inherent ambiguity of their project. On the one hand, Islamic groups appear more disunited than ever before. This in effect opens the Islamic sphere to public penetration, and offers more choice in religious matters to ordinary Muslims interested in taking a stand in the public sphere. Religious discourse is no longer restricted to religious specialists but has become accessible to laymen and public activists. This helped elevate non-orthodox sections of Muslim society. It introduced elements of competition and public representation in Islamic religious discourse, hitherto largely absent. It also constrained religious extremists, forcing them to argue their views in public and listen to adversaries. On the other hand, the emergence of the public sphere and of its Islamic sector helped Islamic groups to coordinate their public activity much better and to achieve greater cohesion. Better communication allowed them to discipline adherents, to delimit doctrinal and other differences more clearly. This

[7]For this debate, see Piscatori (1991), containing a contribution on Pakistan's Islamic parties by Mumtaz Ahmad ('The Politics of War: Islamic Fundamentalisms in Pakistan', pp. 155–85), and Ibrahim and Ferdowsi (1992), including a paper by this author on Pakistan's involvement in the Gulf Crisis (Reetz 1992).

in turn heightened the consciousness of sectarian divisions. It exacerbated existing cleavages and helped radical trends emerge. The formation of the Islamic sector as part of the public sphere promoted a sectarian project relying on anti-minority attitudes that influenced politics in South Asia and beyond to the present day.

But the most important point to be made in this connection is the value of openness in the public sphere. Islamic groups in colonial India, and in other parts of the Islamic world, became public actors through their competition for influence. As long as they form part of the public sphere they cannot close easily themselves to inquiry and political challenge: they must interact with the outside world. The tendency for Islamist formations is to develop a closed mindset of siege, mission and violence, a risk for all ideological groups. This, however, is mitigated through their involvement in the public sphere. While they interact with the public they can claim public legitimacy, fighting marginalization and inferiority: they represent 'insurgent publics'. Where the Islamic sphere closes in on itself, or where Islamist groups are pushed out of the public sphere into a non-public underground, a closed mindset develops, which justifies the pursuit of extremist aims at variance with public interests. The religious extremists could no longer be challenged neither by the public at large nor through religious injunctions that rob them of their legitimacy. Therefore, the concept of the public sphere retains its value for Islamic activism as an analytical tool and as a policy goal. Participation in the public sphere generates, in an extended Habermasian sense, obligations and values that contribute directly to the continued civility of public life.

The concept of the public sphere has not lost its utility provided the focus of the concept is redirected to take full cognizance of diversity in culture, religion, ethnic loyalties, and social status. As Habermas pointed out to his critics, the concept has proved its flexibility by providing the means and norms for its evolution: 'The peculiar feature of this discourse formation is that the rules that constitute the participants' self-understanding at the same time provide the resources for a critique of its own selectivity, of the blind spots and the incompleteness of its own transitional embodiments' (1992: 467). These internal dynamics is what makes the concept resilient and capable of adaptation to a fast-changing world.

Appendix I

THE 'TACK' OF THE DEOBAND SCHOOL

Summarized by the long-time rector of the Dār al-'Ulūm, Deoband, Maulana Qari Muhammad Tayyib, in the Centennial History of the seminary (Rizvi 1980/I: 329–31):

This moderate tack is based on seven basic foundations, which, with brief elucidation of each, are as follows:-

1. Knowledge of the *sharī'a*: Which includes all the branches of beliefs, devotions and worldly dealings, etc. the outcome of which is faith (*īmān*), and Islam; provided this knowledge may have been acquired, being restricted to the sphere of the sayings and practices of the predecessors, through the teachings; training and grace of the company of authoritative divine doctors and discipliners of the hearts whose chain of exterior and interior, knowledge and practice, understanding and taste may have continuously reached through continual authority to the Author of the *sharī'a* (on whom be most excellent blessings and greetings!); and may not be the result of self-opinion or mere book-reading and power of study or mere rational search and intellectual investigation, though it may not be devoid of rational style of description and argumentative proof and demonstration, for without this knowledge, distinguishing between right and wrong, legitimate and illegitimate, permissible and impermissible, the Sunna and the innovation, the abominable (*makrūh*) and the commendable (*mandūb*) is not possible nor is release possible from wild fancies, philosophical theories and blind superstitions in religion.
2. The following of the path: That is, consummation of good breeding, self-purification and spiritual traversing (*sulūk-e bāṯin*) within the auspices of researching Sufis and their well-tried principles (inferred from the Book and the Sunna), because, without this, moderateness in morals, stability of zest and ecstasy, internal insight, mental purity and observation of reality are not possible. It is obvious that this branch is connected with *aḥsān* along with faith and Islam.
3. Conformity to the Sunna: That is, conformance to the Prophetic Sunna in every walk of life and dominance of the permanent Sunna through maintaining respect of the *sharī'a* in every 'state' (*ḥal*) and 'utterance' (*qal*),

every condition of the exterior and the interior; for without it is impossible to be released from the conventions of ignorance, customary innovations and prohibited indecencies, and from the calamity of customarily imitating the ecstatic utterances and sayings of 'men of states' in spite of the lack of spiritual states of giving those utterances the status of a permanent general law parallel to the *sharī'a*.

4. Jurisprudential Hanafitism: The name of Islamic practical doctrines (*far'īyat*) and casuistic interpretations of laws (*ijtihādiyat*) is *fiqh* (jurisprudence). And since the elders of the *Dār al-'Ulūm* are generally Hanafite, the meaning of jurisprudential Hanafitism is compliance with the Hanafite jurisprudence in casuistic practical doctrines, and conformance to its principles of jurisprudence only in the education and preference of propositions and *fatwās*; for without it elusion from the desires of the evil self in educible propositions and, through the way of colligation, operating capriciously under different systems of jurisprudence, excision in the contents of propositions in accordance with the desires of the hoi polloi or guess and conjecture under the awe of emergency conditions and shallow changes and innovations in propositions through unlearnedness are unavoidable. It is obvious that this branch appertains to Islam.
5. Dialectical *Maturidi'ism*[1]: That is, as regards beliefs, the sustentation of the power of certitude and the stability of true beliefs with right thinking in accordance to the laws and principles determined and codified through the method of the *ahl al-sunna wa-'l-jamā'a* and the *ashā'ira* and the *māturīdīya*; for without it escape from the doubts cast by the tergiversators and the conjectural innovations, superstitions and scepticism of the false sects is not possible. It is evident that this branch is connected with faith (*īmān*).
6. Defence against tergiversation: That is, defence against the mischief raised by bigoted cliques and tergiversators, but in the language and expression of the time, with consciousness of the psychology of the milieu and through the contemporary familiar means where the argument or proof may be completed. Moreover, efforts with a crusader-like spirit for stamping them out, for without these the removal of the unlawful things (*munkirat*) and protection of the *sharī'a* from the encroachment of the antagonists is not possible. It includes refutation of polytheism and innovation, confutation of atheism and materialism, correction of the customs of ignorance, and, as per need, polemics, verbal or in writing, and the changing of unlawful things. It is obvious that this branch is concerned with the elevation of the Word of Allah in accordance with 'While Allah's word it was that became the uppermost' and the expression of religion be in accordance with 'He may cause it to prevail over all religion' and the general organisation of the community.
7. The taste for Qasimism and Rashidism[2]: Then while the same tack, with its

[1]After al-Maturidi, Hanafi theologian, jurist and Qur'an commentator, his life dates are unclear, born before 873, died 943/947, see W. Madelung in EI/VI: 846–47.

[2]After the two founders of the Deoband Seminary, Muhammad Qasim Nanaotawi and Rashid Ahmad Gangohi.

collective dignity, appeared after passing through the hearts and souls of the first patrons of the *Dār al-'Ulūm*, Deoband, and the feelers of the pulse of the community, it drew in the demands of the time in it and adopted the form of a particular taste which has been denoted with the word *mashrab* (disposition, nature, temper, conduct). Accordingly, in the basic constitution of the *Dār al-'Ulūm*, Deoband (*Dastūr-e Asāsī-ye Dār al-'Ulūm*, Deoband), which was approved in Sha'bān, 1368 AH, this reality has been stated in the following words: 'The tack of the *Dār al-'Ulūm*, Deoband, will be the Hanafite practical method (*madhab*) in accordance with the *ahl al-sunna wa-'l-jamā'a* and the disposition (mashrab) of its holy founders, Hazrat Maulana Muhammad Qasim Nanaotawi, and Hazrat Maulana Rashid Ahmad Gangohi (may their secrets be sanctified!).' (*Dastūr-e Asāsī*, p. 6).

ARTICLES OF FAITH OF THE BARELWI GROUP

From the Founding Constitution of the All-India Sunni Conference, in '*Tārīkh-i* All-India Sunni Conference: 1925–1947', Qadiri (1999: 42–8), partly abridged:

The founding constitution of the *Jam'īyat 'Āliya Islāmīya Markazīya* (All-India Sunni[3] Conference), that is of the All-India Sunni Conference[4]

Aims of the Jam'īyat 'Āliya Islāmīya

1. To establish relations of unity and understanding among the millions of Muslims who with the blessing of God (*bafazlā t'āla*) are following (lit. under the influence of) thousands scholars and guides (*mashā'ikh*) across the length and breadth of India.
2. To stem the flood of irreligiousness (*bēdīnī*) and atheism (*lā-mazhabī*) with strength and to take effective action for bringing the ranks of Muslims into the realm of religious conduct (*ḥudūd-e shar'ā*).
3. To keep Muslims safe from enemy attacks and advances and to protect them from coming dangers.
4. To give instructions (*dars*)[5] to Muslims on (leading) an Islamic life and to provide religious guidance in matters of living and conduct.

[3]Throughout this annex document 'Sunni' is used in the meaning of representing the Barelwi tradition.

[4]Repetitive wording in the source—DR.

[5]'Be it the promotion of societies for the translation of the Qur'an; or holding Qur'an-reading nights through religious schools (*madāris*); or spreading (religious) tracts about the customs of the time; or sending preachers to the countryside; or establishing libraries holding Sunni [i.e. Barelwi] books, tracts and newspapers; or commissioning manuscripts for this special purpose, which would become part of the curriculum of Muslim students—the (religious) instruction may include all these methods and local organisations are called upon to implement them in due measure step by step' (Qadiri 1999: 42).

5. To adopt practical actions for ending apostasy.
6. To reform beliefs and practices.
7. To remove the common ignorance and for this purpose to make educational resources easily accessible so that Muslims from all strata can benefit from the treasures of knowledge.
8. To create the best conditions for putting in every heart respect and admiration for the greatness of the kind and honourable Prophet, the holy Qur'an and the religion of Islam.
9. To stop Muslims from following bad habits.
10. To free Muslims from the habit of taking loans and teach them how to meet their requirements themselves. To strive for protecting them from extending their hands for loans to non-Muslims (*ghair-aqwām*).
11. To establish a system for the achievement of these aims with the help (lit. advice) of the luminaries (of Islam).
12. To continue the propagation (*tablīgh*) of Islam in an organised manner on a large scale.
13. To undertake well-meaning efforts for the correction and reform of every institution in need of reform.
14. To think about a course of action for the removal of grievances and anxieties of Muslims and implement it.
15. To compile a list of all Sunni Islamic schools (*madāris*) in India. To link them in one association (*silsila*). To create effective curricula for them. To continue necessary reforms among them. To provide them all possible help. To increase the departments of propagation (of Islam—*tablīgh*).
16. To open new religious schools (*madāris*) according to requirements so that religious knowledge can reach Muslims of every strata of society without hindrance.
17. To open a central *Iftā'* office (for judicial advice—*fatāwā*).
18. To strive for the compilation of an effective curriculum for preachers and propagators of Islam (*wā'iẓīn-o-muballighīn*).

Permanent Principles (Ghair-mutabadal Uṣūl)

1. The name of this group will be Supreme Islamic Organisation (*Jam'īyat 'Āliya Islāmīya*), (in English) the All-India Sunni Conference.
2. Any Sunni scholar or Sunni Shaykh belonging to an order (*ṭarīqa*) can become a member of this organisation.
3. A non-Sunni can under no circumstances become a member or office-bearer of this organisation.
4. A Sunni is one who has attested his belief in God, his Prophet and his companions are those who belong to the tradition (*maslak*) of the scholars of religion (*ā'imā-e dīn*), the Caliphs of Islam and the Muslim Shaykhs of the orders and among the contemporary (late, recent—*mutākhirīn*) scholars follow the *Mulk al-'ulamā' Sanad al-faẓilā' Baḥr al-'ulūm* (Abdul Ali)[6] *Ṣāḥib*

[6]See Chapter 2, fn. 22.

Firangī Maḥallī, *Ḥaẓrat* Maulana Fazl-i Haq Sahib Khairabadi[7], '*Alī Ḥaẓrat* Maulana Mufti Shah Fazl-i Rasul *Ṣāḥib* Badayuni, *Ḥaẓrat* Maulana Mufti Irshad Husain *Ṣāḥib* Rampuri and '*Alī Ḥaẓrat* Maulana Mufti Shah Ahmad Raza Khan *Ṣāḥib* Barelwi (*qudsat isrār ham*).

5. Beside the scholars ('*ulamā*') and (Sufi) guides (*mashā'ikh*) membership can also be extended to the friends of the Muslim world (*millat*) and supporters of Sunni Islam.

Rules and Regulations

1. This organisation will create in every province provincial organisations; and district, town and village organisations as their branches.
2. Every small organisation will keep contact with a larger organisation and all organisations will do so with the central organisation.
3. Orders of the centre will be obligatory to implement for all organisations.
4. The branch organisations will have to consult the central organisation on important matters.
5. The central organisation will supervise all the resolutions and methods adopted by the branch organisations, and their implementation, and will be entitled to revise and abrogate them.
6. If some issue or matter cannot be solved by one organisation, or if its members are engaged in some controversy, its solution will rest with the central organisation and the president or the secretary (*nāẓim*) will come forward to issue a decision and their decision will be binding.
7. For the time being, the head office of the Supreme Organisation will be in Muradabad. Its Secretary will be...Maulana *al-Ḥāj* Muhammad Naimuddin... its President...Maulana Maulwi Hafiz Pir Sayyid Jamaat Ali Shah...and the Deputy Secretary...Umar Naimi (Rector of the *Jām'iya Na'īmīyā*, Muradabad).

Rules of Membership

1. The organisation will not set any fixed subscription. On his capacity and conscience every member will determine what annual fee he will contribute. If provincial and district organisations consider it appropriate they can decide on entry fees, a monthly or annual subscription.
2. It is the duty of every member to consider unsparing efforts for the implementation of the aims of the organisation according to his capacity as service to Islam of the highest order.
3. Before accepting membership of any other religious organisation, permission from the *Jam'īyat 'Āliya Islāmīya* [that is, All-India Sunni Conference] has to be taken.
4. If the organisation asks for any advice it should get it, or if it requires the involvement (of its members in any task), participation in (the activities

[7] 1797?–1859.

of) its branches should receive precedence over any other work, in which any delays should also be readily (lit. without pressure) accepted.

5. Special efforts for the expansion of the organisation should be included in its work.
6. It is the duty of every member to show respect to the members and delegations of this organisation in his own living area (*halqā*) and to participate in their work.

Organising Committee (*Jam'īyat-e Muntazima*)
[... Clauses 1–11]

Duties of the President
[... Clauses 1–3]

Vice-President
[... 1 clause]

Duties of the Secretary (*nāzim*)
[... Clauses 1–15]

Duties of the Treasurer (*khāzin*)
[... Clauses 1–2]

Duties of Members
[... Clauses 1–8]

Signature: ...Maulana Muhammad Naimuddin, Secretary All-India Sunni Conference and founder of *Jām'iya Na'īmīyā*, Muradabad

...

[Muradabad, 1925]

OBJECTIVES OF THE NADWA COUNCIL AND SEMINARY

From the report by Abdul Hayy to the session of the Nadwa council on 3 January 1904 (Jalis Nadwi and Tabriz Khan 1983/I: 323–4):

The '*ulamā*' council (Nadwa) has followed five directions for the implementation of its basic objectives:

1. Development of education: It is necessary by any means to stop the degradation which has been brought about by the tribulations of the time which unfortunately has befallen the Islamic sciences ('*ulūm-e islāmīya*) and which is growing day by day. The knowledge must be acquired which has been absent from our curriculum for ages and the absence of which made the educated classes to hold the 'ulamā' in low esteem so that the 'ulamā' can again provide the same service as our pious ancestors (*islāf*) had been doing. The seminary of the '*ulamā*' council is founded on this idea.
2. Reformation of the manner of education: Our lack of knowledge not only pertains to the curriculum but also to the manner of teaching. It should be set up in such a way that there is hope that the students develop lofty

ambitions, noble-mindedness, taste for correctness, awareness of the requirements of the time and allout trust in the country and the nation.

3. Removal of mutual enmity: The pursuit of these objectives should stop those absurd quarrels which have caused extremely shameful strife and bickerings among different Muslim groups.
4. Improvement of morals: Today the morals of Muslims are so much impaired that one can often see examples of ills on display. Some people understand morality in a way that they display artificial and conspicuous behaviour. Immorality is growing day by day. Lies, backbiting, deceit, selfishness, troublemaking and misbehaviour is taking growing root amongst us. So it is the objective of the *'ulamā'* council (*Nadwa*) to make attempts for the removal of these ills with the help of (sending out) preachers (*wā'iẓīn*).
5. General welfare of Muslims: This objective encompasses many issues such as to pay attention to the provision of legitimate and sufficient means for Muslims to earn their livelihood, and to make efforts to remove debased customs etc.

FIRANGĪ MAḤALL ACTIVIST AND SCHOLAR ABDUL BARI (1878–1926)

From his biographical sketch by Maulana Mufti Inayatullah (1988: 173–5):

The Maulana founded the *Madrasa Niẓāmīya* in 1914 (1323 AH) (on the death anniversary of *Ḥaẓrat Ustāẓ al-Hind*) especially for the education of the offspring of the *Firangī Maḥallī* family but also for the whole Islamic community where he established teaching in a modern way. By the grace of God this *madrasa* continues until the present day [that is, through the 1930s] (some time ago it closed down [—the editor]). Currently all its scholars were (Abdul Bari's) students. Besides me [Inayatullah] these include Maulana Qutub Miyan, Maulana Abdul Qadir, Maulana Sibghatullah, Maulana Muhammad Shafi, Maulana Hayatullah, Maulana Ruhullah, Maulana Khwaja Latifuddin, Maulwi Samsam Ali, who were all his students and were filled with the bounty of his knowledge. At present, all the independent scholars of *Firangī Maḥall* who are younger than Maulana (Bari) are his students. From the beginning he was also teaching at the *Madrasa* right up to the end (of his life). He was teaching all books for basic and for advanced level at one time to the extent that he even gave lessons in gardening. For a certain time the Maulana made the *Madrasa* the exclusive focus of his attention. When he was satisfied and in agreement with the work of the *Madrasa* and when he came across such events as the Balkan war, the Kanpur mosque incident, and the shameful 'crime' of Lloyd George against the Turks [regarding his 'broken pledge'], which created a great stir in the Islamic world, and when it became increasingly clear that the power-hungry of Europe and the enemies of Islam were preparing to wipe out the Muslims from the face of the earth, the Maulana joined the righteous *'ulamā'* and completely immersed himself in bold and militant activities in politics and religion. He laid firm foundations of the Society for the Defence of the *Ka'ba*, of the Khilafat committee and of the *JUH*. There is not the slightest doubt that as a founder of the *JUH*, the *Ka'ba* society and the Khilafat conference, as a distinguished teacher he was well ahead of others in the general movement of Islam and its propagation in the whole of India. The initial administrative preparation and founding activity was well placed in his auspicious hands. Only he knows how much in all those boundless activities, which were reflected in the press he spent his own private money on these movements. The whole amount cannot have been less than 40–50 thousand Rupees. From among the '*ulamā*', he was the first who made practical efforts for Hindu–Muslim unity. He developed these to an extent where he often played host to Gandhi and other non-Muslim leaders. When Ibn Saud occupied the Haramain and introduced his Wahhabi innovations (*bid'a*) and turned the places of God and his messenger into a slaughterhouse Maulana (Bari) and political leaders for quite some time strongly opposed this. At this time Maulana (Bari) established the Association of the Servants of the Haramain (*khuddām al-ḥaramain*), which still exists. Maulana (Bari) was so deeply involved in these activities that he often had to work in two, three shifts the whole day and during the night. In support of the Khilafat committee he was so busy that either he himself or his brothers and cousins travelled the whole of India. He went to Bombay every other month. He continued this struggle to the very end of his life. In spite of all his busy activities he never ignored worship and scholarly pursuits. Wherever he was he never neglected prayer with the party. When travelling he took two people with him to be able to conduct a prayer session, also during the Fasting Month of *Ramaḍān* he saw to it that he fulfilled the conditions of breaking the fast.

ARTICLES OF FAITH OF THE AHL-I ḤADĪTH

From Ahl-i Ḥadīth propagandist and historian Muhammad Ibrahim Mir Siyalkoti[8] (1953: 168–72):

The Principles and Religious Doctrines of the Tradition of the Ahl-i Ḥadīth

[Persian couplet:]

The true religion has been sent in the words of God and is honoured for that
But the *ḥadīth* of the Prophet are the real life (spirit) of the Muslims
When you have the sayings of the Prophet, don't pay attention to the words and deeds of any other person.

And that actually is the translation of a sermon by the Prophet. After praising God, the Prophet used to say the following which is included in *Saḥīḥ Muslim* and other collections of *ḥadīth*:

The holy Qur'an is the best book as revealed through the words of God, and the practice of the Prophet is superior to all other behaviour. And the worst deed is what came up new since every innovation is misleading (*Saḥīḥ Muslim*, part I, p. 285).

[8]1874–1956.

So this embodies the beliefs, essence, doctrine and practice of the *Ahl-i Ḥadīth*.

The Removal of Doubt

Now you would say that the observance of the Qur'an and the *ḥadīth* are the principles of every Qur'anic group (*firqa*). Then how can the *Ahl-i Ḥadīth* claim this to be their sign of distinction? No group (*firqa*) adhering to the three principles mentioned can be called modern as all (these groups) understand themselves and claim to be part of the *umma* of the Prophet. And all claim the principles of their beliefs and their practice to be determined by the influence and teachings of the Prophet. Hence everybody declares himself to be an adherent and admirer of Muhammad.

[...] [—Urdu couplet]

To clarify this confusion: apparently every group at the first glance bases itself on the Qur'an and the *ḥadīth*. They consider these the principles of Islamic law (*uṣūl-e shar'a*) and what must be followed in religion (*wājib al-itibā'*) and they don't think of following in their tradition (*maslak*) anyone except the Prophet. But if we look in depth then all sects except *Ahl-i Ḥadīth* are proven to be the translation of this couplet.

[...] [—Arabic couplet]

We are not saying that all other sects have lost total confidence in the *ḥadīth* (sayings) of the prophet like the *Ahl-i Qur'ān* led by Maulwi Abdullah Chakralawi. Rather we are saying that no other sect distinguishes itself by its preference for the *ḥadīth* of the Prophet in the formation of legal opinion in Islam (*rā'e*, *qiyās*, *ijtihād*, *istimbāṭ*) like the *Ahl-i Ḥadīth*. In spite of accepting the authenticity of a *ḥadīth* everyone raises questions while recognising it. Some give the excuse of not accepting the principle of legal analogy *qiyās* and doubt the legal qualifications of the narrator. Some reject it because they view it as opposed to the Qur'an (*m'uāriẓ-e Qur'ān*), some, because it is against logic ('*aql*), and some reject it because the Imam they follow has not recognised it.

According to the saying 'if you argue over the facts you can't narrate the story' they create all kinds of hurdles in the way of following the *ḥadīth*. (As is evident from the books of rules of all sects) and also from the Prophet's saying that 'no one amongst you can be a pious person unless he subjects his desires to what I've brought you (i.e. the Qur'an)' (Mishkat) they have not abandoned their desires and wishes and in spite of belonging to the *umma* of the Prophet they do not relate themselves directly to him but to others.

[Persian verse]

From that it becomes quite evident that these people have erected an internal wall, which prevents them to reach to the *ḥadīth* of the Prophet.

The *Ahl-i Ḥadīth*, in contrast with all others, do not relate themselves to anybody else and do not, by referring to some legal opinion (*qiyās-e-rā'e*), put up conditions for following the honourable *ḥadīth*, but they rather accept the *ḥadīth* in a very straightforward manner as the Prophet wanted to be followed and as his companions, thanks to belonging to his party (*umma*), followed him unquestioningly.

[Persian couplet:]

We are the followers of the *ḥadīth*, don't you recognise us,
on the words of the Prophet we put no doubt nor question.

The *Ahl-i Ḥadīth* regard the *ḥadīth* of the Prophet as a revelation from God as expressed [in the verses of the Qur'an regarding the message of the Prophet]: 'And he speaketh not of his own desire. It is but a revelation revealed.' (Daryabadi, 53: 3, 4) And, as far as his [Muhammad's] narration and his commentary of the Qur'an are concerned, in the following verse: 'And thereafter (after teaching him the words [of the revelation]) verily upon us is the expounding thereof.' (Daryabadi, 75: 19)

In the same sense, *Ḥaẓrat* Hasan has narrated a tradition as quoted in the *Musnad* [collection of traditions] of [Abd Allah b. Abd al-Rahman] al-Darimi [d. 255/869]: 'As Gabriel has brought the revelation of the Qur'an to Muhammad he also brought the revelation of the Sunna.'

Distinctive features of the *Ahl-i Ḥadīth* regarding the observation of the *ḥadīth*:

Except the *Ahl-i Ḥadīth*, all other sects are so defective in their teaching of the *ḥadīth* that, although they have accepted the *ḥadīth* of the Prophet as principles of the *sharī'a*, they have practically turned the sayings of their leaders and Imams into principles [of religion] in two cases: First, if for any reason any pronouncement contradicts a *ḥadīth*, the *ḥadīth* is subjected to further interpretation without giving up support for the pronouncement [of their leader.]

Secondly, if any leader and Imam holds fast to a certain tradition (*ḥadīth*) which according to research is weak [in terms of authenticity], even to be rejected and, by the agreed opinion of the scholars of tradition (*muḥadithīn*), unproven and unfounded or untraceable, still the followers of this Imam even after learning about this situation will not reject his pronouncements. From this it becomes quite clear that practically these people have not accepted the *ḥadīth* as a principle of *sharī'a* even though they verbally and by faith accepted the *ḥadīth*. Another thing is that the latter-day followers of the sects without consulting the *ḥadīth* of the Prophet have accepted the pronouncements of their leaders as principles [of religion] and thus opened the door to reinterpretation so that the ordinary *'ulamā'* have come to believe that these modifications are also the sayings of the Imams [of the law schools] and have to be considered at par with the law (*fiqh*) books as revelation from heaven. From this it is unfortunately clear that the pronouncements of the Imams have come to be regarded as principles [of religion] in the same way as the *ḥadīth*. Shah Waliullah has discussed this in detail in his *Ḥujjat Allāh* (Vol. 1, published in Egypt, pp. 153–161).

But the *Ahl-i Ḥadīth* by belief and practice have never deviated from the eternal *ḥadīth* of the Prophet, and in the presence of an authentic *ḥadīth* have neither cared about opposition from any follower of any sect (*ummatī*)—even if he was a respectable religious elder—nor have they based their objections [against others] on a weak *ḥadīth*. What could be greater evidence than that every sect has compiled certain issues [in their books] and declared these books to be the books of their sect (*madhab*), while in contrast other books are associated with other sects. The *Ahl-i Ḥadīth* do not single out particular issues and do not write books about them which then are made the special books of its sect but they devote their full energy to the whole corpus of the *ḥadīth* of the Prophet, their explanation and description, their critical evaluation and scrutiny. Hence they consider the objective of their life/existence to offer their service to the *ḥadīth* of the Prophet, to publish them, to relay the pronouncements of the Prophet instead of the pronouncements of other people and to keep their distance from every book, which vents opposition to the *ḥadīth* of the Prophet.

Can after this anybody point out to us any literature which the *Ahl-i Ḥadīth* might have written and which was particular to them and which, as principles of the *sharī'a*, the other sects as belonging to the *umma* of the Prophet and recognising the *ḥadīth* of the Prophet cannot implement/follow (*'amal*)? With the blessing of God this circumstance will attract obedient, reasonable and intelligent Muslims towards the *Ahl-i Ḥadīth*. There is no doubt that the way the *ḥadīth* of the Prophet are being respected and followed upon in this sect cannot be found in other sects. This very fact is the particular mark of distinction of the *Ahl-i Ḥadīth* that they have associated themselves with the *ḥadīth* of the Prophet and have made themselves their special servant and keeper (*khādim*).

[Arabic verse] In contrast we can point out the special books of every sect as being the books of that sect (only). The other Muslims have no particular connection with them. Even if (others) have collected some *ḥadīth* it is to create limits and boundaries for their sect. They have subjected those *ḥadīth* to further interpretation, which run counter to their sect (*madhab*), and have reaffirmed those *ḥadīth* and symbols, which are in consonance with their school (*madhab*), even if they are weak or abrogated, so that they are redirected into the river of tradition for people who study the science of *ḥadīth*. [Fn. 1...] In short, the Sunna of the Prophet is being constructed by the Imams and leaders (of the sects) and not derived from the study of the traditions. That is why people have little knowledge of the Sunna (even) when its is generally available through publications.

As a result of this sectarianism [*lit.* drawing of borders] every sect started to claim that unless you join that particular sect you couldn't be considered to have received (divine) guidance (*hidāyat*). Just as it was said (by God) about the Jews and Christians who lived before us that they used to say that you will be guided rightly only if you become Jews or Christians: 'And they say: become Jews or Nazarenes, and ye shall be guided.' (2:135)

But the *Ahl-i Ḥadīth* tell everyone that all these matters do not come from the messenger [the Prophet], rise above them and follow the path of his companions, follow the *ḥadīth* of the Prophet, as the following order (by God) revealed in answer to the Jews and Christians: 'Say thou: Aye! We follow the faith of Ibrahim' (2:135) Those principles by which the holy Qur'an answered the Jews and the Christians are the ones which the *Ahl-i Ḥadīth* tell everyone: 'Follow the unblemished (*ma'ṣūm*) Prophet and don't oblige yourself to follow the corrupt (*ghair-ma'ṣūm*) ones' and leave the circle of factionalism, come on to the main road of Muhammad and raise the slogan in happiness 'when you have the words of the Prophet follow him and nobody else.'

THE SIX ESSENTIALS OF THE TABLĪGHĪ JAMĀ'AT

Chhē batēñ (Six Principles) as formulated by the Tablīghī founder, Maulana Muhammad Ilyas (1997: 114–16):

1. The Declaration of Faith [as done by reciting the formula of] *Kalima ṯaiybā*: There is no God but God and Muhammad is His messenger

To make people correctly recite the Kalima *ṯaiybā*, in which also the proper pronunciation (phonetics) have to be considered, and understand the basic meaning of the *Kalima* and draw attention to its truth (actuality—*haqīqat*) which has two elements: (1) to establish an inner (emotional, of the heart—*qalibī*) relationship with God, (2) turn to God only with pure intentions of the heart which can only be done by following Muhammad [as his messenger]. It means that the *Kalima* embodies the principles of God's unity (*tauḥīd*) and faith in him (*'aqā'id*). Everything through which God becomes known is included in that. It also encompasses profession of faith in Muhammad the Prophet (*shahāda*) and obedience to the Prophet.

2. Prayer (*ṣalāt*)

Among the acts of religion, prayer is the most important act. It is the gate to all other acts. What the *Kalima ṯaiybā* has established in this regard is that I only take my orders from God and obey every of His commands and will mould my life accordingly. This [that is, prayer] is the first step in proof of this (obedience).

Prayer also has two elements: one is external and the other internal. Externally the conduct of prayer has to be correct (*durust*) and graceful (*ḥasan*). For instance, ablution has to be done fully in accordance with tradition (Sunna) and desirable recommendations (*mustaḥabāt*) and every part of the prayer (*rukn*) has to be articulated in accordance with tradition (Sunna). Internally, one should try to say every prayer with utmost humility (*khushū'*), from which the prayer may be marked all by propriety (decency, lit. the complete absence of obscenity—*tanhī 'an al-faḥshā'*). Prayer is a source of light, which lightens up all other acts (of religion)—that is the spirit of prayer.

3. Knowledge and Remembrance of God (*'ilm-o-ḏikr*)

To spend some time in the morning and in the evening on gaining (religious) knowledge and remembering God. The common ritual of commemoration (*ḏikr*) for every person consists of (counting the beads of) one rosary on reciting the third *Kalima* in the morning, one in the evening, and two each on invoking God's blessing (*durūd*) and asking God's forgiveness (*istighfār*). If one is connected to a Shaykh one should follow his recommendation for prayer (*ḏikr*). For (religious) education one should read [from the *Tablīghī* tracts of] 'The Virtues of Prayer' (*faẓā'il-i namāẓ*), 'The Virtues of Commemoration (of God)' (*ḏikr*), 'The Virtues of the Holy Qur'an' (*faẓā'il-i Qur'ān*), 'The Stories of the Companions of Muhammad' (*ḥikāiyāt-i ṣaḥāba*), 'Reward of Good Deeds' (*jaẓā al-a'māl*).[9] If the Qur'an was not read previously it should be studied. For those qualified in religion (*ahl-i 'ilm*) (it is recommended to read) a book on virtuous deeds

[9]Cf. Zakariya (1975).

(*kitāb al-a'māl*), on (religious) knowledge and beliefs (*kitāb al-'ilm-wa-al-e'tiqādāt*), on tradition (*kitāb al-sunnan*), on holy war (*kitāb al-jihād*), on fighting (the Infidels) (*kitāb al-maghāzī*), on revolt (divisions in Islam) (*kitāb al-fitan*), on good behaviour (*kitāb al-raqqāq*), on what is right (and what is wrong) (*kitāb al-amr bi'l-ma'rūf*).

4. Honour and Respect of (Fellow) Muslims (*ikrām al-muslim wa iḥtirām*)

Its essence is the respect of rights. It is everyone's duty to realise the rights of others. Some are general (*'umūmī*). It is everyone's duty to respect the (innate) rights of every Muslim (*muslim kā nafs*), which he holds because of Islam. There are also special rights. For instance, the younger ones can claim special rights, such as much kindness (from the elders), and family members can claim respect and care. Everyone's rights should be respected within his entitlement. The regard for these rights should be turned into a means to express (submission to) religion, it should not become an ends (in itself). Approach the attainment of your rights with composure and don't be in constant pursuit of them. Keep them accumulating for the Hereafter.

5. Correction of Intention and Conduct (*taṣḥīḥ al-niyyat wa al-khalāṣ*)

All this work should be undertaken for the glory of God and for one's self-improvement (*iṣlāḥ*). Don't turn the gaze to any external aim. Also do not pay attention to effect and result (of your action).

6. Going Out (In the Way of God) (*al-nafr*)

While reciting the *Kalima*, praying and commemorating God, realising the virtues of doing so, giving everybody his due rights, and worshipping the Prophet Muhammad to incur God's pleasure, go from door to door, from street to street, from town to town, from country to country (communicating) the essence of being a Muslim; what is most important in religion; what is special to it, as to honour all Prophets; and what the distinction of the community of Muhammad is. Every of its members is its missionary (*dā'ī*) who at the hand of the Prophet (Muhammad) brings Islam to every citizen, with the same vocation and mind which are the root and basis of every aspect of religion. For this purpose as much time is required as is sufficient to keep every branch of the tree of religion fresh and green and lush. If you abandon the earth you yourself are left without branches being reduced to a trunk only.

ARTICLES OF FAITH OF THE AḤMADĪYA

From their statement on the application for membership (Walter 1991: 147–8):

1. God is one, and nobody is or can be his co-sharer in his self, attributes, names or worship.
2. The angels exist.
3. God has been sending from time immemorial his apostles in every country and nation for the guidance of his creatures, and we believe in every one of

them whose names have been mentioned in the Holy Qur'an individually and in the rest collectively.

4. Our Book is the Holy Qur'an and our prophet is Muhammad (peace be upon him), and he is the seal of prophets.
5. The door of inspiration has always been, and will always be, open, and no attribute of God ever becomes useless. As he used to hold communion with his good servants, so he does even now, and will continue to do up to the end of the world.
6. This is our firm faith that divine decree (*taqdīr*) as enunciated by the Holy Qur'an is correct, and that God listens to and accepts the prayers of his creatures, and great deeds are achieved by means of prayer.
7. We believe in the rising of the human beings after their death, and also we firmly believe that the heaven and the hell, as described by the Qur'an and the Traditions, exist and that on the day of Resurrection our prophet Muhammad will be the intercessor.
8. We firmly believe that the man about whom prophecies have been made by the old prophets under different names and of whom the Holy Qur'an speaks in the verse, 'He it is who raised a Prophet amongst the Meccans...and among others of them who have not yet overtaken them,' as the second advent of our Lord Muhammad, and whom our Lord Muhammad calls Messiah the prophet and the Mahdi (the man), is *Ḥaẓrat* Mirza Ghulam Ahmad of Qadiyan, and besides him nobody is the promised Messiah.
9. It is our firm belief that the holy Qur'an is a perfect book and that no new law will be required till the day of Resurrection, and that our Lord Muhammad possesses collectively all the qualities of all the prophets, and that after him none can, for from gaining any spiritual eminence, ever become a true believer except by complete obedience to him. We, not for a moment, believe that any old prophet will come to this place a second time, because in that we will have to admit some defect in the spiritual powers of our Lord Muhammad—but we believe among his followers Reformers have appeared, and will continue to appear, with spiritual knowledge of a very high order. Not only this, but a man can even gain prophethood by the help of our Lord Muhammad's spiritual powers. But no prophet with a new book or having been appointed direct will ever come; for in this case it would be an insult to the perfect prophethood of our Lord, and this the meaning of the seal of prophets, and in this sense the Lord has on the one hand said, 'There is no prophet (i.e., an independent prophet or a prophet with a new law) after me,' and on the other hand has called the coming Messiah a prophet of God.
10. According to this we believe that a man, the Promised Messiah, has gained prophethood in spite of his being a follower of our Lord. We believe in the miracles of the prophets, which, in the words of the Qur'an, are called signs of God, and this is our firm faith that God, for the manifestation of his glory and for proving the truth of his apostles, has been, through his servants, showing signs which are beyond the power of human beings.

STATUTES OF THE MAJLIS-E AḤRĀR-E ISLĀM

From pamphlet: *Majlis-e Markazīya-i Aḥrār-e Islām-e Hind: Dastūr al-'amal* (Urdu: Statutes), Lahore: Suheili Printing Press, 20 January 1934; abridged:[10]

Statutes (Dastūr al-'Amal) of the Aḥrār-e Islām-e Hind

The Central Conference of the Noble of Islam in India (*Majlis-e Markazīya-e Aḥrār-e Islām-e Hind*)

In the name of God, the most beneficent, the most merciful
The Central Conference of the Noble of Islam in India

Its Aims and Objectives

1. To achieve independence for India by peaceful means.
2. To provide correct political guidance to Muslim in the politics of India.
3. To strive for the religious, educational, economic, and social advancement of Muslims.

Means and Ways for the Achievement of the Objectives

1. To create branches (*majālis*) of the *Aḥrār-e Islām* conference throughout India.
2. To organise volunteers corps (troops—*jaish*) of the *Aḥrār-e Islām* in every place.
3. To organise workers and peasants on economic principles.
4. To strive for the development of national production and to increase the demand for *Swadēshī* (national) products.
5. To collect funds for the support (existence—*qiyām*) of the *Aḥrār-e Islām* conference; and to undertake other such measures (for this purpose) as may be considered necessary from time to time.

Statutes (Dastūr al-'Amal)

1. In order to discuss policies for the attainment of the above-mentioned objectives, an annual meeting of representatives of all conferences of the *Aḥrār-e Islām* shall ordinarily be convened during Easter vacations, which shall be called the All-India *Aḥrār* conference. Venue and date shall be determined by the Working Committee (*Majlis-e 'Āmila*), which will be mentioned further below. Besides the annual conference, the Executive Committee shall also be entitled to convene extraordinary sessions of the *Aḥrār* Conference on its own initiative.

[10]Photostat copy received at the central Aḥrār office in Lahore (Pakistan) during interview with Mian Awaiz on 10 December 2002.

The Central Majlis-e Aḥrār-e Islām-e Hind

1. In order to adopt suitable ways and means for the implementation of the decisions taken by the All-India *Aḥrār* Conference and for the achievement of the chief aims and objectives mentioned above, a central body shall be elected by the All-India *Aḥrār* Conference, which shall be named the *Central Majlis-e Aḥrār-e Islām-e Hind.*
2. The members of the *Central Majlis-e Aḥrār-e Islām-e Hind* shall be those comrades (*aṣḥāb*), who have been elected by the *Majlis-e Aḥrār* from every district (*ẓila'*) or part of it (whether belonging to British India or to the princely states). Every of those *Majlis-e Aḥrār* shall elect two delegates while the *Majlis-e Aḥrār* from Lahore, Amritsar, Sialkot, Bombay, Calcutta and Delhi shall have the right to elect delegates in the following numbers:
   Lahore—10, Amritsar—7, Sialkot—7, Bombay—5, Calcutta—5, Delhi—5.
3. Any district in which there is no local (subordinate) Majlis or where the Majlis could not elect its representatives in time, the Working Committee of the Central Majlis shall have the right to select the delegates of that district.
4. After the above-mentioned Central Majlis is being established it will have to see that at least ten per cent of its members are new.
5. The local (subordinate) Majlis shall commonly conduct elections of their representatives for the Central Majlis of the *Aḥrār-e Hind* in December and they shall send information about this to the central office by the first week of January.
6. The Central Majlis shall hold one session in the course of the annual All-India *Aḥrār* Conference during the Easter Holidays, which shall elect all the office-bearers for the next year.
7. The president of the annual session of the All-India *Aḥrār* Conference shall be elected at the advice of the Working Committee and the local *majālis*. This election would take place, as a minimum, one month before the annual session.
8. The Central Majlis shall have the following office-bearers:
   President—one, Vice-Presidents—two, Secretaries (*m'otamad*)—two, Treasurer (*khāzin*)—one, Commander of the troops (*sālār-e jaish*)—one.
9. The term of office of the members and the office-bearers of the Central Majlis shall be one year. Former office-bearers and members can also be elected for the next year.
10. If during the year one of the offices falls vacant, the Working Committee shall elect from among the members of the Central Majlis someone for the remaining period of time. If the place of a member (of the Central Majlis) falls vacant, the Working Committee shall elect someone in his place from among the rank members.
11. The Central Majlis shall for the fulfilment of its duties adopt such rules and principles, which shall not contravene these founding statutes and it shall hold sessions from time to time according to these rules.

12. At the written request of 25 members of the Central Majlis a special session of the Central Majlis shall be convened, on the condition that such demand shall be communicated in writing to the Secretary at least 2 weeks prior to the requested session date.
13. The Trustees of the Central Majlis shall submit a report on the working of the said Majlis for the year and on its accounts at the session of the Central Majlis that shall take place on the occasion of the annual conference.

Working Committee
[... Clauses 17–19]

Local (subordinate) Majlis (*Majālis-e Mātaḥt*)
[... Clauses 20–3]

Membership of the Majlis-e Aḥrār-e Islām-e Hind
[... Clause 24]

Elections of the Delegates for the Aḥrār Conference
[... Clauses 25–32]

Reception Committee (Majlis-e Istiqbālīyā)
[... Clauses 33–5]

Election Steering Committee (*kamīṭī-e intikhāb-e maẓāmīn*)
[... Clauses 36–42]

CREED (14 POINTS) OF THE KHĀKSĀR MOVEMENT

From '*Al-Iṣlāḥ*', Lahore, October 1938:[11]

Announcement of the Supreme Council of India

1. We *Khāksār* will free the human race from all sectarian feelings and religious hatred (*maẓhabī t'aṣṣubāt*) with our dignified and effective action; yet preserving religion as such. We will create a just, tension-free and tolerant yet strong system in which all nations receive a fair treatment and a chance to grow and which would be based on piety, struggle and unlimited justice.
2. The practice of Islam during the founding era of Islam or the first following periods of Islam represented the correct Islam. The *Khāksār* soldiers do not recognise anything as part of the religion of Islam except the way of God's messenger.
3. The way the Maulwis talk today is wrong. The *Khāksār* soldier has risen to remove this wrong religion from the surface of the earth in order to resurrect the religion of the Prophet in its place.
4. There was no group of Maulwis during the founding era of Islam. That's why the *Khāksār* soldier wants to replace it with an organised group of Imams, which will rule the nation by the *sharī'a* (*qaum par shar'ī ḥukūmat karē*) (The

[11]Copy received from the current Khāksār leader in Pakistan, Hamiduddin Ahmad al-Mashriqi, in Lahore on 28 November 2002.

title of 'Maulana' should be removed from the dictionary of Islam as its meaning is 'our God.' Instead they should be called *Shaykh-e Fāẓil* [graduated scholar] or by some other title.)

5. The Khaksar soldier has no concern with the principles of belief of a particular sect. He considers the freedom of belief the religious right of every Muslim and he stands for the unity of action among all sects.
6. The *Khāksār* soldier considers it the religious right of every Muslim to follow every part of the Qur'an and *ḥadīth*—be they practiced or not—and he is ready for any sacrifice to keep (Muslims) free from legal or political pressure [*girift*] of the government of the day.
7. The *Khāksār* soldier stands for due respect of the religious and social feelings of every nation (Hindu, Muslim, Sikh, Parsee, Christian, Jew and Untouchables etc.); for the expression of their particular culture, traditions; and for general tolerance towards them. He is sure that such approach would be key to establishing a thousand year Islamic rule in India.
8. The *Khāksār* soldier considers it the first duty of his organisation to ensure for every nation its legitimate civil rights [*jā'iz shehrī ḥuqūq*] and to defend its internal and external interests. The *Khāksār* soldier approaches all nations with an open heart and is ready to accept them as partners and friends, inviting them for this purpose.
9. The *Khāksār* soldier's objective (motto) is to establish his rule over the entire globe and to achieve political and collective domination of the nation through his effective action.
10. The *Khāksār* soldier's objective is to establish only one *Bayt al-Māl* (Islamic Community Fund) in India, which has been created by the Supreme (*Khāksār*) Council of India; he will resist the creation of separate Community Funds (*Bayt al-Māl*) by force whatever sacrifice this may require. During the first years, the purpose of this Fund can only be to collect money and not to spend anything from it.
11. It is the belief of the *Khāksār* soldier that he can only lead the nations of the world and every individual by no other means but his kind behaviour and honest approach. These noble moral standards are common more or less to every religion and its (major) books.
12. In order to improve the economic conditions of the nation the *Khāksār* soldier considers his duty to increase the trade of every *Khāksār* no matter how much difficulty this may create. He is convinced that without this no progress can be achieved.
13. To the helper (*m'uāwin*) of the *Khāksār* it is recommended from today that for one month six Paisa or for one year one Rupee is to be paid directly into the community fund (*Bayt al-Māl*) of the Supreme Council of India (of the *Khāksār*). When the Supreme Council issues any general order to all the helpers it will be implemented no matter what sacrifice it requires at the time. The *Khāksār* soldier is convinced that the movement cannot win control (*ghalbā*) and its support will not be effective by doing less.

14. We *Khāksār* (*Pākbāz*, *Jānbāz*, or *Ghair—Jānbāz*)[12] are the mortal enemies of all treacherous leaders harming or exploiting the nation, of plunderers, of those in the pay of the enemy, or anti-national editors and newspapers, spreading disinformation) (*ghalat parōpa*), of hooligans, of collaborators with the enemy, of mischief-mongers, spreading hatred among the different nations of India, or sects of Muslims, organisations and groups, no matter to which nation or religion they belong, and we will take extreme revenge from them irrespective of the enormous sacrifice this will require from us.

Inayatullah Khan Mashriqi, issued by Supreme Council of India
Ichhra, Lahore, Announcement No. 226, 15 October 1937 at twelve o'clock.

[12]Categories of Khāksār membership.

Appendix II

STATUTES OF THE JAM'ĪYAT-E 'ULAMĀ'-YE HIND (JUH)

Excerpts from Rozinah (1981/I: 48–9):

Dastūr al-'Amāl (Statutes) (49)

a) To provide...from a religious position to the people of Islam leadership in political and non-political matters which are enlisted as follows:
b) To ward off, from the perspective of the *sharī'a*, harmful influences on Islam, the centres of Islam (the Arabian Peninsula and the enduring location (*mustaqarr*) of the Caliphate), Islamic practice (*shē'ār-e-Islām*) and the Islamic nation (*qaumīyat*);
c) To obtain and defend the shared/agreed religious rights [of all Muslim sects and traditions—DR] and to meet the joint religious and patriotic needs.
d) To bring the '*ulamā*' together in one centre.
e) The organization of the Muslims and their moral and social reform.
f) To establish relations of solidarity and agreement with non-Muslim compatriots as far as Islamic Law (*sharī'a*) allows.
g) (To fight for the) freedom of religion (*i.e.* Islam) and fatherland (*watan*) in accordance with the implementation of the essence (*naṣb-ul-'ain*) of Islamic Law (*sharī'a*).
h) To establish institutions of Islamic law in accordance with the requirements of the *sharī'a*.
i) To propagate (*tablīgh*) Islam in India and in other countries.
j) To establish and strengthen relations of Islamic brotherhood and unity with Muslims from other countries.'

Dastūr al-'Amāl as Adopted by the Session of the Central Committee of the JUH on 27–9 May 1939 (48–9)

a) From an Islamic position, to provide leadership to the Islamic community on the following issues and to fight for them:
b) To defend Islam, the centres of Islam on the Arabian Peninsula (in the

Hijaz), Islamic practice (*shē'ār-e-Islām*) and to ward off harmful influences on the Islamic nation (*qaumīyat*);

c) To obtain and defend the religious and patriotic rights and needs of Muslims.

d) The religious, educational, moral, social and economic reform of Muslims and the propagation and publication of the enormous potentiality of Islam.

e) The establishment and strengthening of relations of Islamic brotherhood and unity with Muslims in Islamic and other countries.

f) To establish relations of solidarity and agreement within the limits of Islamic Law (*sharī'a*) with non-Muslim compatriots.

Appendix III

DUTIES AND POWERS OF THE AMĪR AL-HIND

Resolution of the sub-committee of the Jam'īyat-e 'Ulamā'-ye Hind dated 9 December 1921 (Rozinah 1981/I: 468–79; excerpts)

Members of the sub-committee: Maulanas Kifayatullah—JUH President, Subhanullah, Sayyid Murtaza Hasan, Muhammad Fakhar, Abdul Majid, Muhammad Sajjad, Abdul Halim Siddiqi—deputy nāẓim of the JUH.

CORE PART OF THE RESOLUTION

DUTIES (FARA'IZ) OF THE AMĪR AL-HIND

(1) To achieve the observance of the duties of Islam. To stop the practice of things forbidden in Islam (*manhīyāt-i sharī'a*), that is to establish in practice the regular observance of the commands of Islam (*eḥkām-i sharī'a*).

COMMENTARY/EXPLANATION (*TASHRĪḤ*)

The following duties, prohibitions and commands have been agreed upon:

(2) Provision of community funds (*iqāmāt-e buyūt-e māl*)
(3) Provision of department of Islamic justice (*iqāmāt-e maḥkumā-e jāt-e qiẓā*)
(4) Establishment of administration of (Islamic) trusts (*iqāmāt-e naẓārat-e auqāf islāmīya*)
(5) Establishment of administration of (Islamic) education (*iqāmāt-e naẓārat al-ta'līmāt*)
(6) Establishment of administration of (Islamic) propaganda and guidance (*iqāmāt-e naẓārat al-tablīgh wa al-irshād*)
(7) Establishment of administration of public (Islamic) affairs/works (*iqāmāt-e naẓārat manāf'a 'umūmīya*)
(8) Establishment of a department of accounting and control (*iqāmāt-e maḥkumā-e eḥtiṣāb*)

Note: The *Amīr* can pursue or implement all or only some of these duties, as delegated by the JUH.

POWERS (IKHTĪYĀRĀT) OF THE AMĪR AL-HIND:

(9) The *Amīr al-Hind* is entitled to pursue only those duties which have been handed to him by the *JUH*.
(10) The *Amīr al-Hind* will appoint the leaders of the provincial *sharī'a* administrations and officials for the observance of the commands of Islam (*sharī'a*).
(11) The *Amīr al-Hind* will prepare the annual budget in cooperation with the administration of the *JUH*. He will be entitled to effect its agreed expenditure.
(12) The *Amīr al-Hind* will use all his powers in consultation with a consultative council (*majlis-e shūrā*) to be appointed by the *JUH*.

Signatures: Muhammad Kifayatullah, Muhammad Subhanullah, Faqir Sayyid Muhammad Fakhar, Muhammad Murtaza Hasan.

The duration of the period for which the *Amīr* holds office remains to be fixed.

After (elucidating) the duties and powers (of the *Amīr*) the sub-committee considers it appropriate to express its views on some related issues in connection with the establishment of an Islamic authority (*imārat-e sharī'a*):

- Essential (character) attributes for the *Amīr al-Hind* (...);
- Consultative council of the *Amīr al-Hind* (...).
- [Draft of the] Resolution [to be adopted by the *JUH*] for the establishment of (the post of) *Amīr al-Shariat fi al-Hind* (explanation, conditions, duties, powers, election and removal from office, causes of removal, manner of removal, [manner of] election or appointment of the *Amīr*, role of the *JUH* [in the implementation of an Islamic order under an *Amīr*])

Clause No. 31 makes provisions for the procedure to be adopted for the time when the powers of appointment of an *Amīr al-Hind* go to the *Khalīfa al-Muslimīn*. The latter will confirm the appointment made by the '*ulamā*' of the *JUH* and certify it on their advice.

Bibliography

Archival Material

BLOC L/P&J/6/1696–97. (Various, non-cooperation movement 1920.)

BLOC L/P&J/6/1701. Hijrat in NWFP. Exodus of Muhammadans to Afghanistan.

BLOC L/P&J/6/1731. Volunteer Movement.

BLOC L/P&J/6/1782. Moplah Outbreak. Detailed Reports by Mail.

BLOC L/P&J/6/2002. (Situation in the Punjab.)

BLOC L/P&J/6/2003. Serious Peshawar Riots, File No. 1897/30.

BLOC L/P&J/7/751. Dispute between Ahrars and Ahmadiyyas at Qadian, Punjab. 5 November 1934–12 December 1946.

BLOC L/P&J/8/678. Volunteer Organizations and Volunteer Movement in India. December 1936–October 40, February 42, March–June 43.

BLOC L/P&J/8/679. Steps to Prevent Growth of Private Armies. June 1944–May 1947.

BLOC L/P&J/8/693. Muslim Organizations in India, including All-India Momin Conference, All-India Muslim Majlis, All-Parties Shia Conference. March 1942–January 47.

BLOC L/P&J/12/685–751. Fortnightly Reports by Governors and Chief Commissioners. 1929–34.

BLOC L/P&S/ 7, 10, 12. (Including various Fortnightly Intelligence Diaries or Reports.)

BLOC L/P&S/10/633. Afghanistan: The Silk Letter Case. 1916–1918.

BLOC L/P&S/10/795–8. Turkey: The Future of Muslim Representations—1919. Peace Terms: Representations from Muslims—1920–21. Khilafat Deputation—1919–20. Official Reports of Mohammedan Situation in India—1920. Indian Muslims and Khilafat Deputation's Protest Against Alleged Arrest of Shaikh al-Islam—1920.

BLOC L/P&S/10/895. (Caliphate Question. Kemalists and Khilafatists. 1920–24.)

BLOC L/P&S/11/111. Hindustani Fanatics. 29 July 1912–18 June 1926.

BLOC L/P&S/11/119. The Caliphate: Enemy Propaganda. 18 January 1917–21 January 1919.

BLOC L/P&S/11/170–71, 202. (Afghanistan. Pan-Islamism. Frontier Affairs. 1915–25.)

BLOC L/P&S/12/3125. Tribal Disturbances 1930–31: Peshawar and District Situation. 7 May 1930–14 December 1932, File No. Coll. 23/4.
BLOC L/P&S/18/A184–6. Central Asia, Persia, and Afghanistan. Bolshevik and Pan-Islamic Movements and Connected Information, 1919.
BLOC L/P&S/20/B296/10. (Library of the L/P&S Department, January 1931.)
BLOC P/CONF/50. India Confidential Home Political Proceedings. January–June 1919.
BLOC P/CONF/51. India Confidential Home Political Proceedings. September–December 1920.
BLOC L/R/5/95–99. Selections from Newspapers Published in the UP in 1919–31.
NAI Poll(I) 41–3/11. Question of Releasing, Subject to Suitable Conditions, Prisoners Convicted under the Defence of India Rules in Connection with the Ahrar Civil Disobedience Movement.
NDC 230. Khaksar Frontier. 1937–69.
NDC 242, 268. List on Files on Hijrat Movement, Including Reports reg. returns.
NDC 403–05. Khaksar Movement Started by Inayatullah Khan Mashriqi. 1933–47.
NDC L/I/1/628. Moslems, Including the Khaksar Movement. 1938–45.
NDC L/I/1/629. Khaksar Movement. 1938–41.
NMML B/14. Jam'īyat-e 'Ulamā'-ye Hind: Proceedings of Executive Committee, Working Committee. 1925–78.
UPSA Box 58, /A, /B. Speeches on Non-Cooperation.

Official Publications

Command papers on election results

(Quoted as: UK Parliamentary Papers + Year of Publication, No. of Command Paper)
United Kingdom Parliamentary Papers. 1924. *Return Showing the Results of Elections in India, 1923*. Cmd. 2154. London: HMSO.
____. 1927. *Return Showing the Results of Elections in India, 1925 and 1926*. Cmd. 2923. London: HMSO.
____. 1937. *Return Showing the Results of Elections in India, 1937*. Cmd. 5589. London: HMSO.

Census reports

(Quoted as: Census + Year of Census, Vol., Part)
Government of India. 1903. *Census of India, 1901*. Calcutta: HMSO.
____. 1912. *Census of India 1911, Punjab*. Lahore: Civil and Military Gazette.
____. 1924. *Census of India 1921*. Calcutta: HMSO.
____. 1933. *Census of India 1931, Bihar & Orissa*. Patna: Superintendent Government Printing.
____. 1933. *Census of India 1931, Punjab*. Lahore: Civil and Military Gazette.
____. 1933. *Census of India 1931, United Provinces of Agra and Oudh*. Allahabad: Superintendent, Printing and Stationary.

OTHER

Central Bureau of Information. 1918 (–1935). *India in the Years 1917–18 (–1934–35)*. Calcutta: Government of India. (Quoted as: India in [year of review].)

____. India's Contribution to the Great War. 1923. Calcutta: HMSO.

____. Sedition (Rowlatt) Committee. 1918. *Report*. Calcutta: HMSO.

United Kingdom. Indian Statutory Commission. 1930. *Report of the Indian Statutory Commission*. Vols. 1–17. London: HMSO. (Quoted as: ISC 1930/[volume].)

Periodicals

Aligarh Institute Gazette. Aligarh.

Aligarh Magazine. Aligarh.

Dawn. Karachi, online edition at http://www.dawn.com.

Indian Express. Delhi, online edition at http://www.indianexpress.com.

Tarjumān Dāru'l-'ulūm. Deoband.

The Milli Gazette. Delhi, online edition at http://www.milligazette.com.

The Moslem World. Hartford.

The News. Karachi, online edition at http://www.jang.com.pk/thenews/.

The New York Times. New York, online edition at http://www.nyt.com.

The Times of India Illustrated Weekly. Bombay.

Zarb-i Mumīn (*Dharb-i Mumin*—Urdu: The [Emphatic] Word of a Believer). Karachi/Kabul, online edition at http://dharb-i-mumin.cjb.net/.

References

Abbasi, Mohammad Yusuf. 1987 (1981). *The Genesis of Muslim Fundamentalism in British India*. Delhi: IIAPR.

'Abbāsī, Qāẓī Mu'ammad 'Ādil. 1982. *Taḥrīk-i Khilāfat* (Urdu: The Khilāfat Movement). Delhi: Taraqqī-e Urdū Bureau.

Adams, Charles J. 1983. 'Mawdudi and the Islamic State', in Esposito (ed.), 1983: 99–133.

Ahmad, Akhlaq. 1985. *Traditional Education Among Muslims*. Delhi: BR Publications.

Ahmad, Aziz. 1962. 'Political and Religious Ideas of Shah Wali-Ullah of Delhi.' *Muslim World*, 52 (1): 22–30.

____. 1964. *Studies in Islamic Culture in the Indian Environment*. Oxford: Clarendon Press.

____. 1967. *Islamic Modernism in India and Pakistan 1857–1964*. Oxford: Oxford University Press.

____. 1969. *An Intellectual History of Islam in India*. Edinburgh: University Press.

____ and Gustav von Grunebaum (eds). 1970. *Muslim Self-Statement in India and Pakistan 1857–1968*. Wiesbaden: Otto Harassowitz.

Aḥmad, Ghulām. 1957 (–1968). *Rūḥānī Khazā'in* (Urdu: Spiritual Treasures/Collected Works). Rabwa.

Ahmad, Mahmud. 1924. *Ahmad, the Messenger of Latter Days*. Madras: Addison Press

Ahmad, Mujeeb. 1993. *Jam'īyyat-i 'ulamā'-i Pakistān, 1948–1979*. Islamabad: National Institute of Historical and Cultural Research.

——— 1994. *Tadkira-e faqīh-e a'zam* (Urdu: Biography of the Great Jurist [Maulānā Abū Yūsūf Muḥammad Sharīf]). Muridke: Maktaba-e Ashrafīya.

Ahmad, Qayamuddin. 1966. *The Wahhabi Movement in India*. Calcutta: K. L. Mukhopadhyay.

Ahmad, Shabi. 1977. 'The Making of a Nationalist Muslim: A Study of Maulana Azad and his al-Hilal (1911–1920).' *Islam and the Modern Age*, 8 (4): 54–64.

Aḥmad Khān, Sayyid. 1870. *A Series of Essays on the life of Mohammed and Subjects Subsidiary Thereto*. London: Trübner.

———. 1880. *Tafsīr al-Qur'ān* (Urdu: Commentary of the Qur'an). Vol. 1–6, Aligarh, 1880–95; Vol. 7, Agra, 1904.

———. 1961 (–1962). *Maqālāt-i Sir Sayyid* (Urdu: Works of Sir Sayyid). Lahore.

Ahmed, Munir D. 1975. 'Ausschluss der *Aḥmadīya* aus dem Islam: Eine Umstrittene Entscheidung des Pakistanischen Parlaments.' *Orient*, 16 (1): 112–43.

———. 1977. 'Die Stellung des Koran in der *Aḥmadīya*-Theologie.' *Zeitschrift der Deutschen Morgenländischen Gesellschaft* (Supplement III, 1): 319–330.

———. 1980. 'Die Soziologie der Ahmadiyya.' *Zeitschrift der Deutschen Morgenländischen Gesellschaft* (Supplement IV): 545–7.

Ahmed, Rafiuddin. 1988. *The Bengal Muslims 1871–1906: A Quest For Identity*. New Delhi: Oxford University Press (2nd edn).

Alatas, Farid. 1994. *The Post-Colonial State: Dual Functions in the Public Sphere*. Singapore: Department of Sociology, National University of Singapore.

Ali, Amir. 1922. *The Spirit of Islam: A History of the Evolution and Ideals of Islam, with Life of the Prophet*. London: Christophers.

Ali, Chiragh. 1883. *The Proposed Political, Legal and Social Reforms in the Ottoman Empire and Other Mohammadan States*. Bombay: Education Society Press.

Ali, Muhammad. 1906. *Ahmad, the Promised Messiah*. Lahore: Artistic Print Works.

Ali, Muhammad. 1963. *Selected Writings and Speeches*. 2 vols. Lahore: Ashraf (2nd edn).

All-India Muslim League. 1939. *Report of the Inquiry Committee Appointed by the Council of the All-India Muslim League to Inquire into Muslim Grievances in Congress Provinces* (Pirpur Report). Delhi: Liaqat Ali Khan.

Amjād 'Alī, Muḥammad. 1983. *Bahār-i Sharī'at* (Urdu: The Bloom of Islamic Law). Lahore: Shaykh Ghulām 'Alī.

Andersen, Walter K. and Shridhar D. Damle. 1987. *Brotherhood in Saffron: The Rashtriya Swayamsevak Sangh and Hindu Revivalism*. Boulder: Westview.

Anderson, Benedict. 1983. *Imagined Communities: Reflections on the Origins and Spread of Nationalism*. London: Verso.

Andrews, C. F. 1929. *Zaka Ullah of Delhi*. With an Introductory Memoir by Maulvi Nazir Ahmad. Cambridge: Heffer.

Appadurai, Arjun and Carol A. Breckenridge. 1995. 'Public Modernity in India', in Carol A. Breckenridge (ed.), 1992, pp. 1–20.

Arooran, K. Nambi. 1980. *Tamil Renaissance and Dravidian Nationalism, 1905–1944*. Madurai: Koodal Publishers.

Asad, Talal. 1993. *Genealogies of Religion: Discipline and Reasons of Power in Christianity and Islam*. Baltimore: Johns Hopkins University Press.

——. 1996. 'Modern Power and the Reconfiguration of Religious Traditions' (Interview with Saba Mahmood). *Stanford Electronic Humanities Report (SEHR)*, 5 (1).

Aziz, K. K. (ed.). 1972. *The Indian Khilafat Movement, 1915–1933: A Documentary Record*. Karachi: Pak Publishers Ltd.

—— (ed.). 1993. *Public Life in Muslim India, 1850–1947*. Delhi: Renaissance Publishing House.

Aziz, Zahid. 1997. 'The Ahmadiyya Movement of Lahore: A Survey of the Origins, History, Beliefs, Aims, and Work of the Ahmadiyya Anjuman Isha'at Islam Lahore.' *The Light & Islamic Review* (September–October). (Quoted here after the slightly edited version at the website of the Lahori group of the Aḥmadīya at http://www.ahmadiyya.org/intro/survey.htm.)

Azmeh, Aziz Al-. 1993. *Islams and Modernities*. London: Verso.

Baha, Lal. 1979. 'The Activities of Mujahidin.' *Islamic Studies*, 18: 97–168.

Bakshi, S. R. (ed.). 1989. *Documents of Muslim Politics: A Study of the Khilafat Movement*. Delhi: Criterion.

Baljon, J. M. S. 1961. *Modern Muslim Koran Interpretation, 1880–1960*. Leiden: Brill.

——. 1986. *Religion and Thought of Shah Wali Allah Dihlawi 1703–1762*. Leiden: Brill.

——. 1996. 'Indo-Pakistani and Egyptian Muftis on Medical Issues.' *Muslim World*, 86 (1): 85–95.

Bamford, P. C. 1974 (1925). *Histories of the Non-Cooperation and Khilafat Movements*. Delhi: Deep Publications.

Barrier, N. G. (ed.). 1981. *The Census of British India: New Perspectives*. Delhi: Manohar.

Bauman, Zygmunt. 1999. *In Search of Politics*. Cambridge: Polity Press.

Bayly, C. A. 1996. 'Colonial Rule and the "Informational Order" in South Asia', in Crook (ed.), 1996, pp. 280–315.

Bhatia, Shyamala. 1982. 'Reforms of Mirza Ghulam Ahmad.' *Proceedings* (Punjab History Conference, 15th Session 1981): 230–41. Patiala: Punjab Historical Studies Department, Punjab University.

Blunt, Edward. 1937. *The Indian Civil Service*. London: Faber.

Boyle, Harry C. 1992. 'The Pragmatic Ends of Popular Politics', in Calhoun (ed.), 1992, pp. 340–58.

Brass, Paul. 1974. *Language, Religion and Politics in North India*. Cambridge: Cambridge University Press.

Breckenridge, Carol Appadurai (ed.). 1995. *Consuming Modernity: Public Culture in a South Asian World*. Minneapolis: University of Minnesota Press.

Brown, Judith. 1978. 'War and the Colonial Relationship: Britain, India and the War of 1914–18', in Ellinwood and Pradhan (eds), 1978, 19–48.

Bublitz, Hannelore et al. (eds) 1999. *Das Wuchern der Diskurse: Perspektiven der Diskursanalyse Foucaults*. Frankfurt: Campus.

Bukhārī, Muḥammad Akbar Shāh. 1988. *Akābir 'ulamā-yi Dēoband* (Urdu: The Outstanding Scholars of Deoband). Lahore: Idāra-i Islāmīyat.

Burke, Edmund and Ira M. Lapidus (eds). 1988. *Islam, Politics, and Social Movements*. Berkeley, CA: University of California Press.

Calhoun, Craig (ed.). 1992. *Habermas and the Public Sphere*. Cambridge, MA: MIT Press.

Chandra, Bipan. 1988. *Indian National Movement: The Long-Term Dynamics*. 2 vols. Delhi: Vikas.

Clark, Wayne. 2000. *Activism in the Public Sphere: Exploring the Discourse of Political Participation*. Aldershot: Ashgate.

Crook, Nigel (ed.). 1996. *The Transmission of Knowledge in South Asia: Essays on Education and the Media*. New Delhi: Oxford University Press.

Cumming, John (ed.). 1932. *Political India 1832–1932: A Co-operative Survey of a Century*. London: Oxford University Press.

Dallal, Ahmad. 1993. 'The Origins and Objectives of Islamic Revivalist Thought, 1750–1850.' *Journal of the American Oriental Society*, 113 (3): 341–59.

Douglas, Ian Henderson. 1988. *Abul Kalam Azad: An Intellectual and Religious Biography*. New Delhi: Oxford University Press.

Eaton, Richard M. 1985. 'Approaches to the Study of Conversion to Islam in India', in Martin (ed.), 1985, pp. 106–23.

Edgell, Stephen (ed.). 1995. *Debating the Future of the Public Sphere: Transforming the Public and Private Domains in Free Market Societies*. Aldershot: Avebury.

Edwards, David B. 1993. 'Print, Politics, and Religious Ideology in Afghanistan.' *The Journal of Asian Studies*, 52 (3): 99ff.

Eickelman, Dale F. and Jon W. Anderson (eds). 1999. *New Media in the Muslim World: The Emerging Public Sphere*. Minneapolis: Indiana University Press.

Eisenstadt, Shmuel N. 2000. 'Fundamentalist Movements in the Framework of Multiple Modernities' in Höfert and Salvatore (eds), 2000, pp. 175–97.

Eley, Geoff. 1992. 'Nations, Publics and Political Cultures', in Calhoun (ed.), 1992, pp. 289–339.

Ellinwood, DeWitt C. and S. D. Pradhan (eds). 1978. *India and World War I*. New Delhi: Manohar.

Eminent Mussalmans. 1981 (1926). Biographical and critical sketches of statesmen, poets, reformers, jurists and politicians. Delhi: Neeraj.

Encyclopaedia of Islam. 1986 ff. New Edition, 11 vols. Leiden: Brill. (Quoted as: EI/[volume].)

Engineer, Asghar Ali (ed.). 1987. *The Shah Bano Controversy*. Hyderabad: Orient Longman.

Esposito, John L. (ed.). 1983. *Voices of Resurgent Islam*. New York, Oxford: Oxford University Press.

———. 2000. *Islam and Civil Society*. Badia Fiesolana: European University Institute.

Ewing, Katherine. 1983. 'The Politics of Sufism: Redefining the Saints of Pakistan.' *The Journal of Asian Studies*, 42 (2): 251–68.

——— (ed.). 1988. *Shari'at and Ambiguity in South Asian Islam*. Berkeley, CA: University of California Press.

Farūqī, Ẓīyau'l-Ḥasan. 1988. *Shahīd-e Justijū* (Urdu: Martyr of the Search [of Knowledge?]). Delhi: Maktaba-i Jām'iya.

——. 1996, 'Tadhkirah: Azad's Vindication of Truth.' *Islam and the Modern Age*, 27 (1): 5–16.

Faust, Elke. 2001. 'Die *Jama'at at-Tablīgh* als Teil und Gegenstück der politischen islamischen Bewegung. Untersuchungen in Marokko' in Reetz (ed.), 2001a, pp. 55–78.

Firestone, Reuven. 1999. *The Origin of Holy War in Islam*. New York: Oxford University Press.

Fischer-Tiné, Harald. 2003. *Der Gurukul Kangri oder die Erziehung der Arya-Nation. Kolonialismus, Hindureform und 'Nationale Bildung' in Britisch-Indien (1897–1922)*. Würzburg: Ergon.

——. 2001. 'Character-Building and Manly Games: Viktorianische Konzepte von Männlichkeit und ihre Aneignung in der Ideologie des frühen Hindu-Nationalismus in Britisch-Indien.' *Historische Anthropologie*, 9 (3): 432–56.

Flynn, Barbara W. 1981. 'Cows and Music—Hindu-Muslim Riots as an Instrument of Political Mobilisation', in Robert I. Crane and Bradford Spangenberg (eds), *Language and Society in Modern India: Essays in Honour of Professor Robert O. Swan*, pp. 39–54. Delhi: Heritage Publishers.

Freitag, Sandria. 1988. 'The Roots of Muslim Separation in South Asia: Personal Practice and Public Structures in Kanpur and Bombay', in Burke and Lapidus (eds), 1988, pp. 115–45.

——. 1990 (1989). *Collective Action and Community: Public Arenas and the Emergence of Communalism in North India*. New Delhi: Oxford University Press.

Freitag, Ulrike. 'Clubs, Schulen und Presse: Formen und Inhalte des hadramischen Reformdiskurses in Südostasien und im Südjemen (c. 1900–1930)' in Rothermund (ed.), 1999, pp. 63–84.

Friedmann, Yohanan. 1971. *Shaykh Ahmad Sirhindi: Outline of his Thought and a Study of his Image in the Eyes of Posterity*. Montreal: McGill University Press.

——. 1989. *Prophecy Continuous: Aspects of Ahmadi Religious Thought and its Medieval Background*. Berkeley: University of California Press.

Foucault, Michel. 1970 (1966). *The Order of Things* (*Les Mots et Les Choses*). London: Tavistock.

——. 1972 (1969). *The Archaeology of Knowledge* (*L'Archéologie du Savoir*). London: Tavistock.

Fuchs-Heinritz, Werner, Rüdiger Lautmann, Otthein Ranstedt, and Hann Wienold (eds). 1994. *Lexikon zur Soziologie*. Opladen: Westdeutscher Verlag (3rd edn).

Fusfeld, Warren Edward. 1981. 'The Shaping of Sufi Leadership in Delhi: The Naqshbandiyya Mujaddidiyya, 1750 to 1920.' Ph.D. dissertation. Philadelphia: University of Pennsylvania.

Gaborieau, Marc. 1986. 'Les Ordres Mystiques dans le Sous-continent Indien: Un Point de Vue Ethnologique', in Alexandre Popovic and Gilles Veinstein (eds), *Les Ordres Mystiques dans l'Islam: Cheminements et Situation Actuelle*, pp. 105–34. Paris : EHESS.

——. 2000, 'Le Mahdi Oublié de l'Inde Britannique: Sayyid Ahmad Barelwi (1786–1831), ses Disciples, ses Adversaires', in Mercedes García-Arenal (ed.), *Mahdisme et Millénarisme en Islam*, pp. 257–73. Aix-en Provence: Edisud.

Gangōhī, Rashīd Aḥmad. n.d. *Fatāwā-i Rashīdīya*. Dēoband: Muhammad Ishaq & Sons (Various editions.)

Gani, Haji A. 1988. *Reform of Muslim Personal Law: The Shah Bano Controversy and the Muslim Women (Protection of Rights on Divorce) Act, 1986*. Delhi: Deep & Deep.

Geertz, Clifford. 1971. *Islam Observed*. Chicago: University of Chicago Press.

Gilmartin, David. 1988. 'The Shahidganj Mosque Incident: A Prelude to Pakistan', in Burke and Lapidus (eds), 1988, pp. 146–68.

——. 'Religious Leadership and the Pakistan Movement', in Hasan (ed.), 1993, pp. 196–229.

Graham, William A. 1987. *Beyond the Written Word: Oral Aspects of Scripture in the History of Religion*. Cambridge: Cambridge University Press.

Grandin, Nicole and Marc Gaborieau (eds). 1997. *Madrasa: La Transmission du Savoir dans le Monde Musulman*. Paris: Édition Arguments.

Habermas, Jürgen. 1987 (1984). *Theory of Communicative Action*. Vol. 1: *Reason and the Rationalization of Society*; Vol. 2: *Lifeworld and System: A Critique of Functionalist Reason*. Cambridge: Polity Press. (In German: *Theorie des Kommunikativen Handelns* [Vol. 1: *Handlungsrationalität und Gesellschaftliche Rationalisierung*; Vol. 2: *Zur Kritik der Funktionalistischen Vernunft*]. Frankfurt: Suhrkamp, 1981.)

——. 1990 (1962). *Strukturwandel der Öffentlichkeit: Untersuchungen zu einer Kategorie der bürgerlichen Gesellschaft*. Frankfurt: Suhrkamp.

——. 1992. 'Further Reflections on the Public Sphere', in Calhoun (ed.), 1992, pp. 421–61.

——. 1998 (1989). *The Structural Transformation of the Public Sphere: An Inquiry into a Category of Bourgeois Society*. Cambridge: MIT Press.

Haddad, Yvonne Y. 1983. 'Sayyid Qutb: Ideologue of Islamic Revival', in Esposito (ed.), 1983, pp. 67–98.

Halbach, Uwe. 1991. *Islam, Nation und Politische Öffentlichkeit in den Zentralasiatischen (Unions-) Republiken*. Köln: Bundesinstitut für Ostwissenschaftliche und Internationale Studien (BIOst).

Hamidullah, Muhammad. 1968. *The First Written Constitution in the World: An Important Document of the Time of the Holy Prophet*. Lahore: Ashraf.

Haq, M. Anwarul. 1972. *The Faith Movement of Mawlana Muhammad Ilyas*. London: Allen & Unwin.

Haq, Mushirul. 1995. *Shah Abdul Aziz, His Life and Time: A Study of India Muslims' Attitude to the British in the Early 19th Century*. Lahore: Institute of Islamic Culture.

Hardy, Peter. 1971. *Partners in Freedom—and True Muslims: The Political Thought of Some Muslim Scholars in British India 1912–1947*. Lund: Studentlitteratur.

——. 1998 (1972). *The Muslims of British India*. Cambridge: Cambridge University Press.

Ḥasan, Maḥmūd al-. 1921. *Fatwā Shaykhul-Hind Ḥaẓrat Maulānā Maḥmūd al-Ḥasan Ṣāḥib muta'liq taḥrīk-e tark-e muwālāt* (Urdu: Decrees [from Qur'an] in Support of Non-Cooperation with the Enemies of Islam). Vainyambadi: Khilafat Committee.

Hasan, Mushirul (ed.). 1985. *Communal and Pan-Islamic Trends in Colonial India*. New Delhi: Manohar.

——. (ed.). 1993. *India's Partition: Process, Strategy and Mobilisation*. New Delhi: Oxford University Press.

——. 1995. 'Muslim Intellectuals, Institutions, and the Post-Colonial Predicament.' *India International Centre Quarterly* (Spring): 100–22.

——. 1997. *Legacy of a Divided Nation: India's Muslims Since Independence*. London: Hurst & Company.

—— (ed.). 1998a. *Knowledge, Power and Politics: Educational Institutions in India*. Delhi: Lotus.

—— (ed.). 1998b. *Islam, Communities and the Nation: Muslim Identities in South Asia and Beyond*. New Delhi: Manohar.

——. 2002. *Islam in the Subcontinent: Muslims in a Plural Society*. New Delhi: Manohar.

Ḥasanī, Muḥammad al-. 1964. *Sīrat-e Maulānā Muḥammad 'Alī Monghīrī* (Urdu: The Life of Maulānā Muḥammad 'Alī Monghīrī). Lucknow: Shahi Press.

Hashmi, Syed Masroor Ali Akhtar. 1989. *Muslim Response to Western Education: A Study of Four Pioneer Institutions*. Delhi: Commonwealth.

Haykel, Bernard. 1997. *Order and Righteousness: Muhammad Ali al-Shawkani and the Nature of the Islamic State in Yemen*. Oxford: University of Oxford.

Hegasy, Sonja. 1997. *Staat, Öffentlichkeit und Zivilgesellschaft in Marokko*. Hamburg: Deutsches Orient-Institut.

Heming, Ralf. 1997. *Öffentlichkeit, Diskurs und Gesellschaft: Zum Analytischen Potential und zur Kritik des Begriffs der Öffentlichkeit bei Habermas*. Wiesbaden: Deutscher Universitäts-Verlag.

Hermansen, Marcia. 2001. 'Common Themes, Uncommon Contexts: The Sufi Movements of Khwaja Hasan Nizami (1878–1955) and Hazrat Inayat Khan (1882–1927)', in Pirzade Zia Inayat Khan (ed.), *A Pearl in Wine: Essays on the Life, Music and Sufism of Hazrat Inayat Khan*, pp. 323–53. New Lebanon, NY: Omega Publications.

Herzog, Christoph. 1999. 'Die Entwicklung der türkisch-muslimischen Presse im Osmanischen Reich bis ca. 1875', in Rothermund (ed.), 1999, pp. 15–44

Höfert, Almut and Armando Salvatore (eds). 2000. *Between Europe and Islam: Shaping Modernity in a Transcultural Space*. Bruxelles: PIE Lang.

Höpp, Gerhard and Brigitte Reinwald (eds). 2000. *Fremdeinsätze: Afrikaner und Asiaten in Europäischen Kriegen, 1914–1945*. Berlin: Das Arabische Buch.

Hog, Michael. 1990. *Ethnologie und Öffentlichkeit: Ein Entwicklungsgeschichtlicher Überblick*. Frankfurt: P. Lang.

Hohendahl, Peter U. (ed). 2000. *Öffentlichkeit: Geschichte eines Kritischen Begriffs*. Stuttgart: Metzler.

Hoodbhoy, Pervez. 1991. *Islam and Science: Religious Orthodoxy and the Battle for Rationality*. London: Zed Books.

Hunter, William W. 1969 (1871). *The Indian Musalmans* (Our Indian Mussalmans: Are They Bound in Conscience to Rebel Against the Queen?). Delhi: Indological Book House.

IAR [year/volume], *see* Mitra and Mitra. 1988.

Ibrahim, Ferhad and Mir A. Ferdowsi (eds). 1992. *Die Kuwait-Krise und das Regionale Umfeld: Hintergründe, Interessen, Ziele*. Berlin: Das Arabische Buch.

Ikrām, Shaykh Muḥammad. 1958. *Āb-i kauthar, Rūd-i kauthar, Mauj-i kauthar* (Urdu: The Waters, the Stream, the Waves of Kausar [that is, a spring in paradise], 3 vols. Lahore: FerozSons (numerous editions).

Ilyās, Muḥammad. 1997 (1980). *Irshādāt wa Maktūbāt* (Urdu: Letters of Instruction, Compiled by Iftikhār Ḥusain Farīdī). Lahore: Urdū Bāzār (numerous editions).

Ilyās M [number], *see* Nu'mānī 1993.

IMDR /[volume], *see* Muhammad, Shan (ed.) 1980.

'Ināyatullāh, Maulānā Muftī. 1988 (1930). *'Ulamā'-i Firangī Maḥall: Mabnī bar Taḏkira-i 'Ulamā'-i Firangī Maḥall*. Lucknow: Muḥammad Shahīd Anṣārī—Idāra-i Farogh-i Urdū.

India Office Library and Records. 1976. *Catalogue of Proscribed Urdu Publications in the India Office Library* (Cyclostyled). London: India Office Library and Records.

Iqbal, Afzal. 1974. *Life and Times of Mohammad Ali: An Analysis of the Hopes, Fears and Aspirations of Muslim India from 1778 to 1931*. Lahore: Institute of Islamic Culture.

Iqbal, Muhammad. 1930. *Six Lectures on the Reconstruction of Religious Thought in Islam*. Lahore: Kapur Art Printing Works.

——. 1987. *The Muslim Community: A Sociological Study* (edited by Muzaffar Abbas). Lahore: Maktaba-e 'Aliya.

——. 1995. *Islam and Ahmadism. A Reply to Questions Raised by Pandit Jawahar Lal Nehru* (edited by Zafarul Islam Khan). Delhi: Medie & Publ.

ISC 1930/[Vol.]. *See* United Kingdom. Indian Statutory Commission. 1930. Under Official Publications—Other.

Jain, Naresh Kumar (ed.). 1979. *Muslims in India: A Biographical Dictionary*. 2 vols. New Delhi: Manohar.

Jalal, Ayesha. 1994. *The Sole Spokesman: Jinnah, the Muslim League and the Demand for Pakistan*. Cambridge: Cambridge University Press.

Jalīs Nadwī, Muḥammad Isḥāq, and Maulwī Shams Tabrīz Khān. 1983. *Tārīkh-i Nadwatu'l 'ulamā'* (Urdu: History of the Council of Religious Scholars—Nadwat al-'ulamā'). 2 vols. Lucknow: Maktaba Dār al-'Ulūm Nadwat al-'Ulamā'.

Jam'īyat-i Ahl-i Sunnat (Pakistan). 1989. *Rasā'il-i Ahl-i Ḥadīth* (Urdu: Compilation of Ahl-i Ḥadīth's Literature by Barelwi Scholars). Lahore.

Jinnah, Muhammad Ali. 1976. *Speeches as Governor-General of Pakistan 1947–1948*. Islamabad: Government of Pakistan.

——. 1994. *Quaid-i-Azam Mohammad Ali Jinnah Papers* (Jinnah Papers, edited by Z.H. Zaidi). Vol. I, parts I, II: Prelude to Pakistan, 20 February–2 June

1947; Vol. II: Pakistan in the Making, 3 June–30 June 1947. Islamabad: National Archives of Pakistan. (Quoted as Jinnah papers + vol. + part.)

Jones, Kenneth W. 1976. *Arya Dharm: Hindu Consciousness in 19th-Century Punjab*. Berkeley: University of California Press.

____. 1981. 'Religious Identity and the Indian Census', in Barrier (ed.), 1981, pp. 73–101.

____. 1989. *Socio-Religious Reform Movements in British India* (The New Cambridge History of India, III.1). Cambridge: Cambridge University Press.

____ (ed). 1991. *Religious Controversy in British India: Dialogues in South Asian Languages*. Albany, NY: State University of New York.

Jordens, J. T. F. 1981. *Swami Shraddhananda, His Life and Causes*. New Delhi: Oxford University Press.

Katju, Manjari. 2003. *Vishva Hindu Parishad and Indian Politics*. Delhi: Orient Longman.

Kaye, Lt. Col. Sir Cecil. 1926. *Communism in India*. Delhi: Government Press.

Keddie, Nikki R. 1994. 'The Revolt of Islam, 1700 to 1993: Comparative Considerations and Relations to Imperialism.' *Comparative Studies in Society and History*, 36: 463–87.

Kemper, Michael (ed.). 2000. *Islamische Bildungsnetzwerke im Lokalen und Transnationalen Kontext: Laufende Forschungsarbeiten der Nachwuchsgruppe (Volkswagen-Stiftung) am Seminar für Orientalistik und Indologie der Ruhr-Universität Bochum*. Bochum: Ruhr-Universität.

Kepel, Gilles. 1984. *Le Prophète et Pharaon: Les Mouvements Islamistes dans l'Egypte Contemporaine*. Paris: La Découverte.

Khalilzad, Zalmay. 1985. 'The Politics of Ethnicity in Southwest Asia: Political Development or Political Decay?' *Political Science Quarterly*, 99 (4): 657–79.

Khan, Abdul Rashid. 2001. *The All-India Muslim Educational Conference: Its Contribution to the Cultural Development of Indian Muslims 1886–1947*. New Delhi: Oxford University Press.

Khan, Aga. 1954. *The Memoirs of Aga Khan*. London: Cassell.

Khān, H. B. 1995a. *Taḥrīk-i Pākistān meñ 'ulamā' ka siāsī-o-'ilmī kardār* (Urdu: The Role of the 'Ulamā' in the Pakistan Movement in Politics and as Scholars). Nazimabad: Alhamd Academy.

____. 1995b. *Eighth Amendment: Constitutional and Political Crises in Pakistan*. Lahore: Rana Hameed Law Book House (2nd edn).

Khān, Iqtidār Muḥammad. 1995. *1947 kē ba'd Hindūstān Meñ Islāmī Taḥrikeñ* (Urdu: Islamic Movements in India after 1947). Rampur.

Khan, Mofakhkhar Hussain. 1993 (–94). 'An Early History of Urdu Translations of the Holy Qur'an—A Bio-bibliographic Study.' *The Islamic Quarterly*, 40 (4); 41 (1).

Khan, Shaharyar M. 2000. *The Begums of Bhopal: A Dynasty of Women Rulers in Raj India*. London: Tauris.

Kitchlew, Taufiq. 1987. *Saifuddin Kitchlew: Hero of Jallianwala Bagh*. Delhi: National Book Trust.

Kozlowski, Gregory. 1985. *Muslim Endowments and Sociey in British India*. Cambridge: Cambridge University Press.

Kuwajima, Sho. 1998. *Muslims, Nationalism and the Partition: 1946 Provincial Elections in India*. New Delhi: Manohar.

Landau, Jacob M. 1990. *The Politics of Pan-Islam: Ideology and Organization*. Oxford: Clarendon.

Lang, Sabine. 2001. *Politische Öffentlichkeit im Modernen Staat: Eine Bürgerliche Institution Zwischen Demokratisierung und Disziplinierung*. Baden-Baden: Nomos.

Lavan, Spencer. 1972. 'Polemics and Conflict in Ahmadiyya History: The '*Ulama*', the missionaries, and the British (1898).' *Muslim World*, (62) 4: 283–303.

____. 1976. *The Ahmadiyah Movement: Past and Present*. Amritsar: Department of History, Guru Nanak Dev University.

Lelyveld, David. 1996 (1978). *Aligarh's First Generation*. New Delhi: Oxford University Press.

Levtzion, Nehemia and John Obert Voll (eds). 1987. *Eighteenth-Century Renewal and Reform in Islam*. Syracuse, NY: Syracuse University Press.

Lia, Brynjar. 1998. *The Society of the Muslim Brothers in Egypt: The Rise of an Islamic Mass Movement 1928–1942*. Reading: Ithaca-Press.

Lorey, Isabell. 1999. 'Macht und Diskurs bei Foucault', in Hannelore Bublitz, et al. (eds), 1999, pp. 87–96.

Ludden, David (ed). 1996. *Making India Hindu: Religion, Community and the Politics of Democracy in India*. New Delhi: Oxford University Press.

Ludhīyānwī, Muḥammad Yusūf. n.d. '*Aṣr-yi ḥāẓir aḥādīth-i nabwī kē ā'īnē meñ* (Urdu: The Modern Age in the Mirror of Prophet Muhammad's Traditions). Karachi: Maktaba-i Baiyānāt.

Madanī, Sayyid Ḥusain Aḥmad. 1927. *Tablīghī Taqrīreñ* (Urdu: Speeches on Religious Propaganda). Delhi: Rabbānī Book Depot.

____. 1972 (1939). *Muttaḥida qaumīyat aur Islām* (Urdu: Composite Nationalism and Islam). Delhi.

____. 1974. *Safarnāmah Shaykh al-Hind* (Urdu: Travelogue of the Shaykh al-Hind). Lahore: Maktaba Majmudīyā.

Mahr, Ghulām Rasūl. 1954. *Sayyid Aḥmad Shahīd* (Urdu: Sayyid Ahmad, the Martyr). Lahore: Shaykh Ghulām.

____. 1955. *Jamā'at-i mujāhidīn* (Urdu: The Party of the Mujāhidīn). Lahore: Shaykh Ghulām.

____. 1956. *Sarguzasht-i mujāhidīn* (Urdu: Account of the Movement of the Mujāhidīn). Lahore: Shaykh Ghulām.

Majumdar, R. C. 1962 (–63). *History of the Freedom Movement in India*. 3 vols. Calcutta: Mukhopadhyay.

Malīḥābādī, 'Abdúr-Razzāq. 1960. *Ẕikr-e-Āzād: Maulānā Abū'l Kalām Āzād kī Rafāqat meñ Artīs Sāl* (Urdu: In Memory of Azad: A Companion of Maulana Azad of 38 Years). Kolkata: Daftar-i Āzād Hind.

Malīḥābādī, Sayyid Amīr 'Alī. 1977 (–78). *Tafsīr mawāhibu'r-raḥmān, al-ma'rūf bah, Jāmi'u'l-bayān* (Arabic: Commentary on God's Gifts, Known as Universal Explanation). Lahore: Maktaba-yi Rashīdīya.

Malik, Iftikhar H. 1998. 'Islamic Discourse on Jihad, War and Violence.' *Journal of South Asian and Middle Eastern Studies*, 21 (4): 47–78.

Malik, Jamal. 1989. *Islamisierung in Pakistan 1977–1984: Untersuchungen zur Auflösung Autochthoner Strukturen*. Stuttgart: Franz Steiner.

——. 1996. *Colonialisation of Islam: Dissolution of Traditional Institutions in Pakistan*. New Delhi: Manohar.

——. 1997. *Islamische Gelehrtenkultur in Nordindien: Entwicklungsgeschichte und Tendenzen am Beispiel von Lucknow*. Leiden: Brill.

Malik, Muhammad Aslam. 2000. *Allama Inayatullah Mashraqi: A Political Biography*. Karachi: Oxford University Press.

Manek, M. D. 1961 (1932). *Handbook of Mahomedan Law (Muslim Personal Law)*. Bombay: N. M. Tripathi (6th edn).

Marshall, Gordon (ed). 1994. *The Concise Oxford Dictionary of Sociology*. Oxford: Oxford University Press.

Martin, Richard C. (ed). 1985. *Approaches to Islam in Religious Studies*. Tuscon: University of Arizona Press.

Martyn, John R. C. 1999. Henry Martyn (1781–1812), *Scholar and Missionary to India and Persia: A Biography*. Lewiston, N.Y.: E. Mellen Press.

Mashriqī, 'Ināyatullāh Khān. 1931. *Ishārāt, ya'nī musalmānon kō phir ṯāqatwar banādēne kā wāḥid ṯarīqa aur khāksāroñ kī taḥrīk kī tashrīḥ* (Urdu: Directions, Or the Only Way to Make Muslims Stronger and the Explanation of the Movement of the Khāksār). Lahore: Manzūr-i 'ām Barqī Press.

——. 1972 (1924). *Taḏkira* (Urdu: Treatise). Vol. 1. Amritsar.

——. 1987. *Quran and Evolution*. Islamabad: El-Mashriqi Foundation.

——. 1995. *Khuṭbāt wa Maqālāt* (Urdu: Speeches and Writings.) Lahore: al-Faiṣal.

Masud, Muhammad Khalid. 1995. *Iqbal's Reconstruction of Ijtihad*. Lahore: Iqbal Academy Pakistan.

——, Brinkley Messik, and David S. Powers (eds). 1996. *Islamic Legal Interpretation: Muftis and their Fatwas*. Cambridge, MA: Harvard University Press.

—— (ed.). 2000. *Travellers in Faith: Studies of Tablīghī Jamā'at as a Transnational Movement for Faith Renewal*. Leiden: Brill.

Mathur, Yaduvansh Bahadur. 1968. 'Tanzim and Tabligh Movements in Modern India: Before its Partition into Pakistan and India.' *The Islamic Review & Arab Affairs*, 56 (11–12): 22–4.

——. 1969. 'The Khaksar Movement.' *Studies in Islam* (January): 27–62.

——. 1972. *Muslims and Changing India*. Delhi: Trimurti Publications.

Maudūdī, Sayyid Abū'l-A'lā. 1958 (–71). *Tafhīm al-Qur'ān* (Urdu/Arabic: The Meaning of the Qur'an).

——. 1989. *Tajdīd wa iḥyā-i dīn* (Urdu: The Renewal and Revival of Religion). Lahore: Islamic Publications.

—— et al. 1990 (1960?). *Da'wat-i Islāmī aur us kē mutālibāt* (Urdu: The Renewal of Islam and its Requirements). Lahore: Islamic Publications.

Mayaram, Shail. 1997. *Resisting Regimes: Myth, Memory and the Shaping of a Muslim Identity*. New Delhi: Oxford University Press.

Mehra, Parshotam. 1987. *A Dictionary of Modern Indian History 1707–1947*. New Delhi: Oxford University Press.

Melton, James van Horn. 2001. *The Rise of the Public in Enlightenment Europe*. Cambridge: Cambridge University Press.

Metcalf, Barbara Daly. 1982. *Islamic Revival in British India: Deoband, 1860–1900*. Princeton: Princeton University Press.

____ (ed.). 1984. *Moral Conduct and Authority: The Place of ADAB in South Asian Islam*. Berkeley: University of California.

____. 1992 (1990). *Perfecting Women: Maulana Ashraf Ali Thanawi's Bihishti Zewar* (A Partial Translation with Commentary). New Delhi: Oxford University Press.

____. 1996. 'Meandering Madrasas: Knowledge and Short-term Itinerancy in the *Tablīghi Jamā'at*', in Crook (ed.), 1996, pp. __.

Milner, Anthony. 1994. *The Invention of Politics in Malaya: Contesting Nationalism and the Expansion of the Public Sphere*. Cambridge: Cambridge University Press.

Minault, Gail. 1982. *The Khilafat Movement: Religious Symbolism and Political Mobilisation in India*. New York: Columbia University Press.

Minto, Mary. 1934. *India, Minto and Morley, 1905–1910*. London: Macmillan.

Mirzā, Janbāz. 1970: *Ḥayāt-i Amīr-i Sharī'at* (Urdu: The Life of the Amīr-i Sharī'at [Bukhari]). Lahore: Maktaba-e Tabṣira.

____. 1975. *Karwān-i Aḥrār* (Urdu: The Caravan of the Free). 8 vols. Lahore: Maktaba-e Tabṣira.

Miṣbāḥī, Maulānā Yasīn Akhtar (ed.). 1976. *Imām Aḥmad Raẓā Arbāb-i 'ilm-o-dānish kī Naẓr meñ* (Urdu: Ahmad Raza in the Eyes of Leading Scholars and Intellectuals). Karachi: al-Mujaddid Aḥmad Raẓā Akaidemi—Maktaba Riẓwīya Ārām Bāgh.

Mishra, Vibhuti Bhushan. 1987. *Evolution of the Constitutional History of India (1773–1947) with Special Reference to the Role of the INC and the Minorities*. Delhi: Mittal Publications.

Mitra, H. N. and N. N. Mitra (eds). 1988. *The Indian Annual Register 1919–1947*. 58 vols (reprint). Delhi: Gian. (Quoted as: *IAR* + part + subject year.)

Miyān, Muḥammad. 1976. *Asīrān-i Māltā* (Urdu: Interned on Malta). Delhi: Al-Jam'īyat Book Depot.

____. 1988. *Taḥrīk-e Shaykh al-Hind* (Urdu: Movement of the Shaykh of India). Karachi: Maktaba-e Rashīdīya.

Moḥsinī, Shamsur Raḥmān. 1986. *Hindustāni musulmānoñ kī qaumī ta'līmī tahrīk: Jāmi'a Millīya Islāmīya* (Urdu: Movement for National Education—Jamia Millia Islamia). Delhi: Maktaba-e Jāmi'a.

Moin, Mumtaz. 1976. *The Aligarh Movement: Origin and History*. Karachi: Salman Academy.

Moussalli, Ahmad S. 1992. *Radical Islamic Fundamentalism: The Ideological and Political Discourse of Sayyid Qutb*. Beirut: American University of Beirut.

Muhammad, Shan (ed). 1980. *The Indian Muslims: A Documentary Record, 1900–1947*. 10 vols. Meerut: Meenakshi Prakashan. (Quoted as: IMDR /[volume].)

Muir, William. 1858. *The Life of Mahomet and History of Islam*. London: Smith.

Mujeeb, M. 1967. *The Indian Muslims*. Montreal: McGill University Press.

Mulder, Niels. 1994. *Philippine Public Space and Public Sphere*. Bielefeld: University of Bielefeld.

Munir, Muhammad. 1954. *Report of the Court of Inquiry Constituted under Punjab*

Act II of 1954 to Enquire into the Punjab Disturbances of 1953. Lahore: Supt., Govt. Print., Punjab.

Murshid, Tazeen. 1995. *The Sacred and the Secular: Bengal Muslim Discourses*. Oxford: Oxford University Press.

Muttaqī, 'Abd al-Malik. 1895. *Kanz al-'ummāl* (Arabic). Hyderabad, 1895–97.

Muẓẓatar, A. D. 1985. *Khāksār taḥrīk aor Āzādī-i Hind: Dastawēzāt* (Urdu: The Khāksār Movement and India's Independence: Documents). Islamabad: National Institute of Historical and Cultural Research.

Nadvi, Syed Habibul Haq. 1986. 'The Role of Resurgent 'Ulama' and Sufi-Shaykhs in the Reconstruction of Islamic Education: Foundation of Deoband (1867) and *Nadwa* (1893).' *Muslim Education Quarterly*, 2 (3): 37–56.

Nadwī, 'Abd al-Mubīn. 1988a. *Maulānā Thanā'ullāh Amritsarī* (Urdu). Gujranwālā: Nadwat al-Muḥaddithīn.

Nadwi, Sayyid Abu'l-Hasan Ali. 1979 (1963). *Western Civilisation—Islam and Muslims* (Translation from the Arabic). Lucknow: Academy of Islamic Research and Publications Nadwatúl-'ulamā'.

——. 1980 (1946). *Religion and Civilisation* (Translation of '*Mazhab-o-Tammadun*', 1943). Lucknow: Academy of Islamic Research and Publications, Nadwatu'l-'ulamā'.

——. 1982 (1952). *Makātīb, Ḥazrat Maulānā Shāh Muḥammad Ilyās* (Urdu: Letters by Ilyas). Karachi: Dāru'l-Ishā'at (3rd edn).

——. 1983. *Life and Mission of Maulana Mohammad Ilyas* (Translation of '*Muḥammad Ilyās aur Unkī Dīnī Da'wat*', 1946). Lucknow: Academy of Islamic Research and Publications, Nadwatu'l-'ulamā (2nd edn).

——. 1984. *Tārīkh-i Da'wat wa 'Azimat ya'nī 'ālam-i Islām kī iṣlāḥī wa tajdīdī kōshish kā tarīkhī jaizā* (Urdu: The History of the Propagation and Greatness of Islam, that is, a Historical Analysis of Efforts for Reform and Renewal in the Islamic World). 6 vols. Karachi.

——. 1988b. *Ḥayāt-e 'Abdul-Ḥa'ī* (Urdu: The Life of Abdul Hayy). Pune: Ūrdū-Marathī Prakashan.

Nadwī, Sayyid Sulaimān. 1943. *Ḥayāt-i Shiblī* (Urdu: The Life of Shibli). Azamgarh: Maṭba'a Ma'ārif.

Naregal, Veena. 2001. *Language Politics, Elites, and the Public Sphere*. Delhi: Permanent Black.

Nasr, Seyyed Vali Reza. 1994. *The Vanguard of the Islamic Revolution: The Jamā'at-i Islāmī of Pakistan*. Berkeley, CA: University of California Press.

——. 1996. *Mawdudi and the Making of Islamic Revivalism*. New York, Oxford: Oxford University Press.

——. 2000. 'The Rise of Sunni Militancy in Pakistan: The Changing Role of Islamism and the Ulama in Society and Politics.' *Modern Asian Studies*, 34 (1): 139–80.

Nausharwī, Abū Yaḥyā Imām Khān. 1970 (1937). *Hindustān meñ Ahl-i Ḥadīth kī 'ilmī khidmat* (Urdu: Contribution by the Ahl-i Ḥadīth to (Religious) Knowledge in India). Chicha Watni: Maktaba-yi Nazīrīya.

——. 1971 (1938). *Tarājim-i 'Ulamā'-yi Ḥadīth-i Hind: Mushtāmilbar Tarājim-i Khandān-i Walīullāhī Dihlī wa 'Ulamā'-yi Dihlī wa Sūbā-yi Yū. Pī.* (Urdu:

Dictionary of the Scholars of Tradition in India: Covering the Family of Waliullah of Delhi and the Scholars of Delhi and the Province of UP). Lahore: Markazī Jam'īyat-i Talabā-i Ahl-i Ḥadith.

Nayyar, A. H. 1998. 'Madrasah Education Frozen in Time,' in Pervez Hoodbhoy (ed.), *Fifty Years of Pakistan: Education and the States*, pp. 215–50. Karachi: Oxford University Press.

Naẕīr Ḥusain, Sayyid. 1971 (1913). *Fatāwā-yi Naẕīrīya.* (Urdu: [Collection of] Religious Rulings by Nazir [Husain]). 3 vols. Lahore: Ahl-i Ḥadīth Akādemī, Kashmīrī Bazār.

Niemeyer, A. C. 1972. *The Khilafat Movement in India 1919–1924*. The Hague: Nijhoff.

Nizami, Khaliq Ahmad. 1995. *History of the Aligarh Muslim University*. Vol. 1: 1920–1945. Delhi: Idara-i Adabiyyat-i Dilli.

Niẕāmī, Khwāja Ḥasan. 1913. *Kānpūr kī Khūnī Dāstān* (Urdu: The Bloody Story of Kanpur). Meerut: Tauhid Press.

____. 1923. *Dā'ī Islām* (Urdu: The Preacher of Islam).

Norton, Augustus Richard (ed). 1995. *Civil Society in the Middle East*. Leiden: Brill.

Nu'mānī, Muḥammad Manẕur. 1993 (1950). *Malfūẕāt Shāh Muḥammad Ilyās* (Urdu: Sayings of Muhammad Ilyas). Lucknow: Al-Furqān Book Depot (numerous editions, sayings quoted by their consecutive numbers as: Ilyās M [number]).

Nu'mānī, Shiblī. 1953 (–63). *Sīrāt al-Nabī* (Urdu: Life of the Prophet, with Sulaiman Nadwi). Azamgarh: Matba'-i Ma'ārif.

____. 1965. *Bāqiyāt-i Shiblī* (Urdu: The Legacy of Shibli). Lahore: Majlis-i Taraqqī-i Adab.

Oesterheld, Joachim. 2001. 'Zakir Husain: Begegnungen und Erfahrungen bei der Suche nach moderner Bildung für ein freies Indien', in Petra Heidrich and Heike Liebau (eds), *Akteure des Wandels. Lebensläufe und Gruppenbilder an Schnittstellen von Kulturen*, pp. 105–30. Berlin: Das Arabische Buch.

Orsini, Francesca. 2002. *The Hindi Public Sphere 1920–1940: Language and Literature in the Age of Nationalism*. New Delhi: Oxford University Press.

Pandey, Gyanendra. 1996. *The Construction of Communalism in Colonial North India*. New Delhi: Oxford University Press.

Pati, Budheswar. 1996. *India and the First World War*. Delhi: Atlantic Publication.

Pearson, Harlan Otto. 1979. Islamic Reform And Revival in Nineteenth Century India: The 'Tariqah-i Muhammadiyah.' Ph.D. Dissertation. Durham, NC: Duke University.

Pernau, Margrit. 2000. *The Passing of Patrimonialism: Politics and Political Culture in Hyderabad 1911–48*. New Delhi: Manohar.

Peters, Rudolf. 1979. *Islam and Colonialism: The Doctrine of Jihād in Modern History*. The Hague, Paris: Mouton.

Peycam Philippe Marie, Francois. 1999. Intellectuals and Political Commitment in Vietnam: The Emergence of a Public Sphere in Colonial Saigon (1916–1928).' Ph.D. dissertation, London: University of London.

Piscatori, James (ed.). 1991. *Islamic Fundamentalisms and the Gulf Crisis*. Chicago: American Academy of Arts and Sciences.
Pistor-Hatam, Anja. 1999. 'Die Presse als Instrument der Selbstbehauptung: Persische Kaufleute und ihr Beitrag zur innermuslimischen Modernisierungsdiskussion gegen Ende des 19. Jahrhunderts', in Rothermund (ed.), 1999, pp. 45–62.
Popper, Karl R. 1945. *The Open Society and its Enemies*. 2 vols. London: Routledge.
Poston, Larry. 1992. *Islamic Da'wah in the West: Muslim Missionary Activity and the Dynamics of Conversion to Islam*. New York, Oxford: Oxford University Press.
Pratap, Mahendra. 1947. *My Life Story of Fifty-five Years*. Dehradun.
Preckel, Claudia. 2000. *Begums of Bhopal*. Delhi: Lotus.
Price, Daniel E. 1999. *Islamic Political Culture, Democracy, and Human Rights: A Comparative Study*. Westport, CT: Praeger.
Pylee, M. V. 1967. *Constitutional History of India: 1600–1950*. Bombay: Asia Publishing House.
Qādirī, Arshadul. (1981). *Tablīghī Jamā'at: Ḥaqā'iq wa ma'lūmāt* (Urdu: *The Tablīghī Jamā'at—Facts and Information*). Lahore: Maktaba Nabwiya [n.d.]
Qādirī, Muḥammad Jalāluddīn. 1997 (1978). *Khuṭbāt-i All-India Sunnī Conference: 1925–1947* (Urdu: Presidential Addresses at Annual Sunni Conferences, 1925–1947). Lahore: Islamic Publications.
_____. 1999. *Tārīkh-i All-India Sunnī Conference: 1925–1947* (Urdu: History of All-India Sunni Conference, 1925–1947). Khariyan (Gujarat): Sh'aīd Barādarān.
Qamaruddīn. 1994. *Hindustān kī dīnī darsgāheñ meñ: Kul Hind sarwē* (Urdu: Religious Educational Institutions in India: An All-India Survey.) Delhi: Hamdard Education Society.
Qāsim, Khwāja Muḥammad. 1990. *Tablīghī Jamā'at Apnē Niṣāb kē 'Aināh mēñ* (Urdu: The Tablīghī Jamā'at in the Light of its Preaching Course). Gujranwala: Idāra-yi Iḥyāu'lsunna.
Quddus, Syed Abdul. 1989. *The Challenge of Islamic Renaissance*. Delhi: Atlantic Publication (reprint).
Qureshi, Ishtiaq Husain. 1974. *Ulema in Politics: Activities of the Ulema in the South-Asian Subcontinent*. Karachi: Ma'aref (2nd edn).
Qureshi, M. Naeem. 1999. *Pan-Islam in British Indian Politics: A Study of the Khilafat Movement 1918–1924*. Leiden: Brill.
Raḥmān, Ḥāfiẓ Qārī Feozur-. 1997. *Ḥaẓrat Ḥājjī Imdādullāh Muhājir Makkī aur un kē Khulafā'* (Urdu: Hajji Imdadullah and His Disciples). Karachi: Majlis-e nashrīyāt-e Islām.
Rahmani, Nazir Ahmad. 1972. *Ahl-i Hadith aur Siyasat* (Urdu: The Ahl-i Ḥadīth and Politics). Banares: Al-Jam'īya al-Salafīya.
Ramu, P. S. (ed). 1992. *Khudai Khidmatgar and National Movement: Momentous Speeches of Badshah Khan*. Vol. I. Delhi: SS Publishers.
Rashid, Syed Khalid. 2002. *Awqaf Experiences in South Asia*. Delhi: Institute of Objective Studies.
Raẓā Khān, Aḥmad. 1895. *Anbā al-muṣṭafā be ḥāl i-sar o akhfā* (Urdu: Whether the Highest of All Prophets Can See the Invisible). Lahore: Anjuman Ḥazbul-Eḥnāf.

———. 1905. *Ḥusām al-Ḥaramain 'ala Manhar al-Kufr wa'l Main* (Urdu: The Sword of the Haramain at the Throat of Unbelief and Falsehood). Bareilly.

———. 1921. *Barkāt al-imdād* (Urdu: With the Help of Spiritual Power). Cawnpore: Muḥammad 'Abdul Ḥamīd Fateḥpūrī.

———. 1994. *Fatāwā-i Riẓwīya*. 12 vols. Bombay: Raza Academy.

Redfield, Robert. 1960. *The Little Community; Peasant Society and Culture*. Chicago: Chicago University Press.

Reetz, Dietrich. 1987. 'Besonderheiten der Nationalen Formierung in Nichtsozialistischen Entwicklungsländern am Beispiel Pakistans, 1977–1987.' Ph.D. Dissertation. Berlin: Humboldt-Universität.

———. 1988. 'Enlightenment and Islam: Sayyid Ahmad Khan's Plea to Indian Muslims for Reason.' *The Indian Historical Review*, 14 (1–2): 206–18.

———. 1992. 'Pakistans Engagement in der Golf Region: Islamische Solidarität oder Regionale Machtpolitik?' in Ibrahim and Ferdowsi (eds), 1992, pp. 147–62.

———. 1993. 'Pakistan and the Central Asia Hinterland Option: The Race for Regional Security and Development.' *Journal of South Asian and Middle Eastern Studies*, 17 (1): 28–56.

———. 1995. *Hijrat—The Flight of the Faithful: A British File on the Exodus of Muslim Peasants from North India to Afghanistan in 1920*. Berlin: Das Arabische Buch.

———. 1997. 'In Search of the Collective Self: How Ethnic Group Concepts Were Cast Through Conflict in Colonial India.' *Modern Asian Studies*, 31 (2): 285–315.

———. 1999a. 'Mediating the External: The Changing World and Religious Renewal in Indian Islam', in Katja Füllberg-Stolberg et al. (eds), *Dissociation and Appropriation: Responses to Globalisation in Asia and Africa*, pp. 75–106. Berlin: Das Arabische Buch.

———. 1999b, 'Islamic Activism in Central Asia and the Pakistan Factor.' *Journal of South Asian and Middle Eastern Studies*, 23 (1): 1–37.

——— (ed.). 2001a. *Sendungsbewußtsein oder Eigennutz: Zu Motivation und Selbstverständnis Islamischer Mobilisierung*. Berlin: Das Arabische Buch.

———. 2001b. 'Kenntnisreich und Unerbittlich: Der Sunnitische Radikalismus der *Ahl-i Ḥadīth* in Südasien', in Reetz 2001a, pp. 79–106.

———. 2003. 'Pakistan: Internationaler Partner oder Problemfall?' *FES-Analyse*. Bonn/Berlin: Friedrich-Ebert-Stiftung (http://library.fes.de/fulltext/stabsabteilung/01691.htm).

Rīyāsat 'Alī Riẓwī Barēlwī, Sayyid Muḥammad. 1980. *Muftī-e Ā'ẓam-e Hind* (Urdu: The Great Islamic Jurist of India). Karachi: Idārā-e Ahl-e Sunnat.

Riexinger, Martin. 2004. 'Sana'ullah Amritsari (1868–1948) und die Ahl-i Hadis im Punjab unter britischer Herrschaft': Würzburg: Ergon.

Rittenberg, Stephen. 1988. *Ethnicity, Nationalism, and the Pakhtuns: The Independence Movement in India's North-West Frontier Province*. Durham, NC: Carolina Academic Press.

Rizvi, Sayyid Mahboob. 1980. *History of the Dār al-'Ulūm*. 2 vols. Deoband: Idāra-e Ihtemām. (Quoted as Rizvi 1980/I or 1980/II.)

Rizwī, Sayyid Maḥmūd Aḥmad. 1979. *Sayyidī Abū'l Barkāt* (Urdu: The Noble Father of Blessings [Biography of Didar Ali Shah]). Lahore: Shu'ba-yi Tablīgh Dāru'l-'ulūm Ḥizb-ul-Aḥnāf.

Robinson, Francis. 1994 (1974). *Separatism Among Indian Muslims: The Politics of the United Provinces' Muslims, 1860–1923*. Cambridge: Cambridge University Press.

———. 1996. 'Islam and the Impact of Print in South Asia', in Nigel Crook (ed.), 1996, pp. 62–97.

———. 1997. 'Religious Change and the Self in Muslim South Asia Since 1800.' *South Asia*, 20 (1): 1–15.

———. 2001. *The Ulama of Farangi Mahall and Islamic Culture in South Asia*. Delhi: Permanent Black.

Rogler, Lutz. 2001. 'Zu Erfahrung, Kritik und Selbstkritik im Politischen Selbstverständnis Tunesischer Islamisten', in Reetz (ed.), 2001a, pp. 199–223.

Rothermund, Dietmar. 1970. *The Phases of Indian Nationalism and Other Essays*. Bombay: Nachiketa Publications.

——— (ed.). 1999. *Aneignung und Selbstbehauptung: Antworten auf die Europäische Expansion*. München: Oldenburg Wissenschaftsverlag.

Rozīnah, Parvīn. 1981. *Jam'īyatu'l-'ulamā'-i Hind: Dastāwezāt-i Markazī Ijlās Ha-yi 'ām 1919–1945* (Urdu: Association of Religious Scholars [JUH]: Session Documents of the Central Organization for the Years 1919–45). 2 vols. Islamabad: National Institute of Historical and Cultural Research. (Quoted as Rozīnah 1981/I or 1981/II.)

Ryan, Mary P. 1992. 'Gender and Public Access', in Calhoun (ed.), 1992, pp. 259–88.

Sahāranpūrī, Maulānā Khalīl Aḥmad. 1987 (1907). *Al-muhannad 'alā-al-mufannad y'ani 'aqā'id-i-'ulamā'-i-ahl-i-sunnat* (Urdu: Articles of Faith of the 'Ulamā' of the Sunni Persuasion [in the Deoband tradition]). Lahore: Maktaba-i Madinīya.

Saigol, Rubina. 1999. 'Learning to Hate: Fundamentalism, Modernity and Education.' Seminar Paper presented at the International Seminar on 'Fundamentalism versus Tolerance', Berlin, 17–18 June 1999 (unpublished). Berlin: Humboldt-University.

Salvatore, Armando. 1997. *Islam and the Political Discourse of Modernity*. Reading: Ithaca Press.

Sanyal, Usha. 1996a. *Devotional Islam and Politics in British India: Ahmed Riza Khan Barelvi and His Movement, 1870–1920*. New Delhi: Oxford University Press.

———. 1996b. 'Are Wahhabis Kafirs? Ahmad Riza Khan Barelwi and His Sword of the Haramayn', in Masud, Messik and Powers (eds), 1996, pp. 204–13.

———. 1998, 'Generational Changes in the Leadership of the Ahl-e Sunnat Movement in North India During the Twentieth Century.' *Modern Asian Studies*, 32 (3): 635–56.

Sarwār, Muḥammad. 1967 (1943). *Maulānā 'Ubaidullah Sindhī—Hālāt, Talīmāt, Siyāsī Afkār* (Urdu: Sindhi—His Biography, Education, Political Ideas). Lahore: Al-Maḥmūd Academy.

Schimmel, Annemarie. 1975. *Classical Urdu Literature from the Beginning to Iqbal*. Wiesbaden: Harrassowitz.

____. 1980. *Islam in the Indian Subcontinent* (Handbuch der Orientalistik, II, 4.3). Leiden: Brill.

Scheyli, Martin. 2000. *Politische Öffentlichkeit und Deliberative Demokratie nach Habermas*. Baden-Baden: Nomos.

Schöne, Ellinor. 1997. *Islamische Solidarität: Geschichte, Politik, Ideologie der Organisation der Islamischen Konferenz (OIC) 1969–1981*. Berlin: Schwarz.

____. 2001. 'Islam and Gesellschaft in Sudan. Selbstverständnis und politisches Konzept der Umma Partei,' in Reetz (ed.), 2001a, pp. 153–71.

Schulze, Reinhard. 1985. 'Islamische Kultur und soziale Bewegung.' *Peripherie* 18/19: 60–84.

____. 1990. *Islamischer Internationalismus im 20. Jahrhundert: Untersuchungen zur Geschichte der Islamischen Weltliga*. Leiden: Brill.

Seth, H. L. 1985 (1943). *The Khaksar Movement and its Leader Allama Mashriqi*. Delhi: Discovery.

Shaikh, Farzana. 1989. *Community and Consensus in Islam: Muslim Representation in Colonial India, 1860–1947*. Cambridge: Cambridge University Press.

Shakir, Moin. 1983. *Khilafat to Partition 1919–1947*. Delhi: Ajanta (2nd revised edn).

Sharma, Sri Ram. 1974. *Constitutional History of India*. Bombay: Orient Longman (3rd revised edn).

Sikand, Yoginder. 1996. 'The Emergence of the Tablighi Jamaat among the Meos of Mewat.' *Islam and the Modern Age*, 27 (3): 203–18.

____. 2002. *The Origins and Development of the Tablighi Jama'at (1920–2000): A Cross-Country Comparative Study*. Delhi: Orient Longman.

Siyālkoṭī, Muḥammad Ibrāhīm Mīr. 1953. *Tarīkh-e ahl-i ḥadīth* (Urdu: History of the 'People of the Traditions'). Sargodha: Maktaba-ur-Raḥmān.

Sindhī, 'Ubaidullāh. 1952. *Shāh Walīullāh aur Unkī Siyāsī Taḥrīk* (Urdu: Shah Waliullah and His Political Movement). Lahore.

____. 1970. *Khutbāt-e Maulānā 'Ubaidullāh Sindhī* (Urdu: Speeches and Articles by Sindhi, edited by Prof. Muhammad Sarwar). Lahore: Sindh-e Sagar Academy.

Sinha, Jai B. P. 1995. *The Cultural Context of Leadership and Power*. New Delhi: Sage.

Smith, W. C. 1985 (1947). *Modern Islam in India: A Social Analysis*. New Delhi: Manohar.

Steinberg, Guido. 2002. *Religion und Staat in Saudi-Arabien: Die Wahhabitischen Gelehrten 1902–1953*. Würzburg: Ergon.

Strand, David. 1990. *Civil Society and Public Sphere in Modern China: A Perspective on Popular Movements in Beijing, 1919–1989*. Durham, NC: Asian/Pacific Studies Institute, Duke University.

Talbot, Ian. 1990. *Provincial Politics and the Pakistan Movement*. Karachi: Oxford University Press.

Taylor, David. 1972. 'Indian Politics and the Elections of 1937.' Ph.D. dissertation. London, University of London, SOAS.

Tegart, Charles. A. 1932. *Terrorism in India*. London: Royal Empire Society.

Thānawī, Ashraf ʻAlī n.d. *Tajdīd-i taʻlīm-i tablīgh* (Urdu: Renewal of Education and Propagation of Religion). Lucknow.

———. 1977. *Fatāwā Ashrafīya kāmil* (Urdu: Complete Edition of the Three Parts of his Religious Decrees). Karachi: Sa'id Kampani.

———. 1982. *Iṣlāḥ al-muslimīn: muʻāsharat, maʻīshat aur siyāsat se mutaʻalliq Ḥaẓrat Hakīmu'l-umma kī mujaddidānah taʻlīmāt* (Urdu: The Reformation of Muslims: The Most Up-To-Date Teachings of the Sage of the Umma [Thanawi] on Society, the Economy and Politics). Lahore: Idāra-i Islāmīyat.

———. 1983. *Iṣlāḥ al-muslimīn: Qur'ān o Sunna kī rōshnī meñ zindagī kē tamām shuʻboñ se mutaʻalliq aham dīnī taʻlīmāt* (Urdu: The Reformation of Muslims: The Important Religious Teachings for all Spheres of Life in the Light of the Qur'an and the Sunna). Lahore: Idāra-i Islāmīyat.

———. 1984. *Ifādāt al-yaumiyah min al-ifādāt al-qaumīya, yaʻnī, Malfūẓāt-i Hakīm-u'l-ummat* (Urdu: Daily Utterances for the Benefit of the People, that is, the Sayings of the Sage of the Umma). 10 Vols. Multan: Idāra-i Talīfāt-i Ashrafīya.

———. 1990. *Iṣlāḥī Niṣāb—Tashīḥ-i ʻAqā'id o aʻmāl, Tahẕīb o Tamaddun-i Islāmī, Iṣlāḥ-i Fikr o Nazar* (Urdu: Curriculum for the Reformation of the Muslims—in Faith and Practice, Culture and Civilization, Thought and Views). Karachi: Dāru'l-Ishāʻat (numerous editions).

Tirmiẕī, Muḥammad ibn ʻĪsā ibn Sūrat. n.d. *Shamā'il-i Tirmiẕī. Maʻa Urdū sharḥ Khiṣā'il-i Nabawī Maulānā Muḥammad Zakarīyā* (with the original text in Arabic and Urdu and an Urdu commentary). Lahore: Maktaba-i Raḥmānīya.

Titus, Murray T. 1930. *Indian Islam: A Religious History of Islam in India*. London: Oxford University Press.

Trainor Nicholas, Paul. 1997. 'The Religious Person and the Public Sphere.' Ph.D. dissertation. Oxford: Oxford University Press.

Troll, Christian W. 1978. *Sayyid Ahmad Khan: A Reinterpretation of Muslim Theology*. New Delhi: Vikas.

ʻUthmānī, Shabbīr Aḥmad. 1974 (1924). *Ash-shihāb li-rajm al-khāṭif al-murtāb. Yāʻnī mirẓā'iyoñ kē irtidād kā ṣabūt aor qatal-e murtadd kē sharīʻ dilā'il* (Urdu: Giving the Proof of Apostasy Committed by the Aḥmadīs and the Legal Arguments for the Execution of an Apostate). Karachi: Dāru'l-Ishāʻat.

Vassiliev, Alexei. 1998. *The History of Saudi Arabia*. London: Saqi Books.

Veer, Peter van der. 1994. *Religious Nationalism: Hindus and Muslims in India*. Berkeley: University of California Press.

Verma, B. R. 1986 (1940). *Islamic Law—Personal: Being Commentaries on Mohammedan Law (in India, Pakistan and Bangladesh)*. Allahabad: Law Publishers (6th edn).

Walter, H. A. 1916. 'The *Ahmadiyya* Movement Today.' *Moslem World*, 6: 66–78.

———. 1991 (1918). *The Ahmadiyya Movement*. New Delhi: Manohar.

Watt, W. Montgomery. 1968. *Islamic Political Thought*. Edinburgh: Edinburgh University Press.

———. 1969. *Islamic Revelation in the Modern World*. Edinburgh: Edinburgh University Press.

Weidemann, Diethelm and Lothar Günther. 2002. 'Das indische Infantrieregiment 900—historische Realitäten und subjektive Wahrnehmungen', in Höpp and Reinwald, 2000, pp. 199–208.

Woolman, David Senter. 1969. *Rebels in the Rif: Abd el Krim and the Rif Rebellion.* London: Oxford University Press.

Yandell, Keith E. and John J. Paul (eds). 2000. *Religion and Public Culture: Encounters and Identities in Modern South India.* Richmond, Surrey: Curzon.

Zafarullah Khan, Muhammad (ed.). 1991. The Forgotten Years: Memoirs of Sir Muhammad Zafarullah Khan (edited by A. H. Batalvi). Lahore: Vanguard.

Zakarīyā, Muḥammad. 1975 (1940). *Tablīghī Niṣāb* (Urdu: Course on the Propagation of Islam). Delhi: Madīna Book Depot (numerous editions, later editions under the title: *Faẓā'il-i A'māl*—The Virtues of [Correct] Religious Practices).

Zaman, Muhammad Qasim. 1999. 'Religious Education and the Rhetoric of Reform: The Madrasa in British India and Pakistan.' *Comparative Studies in Society and History*, 41 (2): 294–323.

Index